D0458609

THE GREAT PSYCHOLOGISTS

THE
GREAT
PSYCHOLOGISTS

FROM ARISTOTLE TO FREUD
Second Edition

ROBERT I. WATSON

UNIVERSITY OF NEW HAMPSHIRE

J. B. LIPPINCOTT COMPANY

Philadelphia • New York

To

E. G. B.

my teacher, under whom
I have never studied

PREFACE

WHY AND HOW was this book revised? Five more years experience working with historical problems had made me unhappy contentually and stylistically with certain paragraphs, sections and chapters. I also saw the justice of certain criticisms made in reviews. With these guides, the entire book has been revised, although in differential amounts. Not more than fifty or sixty pages are untouched. Some chapters, notably 3, 7, 8, 9, and the portion of Chapter 20 devoted to Adler and Jung, are almost completely rewritten. A chapter, "Psychology Until 1945," has been added. An effort has been made to see to it that psychological developments outside of the United States were given their due prominence. The Epilogue, "Just Yesterday," was doubled in length and citations to the literature, absent in the first edition, now number over two hundred. For every psychologist included, two others might well have been selected, while twenty others will think they should.

References have been reorganized. In the previous edition many secondary sources were cited for what may be called commonly accepted details, perhaps more accurately referred to as incidents from intellectual folklore. They have been eliminated as unnecessarily pedantic and space-consuming, and, what is more important, as implying, sometimes falsely, that a given author is responsible for what he also drew from a common stockpile of knowledge. Secondary sources are now used primarily for background historical material, such as that concerning a given age or the life of a particular psychologist. Of the over 1,800 citations given, 80 per cent now are to primary sources.

In 1965, *The Source Book in the History of Psychology,* edited by Richard J. Herrnstein and Edwin G. Boring, made its appearance. This important collection of 116 excerpts from the literature on psychology demanded inclusion in the bibliography of as many excerpts as possible. It is either a compliment to our mutual acumen or an alarming indication of our mutual provincialness that sixty-seven of the 116 titles selected by Herrnstein and Boring were referred to in my first edition, although not necessarily to the identical pages or editions. It has been a relatively easy task to assimilate all except about ten of the remaining excerpts. Some primary literature then can be found with a minimum of effort.

I have profited immensely from criticism that I have sought. Robert M. Young of King's College, Cambridge University, was kind enough to loan me his annotated copy of the first edition which contained many cogent criticisms of practically every chapter, and in some chapters, every page. I have profited immensely from his not-so-gentle scoldings which after careful consideration, turned out, from my point of view, to be much more often right than wrong. Theodore A. Mischel of Colgate University, a philosopher very knowledgeable about psychology, helped to correct what was previously an even more amateurish interpretation of the intricacies of Kant. With the help of my friend, James A. Cardno, of the University of Tasmania, the section devoted to the Scottish School, the Mills, and Alexander Bain has been completely rewritten. Heinz Ansbacher of the University of Vermont has aided materially by critically analyzing the pages devoted to Individual Psychology leading to the elimination of certain errors and the inclusion of richer, fuller statements. Mrs. June K. Singer, a practicing analytical psychologist of Chicago, suggested changes in the section devoted to Jung which both clarified certain points and corrected errors in others. In no instance, of course, can these individuals be considered responsible for what is said, especially since on one matter or another I disagreed with all of them.

Permission to quote material in this book is gratefully acknowledged both to the publishers and to the authors or translators: From L. H. Blum, *Psychoanalytic Theories of Personality,* Copyright 1953, by McGraw-Hill Book Company, Inc.; From E. G. Boring, *A History of Experimental Psychology,* 2nd edition, Copyright 1950 by Appleton-Century-Crofts, Inc.; From R. Descartes, *Discourse on the Method of Rightly Conducting the Reason,* translated by E. S. Haldane and G. R. T. Ross, Copyright 1911 by Cambridge University Press; From Theophrastus, *Characters,* translated by J. M. Edmonds, Copyright 1929 by Loeb Classical Library and Harvard University Press.

I must mention again that I am grateful to a number of scholars who initially gave generously of their time in order to read either sections of chapters, chapters, or groups of chapters in order to offer criticism and comment. My thanks go to James R. Barclay, Edwin G. Boring, Donald T. Campbell, Rudolf Dreikurs, Carl P. Duncan, Stephen E. Glickman, Richard S. Ward, James A. Weisheipl, O.P., Michael Wertheimer, and Joseph B. Wheelwright. Their contributions increased materially the accuracy and scope of the book. I also want to repeat that my debt to Edwin G. Boring is the greatest of all. Out of the depth of his enthusiasm for the subject matter and his patience and attention to detail he meticulously worked over my material to improve not only its content but also its style. But my debt to him is greater even than this. It can only be met in small measure by the dedication of this volume. As always, in matters of this kind, my wife gave me help with a thousand and one details for which I would again like to express my thanks. My son, Robert I. Watson, Jr., also helped in seeing to it that materials from the first edition made the transition into the second appropriately and accurately. In the period when checking of quotes, galley and page proof and indexing became paramount, my secretary, Mrs. Valerie E. Herman, and my assistants, R. John Huber, Bradford E. Cook, Marvin Farbman, and Kathleen E. Bonneau rendered valuable service for which they have my heartfelt thanks.

ROBERT I. WATSON

Durham, New Hampshire
March 14, 1968

CONTENTS

xi

THE GREAT PSYCHOLOGISTS

CHAPTER 1

THALES TO HIPPOCRATES:

BEFORE PSYCHOLOGY

T HE FIRST experiment that has come down to us was psychological in nature. As Herodotus tells the story in his *History*, it was prompted by the desire of the Egyptians to demonstrate that they were the most ancient of mankind. To secure exact information, Psammetichus, ruler of Egypt in the seventh century B.C.,

> . . . contrived the following method of discovery: he took two children of the common sort, and gave them over to a herdsman to bring up at his folds, strictly charging him to let no one utter a word in their presence, but to keep them in a sequestered cottage, and from time to time introduce goats to their apartment, see that they got their fill of milk, and in all other respects look after them. His object herein was to know, after the indistinct babblings of infancy were over, what word they would first articulate.[1]

On opening the door two years later the herdsman was greeted by the children rushing to him with outstretched arms, crying, "*Becos*," the Phrygian word for "bread." Consequently, the Egyptians had to yield their claim to priority and admit the greater antiquity of the Phrygians.

We would call this a deprivation experiment. The children were deprived of an important source for the development of human behavior—the speech of others. This intervention, a deliberate manipulation of the variable being studied to ascertain its effect, is the essential characteristic of an experiment. Herodotus says that an even more radical research control had been considered and discarded—having these children brought up by women with their tongues cut out!

Surprisingly enough, the second known research study, also recorded by Herodotus, was quasi-psychological in nature. Croesus, King of Lydia between 560 and 546 b.c., was considering whether or not to go to war against Persia. In his time it was common practice to consult oracles. Since there were various oracles that might be consulted with inevitable differences in the advice given, Croesus decided to test their abilities before asking the crucial question about war with Persia. Messengers were sent to seven oracles with the instructions that, in the words of Herodotus, ". . . they were to keep count of the days from the times of their leaving Sardas, and, reckoning from that date, on the hundredth day they were to consult the oracles, and to inquire of them what Croesus, the son of Alyattes, King of Lydia, was doing at that moment."[2] The Delphic oracle alone reported correctly that he was engaged in the unkinglike task of cooking a tortoise and a lamb in a brazen pot. Reassured by this evidence of prowess, Croesus now asked this oracle about going to war with Persia. When told that, if he did so, a great empire would be destroyed, how was he to know that it was to be his own?

Here again is the attempt to control conditions of inquiry—the asking of the same question of each of the oracles at the same time to determine their accuracy in divining something taking place a great distance away. The manner in which Croesus tested the prowess of the oracles is identical to that in modern distance telepathy studies in parapsychology.

No great significance should be attributed to the few scattered instances that resembled modern scientific procedures. It was national pride in the case of Psammetichus and the question of the desirability of war in the case of Croesus that motivated them. The scientific attitude—that the world is knowable and can be investigated—did not originate with either the Egyptians or the Lydians. Disinterested curiosity about the workings of nature and of man was about to make its appearance elsewhere.

The earliest civilized science came into being about 600 b.c. in that part of Greece on the coast of Asia Minor known as Ionia from whence it spread to the rest of Ancient Greece. It was indebted to some extent to even more ancient civilizations. Fragments of scientific knowledge known to the Egyptians and Babylonians in what we would call astronomy, medicine (particularly surgery), and mathematics had some influence. Attempts to secure scientific knowledge for its own sake, however, which show a continuity with the present, began with the ancient Greeks.[3] The records we have of the achievements of these other civilizations lack continuity, and what have survived are inextricably mixed with magic and superstition. The fragments[4] of the writings of the early Greek thinkers that have come down to us show both the breadth of their interests and their cheery obliviousness to what later came to be divisions among the specialized fields of science. Their conception of nature embraced all that exists. Science and philosophy were one. To be sure, there were a few practitioners—physicians, lawyers, and engineers—but philosopher-scientists took as their province the whole of universe and of man. Men speculated, observed, and thought about the universe or any aspect of it that struck their fancy. Their philosophy was to be distinguished from their science, if at all, only by the broad sweep and vagueness of the philosophical aspects. Man, with the whole glorious world before him, was busy surveying the scene, not working out the details. A synthesis of all knowledge seemed to be their goal.

Psychology's roots are to be found in this amorphous philosophy-science and in medicine. For the beginnings, before psychology emerged as a separate field and even to a considerable extent thereafter, we shall have to draw upon the contributions of men whose major identification to our way of thinking is with philosophy-science or medicine.

THALES

The first philosopher-scientist was Thales. Virtually nothing is known about his life with any degree of certainty. Legends of heroic proportions and facts are intertwined in a confusing mixture. He gained his greatest fame by predicting an eclipse during a battle between the Medes and the Lydians. However, this now seems to have been demonstrated to be just another legend.

Thales of Miletus, born about 625 B.C., was an older contemporary of Croesus and, probably, was in his train when he embarked on his ill-fated attack on Persia. Later, Thales traveled in Egypt, learning much of their methods of measurement and measuring, it is said, the heights of the pyramids by the length of their shadows. In Miletus, where he returned to spend most of his life, he led what was apparently a very active and, to some extent, a very practical life. Aristotle[5] himself is the authority for the story that, taking advantage of his knowledge of the stars which told him that there would be a great harvest of olives in the coming year, Thales managed very cheaply to make deposits on the use of all the olive presses during the time of harvest. When all of his fellow citizens wished to use these presses at the same time, he rented them for whatever he pleased, thereby making a large sum of money.

Aristotle draws the somewhat disingenuous conclusion that Thales did this to show that philosophers could easily be rich if they so desired, but that their true ambitions were of another sort. On the other hand, Thales might have carried out the transactions in order to make a living! Neither he nor his successors were paid for their philosophical or scientific efforts. They either worked at something else or were supported by inherited wealth. The even more apocryphal story of his once falling into a well because he was so intent upon gazing at the stars may well be seen as counter-balancing the somewhat shrewd practice of the earlier story. At any rate, this anecdote launched the first absentminded-professor joke.

It is to Thales we owe the recognition that while one must solve problems, one must also find the principles on which they are based. In this spirit he approached the problem of the nature of the world itself. In spite of multiplicity of appearances, he assumed that there must be some basic unity of substance in the universe. He reached the conclusion that water is the original substance that he sought, since from water all other things—earth, air and living things—were derived. The reasons for his choice cannot be established with any assurance, although some can be suggested. Water is the only substance readily known to man in the three states of solid, liquid, and gas. Rising steam was recognized as the same substance as the water within the kettle on that historic occasion when the first kettle boiled over. The manifestations of water in snow, ice, clouds, fog, dew, rain, hail, and in the seas and rivers are not difficult to conceive of as the same substance. Moreover, water appears to be everywhere.

What so far has been said about water as the primordial substance, leaves the impression, often fostered by later scholars, that Thales concerned himself with inanimate objects alone and that he could not be claimed by biology and by psychology as pertinent to their beginnings. This is not the case. The early Greeks held the conviction that man is of the same substance as other things, and, along with other animate beings, was part and parcel of the material world. Man's characteristics were used by them to help to explain the world, just as the nature of the world in the earlier cosmological discussions was shown to help to explain the nature of man. The world is the macrocosm; man is the microcosm, and they serve to explain one another reciprocally. It is not surprising then that Thale's choice of the ultimate matter was influenced by biological observations.

Several considerations show that Thales was also advancing that which is of more direct concern—a biological-psychological point of view. A passage from Aristotle[6] shows that Thales viewed the whole world as alive and animated. Aristotle also believed that Thales held his view about water as the ultimate substance because all living things depend on water for nourishment, and the sperm is moist. From Greek mythology considerable evidence has been marshalled[7] showing that water was conceived by the Greeks to be the generative or life-giving fluid. Aristotle also commented that Thales thought that the magnetic stone possesses life because it is able to move iron and added that, for Thales, the soul was something motivational in nature. Elsewhere[8] it is added that Thales reached this view not only from knowledge of the properties of a magnet but also from studying the attraction of amber for straw and dried leaves when rubbed briskly. After working with both the magnet and amber and finding the same manifestation of movement, he could have reached the conclusion that *all* objects, provided that one knows how to bring it about, had the power of movement, *i.e.*, apparently inanimate objects, because of having the power of movement, are therefore alive. There is the other side of the coin. Instead of seeing this as an instance of his scientific acumen, his belief in the magnet being alive might represent nothing more than an animistic strain in his thinking. At any rate, Thales seems to have been interested in animate as well as inanimate matter.

Coming after Thales, others argued for a different primary substance or substances—Anaximenes (c.540 B.C.) for air, Heraclitus (c.500 B.C.) for fire, and Empedocles (c.440 B.C.) for earth, air, fire and water.[9] It is by raising the question at all of a primary substance and by agreeing that this substance was material, that these men contributed to psychology.

DEMOCRITUS

It was the philosopher-scientists coming after Thales who showed specific interest in psychological problems. Much of their work centered on the problem of epistemology, *i.e.*, how knowledge is obtained. One answer was empiricism, a doctrine destined to have a long history in psychology. Empiricism holds that all contents of the mind are derived from experience. The Greeks expressed their attitude toward empiricism in various ways. In speaking of knowledge being derived only through the doorway of sense, Heraclitus[10] introduced an element of empiricism but went on to say that, while the senses are necessary, the mind alone can apprehend the law that governs change. Protagoras (c.430 B.C.), a Sophist and an older contemporary of Plato, reduced all psychic life to sensations, and based on his famous saying, "man is the measure of all things,"[11] it has been deduced that he held that a given individual's perceptions are true for him, but if there are several opinions about the same external object, there is no way of deciding which is the true one.[12]

Democritus, who flourished about 420 B.C. and also an older contemporary of Plato's, could not agree that all sensations are relative to the sentient subject, that an object could be truly sweet for X and truly bitter for Y. *All* sensations are false, declared Democritus, for there is nothing real corresponding to them outside the subject, nothing that we can know for sure. There is color, sweet, cold, and the like, true enough, but they are caused by something else, the atoms in the void, which are not sense.[13] The senses give us no information about reality. The tastes and smells are subjective. Many, many centuries later these were to be christened the secondary qualities and become important for Galileo, Descartes, Locke and other moderns. To this issue of the fallibility of the senses we shall return after giving more details about Democritus' theory of atoms.

In his search for the basic substance he postulated the existence of atoms—tiny particles of matter in ceaseless motion.[14] He conceived the matter of the universe as entirely made up of these atoms with all of the rest being merely empty space. The interaction of atoms was the exclusive source of all phenomena. The world of Democritus ran itself. Movement alone was sufficient; there was no necessity for postulating a prime mover. The service of atoms accounts for and determines all movements. Because he postulated that the cause of all activity was the movement and contact of atoms, there is little doubt that he must be identified as a determinist.

Democritus' mechanical conception when applied to the problem of perception gave us what may be called the first psychological theory. Empedocles had supposed that objects gave off effluences which act upon the senses to furnish knowledge.[15] Following this lead, Democritus described their projection as faint images. Sensation and perception involved contact of non-bodily atoms with those of the body. The impression that their interaction produced spread or reverberated through the body. An external thing is perceived because the atoms from the object pass through organs of the body to the "mind."[16] The mind, itself, is made of atoms distinguishable from other atoms in terms of degree only, being of a spherical shape, having greater rapidity of motion, and showing a "subtlety" of action.[17] For an impression by the atoms of the external object to be made on those of the body, the former must be above a certain minimum strength. Of course it was not understood in this fashion at the time, but much later this was conceptualized as the sensory threshold. (See Fechner, page 237.) The mind, itself, rises from the senses and there is no absolute separation of sense and thought.[18]

The various senses reduce to touch in that no matter whether it be vision, smell, taste, or whatever, the atoms of the object that is being sensed come into contact with the atoms of the body of the perceiver. Objects produce tastes in accordance with their shapes: sour, for example, being produced by atoms which are angular, thin, small, and winding.[19] Vision, with the original source of the sensation at a distance from the observer, demanded and received a more elaborate account from Democritus. The object seen sends off images which act on the air to mold the atoms of the air to the shape of the object and this air "figure-copy" touches the atoms of the eye whence it is conveyed to the mind.

This is the first statement of the representative theory of perception, that perception represents an object by being similar to it. A faint representation of the object emanates from the object and is conducted to the experiencing element of the body, the mind. The projections, images, or representations given off from the object are perceived and communicated to the mind. Variants of the theory that perception of an object is similar to that object proved so appealing as to persist thereafter in scientific circles until the end of the last century, despite repeated cogent objections. It still is the view of the man in the street who supposes an object gives off some sort of emanation which forms a pattern of size, shape, and color; this pattern once impressed on the eyes is carried to the brain where this unchanged pattern is "seen."

Now to return to the question of the trustworthiness of the senses. As we have seen, Democritus argued that not only were the senses deceptive, but, contrary to Protagoras, that they were not "true" even to the individual having the perception. His reasoning took the following form: since all matter is atoms, there are atoms other than those of the object in immediate proximity to it, and the atoms from the sounding object, for example, may mix with extraneous atoms which lie between the perceiver and the object, so that the person's perception does not represent the object faithfully. The senses are deceptive in that neither always, nor under all circumstances, do they portray the external world correctly.

These early Greek philosopher-scientists, to a limited extent, had considered the senses singly and collectively and in relation to reason. What we would call feeling, in the meaning of experiencing pleasure and pain, was neglected by them or, rather, not recognized as an issue worthy of attention. There was no single word in ancient Greek for feeling as an affective experience.[20] One word carried not only the affective or pleasure-pain motif but also a cognitive meaning, similar to that which in English is still expressed by "feeling" when we combine the two as in the expression, "I have a feeling of danger," when a sense of impending danger, plus an unpleasant feeling tone is meant. These early thinkers did explore cursorily the nature of man's desires while specific emotions, such as courage, were dealt with in passing, as it were. By and large, however, the affective life was neglected.

Nothing approaching a detailed systematic or ordered view of the inter-
relation of sense, thought, desire, and emotion was presented by any of these
early thinkers. Meanwhile, significant events were taking place in that other
source for psychological thinking—medicine.

ALCMAEON OF CROTON

Medicine and psychology share an interest in the functioning of human body
and mind, and, by the very nature of their art, medical practitioners must
pay attention to the individual. Since psychology, too, has a concern with
what may be broadly called psychosomatic relations as well as an interest
in the psychological functioning of individuals, some aspects of the advent of
medicine become relevant to that of psychology. This relation between the
two fields is reinforced when one remembers that, today, clinical psychology
and psychiatry are uneasy blood relatives.

It is in the *Odyssey* that we first hear of Greek medical practitioners. They
made their way through the land, coming into homes to sell their services
to those who had use for them, and then moved on.[21] The sign of a highly
successful practitioner was that his fame preceded him wherever he went and
that he lived on in memory until his return. In the time of Homer, Asclepius,
the first Greek physician of whom we have knowledge, was not a god, but
just such a physician. As the years passed his fame became so great that he
was deified, and over 300 temples were erected in his honor. His priests
jealously guarded their knowledge, passing it on only to those of the next
generation whom they initiated into its mysteries. People from all walks of
life went to the Temples of Asclepius. Indeed, Socrates' last words had to
do with a debt to Asclepius, "Crito," he said, "we owe a cock to Asclepius;
will you remember to pay the debt?"[22]

Although instances of surgical operations were not uncommon in their
records, the percentage of cures of blindness and of lameness seem to be very
high which suggests a psychosomatic basis to many of these cures. Among
the factors operating to produce a favorable receptivity to the suggestive
influences of temple healing were the reports of wonderful cures, the waiting
to be received, the period of purification before admission to the sanctuary,
the wearing of special robes, and the drinking of sacred waters.[23] The peak
of treatment was the incubation, or a period of sleep in the sanctuary. Several
characteristic phenomena were associated with incubation. While still awake,
apparitions might occur in which the patient saw the God and received a
message specific to his illness. Or he might have a dream in which a priest
or a God told him what to do (an oracle), or he might have a dream foretelling

the future (a vision) or even one in which the cure itself came. A certain amount of rational treatment, such as occasional use of drugs, was combined with these magical practices, but surgical treatment, bleeding, and massage were left to lay hands. As a consequence, the medical experience accumulated by the priests was almost exclusively "psychological" in nature. Faith healing, tempered a bit by scanty scientific observation, epitomized the approach of temple medicine.

Gradually, a new more scientifically based medicine, relatively divorced from the irrational aspects of temple medicine, began to emerge. One of its founders was Alcmaeon of Croton, a physician who flourished at the beginning of the fifth century B.C. Almost nothing is known of his life and only sparse fragments of his writings remain. Many of these fragments are of psychological-physiological import.[24] After discovering passages from the eyes to the brain, Alcmaeon boldly concluded that the brain both received perceptions of vision, audition, and olfaction, and was also the seat of thought. The brain, being the seat or central organ of intellectual activity, he called the soul. It was his way of naming the vital principle or life source. Alcmaeon did not use the word "soul" in a theological sense and there was no necessary connotation of immortality. Soul was a convenient name for the central psychological agency. As a matter of fact, he did accept the immortality of the soul because he considered it to be self moving,[25] but its naturalistic description was divorced from his speculations about immortality.

It cannot be overemphasized that "soul" is one of the most elusive and complicated terms in the history of thought. Among the Greeks of this time the soul was regarded as the source of consciousness and life. A man is alive if he can move his limbs and other parts of his body; fainting means that his soul has withdrawn temporarily, and death means that his soul has withdrawn permanently.[26] Soul often was given the meaning of vital principle or life force and had no necessary connection with theological considerations. Their view of soul gave their perspective on the process of living things. Succinctly, conscious experiences are seen as related to a source, soul, which initiates movement.

Speaking more strictly, the Greeks accepted what came to be called a two-aspect theory of soul, although sometimes it would appear that it was two separate souls they were talking about.[27] One aspect of the soul, *thymos*, with which we, as students of psychology, are concerned because it is involved in thought and emotion, perished with the body. The "diaphragm" or the lungs were the organs of consciousness. How could such a view be held? As Onians[28] puts it, to the ancient Greeks, thoughts are words, words are breath (*pneuma*), and the organs of the mind consequently are the lungs. This is even more plausible when it is remembered that anyone unfamiliar with writing would find words always spoken.

The other aspect of the soul, *psyche,* was immortal, but in the earliest traditions, as in Homer, it maintained no memory of its earthly existence and, indeed, had no concern with waking experience. Psychologists, whose very name is derived from the latter meaning of soul, more accurately should have been called "thymotologists," since conscious experience is definitely the concern of psychologists, while immortality is not!

To return to Alcmaeon, he made the advance of unifying these two entities or aspects of the soul, formerly localized in the head and lungs, into one entity centering in the head. One soul performs all of its functions. Alcmaeon taught that the brain contains the governing faculty of the soul where all sensations are "somehow fitted together." [29] The brain is also the seat of thought; it serves for the storing and arranging of perceptions, and gives memory and belief. Alcmaeon held that sensations reach the brain through the medium of channels which start with the organs of sense. These passages were not the nerves, as such, but rather channels for breath, the *pneuma,* mentioned earlier in connection with the *thymos.*

Thinking and perceiving were recognized as separate processes. To put it in his terminology, Alcmaeon made a distinction between intelligence and sensation, claiming that man alone understands, whereas other creatures have sense perception but are without understanding.[30] This distinction, between perception, or what is given by sensory experiences, and thought, independent of sensory experience, was to become a major concern for the Greeks, reaching its culmination in the formulation of Plato.

Alcmaeon was not the first to relate bodily functioning and the soul. As a matter of fact, Anaximenes had earlier assigned a bodily function to the soul, thinking of it as the life-giving principle of breath.[31] Others before Alcmaeon had also used their cosmological principles to assign the soul's locus of function. In searching for unity in diversity which makes up the world, Heraclitus found the essence of all things in fire—transforming and consuming as fire does, heterogeneous matter onto itself. This fire is also soul[32] to Heraclitus. Aristotle, the authority for this last, adds, that, in keeping with the prevailing opinion, Heraclitus relates soul to movement. Heraclitus, however, is not known to have given soul a specific bodily locus.

Other views, particularly folk traditions, had located the soul in the blood, in the heart, or in the spinal marrow. Alcmaeon's views were a definite advance over both those in the philosophic and folk traditions.

Alcmaeon's work on the senses was based upon observation of surgical operations. Tradition has it that he was the first one to dare to undertake

whence it originates. . . . hereditary, like that of other diseases."[39] He goes on to indicate that epilepsy is caused in the brain. Even more specifically he relates it to a humoral congestion in the brain which results in affected individuals becoming phlegmatic, which, in turn, brings on epileptic attacks.

The functioning of the humors, just alluded to, gave rise to the major theory of bodily function that was to dominate for many centuries to come. Polybos, son-in-law of Hippocrates, is supposed to be the author of the Hippocratic treatise concerned with the theory of humors, the *Nature of Man*.[40] In propounding the theory, this Hippocratic writer implicitly accepted the view of Empedocles that the universe is composed of air, earth, fire, and water, which combined to produce all substances, although he spoke of them not as elements but as "roots of all."[41] They are unchangeable, water cannot become earth, nor earth water. By mingling, they form concrete objects. Corresponding respectively to these elements, he held, are the four combinations of qualities, warm-moist, cold-dry, warm-dry, and cold-moist. With this as its base, these elements and qualities took bodily form in the respective humors, blood, black bile, yellow bile, and phlegm. These humors make up the constitution of the body and cause both disease and health. Deficiency or excess of one or another of the humors causes pain. Some disorders are evidenced by the various appearance of liquid excretions from the body of the sick person, as from a cold in the head, and when the skin is broken, blood comes forth, while in the case of severe injury, other fluids of the body become visible. Relatively direct reasoning would lead them to conclude that these fluids are of considerable importance in the economy of the body. To Hippocrates, the theory of humors was a theory of disease. Only much later was it related to personality by Galen (see page 83) who added in a relatively systematic fashion the theory of temperaments to this four-fold classifacatory system.

On this basis, Hippocratic thinking considered disease to be created by disturbance of the harmony of the relation of the elements as manifested in the humors. In agreement with Alcmaeon, cures depended upon restoration of the disturbed harmony. The humors, in fact, tend naturally to equilibrium and, if left to themselves, often will be brought to this state by the body's inherent tendency to recover from disease or injury. The concept of the crisis, or critical turning point, was utilized and it was the task of the physician to assist nature by bringing his remedies to bear upon the patient at these critical times.[42]

Hippocrates was the first to relate to the brain the conscious life in its entirety, including the emotions.[43] He discusses this relation of the emotions to the brain in specific terms. Overheating of the brain causes terror and fear, as shown by the flushed face. When the brain is unduly cold, anxiety and grief are shown. Too much bile causes overheating; too much phlegm causes overcooling.

Nerves had no place in the Hippocratic writings, and there was no distinct concept of the functioning of muscles, and a confusion of tendons and muscles.[44] The coordination of parts of the body in movement was explained by the doctrine of "sympathy," or "consensus"; an immaterial connection between parts of the body which brought about movement. Knowledge of the structural basis of sympathy was absent, and it even did not occur to them that such structure might be sought.

OVERVIEW

The philosopher-scientists and physicians of ancient Greece made the decisive choice of the natural order of existence over the supernatural. They reached the conviction that the world and man within it could be understood as acting according to natural laws, free from mythology. Aristotle,[45] looking back to these beginnings some 250 years after Thales, held that theologians had treated science in the form of myths while the philosopher-scientists set forth their reasons in a demonstrative form. Life for Thales and those who came after him was not, as it was for Homer, explained by the capricious whims of the gods. Thales offered a general explanation of nature—all things came from water—without an appeal to anything outside of nature. The Hippocratic writers similarly rejected supernatural influence in disease. The cause of things, he and the others were saying, is to be sought, not in the gods, but in nature itself. A naturalistic spirit was becoming evident.

Thales and the other Greek pioneers were the first to be interested in nature for its own sake. Before them, other Greeks, such as Hesiod, the poet, had been interested in natural events, as undoubtedly had farmers and sailors. But in these people the interest in nature was secondary, being dominated by other more important interests. In stripping off the mythological and theological trappings to give their accounts of the universe, however immature and incomplete, these scientist-philosophers were trying to get at the facts and to offer rational explanations of these facts. Without doing too much violence to the meaning of "demonstrative form," by which Aristotle characterized their work, it could be said that they based their contentions on observations of natural phenomena.

The experimental method with its empirical and inductive procedures akin to those followed by Psammetichus and Croesus was used only occasionally.[46] These pioneers had to depend upon "nature's experiments," the phenomena of earth, the stars, and of man, which occurred naturally. Observation, as yet almost unaided by instruments, was the method from which came most of our first scientific knowledge. But observations could and did do much to increase scientific knowledge. After all, the function of experiment is to supplement, or rather, to direct observation, not to take its place. Observation may occur without experimental variations of conditions, and the Greeks certainly included some acute observers. Hailing them as the first scientists in the modern connotation of the word would be a mistake; they did not generalize cautiously from observation and experiment. On the contrary, they proceeded by analogy to reach fantastically extensive generalizations. Sometimes there was a lucky hit, sometimes not. Democritus, for example, allowed his reason to outrun his senses, having no means of observation by which to verify his views concerning the atom.

It may have been unfortunate that in the nineteenth century John Dalton in his research on chemical combinations used "atom" to specify his particles, since his was an almost completely different theoretical position. His particles were of different *weights*, thus differentiating his theory from that of the Greeks.

Their criterion of the scientific truth of their hypotheses was their intrinsic plausibility.[47] Philosopher-scientists were convincing to one another to the extent that their arguments agreed with the other person's experience. Philosopher-scientists of this age could do little more than accuse others of inconsistency when they disagreed with their views; they could not prove them wrong. Nor could they prove their own views to be correct, no matter how personally convinced they might have been. Nevertheless, they took the decisive first step toward science in using what methods they had at their command.

The first inquiries about scientific problems had been made. These scientist-philosophers wanted to account for the basic nature of the world, which they interpreted as being material. Democritus' answer was the most significant for the future—atoms differing only in size and shape, their contact accounting for movement. His answer included the first theory of perception and was to have a profound effect on the scientific thinking, starting at the very beginning of the modern period, which centered upon the distinction between so-called primary and secondary qualities. (See page 184.) Even those who were to reject materialism, as did Berkeley, had to deal with its arguments by presenting alternative theories. (See page 190.)

Materialism was not yet involved in the separation and contrast between matter and mind, and for a very good reason—this distinction was only beginning to be articulated. Only the first gropings toward a dualistic contrast of man and world or body and mind was evident. The predominate view is exemplified by the lack of distinction between matter, and what we today would call the qualities of matter. To them, "the hot," "the cold," "the dry," *are* the stuff of things. Heat is as much "out there" as is motion. Heraclitean fire and soul being identical is illustrative of both lack of separation and lack of opposition between body and mind.

This, the first and formative period of Greek science and philosophy, extended from about 600 to just before 400 B.C. The new century was to be that of Plato and Aristotle.

REFERENCE STYLE

A FULL REFERENCE is given, including the particular edition consulted, the first time a work is cited. Whenever possible, the date of original publication follows in parentheses at the end of the reference. When the work is cited again, either the author and a title abbreviation, or the author's surname is repeated. The conventional *op. cit.* is used except for the works of men thematically central to the chapter, where the brief title is cited (*e.g.*, "Timaeus," not "Timaeus, *op. cit.*" in chapter on Plato).

Editions from *The Great Books of the Western World* were used, except when more suitable editions were found (*e.g.* with Berkeley). Psychologists should feel a certain touch of pride about their field since 15 of the 50 volumes in this series are directly relevant. Moreover, James and Freud are the most modern included.

If more specificity seems appropriate, the authors' divisions in terms of part, section, chapter, and part chapter are given. Direct quotations carry a page reference to the particular edition cited. References to Plato are given in the numbering system of Stephanus which is standard in almost all editions and translations. For works of Aristotle, the page and column are of the Berlin edition of the Greek text edited by Immanuel Becker.

Excerpts from the collection of readings, R. J. Herrnstein and E. G. Boring (eds.), *A Source Book on the History of Psychology* (Cambridge: Harvard University Press, 1965) are cited whenever pertinent. The full reference is not repeated; only the numbers of the excerpt are given.

REFERENCES

1. HERODOTUS, The History. (Translated by G. Rawlinson) In R. M. Hutchins (ed.). *Great Books of the Western World.* (Vol. 6) Chicago: Encyclopaedia Britannica, 1952, pp. 1–341. (450 B.C.); Book 2, Part 2, p. 49.

2. *Ibid.,* Book 1, Part 47, p. 10.

3. A masterly exposition of Babylonian astronomy and mathematics is that of Otto Neugebauer in *The Exact Sciences in Antiquity.* (2nd ed.; Providence: Brown University Press, 1957). He shows that there was relatively little contact with the Greeks before the diffusion created by the conquests of Alexander the Great which did not begin until the third century B.C.

4. The primary sources are most completely and carefully collected in H. Diels, *Fragmente der Vorsokratiker,* ed. W. Krantz (5th ed.; Berlin: Weidman, 1934–1938). An English translation of the fragments by Kathleen Freeman is available in her *Ancilla to the Pre-Socratic Philosophers.* (Cambridge: Harvard University Press, 1957). She also gives a detailed exposition of these fragments and early reports in *The Pre-Socratic Philosophers: a Companion to Diels, Fragmente der Vorsakratiker.* (3rd. ed.; Oxford: Basil Blackwell, 1953). The most complete and therefore the most important work on the lives of the Greek philosophers that has survived from antiquity is Diogenes Laertius' *Lives and Opinions of Eminent Philosophers* (Translated by R. D. Hicks. Cambridge: Harvard University Press, 1925, III, A.D.). Unfortunately it is frequently inaccurate but it is still our only source for many details. Most of what is given about the lives and works of Thales, Democritus, Heraclitus, Parmenides, Empedocles and Alcmaeon is derived from these sources and from Plato and Aristotle cited below.

5. ARISTOTLE, Works. (Translated under direction of W. D. Ross) In R. M. Hutchins (ed.), *op. cit.,* Vols. 8–9, (*c.*340–322 B.C.); *Politics,* 1259a 8.

6. *Ibid., On the Soul,* 411a 8.

7. B. B. ONIANS, *The Origins of European Thought, About the Body, the Mind, the Soul, the World, Time and Fate.* Cambridge: Cambridge University Press, 1951

8. Thales, in Freeman, *Companion, op. cit.,* p. 53.

9. Anaximenes, in Freeman, *Ancilla, op. cit.,* p. 65.

10. Heraclitus, *Ibid.,* p. 118.

11. Protagoras, in Diels, *Vorsokratiker, op. cit.,* No. 1.

12. Protagoras, in Freeman, *Companion, op. cit.,* p. 348.

13. Democritus, in Diels, *Vorsokratiker, op. cit.,* No. 9.

14. FREEMAN, *Ancilla, op. cit.,* pp 299–303.

15. Theophrastus, *De Sensu,* (Sec. 49–83) G. S. Kirk, and J. E. Raven, *Presocratic Philosophy.* Cambridge: Cambridge University Press, 1957.

16. Aristotle is the authority for Democritus alleging that mind and soul are one and the same (*On the Soul, op. cit.,* 405a 8–13).

17. *Ibid.,* 403b 28–404a 16.

18. Democritus, in Diels, *Vorsokratiker, op. cit.,* No. 125.

19. Theophrastus, *De Sensu, op. cit.,* Sec. 49–83.

20. J. I. Beare, *Greek Theories of Elementary Cognition from Alcmaeon to Aristotle.* Oxford: Clarendon Press, 1906.

21. H. Gomperz, Problems and Methods of Early Greek Science, *J. Hist. Ideas,* 1943, 4, 161–176.

22. Plato, Dialogues. (Translated by B. Jowett) In R. M. Hutchins (ed.), *op. cit.,* Vol. 7, (*c.*390–348 B.C.); *Phaedo,* 118a.

23. H. Ellenberger, The Ancestry of Dynamic Psychotherapy, *Bull. Menn. Clinic,* 1956, 20, 281–299.

24. Alcmaeon, in Diels, *Vorsokratiker, op. cit.,* No. 5–11.

25. Aristotle, *On the Soul, op. cit.,* 405a 29–34.

26. Kirk and Raven, *Presocratic Philosophy, op. cit.*

27. Onians, *Origins, op. cit.,* 1.

28. *Ibid.*

29. Alcmaeon, in Diels, *Vorsokratiker, op. cit.,* No. 5.

30. Alcmaeon, in Freeman, *Ancilla, op. cit.,* No. 1a.

31. Anaximenes, in Diels, *Vorsokratiker, op. cit.,* No. 22, 23.

32. Aristotle, *On the Soul, op. cit.,* 405a 25–28.

33. Alcmaeon, in Diels, *Vorsokratiker, op. cit.,* No. 10.

34. G. M. Stratton, *Theophrastus and the Greek Physiological Psychology.* New York: Macmillan, 1917.

35. Plato, *Protagoras; Phaedrus,* 311.

36. E. T. Withington, The Asclepiadae and the Priests of Asclepius. In C. Singer (ed.), *Studies in the History and Method of Science.* Oxford: Oxford University Press, 1921, 192–205.

37. Hippocrates, Writings. (Translated by F. Adams) In R. M. Hutchins (ed.), *op. cit.,* Vol. 10, pp. 1–160. (*c.*400 B.C.)

38. *Ibid., On the Sacred Disease,* pp. 154–160.

39. *Ibid.,* p. 155.

40. Hippocrates, The Nature of Man. In J. Chadwick & W. N. Mann (eds.), *The Medical Works of Hippocrates.* Oxford: Blackwell, 1950, pp. 202–213.

41. Empedocles, in Diels, *Vorsokratiker, op. cit.,* No. 7.

42. Hippocrates, *Of the Epidemics, op. cit.,* pp. 44–63.

43. Hippocrates, *On the Sacred Disease, op. cit.,* pp. 159–160.

44. F. Fearing, *Reflex Action.* New York: Hafner, 1930, p. 10.

45. Aristotle, *Metaphysics, op. cit.,* 980a–993a.

46. For discussion of this point see W. A. Heidel, *The Heroic Age of Science.* (Baltimore: Williams & Wilkins, 1933), and M. Clagett, *Greek Science in Antiquity.* (New York: Abelard-Schuman, 1955).

47. Gomperz, *op. cit.*

CHAPTER 2

PLATO:

BEFORE PSYCHOLOGY

B Y THE time of Plato, Athens had been established firmly as the center of intellectual activity of the Greek world. Thales, the earliest of the great men of science and philosophy, had already become a figure of legend. Plato's life all but bridged the span between the death of Pericles and Athenian acceptance of Macedonian domination.[1] Plato lived in the Golden Age of Greece and saw it crumble. Philosophy, poetry, playwriting, sculpturing, and architecture flourished as never before and, perhaps, since. Plato was a contemporary of Sophocles, Aristophanes, Hippocrates, Thucydides, Pericles, and Phidias; and the quickening of the intellectual life they produced was paralleled by a great deal of political and military activity. Trade and commerce flourished, despite military interruption. The Peloponnesian War was fought during his youth, and the struggle between the democratic and oligarchic factions in Athens later involved him.

SOCRATES

His teacher, Socrates, who was born about 470 B.C., was the son of a middle-class couple, possibly a sculptor and a midwife. He dedicated his life to seeking knowledge wherever it might be found, drawing men out to talk with him on the street, in the gymnasium, in the market place, at dinner, and wherever else he could find men willing to respond to his questioning.

His style of seeking knowledge gave us what later came to be called the Socratic method. It took the following form. Some general term used widely but without necessarily much reflection as to its true meaning, say, "friendship," "justice," or "piety," would be advanced in the course of one of the conversations which Socrates sought so eagerly. Socrates would then ask for a definition of the idea. After a definition had been given by his opponent he would draw him out in such a way as to get him to admit exceptions to that particular definition. A cross-examination of questions and answers would follow until either a clear final definition was reached on which both could agree or, seeing the shortcomings of his particular definition, Socrates' companion acknowledged that which he had unquestioningly accepted as true was not true at all.

The Socratic method combined induction and deduction, as they are called today. Thinkers before him had so uniformly started with general propositions from which they deduced particulars that Socrates' insistence on considering particular instances to arrive at a general statement made him a founder of the inductive method, although he also used deduction.

His particular opponents in Athens were the Sophists, professional itinerant teachers who for a fee, professed to teach virtue while simultaneously promising worldly success, and, at the same time, holding that true knowledge was impossible because sensory life is entirely subjective. The Sophistic contention of Protagoras, cited in the previous chapter, that man is the measure, was interpreted to mean that what men think determines what is true for them. Socrates differed from the Sophists in two major respects. He held he could not teach virtue and directed his inquiries toward universal and constant moral norms. The dialogue of Plato which bears the name of a major Sophist, Protagoras, shows Socrates and he locked in an argument over whether or not men can be taught basic values.[2] In order to combat their doctrines, Socrates sought knowledge within the person himself. Knowledge to him was an activity of the mind. Self-knowledge resulted from the discovery of one's own ignorance. Once this discovery had been made, one may go on to knowledge by use of the Socratic method since truth is innate in the mind all along. He used his method not primarily for destructive sceptical reasons, but because he was convinced that, for example, the acts we call courageous share a common reality, and he was seeking for this common reality. The Socratic method, he felt, permits one to find the truth, the abiding reality which lies behind the apparent flux and relativity that the Sophists made so much of.

Socrates made self-examination a philosophic method. "Know thyself" took on the meaning that the mind could turn to itself for knowledge. From the perspective of psychology it was one of the first instances, if not the first, turning to their homes. They undoubtedly paid dues of a sort, but certainly not tuition, since Plato showed an aristocratic disdain for the Sophists who taught for a fee. Undoubtedly the Socratic method was used by Plato for much of his teaching. Despite doubts that have recently been expressed, it is probable that Plato also gave formal lectures in which a systematic and continued exposition of a given topic took place. There is indirect evidence of teaching at more than one level. Some lectures might well have been of an advanced nature and others more popular in character. For example, there is the anecdote[10] that when Plato was announced as lecturing, "On the Good," many persons came expecting to hear how they might secure more wordly goods. Under these circumstances their disappointment on hearing about mathematics and such abstruse topics as the "Definite" and the "Indefinite" can be imagined. This story also suggests that there were members of his audience who were relatively unfamiliar with what they might expect to hear from Plato. This would not have been the case with his disciples.

Very little is known with any degree of certainty about the activities of Plato's later years. On the basis of the *Seventh Letter*,[11] he is supposed to have become involved in Syracusian politics as the supporter of a former pupil who aspired to the throne. However, Plato could only dream that a philosopher might be king, for grief, not victory, was the final result. Plato died in 347 B.C. at over 81 years of age. He is supposed to be buried in the ground of the school in which he served for forty years.

The Philosophical Basis of Plato's Psychology

Plato's psychological views are neither systematically presented, nor isolated in particular dialogues. His views on ethics, religion, metaphysics, politics, social theory, psychology, and indeed, all facets of his thinking are intermingled. Moreover, the dialogue form, a conversation cast in a dramatic setting, is hardly conducive to systematic presentation. His psychological contentions were always subordinate to what he considered to be much more important and fundamental problems. Indeed at one point he practically apologized for turning away from the eternal to indulge in the recreation of dealing with psychological matters, such as sensation.[12]

There are two major themes which form the basis for his interest in what were to become matters of psychological concern. Plato wished to find knowledge about which he could be certain. He decided those ideas or forms which he sought are to be found in a reality that lies behind the shifting phenomena of human conduct and physical processes, and he was eager to demonstrate the immortality of the soul.

In formulating these views he was influenced by Socrates' admonishment to care for the soul and his insistence that by using his method there was a definite meaning of things to which one could penetrate. Plato was also influenced by the Pythagoreans, a religious cult, who taught, contrary to those who conceived of the after-life as pallid and bloodless, that the soul was immortal and that death was a release from the bonds of flesh and that after repeated reincarnations a man could rise to know the Divine. The Pythagoreans attached considerable importance to number, and, more or less incidentally, they made a not inconsiderable contribution to mathematical knowledge. Aristotle [13] is the authority who tells that the Pythagoreans devoted themselves to mathematics and held that they thought its principles were the principles of all things. All things are numerable. The relation between things are also expressible numerically, such as their discovery that the musical intervals between the note on the lyre may be so expressed. Just as the musical harmony is dependent upon number, so too, is the harmony of the world itself. It was their contention that the first principle or the very basis of the universe (instead of water, atoms, and the like) *is* number—that the world in a sense is *made* of number.

In his reaction against the dawning materialistic emphasis, Socrates had rejected science in favor of a new emphasis upon spiritual concerns. Plato shared this view. His view toward science can best be characterized as ambivalent. He denied explicitly the possibility of experiment.[14] He had been speaking of color mixture, and, in conclusion, he said that those who would attempt to verify this by experiment would be ignoring the difference between human and divine nature, since only God has the knowledge and power to either combine or to resolve color mixtures. The astronomer is warned[15] that his knowledge of the heavens is not to be from observation but from *a priori* deduction from the heavenly ideal. His apparently harsh rejection of scientific observation can be softened if he is interpreted to mean that the astronomer's task should be to record real and not merely the apparent movements of the stars.

In the *Timaeus*[16] he says explicitly that an account of the material world should not be expected to be more than "likely" not exact or even self-consistent. Moreover, while he conceived the world as showing mathematical relationships, no more than the Pythagoreans before him did he conceive of this world being measurable.

It would seem that he rejected quantitatively and inductively derived empirical knowledge. But this is only one side of the coin. While this may have been his attitude toward what many of us today would consider crucial aspects of modern science—induction, quantification and empiricism—he also was already present since birth. Learning, in other words, is the drawing out of what is already present. Education is recollection.

This doctrine is not that of innate ideas. Knowledge is not ready made; it requires effort and to remember is hard work. Nor is reminiscence a register of past experiences or learning from the senses. Plato admitted that a certain amount of remembering does take place this way, but it is negligible. In this connection he introduced the famous simile of the wax tablet.[26] The minds of men are akin to wax tablets that vary in size, hardness, moistness, and purity, just as the minds of men vary in accuracy of recognition, retentiveness, and ease of learning. However, he not only minimized the importance of such learning in favor of reminiscence but also further along in the same dialogue[27] rejected his own wax tablet theory as being unable to account for error. The

and error. Since many errors, such as adding 6 + 5 to get 12, are not misinterpretations of experience, the wax tablet does not account for all errors. Consequently, it is but a relatively unimportant explanatory device.

More specifically, it is reason, as an aspect or part of the soul, that makes the Forms intelligible. Discussion is best presented in consideration of his psychological views.

PSYCHOLOGICAL VIEWS

That the soul is independent of body was an inference Plato was shown to have drawn on the basis of reminiscence in the slave-boy. Since the soul is independent of body, it follows that Plato's psychological views rest upon a dualism.

Soul and Body

To Plato, the body may be a hindrance to the functioning of the soul when it becomes an unruly instrument.[28] Strong natural appetites of the body may upset the functioning of reason. Through action of the humors of the body, the mind may be affected. Madness and ignorance are diseases of the mind brought about by the body. But excessive pain and pleasure are the greatest diseases of the mind since a man in great joy or great pain cannot reason properly. Sense perception, desire, feeling, and appetite are of the body and at war with the mind, in this connection interfering with apprehension of the Forms.

Plato considered the organic seat of or physical link between the three souls (or three aspects of the soul) of reason, feeling and appetite to be the cerebral-spinal marrow on which they were strung.[29] The immortal (rational) soul had a separate place in the brain while the mortal (irrational) souls of feeling and appetite were located in the thoracic and abdominal cavities.[30] The heart served as an advance post of the immortal soul, so that when wrong was committed, it stimulated anger in the heart, whence this emotion is carried by the blood vessels to all parts of the body. The blood vessels serve as the means for conveying sensations through the body.

The question of the independence or dependence of the body and soul may be now clarified. As an entity, the soul is independent; when it is within the body, it has to be connected to it. The soul, itself, is immortal, but certain relations and functions it has when it is related to the body are not.[31] The vital principle is imperishable; some of the ways the soul functions in the body are temporary, disappearing when the soul is independent of the body.

Motions and the Soul

In explaining sensory and other bodily processes, Plato made use of a somewhat vague concept of motion.[32] It will be remembered that, philosophically speaking, the essence of soul is movement. Nevertheless, in discussing movement he was making use of a concept having status which was to some degree independent of his theory of the soul. This concept of movement was the nearest Plato came to naturalistic theory. In dealing with the psychology of Plato, one always finds oneself returning to soul, and this instance is no exception. Plato said that psychological activities are related to various kinds of inner motions. It was probably arrived at by analogy to motion in the external world, which Plato observed preceding sensations. The instrument is the body; the function and source belongs to the soul which directs the acts of the body. A sensory organ is the means whereby the motion of the external world interacts with the motion of the soul so that external nature is apprehended. Sensation comes about because some motion impinged on a sense organ. This outer motion is communicated to an inner motion which is carried to the seat of consciousness in the soul. Sense qualities, such as color, are emergent from the interaction of the motion from the environment with the internal motion of the body. Diversity in the qualities sensed is caused by the diversity in the motions which the impression communicates to the body and which the body communicates to the soul.

More than merely passive internal reception of external motion takes place. Mind, an inner activity, acts upon sensation. For example, there is a light or fire in the eyes which goes forth to meet the light coming from the object.

(Presumably the presence of "fire" in the eye is inferred from the reflection seen on the cornea.)

The movements of the soul include various kinds of motions other than those related to sensations—will, pleasure, consideration, deliberation, pain, confidence, fear, hatred, love, and other "similar" motions. Thinking (mind) also is a functioning (motion) of the soul,[33] in that it is selective, spontaneous, and self-moving. Emotion and drive are also explained on the basis of motion. That sensation is movement and that emotion is merely violent movement was a doctrine advanced by thinkers before Plato. This relative and mechanical doctrine Plato[34] could not accept as it stood. As he modified it, sensation is accompanied by emotion when the more violent degree of motion occurs, but the direction of movement, whether it be toward the natural or unnatural, decided whether it be pleasant or painful. If the violent motion conformed to nature, it was pleasant; if it did not, it was painful. When it is added that natural meant to Plato productive of the Good and unnatural productive of the Bad, we see that here again psychology as subordinate to other considerations, in this case to ethics. What is called *drive* today is also related by Plato[35] to motion and to the soul. Inner motion is spontaneous or self-active. The highest form of such movement is reserved for purposeful action directed toward an end of some sort. Hence, purposive behavior is derived from the soul and expressed in movement.

The Composition of the Soul

Plato expressed three pertinent views on the composition of the soul. In the *Phaedo*[36] the soul is unitary and simple. In one place in the *Timaeus* the soul is described as having a two-fold division:[37] the rational soul, concerned with the reasoning aspect, or mind, and the irrational soul, consisting of desire and appetite. A little later in the *Timaeus*,[38] in the *Republic*,[39] and in the *Phaedrus*[40] the soul is tripartite—reasonable, spirited, and appetitive. Although some authorities find these three ways of describing the soul contradictory, it is possible to reconcile them by considering the first view as emphasizing the essential unity of the soul, while the second and third views are descriptions of *aspects*—not parts—of this unitary soul. The soul as a vital principle is unitary, but, as before, certain aspects or modes of functioning come into being when the soul is present in the body. Plato used either the classification of reasonable, spirited, and appetitive or that of rational and irrational as circumstances seemed to dictate. The emphasis that Plato placed upon the unity of the soul is important because consistency and integration of psychological functions is thereby made explicit.

Reasoning in the Dual and Tripartite Soul

The first and highest aspect, reason or the mind, is the intellectual facet of the soul. Mind, reason, and thought are practically equivalent terms for Plato. Reason, hereafter, will be the preferred term. Mind will be reserved for discussion of later psychologists when it replaces soul as a guiding concept. In this and later discussion, thought is seen more as a *process* rather than as an aspect of the soul. To Plato, reason is the very essence of man; he is a man insofar as he is rational. This does not mean that rational man does not possess the lower aspects of the soul but that he is to be guided by reason. Certain functions of reason are familiar from the statement of the theory of Forms and the theory of reminiscence. To review, reason is the means whereby we intuitively know the Forms. Reason, as reminiscence, is only indirectly dependent upon the natural world or its phenomena.

To go more deeply into Plato's conception of reason, it is necessary to compare and contrast it with sensory experience. As we saw in discussing the Pre-Socratics, the controversy over reason or sense as the means of securing knowledge existed before Plato. Plato admitted that the data of sensation are the material of knowledge, but then denied that sensation is knowledge. Reason (not sense perception) is the means of synthesis of our experiences. We do not see with the eyes but *through* them. We do not hear with the ears but *through* them. Common characteristics of diverse objects are not perceived by the separate organs of sense but by reason.

As known from the theory of Forms, the senses present us with a world of particular events. If left to the senses alone, their meaning would never be unraveled. The perceptible world does reflect, albeit dimly, an interrelated reality. The "constituents" of this interrelated reality are the means by which, through tracing the tangled web of particulars, one may reach some view of the Forms. Sense perceptions give only particulars, but these particulars when formed in a pattern, by the nature of that pattern, give some intelligibility. Reality is revealed by reason through making possible *interpretation* of perceptual experience. Sensory processes simply supply some of the occasions for knowledge or serve as one of the tools of knowledge. An activity of the mind, the faculty of reason, reveals the Forms behind them, and it is the soul which makes one aware of perceiving.

Reasoning is related to other processes besides reminiscence and sense. Memory plays a role in reasoning, although from what is already known of Plato it is not surprising to find it is a relatively minor one. Plato[41] says the soul is like a book in which memory inscribes the perceptions in our souls. He goes on to indicate that this record may be true when the "secretary" inscribes correctly but false when the opinion expressed is false. But there is another artist at work—the painter, imagination, who uses the records in his own characteristically creative way. Reasoning is completed or worked through by a process of dialectic essentially similar to that of Socrates. Using the three processes of reminiscence, memory, and imagination, reasoning is carried out by dialectic.

Spirit and Appetite in the Tripartite Soul

The second aspect of the tripartite division of the soul is concerned with spirit. Spirit is contentious, assertive, pugnacious, and forceful. In its drive to action, it carries out the directives of reason. In so doing, spirit has the role of mediator between reason and the third aspect of appetite.

Both the role of spirit as a mediator and the necessity for its separation from appetite is best shown by using Plato's own illustration.[42] One, Leontius, was at a place of execution. He felt a desire to see the dead bodies and yet had an abhorrence and fear of them. He struggled for a time, but desire won, and Leontius "ran up to the dead bodies saying, 'Look, ye wretches take your fill of the fair sight.'" He was angry with himself for his action, showing that spirit was on the side of reason, but nevertheless, appetite won out. This is proof positive to Plato of the existence of different aspects of soul, for how otherwise could he want to look and yet not want to look at the bodies? The spirited element is not the same as appetite since it can be used against it. Although spirit and appetite are sometimes antagonists, they must be distinguished.

Appetite, the third aspect, above all, is indiscriminating desire. Appetite wants something, and it wants it now, without delay, and without any consideration for the other aspects of the soul. The goal of appetite, as Plato sees it, is attainment serving as a replenishment. Thrist, for example, arising from deprivation of water, leads to striving for water which, when achieved, results in repletion. Appetite expresses a level of pleasure centering upon a felt depletion which needs to be replenished.[43]

Conflict and Harmony and the Tripartite Soul

The fact that soul is unitary does not mean that it cannot have aspects which may be at odds with one another.[44] Awareness of the nature of conflict on the part of Plato is shown in the story of Leontius, but an even more dramatic illustration is given in Plato's figure of the charioteer in the *Phaedrus*.[45] Plato likened man to a chariot team. In the team there is a powerful unruly brute of a horse intent on having his own way at all costs (appetite). The other horse is a thoroughbred, spirited but manageable (spirit). On catching sight of his beloved, the charioteer (reason) attempts to direct the two horses, although with some difficulty, to work toward the goal which he alone (not they) can comprehend.

What Plato seems to be teaching is a theory of conflict based upon reason, emotion, and drive. Man's behavior toward goal objects is swayed by affective impulses and inhibitions over which reason, the charioteer, has some control. Reason acts as a check upon the affective aspect. For the ends of spirit or appetite to be met, reason must guide. But reason and thought is more than a means to serving their ends. For self-realization, reason, too, has its share. Thinking just for fun is important, but thinking as a seeking for truth is more important. Spirit or appetite are not to be eliminated; instead they are to be controlled. Reason attempting to oust emotion or drive would be as irrational as emotion or drive seeking to banish reason. Although there is conflict among the aspects of the soul, sometimes they agree.[46] Reason is the natural harmonizer. Balance and proportion among the aspects is sought, with the others subordinate to reason. Order is in harmony and subordination.

Drive and the Tripartite Soul

Drive characterizes all three aspects of the soul. Reason, spirit, and appetite each is a drive, of and by itself, an endeavor toward a thing, a striving toward attainment of a goal.[47] The reflective aspect seeks understanding and wisdom; the spirited seeks success; the appetite, the lowest form of desire, seeks bodily pleasures or means to them, especially money, food, drink, and sex. Reason may long for the realization of its own drives and assent to them. On other occasions reason dissents, as it does to many of the drives of spirit or appetite. But this should not obscure the fact that the reason has a drive characteristic of its own.

The *Symposium*[48] of Plato is concerned with *Eros*, each participant in the dialogue offering his own interpretation. Plato's position seems to be that of a division into two kinds of love—profane and sacred. The first sort is concerned with the body and the second with the soul, mind, and character. Physical sexual desire is interpreted, not as a desire for intercourse, but as a masked desire for parenthood, an attempt to perpetuate oneself. This passion for physical parenthood is the most elementary or rudimentary fruition of the good and eternal.

Only the higher love can lead to happiness. Love, as Plato conceived it, is in its highest form, the love of wisdom. Whether one knows it or not, what one seeks is the beauty of the eternal Forms. This love is a longing for union, not only with the partner through reason, but, beyond this, a love of pure Form, or the essence of love itself. Thus the higher or immortal soul had its own enjoyment, its particular *Eros*. *Eros* is popularly translated as "love" but often may be more meaningfully called *libido*, in the sense that this means life force. This is something akin to the biological will to live, the life energy, a concept of which we shall hear again. Although this qualification should be kept in mind, the term, love, will be used in that which follows.

Drives have an affective coloring of pleasure and pain. Pleasure and pain are considered by Plato in a fashion closely related to that of emotion. As we have seen, pain is that which is contrary to nature, pleasure that which is in accord with nature. One class of Pleasures derives from the restoration of the natural state of equilibrium. At the level of the appetite, depletion causes need (lack of pleasure) which when satisfied is followed by repletion (pleasure).[49] This process of return to the normal on the part of the organism is one form of pleasure.[50] Under excess heat or chilling there is a disturbance of equilibrium, and recovery or return to the natural state is pleasant. This is a form of pleasure in which there is an agreeable return to a normal bodily condition.[51] There is a second class of pleasures depending upon mental processes themselves, not upon a balance within the organism, such as the pleasures to be found in remembering and in anticipating. These are pleasures which we anticipate or remember mentally, such as anticipating recovery from a painful illness and remembering past pleasures which we look forward to enjoying again.

The Irrational in the Dual Soul

While not the first to recognize an irrational aspect in man, Plato considerably amplified, extended and gave a rationale for it. He located this lower or irrational aspect within the soul itself, thinking of it in terms of psychological conflict. The already familiar accounts of the passions, the tripartite division itself, and the story of Leontius, all point to an appreciation of this aspect.

Emotions are related to the mortal (irrational) soul, which is endowed with courage, passion and love of strife. The wild beast in man may slumber or be restrained but never tamed. Passion is irrational, liable to excess, expanding until it becomes a form of mania. A graphic illustration is given by Plato when he speaks of the "unnecessary" pleasures and appetites which everyone seems to have, although some can control them by reason. With everyone, when reason

. . . is asleep, then the wild beast within us, gorged with meat or drink, starts up and having shaken off sleep; goes forth to satisfy his desires; and there is no conceivable folly or crime—not expecting incest or any other unnatural crime or parricide, or the eating of forbidden food—which at such a time, when he has parted company with all shame and sense, a man may not be ready to commit.[52]

OVERVIEW

Plato's rationalistic theory of Forms decided his attitude toward science. Then, as now, science dealt with the physical world. By definition, its phenomena belong to what Plato saw as the shifting relatively unintelligible world of sensation. According to Plato one could never trust these phenomena to give true knowledge. His distrust of the physical world, including the sensory processes, helped to turn individuals away from science, including psychological science. Only knowledge of the Forms, another class of existence entirely, could give us truth. The Forms are the object of knowledge, not material things, and inductive science belonged to the material world.

But this was a rejection of science as empirical and inductive, not science as rationalistically drawing conclusions from axioms. This approach would have been acceptable to him. In his rationalism Plato gave us the beginning of law as something imminent—law as basic nature far removed from mere phenomena. When we understand the Forms, Plato was saying, we understand their natural relationship one with another. This interrelationship was later conceptualized as natural law. It should be evident that Plato did not himself formulate anything approaching this modern conception. He did lay the groundwork from which it was to emerge.

Ironically enough, he who glorified reason showed keen insight into the functioning of the unconscious irrational aspect of man. His distinction between the rational and irrational aspects of living function (soul); his appreciation of the nature of conflict and, correlatively, of the nature of harmony; his primordial concept of Eros; his conception of drive as related differentially to the various aspects of living function; his realization of the perniciousness of repression and advocacy of controlled expression are indicative of his deep insight into the irrational aspect of human nature. This understanding, however, was but one among a few isolated instances occurring before the modern period and without immediate impact. Its significance was not to be appreciated until the time of Jung and Freud. Jung's conception of libido is actually closer in spirit to that of Plato than is that of Freud, in that he stressed its general non-specialized drive character. (See page 500.) Freud signalized his more specific debt to Plato by utilizing the very term, "Eros" in his systematic formulation. He also saw personality as subject to reciprocal urging and checking forces akin to Plato's reason, emotion and drive in his theory of personality structure as dependent upon id, ego and superego. (See pages 476–479.)

Side by side with this view of irrational aspects of the soul was the transcendental one of a rational soul whose unity is a guarantee of immortality. This gulf between immortal (rational) and mortal (affective) aspects of soul corresponds to the gulf Plato saw between man as he is and as he should be. Dodds[53] sees these strains as two diverse tendencies in Plato's thinking about the nature of man. He had a pride and faith in human reason, a heritage from the Golden Age. He had also a recognition of human worthlessness forced by his experiences in Athens and Syracuse. Dodds goes on to indicate that a psychologist might see this not as a simple opposition but as a compensation in which the first tendency became a compensation for the second—the less Plato cared for men in the flesh, the more noble he thought the soul to be.

The influence of his far-reaching and multifaceted dualism has yet to be mentioned. In espousing his theory of Forms, Plato broke away from pre-Socratic materialistic monism. He acknowledged a reality that could be apprehended by the senses, but described an immeasurably higher realm where intelligible beings gained true knowledge by understanding the Forms. Plato established the character of dualism to prevail until modified by Plotinus (see page 92) and even more thoroughly by Augustine (see page 99) into Christian Augustinianism. In this guise it became the predominant philosophy of the West until challenged by Aristotelianism in the Thirteenth Century.

The soul, not the body, was the means of apperceiving the intangible realms, and a more specific dualism, that of mind and body, began to take shape which was to persist well into the modern period.

The Platonic tradition reached still another climax and redirection in the hand of Descartes. (See page 154.) With the same goal of intuitive insight concerning knowledge, for Descartes it was to be found, not in the Forms or Ideas of Plato, but in innate ideas within the mind, a concept that for Plato was hardly more than an illustration of his broader dualism.

With Plato, psychology still had not emerged as a separate discipline. His interest in psychological matters was always subordinate to other issues. This is abundantly clear from his espousal of the theory of Forms, his desire to demonstrate the immortality of the soul, his conviction of the subordination of the body to the soul, and his distrust of the evidence of the senses which so channeled his thinking as to make psychology incidental to, and subordinate to, these other problems. He considered psychology only to the extent that it was necessary for him to do so in dealing with these other, to him, more important problems. So, Plato, momentous though he is in the history of thought, lived and worked before psychology began to emerge as a separate field. Aristotle, his pupil, was the first psychologist.

REFERENCES*

1. Major sources for the lives of both Socrates and Plato are Diogenes Laertius, *Lives and Opinions of Eminent Philosophers.* (III A.D.; Translated by R. D. Hicks. Cambridge: Harvard University Press, 1925); G. C. Field, *Plato and His Contemporaries.* (London: Methuen, 1920); A. E. Taylor, *Plato: the Man and His Work.* (6th ed; New York: Meridian, 1956); and G. Boas, Facts and Legends in the Biography of Plato. (*Phil. Rev.*, N. Y., 1948, 57, 439–457).

2. PLATO, Dialogues. (Translated by B. Jowett) In R. M. Hutchins (ed.), *Great Books of the Western World.* (Vol. 7) Chicago: Encyclopaedia Britannica, 1952, pp. 1–799. (*c.*390–348); *Protagoras.*

3. CICERO, *Tusculan Disputations.* (Translated by J. E. King) Cambridge: Harvard University Press, 1927, Vol. 4, 10.

4. J. BURNET, The Socratic Doctrine of the Soul, *Proc. Brit. Acad.*, 1916, 7, 235–259.

5. *Dialogues.*

6. *Phaedo.*

7. *E.g.*, Taylor, *op. cit.*

8. *E.g.*, Boas, *op. cit.*

9. PLATO, The Seventh Letter. (Translated by J. Harward) In R. M. Hutchins (ed.), *op. cit.*, Vol. 7, pp. 800–814. (*c.*367 B.C.)

10. FIELD, *op. cit.*

11. *Seventh Letter.*

12. *Timaeus.*

13. ARISTOTLE, Works. (Translated under direction of W. D. Ross) In R. M. Hutchins (ed.), *op. cit.*, Vols. 8–9, (*c.*340–322 B.C.); *Metaphysics*, 985b 23–986a 3.

14. *Timaeus*, 67–68.

15. *Republic*, 530.

16. *Timaeus*, 27d 5–28a 4; 29b 3-d 3, p. 447.

17. *Phaedo*, 79.

18. *Parmenides*, 132.

19. *Republic*, 596a 6–7.

20. *Republic*, 510.

21. *Phaedo*, 66b and *passim; Phaedrus*, 247c.

22. Plato affirmed the immortality of the soul on several occasions, *e.g.*, *Phaedo*, 85e–86d and *passim; Phaedrus*, 245cff; *Laws*, 893b–896d; and *Timaeus*, 69c–e.

23. ARISTOTLE, *Metaphysics, op. cit.*, 987b 27.

24. *Republic*, 514–521.

* See page 16 for description of reference style.

25. *Meno,* 82–86.

26. *Theaetetus,* 191.

27. *Ibid.,* 194–196.

28. *Timaeus,* 86.

29. *Ibid.,* 85–86.

30. *Ibid.,* 69d–70a.

31. *Phaedo,* 64ff.

32. *Laws,* 894–896; *Cratylus* 400e; *Phaedrus,* 245b–c.

33. *Laws,* 896.

34. *Timaeus,* 64–65.

35. *Phaedrus,* 245c–246a.

36. *Phaedo,* 78ff.

37. *Timaeus,* 69.

38. *Ibid.,* 70–71, 77.

39. *Republic,* 439–440, 580–594.

40. *Phaedrus,* 253–254.

41. *Philebus,* 38.

42. *Republic,* 439–440, p. 353.

43. *Philebus,* 31.

44. *Republic,* 436, 440, 588.

45. *Phaedrus,* 253–254.

46. *Ibid.,* 237.

47. *Republic,* 580ff.

48. *Symposium.*

49. *Timaeus,* 81.

50. *Philebus,* 31.

51. *Ibid.,* 72.

52. *Republic,* 571, p. 416.

53. E. R. Dodds, *The Greeks and the Irrational.* Berkeley: University of California
     Press, 1951.

CHAPTER 3

ARISTOTLE:

THE FOUNDING OF PSYCHOLOGY

K NOWLEDGE of the earliest Greek speculations on psychological problems is both fragmentary and found imbedded in nonpsychological frameworks. Later, Socrates insisted that the proper study of mankind was man, but he did not frame a science of human experience and behavior nor, for all his brilliant excursions into many aspects of knowledge, did Plato. Aristotle was the first to develop a systematic psychology and consequently was the first psychologist.

No more than to Plato can one do justice to the wide ranging thought of Aristotle. Selection is inevitable. If this was a treatise on the history of philosophy, his "first philosophy" would be selected for emphasis; if this was a book on logic, his "Organon" would be made central. Here attention is primarily devoted to Aristotle, the biologist and psychologist.

ARISTOTLE'S LIFE AND WORKS [1]

In the year 367 B.C., Aristotle, a young man of seventeen, arrived in Athens. Socrates had been dead for thirty-two years, Plato himself was sixty-one, and the Academy had been in existence for nineteen or twenty years. His birthplace in 384 B.C. had been Stagira, a provincial town in northern Greece. Aristotle's

father, physician to the King of Macedon, following the Ascepliad tradition
of his family, probably had begun training his son as a doctor. After his father's
premature death, Aristotle's early education was continued by a friend of the
family.

Aristotle remained in Athens for twenty years, until he was thirty-seven.
Less is known about these years than any other period of his life. It is even
a matter of scholarly dispute as to what it means when the statement is made
that he "studied" with Plato. Aristotle, himself, makes no mention in his
extensive writings either of the Academy or of actually studying with Plato.[2]
It is probable, however, that either immediately on arrival in Athens or shortly
thereafter, he entered the Academy and that sometime during these twenty
years he became a "colleague" of his former teacher. Certainly during the
latter part of this period he produced his first writings.

A literary myth exists that Aristotle in his writings was static and unchanging.
It is the view of recent scholars[3] that, as a matter of fact, Aristotle went through
more or less definable stages in his thinking. The neat, systematic order of
his works in which they appear in collected editions to this very day with
all works on logic, biology, and the like, each in its "proper" place was
the result of the work of later editors who arranged the works as they saw
fit. The legend grew up that his works were written by him in the order used
by his editors and that they were written almost entirely in his second stay
in Athens during the years yet to come. Until very recently this served to
mislead scholars. Contradictory views, in different works or in different parts
of the same work, not the least of which center on the soul, were once treated
by scholars as contemporaneous. Did he or did he not accept the Platonic
theory of Forms? When his writings were treated as contemporaneous with
one another, this became an insoluble question since both affirmative and
negative answers are present in his writings. When his views are treated as
showing development and change with time, such problems become much
more capable of being solved.

In his early years, Aristotle was an enthusiastic Platonist. His works were
written in the popular form of the dialogue during these days at the Academy.
In his hands it was no longer the interplay of Socratic cross-examination, but
a series of long speeches with each book having a special introduction with
Aristotle, himself, a speaker. None of these early dialogues have survived except
through fragments.

Devotion to the Platonic theory of forms, and all that this implies, seems to
have characterized his early stage of intellectual development. Aristotle expresses a yearning for death, treating it as a release of the immortal soul from
the body. The soul exists before the body, leads an unnatural existence when

connected with the body, and is released by death to return to its real existence.

In 347 B.C. Plato died at the age of eighty-one. He was succeeded as the leader of the Academy by Speusippus, a second-rater, but Plato's nephew and legal heir. Speusippus had strongly mathematical and Phythagorean leanings, which Aristotle probably found uncongenial to his developing new point of view.

Whatever the reason, Aristotle left Athens for Asia Minor at this time, remaining away from Athens for a period of twelve years. During this time he traveled, first settling in the town of Assus, near Troy, where he became part of the court of the Tyrant of Assus, Hermias. During his three-year stay, Aristotle not only continued his studying, writing and collecting biological specimens, but he also married Hermias' niece and adopted daughter, Pythias. The story that he devoted his honeymoon to collecting seashells, if it be true, certainly betrays a severely scholarly turn of mind.

After leaving Assus he went to Mitylene in Lesbos where he lived until 343–2 B.C., continuing his teaching and writing. He also went on with his factual researches on animals. Here or even earlier he was joined by Theophrastus, destined to follow him years later as head of his as yet unfounded school.

Under the influence of Hermias, whose territory was at the edge of the Greek world bordering lands under Persian influence, Aristotle had become a Pan-Hellenist, a protagonist for a Greece united against the Persian Empire. He was invited to Pella, court of Philip of Macedon, where his father had been physician to the father of the present ruler. Although we cannot be certain of the reason, it was apparently not as a philosopher, but as a learned Pan-Hellenist patriot that Philip called upon him to become tutor of his son, Alexander.

He served as tutor to Alexander for some years. His tutorship seems to have made some impression because legend would have it that it was Aristotle who had a great deal to do with Alexander's strong, but short-lived, passion for spreading Greek ideals on his monumental march of conquest in the East, during which Alexander gave instructions to his subordinates that biological specimens were to be sent back to his old teacher. Aristotle's tutorship ended when Alexander became Regent for his father. In 336 B.C. Philip was assassinated. The court at Macedon was thrown in a state of turmoil with intrigue and counter-intrigue rampant. It was during these stirring times in 335 B.C. that Aristotle decided to leave Pella and to return to Athens.

During the years away from Athens, Aristotle's thinking began to differ from that of Plato's. There are differences of opinion among experts as to precisely when these divergences took place, but there is general agreement that they arose during these travel years and the first few years after his return to Athens. In broad outline Aristotle's thinking progressed from the Platonism of the dialogues and other earlier works to the point where eventually he was much more concerned with empirical research. Hereafter when empirical convictions contradicted Platonic or other philosophical thinking, he did not hesitate to modify them in an empirical direction, even if they disagreed with the position of his former master and belied his former major interests and convictions.

Insofar as he was a scientist, Plato had been a mathematician and an astronomer inspired by Phythagorean teaching which demanded *a priori* conceptions of a fixed universal character. As a biologist, Aristotle was more interested in particulars—particular species of animals and particular physical phenomena. Aristotle, himself, suggested one major aspect of this difference in attitude. In his *Physics*[4] he raised the issue that mathematics deals with planes, lines, and points, and the physical sciences also present in their objects of interest planes, lines, and points. How then is one to distinguish the procedures of mathematics from those of physical sciences? He replied that in studying planes, lines, and points, the mathematician does so not as the limits of a physical body (which in reality they are) but as abstractions. He ignores for his purposes that physical body itself. Not so the physical scientist who deals with physical bodies which show motion, *i.e.*, change. Change is an essential part of both animate and inanimate nature. Change can be ignored in mathematics making one unit exactly like another forevermore; in science change prevents nature from ever repeating itself. In this same section of his *Physics* he makes a side reference to those "holders of the theory of Forms"[5] following the same procedure as the mathematicians, although, he says, they have even less justification for doing so.

Aristotle, perhaps first influenced by his medical training, had become more and more convinced of the necessity of using observations through the senses. Thus he disagreed with Plato about trustworthiness of the senses.[6] Plato's other-worldly and idealistic view stands in sharp contrast to Aristotle's empirical outlook. It is natural that instead of the perfect but static and lifeless mathematics that was the science of Plato, Aristotle turned to biology with its imperfect but living and changing organisms.

Aristotle repeatedly criticized Plato for incorrectly separating form from matter and for giving some sort of separate existence to universals.[7] Universals, in contrast to individual subjects, are class names, that which are of such nature as to predicate many subjects. To Aristotle the subject matter of physics is *both* form and matter,[8] that is, form embodied in matter.[9] Although substance is individual, we can treat a universal or a general type, *i. e.*, the form, as if it were a substance in dealing with it. After all, we can speak of human nature, for example, and have meaning in the statement. A universal may be arrived at by abstracting from a class of objects what they have in common. Thus a general notion is a useful tool in science despite the fact that only the individual, as such, is that which has separate existence. Plato had insisted on the reality of ideas apart from objects; Aristotle found Form resident in physical bodies. Aristotle denied the existence of the Forms apart from the particular and tangible things embodying them.

A lump of wax will serve as an illustration. Always the material has some shape; the shape has material. The shape of a lump cannot perish without the material also perishing; if form ceases, the material ceases. The lump may change its form, but form, as such, cannot disappear without the material disappearing. Form and matter may be conceptualized separately by an act of abstraction, but we cannot imagine a substance without form or a form without substance.

Form, to Aristotle, existed in the particular, not apart from it as it did for Plato. As in common sense, the substantial reality of things resided in these things. A thing cannot exist without matter, nor can matter exist without form. The individual object as we know it, is that which has separate existence—this man, this horse, this plant. They are a man, or horse, or plant, insofar as each has both matter and form.

The substantial reality of things is in the things themselves, not in another order apart from these things. Aristotle argued that by attributing an independent existence to Forms, Plato had made it impossible to explain the changing moving character that objects exhibit. Platonic Forms do not contribute to the exploration of changes in the sensible world. What exists is not the ideal, but the imperfect drawing marked off on the ground, not the ideal of justice but the faulty justice carried out by men. The forms exist when realized in matter. For each form there corresponds, as Aristotle put it, "a special matter." [10]

Aristotle thus denied Plato's dualism of two worlds as an unnecessary duplication. For him, there was but one world, that of actual things, with the role of form merely an aspect of this world. The reality of forms was not denied and could be studied, but as a task of philosophy, not of science.

Although one of his logical works dates from the earlier period, the rest quite possibly were written during these years as were those on ethics. Aristotle founded the field of logic to such an extent that to this very day to represent developments not starting with him, the expression "non-Aristotelian" logic is used. Collectively his works in this field are referred to as the *Organon*,[11] meaning instrument in the sense that it was a tool for philosophic and scientific investigation. The ethical treatises of Aristotle were the earliest *formal* works of this kind. Ethical considerations had been discussed before by Plato and even earlier. But these accounts were not systematically organized. It was Aristotle who performed this service. Some of his biological works date from this period but it is more convenient to examine them later as a whole.

Aristotle was forty-nine years of age and at the height of his powers when he returned to Athens. Shortly after his return he founded his school, the Lyceum. The name, "Peripatetic," [12] which came to be attached to his point of view arose from his habit of walking and talking with his pupils in its covered walk.

We seem to know somewhat more about the organization of the Lyceum than we do of the Academy. It is held that Aristotle devoted the mornings to lecturing on logic and metaphysics. During the afternoons he is supposed to have given public lectures on ethics, politics, and rhetoric. Along with this teaching, he and his students actively engaged in research. The school had a rudimentary organization and something of a staff, a library and specimen collections, and even regular dinners with its special dinnerware.

The atmosphere of the Lyceum, in the modern sense, appears to have been more scientific than philosophical. Aristotle had collected zoological specimens during his travel years, but he engaged most extensively in research on his return to Athens. Observational studies were made, his students prepared collections, and in general the research resources were augmented quite deliberately. The *History of Animals* shows clear traces of different authors. The work was apparently distributed among various persons, each having an assignment that had been schematically developed in advance.

Aristotle was a powerful scientific organizer in addition to his great scientific prowess. He was the first of a long line of individuals who, quite apart from their own direct contributions to science, are able to direct and to stimulate scientific work in their associates.

During these years, although engaged in a great amount of intellectual labor, he found time to exercise other interests and concerns. He adopted the orphan son of his former guardian. After the death of his wife he formed an attachment to Herpyllis, a native of Stagira. Although they never married, apparently their union was a happy one and he lavished care on Nicomachus, the son he had by her.

In his later days, his encyclopedic drive for knowledge inspired him to set his students to work upon some of the remaining intellectual worlds to be conquered. He attempted to have prepared a systematic history of philosophy and sciences, a collective work divided among several workers. Theophrastus was given the task of writing the history of the physical and metaphysical systems, while others were to write the history of arithmetic, geometry, artronomy, and medicine. Of those written none survive except in fragments.

His past tutorship and his continued connection with the court of Alexander had made Aristotle unpopular with the very strong nationalist party in Athens. In 323 B.C. the news of the death of Alexander was received in Athens while Aristotle's political protector was absent from the city. Anti-Macedonian feeling ran strong in the city. Rather than allow the Athenians "to sin twice against philosophy," [13] Aristotle retired to his mother's former country estate in Chalcis, a stronghold of Macedonian influence. Here he died of some form of stomach disorder in 323 B.C. at the age of sixty-two. His will, which is extant, shows his concern for every relative and dependent, including provision for the emancipation of several of his slaves.

Much of Aristotle's scientific work in a stricter sense was completed during these later years after his return to Athens. These years saw also the completion of many sections of his major philosophical work, *Metaphysics*. His biological treatises were, in some instances, products of the earlier transitional period but discussion of them was deferred until this point. His research in botany, zoology, and anatomy, through which he concerned himself with many of the fundamental problems of biology, clearly established him as a great pioneer. For example, he carried on studies of comparative embryology and developed a classification of animals. His research on the structures and function of living things was more exhaustive and greater in scope than that of anyone who had lived before. He was familiar with more than 500 different species of animals and had dissected or investigated fifty of these in considerable detail.

In fact, in examining the surviving complete works as a whole, one cannot but be impressed by the amount of space devoted to the biological-psychological works. A calculation[14] of the percentage of space devoted to biology and psychology shows that 30 per cent of the pages are given over to these subjects. No other topic is treated so extensively.

It was during this second stay in Athens that most of his definitive works on psychology were written or completed.[15] The predominantly psychological works include the master work, *On the Soul,* and shorter works, known collectively (and misleading) as the *Short Physical Treatises*, bearing such titles as *On the Sense and Sensible, On Memory and Reminiscence, On Sleep and Sleeplessness,* and *On Dreams.*

De Anima, On the Soul, is the first systematic treatise on psychology in that it deals with the functioning of the individual organism as a whole. It is, therefore, the first book concerned with psychology as a systematic science. The emphasis in *On the Soul* on the *whole* organism[16] serves to differentiate psychology from its biological neighbors, particularly physiology, the study of the functioning of organs; the focus in *On the Soul* on the *individual* differentiates psychology from what later were to be its social science neighbors. With this book, psychology as a discipline, consciously differentiated from other fields, comes into being. In writing it Aristotle became the first psychologist and the founder of psychology.

Aristotle's account of the earlier Greek thinkers in Book 1[17] gives us our first history of psychology and philosophy. Detailed and sharply critical, this analysis is most important for bringing out clearly his conviction that these previous thinkers had ignored the unity or oneness of the *psyche* or soul by dividing it into parts. They had also misstated the soul's relation to the body by separating one from the other. Moreover, they had limited the soul to man instead of extending it to all living things.

THE AIM OF ARISTOTLE

Above all, Aristotle claimed, he sought knowledge.[18] All kinds of knowledge are to be prized.[19] There is a sheer delight in exercise of the senses, quite apart from their usefulness in other matters.[20] (This last, by the way, is a point which it is impossible to imagine Plato making.)

All men, he held, begin by wondering that things are as they are.[21] It was from this human need of wonder that men began to philosophize.[22] Knowledge, more specifically understanding the cause of things, removes this wonder by abolishing ignorance.[23] The very definition of soul or *psyche* is that it is "a substance capable of receiving knowledge."[24] More specifically, intelligence is the faculty of *psyche* which gives this grasp.[25] Man alone is capable of intelligence or deliberation.[26] It follows that man is the only animal capable of acquiring knowledge.[27] It appears amply demonstrated that the aim of Aristotle was to seek knowledge.

Not only was Aristotle's aim to seek knowledge, he saw man as uniquely fitted for its pursuit. The very function of man's performance is to be in tune with his particular excellence, that of following the rational principle.[28]

While his goal was always to be knowledge, one might say knowledge of any sort, various kinds still need be distinguished—theoretical, practical and productive knowledge.[29] The theoretical sciences, in turn, were three in number. Pride of place goes to "first philosophy" which in the Middle Ages came to be called "Metaphysics" for no more reason than that Aristotle's lectures on the matter at hand were so placed by his editors that they came after those of physics. The other two theoretical sciences are mathematics and physics. This last, concerned with material nature, included what we call biology and psychology.

Knowledge, which involves the explanation of things (theoretical science), is more to be prized as on a higher intellectual plane than knowledge based on sense perception exclusively or on the skills of workmen.[30] Theoretical science seeks truth; practical knowledge eventuates in action.[31] Even more important, theoretical science involves that which could not be otherwise,[32] that is to say, science admits of but one true answer to a particular problem. Art and practical wisdom involves situations which are variable, those in which more than one solution is possible. This emphasis upon one true answer, something occurring without exception, was indicative of Aristotle's groping toward a concept of scientific law. In this area, however, law in terminology and concept to Aristotle was still a matter of jurisprudence and ethics, not of science. Not only is scientific knowledge universal in character, it follows from first principles and comes about as inclusions from demonstrations.[33] There are basic and indispensible characteristics of science. In discussing them we are turning to the issue of scientific method.

KNOWLEDGE AND SCIENTIFIC METHOD

In a remarkable introductory paragraph to his *Physics*, his major account of scientific inquiry, Aristotle wishes to consider what the scientist first encounters when he begins to think scientifically:

Now what is to us plain and obvious at first is rather confused masses, the elements and principles of which become known to us later by analysis. Thus we must advance from generalities to particulars; for it is a whole that is best known to sense-perception, and a generality is a kind of whole, comprehending many things within it, like parts. Much the same thing happens in the relation of the name to the formula. A name, e.g., 'round', means vaguely a sort of whole: its definition analyses this into its particular senses. Similarly a child begins by calling all men 'father', and all women 'mother', but later on distinguishes each of them.[34]

He is saying that out of this welter of sense experience there emerges the first one of the basic or indispensible characteristics of science, principles or basic truths. They serve as starting points from which one proceeds to particulars. While sense perception is concerned with particular instances, their content yields the rudimentary general principles from which we proceed inductively to higher and higher levels of principles, until the "true" principles are established. Knowledge is not possible through sense perception alone, since the senses give us only particulars without demonstration.[35] Sense perception is nevertheless necessary for knowledge acquisition.[36] To have knowledge, we must grasp the primary or first principles or, as he puts it elsewhere, the "'why' of it."[37]

In keeping with his definition of the soul or *psyche* as a substance capable of receiving knowledge, it is the locus for the growth of knowledge of the primary principles.[38] First principles themselves, he says elsewhere,[39] neither do nor could require demonstration.

Induction provides deductive reasoning with its basic principles (as do also sense perception and habit).[40] Thereafter, sometimes one proceeds from induction and sometimes from deduction.[41] There is no question, however, that Aristotle emphasized deduction, although seldom using the word as the name for the phase of thought complementary to induction. Instead, he spoke of demonstration, already identified as an indispensible characteristic of science.

The basic premises of demonstration are definitions.[42] Intuitive definition already exempted for reasons just given, he proceeds on the assumption "that all (scientific) events we do know by demonstration."[43] What is demonstration?

Demonstration is a kind of syllogism (although not all syllogisms are demonstrations).[44] A syllogism, in turn, is defined as a "discourse, in which certain things being stated, something other than what is stated follows of necessity from their being so."[45] This is a very wide definition covering any valid deductive argument, including, for example, Euclid's theorems. Passing over certain slight inaccuracies which need not concern us, we might use as an illustration of a syllogism: [46]

All theories based on empirical evidence deserve rational consideration. All psychological theories are based on empirical evidence. Therefore: All psychological theories deserve rational consideration.

All sciences have communion with one another because of this common element of demonstration.[47] However, the scientist needs to answer only questions that fall within his own field and not range over all of them indiscriminately.[48]

Despite his allegiance to logic and his tremendous contribution to the field, in actual practice he often disregarded logical considerations (which was fortunate for science). He was fully aware that besides syllogisms, induction, as such, may give proof. Shown by his frequent use of letters of the alphabet for major, minor and middle terms, and by explicit statement,[49] Aristotle was also aware that the subject matter content of deductive arguments is quite irrelevant to their validity. In other words, if false premises are used, the conclusion is untrue. "True," "false," or "empty" statements, such as the letters, may be used without the form of deductive argument being vitiated. His critics in the centuries to come were to disregard this and triumphantly proclaim that poor Aristotle never knew that by syllogistic reasoning one could not go beyond the truth of one's original premises.

Experience and observation are tests of his theories, astronomical and biological. Observation of hundreds of species of animals were carefully reported in his biological treatises. He even contrasted observation and theory. Concerning the method of generations of bees, for example, he comments that if we ever learn the truth of the matter, credit must be given to observation, not to theories, which we will accept only if they agree with the observation.[50]

In practice Aristotle sometimes would rush in with the few available facts and make sweeping generalizations. Naturally, he made mistakes. When working on a specific problem, his driving search for all knowledge did not allow him time to make sure of the ground before proceeding on to the next question. Moreover, sometimes he was not too critical of the facts he accepted. He was not above believing, without any attempt at verification, old wives tales and the accounts of credulous or sensation-seeking travelers. However, the major source of his difficulty was that enough facts simply were not available to him or to anyone else.

His emphasis upon classification, later often considered by historians of science to be a stage of science which must precede experiment, bears out this sheer lack of other information. Membership of an object in a given class was of crucial importance to him. This knowledge decided its essential nature or essence and marks his distinctive contribution to biology.[51]

SCIENCE AND CAUSE

We also know by means of cause.[52] In fact knowledge of them is the essence of scientific knowledge. Four causes underline everything—the material, motor or efficient, formal, and final.[53] Aristotle describes in considerable detail the nature and interrelation of each cause.[54] The material cause is that thing out of which it is made (*e.g.*, bronze of a statue); the motor or efficient cause is that which sets going the process leading to its production or making it move (*e.g.*, sculptor); the formal cause, is that which gives the definition of its essential character (*e.g.*, a horse); and the final cause, is that aim or end toward which a thing develops (*e.g.*, serving to decorate a temple). This position concerning causes was his solution to the problem posited by the Pre-Socratic philosophers over the causes of the world. He argued that his predecessors had given inadequate answers because of their preoccupation with the material cause only to the relative neglect of the other causes.[55] A major issue for Aristotle is whether the final or the efficient cause has priority.[56] Clearly, he asserts, it is the final cause, that for the sake of which the thing is formed. Hence, purpose is central.

Today, the efficient cause is generally what we mean by cause. Matter and form are not conceived as causes, but as static aspects to be found in a thing or object. This restriction arises because we require the meaning of cause to be that which is both "necessary and sufficient" to produce an effect. This meaning applies only to the efficient and the final causes. To Aristotle none of the four causes alone is sufficient; all are necessary. Thus to him "cause" meant conditions, none in themselves sufficient to account for the exist- ence of something. If his interpretation be followed, it is not surprising matter and form are causes, since, without them, nothing could be or come to be.

To call final cause, "purpose," as has often been done, sometimes is misleading because not all final causes have consciously foreseen ends, an implication of purpose often considered to be essential today. To Aristotle, human purposes do exist, people do display foresight and conscious intention, but purpose was but an aspect of final cause. No conscious purpose existed outside of human actions. Natural processes are final ends, purposes if you wish, but not conscious intents.

The prominence of end gives Aristotle's views a thoroughgoing teleological character. To say that Aristotle was a teleologist is to say that he held there was a plan or design to the universe. All things, including man, develop and move to an end, the final cause of their motion. Every instrument, including the human being, depends upon the nature of that for which it is designed. Anaxagoras had said that man was the most intelligent animal because he had hands; Aristotle reversed the statement saying that man had hands because he was an intelligent animal.[57]

Today, as a means of explaining a teleological position, a contrast often is offered between it and an explanation by efficient cause. Those who accept the teleological position are portrayed as denying efficient causes; those who accept efficient causes are said to deny final causes. In accepting both final and efficient causes (as well as formal and material causes), Aristotle was clearly more than a teleologist.

Insofar as he was a teleologist, Aristotle was also a functionalist. (See page 66.) That is to say, a search for end is also a search for function or what something does. For example, the eye, to Aristotle, seemed designed for seeing. The explanation of its structure which he gave lies in its function. It exists for seeing. The organism as a whole in its life history seems decided from the outset by a prevision of the form which is this actual outcome. Little acorns grow into mighty oaks if nothing hinders that growth. There is no wrong turning, and no beech or maple comes from the acorn. This functional cast dominates the discussion of his views of biology and psychology which is to follow.

BIOLOGICAL AND PSYCHOLOGICAL FUNCTIONS

In connection with Aristotle's classification of knowledge (see page 45), it was mentioned in passing that physics, one of the theoretical sciences, included biological and psychological aspects. Generally speaking, physics concerns natural things that are in motion.[58] What physical sciences, in general, have in common is that they concern things which have in themselves a principle of movement.[59]

Living things have a particular movement which arises from *psyche,* or soul.[60] "Movement" in this case should not be interpreted literally. *Psyche* is not self-moved; it does not transport itself in space (except incidentally as the body moves about). Movement is more figurative, more a principle than a literal movement, though *psyche* manifests itself in movements of various sorts. This movement shows varied manifestations, for example, locomotion, alteration, diminution, growth, sensation, and thinking.[61] Inclusion of what we would call both biological *and* psychological activities is evident. *Psyche* is of primary interest to Aristotle who wrote, in the same sentence where he claimed all knowledge to be valuable, that knowledge of the *psyche* is to be prized above all. (See page 45.)

The word *psyche* means both more and less for Aristotle than "soul." It means more in that *psyche* is integrated with matter. It means less in that *psyche* later acquired a variety of religious significances which are quite absent from Aristotle's thinking. Although soul is the customary translation of *psyche,* it is best to use the word without translation so as to avoid both the subtractions and the whole host of accretions "soul" has acquired over the centuries since Aristotle used it in his own way.

His particular conception of life as *psyche* marks Aristotle as a *vitalist.* (A vitalist believes that there is a principle peculiar and essential for the exhibition of the phenomena of life.) Vitalism stands in contrast to a mechanistic view. For example, Democritus was a mechanist, since his theory of atoms encompassed living and non-living objects alike; life was capable of mechanical expression. This was not the case with Aristotle who postulated a special principle, *psyche,* necessary for life and absent from non-animate things. The opposition of vitalistic and mechanistic views was one destined to extend throughout the history of science and still serves to trouble biologists to this very day.

Body, to Aristotle, is that of which living is composed, the *psyche* that which gives living its essential character. What is its essential character? Life in this perspective is defined in terms of entelechy. *Psyche* is first defined by Aristotle as "the first grade of actuality of a natural body having life potentially in it."[62] This is the first entelechy. In similar fashion, Aristotle then defined the second entelechy which is the operation of the function. The first entelechy has to do with possession of a function not being exercised or the potentiality of function: the second entelechy has to do with exercising that function. Illustrative of the first entelechy would be possessing knowledge when asleep, of the second entelechy exercising that knowledge when awake. It is the latter sense of performing the function with which we are primarily concerned. In this connection the sequence of first and second entelechies may cause confusion, since, in effect, the more important entelechy is the second, not the first. Yet Aristotle was being quite logical since the capacity is, after all, chronologically prior to actual exercise of a function. Moreover, the first entelechy (*psyche*) is the subject and source of operations, but they are known through the operation of living. *Psyche* is the principle of these operations.

Entelechy, as exercised in some function, has been variously defined in translation—the last stage in the process from potentiality to reality, the fullest realization, the culminating end, and the actuality. In the present setting, the complete expression of some function would seem to be the most apt way to express its meaning. The teleological implications of the way of thinking are plain in that it is the end toward which the *psyche* moves which Aristotle stressed.

To Aristotle, *psyche* basically meant living. It is again evident why psychology is an aspect of biology since all psychological phenomena are included among living activities. This view is what Nuyens[63] calls the biological conception of *psyche*. *Psyche*, it also becomes clear, is operative, then, throughout the whole scale of animate things and is not confined to man alone. *Psyche* marks not the distinction between thinking and unthinking beings, but that between living organisms and inorganic things. Hence, Aristotle's view is not mentalistic.

It will be remembered (see page 41) that Aristotle distinguished between matter and form. In this context, the body is the matter; the *psyche* is the form.[64] The illustrations used before of man, horse, and plant as matter and form now become illustrations of body and *psyche*. The constituents of the body are the matter; the form is the *psyche*. The living individual consists of both of them together. A dead body is only matter having no form of man.

In this setting a recasting of the traditional four causes is indicated. Instead of keeping them distinct and separate, Aristotle indicates that *psyche* functions not only as the formal, but also as the efficient and final causes of the body.[65] *Psyche* is the efficient cause since it sets the process going in the body; it is the formal cause since the being of the body means life; and it is the final cause since a body exists for living. So far as the final cause is concerned, it is Aristotle's way of saying that the body was made for *psyche,* that it exists for the sake of *psyche. Psyche* coincides, then, with three of the causes. The final, formal, and efficient causes all function as form and thus in an extended sense are formal, while the material cause is the passive recipient of form.

It follows from all of this, that when a natural state of affairs prevails, *psyche* dominates the body; when corrupted, the body dominates *psyche.*[66] Although he refers to it only casually and incidentally, Aristotle goes so far as to compare movement originated by *psyche* to that which animates automatic puppets.[67] This idea was to be developed by Descartes many centuries later, without, however, citing Aristotle as the source of inspiration. (See page 157.)

Body and *psyche* are not in dualistic contrast; they are unity.[68] They are aspects of the same living thing. This again is in disagreement with Plato. It will be remembered that Soul was not Form, according to Plato. (See page 26.) To Aristotle, *psyche* was essentially form in his own sense of the word. There is a unity and inseparability of body and *psyche* as an instance of matter and form.

The *psyche* as form and the body as matter, then, is unified, single, and indivisible. The form of body cannot exist without body with which it has an organic connection. What happens then to the *psyche* when the body is gone? One interpretation of Aristotle's views on immortality is dependent upon body and soul being a complete unit in which one cannot survive without the other. Soul cannot exist disembodied. This straight-forward, logically derived, and not unexpected view is to be found clearly stated in Aristotle in Book 1 of *On Psyche* which is devoted to a dialectical examination of the various views of *psyche* which weakens the argument somewhat.[69] Moreover, there is another view which is logically discordant with this position that is also to be found in Aristotle. This is the part of *On Psyche* considered as having been written in the earlier, Platonic phase of his thinking, and, consequently, it is not representative of his mature position. In it the highest element in man, *Nous,* not dependent upon the body, seems to have been thought of by him as immortal in that it survived the body. Here, however, we get into one of the most tangled webs, both of the thinking of the Middle Ages and of modern scholarship. Suffice it to say, that the elimination of the immortality of the psyche is *one* defensible interpretation of Aristotle.

The view of Aristotle concerning the relation of *psyche* and body should not be mistaken for a modern materialist or epiphenomenalist position. Life, according to this position, is an emergent characteristic—a resultant of the particular composition of the body. Life is thus subordinate to, and antecedent in time to, body. In Aristotelian terms this view would mean that form is subordinate to matter. Despite the fact that in the generative process[70] the matter of the body exists prior to *psyche,* this view is one Aristotle could not accept.

A body is composed of organs needed for the body's functions.[71] An organ, in turn, is made to fulfill a function.[72] This concept of "organic" we owe to Aristotle. Even plants, Aristotle said, have rudimentary organs, since roots are analogous to the mouth and serve to take in nourishment.[73] In contrast to Aristotle's functional definition, today we use the distinction between organic and inorganic structure to differentiate animate from inanimate things. This distinction on the basis of structure to Aristotle was but an incidental bit of information helping in his differentiation of life from non-life. He remained consistent in emphasizing the different ways living and non-living things behave over the existence of differences in bodily structure.

Aristotle does not seem to have made clear the physical means by which movement of the body was brought about. He did distinguish voluntary and involuntary motions. Motions of heart and sex organs "without the express mandate of the reason"[74] are illustrative of involuntary motions.

Psyche is found in every part of the body, argues Aristotle. This diffusion of *psyche* becomes less marked; the greater the degree of organization in the animal, the greater the degree of centralization and the less need for *psyche* in each part.[75] Despite *psyche* being diffused throughout the living body, a center in the body is necessary. Searching for a center, the point at which it actuates the body, Aristotle[76] found it in the heart, for the following reasons—diseases of the heart are fatal; psychological experiences, such as joy or sorrow, cause a disturbance of the heart; the heart is the first organ formed in the embryo (as in the egg, and its starting to palpitate shows that it has life). In identifying life with the *psyche* and this, in turn, with the heart, he also rejects the Platonic doctrine of the brain as the organ of the soul. He used as one argument for doing so the fact that he found the brain to be insensible to direct stimulation.[77] It is ironical that Plato was right for the wrong reasons. Plato assigned reason to the brain on the basis of several irrelevant reasons typical of which is the fact that the brain was the part of man nearest the heavens. Aristotle, on the other hand, was wrong for the "right," *i.e.,* naturalistic reasons.

Aristotle referred, just as did Plato, to "parts" of the *psyche*. Neither thinker meant "parts" in a literal sense. For the same reason that the term "aspects" was used instead of "parts" in discussing Plato, "general functions" will be used hereafter in discussing Aristotle's views on the matter. "Aspects" reflected the static view of Plato while "general functions" catches more accurately the dynamic view of Aristotle. The functions of *psyche* are exhibited in inclusive or general functions, which, in turn, may be broken down into more specific functions.

Aristotle makes clear that the various ways in which the *psyche* may be divided into general functions are indefinite in number. In practice the number of divisions most often used by him seemed to range from two to five, dependent upon his intent in discussion. Earlier in the chapter the general function of growing was used in precisely this way. Other divisions of function used by Aristotle are into rational and irrational; into growing, sensing, desiring, reacting, and knowing; and growing, sensing, and knowing. This last tripartite division referred to in a somewhat less functional way—nutritive, sensitive, and rational *psyche*—is the one most commonly used in summarizing the views of Aristotle.[78] However, the more functional growing, sensing, and knowing often will be used in the account to follow, especially when a convenient, quick way to summarize the functions of *psyche* is desired.

In living things there is an unbroken developmental hierarchy among levels of functioning; each higher level includes the lower levels of functioning in that it does not take place without them. The lower functions exist potentially in the higher function, or, to use Aristotle's own illustration, they function in the same manner as does the triangle existing potentially in the quadrilateral.[79] The highest act of thinking is in a chain of continuous development with sensing as the lowest form of discrimination.[80] This hierarchy serves to demonstrate that *psyche* has a unity with several related functions. This argument for the unity of *psyche*, in a slightly different perspective, may be seen as a theory of development. The growth *psyche* is included in the sensing (or animal) *psyche*, the sensing *psyche* in the knowing (or human) *psyche*.

It would be a serious misunderstanding of his point of view to conclude that Aristotle had arrived at a theory of evolution. Two major considerations show he did not anticipate a theory of evolution. The modern view of evolution teaches that species are not fixed, but mutable. Furthermore, the more complicated structures are seen as coming later than the simple ones and developing from them. On both these counts Aristotle took a diametrically opposed stand. Species had no origin for Aristotle; they were existent. A fully developed member of a species existed before young of that species were generated. In terms of that old puzzle, "Which came first, the hen or the egg?" Aristotle's answer would have been unequivocal—the chicken came before the egg. Aristotle's conception of the developmental hierarchy reverses present day evolutionary thinking. Aristotle said that the simpler function exists potentially in the more complex; evolutionary theory would say the more complex exists potentially in the simpler one. Reality precedes potentiality in that the simpler function exists potentially in the more complex reality. The higher, more developed function stands first. This view of Aristotle is not only non-evolutionary, it is teleological in that the higher stage represents the realization of the lower; it is its end. In every sphere of reality the higher levels include the lower.

While living was the fundamental activity, the master function as it were, there were different expressions of *psyche*. The more specific biological-psychological functions of growing, sensing, remembering, desiring and reacting, and thinking now merit examination.

Growing

Development of the organism is brought about by somewhat more specific activities which are included under the general function of growing. Briefly, these specific functions of growing are persistence of the living thing, its accession of things from its surroundings, and the increase in size of every particle of it.[81] Growing is the most widely distributed general function being shown by plants, animals, and men. It differentiates plants from other living things in that plants possess this general function and not sensing.[82] It is because of this relation to plants that a term popular in the Middle Ages, "vegetative soul," was applied to this general function.

In forms of life higher than plants growing is essential for the appearance of sensing and knowing. The specific functions of the general functions of growth are the necessary activities without which the higher general functions of sensing and knowing could not be carried out. It assures the conditions that make them possible. Although with psychological implications to Aristotle and to us, growing is sufficiently biological in nature to pass on to the functioning level of sensing as a specific function.

Sensing [83]

The specific function of sensing is possessed by animals and men, but not by plants. Indeed, the presence or absence of sensing (in what Aristotle considered to be its most primitive manifestation of touch) is the means of distinguishing what is and is not an animal.[84] In speaking of sensing objects, Aristotle meant in modern terminology that perceiving is involved. The function of sensing includes what is called *perceiving* today.

External senses are specified by Aristotle to be what has become the traditional five—sight, hearing, smell, taste, and touch—and no other. Aristotle's argument for there being but five external senses runs somewhat as follows: If we assume that all objects in this world are known to us through these external senses, then the assumption of a further sense would mean either it merely duplicates an existing sense or that it would have no object. These are both unthinkable consequences in a world in which each thing is designed for an end.

The senses each received detailed consideration. Aristotle saw touch as more complex than the others, a contention still followed, no matter how we subdivide the original five senses. Each sense organ is sensitive to one or more sets of qualities. For example, the eye is sensitive to color, including black and white.[85]

Sensation, as does growing, depends upon alteration or movement from without.[86] Sensitivity is an activity aroused in the organism by the environment. This necessity of dual functioning of organism and environment is based upon Aristotle's basic premise of movement or change which demands that the senses be related to the environment. However, the relation with the environment in sensing is different from that taking place in nutrition. Nutrition takes in the material object from the environment; plants and animals devour the nutritive object. A sweet fig nourishes the organism through the matter of fig: the form, sweetness, does not enter. In sensing there is received from the environment, not the object itself but its form, just as the wax received the form of the seal without assimilating the metal of which it is composed.[87] In sensing, the body responds to the *form* of the external object without being acted upon by the *matter*.[88] The environmental effect is formal, not material.

Sensing is actualized by the sensible quality of the object.[89] But it is not merely a passive process in assimilating form. At this point the sensing of the organ becomes "like" the sense object. The sense quality which is a potentiality of the object becomes actual through the action of the sense organs. The sky has the power of being seen as blue; the power of vision by means of the eyes of seeing blue. Hence, for Aristotle one does not see in the eyes but *with* the eyes.

The particular nature of sensing needs further specification. In commenting on Aristotle's view of the nature of sensing, Guthrie states it admirably. He writes: "The peculiarity of life is that *when* the bodily organ is materially altered by an external object, *then* another, totally different result supervenes, which we call sensation."[90] The objective stimulus is the cause of motion, *i.e.*, a change which proceeds through a medium in the sense organ or some other part of the body becomes transformed or, to use Aristotle's term, is actualized into consciousness. The sounding in the object and the hearing of the animal are different, as has just been explained, but when the process occurs, they are merged into one.[91]

Aristotle was struck by the fact that, although each of the senses had special organs and although each had special sensory qualities, nevertheless, when seeing white with the eye and hearing a sound with the ear, these sensory qualities from different senses are localized in the same perceived object in the environment. The question arose how do sensations of *qualities*, white, sweet, and so on, give a perception of concrete *things?* Moreover, there are perceptions which are not peculiar to any one of the senses. Movement, rest, shape, size, number, and duration are not experienced by any one sense alone. How, then, does one experience these so-called "common sensibles"? They seem to belong to or to be common to all senses, but not exclusively to any one of them. Moreover, there is the fact that one is aware of sensing as when one says, "I smell smoke," he means not only that the smell is experienced but also that he is aware he is smelling it. These considerations led Aristotle to postulate that there was a "common sense." The common sense was thought to carry out the functions of synthesizing the sensory elements into perceptions of units, the perception of common sensibles and consciousness that one is perceiving.

The particular argument of Aristotle for a composite functioning of the special senses in sensing self-perception may be stated as follows: If I do not perceive that I perceive in a single indivisible act when perceiving the stimulus, then there would be required another sense in order for me to know I was sensing. But this would require a third to unite the previous ones. But this, in turn, would require another sense to unite the three, and so on, by infinite regress. To cut this short, Aristotle asserts that the sense perceives itself. Hence the common sense depends on the functioning together of the various senses to account for what it does.

This distinction of form and matter has been applied to the relation of *psyche* and body, and to sense and sense organ now may be applied to self-perception itself, wherein the knower receives the qualities of an object. *Psyche* has form and apprehends form; the sense organ has form and apprehends form; the person has form and apprehends form.

Aristotle concerned himself with the question of a common sense being either a sixth sense or a composite of the single senses.[92] Despite some disagreement among authorities, it is in keeping both with Aristotle's naturalistic spirit and his argument about perceiving that one is inclined to accept the view that he thought of it as a composite and not as another sense.[93] The common sense functions through the common nature of all five senses assuring that there is one world we perceive, not one for each sense. It is not another or sixth sense, it is a name for certain functions for the five senses collectively. The other interpretation which would make common sense distinct from the five external senses is taken up in the chapter devoted to Aquinas.

The conscious being is always active. An admirable illustration may be found in Aristotle's account of sleeping,[94] a function which he considered related to the common sense. After all, one does not sleep with some senses awake (*i.e.*, active) and the others asleep. Hence, they function in common. Sleep is caused by fatigue of the common sense which loses vitality. Sleep, then, has a restorative function.

Aristotle was a shrewd observer who let few details escape him. For example, he argued, that sleep may also be brought about by food in the stomach. It seems compelling that this last point is based upon an observation open to all concerning the effects of a heavy meal. Instead, however, of attributing sleep to blood being withdrawn from the brain, Aristotle had to account for it in terms of his center for *psyche*, the heart. He did so in the following fashion. Digestion causes gases to descend to the heart, which in turn cause the heat of the body to collect around the heart. In a sense, then, sleep, according to Aristotle, is due to "heart burn"!

In sleeping only the growth functions are active; sleep is inhibition of conscious functioning. How, then, is a dream to be accounted for?[95] It is similar to sensation, Aristotle held, yet not the same since there is no object sensed. He concluded that in dreaming there is a persistence of the effects of sensory stimulation that occurred during the waking state carried over into sleeping.

Remembering [96]

Memory is related to sense perception.[97] There is a persistence of the effect of sense impressions. These perceptions allow us to exercise knowledge already acquired.

Remembering, just as in dreaming, arises from the effects of sensing that persist after the object is removed. Sensory stimulation "stamps in," as it were, an "impression of the percept."[98] These traces of former movements, called images, are one of the bases for remembering. There is a continuation of the original movement based on images. One also recognizes memory for what it is by the fact that one remembers having originally sensed the object or event. Memory consists, then, of remembering a perception of some event which had occurred before. To have memory one must have awareness of duration (time) and this perception. Remembering, as such, is related primarily to the general function of sensing and, hence, is shared with animals. But memory is also a faculty in and of itself. This is because its object is distinct and separable—the past precisely as past.

Recollecting (recalling) is not the same as remembering.[99] Remembering is the spontaneous reproduction of past perceptions, *i.e.*, a retention of the effects of past experience. Recalling is the active search to recover these past perceptions. This demands hard thinking, called deliberation by Aristotle in this context, since it involves a search in which one reasons he had the experience in question before. Hence, recollection unlike remembering, is limited to man, who alone has the power of deliberation.[100]

It was in connection with recalling that Aristotle introduced the now famous doctrine of the laws of association. Recalling occurs because we are able to call up a series of associations "in regular order," [101] *i.e.*, according to specified principles. Plato in an off-hand fashion had referred to two of the ways recollection operates as being through similarity and continuity, without, however, developing the notion further.[102] It fell to Aristotle, if not to be the first to recognize these principles, to be the first to develop them systematically. He considered that three sorts of relationships serve as links in the chain of associations—similarity, contrast, and contiguity.[103] Recalling occurs in that experiences succeed one another in memory. This is to say that the recalling of an object tends to be followed by the recalling of what is like (similar to it), contrary (contrasted with) to it, or accompanied (contiguous with) it in the original learning.

Although similarity, contrast, and contiguity were historically to form the basis for the doctrine of association in the centuries to come, three other factors relevant to modern learning theory also are mentioned by Aristotle. Aristotle was aware of the contention that the more often an experience is repeated, the better it will be remembered.[104] He spoke of "some" experiences as being better remembered after a single experience than others experienced many times. Remembering after only a single experience is a qualification of a more general norm, not specifically verbalized, that the more an experience is repeated, the better it will be remembered. "Bonds of association" also are seen by Aristotle as acquiring special strength from emotion. He indicated that when excited by love or by fear, the person can see his desired one or the feared one approaching despite there being little resemblance.[105] He goes on to state that the more one is under the influence of emotion, the less "similarity" is necessary for this to happen. Aristotle also spoke of things arranged in a "fixed" order as more easily recalled than "badly" arranged items.[106] Something approaching the distinction between meaningful and rote materials is suggested in this identification of order of materials as a potent factor in recall.

Desiring and Reacting

In some of his writings Aristotle lifted desiring (appetite, conation) to equal status with growing, sensing, and knowing and spoke of four general functions.[107] Desiring is related to sensing and pleasure-pain, which gives rise to it, and has consequences in reacting.

Sensing, pleasure-pain, desire, and self-motion form a sequence. The process is as follows: pleasure and pain follow upon sensing, although not a part of sensing itself. Rather, they are consequences of sensory experiences.[108] As explained earlier, sensing is the means whereby objects in the environment are perceived. Now some of these objects are perceived as pleasurable, others as unpleasurable. After sensing has taken place, these feelings may be experienced. Once these feelings are experienced, desire is introduced. Where there is sensing, there is pleasure and pain; where there is pleasure and pain, there is desire.[109] Ignoring pain for the moment, craving or desiring in the organism is for the satisfaction that the perceived object will give. It should be noted that desire is related to sensing in a circular fashion since sensing is followed by pleasure and pain, which in turn arouses desire, and desire is a craving for the pleasant and avoidance of the painful. So far, sequentially accounted for are sensing, pleasure-pain and desiring, which leaves reacting to be brought into the sequence.

Desire, says Aristotle, is the immediate and efficient cause of movement.[110] Locomotion is also related through pleasure and pain to desire since it takes us toward an object we desire or away from one we desire to avoid. As Aristotle puts it, only in seeking pleasure and in avoiding pain is the animal moved, unless moved by compulsion.[111] Pleasure and pain are not simple impressions following sensing; they incite to desire which brings about local movement or locomotion. This completes the process from sensing to self-movement. This sequence, however, is subject to an important qualifying addition in that thinking, too, is a source of movement. (See page 62.)

Aristotle's theory of the nature of pleasure and pain was an extension and modification of the old familiar doctrine that pleasure is that which is according to nature and pain that which is contrary to nature.[112] Pleasure and pain, as has already been said of his views, are the concommitants or accompaniments of activities. Aristotle held that pleasure accompanies the free expression of activity, an unimpeded exercise of the functions of the *psyche*. If the experience is painful, it is so because it conflicts with the natural state of the functioning of the *psyche*. The exercise of realization of any natural function of living is pleasurable and, to add a new aspect, the pleasure is proportional to the completeness of the realization. Pleasure, moreover, is related to exercise of a function. When an activity is pleasurable, it tends to be exercised—those who delight in geometry become geometricians.[113] The presence of instances of pathological pleasure is not an objection to this claim that freedom and naturalness characterize pleasure since Aristotle held that these abnormal pleasures come about from one sort or another of a diseased condition of the body and not from psychological activities.

In his analysis of psychological motion, or to put it in more modern terms, his analysis of psychological field forces, Aristotle appealed to a concept of "unmoved mover."[114] Its use in connection with desire was straightforward and objective. In the relation of desiring individual and desired object, the latter served as a stimulus, or "mover," as he called it. But this mover was not similarly affected by desire. Consequently it was an "unmoved mover." In a sense, then, the object of desire, the unmoved mover, is outside the process of the functioning organism. Aristotle argued that every action has an "unmoved mover." As a consequence the number of "unmoved movers" would be impossible to count.

The "unmoved mover" was seized upon by scholars in later ages in their search for God in Aristotle and a single "supreme unmoved mover" was lifted to theological heights. Many of his remarks lend credence to this position.[115] In the analysis of the number of kinds of motion his highest order attempt at unification reached only either forty-seven or fifty-five kinds of unmoved movers. But in this same discussion he spoke of one eternal mover whose essense was actuality. It would seem as if this analysis of unmoved movers occurred in two different realms—one concerned with kinds of motion, the other with a theological necessity. Whatever the significance of it for philosophy may be, his use in psychology of the concept of the "unmoved mover" was singularly free from these complications. In baldest terms he seemed to mean that for every reaction there was a stimulus.

Aristotle resembles Plato in that, in the main, his interest in pleasure and pain are placed in a setting of other than psychological issues. It is convenient to add emotions at this point to the further discussion of pleasure and pain, since this was true for them as well. Despite their setting being elsewhere, Aristotle often gave a psychological turn to discussion of these topics. His *Rhetoric*[116] and his *Nichomachean Ethics*[117] contain the major relevant material.

Illustrative of how he relates psychological implications to philosophical concerns is to be found in his treatment of emotions and desires as they relate to the moral virtues. These virtues include courage which necessitates a psychological discussion of fear, temperance which requires that desires be considered in a psychological setting, and good temper which demands consideration of the psychology of anger. Other psychological matters are discussed in a similar vein. The various emotions are analyzed in terms of the disposition which gives rise to the particular emotion, the person towards whom it is directed, and the occasions which give rise to it.[118] A descriptive view of the emotions which is essentially practical in nature emerges. Since it lacks the systematic significance of his other psychological work, there is no need for details.

His comments concerning emotion extended even into his theory of the fine arts, including the theatre. In discussing the nature of tragedy as shown in plays, he indicated that its function is to arouse pity and fear but in such fashion and in such amounts that will allow us to purge ourselves of these emotions.[119] This is the famous doctrine of catharsis. Catharsis is brought about by transfering to the tragic hero our own sufferings. In him we see ourselves, and, in his fate, our doom. But since this is not the actual situation, since his particular fate is not ours, we shift our fear into fear for him. This emotional use of the play allows us to release our apprehensions and to deflect our psychic burdens to another's shoulders. Self-pity gives way to compassion, and we are the better for the experience.

Thinking

Man may behave in this fashion with desire leading to activity; he may also take thought,[120] which may or may not be followed by action. In other words, not only appetite but also thinking, in which calculation of means to an end becomes part of the sequence, may precede action.

Action is by no means all sorts of movement. Consistent with what was just said, action is a kind of movement in which an end is involved.[121] All other movements are just that and nothing more, since they are not complete in that they do not involve an end. Again Aristotle is seen to be both functional and teleological in approach.

Some animals not only have the functions of sensing but also that of imagining, but they do not have that of thinking. The presence of imagining in animals marks it as the *highest* of their functions. As Aristotle conceived it, man is the only animal that thinks.[122]

Thinking, to Aristotle, is a process which is dependent upon the hierarchically lower general functions. It is not completely separable since each higher level presupposes the lower ones. Those functions which bear a hierarchical relation to thinking are sensing, imagining, and remembering. Thinking requires sensory experiences with which to work and sensing leads to its derivative, imagining, and this in turn to the latter's special expression in remembering. The materials of thinking are supplied by imagination. In this case, images serve as if they were perceptions.[123] Without retaining images, thinking could not function. These images are moulded by thinking into relations and patterns, so that there is not merely a flux of images but meaningful organization.

Aristotle's insistence that images are an inevitable necessity for thinking is worth stressing. On his position he left no doubt—thinking takes place in images[124] and never without them.[125] His influence was such that dependence on this Aristotelian dogma of no image-no thought, was to last well into the modern period, indeed, until the turn of the twentieth century and the Wurzburg School. (See page 292.)

By a shift of perspective from remembering to thinking, association becomes an integral aspect of the latter. (See page 59.) Similarity, contrast contiguity and the rest bring about associations that we refer to as thinking.

Thinking was not seen by Aristotle to function to suppress natural impulses. Suppression of any natural human function was considered a deficit.[126] It was distortion of the natural. Fear and anger and other emotions had their suitable occasions when they were appropriate. There are things we ought to fear, and there are occasions when we should be angry. Thinking does not suppress the emotions; they help to determine right conduct.

Quite explicitly Aristotle says that thinking as a higher function does not exist apart from the lower, but that the lower can exist apart from the higher functions.[127] However, in all justice it must be added that he goes on to say that knowing, "with immediate intuition presents a different problem." [128] This last comment takes us to the problem of knowing itself.

Epistemological Analysis of Knowing

Going beyond thinking, as the term has been used here, carries us into the disputed books of *On the Soul*. With Jaeger[129] it is accepted that the doctrine of *nous*, or knowing, was formulated by Aristotle before his interest in empirical psychology. Moreover, even if these books are accepted as representing the acme of Aristotle's thinking, as many scholars do, it may be argued that from present perspective, their content goes beyond psychology into epistemology.

The study of knowing is not psychological in the sense the study of thinking is, but it is an epistemological issue, a problem in the nature and validity of knowledge. Despite the fact that knowing is not considered to be part of his formulation of psychology, it nevertheless is discussed because it became very important to the interpreters of Aristotelian psychological doctrine in later ages.

It will be remembered that the form of particular objects was perceived in the sensory process. The form that was assimilated in sensing was of particular objects. In other words, particulars are perceived through sensing and used in related functions, such as thinking. Sensing is always aroused by a particular object. This is not the case with knowing.[130]

Nous, or knowing, essentially is a capacity to actualize pure forms, to make universals capable of being apprehended by human beings. As soon as we pass beyond color or magnitude or man and begin to ask what *is* color, magnitude, or man, we are considering universals, not particulars. Universals are not objects and cannot be brought about by the perceiving process. They must be explained by something else. This process was called "knowing" by Aristotle. Knowing serves the same critical discriminating function as did sensorially based thinking. Knowing in this sense is a general term to denote the non-sensorially derived activities of the critical discriminating capacity of the person.

Through knowing, the *psyche* explores the completely immaterial—the realm of pure forms. Aristotle reasoned that to know the immaterial there must be similarity between receiver and received; hence, the receiver, too, must be immaterial. There are passages[131] that seem to imply that when *nous* is knowing, knowing is identical with the form known and that knowing as actualized is identical with the form.[132] One writer[133] in considering this particular point, indicates that one could hardly imagine a closer relation between organism and environment.

From what was said earlier about a part of the *psyche* itself must be potentially the same as the object of thought,[134] it follows that knowing has no actual existence except when in operation. The *nous* as a capacity is the place of forms and is not actualized except when knowing. The *nous* as capacity cannot be said to know at times and at other times not to know.

Knowing is "active" in that it is never passive, only existing when acting.[135] "Passive reason" as distinguished from "active reason," on the other hand, receives from without and corresponds more or less to thinking as previously described. All knowledge in one sense is perceptually derived, but this material cannot be converted into knowing without the supplementary activity of creative reason. In this way it is *created*.

Sensing, being directly dependent for its data upon sense organs, is capable of being distorted. A sensation can be too intense, a sound too loud, a light too bright so it is not perceived. They are too strong, not for the *psyche*, but for the physical organ's capacity to receive. Thinking, too, may be wrong, but true knowing is incapable of error. *Nous* assimilates pure form precisely to the degree that, in sensing, the form of objects is assimilated. Since knowing assimilates pure form, error is impossible when the process is genuinely carried out. True knowing, as differentiated from thinking as the latter term is used here, is not subject to error.

In spite of this separation of the processes, sensing and thinking do bear relations to knowing. Aristotle is quite clear and explicit on this point; without passive reason (thinking) there is no thought of any sort.[136] Although one does not know the reason for things from sense, one draws them from sense experiences. After a certain number of experiences of a fact, *i.e.*, perceiving that fact, the universal explanation or reason comes by an act of knowing.[137] To use Aristotle's own illustration, it is not Callias, but Callias as a man, that we perceive. Knowing seems to be immediate and intuitive, an immediate act of consciousness. Sensing takes us so far and no further; the new process that then takes over is curiously akin to what today might be called insight or even "intuition."

Knowing is not a cause of movement.[138] This is in sharp distinction from thinking which is concerned with desire and movement. Knowing thinks nothing that is practical; it is not concerned with objects to be avoided or to be pursued. This characteristic, alone, is enough to eliminate knowing from the field of psychology as we see it today, since it involves experience without the possibility of effecting movement. Hence, knowing is referred to as pure reason, while thinking, psychology's concern, is called practical reason.

Although not integral parts of the theory, three important implications of knowing for other doctrines must be discussed. The first issue is the question of whether or not there is implicit in knowing a return to Platonic Forms. This implication may be disposed of quickly. This formulation does not bring about a return to the theory of Platonic Form in disguise. There is a critical difference. The universal, although real and objective, has no *separate* existence.[139] Forms, to Aristotle, are still individual.

The second implication has to do with the theological-philosophical significance of the theory for workers in later ages. It has already been established that knowing is independent of bodily activity. Aristotle also says of knowing that "this alone is immortal,"[140] merely adding that we do not remember its former activities because the passive knowing (as in thinking) is destructible with the body. Aristotle insisted that knowing was a "part" or a function of *psyche,* but, being independent, it bore no hierarchical relation to the other functions. This resulted in a break in the continuity so much insisted upon before. The immateriality of knowing as differentiated from the materiality of other functions of *psyche* is signalized by knowing being eternal and not perishable as were the other functions. Thus, Aristotelian commentators in the Middle Ages and later were in a position to interpret that he was saying a part of the soul was immortal.

The third implication concerns knowing or *nous* and the mind-body problem. Sometimes *nous* is translated into English as "mind." Just as there were objections to translating *psyche* as "soul," so too are there objections to translating *nous* as mind. Mind, since Descartes, had been involved in the so-called mind-body problem. In this controversy, mind and body are contrasted in various ways. *Nous,* as functioning with universals, is contrasted by Aristotle not with body, but with particularity. The issue at hand is that of the relation of particularity and universality, not that of body and mind. There is still another major objection to translating *nous* as mind. Mind, as it is conceived today, involves both sensing and thinking. With Aristotle it bore only a slight overlapping relation with the former and was confined almost entirely to thinking as expressed within the meaning of knowing. It would seem that "mind" and "*nous*" should not be considered synonymous.

OVERVIEW

Aristotle gave us the first functional view of mind. Mind still was sometimes treated as a substance (his *Metaphysics,* in fact, is a great treatise on substance), but psychological mind has its source in a principle of movement. In this way function predominates. The *psyche* is not isolated from the thing known. This yields a functional definition. *Psyche* is a *process; psyche* is what the *psyche* does. The inner structure of *psyche* is supported and partly guided by a field of external relations. This field, this environmental world, cannot be defined unless we consider as an integral part of it what we do in response to it. Organism and environment are two aspects of the same interacting process. Psychological functions are understood in terms of some object or objective toward which they are directed. A psychological activity is a response directed to this object or objective; desiring is understood in terms of that which is desired; thinking is understood in terms of that which is thought.

Although no doubt it would be pleasing to be able to claim Aristotle as the first psychologist interested in the scientific study of behavior and, therefore, a precursor for the present behavioral emphasis, this hope must be dashed in view of his contentions concerning "action" which, as we already know, are the only motions of psychological significance. Actions are always particular[141] and, as we have seen, science is not concerned with particulars, but universals. To put the same point in a somewhat different way, he holds that actions are concerned with individuals, and to drive home the point further, he adds that knowledge of all actions is the result of experience and not theory.[142] Further, actions involve practical and not philosophical wisdom.[143] Behavior, as such, was not open to scientific study from Aristotle's point of view.

The continuity of psycho-biological development is another major guiding concept in the thinking of Aristotle. If one disregards his doctrine of knowing, his account of psychological functioning from thinking, the highest level, down to growing, the lowest level, has been found to be consistent throughout all of his teachings.

He also did much to advance an empirical point of view. Before Aristotle, some of the Pre-Socratics and Sophists had taken a position of extreme sensationalism; Plato had taken a position of extreme rationalism. Reconciling these two, Aristotle took a mediating position of empiricism. Aristotle held that knowledge was gained from sense experience *and* thinking. In contrast to Plato, Aristotle was naturalistic in outlook. He kept within the realm of the natural world, within the natural processes of living, sensing, and thinking. When he ventured "beyond" physics, as did all the Greeks, his position was commendably cautious although not without fire and conviction.

Aristotle did much to lay the groundwork for later conceptions of memory and thinking. His associative principles of memory and thinking of similarity, contrast, contiguity, frequency, emotional effect and degree of meaningfulness were to have a most remarkable vitality since in modern guise they are still very much a part of psychology today.

In the centuries to come Aristotle's teachings on psychology were to be adopted by the Church, particularly through the promulgation and reconciliation with theological doctrine provided by Aquinas. (See chapter 6.) With various shifts of fortune they tended to dominate up to the beginning of the modern period.

More than any one other factor, his insistence upon the primacy of final cause over efficient cause was to result in his overthrow during the scientific revolution of the sixteenth and the seventeenth centuries in which the physical description of natural processes concerned itself more with efficient cause and consequent effect. To be sure, this was not the case with the more biologically minded Leibniz and Harvey who fought a valiant rear-guard action in defense of purpose and teleology. Gradually thereafter this doctrine disappeared or rather merged with a more general functional viewpoint.

Study of Aristotle is rewarded by a feeling of wonder at the newness, the freshness, the modernity of much of what he was saying. It is with Aristotle that, for the first time, we have a reasonably complete, rounded picture of psychology as a whole. He was, of course, wrong in many of his "facts" and he omitted important topics; but the overall frame with but a few changes can be discerned to bear more than a resemblance to that of modern psychology. Aristotle was the first psychologist.

REFERENCES [*]

1. The account of Aristotle's life and works leans heavily upon those by J. H. Randall, *Aristotle* (New York: Columbia University Press, 1960) and by W. Jaeger, *Aristotle: Fundamentals of the History of His Development.* (Oxford: Claredon Press, 1934). The chronology of his works given by Jaeger (*ibid.*) is followed and supplemented by that of F. J. Nuyens, The Evolution of Aristotle's Psychology. (*Proc. Xth Int. Cong. Phil., Amsterdam,* 1948, pp. 1101–1104).

2. T. W. Organ, *An Index to Aristotle: in English Translation.* Princeton: Princeton University Press, 1949.

3. Jaeger, *op. cit.*; Nuyens, *op. cit.*

4. Aristotle, Works. (Translated under direction of W. D. Ross) In R. M. Hutchins (ed.), *Great Books of the Western World.* (Vols. 8–9) Chicago: Encyclopaedia Britannica, 1952. (*c.*340–322 B.C.); *Physics,* 193b 22–194a 18.

5. *Ibid.,* 193b 35, p. 270.

6. *On the Soul,* 428a 11.

7. *Metaphysics,* 990a 33–993a 16, 1040a 9, 1078b 6–1079b 11, 1086a 18–1087a 25; *On Interpretation,* 17a 38.

8. *Physics,* 194b 12.

9. *Ibid.,* 324b 5–22.

10. *Ibid.,* 194b 9, p. 271.

11. *Categories; On Interpretation; Prior Analytics; Posterior Analytics; Topics; On Sophistical Refutations.*

12. From *peri,* a prefix meaning "around," and *patos,* meaning "a path."

13. W. D. Ross, *Aristotle: a Complete Exposition of His Works and Thought.* (5th ed.) New York: Meridian, 1959, p. 14.

[*] See page 16 for description of reference style.

14. In the edition used (*op. cit.*) the total of his complete works are given in 1415 printed pages. The so-called "Biological Treaties" occupy 331 pages, while *On the Soul* and the other psychological works occupy 98 more for a total of 429 pages or 30 per cent of the total. The obvious danger that the contents may belie the titles given is obviated by the fact that Aristotle was remarkably consistent in sticking to the subject about which he said he was writing.

15. For the purposes of this presentation Jaeger's (*op. cit.*) opinion about the dating of the books of *De Anima* is followed instead of that of Nuyens (*op. cit.*) This means that the discussion of *Nous* in *De Anima* III, Chapters 4 and 5, is considered as an earlier position in harmony with earlier ethical and metaphysical views, but not expressive of his final thinking. The doctrine of the *Nous* as making all things and being separate, deathless, eternal and impersonal is questioned. This is a matter of a judgment with which, at least, Nuyens would disagree—and he has some cogent arguments for arguing that this doctrine represents a final phase of Aristotle's thinking. It is agreed with both Nuyens and Jaeger that some of the physical treatises date from the transition period.

16. *Metaphysics,* 1040b 5.

17. *On the Soul,* 404a 1–411b 30.

18. *Metaphysics,* 980a 1.

19. *On the Soul,* 402a 1–4.

20. *Metaphysics,* 980a 22.

21. *Ibid.,* 983b 14.

22. *Ibid.,* 500a–501a.

23. *Ibid.,* 501b–c.

24. *Topics,* 151b 1 p. 206.

25. *On Dreams,* 458b 3.

26. *On the Soul,* 443a 12; *On the Parts of Animals,* 642b 18; *Politics,* 1332b 5.

27. *Topics,* 130b 8, 132a 20, 133a 21, 134a 15, 140a 36.

28. *Nicomachean Ethics,* 1097b 25–1098a 20.

29. *Metaphysics,* 1025b 25ff.

30. *Ibid.,* 981a 12–982a 4.

31. *Metaphysics,* 993b 21.

32. *Nicomachean Ethics,* 1140b 2.

33. *Ibid.,* 1140b 31–1141a 1.

34. *Physics,* 184a 21–b 14, p. 259. This description of psychological "individuation within a total mass" as it might be called, showed Aristotle's appreciation of the Gestalt properties of perceptual wholes long before that point of view became prominent on the psychological scene.

35. *Posterior Analytics,* 87b 28–88a 17.

36. *On Dreams,* 458b 2.

37. *Physics,* 195b 19, p. 271; *Metaphysics,* 983a 25, 993b 23, 994b 29.

38. *Prior Analytics,* 99b 15–100b 17.

39. *Nichomachean Ethics,* 1141a 8.

40. *Ibid.,* 1098b 1–8.

41. *Ibid.,* 1139b 18–35.

42. *Posterior Analytics,* 90b 24.

43. *Ibid.,* 72b 16, p. 98.

44. *Prior Analytics,* 25b 28.

45. *Ibid.,* 24b 18–20, p. 39.

46. J. Lukasiewicz, *Aristotle's Syllogistic.* (2nd. ed.) Oxford: Clarendon, 1957, Chap. 3.

47. *Posterior Analytics,* 77a 26.

48. *Ibid.,* 77b 7.

49. *Rhetoric,* 1356b 8.

50. *On the Generation of Animals,* 760b 70.

51. *E.g., On the Parts of Animals,* 639a 1–642b 4.

52. *Posterior Analytics,* 94a 20.

53. *On the Generation of Animals,* 715b 3–5.

54. *Physics,* 194b 16–195b 30; *On the Soul,* 415b 8–11; *Metaphysics,* 1013a 24–1014a 25.

55. *Metaphysics,* 983b 7–985b 22.

56. *On the Parts of Animals,* 639b 12–640a 12.

57. *Ibid.,* 687a 8.

58. *Physics,* 185a 12.

59. *Metaphysics,* 1064a 17.

60. *On the Soul,* 415b 8–28, 432a 14–434a 22; *On the Motion of Animals,* 700b 4–701a 6, 701a 35, 702a 35, 703a 2.

61. *On the Soul,* 406a 13, 413a 24, 415b 19–27.

62. *Ibid.,* 412a 30, p.642.

63. F. J. Nuyens, *L'evolution de la Psychologie d'Aristotle.* Louvain: Institut Supérieur de Philosophie, 1948.

64. *On the Soul,* 412a 12–413a 10.

65. *Ibid.,* 415b 8–11; *On the Parts of Animals,* 645b 15; *On the Generation of Animals,* 715b 3–5; *Metaphysics,* 1044a 37–1044b 1.

66. *Politics,* 1254a 31–b 4.

67. *On the Motion of Animals,* 701b 1–5.

68. *On the Soul,* 412a 12–413a 10.

69. *Ibid.,* 403a 2–b 19.

70. *Politics,* 1334b 20.

71. *On the Generation of Animals,* 716a 25.

72. *On the Parts of Animals,* 687a 11.

73. *On the Soul,* 412b 3.

74. *On the Motion of Animals,* 703b 3–704a 3, p. 239.

75. *Ibid.,* 703a 38.

76. *On the Parts of Animals,* 657a 25, 656a 30; *On the Motion of Animals,* 703b 24; *On the Generation of Animals* 734b 26.

77. *On the Parts of Animals,* 656a 18–28.

78. *E.g., On the Generation of Animals,* 736b 15.

79. *On the Soul,* 414b 29.

80. *Posterior Analytics,* 99b 35.

81. *Generation and Corruption,* 321a 19-b 12.

82. *E.g., On the Soul,* 424a 33; *On the Parts of Animals,* 666a 35.

83. The major discussion of the five senses occupies chapters 5 through 12 of Book II of *On the Soul,* 416b 31–424b 19. (Herrnstein & Boring's Excerpt No. 1 gives a major portion of these chapters).

84. *On the Sense and Sensible,* 436b 10.

85. *On the Soul,* 418a 27ff.

86. *Ibid.,* 415b 24–416b 32.

87. *Ibid.,* 424a 16–24.

88. *Ibid.,* 425b 22–24.

89. *Ibid.,* 417a 10–418a 6, 418b 27–419b 11.

90. W. K. GUTHRIE, *The Greek Philosophers: from Thales to Aristotle.* New York: Harper, 1950, p. 149.

91. *On the Soul,* 425b 27.

92. *Ibid.,* 424b 20–427a 15.

93. *E.g., ibid.,* 424b 20–22.

94. *On Sleep and Sleeplessness,* 953b 12–958a 32.

95. *On Dreams,* 458b 1–464b 18.

96. *On Memory and Reminiscence,* 449b 1–453b 11. (Herrnstein & Boring Excerpt No. 65 gives the portion devoted to associative memory).

97. *Ibid.,* 450a 14, 541a 16; *Posterior Analytics,* 99b 36–100a 8; *Sense and Sensible,* 441b 23–24.

98. *On Memory and Reminiscence,* 450a 31, p. 691.

99. *Ibid.,* 451a 21–453b 11.

100. *Ibid.,* 453a 13.

101. *Ibid.*, 451b 11, p. 693.

102. PLATO, Dialogues. (Translated by B. Jowett) In R. M. Hutchins (ed.), *op. cit.*, Vol. 7, (*c*.390–348 B.C.); *Phaedo*, 73c.

103. *On Memory and Reminiscence*, 451b 19–21.

104. *Ibid.*, 451b 11.

105. *On Dreams*, 460b 2.

106. *On Memory and Reminiscence*, 452a 3.

107. *On the Soul*, 432b 3.

108. *Ibid.*, 414b 5.

109. *Ibid.*, 413b 23.

110. *Ibid.*, 433a 5–434a 22; *On the Motion of Animals*, 701a 35, 703a 5.

111. *On the Soul*, 432b 17.

112. *Nicomachean Ethics*, 1174b 4.

113. *Ibid.*, 1175a 34.

114. *On the Soul*, 434b 33.

115. *E.g. Metaphysics*, 1071b 3–1075a 14, *passim; On the Motion of Animals*, 699a 12–700a 26.

116. *Rhetoric*, 1378a 20–1388b 30.

117. *Nicomachean Ethics*, 1105b 19–1106a 14, 1108a 30–1109b 27, 1111b 4–18.

118. *Rhetoric*, 1378a 20.

119. *On Poetics*, 1149b 27.

120. *On the Soul*, 433a 5–434a 22; *On the Motion of Animals*, 701a 1–b 33.

121. *Metaphysics*, 1048b 22.

122. *On the Soul*, 433a 12.

123. *Ibid.*, 432b 14.

124. *Ibid.*, 431b 2.

125. *Ibid.*, 431a 16.

126. *Nicomachean Ethics*, 1103a 14–1109b 27.

127. *On the Soul*, 415a 7.

128. *Ibid.*, 415a 11.

129. JAEGER, *op. cit.*

130. *On the Soul*, 417b 10–27.

131. *Ibid.*, 429b.

132. *Ibid.*, 430a.

133. C. SHUTE, *The Psychology of Aristotle*, New York: Columbia University Press, 1941.

134. *On the Soul*, 431b 17.

135. *Ibid.*, 429a 10–430a 25.

136. *Ibid.*, 430a 25.

137. *Posterior Analytics*, 87b 27.

138. *On the Soul*, 430b 27.

139. *Metaphysics* 1086a 18–1087a 25.

140. *On the Soul*, 430a 23.

141. *Nicomachean Ethics*, 1110b 6.

142. *Metaphysics*, 981a 1.

143. *Nicomachean Ethics*, 1141b 21.

CHAPTER 4

THEOPHRASTUS AND GALEN:

THE HELLENISTIC AND ROMAN PERIODS

THE HELLENISTIC PERIOD

WITH the death of Aristotle and Alexander, Greek history, science, and philosophy entered its third phase, the Hellenistic Period, which extended from about 300 to 100 B.C. Following its conquest by Alexander, Greek culture began to spread over the Near East with profound effects upon subsequent political and intellectual history. Aspects of Greek culture were carried eastward; aspects of Oriental culture were carried westward. The Hellenistic Period is often referred to as the twilight of Greek thinking, but this does not mean that the decline was abrupt. Progress was made by men who came after, but they were cast in the shadow created by their proximity to Aristotle. So far as psychology was concerned, a lesser man advanced it in the sense that his views were more modern in spirit than his master. This man was Theophrastus.

THEOPHRASTUS

When Aristotle was obliged to leave Athens in 323–322 B.C., he appointed Theophrastus his successor as head of the Lyceum. Only twelve years or so younger than Aristotle, being born about 372 B.C., Theophrastus had first come to Athens to study under Plato, and had become a friend of Aristotle, and joined him in his travels and shared in the study of natural history. Despite his closeness in age to Aristotle, Theophrastus lived long enough to serve as head of the Lyceum for thirty-five years. He died in 287 B.C., complaining that life was so short that a man must go just when he is beginning to understand life's mysteries.

During the lifetime of Aristotle, Theophrastus had paid special attention to the study of botany, and he continued this work after his master's death. His two treatises on plants made him the founder of botany just as Aristotle's works founded zoology. As if this were not enough for one man, no less than 227 treatises on such varied topics as religion, politics, education, rhetoric, mathematics, astronomy, logic, natural history, meterology, ethics, and psychology are ascribed to him![1] He showed an unflagging zeal in his scientific inquires and continued the pattern laid down by Aristotle of systematically collecting and reviewing the material, sometimes with the aid of other experts.

In most matters he followed Aristotle faithfully but tended to be even more empirical. He sought for an empirical basis for scientific theories and argued that the facts should not be forced artificially into a theory.[2] Reacting against the major role assigned by Aristotle to the search for final causes, he held that science was concerned more with efficient causes than with teleological causes, although the latter are accepted explicitly.[3] This was an anticipation of the advance not actually made until the time of Galileo, when it was realized that final causes are scientifically irrelevant.

In expressing these objections and reservations he shows an even more naturalistic, modern spirit. Theophrastus went into much more detail in describing the observable processes of the mind—sensation, perception, pleasure and pain, emotion, and temperament—than had his master. All of these are more important for modern psychology than the *psyche* which so preoccupied Aristotle.

These tendencies of Theophrastus were expressed in his work on physiological psychology, *On the Senses*.[4] Contrary to Aristotle, he returned the seat of the intellect to the brain. His treatise contains both valuable criticisms of earlier workers and a statement of his own views. His specific findings and assertions on vision, hearing, smell, taste, and touch are given by him in such detail as to defy summarization.

Throughout this work, he shows the spirit of critical scientific thinking that characterized his general attitude. He adopted the only position open to a scientist, that in the usual course of things perception is in accord with nature, not the contrary, as Plato had held. Perceptions reveal external nature which has existence independent of our senses. He also recognized that it was not enough to pay attention to the stimulus alone; the same stimulus may have different effects according to the conditions present in the sensory organs.

How does an object act upon the sense organ? He rejected the theory of emanations for several reasons, among them that effluences would not explain taste, touch, and smell; since this would require a wasting away of such objects, and many objects that are sources for these experiences are noted for the duration of their sensory impressions. He also rejected the theory that the sensed object comes into contact with the sense organ directly. Nothing actually penetrated the organ. He then adopted Aristotle's view that sensory objects act upon the senses through media and not by direct presence. He disagreed with him, however, concerning the locus of sensory qualities. Theophrastus argued that, whatever the effects of the objects on the sense organs, these effects are carried to the brain before having the quality of sensory experiences. Aristotle had held this to be correct only for some sense modalities, while for others the sensory qualities were generated in the sense organs themselves. From a modern standard, Theophrastus had rather the better of this argument.

Pleasure, according to Theophrastus, is a natural accompaniment of that which is in accord with nature. Pain is not involved in all sense perceptions as some of his predecessors had held. He based his denial on what he called the plain facts of observation. Excessive stimulation sometimes caused pain because it disturbed the correspondence between sense organ and object, but this is not usually the case. He had no patience with the view of Plato that one's pleasures may be false. All pleasures are true in the sense that they are pleasures, no matter what may be our ethical or other judgments about them.

Although it was a quasi-literary contribution, Theophrastus is best known for his collection of personality sketches called, "Characters."[5] Before considering them, a word should be said about earlier work.

Centuries before, Homer had used the device of attributing a master personality trait to certain of his characters as "crafty Ulysses" and "brave Hector." Aristotle had rather casually inserted descriptions of character types in his *Ethics* and *Rhetoric*. But what to his master was a passing illustration became in the hands of Theophrastus a new psychological genre—the description of types of character. Nor was he content to use a single descriptive term for a person, as did Homer, but deduced from a personality attribute the variety of consequences which would follow in diverse circumstances in which that attribute might be exhibited. Consequently, there was an interdependence among the behaviors described. But by sheer freedom of selection, within the limitation of the personality attribute, there were neither incongruities nor combinations or more than one master trait. It followed that he imposed unity upon the personality but did not allow incongruity. In this respect, at least, the Greek dramatists, Aeschylus and Sophocles, were immeasurably superior in giving subtlety to personality portrayal. Nevertheless, it would appear that this subtlety was utilized only with literary aims in view while the efforts of Theophrastus, relatively one-dimensional though they may be, were carried out with full awareness of their scientific interest. He says as much in his dedicatory letter to the *Characters,* indicating that his interest in the subject was aroused when he considered that, while the whole of Greece had the same climate and all Greeks have the same upbringing, they do not have the same character.

Each character is a vignette emphasizing one or another major trait. Dissembling, flattery, garrulity, boorishness, penuriousness, tactlessness, and surliness are some of the thirty characters he sketched. That on flattery follows:

Flattery might be understood to be a sort of converse that is dishonourable, but at the same time profitable, to him that flatters; and the Flatterer will say as he walks beside you "Are you aware how people are looking at you? No man in Athens gets such attention"; or this, "You were the man of the hour yesterday in the Porch; why, although there were more than thirty present, when the talk turned to who was the finest man there, the name that came to every lip both first and last was yours." And while he says such things as these, he picks a speck from your coat; or if so be a morsel of chaff be blown into your beard, plucks it out and then says with a smile "D'ye see? because you and I be not met a whole day, your beard's full of grey hairs—though I own your hair is singularly dark of your age." He will desire silence when his friend speaks, or praise the company for listening to him; when he comes to a stop, he will cry in approbation "Quite right"; and if he make a stale jest will laugh, and stuff the corner of his cloak in his mouth as if he could not hold his merriment. Moreover, any man that comes their way is bidden stand awhile till the great one be gone past. He will buy apples and pears and bring them in for the children, and giving them before their father will kiss them and cry "Chicks of a good strain." When he buys shoes with him at the cordwainer's, he will tell him that the foot is shapelier than the shoe. And if he go visiting a friend of his, he will run ahead and tell him he is coming, and then face round and say "I have announced you." He is the man, you may be sure, to go errands to the women's market there and back without stopping for breath; and of all the guests will be first to praise the wine; and will say in his patron's ear "You are eating nothing"; or picking up some of the food upon the table exclaim "How good this is, isn't it?" and will ask him whether he is not cold? and will he not have his coat on? and shall he not draw his skirts a little closer about him? and saying this, bend forward to whisper in his ear; and will speak to another with his eye on his friend. He will take the cushions from the lackey at the theatre and place them for him himself. He will remark how tasteful is the style of his patron's house; how excellent the planting of his farm; how like him the portrait he has had made.[6]

It may have been noted that this and the other characters mentioned tend to be concerned with the less admirable aspects of human nature. Lest a misanthropic point of view be attributed to Theophrastus, there are several references in the ancient literature to a lost companion volume, devoted to the "Good" characters.

On the death of Theophrastus, his successor as head of the Lyceum was Strato of Lampsacus. Strato was also a worker faithful to the naturalistic spirit of Aristotle. His numerous writings, now lost, dealt with so many of the problems of natural science that he gained the title of "the Physicist." The many successors who were to follow Strato appear to have been of relatively little importance. More and more they became involved in specialized investigations in grammar, literature, and ethics, while the earlier keen interest in the sciences disappeared almost completely. It was not until the sixth century after Christ, however, after a stretch of 860 years, that the school finally closed its doors. Even during the lifetime of Theophrastus and Strato the intellectual center of the Hellenic world was shifting to Alexandria, and in so doing changing its character.

ALEXANDRIA AND SCIENCE[7]

The great Empire of Alexander had disintegrated on his death, with various parts falling into the hands of his generals. A few large monarchies replaced the Empire. Of particular importance in the history of science was Ptolemaic Egypt. Ptolemy I, a Macedonian general, proclaimed himself king and founded the Ptolemaic dynasty which was to last for three centuries, ending with Cleopatra, when Egypt fell to the Romans. Ptolemy's capitol was Alexandria, founded a few years before by Alexander. Under Ptolemy's leadership and that of his son, Ptolemy II, during the first half of the third century B.C., there were organized in Alexandria two great institutions, the Museum and the Library. The great Library, the largest in the ancient world, was probably associated with the Museum since both were within the Royal City. The Museum of Alexandria was primarily a research institute. When fully developed, it comprised living accommodations for the scientists and their assistants, seminar rooms, laboratories, botanical and zoological gardens, and an observatory. The Ptolemys made still another indirect but not unimportant contribution to science. The stipends they paid the Museum scientists was the first financial support scientists had received!

The first intellectual leadership for the Museum was supplied by the same Strato who returned to Athens from Alexandria on the death of his master to lead the Lyceum. In his dozen or so years in Alexandria, he so emphasized science (at the expense of philosophy) that its future course was assured.

During the first century of its existence much important scientific work was done. Most of the sciences as we know them had had their beginnings and their pioneers, and Alexandria became a center of specialists. The opportunity for sustained work in a narrower area, which specialization demands, was to be an approach that was to disappear in a short time, not to reappear on such an extensive scale until the modern period. Mathematical workers at the Museum included Euclid. Archimedes, who may have visited Alexandria from Syracuse, was directly influenced by its school of mathematics. Advances in mechanics, astronomy, geography, medicine and physiology were also made in profusion.

A certain amount of indifference to philosophical issues rather than an animosity marked the workers in these specialities. This indifference increased the more it appeared that fruitful advances were being made in the special sciences. In this characteristic they were the first modern scientists! A realization that heretofore there had been attempts at premature syntheses of knowledge seems to have come to these men. As scientific Candides they resolved to cultivate their own gardens, while still talking with their neighbors over the fences they were erecting. Nevertheless, even in the Museum there was still a much closer connection between science and philosophy than there is today. Outside of it, the connection was even more pronounced, particularly among the physicians who were often explicitly pledged to a school of philosophy and related it to their medical doctrines.

From the Alexandrian point of view, psychology was not a science. Apparently, it was considered to be outside the realm of natural law, while anatomy and physiology were not. In the separation of the several sciences, psychology and physiology, heretofore intermingled, now were separated—a separation which was to continue for many centuries. Therefore, the work of Herophilus and Erasistratus now to be considered, must be referred to as work in anatomy and physiology. It is still relevant to psychology in present perspective, though not in that of Alexandrian science.

Herophilus of Chalcedon, who flourished about 300 B.C. and was a contemporary of Euclid, was one of the founders of anatomy. In the scientifically free atmosphere of Alexandria, he not only dissected the human body, but did so publicly. The anatomy of man he compared explicitly to that of animals. The brain was recognized as the center of the nervous system and as the seat of intelligence. He distinguished tendons from nerves and through the name given to the latter (*neura-aisthetica*) implied a recognition of their function of sensitivity.

Erasistratus, a younger contemporary of Herophilus, distinguished clearly among the arteries, veins, and nerves, regarding the last as vehicles for carrying the *pneuma* for sensation and motion. The shortening of muscles he regarded as due to distention of the animal spirits as conveyed by the nerves. He distinguished motor and sensory nerves, but this finding was lost to those who came after him and had to be independently "discovered" all over again.

One contribution from a physician, unknown as to name but probably from Alexandria, deserves mention. It is contained in a *Book of Medicine*,[8] a series of lectures in which he refers to nerves having exits from the spinal cord and radiating throughout the body. In these nerves is located the power of sensation and motion. Voluntary powers are distinguished from what is called natural powers, which include attraction, growth, digestion, and expulsion, *taking place whether we wish it or whether we do not*. This view contains an anticipation of the concept of reflex or involuntary action. It also serves as a blow to the vague theory of sympathy.

The Background of the Hellenistic and Roman Periods

While these advances were being made in Alexandria, the rest of the Mediterranean world was showing a slow intellectual decline. Indeed, these same deteriorative elements existed in Alexandria, if not in the Museum itself, but they have been slighted in sketching the positive changes taking place. Indicative of the decline among the intellectual activities taking place in Alexandria was the first concerted interest in alchemy.

The causes for this decline are too peripheral for more than a short summary. There was a growth of skepticism, a growing sense of futility, and intellectual disillusionment. Above all, there was increased acceptance of supernaturalism in its more extreme forms. As was said of the Greeks of centuries before, superstition and irrationality were part of their daily existence. Their influence was increased by even more disastrous blows being struck against Greece. Military and political disasters and epidemics, particularly of malaria, swept their lands and peoples. Alongside the ancient Greek religion flourished various Oriental mystery religions. The easy-going old Greek paganism did not meet their new problems. The growth in appeal of the mystery cults, astrology, and magic, emanating mostly from the East, either as cause or effect, were related to the shifting perspectives of Hellenistic man.[9]

The Roman Period

During these years the Roman conquest of the Hellenic world had been taking place, ushering in the fourth and last phase of ancient science. It is commonly called the Graeco-Roman period and extended from about 100 B.C. to A.D. 600.

It is remarkable that it is only at this relatively late date that the Romans are first mentioned. The Latins first emerged into history in the seventh century B.C., went through the period of their early kings and the republican era, always steadily increasing their prosperity, military, and governmental power, with only silence about science and philosophy. This is not difficult to explain. Just as in their drama and art, which were inspired by Greek sources, their science and philosophy were basically derivative. This does not mean that no changes took place. When the Greeks were incorporated into the Roman Empire, Greek thought assumed a Latin dress.

The general intellectual climate was intensely practical. The Romans had little interest in the theoretical issues which had so excited the Greeks. Almost all of their engineers and architects, who covered the hills of Rome with mighty buildings, roads, and aqueducts, were essentially practical in outlook, not consciously applying scientific principles, but using rules of thumb.[10] The Romans also had a definite flair for law, for the maintenance of order, and for conquest. Their sense of order did extend to commenting upon and epitomizing Greek science but hardly to advancing it in either scope or depth. The period of the Roman Empire, to use the words of Russell,[11] was the period of "subjection and order." The winds of doctrine sweeping in from Greece and the East excited a few of them but a large proportion of their leaders went about their business—economic, military, and governmental—more or less unheeding. Since there was no applied psychology as yet, psychological matters would have put almost all of them to sleep.

Roman philosophy, as represented by Stoicism and Epicureanism, was directed to providing a means of personal escape from the evils of the world. "Wisdom for the conduct of life," to use a phrase of Windelband's,[12] became the fundamental philosophical problem. In trying to solve this problem these two schools of thought contributed incidentally to psychological thinking, for example, through maintaining the representative theory of perception promulgated by Epicurus[13] which had been derived from Democritus. (See page 7.) In a more detailed statement than this they would deserve some consideration.

The last great contributor to psychology in the ancient pagan tradition was Galen. He preserved in his person much of the medical and related knowledge of the earlier years, while making considerable contributions of his own.

GALEN

Some 600 years after the birth of Hippocrates, Galen, the next great figure in the medical-psychological tradition, was born. A Greek subject of the Roman Empire, he was born in Asia Minor about 130 A.D. A considerable amount of information is available about his life.[14] His natal town, Pergamon, was then second only to Alexandria as a center of learning in the Western world. He received as complete an education in both philosophy and medicine as the time and place afforded. At twenty he began traveling and studying abroad including a stay in Alexandria, where he concentrated on anatomy. Dissection of the human body was no longer allowed in Alexandria, but the anatomy of apes and other large mammals was studied. Many of his errors, perpetuated over the centuries, were based upon attributing one organ or another to the human which in fact were to be found in only non-human species. At this same age he began writing, remaining a prolific writer for the rest of his life. When twenty-eight years of age, he returned to Pergamon where he was appointed surgeon to the gladiators. This gave him an excellent opportunity to further his knowledge of anatomy on living and dead patients. At the age of thirty-two in 161 A.D., he migrated to Rome to practice. A spectacularly successful cure of a prominent citizen brought him to the attention of the great philosopher-emperor, Marcus Aurelius, who made him his personal physician. From then on, his fortune and his movements were bound to the court and to a whole series of emperors. Meanwhile, his eminence as a medical teacher was recognized, and he lectured to large crowds. A whole series of works on anatomy and physiology and kindred subjects were written in these years.

Before turning to the presentation of his systematic views, it should be emphasized that he was a skilled, astute practitioner. An anecdote[15] that illustrated Galen's clinical shrewdness anticipates by nearly two thousand years a measure now used in so-called lie detection. One day, Galen observed that a female patient of his had a quickening of the pulse when someone mentioned the name of a male dancer. On her visit the following day Galen had arranged for someone to enter and report by name of having seen the performance of still another dancer. A similar test was performed on the third day. Neither the second nor third name produced a quickening of the pulse. On the fourth day it became more rapid when the dancer's name of the first day was again mentioned. The sickness of love was his diagnosis of her malady, and he went on to comment that physicians seem to have no conception of how bodily health can be affected by the *"psyche's"* suffering.

The basic Galenic physiological principle of life was spirit or *pneuma*, a belief encountered before. Galen used it in connection with a division of all living things into plants, animals, and men, a classification familiar from the work of Aristotle. He held that plants showed growth, animals exhibited not only growth but also locomotion, while man had reason in addition. These grades of life had their three characteristic adaptations of the *pneuma*.[16] The first adaptation became natural spirit and brought about growth; the second became vital spirit and caused locomotion; the third became animal spirit and caused thought. Lest there be confusion between the second and third adaptations, "animal" spirit, possessed by man alone and not by animals, was derived from the word, *anima*, the soul. Regarding the seat of the soul, Galen remained faithful to Plato, for in man the liver and veins were the principle organs of growth; the heart, lungs, and arteries were those of locomotion; while the brain and nervous system were those of his distinctive intellectual life.

Galen brought together the then current knowledge of anatomy and physiology.[17] In cutting open the solid-looking organ that is the brain of the ape or man, Galen was struck by the four hollow intercommunicating chambers containing a clear fluid.[18] They must serve some function, and Galen decided it was the place of generation and assembly of the animal spirits of the Soul (mind). Throughout the body the animal spirits flowed along the nerves, in accord with the now general acceptance of nerves, as essential for motion.[19] That the animal spirits were the cause of movement was reinforced for Galen by his observation that the living brain rhythmically pulsated. This dogma was not successfully challenged until the Renaissance. This doctrine of animal spirits was related to and expressed by sympathy or "consent." Communication in this manner, allowing animal spirits to flow from one part of the body to another, accounted for the appearance of symptoms in one organ upon disease in another.[20]

It fell to Galen to complete Hippocrates' four-fold classificatory system by his theory of the four temperaments.[21] It will be remembered that, utilizing the Empedoclean theory of the four elements, Hippocrates had related them to the humors; blood, black bile, yellow bile, and phlegm. A vaguely formulated theory of four temperaments was known more or less incidentally before Galen, particularly among the Stoics, but he handled it systematically and gave to it a much wider sphere of influence. According to Galen, a man with predominance of the blood is said to be sanguine (warm-hearted, volatile) in temperament. When there is an excess of black bile, he is melancholic (sad); when yellow bile is prominent, he is choleric (quick to anger and to action); while the connotation of the fourth humor (phlegmatic) has so little changed over the centuries it needs no description. With these additions to the Hippocratic doctrine from Galen, we have the theory of humors completed.

Later workers in dealing with the theory of temperaments teased out and separated the psychological aspects to such an extent that sometimes the theory is not recognized for what it was to Galen—a system of medical pathological types.[22] He was not consciously developing a psychological theory; it was a part of his systematic theory of disease causation, the other two aspects being external factors and the climate. To use typical medical examples of the system, he argued that foods which are naturally warmer produce more bile and that a person of warmer nature is more subject to biliousness. A secondary consideration for Galen was the explanation of individual differences in behavior and emotion. He claimed not only that the temperaments but also such characteristics as intelligence and boldness could be identified through extensions of humoral theory.

The theory of four temperaments formed a part of the dominant intellectual stream until the rebirth of medicine in the Renaissance, 1,400 years after Galen. Although the doctrine of humors has now faded from the medical scene, vestiges in expressions such as "good humor," "humorous," and their derivatives show its persistence. Also, in "type" theories of personality in which a person is said to be characterized by the possession of a particular temperament, it survives today.

What occurred in connection with the Galenic theory of humors is illustrative of his influence during the centuries that followed. A variety of circumstances fostered a reliance upon Galen's work over many centuries after his death in 200 A.D. His strongly devout theistic attitude appealed to both Christendom and Islam alike. He held all things were determined by God and the structure of the body was formed by Him for an intelligible end, which was consonant with Christianity. He was not a Christian, although for centuries many people believed he had been. Moreover, his writings were confident and dogmatic in tone. They are studded with strong characterizations of those whose views he opposed—stupid, if not insane, shameless, nonsense, absurd, and foolish are but a few of the terms he used.[23] His bulky writings, far too difficult for general study, were summarized and epitomized and commented upon by many lesser and much more ignorant men, and it was their words, not his, that were read. Wretched treatises, whether or not based on his works, flourished so long as they bore his magic name. Meanwhile his best works were lost or fell into oblivion. This compounded the errors and further reduced the general low level to which medicine sank.

Overview

Greek science extended over a period of 800 years, beginning with the speculations of the earliest philosopher-scientists of the sixth century B.C., and maintained its course until the second or third century of the Christian Era. The rate of progress slowed, finally stopped, and, some would say, went backward. Greek science did not die, however, but was transmitted to the Arabs to return to European paths centuries later in the late Middle Ages, modified and changed, but still recognizable and forceful.

REFERENCES *

1. DIOGENES LAERTIUS, *Lives and Opinions of Eminent Philosophers*. (Translated by R. D. Hicks) Cambridge: Harvard University Press, 1925. (III, A.D.)

2. Theophrastus. In C. J. DeVogel. *Greek Philosophy: A Collection of Texts with Notes and Explanations*. (Vol. 2) *Aristotle, the Early Peripatetic School and the Early Academy*. Leiden: Brill, 1953, pp. 230–240. (*c.*300 B.C.)

3. *Ibid.*

4. Theophrastus. In G. M. Stratton, *Theophrastus and the Greek Physiological Psychology*. New York: Macmillan, 1917.

5. THEOPHRASTUS. *The Characters*. (Translated by J. M. Edmonds) London: Heinemann, 1929, pp. 13, 15.

6. *Ibid.*, pp. 43, 45.

7. Sources for this account of Alexandrian science were two books by G. Sarton, *Ancient Science and Modern Civilization* (Lincoln: University of Nebraska Press, 1947); and *A History of Science and Culture in the Last Three Centuries* B.C. (Cambridge: Harvard University Press, 1959); B. Farrington, *Science in Antiquity* (London: Home University Library, 1936); and two more general books that nevertheless contained valuable material on this period, C. Singer, *A Short History of Medicine, Introducing Medical Principles to Students and Non-medical Readers*. (New York: Oxford University Press, 1928); and W. Windelband, *A History of Philosophy* (Vol. 1) *Greek, Roman and Medieval* (New York, Harper, 1901).

8. *Book of Medicine*, (Translated by E. A. W. Budge.) London: Oxford University Press, 1913. (*c.*300 B.C.)

9. W. C. DAMPIER, *A History of Science, and its Relations with Philosophy and Religion*. (4th ed.) Cambridge: Cambridge University Press, 1949.

10. M. CLAGETT, *Greek Science in Antiquity*. New York: Abelard Schuman, 1955.

11. B. RUSSELL, *A History of Western Philosophy*. New York: Simon and Schuster, 1945, p. 218.

12. WINDELBAND, *op. cit.*, p. 157.

13. EPICURUS, Letter to Herodotus, from the Original Text of Diogenes Laertius. (Translated by C. Bailey) In W. J. Oates, (ed.), *The Stoic and Epicurean Philosophers: Complete Extant Writings of Epicurus, Epictetus, Lucretius, and Marcus Aurelius*. New York: Random House, 1940. (*c.*300 B.C.) (Herrnstein & Boring Excerpt No. 22).

14. Sources include C. Singer, *A Short History of Medicine, op. cit.*; H. E. Sigerist, *The Great Doctors: a Biographical History of Medicine*, (London: Allan and Unwin, 1933); and G. Sarton, *Galen of Pergamon*, (Lawrence: University of Kansas Press, 1954).

* See page 16 for description of reference style.

15. L. THORNDIKE, *A History of Magic and Experimental Science During the First Thirteen Centuries of Our Era.* (Vol. 1) New York: Macmillan, 1923.

16. B. FARRINGTON, *Greek Science: its Meaning for Us.* London: Penguin, 1953, pp. 297–298.

17. GALEN, *On Anatomical Procedures: Translating the Surviving Books With Introduction and Notes.* (Translated by C. Single) London: Oxford University Press, 1956; Galen, *On Anatomical Procedures: the Later Books.* (Translated by W. L. H. Duckworth.) M. C. Lyons & B. Towers, (eds.), Cambridge: Cambridge University Press, 1962.

18. C. S. SHERRINGTON, *Man on His Nature.* (2nd ed.) London: Cambridge University Press, 1951, pp. 198–199.

19. F. FEARING, *Reflex Action: a Study in the History of Physiological Psychology.* Baltimore: Williams & Wilkins, 1930, p. 12.

20. J. F. FULTON, *Physiology of the Nervous System.* (3rd ed. rev.) London: Oxford University Press, 1949, p. 202.

21. According to MAY SMITH, in The Nervous Temperament. (*Brit. J. Med. Psychol.,* 1930. 10, 99–174), it is more correct to speak of nine temperaments, the four above, each of which is based more precisely, not on the humors, but on the preponderance of one of the *pairs* hot-wet, hot-dry, cold-wet, cold-dry: one perfect balance of hot, wet, cold, and dry; and four more based on the preponderance of one or another of the qualities hot, wet, cold and dry not in pairs, but alone.

22. GALEN, On the Natural Faculties. (Translated by A. J. Brock) In R. M. Hutchins (ed.), *Great Books of the Western World.* (Vol. 10) Chicago: Encyclopaedia Britannica, 1952, pp. 163–215. (200 A.D.)

23. *Ibid.*

CHAPTER 5

PLOTINUS AND AUGUSTINE:

THE PATRISTIC PERIOD

Before considering the work of the next two great psychologists, it becomes necessary to turn back in time from Galen, some two centuries, to when the Christian Era began. An examination of the link between philosophy and early Christianity, and the presumed influence of religion on the fall of science provides a vital introduction to Plotinus, the greatest exponent of Neoplatinism. In spite of being a pagan, Plotinus profoundly influenced Augustine who became the greatest "psychologist" during the following span of nearly a thousand years.

CHRISTIANITY AND THE FALL OF SCIENCE

Christianity had no direct relation to the fall of science. The decline had started before the advent of Christianity. Moreover, science was at almost as low a point as it ever descended at the end of the second century when Christianity still formed a small obscure sect with no influence one way or another on the class of individuals who might be expected to study science. The maintenance of the low estate of science is a different matter. In the centuries that followed, Christianity did nothing to promote science and in many ways discouraged its revival. The practical attitude of the Romans and later the invasions of the Barbarians contributed to this fall, and the Church then maintained the situation and, to some degree, increased it. Early Christian teaching indirectly abetted this decline by diverting to theological speculation individuals of scholarly temperament who might otherwise have turned their interests to science.

PHILOSOPHY AND THE BEGINNING OF CHRISTIANITY

Jesus, the Apostles, and their immediate successors were concerned with spreading the Gospel, not in promulgating philosophy, let alone science. Jesus, a man of simple faith with an intuitive vision into the hearts of men, had no interest in formalizing and systematizing the implicit assumptions behind his practices. An artist in the broadest sense, even a psychotherapist, if you will permit such a term, he epitomized the point of view of art, not science.

Once the period of comparative obscurity was over, Christians did find a need to defend the new religion against non-Christian thinkers. Philosophy, insofar as it was studied, was used for defense of religion, or "apologetics" as it was called. Several writers of the second century address these apologetics to the Roman emperors. This century began the period of the Church Fathers, whose writings in later ages were used as sources of reference for points of doctrinal orthodoxy. The names of Justin, Clement of Alexandria, Origen, Tertullian, Cyprian, Gregory of Nyassa, Augustine of Hippo, Jerome, Cassiodorus, and Pope Gregory I are among them. The Patristic Period, as it came to be called, covered the centuries devoted to the formation of Christian orthodoxy.

A detailed history of the early Christian views would show that it was a history of Christian dogma, not a history of philosophy. At least one Church Father, Tertullian, not only held that his faith was unphilosophical, he was proud of this fact.[1] He took the position that the content of revelation is not only above reason, but in one sense, contrary to reason. The gospel is incomprehensible in terms of worldly discernment. Therefore to such thinkers as Tertullian, Christianity has nothing to do with philosophy. A period of anti-rationalism had set in.

It was not until the beginning of the third century that a consciously thought-out system of theology was seen to be a necessity. Origen, born in Alexandria in 185 A.D., was one of the intellectual leaders of that time. While his theological views are of no concern, his attitude toward science and philosophy is noteworthy because it showed a contrast to the earlier anti-rationalist view. He held that all knowledge was good since it was a means toward perfection and that philosophy and science were in no way incompatible with a Christian life.[2] The Edict of Milan, issued by Constantine in 313, securing the toleration of Christianity, and official recognition that followed soon thereafter made even more imperative the development of an authoritative system of theology.

The official sanction of Christianity brought with it one paramount intellectual consequence. Heresy was born. Unlike the "easy going" religions of old whose guardians were content to allow one to worship how and when one pleased if only a token obeisance be made to the gods of city or state, Christianity demanded uncompromising adherence to the one God who through the voices of the Hebrew prophets and through Christ had made manifest the Truth. This revelation could not be gainsaid. To do so was heresy. No longer was one free to speculate on any and all matters. Certain truths were revealed, and one could not challenge them without being accused of heresy.

Philosophers could no longer inquire about a given point, once dogma was settled by the ecumenical councils. These councils decided by majority vote what was henceforth to be regarded as revealed Christian truths. The minorities on these votes, now faced with heresy, could either agree or, as sometimes not unremarkably happened, break off to form heretical sects. These heretics were still Christian in that they drew their inspiration from the same source, but they denied some point of dogma. Sometimes these differences were introduced by continued adherence to one or another now banned aspect of the old religions of the classical twilight, such as a belief in magic. Often they arose over the interpretation of the Trinity, especially the particular nature of the relation of the Son to the Father.

The Church Fathers forged the restraints of dogma which thereafter circumscribed philosophy. Within these limits there was, contrary to the opinion sometimes expressed, considerable room in which philosophy could move freely. As Gilson reminds us, no one can seriously maintain that all philosophy of these years was Christian—any more than that all literature, art, and architecture of these centuries was exclusively Christian.

The predominant world view of moral sickness influenced the psychological thought of the Church Fathers.[3] Intense preoccupation with problems of sin and guilt marked the theological aspects of the reaction to the same feeling of helplessness and doom that had influenced the non-Christian mystics. For psychology there were three major results. First, soul-body dualism was elevated to the central problem of psychology. Second, a frantic attempt occurred to divorce human nature from any suggestion of relation to the animal kingdom. The animal was degraded, and a sharp dichotomy was drawn between mankind and the beasts that perish. This position was demanded since, otherwise, animals might be seen as having reason which in turn might imply moral responsibility.

Third, a preoccupation developed with the world to come. Naturalistic interests, being of this world, were held suspect.

Philosophy was dominated by the Neoplatonists, those thinkers who claimed to subscribe to Plato's doctrines, especially his theory of Forms. From this base they had proceeded in many curious directions, most often highly speculative and always mystical. One of these philosophers, the pagan Plotinus, had a profound effect upon the greatest of the Patristic philosophers, Augustine, and through him upon all Christian philosophy.

PLOTINUS[4]

Plotinus was the greatest exponent of Neoplatonism. Born in Egypt about 205 A.D., five years after the death of Galen, he became a disciple of Ammonius Saccas in Alexandria and remained with him for eleven years. He and other students entered into a compact to keep secret their master's teachings, which had not been reduced to writing. At the age of thirty-nine, Plotinus left Ammonius with the intention of traveling to the East in order to learn Persian and Indian philosophy. The expedition of the Emperor Gordian, which he joined for this purpose, reached Mesapotamia, but the trip was cut short by the assassination of the Emperor. This was the occupational hazard of emperors at the time of Plotinus, no less than eleven dying in this fashion during his sixty-five years.

Plotinus arrived in Rome in 245, to remain there for the rest of his life. His teaching, austere and ethical in character, soon gained him influence over many of the leading Romans of his time. He functioned not only as a teacher of philosophy, but also as a counselor on ethical problems. Of high moral principles and unimpeachable character, his advice on moral problems was eagerly sought.

During the first years in Rome he wrote nothing. Probably due to the failure of fellow students of Ammonius to keep their pledge of secrecy, he began to record his own views. Indifferent toward his own writing, it was only under the repeated urging of his student and biographer, Porphyry, that he wrote the major portion of his only work in what proved to be the last six years of his life. After the death of Plotinus in 270 A.D., Porphyry, following a numerological quirk, arranged the essays in six groups or sets of nine works each, as a consequence of which he gave them the name of *The Six Enneads* (six groups of nine).[5]

The central theme of the teaching of Plotinus was mystical reunion with the world soul. Plotinus seems to have been dominated by a desire to map out the world beyond sense reality and to try to live in that world as fully as the bonds of flesh would permit. It would be easy at this point to dismiss Plotinus as a mystic and move on. And yet, he was something more than this. His was not a crude mysticism based merely on habitual existence in a state of trance. In fact, according to Porphyry, he attained a state of vision only four times in his sixty-five years. In these states he felt himself to have risen above the world of experience to the world beyond. In the meantime, although careless of dress and hygienic considerations, he was in great demand as the executor of estates of minor children! The practical Romans would hardly have so trusted him if he fitted the stereotype of the mystic. When chided for performing this business service, seemingly discordant with his philosophical teaching, Plotinus is said to have remarked that the children would need the money if they did not find philosophy. It was not that he was oblivious to the world; rather he valued things other than those which the majority of men held dear. Material life he saw as a play acted out by the shadows of men.[6] Their comings and goings were irrelevant.

There is a calmness to his writing, not the heat that so often is accompanied by confusion. Consider how he describes his mysticism:

But there are earlier and loftier beauties than these [from sense]. In the sense-bound life we are no longer granted to know them, but the soul, taking no help from the organs, sees and proclaims them. To the vision of these we must mount, leaving sense to its own low place.[7]

Not that he was a scientist, far from it. His use of the things of this world was as casual illustrations of his philosophical doctrine. Nevertheless, when he used introspection, his genius for this inward turning was very prominent. Naturally, he divorced introspection completely from underlying physiological processes. Psychology, to Plotinus, was pure experience.

The intent of his teachings was to demonstrate to those who do not have these transcendental experiences that there are realities beyond the world of sense.[8] Consequently, he had to appeal to experiences that were open to understanding, and this made his thinking relevant to the history of psychology. He adopted, as his method, the analysis of the forms of mental activity. This was the logical method to give him information about the soul, since, by definition, the soul was not material. This analysis was only incidental to his major thinking, and not part of an attempt to systematize a psychology. Nevertheless, throughout all of his work he used an introspective method, thereby helping to establish this approach to psychology. In spite of himself, he made a modest contribution to psychology in an age otherwise barren of advance.

He espoused a doctrine of the development of man toward perfection. The independence of the soul from the body, or as close an approximation to this as possible, was his goal. Matter was the obstacle to its perfect realization. The Platonic doctrine of the body as the prison of the soul was made central to his thinking, although he altered the relationship between the two. Where Plato had conceived of the soul as being in the body, Plotinus believed the body to be in space, since space is that which contains body, but the soul not being corporeal could not be so contained.[9] It gives the body life but does not combine with it. The soul and body are united but they are never fused, mixed, or spatially connected. The soul used the organs of sense of the body, and the motions that are forthcoming are motions of the body, not of the soul. That the soul is correlative with, but independent of, the body, was his central point. The emotions, for example, are known to the soul, but it is the body which is perturbed.[10] The body experiences the emotion; the soul perceives it.

The soul has three major classes of activity. First, the soul performs the functions of perceiving the world of sense. Second, the soul reflects, that is to say, there is a division of consciousness into subject and object. The soul not only thinks, but it also thinks it thinks. To speak of the first and second kinds of mental activity, there is a state of excitation which is sensation; reflection is conscious perception of this excitation. Third, there is the pure activity of contemplation without such a separation of subject and object in which the soul transcends its immediate location to dwell on the eternal and changeless. This "changeless" was the goal of Plotinus, the ineffable state toward which he strove. It is at its highest level the experience of the "one." [11]

Psychological interest centers, however, not on his goal, but on the second function. His distinction of this function where "we," his word for self, was operating, gives us the first clear and explicit statement of self-consciousness.[12] At this level, unlike union with the "One," without consciousness of self, "we" are aware of the object and, separate from this, of ourselves. We are self-conscious in that the object and the thinker are distinguished by us.[13] As he puts it, "we know, and it is ourselves that we know. . . ."[14] He even used blushing as an illustration of heightened self-consciousness. To Plotinus, self-consciousness was but a means of contrast with his major interest at an ineffably higher plane. Self-consciousness was hit upon as an effective means of contrast with his higher level and, once it served its purpose, he said no more about it.

St. Augustine

St. Augustine lived in a Christian and Roman world overwhelmed with troubles. In his youth the barbarians were pouring into the Empire; in his middle age he experienced the effects of the sack of Rome by the Goths; and his declining years he spent preparing for the defense of his own city, Hippo, against the Vandals, while all around him the whole Western Roman Empire faced final ruin. Augustine did not advance science generally, and probably even impeded its development, but his subjective attitude, with its consequent attention to the self and to introspection, and his stress on the functioning of the will make him important in the history of psychology.

Life of St. Augustine[15]

Aurelius Augustine was born in 354, during the reign of Constantine II, at Tagaste, a small town in the Roman province of Numidia in northern Africa. His father, a minor Roman functionary, was a pagan (although baptized just before his death). His mother, Monnica, was a devout Christian who exercised a profound influence over Augustine. However, Augustine was not baptized at birth, it being a not uncommon custom of his time to defer this step until later years, in order to wash away the sins accumulated before receiving the sacrament and because it was felt that only those of mature years and understanding could worthily receive baptism.

Many years later, he described his childhood and youth in his *Confessions*.[16] Through this psychological work of insight, it is possible to trace his physical and spiritual autobiography. He learned something about Christianity from his mother at an early age, but her teachings made little impression at this time. When he did well in his first schooling, his father aspired to make him a lawyer; so he was sent to Carthage at about the age of sixteen to study rhetoric. Again he did well in his studies, but the frivolity of student life led him into dissipation of various sorts described in detail in his *Confessions*. Since he was now sixteen, he took a mistress to whom he remained faithful for ten years. She bore him a son, named "Adeodatus," meaning "Given of God." The custom of taking a concubine, sanctioned by pagan morals and Roman law, was thought to be a step above promiscuity. Then and later, he had a deeply passionate nature. "Give me chastity and continency," he cried out, "only not yet."[17] This plea occurred many years later in Milan after his mistress had returned to Africa, and before his planned but never contracted marriage to another.

His intellectual life too, was intense. The reading of a now lost work by Cicero, *Hortensius*, led him to a love of philosophy. Over the years he became increasingly conversant with the Roman pagan literature. He disliked Greek and never mastered the language, although he became fascinated by Plato and the Neoplatonists. Roman Africa of his time was a place where many diverse Christian, heretical, and pagan religious strands intertwined. With these Augustine involved himself. At the age of nineteen, he embraced one of these strands, Manicheanism, which told of a world of opposed substances of light and darkness. The external opposition of good and evil was a battle fought on many levels. Man on earth strove to become part of the kingdom of light and could become part of that body. This doctrine was submerged in a morass of esoteric teachings, including, for example, dietary prescriptions: meat belonged to darkness and was forbidden; vegetables were of light, so should be eaten. Since Manes, the Persian, who was the founder of the system of thought, claimed his authority directly from Jesus Christ, technically his doctrine was a perverted form of Christianity and, from the Christian point of view, a particularly offensive form of heresy. During Augustine's time, Manicheanism had a large number of adherents and exercised considerable temporal power.

On the completion of his studies in Carthage in 373, Augustine decided to follow the career of a teacher of rhetoric, rather than that of a lawyer. He established himself as a teacher in Carthage for a period of years, and, then in 383, to further his career, Augustine went on to the larger world of Rome. He left behind his mother, who wished to accompany him, by the simple expedient of slipping aboard ship without her. After a year in Rome, during which time his students cheated him, he accepted the municipal post of rhetoric in Milan. This post was in the control of the Manicheans and was secured for him precisely because he was an adherent—a doctrine which by this time he was in process of discarding.

An increasingly sceptical view was becoming forced upon Augustine. That is to say, he was experiencing doubts as to whether reality could be known at all. Meanwhile, he had been reading assiduously in Platonic and Neoplatonic sources, not always, however, correctly understanding what he read.[18] Augustine, now a sceptic, had found it hard to conceive of God as immaterial. Neoplatonism freed him from this difficulty. Through the Neoplatonists he was led to accept as legitimate an order of reality beyond the material world.

In his later writings the Neoplatonic conception of reality was adapted to a Christian context.[19] This was to have a profound effect upon all subsequent Christian theological and philosophical thinking. Many of his doctrines—God, matter, the ascent of the soul, freedom and evil, the relation of God to the world—show the impress of Neoplatonism, especially as earlier expressed by Plotinus. It was this conception of reality which he inserted into Christian theology and philosophy. His views on the spiritual nature of reality accessible to the human soul were derived from them. There was a shared belief that there was a supreme author and a common desire to transcend the material world. There were, of course, differences in outlook. Contrary to Neoplatonism, Christian thinkers insisted on a voluntary act of creation by God; existence was in time, not eternal; and God was at an entirely different level than that of his creatures.

It was in Milan that Augustine came under the influence of Ambrose, Bishop of Milan. In his relationship with Ambrose we have one of the decisive factors in the development of his thought. Dissatisfied with what he saw as an incompleteness of Neoplatonism and philosophy, he found in Ambrose someone to fill his needs, someone to help him find peace. In his *Confessions* he says, "That man of God received me as a father, and showed me an episcopal kindness on my coming. Thenceforth, I began to love him at first, indeed not as a teacher of the truth but as a person kind toward myself."[20] He is saying that first came a human relationship to Ambrose. Friendship would be too strong a word to characterize his relationship to the busy Ambrose, who although kindly enough, could not spare much time for the youthful student. An important step in the intellectual forces of Western Christendom started first in an interpersonal relationship, later to flower into a religious conversion.

There were other influences at work to help to bring him to join the Church. The pleading and the faith of his mother, who by this time had caught up with him, was also a potent force in his conversion. There was also the scene in the garden of his house in Milan, movingly described in the *Confessions*.[21] Of this incident, he tells, in words of fire, of his conflict of will over whether or not to renounce the joys of the flesh for the sake of God. After an intense struggle the conflict was resolved when, after being commanded by a voice as if from a neighboring child, chanting over and over again, "Take up and read," he had taken up the Bible and read from Paul: "Not in rioting and drunkenness, not in chambering and wantonness, not in strife and envying; but put ye on the Lord Jesus Christ, and make not provision for the flesh to fulfill the lusts thereof."[22] He reread Paul's *Epistles* finding in him a kindred spirit who had passed through a thousand doubts to the Divine Word. This was not a pale abstraction of Platonic *logos* but something that was to him, as it was to Paul, much more vital, warm, and deep.[23]

After a period of intellectual and spiritual preparation, he was baptized in Milan by Ambrose, in 387. The year before, primarily because of dissatisfaction with what he had to teach, but partly because he was suffering from a chest ailment, he had resigned his professorship of rhetoric. Although never again formally a teacher, he did not cease teaching, though now he pursued a different goal. After his conversion, accompanied by his mother, Monnica, his son, Adeodatus, and some friends, he left for Rome preparatory to embarking for Africa. At Ostia, the port of Rome, his mother died. She died in peace; her prayers had been answered. Augustine stayed on in Rome for almost two more years before returning home to Africa. Upon his return, he sold his property and gave the proceeds to the poor. He and some friends organized a monastery in Tagaste, where he lived the life of an ascetic. In 389 his son, Adeodatus, on whom he had lavished great care and affection, died. Augustine shortly thereafter was ordained a priest in Hippo. Here, in what was to be his home for the rest of his life, he founded another monastery.

Sometime in 395 or 396 Augustine had been consecrated a bishop—a post he held until his death. His quiet monastic life was now over. The successful administration of a bishopric in the fifth century in northern Africa among pagans and heretics was no light task. Practical shrewdness and forceful leadership, as well as piety, were necessary for the task. Above all, it required skill in human relationships. Religious controversies within the church, church councils, combats against heresy, and even lay legal activities occupied much of his time, and he continued to be in poor health. Nevertheless, he was able to find time to engage in enormous literary activity as well as a prolific correspondence with other church leaders.

With the Vandals at the gates of Hippo on August 28th, 430 A.D., at the age of seventy-six, Augustine died. A few months after his death his parishioners were either slain or scattered. Less than fifty years later, in 476, the Western Caesar was abolished.

His major works were written during the later part of his life, that is to say, in the first quarter of the fifth century. The two best known are his *Confessions*[24] finished in 406, and the *City of God*[25] completed in 426. Augustine gave the classic statement of the Christian philosophy of history in his *City of God* in the form of a contrast and comparison of the earthly and the heavenly city. Eventually the terrestrial city must yield to the heavenly city, and the course of history is the struggle of these two cities.

Attitudes Toward Science

The attitude Augustine took toward faith is responsible for his philosophical and scientific views. He held that it is necessary to believe in order to know; understanding comes from faith. Nevertheless, there are many things we cannot believe unless we understand them. So, supplementing the primacy of belief was the subordinate principle that we also know in order to believe.

Knowledge is valuable to Augustine only to the extent that it will bring him closer to his aims of understanding God and the soul and self of man. God is the source of all causation. Miracles are simply unusual occurrences, requiring no more and no less explanation than that for any other event.[26] If only they were not rare, they would not cause surprise. Often knowledge of this fact is enough, thereby obscuring any need for understanding rationally. Eyes fastened on God have little care for the transitory mundane affairs of the world.

His views of science as science must be described as ambivalent. Deprecatory remarks are to be found in abundance. For example, scientific knowledge, such as prediction of eclipses, may puff up man with pride.[27] After a short account of the work of Thales, he complains he did not relate this to the divine mind,[28] yet he made laudatory remarks as well. The apparent discrepancy is considerably dissipated when it is remembered that science was good when it served religious ends; irrelevant and, hence, bad, when it did not. In this connection when comparing profane knowledge with Scripture, he writes, "For whatever man may have learnt from other sources, if it is hurtful, it is there condemned; if it is useful, it is therein contained."[29] By and large, the effect of Augustine upon science was to impede rather than advance its progress. This ambivalent attitude toward science in general went hand in hand with a firm conviction of the certainty of inner experience.[30] As a consequence he is important in the history of psychology, although not in the other sciences.

Philosophical and Personal Background to Augustine's Psychology

For Augustine, revelation and inner experience were the two sources of truth. His most systematic statement of the principles of sacred theology, a guide to interpretation of Scripture which center on revealed truth, is his "On Christian Doctrine."[31] References to inner experience are scattered and will be cited in developing its particular aspects. In his dependence upon subjective knowledge, the second source, he made use of a concept of self, and focused upon the issue of the freedom of the will as an experienced phenomenon. How self and freedom of the will were related to his philosophical views now can be specified briefly.

Augustine wished to rise to the heavenly city by the love of God. In order to do this there must be contempt of self.[32] This ascent of soul to God vividly described in his *Confessions*[33] required various steps involving passing from body, to sense, to inner sense, and by several more steps to the final place of abiding with disregard of self. The direct relation of his thinking to that of Plotinus is obvious, while his indirect debt to Plato may also be discerned.

From Augustine's point of view, there were several compelling theological reasons that made the problem of will a primary issue.[34] For one, Adam's fall, although in a sense brought about by Satan, would not have occurred had Adam not already had a deficient will. Moreover, the problems of the relation of absolute predestination to freedom of the will, Divine Grace, and sin all occupied central positions in his theological thinking. Fortunately, it is unnecessary to unravel their intricate interrelationships. Equally compelling were his experiences as a youth when passion overwhelmed his will and for which he later reproached himself severely. In one dramatic instance, he recounted his remembering with shame that in his youth he, along with some friends, had stolen some pears, only to throw them away uneaten. He did more than register his harrowing repentance. He analyzed his motives for what today might be called a typical act of juvenile vandalism.[35] In the first place he recognized that he committed this act because he was with his friends. If alone, it would not have occurred to him to set out to steal the fruit. More important for our use of the illustration, he believed that he did it precisely because it was forbidden; he experienced a sense of power in doing that which he should not. Will, or motivation, as it may be called, is the crux to the understanding of the episode.

Concerning these matters, Augustine held to an introspective and phenomenological view. But why, it may be asked, was Augustine interested in the inner man—in psychological topics? The direction his interests took, focusing as he did upon the inward man, came about from the sort of man he was and the experiences he had had. Augustine illustrates in an admirable fashion that a man turns to introspection when he becomes aware of difficulties within himself.

Augustine had no conception of psychology as a separate discipline, so what is to follow may give an impression of greater integration than is warranted by his own presentation. His goal of relation of man to God does not require, even contradicts, a self subsistent view of man.

Some Aspects of the Psychology of Augustine

Augustine's introspective approach is illustrated by his psychological description of time.[36] Time was created when the world was created, having no reality apart from created existence. Neither the past nor the future really is, in the sense of being experienced, when they are in the past or in the future. Yet there is time past and future. This contradiction is solved by Augustine arguing that time is thought of in the present; the past is identified with memory, the future with expectation. There are three times, a present of things past, a present of things present, and a present of things future. Time is not of the external world but an inner experience as one measures and compares. Time is psychological.

His subjective emphasis led naturally to consideration of proof of the reality of self-existence. Assume, Augustine said, that one doubts his existence. But to do so is to assert existence, since to doubt is to think, and to think is to exist. Under these circumstances, then, a man cannot doubt his existence for to do so would be to talk nonsense. Instead of the expression of Descartes, "I think therefore I am," (see page 150) Augustine's formula was "For if I am deceived, I am." [37] Of all knowledge, the existence of one's own thought is most certain. Sense perception does not give us knowledge. The mind knows the external world only indirectly. What it does know directly is awareness of self, not from the contact with the world but by itself, knowing itself. The mind produces its experiences from within the self. Life is a unity known through self-consciousness. One important consequence of this view is that the automatic functions of the body, grouped together as lower functions, were not part of this self, but were considered to be negligible and safely to be ignored.

From this primary awareness of existence one can advance to an awareness of ideas in the mind. These ideas are universal and real concepts—goodness, being, number, and the like. In his way of expressing universals, Augustine was following Platonic lines, but differed beyond this point. Their source was in God; these ideas were grasped by God's gift of illumination. The mind, when considering things of this world, including the body, can recognize its own superiority to them, but at the same time, it realizes that it falls short of knowledge of things eternal and thereby recognizes its own shortcomings.

Soul was regarded by Augustine as an immaterial spiritual entity, and man as a dualistic union of body and soul. Body and soul make up human nature. [38] The soul was considered immaterial and indestructible. Moreover, the soul had not pre-existed from eternity but was a product of creation. Since nothing was created after the six days of creation, the body and the soul, too, must have been created then.

The soul was immaterial but it acted in and through the body, animating and directing. It was the form of the body but could be separated from the body after death and become immortal. [39] Both the immateriality and immortality of the soul are demonstrated by its power of grasping the eternal. The proof of the existence of the soul is an extension of what has already been said about self-existence. To put it in small compass, to have a thinking existence is to have a soul.

Although the mind is unitary, this does not preclude coexistence of various parts or, more strictly, diverse functions. In connection with the mind he attributes to it three faculties—reason (understanding, intellect), memory, and will, albeit in scattered and unsystematic fashion.[40] Imagination, mediating between memory and reason, although not quite at the same level of importance as the other three, seems to be treated as still another faculty. Each of them is a relatively independent function of mind. These faculties seemed to be handled by Augustine as if they were entities which explained the facts in and of themselves. This is especially the case with will as faculty. His view is brought out clearly in the following illustration. In speaking of a youthful temptation he wrote: "My will the enemy held, and thence made a chain for me, and bound me. For of a froward will was a lust made; and a lust served a custom; and custom not resisted became necessity."[41] The will created a habit; habit became necessity. In so doing will functioned as an entity in itself.

The reality of the freedom of will has already been affirmed in the quotation just given. It is the human will which makes for choice of good or evil.[42] On more than one occasion he affirms will as a matter of freely determined choice,[43] while particularly concerning himself with human freedom in relation to the will of God,[44] and its relation to sin and salvation.[45]

The psychological faculties of reason and memory also receive attention from Augustine. A partial summary of their functioning may be offered in terms of one of the forms of interrelationship of the three faculties. Even the simplest act of apprehension has three components, the mind is conscious of itself (memory); it is aware of the possibility of many objects potentially available to attention (understanding, intelligence); and it selects one with which it becomes involved (will).

OVERVIEW

Until the rise of scholastic Aristotelianism 800 years later, Augustine was the chief authority on "psychological" matters. His insistence upon the accuracy of findings based upon the immediate certainty of inner experience did much to foster an introspective approach to psychological problems. His defense of the primacy of will helped to counteract too exclusive a stress upon the intellectual phase of human experience. On the other side of the ledger, when combined with his negative attitude toward science, the sheer charm of his writings, his brilliantly insightful expression, and his striking metaphors served to help slow down and delay the advance of psychology as a science. In turning his back upon scientific advance, he did psychology a disservice.

REFERENCES*

1. W. WINDELBAND, *A History of Philosophy*. Vol. 1. *Greek, Roman and Medieval*. New York: Harper, 1901.

2. A. C. CROMBIE, *Medieval and Early Modern Science*. 2 Vols. (2nd rev. ed.) New York: Doubleday, 1959.

3. G. MURPHY, *Historical Introduction to Modern Psychology*. (rev. ed.) New York: Harcourt, Brace, 1949.

4. Sources for the account of his life are those of his student, Porphyry, On the life of Plotinus and the arrangement of his works. In *The Enneads*. (Translated by S. MacKenna.) New York: Pantheon, undated and J. Katz, *The Philosophy of Plotinus* (New York: Appleton-Century-Crofts, 1950).

5. PLOTINUS, *The Six Enneads*. (Translated by S. MacKenna & B. S. Page) In R. M. Hutchins (ed.), *Great Books of the Western World*, (Vol. 17) Chicago: Encyclopaedia Britannica, 1952, pp. 1–360. (*c.*270 A.D.)

6. *Ibid.*, III, Trac. II, 15.

7. *Ibid.*, I, Trac. VI, 4, p. 23.

8. This view permeates his discussion. A good secondary discussion is to be found in J. Katz. *op. cit.*

9. *Enneads*, IV, Trac. III, 20.

10. *Ibid.*, IV, Trac. IV, 28.

11. *Ibid.*, V, Trac. I, 2.

12. *Ibid.*, IV, Trac. III.

13. *Ibid.*, III, Trac. IX, 3.

14. *Ibid.*, p. 137.

15. AUGUSTINE, The Confessions. (Translated by E. B. Pusey) In R. M. Hutchins, (ed.) *op. cit.*, Vol. 18, pp. 1–125. (*c.*400). This is the major source for details about his life. It is supplemented by R. W. Battenhouse, The Life of St. Augustine. In R. W. Battenhouse (ed.), *A Companion to the Study of St. Augustine*. (New York: Oxford University Press, 1955, pp. 15–56); V. J. Bourke, *Augustine's Quest of Wisdom*. (Milwaukee: Bruce, 1945); and B. Russell, *A History of Western Philosophy*. (New York: Simon & Schuster, 1945).

16. *Confessions*.

17. *Ibid.*, VIII, 17, p. 57.

18. *E.g.*, Augustine, The City of God. (Translated by M. Dods) In R. M. Hutchins, (ed.) *op. cit.*, Vol. 18, pp. 127–618, (*c.*413–426), VIII.

19. M. H. CARRE, *Realists and Nominalists*. London: Oxford University Press, 1946.

20. *Confessions*, V, 23, p. 33.

* See page 16 for description of reference style.

21. *Ibid.*, VIII, 19–22, 30.

22. *Ibid.*, p. 61.

23. *Ibid.*, VII, 27.

24. *Ibid.*

25. *City of God.*

26. *Ibid.*, XXI, 8.

27. *Confessions*, V, 3–5, 8.

28. *City of God*, VIII, 2.

29. AUGUSTINE, On Christian Doctrine. (Translated by J. F. Shaw) In R. M. Hutchins (ed.), *op. cit.*, Vol. 18, pp. 619–698, (*c.*427), p. 656.

30. AUGUSTINE, The Trinity. (Translated by S. MacKenna) In J. Deferrari (ed.), *The Fathers of the Church: A New Translation*, (Vol. 45) Washington, D.C.: Catholic University of America Press, 1963, pp. 281–282. (*c.*416)

31. *On Christian Doctrine.*

32. *City of God*, XIV, 28.

33. *Confessions*, VII, 23.

34. *On Christian Doctrine*, II, 46.

35. *Confessions*, II, 9–18.

36. *Ibid.*, XI, 17–40.

37. *City of God*, XI, 26, p. 337.

38. *Ibid.*, XIV, 5.

39. *Ibid.*, XIII, 19, XIV, 2–3, 5–6.

40. *Confessions*, X, 6, 10–11, 18, 17, 26–27, 37; *City of God*, IX, 4–5, XIV 6–9, XIX, 18.

41. *Confessions*, VIII, 10, p. 55.

42. *City of God*, XIV, 6.

43. *Confessions*, IX, 1; *City of God*, XXII, 30.

44. *Ibid.*, II, 14; *City of God*, I, 36, IV 33, V, 1, 9–10, XVIII, 2.

45. *Confessions*, VII, 5; *City of God*, V, 9–10, XII, 21, XIV, 11–12, 15, XXII, 1, 30.

CHAPTER 6

AQUINAS:

THE MIDDLE AGES, REASON, AND FAITH

A LONG period of preparation was necessary before Thomas Aquinas could emerge as the great psychologist of the Middle Ages. Consideration of the Dark Ages, the rise and fall of Islam and the intellectual climate of the later Middle Ages will provide some background must precede discussion of his contributions.

THE DARK AGES

After the classical twilight and the Patristic period came the early Middle Ages extending from about 400 or 500 to 900 A.D., and often spoken of as the Dark Ages. Although there were still some Fathers of the Church yet to come, some scholars argue[1] that the creative Patristic epoch had closed with the death of Augustine in 430. In the fifth century the world empire of the Romans collapsed and was broken up. Hereafter, the West was to be divorced from the empire in the East. It was in 529 that Emperor Justinian closed the Academy of Athens. One may find this event even more emotionally satisfying as the date which brings to a close both the Greek and the early period of Christianity itself.

During the Dark Ages, the material pre-conditions for scientific advance no longer existed. Misgovernment, top-heavy bureaucracy, civil wars, and the inroads of neighboring barbarian peoples led to a steady decline. The uniformity of Roman law gave way to a maze of discordant local customs. The universal monetary system of the Romans disappeared. Land became the basic unit of value. Lack of order among the new kingdoms, further inroads of barbarians, and the utter lack of culture among the rulers produced disordered systems of government and low standards of living. There was little leisure time, little literacy, and few towns, let alone cities. Science and culture inevitably suffered. To be sure, there were little pockets in Ireland and Monte Cassino where scholarship of sorts survived. Almost needless to say, there were no psychological advances made during this period. Insofar as there was any interest in psychology, and there was precious little, it was Augustinian doctrines which were known. Aristotle and Plato, by and large, had been lost, to be restored only later from the East through the rise of a new cultural power, the Arabian people, with their new religion founded by Mahomet.

ISLAM

Mahomet was born in Mecca in Arabia in 570. In middle age, he received a revelation from God on which thereafter he preached. He fled to Medina in 622 to escape persecution for his teachings. This date, the Hegira, or flight, marks the beginning of the Mohammedan era. He called his religion, Islam, meaning a surrender to God, and his followers, Muslims. His message is contained in the holy book, the Koran. The spread of Islam became the aim of his followers.

The gigantic and rapid development of Islam was remarkable.[2] From the Hegira in 622 and the death of the prophet ten years later, to the conquest of not only Arabia and Syria but also of Egypt and Persia in another twenty years, an irrevocable change was wrought upon the face of the Near East. Sicily and Spain soon came to be under the domination of Islam. One hundred years after the death of Mahomet, the Muslim Empire extended over an area larger than that of the Roman Empire at its height.

Muslims assumed positions of leadership in governmental, military and religious affairs, but, at first, scholarship fell to non-Muslims. A series of historical forces had been at work making these non-Muslim scholars available in lands that fell under the Muslim sword.[3] Egypt and Syria had been Hellenized and had Greek-speaking schools and strong philosophical traditions. In Persia an ancient Oriental culture came under Muslim domination. The scholars of these lands, with unbroken ties to the ancient civilizations, contributed a great deal to the cultural and scientific advance of the area. More-

over, pagan and heretic Christian scholars, especially the Syrian Nestorian
Christians and the Greeks of the Byzantine Empire, fled the Christian Empire
in the West to take refuge in this region, and helped in the spread of Hellenic
civilization to Muslim culture. Christian physicians, when driven out of
Constantinople, carried their knowledge to the Arabs.

The jostling proximity of many tongues made translation an extremely
important source for the diffusion of knowledge. Naturally the most important
translations were from Greek sources. Material from Greek philosophy and
science was available to the Arabs from their newly conquered lands. By the
end of the fifth century much of Aristotle and some of Plato had been translated
into Armenian and Persian. In the eighth century this non-Muslim material
became a major portion of the secular intellectual provender of the Muslims.
Aristotle held a particular fascination and his writings were very popular, along
with Neoplatonic works often not clearly attributed to their correct sources.
Aristotle, himself, in going through several translations was often, if not always,
garbled. To add to the confusion, many works were falsely attributed to him.
For example, the so-called *Theology* of Aristotle was actually an abridgement
of the last three books of Plotinus' *Enneads!* Moreover, he was often known
through the coloring given him by commentators, rather than from first hand
study. Hippocrates and Galen were also much translated. Despite the confusion
in the materials available to them, from the middle of the eighth century until
the twelfth century Muslim culture completely overshadowed that of the Latin
West.

The Muslims assimilated the Greek and Hellenistic material and then went
on to make distinctive contributions of their own. The philosophical speculation received from the Greek world had much the same effect upon Islam
that it was to have upon Christianity. Attempts at reconciliation of revelation
and reason became a major problem. Hotly contested arguments and action
arose concerning the question of heresy. Mystical movements, similar in spirit
to those among the Christians, also appeared.

Our knowledge of the original contributions made to psychology by Islam
is only superficial. It would appear that, by and large, even the greatest of
the Muslim philosophers, Alkindi, Avicenna, Alfarabi, and Averroes[4] (giving
their Westernized names) were primarily imitative of the Greeks, often showing a strong Neoplatonic strain. Insofar as they were naturalistic, they tended
to follow Aristotle. None of the Muslim scholars can now be seen as qualifying
among the great psychologists. Nevertheless, their contributions to psychology deserve more study than has so far been given them.

This same neglect has befallen the Jews who lived during these centuries
in the Muslim world. Treated by the Muslims rather more often in an enlight-

ened fashion than not, they experienced one of the high points of their scholarship. Between the ninth and the thirteenth centuries, especially in Spain and Egypt, lived several Jewish scholars who presented psychological thinking of originality and power. The psychological views[5] of the Jewish philosophers, such as Abraham Ibn Daud, Solomon Ibn Gabirol, Abraham Ibn Ezra, Ibn Zaddik, Isaac Israeli, and especially Moses Maimonides, have been shamefully neglected. Although their influence on later developments in psychology is, to say the least, obscure, and their work will not be examined here, they are well worth serious study.

In fields other than psychology and philosophy, the Muslims made some scientific advance.[6] Fired with enthusiasm by Greek and Hindu sources of knowledge, they made contributions in mathematics, astronomy, chemistry, technology, and medicine. Instead of being members of the clergy, as they were in the West, Muslim scholars were often physicians. With them the study of philosophy, medicine, and some of the rudiments of natural science went hand in hand. Advances continued even until the fifteenth century, but by the twelfth century Muslim supremacy had come to an end.

THE HIGH MIDDLE AGES[7]

By the eleventh century the social characteristic often associated with the Middle Ages had emerged more or less clearly. The spread of feudalism gave a measure of personal safety to individuals of all social classes and tended to stabilize social relations among them. There were three major social classes: the clerics, the aristocracy, and the rural farm workers. The church was influential not only because of its spiritual authority but because of its extensive land holdings. It was beginning to challenge successfully the secular influences upon its affairs which had existed heretofore and to make its appointments increasingly free from these influences. Moreover, it wielded considerable political power. The aristocracy was, by and large, a military caste depending for its revenues upon its estates. The institution of knighthood with its chivalric conventions had emerged. The rural population worked the estates and was levied for war service, receiving protection in return from their liege lords. In the eleventh century, due to a growth in population, greater political stability, more extensive trade, and increased social mobility, the towns became increasingly important. These conditions made possible a surge in scholarship.

Common Characteristics of Thinking

The thinking of the Middle Ages must be understood against its background. Greek philosophy-science had been based upon an attempt to see the world rationally; Christian doctrine is based on faith. One solution, popularly the only one attributed to the men of the Middle Ages, was to deny reason and embrace faith. Although this attitude prevailed, among some churchmen there was also an attempt to reconcile faith and reason. But of the two, one was primary and fixed; the other was secondary and precarious. The dominance of one over the other was never in doubt. No matter how precise the reasoning, if the conclusion did not conform to revelation, it was not true. Errors in faith, no matter how introduced, were heretical. Conformity was expected and enforced.

This common, general attitude, for such it can be called, led to a considerable amount of uniformity in intellectual life. There was a preoccupation with death. The pilgrimage of man to the grave, with life but a fateful probation either for blissful life everlasting or eternal woe, was a dominant theme. Large segments of the intellectual life were guided by a contempt for earthly matters, a despising of human joy, a gazing at eternity, a sense of *memento mori*. But not all life was uniformly gloomy.[8] There were rays of simple joy penetrating that dark gray, making the period of the Middle Ages less grim than it is often supposed to be.

Medieval thinking was not all of a piece. To speak of medieval philosophy does not mean there was one integrated system any more than it would be correct to reach the same conclusion concerning modern philosophy. The uniformity of thinking was greater than today, but it was not all pervasive. As Gilson[9] has reminded us, not all Christian philosophy was either Christian or philosophy. It was fortunate that there were many authorities, moreover, authorities who disagreed with one another. There was variation and change according to the style of the writer and particular problem. Furthermore, as will be demonstrated shortly, the scholastic method, contrary to popular opinion, did allow for some freedom of thought.

On the whole, the spirit of the age was not conducive to psychological concerns. The union of theology and philosophy that gave us Christian philosophy in its spirit of otherworldliness was foreign to psychology. Most of its problems dealt not with man, but with the relation of God and man, a quite different proposition. Only incidentally did the question of man, as man, occupy these thinkers. In this small fragment, in this isolated part of the pattern, there were some matters of psychological concern.

Sources of Knowledge

Until the twelfth century the West was lacking almost all of the works of Aristotle, knew but one dialogue of Plato, had incomplete knowledge of

Neoplatonism and lacked contact with Arabian thought. Most of its heritage was derived from the scriptures, from the writings of the Church fathers, including St. Augustine, and from a smattering of Neoplatonism. In the early Middle Ages the largest and most important compilation of fact, and fiction masquerading as fact, was the *Natural History*[10] of Pliny (23–79 A.D.). This work served as a textbook and encyclopedia for the medieval scholar, having within it all sorts of miscellaneous information on what might be called "facts" about nature.

The Latin writer, Chalcidius, living at about the same time as Plotinus, translated part of the *Timaeus* into Latin and commented upon it. This was the only work of Plato known to the Latin world until the twelfth century. Otherwise, Plato was known through Neoplatonic writers rather than directly. Only much later in about 1150 were two other dialogues, the *Meno* and the *Phaedo* made available in Latin, while the remainder of Plato's works received little attention until the humanist translations of the fifteenth century.

The *Timaeus* contains Plato's version of the creation of the world and universe and the relating of the world's creation to God. It was his poetic vision of the world and of the universe and of God. The central theme is that the world and man are but incidents or manifestations in the ideal patterns in the mind of God. The individual mind will be home again in the world of Mind and will reach the summit in God. The things of this world, the visible things, are not real. Only to the extent that they conform to the perfect conception have they any significance.

The trouble is that the *Timaeus,* his least typical dialogue, is a mixture of what Plato took seriously, mixed with plays of fancy. What he expected to be taken seriously and what was satire is not always easy to separate. Moreover, its excursions into astronomy—each soul having a star and a numerical relation among the planets—later produced a liberal dose of astrological nonsense which was to do considerable harm. There are also problems of interpretation because of the style of the dialogue. Indeed, this makes it so baffling that the interpretation of the *Timaeus* still causes as much, if not more, perplexity among scholars than does any of his other dialogues. From the perspective of scientific advance, Sarton,[11] goes so far as to say that the influence of the *Timaeus* was largely a negative one.

Aristotle, insofar as he had been known to the earlier Christian thinkers, was seen as definitely secondary to Plato and in fundamental agreement with him. The one area in which Aristotle was acknowledged to be original was that of logic. The earlier and more elementary portion of Aristotle's *Organon,* the logical works, had come down from the early Middle Ages in the direct tradition. It was studied along with a widely-used commentary by Boethius.

These works were staple of the dialectic training received, forming one of the three subjects of the *Trivium,* the other two being grammar and rhetoric. The rest of the *Organon* were translated as early as 1150, two generations earlier than those of Aristotle's works of more direct psychological interests. In the Middle Ages there was a search for the premises about which one can be certain. This, according to Schiller[12] went far to account for a relative neglect of experience during the 2,000 years after Aristotle.

Platonic sources from which Greek ideas came to Christianity dominated in its philosophy. The fundamental theme in Platonism—the dualistic contrast between things of the mind and those of the senses, between body and spirit—was preserved. Man, ever the resident of two realms, can either choose one or the other—either to take the tangible but temporal things of the senses or to turn upward to God and eternal life. For the Christian the choice was clear.

Scholasticism

The Patristic period, whose task had been the formation of orthodoxy, had passed long before scholasticism made its appearance. The task of scholasticism was to elaborate a recognized and accepted orthodoxy, to build upon recognized dogma a system of principles. The scholastic began with this doctrine and then traced its implications for various theological questions. Along with consciousness of a need for divine salvation, Henry O. Taylor[13] considers two of the common characteristics of medieval thought to be a deference to authority and an all pervasive scholasticism, leading to work that was diligent and receptive rather than original. Reverence for the past was a predominant attitude of the scholastic.

The scholastic method in its generic form is defined by Windelband as follows:

. . . a text used as the basis for discussion is broken up by division and explanation into a number of propositions; questions are attached and the possible answers brought together; finally the arguments to be adduced for establishing or refuting these answers are presented in the form of a chain of syllogistic reasoning, leading ultimately to a decision upon the subject.[14]

Naturally, there was variation in detail from writer to writer. In more general terms, oral discussion of question and answer, a form of dialectic, characterized the scholastic method. Scholasticism was especially congenial to the medieval mind because it permitted acceptance of authority and yet proceeded from that point on by dialectic. It was their version of eating their cake and having it too.

The scholastic had considerable freedom within the framework of his method, limited in latitude by the fact that dogma in no way must be put to question. It should be noted that the scholastic did not merely make an appeal to authority, as is sometimes alleged. As McKeon[15] indicates, a good scholastic could find authority for either side of a question and then proceed to find truth by examining their interplay. The scholastic might know the ultimate correct answer on the basis of revelation and faith, but he did not necessarily, or even often, cheat to make it come out "right." If his claim led to erroneous conclusions, he did not claim that it did not. Instead he went back over his earlier arguments for the sources of his error, and, perhaps, sometimes he couldn't find it! Moreover, being human, he could delude himself that his doctrine was not contrary to dogma and proceed to argue the point. He, of course, did so at his peril because his position might eventually be judged heretical.

During the Middle Ages philosophers were so often also theologians that sometimes it is overlooked that there were some problems which had no theological import whatsoever which they considered. A philosopher as philosopher, then, could depend upon reason alone, limited only by his skill and the knowledge available to him.

The Universities

Although some were founded in the century before, it was the thirteenth century that saw the universities come into prominence.[16] The universities had not been important before because there was simply not enough learning to justify their existence. With expansion of knowledge they came into being. The conditions for their presence also had become available. Gathering of the people into larger communities and increased ease of travel helped set the stage for their appearance. The youth of the eleventh century entered the monasteries; those of the thirteenth attended the universities. It is necessary to pass over the origins of the universities, which are frequently obscure and always intricate. Suffice it to say that some of the universities can trace their origin to the so-called cathedral schools. The newly organized universities at Bologna, Paris, and Oxford were certainly among the most important. Paris was a truly international university; men came to study not only from the many different regions now called France, but also from the Low Countries, and from Italy, England, and Germany as well. There were, of course, other universities: Cambridge in England; Padua and Naples and the medical school at Salerno in Italy; Montpellier, Toulouse, and Orleans in France; and Salamanca, Valladolid, and Lisbon in Spain and Portugal.

Their curricula consisted of an arts course and higher courses of theology, law, and medicine, each with separate faculties. The arts course usually involved a study of the seven liberal arts and the "three philosophies"—natural philosophy (natural science), ethics, and metaphysics. Masters and scholars were usually clerics, although not necessarily in holy orders. Almost always the church predominated. The newly founded orders of friars, the Dominicans and the Franciscans, both controlled professorships and did much to further the cause of the Church. They also served to supply many of the most distinguished professors.

The universities became a potent intellectual force. They aided intellectual progress by supplying a setting that made time and resources for study possible and provided a less involved, more disinterested point of vantage from which to approach fields of knowledge.

The Recovery of Aristotle

It was to Spain and Sicily, recently recovered to the Christian world in the twelfth and thirteenth centuries, that scholars from the West came to work on translation from the Arabic.[17] These translations could have been done directly from the Greek sources and, as a matter of fact, some such translations were made at this time. However, by and large, Arabic sources were used. This reflected luster upon the accompanying Arabic commentaries and original works. Along with the recovery of Galen and Hippocrates, the West received the medical works of Avicenna and the philosophical teachings of Averroes, which immediately became important. In medicine the Arabic scholars had added valuable observations, and in philosophy they had given a variety of distinctive new slants. The works translated from Arabic sources included not only religious, philosophical, and medical works, but also works in the fields of science, such as optics, geology, and mathematics. Original contributions in alchemy, magic, and astrology (sometimes attributed to Aristotle) had a considerable effect both for good and for ill. From the end of the twelfth century, extending over the next hundred years, the proportion of texts translated directly from the Greek gradually increased, and in the fourteenth century translations from the Arabic virtually ceased.

The introduction of these texts into the West, Renan[18] goes so far as to claim, divided the Middle Ages into two distinct periods: the earlier one without Greek knowledge, the later with ancient science restored. This sweeping generalization is not without merit as a summarization. Certainly a major task of the scholars was to assimilate and learn ancient knowledge and reexpress it in a fashion that would be acceptable when viewed against the imperatives of the time.

As important, perhaps, for the intellectual history of the West as all other works combined was the recovery of the works of Aristotle. The first medieval scholar supposed to be familiar with Aristotelian treatises was Alexander of Hales (d.1245). In the course of the years between 1200 and 1270, the body of his writings was imported into the universities of Paris and Oxford. With his recovery the times were ready for the appearance of Aquinas.

THOMAS AQUINAS

Reconciliation of faith and reason was the task of Aquinas. He carried on this task with intricate but massive tools, the teachings of the Church and the recovered works of Aristotle.

Life and Labors of Aquinas[19]

It is perhaps fitting that so far as places and events are concerned, the life of Thomas Aquinas bears an impersonal stamp, an objectivity without many of the towering heights and dark shadows of other great men. The fire was there, but it burned with a steady glow, not in a great shower of sparks and flame. For example, he was known to be really angry only twice in his life. It was not for him to wear his heart on his sleeve or to show his feelings in order to achieve sympathy or even to find understanding from his fellows. He led an intense intellectual life, and his solitary mind was always hard at work beneath a placid bulk that achieved for him the nickname of the "Dumb Ox" from his fellow students at the University of Paris. A story is told which characterizes his imperturbability and abstractedness in the service of scholarship, irrespective of circumstances. Obedient to the orders of his superiors, he had gone to a state dinner at the Court of the King of France, Louis IX, later to be known as St. Louis. Here he was, a huge man in the black and white habit of the Dominicans, quietly sitting at table. Unheeded and unheeding, all around him eddied the pomp, the colors, and the jewels of the most brilliant court of Europe. All around him was gossip, intrigue, and idle inconsequential chatter. He sat, saying little or nothing to those around him. Suddenly came a crash as a huge fist came down on a table, and his voice rang out clearly above the discreet hubbub, "And *that* will settle the Manichees!" He had been elsewhere, using his time for his task in life.

Besides being a great scholar, Aquinas was also to be a Christian saint. This sketch does not pretend to be concerned with this side of his nature. This omission is mentioned as a warning since some[20] would say that Thomas the scholar cannot be understood apart from Thomas the Saint.

face another disconcerting problem. Even in the passage in *On the Soul*[31] where Aristotle speaks of *nous* (mind) as imperishable, he seems to indicate that memory and love perish because they are parts of a complex, the body-psyche as a unit, which perishes. Hence, *personal* immortality seems to be denied in the very passage that is crucial to the argument of some form of immortality for living beings as individuals. Such, then, might be one interpretation of the material.

In broad perspective, Aristotle was not concerned with the problem of the immortality of the human soul, but of *nous* as a human function capable of knowing truth, of rising above man's animal limitations to a direct vision of universals. He was arguing for the existence of some dominating source of intelligence outside of the Universe. However, in considering what he has to say about movement and the unmoved mover, it is hard to read religious overtone into it.[32] Motion is eternal—it always has been and always will be. We can trace movement back from one mover to another—A moves B, B moves C, and so on. Eventually we have to postulate a mover himself unmoved, a transmitter of movement, not moved by an anterior movement. This unmoved mover Aristotle calls "God." The unmoved mover is not an object of worship. He is not aware of man, nor in any way concerned with him. Divine providence is completely absent. God is a metaphysical necessity, not an object to be loved and worshipped. What modern science disregards as irrelevant to its enterprise, the cause-uncaused, Aristotle considered he had to solve, because metaphysics could not, in his view, be divorced from physics.

Aristotle's theory of development in which each higher level included the lower levels, sketched in Chapter 3, was one of his greatest contributions. In this earlier discussion, progression from lower to higher stopped with man. But in the part of his theory, alleged to be earlier and Platonically based, he discussed a higher form of existence than man. Man's existence, in this extension, has its origin in a supreme existence.

The striving toward higher existence was seen in the Middle Ages as a striving toward God. That this phase of Aristotle's thinking may have been something which in his later thinking he discarded was not and could not have been known in the Middle Ages. Aristotle appealed to the Christian thinkers precisely because this appeal to supreme intelligence was considered by them to be an integral part, nay, the capstone of his thinking. His thinking, stressing that all living creatures are subject to law, was seen by them as demonstrating that this law was by personal guidance of God. The only alternative known to thinkers of the Middle Ages was pure chance. It was not until the time of Galileo and Newton that natural laws were seen as still a third alternative.

Aristotle had advanced four meanings of cause: the material, the motor, the formal, and the final cause; and had given weight to each of them. (See page 48.) It was possible for those who came after him to stress one or the other, according to their interests. His teleological strain, in his sponsorship of final causes, was lifted by Aquinas to a position of primacy. There is an intelligent being who directs all things to their ends—and this is God.[33] The other causes Aristotle had used to complete the analysis were subordinated to it. Efficient causes, said Aquinas, are subordinate to final causes, corresponding to a soldier's tactical disposition by a subordinate commander, while being directed to victory by the high command.[34]

Aristotle was interpreted as holding all that exists and all that happens does so for the sake of some end. Every activity, all change, and all growth are to be understood in relation to the ends they serve. All things are pervaded with change, and no change is meaningless. Change implies preparation, and preparation implies becoming. Hence, Aristotle's view was considered in the Middle Ages to be uncompromisingly teleological.

All we have just said was interpreted by Aquinas in a fashion which would reconcile it with Christian dogma. His great glory was that he could do it in a fashion such that not an inconsiderable number of thinking men today could find their personal application of the test of reason was met.

Nous, or Active Reason, minimized in the earlier, naturalistic account of Aristotle was lifted by Aquinas to the highest pinnacle of his views of man in general and of psychology in particular. Moreover he did not divorce metaphysical considerations from those of psychology. The "unmixed" separable character of *nous* was taken by religious Aristotelianism, especially that of Aquinas, to mean that *nous* was capable of separate existence. Hence, it was considered to be the Aristotelian counterpart of the immortal soul.

As a consequence of his espousing Aristotle, Aquinas laid himself open to attackers on two fronts. On one side the Church conservatives saw his furtherance of Aristotle as an attack on Augustine and the other Church fathers and the strains of Neoplatonism with which they had been so intermingled as to have lost their source.

From Aquinas' point of view the second source of attack was the crucial one because it came in the form more in what seemed to be agreement with him than it did in opposition. For his opponents were Aristotelians. Siger of Brabant, their leader, following to some extent the interpretation of Aristotle by Averroes, taught that *nous* was separable, but in the individual was conjoined with a "material intellect," both *nous* and material intellect being necessary for thinking, and, since the material intellect was corruptible, this prevented personal immortality; that matter existed from eternity; and that the impersonal *nous*, after leaving the matter of the body, became part of a universal and common intelligence. Irrespective of one's own interpretation of Aristotle's views about personal immortality and the exact nature of *nous* (and it would seem as Russell[35] said, that Siger may have had a case), it is possible, as was stated earlier, to take the position of Aquinas and argue for the soul's immortality. The views of the Averroists, as they were called, concerning the eternity of matter, although definitely contained in Aristotle, disagreed with the teaching of the Church on creation. On all three counts the position of the Averroists was incompatible with Catholic doctrine. When this was called to their attention, Siger and his followers agreed that perhaps these teachings of Aristotle did contradict the teaching of faith. So, ostensibly in the interests of defending reason and faith, Siger suggested the compromise known as the doctrine of two truths. This doctrine of the two truths had originally been advanced by Averroes, himself, under much the same circumstances, when he had been called on to reconcile his teachings with orthodox Islamic theology. Siger argued that there were two truths: the truth of the material world and the truth of the supernatural world. He argued that, when being naturalistic, one may hold in abeyance the other truth; on turning to religion, one accepts this truth. Aquinas, too, followed Averroes in separating faith from reason. To Aquinas, Siger said in effect, "You speak of reason and faith as both giving truth; so, too, do we, but with only this difference, one does not need to trouble about reconciling the two truths." "This fine distinction," Siger said, "is all that divides us."

This doctrine, seeming so near and yet actually so far from what he was teaching, was a flat contradiction to all that Aquinas stood for. To Aquinas, the doctrine was a mere subterfuge. For the second time in his life he was aroused in anger.[36] Such expressions as "puffed up with false knowledge," "if he dares," and "false teaching" were used in his reply to Siger, instead of his usual temperate and balanced style.[37]

It is to his eternal credit that he also opposed the reverse form of error. It is thoroughly unsound, he held, to believe views about other matters are irrelevant so long as one's religious attitude is correct.[38]

What Aquinas represented was the doctrine of the *one* truth. There were two paths to the *same* truth, not two truths. Nothing that was philosophically demonstrated would ever contradict or ever be contradicted by anything taught to man through revelation. This position of Aquinas may be made clearer if we deal more specifically with the issue of reason and faith as he saw it. That truth in reason and faith (in science and religion) are one, is so important to him that it is on this theme he opens the *Summa*.[39] Theology's position is that of the noblest of the sciences because of the worth of its subject matter. Natural knowledge derived from sense is not enough to know the essence of God but things from sense do come from God and this allows us to know he exists.[40] Not that there is no distinction between theology and philosophy, there is. One concerns faith, known immediately and without doubt; the other opinion, known only with consideration about the other possible alternatives.[41] Some truths are proper to theology alone since they can not be known by reason, *e.g.*, the mystery of the Trinity, other truths obviously are concerned with reason alone, but there are many truths which are common to both reason and revelation.[42] In these instances the philosopher and theologian consider the same truths, each in a different manner, the theologian as revealed, the philosopher as the result of a chain of reasoning. God the Creator may be the consequence of a chain of reasoning to the philosopher; God the Creator is accepted as revealed by the theologian. The same truth will be found in these instances, but arrived at in different ways.

Aquinas decisively disposed of the arguments of Siger, so far as Church orthodoxy was concerned, in a manner that need not be of concern. However, on more than one occasion during his lifetime and after, Aristotelian teachings were brought up for condemnation by Church authorities.[43]

Psychology

Three factors conspire to make it possible to be more brief in discussing the psychological views of Aquinas than has been the case with some of the other great psychologists. The previous discussion of reason and faith is directly relevant to Thomistic psychology. Moreover, there are much more complete modern statements readily available which was not the case for the earlier men.[44] Most important of all, Aquinas followed Aristotle in much of his psychology, and Aristotle already has received rather detailed treatment. A possible misunderstanding must be disposed of in this connection. To put it succinctly, Aquinas followed Aristotle, not because he was Aristotle, but because he thought much of what Aristotle had said was true. Aquinas did not hesitate to disagree with him if he thought what he wrote was incorrect. Since the terminology of Aquinas is different from that of Aristotle, some restatement has to be made even of points on which they were in agreement.

As a species, man, to Aquinas, has one substantial form, the rational soul.[45] Man is neither soul alone, nor body alone, but soul and body, a united or composite substance. There are no vegetative or sensitive substantive forms or souls. The person is a unity in that the rational soul has not only the function particular to itself but also the vegetative and sensitive functions. The human soul exercises the functions of the lower forms of life which have vegetative or sensitive souls. The rational soul as a unity is united with its body to carry on its natural functions. In distinction from what was held by some earlier thinkers, Aquinas taught that the soul is neither imprisoned nor carrying out a sentence of punishment; it is doing that which is natural and good. The uniting of the body with the soul is not to its detriment but to its enrichment.[46] It completes human nature and also confers the accidental benefit of allowing achievement of knowledge through the senses. The soul is acting according to its nature, in which matter exists for form, and not *vice versa*.[47]

This view is neither materialistic in the sense that soul or mind is made to depend upon material substances or, if you prefer, cortical substances, nor is this view, to use a Thomistic term, angelectic, in which mind or soul is interpreted as a purely immaterial entity, or as an independent spiritual being.

For Aquinas there were a multiplicity of corporeal substances; that is to say, a multiplicity of substances that have matter in their nature. Four species may be distinguished—non-living bodies, plants, animals, and men.[48] Inanimate things have material activities alone, plants show material activities and vegetative activities, animals these two and sensory activities, and man shows rational activities in addition to the three lower activities.

In one of the most sustained and detailed psychological statements a distinction is made by Aquinas between the unity that is soul, its faculties or powers, and further distinctions among these faculties or powers.[49] The soul is not its faculties. The soul does not exercise these functions directly through its essence as such, but has powers with which it is endowed and which are distinct from its essence. There is an order or priority among these faculties related to the corporeal substances of which they are composed. The rational faculties are conceived to be higher than the sensitive and, therefore, embracing and controlling the sensitive, while the latter is above the nutritive faculties. The vegetative faculty embraces the powers of nutrition, growth, and reproduction. The sensitive faculty embraces the five exterior senses, the four interior senses (to be described in a moment), sensitive appetite, and locomotion. The rational faculty comprises the active and passive intellect and the will. The vegetative faculty has as its object the subject's own body-soul combination. The sensitive faculty has as its object, not the body of its sentient subject alone, but every sensible body. The rational faculty has as its object, not only sensible body, but being itself. The higher the faculty, the more comprehensive its scope, extending from a particular body-soul composite, to sensed bodies, to being in general.

There is no need to review the powers of vegetative faculty or the exterior senses of the sensitive faculty since they are treated in a manner similar to that of Aristotle. This is not the case with the interior senses of the latter faculty. In using the expression, interior "sense," Aquinas was using it in a fashion that might seem strange today. Aquinas was referring, not to additional sense modalities arising from stimulation within the organism, but rather, to operations at the level of sensitive life and, consequently, psychological functioning which did not involve reason. For example, a bird goes beyond the outer senses in using vision in selecting twigs for nest building because, while the exterior sense gives awareness of color, it does not inform him that the twig is useful for the particular task. Since the bird does not reason, he must have an "interior sense" by which to apprehend the utility of the twig.

Reception of sense data involves the already familiar common sense for reception of those qualities, such as softness, which cannot be perceived by one sense modality alone. But reception also includes the particular interior sense that was just illustrated in the preceding paragraph. It becomes necessary because the data received transcends the qualities of the common sense. It is called *via aestimativa,* or estimative power. Animals are dependent upon it, being, as they are without the aid of reason. When a lamb sees a wolf and "estimates" it is to be avoided, this is done, to use a modern term, by instinct. That is to say, estimating is a power of sensing that which is harmful or useful to the organism without previous experience or training. In man, estimating is allied to mind, since there is always a background of abstract knowledge and universal principles derived from reason with which it interacts. While analogous to instinctive estimating, since it is effected by reason, must be distinguished from it. Hence, it is given a distinctive name, *via cogitativa* or cogitative power.

In addition to reception of sense expressed in the common sense and estimative or cogitative power, both animals and the humans conserve the data of sense. The conservation of data of sense Aquinas referred to as the imagination in that it produces the sense images. For the conservation of estimative or cogitative powers transcending sense as in recognition of an image as an item of personal experience in past time, still another power is necessary. This is called sensory memory. Thus the four interior senses are the common sense, the sense of estimation and cogitation, imagination and memory.

To sum up the processes involved, it is hardly surprising that Aquinas all but repeats Aristotle in considering sensation. He wrote that sensed material things exist only in the sensing individual, not as material but as immaterial, and the ability to sense is the ability to receive form (species) without matter.

The power of appetite is two-fold, according to Aquinas, involving sensitive appetite at the sensitive level and volition or will at the rational level. Sensitive appetite desires objects that are sensed. There are two major kinds of sensitive appetites, the *concupiscible,* so called because they desire the objects of sensible pleasure, and the *irascible,* whose function is the urge to fight for the objects in question when there are difficulties in securing them. The *concupiscible emotions* include love, desire, joy, hatred, aversion, and sorrow, while the *irascible* embrace hope, despair, courage, fear, and anger. The act of a sensitive appetite is called by Aquinas a *passion.*

In keeping with his teleological emphasis, Aquinas argues that at least some knowledge of purpose must be present for an activity to be called voluntary.[50] Perhaps the most typical of the solutions that Aquinas advanced for freedom of the will was that it arose from freedom of the intellect, or, as he puts it, free choice is free judgment. There are some activities forced on one which give rise to coercive necessity, but these are involuntary. Free will is shown in performing voluntary activities about which judgments are made.

The will, since it is an appetitive faculty, cannot be understood apart from its natural object. We desire happiness which is to be found in the good by our very nature, proceeding from the will in itself. This means the desire comes from the will itself and is not imposed upon us from without, as by violence. We cannot help desiring because we are the creatures that we are. This naturalness of desire for happiness does not mean one is not free to make his own individual choices. In the relation of will and intellect, will is subordinate. Intellect is dominant. "Nothing is willed unless known," is a dictum of Aquinas.

The functioning of the rational faculty, as such, needs to be considered. The power of the so-called agent intellect or active intellect is concerned with abstraction; and the power of the possible intellect is concerned with understanding, judgment, and reasoning. The first power is active or creative; the second is passive or receptive. A sensible object is only potentially intelligible since it is material. Aquinas was empirical in that he held with Aristotle that natural knowledge begins with sensation.[51] But in order to make sensory experience intelligible, the activity of the active intellect of the mind is necessary. With the operation of the active intellect we extract the form from the individual substance in which it is embedded and experience "color" or "horse." When the agent intellect acts, the concrete nature of the datum is laid aside and what remains is something capable of being understood. It is no longer material but is intelligible, an object of intellect. The agent intellect renders sensible natures intelligible by "abstraction" for use by the possible intellect. Sense experience provides the stimulus for setting in operation the agent intellect. It makes "possible" the realization of the truth that the possible intellect potentially contains. Before sensory experience the possible intellect was a *tabula rasa,* devoid of ideas. To a certain extent this task is performed by the senses themselves in that through them we perceive the *species* to which the objects belong, *i.e.*, a green flower and a green glass have the color green, which is its species. To understand, however, we must penetrate sensible species to intelligible terms.

In closing discussion of these aspects of the psychology of Aquinas, a return to theology is particularly fitting. So far as the teachings of psychology are concerned, a reconciliation with dogma becomes most imperative in connection with revealed doctrines about the resurrection of the body and its eventual reunion with the soul. This, in turn, requires the immortality of the soul. The issue at hand is how Aquinas reconciled his previously stated views on psychology with these theological imperatives. To do so Aquinas drew upon previously established teachings. It will be remembered that Aristotelian *nous,* the active reason or active intellect, has been interpreted by Aquinas as deathless. Aquinas extended this contention of immortality to the rational soul as a unit. It will also be remembered that Aquinas, himself, made a distinction between the soul and its faculties. Both of these points are made use of in the reconciliation.

To Aquinas, some of the faculties belong to the soul, as such. These faculties transcend the power of matter. For the rational faculties, the body is not necessary as the *organ* of activities. The rational faculties are not intrinsically dependent upon body, even though when united with the body they draw upon sense experience, which is dependent upon the composite. Other lower faculties, when in the soul-body composite, do depend upon the body for the way in which they are exercised in the composite, and cannot be exercised in that way without the body. Depending as they do upon the body, the sensitive and vegetative faculties, in the form they functioned in the soul-body composite, perish with the composite. But the soul is a unity. It, therefore, follows that the human soul cannot be said to depend intrinsically upon the body for its existence. Consequently, the whole substance of the soul shares in the deathlessness of the active intellect (the *nous* of Aristotle). The soul, as distinguished from its faculties, is a unity, and this unity survives separation from the body. All the powers of the soul, whether exercised by the soul and body in combination or by the soul alone, flow from the essence of the soul, and this essence is deathless. It also follows that not only do the faculties not dependent upon the body for functioning remain in the soul, separated from body, but likewise, those faculties dependent upon body for their particular way of functioning also remain in the soul, even when separated from the body. They function only potentially; reunited with the body they could act again, as upon resurrection. While death is a transforming experience of the rational faculties, their purely intellectual capacities are not destroyed.

Moreover, the fact of self-consciousness, that is to say, the ability of the active intellect to reflect upon itself, shows the immateriality of the rational soul as contrasted with the body. So it may be added that while the lower functions may be lost, *we* do not perish. Self-awareness, reason, and the will, integral aspects of the rational soul, do survive.

The Influence of Aquinas

Our view back over the centuries leads some to call this period the Age of Thomism.[52] In his own time Thomas was well known, to be sure, but he certainly was not universally acclaimed. On the contrary, his views met considerable opposition. His novelty was recognized, but often this realization was accompanied by the suspicion that his ideas were dangerous as well.

The victory that came to Thomism did not happen overnight. His fellow Dominicans were the first to accept him in a more or less official fashion, but opposition continued to be vigorous. As Sarton[53] reminds us, the gradual triumph was an advantage, stirring less jealousy and opposition when it reached the stage of almost being taken for granted. The victory of Aquinas, when it came, was complete. It set the prevailing position of later Catholic philosophy to this very day.[54] The Thomist philosophy was eventually established as the official philosophy of the Roman Catholic Church.[55] The Papal Encyclical of 1897 confirmed the teachings of St. Thomas Aquinas as the true Catholic philosophy. This does not mean, as it is sometimes mistakenly alleged, that his views must be accepted by Catholics. Rather, serious consideration of his teachings is required, but not unthinking obedience.

From the modern perspective, the reconciliation of faith and reason performed by Aquinas still has an intellectual appeal. For those to whom it is important and relevant to do so, he still provides a means of reconciliation of faith and reason without compromising the value or nature of either one or the other. Make no mistake. According to this view, experimental psychology, even psychophysical investigation, is legitimate. In no way does psychology detract from faith, and faith is neither subordinated nor contradicted by psychology.

Reason was given an enhanced stature through the work of Aquinas. The senses were the means by which man attained the basis of knowledge. In accepting the senses, Aquinas was accepting man's ability to use knowledge that he obtained in this manner, and, hence, saying that man's reason was sovereign for him when he was in the human state. The world may be transitory, but reason does have its own domain. Reason supplements faith; it does not deny it.

The appeal to reason argued so eloquently by Aquinas was highly successful even though sometimes in ways not intended by Aquinas or the Church. Others after him could and did draw the conclusion that the two—reason and faith —could exist side-by-side as two separate realms. Insofar as this happened, it was not intended by Aquinas. Nevertheless, it did happen on many occasions that his work was used to help to justify the separation of faith and reason, a separation of religion and philosophy. This controversy foreshadowed the separation of science and theology that was to come.

SCIENCE IN THE LATER MIDDLE AGES

The recovered works of Aristotle played a double and antithetical role in scientific developments in the later Middle Ages. It was as if thinkers could not let him alone—they were either for Aristotle or against him but ignore him they could not. In these developments his different works served different purposes. On one hand, the contentual works formed the basis of a statement of knowledge for many scholastics. On the other, his newly recovered methodological works, with their teachings of logic, gave the opponents of the first group of "Aristotelians" a weapon which, when complemented by the recovered Greek and the new Arabic mathematical works, became a potent tool for the development of new ideas on induction and experiment and the use of mathematical demonstration.[56] This was especially true in the field of physical dynamics where the greatest scientific advances were made in these centuries. It was precisely Aristotle's views of motion and space that were the ones most sharply criticized. In terms of the present-day index numbers of semantics, $Aristotle_1$ was used to demolish $Aristotle_2$.

In general, the gist of the great advance of the twelfth century had been a dawning realization "that a particular fact was explained when it could be deduced from a more general principle."[57] A mathematical-deductive method was beginning to emerge, reinforced by the mathematical advances taking place in the thirteenth and subsequent centuries. At Oxford there had been a reaction against the almost exclusive attention to theology, logic, and philosophy. Robert Grosseteste (c.1170–1253) was the most prominent teacher and the founder of the mathematical-scientific tradition of that great institution.[58] He had realized, albeit dimly, that a distinction could be made among the inductive, experimental, and mathematical approaches to science.

Developments within philosophy thereafter made it more possible to apply the scientific approach to nature. This was the developing gap between reason and faith as expressed in the rise of scepticism. Duns Scotus[59] and William of Ockham,[60] two Franciscan friars of Oxford at the end of the thirteenth and the beginning of the fourteenth centuries, were very important in this connection. They both contributed to the trends then dominating thought centering around a desire to separate reason and faith. At opposite poles in the struggle between realism and nominalism, though Scotus and Ockham may have been sharing in the belief that they were working toward increased glory of faith, their effect was to make faith and reason easier to be seen as separate, and not as unitary. As a consequence, scepticism toward faith went hand in hand with a greater independence of faith. Thereafter it was increasingly possible for reason to go one way and faith another.

The Experiment

In view of the grip that scholasticism had upon the thinkers of the later Middle Ages, it is hardly surprising that observational study of the phenomena of nature was almost non-existent during these years. A few, but very few, isolated observations were made by some scholars. The work of Albert the Great on botany would be a case in point. More significant for the future than observational excursions were the scattering of halting, imperfectly understood attempts to develop an experimental approach to the problems of nature and man.

True experiments were rare in the Middle Ages and continued to be rare in the Renaissance.[61] Working in almost complete isolation from one another, a number of scholars, each in his own way, were trying to formulate in their writings this "new" way of studying nature. These lonely pioneers included Roger Bacon, Peter of Spain, Raymond Lull, Arnold Villanova, Peter Olivi, Peter the Stranger, John of St. Almond, Pseudo-Galen, and Peter of Abano. Roger Bacon[62] is, by far, the best known of these men today. In fact a myth of his singularity grew up among those who came after Bacon who also believed that he alone of his day had a true appreciation of the scientific spirit. It is partly as a corrective for this that Peter of Spain, rather than Roger Bacon, is chosen for exposition.

Peter of Spain (c.1215–1277) was a remarkably versatile man. He was educated at Paris, became Rector of Medicine at the University of Sienna, physician to Gregory X, Archbishop of Braga, and, in 1276, was elevated to the Chair of St. Peter, as John the XXI. He wrote a textbook in logic[63] in use for centuries and a compendium of medicine, likewise very popular. But it was for two other accomplishments that he deserves to be rescued from the complete neglect that psychologists have shown him. Somewhere between 1245 and 1250 he wrote an original account of psychology, De Anima.[64] It must be emphasized that this was not a commentary on Aristotle. (As a matter of fact, he also wrote a commentary on Aristotle's *De Anima*.) Instead, it was perhaps the first avowedly independent work on psychology for over a thousand years in the sense that it was concerned with psychology and psychology alone. It even contained a chapter on the history of psychology! Moreover, he devoted some attention to the psychological and medical relations of the field. The "psychologist Pope" by no means has received the attention that he deserves.

The second of the two accomplishments making Peter of Spain worthy of attention was his account of the experimental method. In his *Commentaries on Isaac*,[65] a work on diets and medicines, Peter formulated his plea for something resembling an experiment. He spoke of two methods by which dietary science may be investigated, *via rationis* and *via experimenti*. The path of reason and the way of experiment (or experience) are both necessary but different. The path of reason proceeds through the use of the intellect, studies causes, and uses syllogistic methods; the way of experiment proceeds through sense, studies effects, and applies induction. Reason again is a necessary step beyond experiment to confirm what was found by it. Peter gives a series of six steps or conditions which he considered necessary to carry on medical experimentation. (1) The medicine should be free of foreign substances. (2) It should be established that the patient has the disease for which the medicine is intended. (3) It should be given without admixture with other medicines. (4) The medicine should be of the degree opposite to the disease. That is to say that if the disease causes an excess, the medicine should be such as to decrease it, as when a medicine is cooling of a heated condition. (5) It should be tested, not only once but many times. (6) The proper body should be used, the body of a man, not an ass. Through its simple and concrete language shines a remarkable grasp of some of the implications of how an experiment is conducted today.

Medicine

After the classical twilight, medicine had become largely a matter of folk-medicine.[66] The historical situation in this area repeated that for ancient knowledge in general, some medical knowledge persisted particularly in commentaries on Galen, and much more had come back from the Arabs. The revival of Western medicine began in the eleventh century when the medical school at Salerno, founded a century or two earlier, came into prominence, perhaps stimulated in its pioneering by contact with Arabian medicine of nearby Sicily. In the twelfth and thirteenth centuries the university medical schools of Montpellier, Bologna, Padua, and Paris gained prominence. How-

ever, the church prohibited its clergy to carry out surgery on the principle
of its abhorence of bloodshed. This coupled with a contempt for any form
of handiwork led to the barber-surgeons making their appearance as assistants
to the professors. Moreover, so-called monastic medicine appears to have been
"a gigantic delusion." Certainly knowledge of anatomy was in a poor state,
and most university medical teaching was of a theoretical and dogmatic
character.

Science and Superstition

In the late Middle Ages the irrational still had great appeal. The history
of medieval science was inextricably bound with magical, superstitious practices. Differences among men of the age were only a matter of degree. Magic
was so pervasive that Lynn Thorndike,[67] the historian of science of the Middle
Ages, found it eminently fitting to write a history of magic *and* experimental
science.

Belief in demons and witches was widespread in the fourteenth century
although not to the terrifying extent to which it swelled in the fifteenth and
sixteenth centuries. Astrology had many devotees; magic was performed
everywhere. Divination by dreams was taken very seriously. These and similar
superstitions were not confined to the ignorant peasant; a king might be as
superstitious as his lowliest subject. Nor was the scholar-churchman exempt.
The official policies of the church toward such matters took a complicated
and circuitous course, impossible to trace in short compass. Suffice it to say
that in earlier centuries it was something tolerated but generally discouraged,
but in later centuries superstition became a matter of considerable concern
and brought massive persecution of alleged witches on the part of Catholic
and Protestant authorities alike.

An apt illustration of the combination of science and superstition of these
times is to be found in the medical teachings of Arnold of Villanova (*c.* 1235–
1316).[68] At one and the same time, he was a thorough Galenist and believed
in the Devil and demons. He proceeded to combine Galenic humoralism with
demonology in his diagnostic and etiological considerations. Because the Devil
likes warmth, the presence of warm humors in the body makes the individual
susceptible to seizure by the Devil. Hence, warm humors are to be avoided.
Arnold, likewise, brought Galen into accord with astrology. Accepting the
Galenic contention that epilepsy is caused by the humors, he related the
particular humor bringing on the attacks to the particular quarter of the moon
in which it occurred. The planet Mars he considered to be responsible for
melancholia because the planet's color and supposed heat had affected the

color and heat of the bile, which brought on melancholia. While bleeding was recommended as a treatment, he argued it must be applied in accordance with astrological portents involving consideration of the phases of the moon and constellations.

THE END OF THE MIDDLE AGES

The period of the medieval revival of learning seems to have spent its force by the close of the first quarter of the fourteenth century.[69] Its contributions were again and again reproduced in the fourteenth through the sixteenth centuries, first in manuscript and then in printed form; but very little creative or original work was done until the new period of the scientific Renaissance came into being.

To be sure there were changes presaging the future. In the second half of the fourteenth century there was an increase in the number of scholars who were not clerics.[70] This was significant of the changing times. Works also began to be written in the native tongues instead of in Latin.

The fourteenth century and the first years of the fifteenth century in general historical perspective saw many stirring events whose general effect was to destroy the synthesis of the thirteenth century. The Black Death wiped away perhaps a fourth of the population. The One Hundred Years' War involved the usual wastefulness of war, which was heightened in this case by sheer length. There was the rise of the commercial classes, the decrease in importance of the feudal aristocracy, the rise of strong national monarchies, and a decline in the moral prestige of the papacy. The Babylonian captivity, the Great Schism, and the power politics of the Church hierarchy helped to persuade people that papal autocracy must be held in check.

But when did this period end and a new one begin? Various dates have been advanced, but it is relatively unimportant to be precise here. With Sarton[71] it is agreed that about 1450 is as good a date as any. This date saw the appearance of printing in the West, a discovery the importance of which is self-evident.

REFERENCES*

1. *E.g.,* H. O. TAYLOR, *The Mediaeval Mind.* (4th ed.) Cambridge: Harvard University Press, 1959.

2. P. K. HITTI, *Arabs, a Short History.* Princeton: Princeton University Press, 1946.

* See page 16 for description of reference style.

3. The influence of non-Muslim scholars and the assimilation of Greek and Hellenistic material is recounted by A. C. Crombie, *Medieval and Early Modern Science*. (2 vols.); 2nd rev. ed. New York: Doubleday, 1959; M. Desruelles, & A. Bersot, L'assistance aux alienes chez les Arabes du VIIIe au XIIe siecle, (*Année med. psychol.*, 1938, 96, 689–709); and D. L. O'Leary, *How Greek Science Passed to the Arabs*. (London: Broadway House, 1948).

4. AVERROES is perhaps the only one of the group who has been studied from a psychological point of view. J. Bákoš, *Psychologie d'Ibn Sīnā (Avicenne) d'après son oeuvre aš Sifā'*. (Prague: Editions de l'académie Tchécoslovaque des Sciences, 1956). More peripheral but still interesting is the volume by E. Renan, *Averroes et L'Averrosime*. (Paris: Alcan, 1869).

5. Dimly discernible in such works as I. Husik, *A History of Mediaeval Jewish Philosophy*. (New York: Meridian, 1958).

6. G. SARTON, *Introduction to the History of Science*. (3 vols. in 5) Baltimore: Williams & Wilkins, 1927–1948.

7. Major sources helpful in understanding the relevant aspects of high Middle Ages were Taylor (*op. cit.*); Sarton (*op. cit.*); G. Leff, *Medieval Thought: St. Augustine to Ockham*. (Baltimore: Penguin, 1958); E. Gilson, *The Spirit of Medieval Philosophy*. (New York: Scribner's, 1936); the introductions to *Selections from Mediaeval Philosophy*. (ed. R. McKeon, 2 vols., New York: Scribner's 1929); the article by the same writer, Aristotelianism in Western Christianity. (*Environmental Factors in Christian History*, ed. J. T. McNeill, et. al., Chicago: University of Chicago Press, 1939, pp. 206–231); and R. Klibansky, *The Continuity of the Platonic Tradition During the Middle Ages*. (London: Warburg Institute, 1939).

8. E. K. RAND, Medieval Gloom and Medieval Uniformity, *Speculum*, 1926, 1, 253–268.

9. GILSON, *op. cit.*

10. Pliny the Elder, *Natural History*, 6 vols. (Translated by J. Bostock & H. T. Dilly). London: Bell, 1855–1890. (A.D. 77).

11. SARTON, *op. cit.*

12. F. C. S. SCHILLER, Hypotheses. *Studies in the History and Method of Science*. In C. Singer (ed.), London: Oxford University Press, 1917, pp. 414–446.

13. TAYLOR, *op. cit.*

14. W. WINDELBAND, *A History of Philosophy*, Vol. 1, *Greek, Roman and Medieval*. New York: Harper, 1901, pp. 312–313.

15. McKEON, *op. cit.*

16. A standard source is H. Rashdall, *The Universities of Europe in the Middle Ages*. (2nd ed.) (eds.) (R. M. Powicke, A. B. Emden) Oxford: Clarendon Press, 1936.

17. A good succinct account may be found in O. H. Haskins, Arabian Science in Western Europe, (*Isis*, 1925, 7, 478–485).

18. RENAN, *op. cit.*

19. The major source for details and for all dates is the account of his life by V. Bourke, *Thomistic Bibliography, 1920–1940.* (St. Louis: St. Louis University, 1945). Some material has also been drawn from F. C. Coplestone's *Aquinas.* (Baltimore: Penguin, 1955), G. K. Chesterton, *St. Thomas Aquinas.* (Garden City: Doubleday, 1958), and M. Grabmann, *Thomas Aquinas: his Personality and Thought.* (Authorized translation by V. Michel, London: Longmans, 1929).

20. *E.g.,* GRABMANN, *op. cit.*

21. CHESTERTON, *op. cit.*

22. Particularly relevant to psychology are his *Summa Theologiae* and *Summa de Homine* which form volumes 31–33, and 35 respectively of *Opera Omnia* (Ed. by A. Bourget, Paris: Vives, 1890). A good secondary source is G. C. Reilly's, The Psychology of Saint Albert the Great, compared with that of St. Thomas. (*Phil. Stud., Cath. U. of America,* 1934, No. 29)

23. T. AQUINAS, *Summa contra Gentiles.* 5 vols. (Translated by the English Dominican Fathers) New York: Benziger, 1928–1929. (1258–1264).

24. *Aristotle's De Anima in the Version of William of Moerbeke and the Commentary of St. Thomas Aquinas.* (Translated by K. Foster & S. Humphries) New Haven: Yale University Press, 1951. (1269–1270)

25. T. AQUINAS, The Summa Theologica. (Translated by English Dominican Fathers & rev. by D. J. Sullivan) In R. M. Hutchins (ed.), *Great Books of the Western World.* (Vols. 19–20) Chicago: Encyclopaedia Britannica, 1952. (1266–1273).

26. *Ibid.,* First Part, QQ. 75–100, Vol. 1, pp. 378–522.

27. *Ibid.,* Part 1, Second Part, QQ. 1–48, 49–89, Vol. 1, pp. 644–826, Vol. 2, pp. 1–204.

28. K. FOSTER, *The Life of St. Thomas Aquinas: Biographical Documents.* Baltimore: Helicon, 1959.

29. ARISTOTLE, Works. (Translated under direction of W. D. Ross) In R. M. Hutchins (ed.), *op. cit.,* Vols. 8–9, (*c.*340–322 B.C.); *On the Soul,* 429a 10–430a 25.

30. F. NUYENS, *L'evolution de la psychologie d' Aristote.* Louvain: Institut supérieur de Philosophie, 1948.

31. ARISTOTLE, *On the Soul,* 408b 17–32.

32. ARISTOTLE, *Physics,* 241b 24–245b 2, 252b 10–267b 26; *On Generation and Corruption,* 334a 8–15; *Metaphysics,* 1012b 22–31, 1018b 8–35, 1049b 4–1050b 5, 1072a 30–3, 1074b 14.

33. *Summa Theologica,* First Part, Q. 2, 3.

34. *Ibid.,* Part 1, Second Part, Q. 109, 6.

35. B. RUSSELL, *A History of Western Philosophy.* New York: Simon & Schuster, 1945.

36. CHESTERTON, *op. cit.*

37. T. Aquinas, The Unicity of the Intellect, *"The Trinity" and "The Unicity of the Intellect."* (Translated by R. E. Brennan) London: Herder, 1946. (1270)

38. *Summa contra Gentiles*, Vol. 2, 3.

39. *Summa Theologica*, First Part, Q. 1, 1–3.

40. *Ibid.*, Q. 12, 12.

41. *Ibid.*, Part 2, Second Part, Q. 1, 4.

42. *Summa contra Gentiles*, Vol. 1, 3.

43. F. Van Steenbergen, *The Philosophical Movement in the Thirteenth Century.* New York: Nelson, 1955.

44. R. E. Brennan, *Thomistic Psychology, a Philosophic Analysis of the Nature of Man.* New York: Macmillan, 1941; G. P. Klubertanz, *The Philosophy of Human Nature.* New York: Appleton-Century-Crofts, 1953.

45. *Summa Theologica*, First Part, Q. 75, 1–7, Q. 76, 3; *Summa contra Gentiles*, Vol. 2, 56, 57.

46. *Commentary on Aristotle's De Anima*, 1 ad 7, 2 ad 14. (In reference 24)

47. *Summa Theologica*, First Part, Q. 76, 41.

48. *Summa contra Gentiles*, Vol. 4, 11.

49. *Summa Theologica*, First Part, QQ. 77–90. (With exceptions specified below, this is the source for discussion of his psychological views hereafter.)

50. *Ibid.*, Part 1, Second Part, Q. 6.

51. *Ibid.*, First Part, Q. 12, 12.

52. Leff. *op. cit.*

53. Sarton, *op. cit.*

54. Crabmann, *op. cit.*

55. Sarton, *op. cit.*

56. A. C. Crombie, *Medieval and Early Modern Science.* Vol. 2. *Science in the Later Middle Ages and Early Modern Times.* (2nd rev. ed.) Garden City: Doubleday, 1959.

57. *Ibid.*, p. 3.

58. A. C. Crombie, *Robert Grosseteste and the Origins of Experimental Science, 1100–1700.* Oxford: Clarendon, 1953.

59. John Duns Scotus. Selections from the Oxford Commentary on the Four Books of the Master of the Sentences. In R. McKeon (ed.), *Selections from Medieval Philosophers.* (Vol. 2) New York: Scribner's, 1930, pp. 313–350. (*c.* 1300)

60. William of Ockham, *Studies and Selections.* (Edited & translated by S. C. Tornay) Chicago: Open Court, 1938. (*c.*1322)

61. Sarton, *op. cit.*

62. Roger Bacon, Selections from the *Opus Majus.* In R. McKeon (ed.), *op. cit.*, Vol. 2, pp. 7–110. (1268)

63. PETRUS HISPANUS, *The Summulae Logicales of Peter of Spain.* (Edited & translated by J. P. Mullally) South Bend: Notre Dame University Press, 1945. (1268)

64. PEDRO HISPANO, *De Anima.* (Edited by P. Manuel Alonso, S. I.) Consejo Superior de Investigaciones Cientificas. Instituto Filosofico "Luis Vives." Serie A. Num. 1, Madrid: 1941.

65. L. THORNDIKE, *A History of Magic and Experimental Science, During the First Thirteen Centuries of our Era.* (Vol. 2) New York: Macmillan, 1923.

66. CROMBIE, *op. cit.*

67. THORNDIKE, *op. cit.*

68. G. ZILBOORG & G. W. HENRY, *A History of Medical Psychology.* New York: Norton, 1941, p. 137.

69. THORNDIKE, *op. cit.*

70. SARTON, *op. cit.*

71. G. SARTON, *Six Wings: Men of Science in the Renaissance.* Bloomington: Indiana University Press, 1957.

CHAPTER 7

DESCARTES:
THE RENAISSANCE AND THE BEGINNING OF THE MODERN PERIOD

THE 150 years from the appearance of printing in the West in about 1450 to about 1600 has come to be called the Renaissance. Choice of limiting dates such as these for a given historical period is essentially a matter of adaptability to the task at hand. The beginning date, when learning could be transmitted in a stable fashion, is a plausible one for a presentation of the history for psychology, especially when some attention is devoted to the larger scientific and cultural history of which it is a part. The terminal date of the period of the Renaissance, although often selected for other reasons, has special appeal for psychology since it was in 1596 that Descartes, the first psychologist of modern times, was born.

THE RENAISSANCE[1]

In the main the Renaissance was a period of general and literary preparation rather than specific and scientific accomplishment. Nevertheless, the spirit of the age, literary though it may have been, brought differences in outlook which were to influence science, including psychology.

Anticipation of the new outlook it was to express may be found in the work of Petrarch,[2] a lonely pioneer who died in 1374, only one century after Thomas

Aquinas, but nearly a century before the date of convenience that is being used for the beginning of the Renaissance. This dawning outlook was expressed in the humanistic attitude—an interest in freedom of the human spirit and freedom from the medieval traditions of scholastic theology and philosophy. Petrarch was filled with a sense of being in a transitional period and an eagerness to recover and know the Latin Classics. The Renaissance movement as heralded by Petrarch had not yet become pagan, nor had it cut itself off from the Middle Ages, as it was later to do. Although Petrarch may have loved Cicero best, he quoted Augustine in his writings many, many times. A loyal Churchman, he regarded the study of the classics not as an enemy, but rather as an ally to Christianity. From the start, however, he had a contempt for scholasticism. In speaking of these interpreters of the works of others, Petrarch scoffed, "Like those who have no notion of architecture, they make it their profession to whitewash walls."[3]

The concern of the humanistic scholars of the Renaissance was the development of a cultural-educational ideal in imitation of that of classical antiquity. Concern for the humanness of man was primary, that is to say, the value of man as an earthly being and as an integral part of the world of nature was held paramount at the expense of consideration of his destiny in the life beyond. In their enthusiasm for classical knowledge, the men of the Renaissance could not escape noticing that the Greeks and the Romans had led good and happy lives and had developed a magnificent civilization without the aid of supernatural revelation.

The discovery, preservation and translation of ancient manuscripts, textual criticism, letter writing in the manner of Cicero, and concern with epigraphy, archaelogy, grammar, and rhetoric occupied their time. A paradox of the rebirth of classical humanism, with its emphasis on Latin and Greek, was the concurrent popularization of the vernacular tongues as vehicles of the literature of the day. Rabelais and Montaigne, for example, fought for the growth of French as a language of literature. The fear of novelty, so characteristic of the Middle Ages, gave way in the Renaissance to an actual seeking of novelty for its own sake.

During the Renaissance another form of discovery was also taking place— that epitomized in the voyages of Columbus, Dias, de Gama, and the captains of Prince Henry the Navigator. In this way the known world was enlarged. Characteristically, other Renaissance men were rediscovering ancient geography through translations of ancient manuscripts.

The "New Education" was one of the innovations of Renaissance men. Impatient with the *Trivium* and *Quadrivium* of the Middle Ages, and eager to transmit the newly discovered heritage to their fellow men, they developed a new curriculum. More and Ascham, both Englishmen, and Vives, a Spaniard, were leading figures in espousing this brave new curriculum. There is perhaps more than a touch of irony in the fact that the curriculum which emerged resembled in many ways the classical liberal education of Latin and Greek, now so much decried by modern education. As Randall[4] puts it, this curriculum proved so attractive as to be paid for dearly since it effectively blocked wide-spread teaching of science for centuries to come.

The leading humanists, although well read in the ancient classics, were not concerned with working toward new developments in philosophy. This does not mean that there were no philosophers. In fact, every school of ancient philosophy had its champions during the Renaissance.

Under the patronage of Cosimo de Medici a Platonic Academy was founded in Florence in 1462. It was dominated by Marsilio Ficino (1433–1499), who along with others typical of this time, attacked the Aristotelianism of the Scholastic.[5] Since Ficino[6] regarded Plato not as inferior but equal in authority with divine law, he set out to combine Platonic doctrine as a complete organic whole with Christian teachings. In the endless battle of Plato versus Aristotle, Plato triumphed during this period. After all, Aristotle had been the philosopher of the schoolman. Moreover, Plato was in the process of being rediscovered, as Aristotle had been earlier, and his views seemed fresh and new while Aristotle's views seemed musty and old-fashioned. Some students of the period[7] have gone so far as to say that it was due largely to the influence of Plato that the early humanists were not scientific. Whatever the reason, many of the great men of the Renaissance were hostile to science. Petrarch, Erasmus, Rabelais, Ficino, and even Vives at one time or another had something disparaging to say about science.[8]

Neither philosophy nor science of that time owes anything to the religious revolution of the sixteenth century, the Reformation. Many of its leaders detested "natural reason" and were hostile to science. Luther denounced reason as the mistress of the Devil; taught that Aristotelian metaphysics, science, and ethics were false, and even that his logic was inconsistent with theology.[9] Although it was a convenient pretext, Calvin condoned the burning alive of Servetus, the discoverer of the pulmonary circulation of the blood, for describing the barren topography of the Holy Land as it was, contrary to the scriptural teaching of it being a land flowing with milk and honey. The same lack of positive contribution to philosophy or science must be said of the counter-Reformation within the Catholic Church.

Although no great psychologist emerged during the period, there were some contributions of lesser rank. Arranged in order of birth date there was the interpretation of Aristotle by Pomponazzi[10] (1462–1525) as being agnostic concerning the immortality of the soul; the forceful presentation by Niccolo Machiavelli[11] (1469–1527) of how men are more controlled by passion than by their reason; the espousal by Juan Luis Vives[12] (1492–1540) of education of women, of the direct examination of our experience and of the use of psychology in education; the identification by Paracelcus[13] (1493–1541) of the influence of unconscious motivation; the advancement by Jean Fernel[14] (1497–1558) of the view of man as a work of nature; the bringing by Philipp Melanchthon[15] (1497–1560) of affectivity into the interpretation of consciousness and the first use of the term, "psychology"; the specification by Huarte of San Juan[16] (*c.*1530–1592) of the connection between psychology and physiology, and the examination of differential capacities; the emphasis by Michel de Montaigne[17] (1533–1592) upon individual differences and variability of human nature; and the first use in 1590 by Rudolf Goeckel[18] (1547–1628) of the word "psychology" in the title of a book. Despite the lack of great men, there seems to have been a noticeable broadening of the general field of psychology during the Renaissance. A certain amount of freedom from theological concern can also be observed even from this very short statement. In psychological thinking about the soul and body, chief reliance was placed upon the division of the soul into vegetative, sensitive, and rational faculties intertwined with some version of Galenic humors.

It is hardly surprising to find that the most important scientific work during the Renaissance appeared relatively late in the period. The year 1543 saw the appearance of both of the scientific works heralding the modern period, the *De Fabrica corporis humani* of Vesalius[19] and the *De revolutionibus orbium Coelestium* of Copernicus.[20] Although for generations afterward the characteristic medieval scientific doctrines continued to be taught in the schools, the ideas that Vesalius and Copernicus represented steadily gained wider and wider acceptance and extension. In his work on anatomy derived from dissection, Vesalius was finding reason to disagree with ancient authority, or more specifically with the anatomical teachings of Galen, despite Vesalius' almost reverent attitude toward him; in his treatise on celestial mechanics Copernicus was revolting against Ptolemy. In a positive and, therefore, even more important way, Vesalius was giving a new emphasis to the use of direct observation for securing scientific data and Copernicus was giving the world a new cosmology.

In spite of the importance of the work of these men there still existed a severe limitation upon scientific work during the Renaissance in the absence of a clearly understood scientific method.[21] It was the scientific movement of the seventeenth century which gave us the modern period in science.

THE BEGINNINGS OF THE MODERN PERIOD IN SCIENCE

The modern period in science was coming into being at the turn of the seventeenth century. A distrust of the past and a desire for the new were prominent characteristics of the age. Whether merited or not and whether scientific or pseudo-scientific, a remarkably large number of works published in this century either in title or in preface claimed to be "new."[22] Even as we do today, the men of the seventeenth century prided themselves on their modernity, and, even as we, they were trapped in the old.

The scientists of the century did show a reluctance to accept sacrosanct first principles on the bases of which one was to deduce conclusions on what must happen. They were groping toward freedom from philosophical presuppositions. However, there is no unanimity of opinion concerning their lack of philosophical presuppositions. Burtt[23] has alleged that the Platonic and Pythagorean tradition can be shown to be the foundation for, and justification of, the beginning of modern science in these years. Against this view on the other hand, Strong[24] has arrayed an impressive mass of evidence. He took the position that the choice of method by the scientists of this time was prior to whatever metaphysics they might have used thereafter to justify the position. Philosophical precedents and distinctions, instead of being fundamental to their work, were merely incidental and supportive. Strong argued that it was not knowledge of the Pythagorean-Platonic tradition which turned these scientific workers from classification to measurement. Rather, theirs was the methodological problems of how to do the job at hand, not the metaphysical task of justifying it. They were "pragmatic" in that they developed working distinctions and definitions in order to handle the specific subject matters with which they were concerned. Reluctance to accept first principles meant specifically that appeal to the authority of the ancients had lost its former almost paralyzing hold. It followed that, if the authority of the ancients be abandoned, a new procedure must replace it. This procedure was found in mathematics.

A variety of circumstances conspired to make mathematical operations characteristic of the science of the time. For one thing the appeal of the Aristotelian conception of nature as a hierarchy of being, based upon qualitative differences, had lost its hold. The influences of Aristotle and his emphasis on classification was at its lowest point in centuries. This gave an opportunity for mathematics as a quantitative method to regain its importance. There were other, more positive factors at work that strengthened the appeal of mathematics. The Greek mathematics of Alexandria had been rediscovered. Moreover, mathematics had gained in generality and complexity over the centuries and now had the very useful tool of the "Arabic" notation.

A tremendous variety of practical problems in navigation and gunnery, for example, stimulated craftsmen and others to apply mathematics. Without mathematics, the scientific advances of the seventeenth century would have been impossible.

The mathematically oriented scientists of the sixteenth and seventeenth centuries followed the procedure of relating their measurements to the properties or motions of the bodies they studied.[25] These they generalized as the rules of operation in nature. The demonstrations of physical relations in mathematical formulation was their contribution to physical science.

Galilei Galileo was perhaps the most important of these early modern scientists. In his *Dialogues Concerning the Two New Sciences*[26] which contain his most important studies, he used mathematics and concerned himself with the quantitative conditions of variations in quality. The constants he assumed in his work were not absolute, but subject to correction by empirical means. If so and so were true, then a certain specified result should eventuate. He then proceeded to verify whether his conclusions did or did not hold true. This is a far cry from making these constants metaphysical ultimates.

One facet of the emergence of physical sciences during this time was to have a considerable effect upon psychology. Today everyone is so accustomed to thinking of physics and psychology as separate disciplines that no perplexity whatsoever arises from the fact that sound, light, heat, and similar properties are the concern of *both* physics and psychology. It was during the seventeenth century that a division of labor took place. Representative of the problems investigated during the period in question are studies on the pitch, velocity, and transmission of sound; the origin of light and color: the wave-like properties of light; and the corpuscular theory of matter.

Those aspects of sound and light that were trustworthy, in the sense that they were open to investigation, were considered parts of physics; the aspects which were subjective in character were relegated to the study of the mind and philosophy. Moreover, cogent reasons to distrust the unaided senses had become apparent to thinking men, whether or not they were influenced by Platonism. To those accepting his findings, the very discovery by Copernicus that the earth moved showed them at the same time that the senses were unreliable. This phase of the emergence of the physical sciences was to help to delay the appearance of a more modern psychology.

The reaction of many physical scientists to psychological phenomena then and later was neatly epitomized by Galileo's attempt to deal with the separation of what we now call physics and psychology. He noticed distinct differences which from the time of Locke were to be called primary and secondary qualities.

Galileo seized upon Democritus' distinction between the perceptual world of sensory appearances and the conceptual real world. (See page 7.) Galileo[27] objected to considering qualities specified as heat (in the subjective sense), tastes, smells, and colors as having this same reality as shape and motion. They are names for qualities having their locus, not in the object, but in the responsive body. Remove the body, and these qualities would be annihilated. They are different from the primary and real. They do not exist as truly and as genuinely as do the phenomena with which a physical scientist deals. It can be seen that Galileo was in the process of excluding man's experience from the world of nature. This attitude, to be continued by many other scientists of his time and later, goes a long way to explain the caution and suspicion with which psychology, as a science, is viewed by physicists and others to this very day. Somehow what a psychologist deals with is not as "real" as that with which the physical scientist works.

Sensory experiences rejected at the front door went round to the back, since Galileo and all later scientists accepted the trustworthiness of the evidence of their senses to conduct their experiments and observations! They, after all, did look through their telescopes and derided those who would not look with them.

Another form of rebellion against dependence upon philosophical presuppositions was expressed by Francis Bacon (1561–1626) who in *Novum Organum*,[28] *Advancement of Learning*[29] and *New Atlantis*[30] sketched his views of what he thought science should become. In *Novum Organum* and the *Advancement of Learning*[31] his procedural proposals for science are given. His target was Aristotle, or, rather, the Aristotle of the *Organon*, the Aristotelian logic. He did not see that Aristotle had insisted upon the priority of induction in carrying on research, although by no means to the exclusion of deductive logic. Bacon eagerly espoused induction, almost to the point of excluding deductive procedures. He did not, however, hold mathematics in particularly high regard as a scientific tool,[32] and in failing to stress mathematics, he was out of tune with most of the great scientists of his time. He realized that the mathematical method is essentially deductive,[33] while the appropriate method to him was primarily inductive, being based upon the patient collection of instances.

Bacon insisted on going beyond simple enumeration of instances, a method which was well known long before this time. His goal was to bring into use a new, particular form of induction. He would have drawn up lists of facts, not only lists of things that had a given quality in common, but also lists of things lacking it, as well as lists of those that possessed the quality in varying degrees. In this way the particular character of a given quality could be expected to emerge from study of the lists. His was a sweeping inductive method; the observation of many facts would lead eventually to a generalization. His reaction against rationalism was so extreme and his dependence upon empiricism so intense, that he could not convince himself that even tentative hypotheses should guide a scientist in selection of facts. He had faith, too much faith, that laws would emerge from the welter of particular instances if one were but reasonably observant.

In his espousal of induction he was anticipating fields where mathematics had as yet but little use. It was in biology that inductive procedure was to be most faithfully followed. But to use induction properly, one must have preliminary hypotheses as a guide in selecting instances, something which Darwin and the other great biologists recognized. In the long run, of course, both induction and deduction were found to be essential to the scientific enterprise.

Bacon enthusiastically but uncritically endorsed the use of experiments.[34] Experiments, he argued, by prodding nature so that she takes off her mask, make her reveal her struggles and help to decide causes. One goes from experiments to the isolating of causes, and, conversely, to relate the matter back to his inductive method, goes from causes to the invention of new experiments.

In service of his method, Bacon advanced his famous account of the *Idols*, the preconceptions that blind men to the truth.[35] There are four kinds of these preconceptions: *Idols of the Tribe*, inherent, generally agreed-upon ways of thinking, such as our ways of perceiving; *Idols of the Den*, prejudices created by an individual's environment and education; *Idols of the Market Place*, deceptions arising from loose use of words; and *Idols of the Theater*, blind acceptance of authority and tradition (so-called because all previous systems of philosophy created theatrical worlds, not the real one).

Bacon also best expressed another aim which became characteristic of the age—the seeking of useful knowledge.[36] Power over nature in the service of man expressed the Baconian spirit of the age, so important to him that he expressed it in the very first aphorism of *Novum Organum*: effects cannot be produced without knowledge of causes; with this knowledge power and knowledge become one. This view of power as the fruit of knowledge was shared with others of his time, including Descartes, who in his *Discourse on the Method of Rightly Conducting the Reason*,[37] spoke of a practical philosophy that masters nature.[38]

Generally speaking, Bacon's forceful writings, his enthusiasm, and his position as one of the eminent figures of his time (he was Chancellor under James I) led to wide knowledge of his writings and to increased knowledge of, and respect for, scientific methods. Especially prominent in this connection was his influence in pleading for the usefulness of science. From his time onward, scientific study was to be judged by its usefulness to some extent, sometimes unduly so.

The opening stages of the scientific revolution in biology lagged behind that of the physical sciences.[39] Contributions in biology in the sixteenth century were still hampered by dependence upon the soul as the place of origin of bodily action. The reason for a relative neglect of biology and psychology during these years was not entirely the lack of workers in these fields, but, rather that the general scientific climate of the age was dominated by the work in the physical sciences. Indeed, the emulation of physics by psychologists to come into prominence in the nineteenth century had its roots in the seventeenth century.

Before the seventeenth century, the naturalist had no more than the unaided senses to guide him in his work. Thereafter, he had the microscope; but it was not until 1674 that Leeuwenhoek could use it to discover micro-organisms and spermatozoa.

Some noteworthy researches were carried out. As a natural extension of his interest in that primarily visual science of astronomy, Kepler[40] studied vision directly. On examining the eye he found that an *inverted* image is cast upon the retina. This flatly contradicted the Epicurean representative theory of vision (see page 81) which called for objects to give off images of themselves that impinged directly upon the sense organs. How could this be if the image was inverted, not right-side up? Kepler was content to demonstrate the phenomena and to leave to others reconciliation of his finding with a theory of perception. (See page 177.)

Even more important was the demonstration of the circulation of the blood by William Harvey.[41] Before his time the thousand-year-old Galenic theory had prevailed which called for pulsation of the blood with the body consuming it as nutriment. In this theory the blood itself was not the substance we know, but involved animistic, and super-natural entities, the "animal spirits." Harvey not only conclusively demonstrated that the blood moved, *"as it were, in a circle,"*[42] but also measured the amount of blood passing through the heart in one-half hour and found that would exceed by more than three or four times the body weight, thus destroying the consumption theory. However crude though it may have been, he measured a bodily function and thus brought a quantitative cast to physiology. He also did much to weaken the belief in the occult qualities that had been attributed to the blood. What made Harvey's work outstanding was the fact that he integrated scattered facts into a comprehensive generalization.

The biological sciences were still seen as part of medicine, not as sciences in their own right; and no other comparable advances were to be found. Hall,[43] in his careful study of scientific development between 1500 and 1800, concluded that the biology of today as pursued in laboratories and in field stations is essentially a creation of the nineteenth century. Moreover, the closest of kin to modern psychology, the field of physiology, had to await advances in knowledge of anatomy before it could come into its own.

RENÉ DESCARTES

René Descartes was the first great psychologist born in the modern era. This is not the same as saying that he was the first modern psychologist. His views on psychology were still rooted in his metaphysical assumptions, and consequently his psychology was subservient to his philosophy. Nevertheless, for the first time since Aristotle, a philosophic system *de novo* was attempted.

He fondly believed himself to be independent of past authorities. Starting out to find truth from rock bottom, as it were, was one of the ways he expressed the modern spirit. He prided himself in reading relatively little, wanting, as he did, to turn away from the classics to "the great books of the world."[44] He referred little to the past either to acknowledge borrowing or to criticize. Of course, no more than any man could he entirely escape the past, and his thinking shows the effect of the past more than he was prepared to acknowledge.

A remarkable amount of scientific work had taken place during the early years of the century when Descartes was growing up and attending school. Specifically, what scientific knowledge was available to young Descartes in 1628 when he was thirty-two years of age and ready to begin his epoch-making writings? Over eighty years had elapsed since Vesalius and Copernicus had published their works. Gilbert had described his experiments in electricity and magnetism twenty-eight years before. Francis Bacon, with his deep concern for enlarging the scope of knowledge, through his form of induction particularly for the sake of the control of nature it gave, had died two years earlier in 1626. Tycho Brahe, whose observatory Descartes had already visited, had made his meticulous astronomical observations. Kepler, who had worked with Brahe, had advanced his three basic laws of planetary motion, and was to die two years later in 1630. Galileo's secret condemnation of 1616 by the Church for advancing evidence concerning the heliocentric theory was probably already known to Descartes; and if not, he had but to wait five years for the public condemnation of 1633. Harvey, born before him but destined to outlive him, had published the demonstration of the circulation of the blood that very year. Of the great scientists of his time, only the greatest of all, Isaac Newton (1642–1727), with his general theory of dynamics embracing his laws of motion and accounting for the motions of the whole universe, the planets, their satellites, and the comets, was not contemporaneous with Descartes.

The Life of Descartes[45]

René Descartes was born at La Haye in Touraine in March 1596. The economic circumstances of his father and mother, both from professional families, was such that they left him with an income sufficient to assure a modest financial independence throughout life. He never occupied ecclesiastical or academic office.

In the spring of 1606, René entered the college of La Flêche, which had been founded a year or two before by the Jesuits. As he was in frail health, he was excused from morning religious duties and allowed to stay in bed. While abed he did his lessons and developed the habit of long sustained reflection and analysis. He continued both the habit of remaining in bed in the morning and working out his thinking through sustained reflection for almost the rest of his life. The program of studies at La Flêche can be seen as aimed at reconciling the classical learning of the Renaissance with the scholastic learning of the Middle Ages. The program consisted of languages, mathematics, humane letters, physics, ethics, logic, and metaphysics. Even before he began his travels, he tells us in his *Discourse* that he took the first step on his intellectual journey. With only one clear exception, the subjects he studied left him ". . . embarrassed with so many doubts and errors that it seemed to me that the effort to instruct myself had no effect other than the increasing discovery of my own ignorance."[46] Mathematics was the only exception, ". . . because of the certainty of its demonstration and the evidence of its reasoning."[47]

Little is known about his life for the six years following his departure in 1612 from La Flêche. It would seem he went to Paris and that after a brief period of sampling the pleasures of Paris, he found that they palled on him. As a result he went into studious seclusion. Then and later, the proximity of friends proved to be too much of a distraction. It was in pursuit of even more privacy that he went to Holland sometime in 1618.

He enlisted as a gentleman volunteer in the army of Prince Maurice of Nassau but apparently did not see combat. In November of that year he met Isaac Beeckman, a mathematician and the rector of a small college. They became warm friends, and Beeckman's influence turned Descartes to purely theoretical problems. Before he left Holland, Descartes had written, although not published, works on algebra and music. The following year (1619) René, ostensibly in military service, spent many months traveling to Denmark, Hungary, Austria, and, perhaps, to Bohemia. His 1619–20 winter quarters were in a small village near Ulm. There he spent his time in study and speculation. The next step of his intellectual journey was taken during this winter. It was at this time that an inspiration came to him. It appeared to be enough of a mystical experience to result in a vow to travel to the shrine of the Blessed Virgin in Loretto. The gist of the inspiration was the conviction that mathematical methods could be the basis of all rational knowledge. He resolved to devote the rest of his life to the cultivation of reason through the method revealed to him.

In the spring of 1620 he again took to traveling for the study of *le grande livre du monde*. He continued to travel until 1628, spending the winter of 1622–23 and the years 1625–28 largely in Paris. Between 1628 and 1649, Descartes lived in various places in Holland. Although he lived quietly, his thinking attracted considerable attention which he sought to avoid so far as personal contact is concerned. He was, however, a voluminous correspondent. He moved often from town to town, requiring for his needs only proximity to a Catholic Church and to a university.

Most of his important works were written and published in Holland, although much preparation preceded this period. During his first years of residence in Holland, he wrote *Rules for the Direction of the Mind*,[48] to be referred to often later in the account of his views. By 1633 he had nearly completed his *Treatise on the World*, his account of the world and man. This work contained two heretical doctrines—defenses of the earth's rotation and espousal of the infinity of the universe. In this year he stopped work on the *Treatise*, and what he had already written was not published during his lifetime. The reason or reasons for this decision cannot be known. With the example of the condemnation of Galileo before him, was he merely timid? Was he desirous for peace to continue his work undisturbed? Or did he form a resolve to justify both science and religion and consequently deferred publication until he could do more work? We simply do not know. His life-long religious orthodoxy may have been merely politic, but the evidence seems to indicate sincerity.

A portion of *The World*, called *L'Homme*, [49] by Descartes, was posthumously published. It has been called the first textbook on physiology. It is also useful for the information it gives on his views on physiological psychology. In 1637 he published his *Discourse on Method*[50] accompanied by three shorter pieces including *Dioptric,*[51] a study of optics, which gave the first published statement of the law of refraction.

He followed these works with the circulation in manuscript form of his *Meditations of the First Philosophy*[52] for the sake of securing criticism. In 1641 he published the book along with his answers to the criticisms that had been submitted. *The Discourse* and the *Meditations* included an account of his methodology of science as based upon his particular philosophical presuppositions.

An otherwise relatively minor point in connection with the *Meditations* helps to throw light on the shift in attitude toward theological and philosophical matters since the Middle Ages. At the time he published his *Meditations,* Descartes was especially anxious to placate the Church. Accordingly, he dedicated the book to the Dean and members of the Faculty of Theology of the University of Paris. However, in the second paragraph of this dedication,[53] he remarked that he had always considered the question of God and soul to be matters of philosophical concern rather than theological argument. Although he was not successful in getting their desired support, this remark did not in any way seem to put him in a poorer position. An assertion such as this would have been impossible in the Middle Ages. This remark could not have been expected to endear him with the clergy; however, at this time, he surely would not have included a remark that would have inevitably weakened his case. Indeed he had reason to feel anxious about the attitude of the Church toward him, then and later. The age may have been somewhat more tolerant, but this is far from saying one could not get into trouble through philosophical and scientific teachings. Indeed his works in general produced criticism as subversive and contrary to religious teachings from Catholic and Protestant religious circles. As a consequence of his living in a Protestant country, he learned that Protestant dogmatism could be as unyielding as others had found the Catholic. Intervention of powerful friends prevented, however, any serious consequences.

In 1649 he published the *Passions of the Soul.*[54] In accord with the times, psychological discussion early in the volume was followed by a development of the ethical significance of his psychological ideas. He considered that it is the passions which give rise to all good and evil of this life, and he wished to show how the mind might control the passions.

Queen Christina of Sweden had become interested in his views, and a correspondence had developed which, when reworked, had become part of his *Passions of the Soul.* In the fall of 1649 Descartes took up residence at her Royal Court. This change was to prove both incongenial and fateful. For a man accustomed to spending mornings in bed, the hour of his tutorship of his not very apt but energetic pupil, set by her command at five in the morning, must have been painful. It was an unusually cold winter in Stockholm, and the castle was drafty. Before six months had passed, on February 11, 1650, he died of pneumonia. His certainty that he had proved the existence of God was akin to that which he held toward his beloved mathematics. Less than fifteen years later his works were placed in the *Index.*

The Method of Descartes

The method of Descartes has several intertwined facets or aspects. To put it briefly, at one and the same time, the method was mathematical, deductive, procedural, and rationalistic.

He came upon the method in its mathematical guise first during that winter spent near Ulm. His discovery was to emerge as analytic geometry, the reciprocal application of algebra and geometry. In this he was not the first. [55] However, his predecessors, working with algebra combined with geometry in solving particular problems, had used *ad hoc* methods. Descartes helped to systematize and extend the relation between these two formerly disparate fields of mathematics to form a unity. He made it possible to express the properties of whole families of curves by means of simple algebraic equations. But Descartes went even farther. If two apparently disparate fields of knowledge could be combined, could not all fields of knowledge be combined? Could not the method of analytic geometry be applied to other fields of knowledge in such a fashion as to make a unity of all science? Were not the methodological assumptions of the physical sciences a unity which he was making explicit and could defend with examples? To anticipate later developments he was close to seeing that the properties not only of numbers but also of shapes and dimensions are expressible in equations. In a more general fashion, qualitative difference, intensive as well as extensive, may be related to variations in shape and dimensions expressed in numerical symbolism. Descartes was fortified in this view of unity to the sciences by a conviction that it is more efficient to study them all together, than to deal with them one at a time.[56]

Turning now to the deductive aspect, the particular value of the mathematical method, as Descartes saw it, was the possibility of starting with the simplest ideas and then going on to draw from them careful inferences. He contrasted this deductive method, explained in more detail in a moment, with the syllogism and with dependence upon raw experience. Descartes recognized that the syllogism did not directly adapt itself to learning what was new, but was more useful in restating and in clarifying that which was already known.[57] Consequently, it was unsuitable for discovery of new facts. The use of experience as a source of scientific knowledge allows deduction but it is otherwise methodologically weak. In his view if one depends upon experience, one must, of necessity, start with highly complex objects. Inferences, although they may be drawn, may easily go wrong. Mathematical deductions, starting as they do, from simple clear self-evident truths, cannot, in his view, go wrong.

How does one proceed to use this deductive method? He answered in more than one way. His *Rules for the Direction of the Mind*[58] gives a version in terms of twenty-one rules. He also answered in the *Discourse on Method*[59] in terms of what is explicitly stated to be the four most essential rules of procedure. These four rules were: (1) never accept anything as true which is not known clearly to be such; (2) divide difficulties into as many parts as possible; (3) proceed from the simplest and easiest to understand to the more complex knowledge; (4) make the connections so complete and the reviews so general as to insure that nothing is overlooked. His manner of presentation of abstract argument, here and elsewhere, was clear and simple in form and was a far cry from scholastic technicalities. Only occasionally did he slip into the terminology of what he called the language of the schools. Of course, these rules are neither as self-evident nor as free from the possibility of error as Descartes thought, but to explore this further would take us too far afield.[60]

Descartes placed the problem of knowledge in the center of his inquiry. He held a rationalistic theory of knowledge, that is to say, by reason one can know truth. In his writings he seems to be saying that men have, to an equal degree, the power of reason by which to distinguish the true from the false.[61] However, he also admitted that individuals are born with different degrees of discernment of clear truth.[62] Even here, he goes on to add this discernment can be made much more expert by practice, and he insisted that all of the sciences proceed from those which are easy to understand.

Truth and falsity come from thinking alone.[63] This, then, is his plea for rationalism: by taking thought one can know truth. Experience, to be sure, is present but fallible.[64] His paradigm of geometry misled him however into thinking that clarity and distinctness is a guarantee of truth. Then and later, the history of science is littered with the self-evident certainties which have had to be abandoned. The Ptolemaic hypothesis of the movement of the sun around the earth, if one may be forgiven for stating it thus, is a shining example. He failed to see, as Galileo did, that hypotheses are tentative, the test of which is whether or not the consequences deduced from them agree with the observations made. In short, he did not insist in his methodological account upon the experimental check required by Galileo.

The Search for Certainty

In keeping with the temper of his age and with his distrust of knowledge inherited from his predecessors, Descartes asked himself as a major theme throughout his *Discourse on Method*[65] of what could he be certain without any possibility of doubt? His position is not that of the skeptic, but, rather, he insisted that doubt is the proper starting place for constructing a system that would answer the skeptic. He did not wish to deny the reality of everything; he insisted merely that we may be in error. He wanted to doubt in order to find that about which he could be certain. As he indicated, the senses deceive, men can deceive themselves through faulty reasoning, and even in sleep one may have the same thoughts as one does in waking without their being true.

... I resolved to assume that everything that ever entered into my mind was no more true than the illusions of my dreams. But immediately afterwards I noticed that whilst I thus wished to think all things false, it was absolutely essential that the "I" who thought this should be somewhat, and remarking that this truth *"I think, therefore I am"* was so certain and so assured that all the most extravagant suppositions brought forward by the sceptics were incapable of shaking it, I came to the conclusion that I could receive it without scruple as the first principle of the Philosophy for which I was seeking.

And then, examining attentively that which I was, I saw that I could conceive that I had no body, and that there was no world nor place where I might be; but yet that I could not for all that conceive that I was not. On the contrary, I saw from the very fact that I thought of doubting the truth of other things, it very evidently and certainly followed that I was; on the other hand if I had only ceased from thinking, even if all the rest of what I had ever imagined had really existed, I should have no reason for thinking that I had existed. From that I knew that I was substance the whole essence or nature of which is to think, and that for its existence there is no need of any place, nor does it depend on any material thing; so that this "me," that is to say, the soul by which I am what I am, is entirely distinct from body, and is even more easy to know than is the latter; and even if body were not, the soul would not cease to be what it is.[66]

Along with indications of his thinking on other matters taken up later, this quotation brings out that the central core of his solution to his search is the certainty of his thinking and, therefore, of his existence. He found the last limits of doubt and the starting point of his system in the application of his first procedural principle, to accept nothing as true unless it be clearly evident.

In the *Meditations*[67] he used a somewhat different but closely related approach to the same problem. He first asked what he formerly had considered himself to be. To paraphrase, he answered he had believed himself to be a man—a man with face, hands, arms, flesh, and bones; that he had been nourished; that he had been able to walk; and that he had been able to think and to feel. He had referred these in the past to the soul, and then either did not stop to ask what the soul might be, or considered that it was something subtle or rare akin to a flame, or the wind, or the ether, spread throughout his grosser parts. As for the body itself, he had been sure he had known that it was a figure confined in a certain place, filling a given place from which other bodies were excluded. This body, he had thought, could be perceived by the senses, touch, sight, and the like, and it could be moved, not by itself, it is true, but by something different from the body itself by which it was touched (and also from which it received impressions). This power of self-movement and also thinking and feeling were not of the nature of the body itself. Such then is what he had believed himself to be.

He proceeded with his argument by asking one to suppose that there was a certain powerful "genius," or demon, who was intent on deceiving him. Under these circumstances, could he, Descartes, affirm as certain these things, which pertain to the nature of the body which he has just enumerated? After thinking this over carefully, he said he realized that of none of these things said of the body could he say they pertained to his awareness of "me." Moreover, if he had no body about which he could be certain, he can not be certain about walking or taking nourishment or perceiving. But what of thinking? Here is something, he says, about which I can be certain.

. . . I am not more than a thing which thinks, that is to say a mind or soul, or an understanding, or a reason, which are terms whose significance was formerly unknown to me. I am, however, a real thing and really exist; but what thing? I have answered: a thing which thinks.[68]

This is the starting point of the system of Descartes, the certainty, open to each of us, of one's own existence. In conformity with his procedural principle this is so clearly recognized, that it cannot be denied. Even if one is being deceived by the malicious demon he is still a thinking being. Doubt, itself, is an act of thinking. I doubt, but in doubting, I think. I know I exist because I perceive the fact distinctly. This doubting self is conscious. It is not identical with one's thought, even the sum of them. Descartes was not affirming self and thought taken separately as in a subject and verb, but a thinking self as a unity, something whose "essence" consists in thinking. This is not thinking in the abstract; it is a person he was talking about. One is reminded of Augustine's somewhat similar expression. (See page 99.) However, Augustine advanced the principle only incidentally, while Descartes used it to deduce principles fundamental to his over-all position.

His doubt was provisional, not fixed. He retrieved the world by first proving to his satisfaction the existence of God starting from his axiomatic self-certainty. Going beyond this primary axiom, that man is a being whose nature is to think, suffice it to say, he proceeded to examine another clear idea, that of perfection, which leads him to the perfect being and the consequent proof that God exists. Although this proof of the existence of God is complicated in detail, his major points are clear: [69] (1) everything has a cause, including our ideas; (2) we have the idea of God; (3) to cause us to have an adequate idea of God nothing less than God is necessary; therefore, (4) God does exist. God, he goes on, the most perfect of all beings, would not deceive, and, hence, we proceed with confidence to examination of natural reality which must also exist. [70]

While not denying its reality, he held that final cause or purpose could not be utilized in science. [71] We can form no clear idea of the end to which God made the world, so we have no right to attribute to him some special reason for creating it. Final causes in science—explaining things by attempting to ascertain God's purpose—is worse than useless. It is apparent from Descartes' discussion that inadmissibility of final cause extends beyond physical to include biological and physiological events. Organs may perform their function admirably but this does not entitle one to draw the conclusion they were created to serve this purpose.

Comparing himself to Archimedes who had said that, given a fixed point in space, he could lift the earth, Descartes claimed that he had found the bedrock upon which to construct a whole system of science. [72]

His system of science was built upon what he considered to be essential, basic philosophical assumptions. Despite the originality of his system as such, in his demand for basic philosophical assumptions, he can be seen to resemble his philosophical predecessors, rather than the first great modern scientists who were his contemporaries.

Mind and Body

To Descartes this "thinking thing" was a mind. He also affirmed that it was a substance, that this substance was immaterial, and that it was entirely different from the body. In other words, Descartes was stating a view of the dualism of mind and body. He was saying that there is nothing at all common to matter (body) and mind. Matter is extended substance; that is to say, it has the property of extension in length, breadth, and depth. [73] Animals and the bodies of men are matter. The Aristotelian distinction between inorganic and organic matter was being swept away. Matter is matter, with no difference between the matter of living and that of non-living things.

His major argument for the separation of mind and body has already been given in the subjective certainty of self, but Descartes also offered[74] the suggestion that one way we know that mind and body are separate is that if you take something away from the body, say a foot, nothing is considered to have been lost to the mind. Since we clearly perceive mind as different from body and *vice versa*, there is a real distinction between them; and they can exist apart from one another.[75] To put it in terms of their fundamental difference, created reality is composed of two materially exclusive natures—extension and thought. Since they are of different natures, distinct in kind, it follows that they are subject to different laws. Mind is free; matter is subject to natural law. Moreover, this dualism implies two parallel worlds either one of which may be studied without reference to the other.

The rational soul and the mind are synonymous. Mind is the soul that thinks.[76] In order to avoid ambiguity, Descartes considered mind to be the preferred term, instead of soul. His choice if followed hereafter.

In various places he gave several succinct statements on the nature of mind which may help us to grasp more clearly what it is that he meant. Mind, he said, is a thing which thinks, and it is identical with the thinking thing;[77] this thing is unextended substance;[78] this non-bodily substance has the characteristic of thought;[79] the power by which we know things is purely spiritual;[80] the purely spiritual is called mind.[81] The mind is outside of the physical order of matter and in no way derived from matter.[82] Such, then, is the nature of mind.

The mind is a unity, but it does have functions, powers, or faculties.[83] The faculties are not parts since it is one and the same mind that employs itself in these faculties. He most often spoke of thought as embracing the functioning of mind. He used the term broadly, considering it to include all kind of mental experience: doubting, denying, willing, imagining, and feeling.[84] In fact, thought, as he used the term, included all that of which we are conscious.[85] In almost all occasions other than that which follows below, he preferred to discuss the mind as involving thought or understanding, imagination, memory, and sense, without relating it to the will. Mind, it will be found, involves all of these factors, but also encompasses will.

What amounts to his most fundamental classification of the modes of thought is the dual classification into will on one hand and understanding in all of its ramifications on the other.[86] Volition, or will, then, is one of the two basic powers of the mind; the other is understanding. To Descartes, one of the innate ideas (the nature of which is discussed in a moment) that we have is of freedom of will.[87] Will is related to understanding as a means of accounting for error.[88] The will is unlimited and has freedom of choice; understanding, on the other hand, is limited. This dominance of will is demonstrated in that we do not always connect the same action with the same thought. Willing has intervened, causing movement in the way required by the act of will. The will then directs the action. Will gives assent or dissent to what has come into our understanding. This is a free choice.[89] One errs, not in failing to understand properly, but in willing, which is wider in compass and range than is understanding. One may not will properly and, hence, fall into error. For example, if the principle of clarity is disregarded and will is allowed to precipitate a decision, error can occur. In a way this makes understanding subordinate to will. But in the same context he speaks of choices made by necessity, thereby making the issue somewhat obscure.

In view of the relation of the self to will, it is plausible to consider at this point Descartes' conception of self. The self, as was established to Descartes' satisfaction by considerations given before, is known directly, since he could conceive of not having a body but not of a mind aware of itself. The self participates in the willing (as well as in discriminating and judging) shown by the experience of having made a choice. Self is known through consciousness.

Thought gives rise to ideas. Ideas are of two sorts: those which might be called derived ideas and innate ideas. The derived ideas arise on the occasion of external stimuli, but vastly more important are the innate ideas. Innate ideas are a special class of ideas, those of universal truths.[90] Unlike ideas arising from sensations, they are not preceded by organic impressions. Ideas are innate because they are developments of consciousness alone, not transmitted by the objects in the eternal world. It should cause no surprise that to Descartes the idea of self, of God, and the axioms of geometry are among the most important innate ideas. Perfection, substance, quality, infinity, and unity are also innate to the mind, not needing sensory experience in order to exist. Sensory experiences may remind us of these ideas, to be sure, but they are not due to the sense perceptions. These ideas are innate in the sense that they are potentially capable of being developed into a form of conscious experience. They exist potentially and become actual in the presence of experience. Descartes had little occasion to consider memory or association as mental processes since this doctrine of innate ideas solved for him these problems as well.

Understanding is the basic instrument of thought, while imagination, memory, and sense are aids to this understanding.[91] Understanding alone is capable of perceiving truth, but the others may aid when used correctly. Understanding derives directly from mental activity, uninfluenced by the body. Although imagination, memory, and sense are also purely mental in themselves, they are influenced by bodily activities and, hence, are a product of the interaction of body and mind. In the section that follows, it is their mental nature which is being considered. In so far as body is concerned, discussion is deferred until consideration of interaction.

We are exposed to error in direct experience, not through failure of the understanding, but in a fashion similar in spirit to that occurring in the case of will. We fail to take into account that sense, imagination, and memory may err. The setting for handling the problem of error due to the senses is that of his search for certainty. It will be remembered that he concluded God would not deceive us about the reality of the world of matter. In a sense Descartes' argument has proved too much, for, after all, errors and illusions do exist. How, then, to account for them? Here he falls back on his procedural rule concerning clarity. We can be sure of that which we apprehend clearly. Error comes when we neglect this precaution. Sensory qualities are not among the clearly thinkable ideas and hence, are among those prone to error. Similarly, imagination and memory share in this lack of clarity and are, therefore, also subject to error. If we forget that these three may err, our conclusions may be wrong because we failed to take their tendency to error into account. If we had done so, our understanding would have served us correctly.

Sensing, as distinguished from understanding, is the perception of qualities, colors, sounds, odors, and the like.[92] These sense experiences are less than real, but are convenient as signs to allow us to get about in the world. Thus the sound of horses' hoofs warns us of the approaching object, and we can step out of the way; but it has told us nothing about the true reality of matter. The image we have of the horse does not copy the natural object, as men before Descartes believed; rather, our image signifies or stands for the object. This was a considerable step forward from the naïve representative theory of perception which would have our experience nothing more than a copy of a picture of the object.

Sensations are of the mind and cannot be qualities of objects. The perceived qualities of natural bodies are variables of sense experience. They have no existence in things but are qualities of sensory *experience*. This Descartes demonstrates in the following manner. Heat could not be a quality of a burning object, for if it were so, it would mean that as we approached, the object itself got hotter, as we went away from it, the object got colder. If the object bore the qualities of sensory experience, it would also have to bear the pleasurable or painful qualities of it which we experienced according to our distance from it. At one distance the object would have to have the quality of pain, at another distance the quality of pleasure. Thus, the same object would have to have alternating and contrary qualities. Moreover, objects change in their sensory qualities without changing essentially. Beeswax, in its natural state of taste, color, fragrance, and hardness may lose or change these qualities when it is heated and melted without the beeswax becoming any the less beeswax. The thing that is the wax cannot be sensible, since it appears in various guises. Remove these sensory qualities, and it will still have length, breadth, and depth and will still be in a state of motion or rest. This is its true nature, known only to the mind and not to the senses. As was established before, sensory qualities, such as odor and color, are not among those clearly thinkable. Extension and motion, on the other hand, are clear and distinct in thought. All of this can be seen as support for a mechanical interpretation of nature but at the same time a disparagement of mental consequences of that nature.

What he says about the specific senses needs only brief summary. There were seven senses to Descartes, the usual five, plus the internal sense by which we localize sensory happenings within the body, and the passions. Further discussion will be foregone until the consideration of body and the interactions of mind and body.

Discussion of the body of man will be preceded by a discussion of animals. The subject of the brutes belongs entirely in the area of physical phenomena.[93] A host of consequences result. Without rational souls, animals have no immortality, are incapable of thought, and, since they lack will itself, have no freedom of will. Descartes, as his thinking progressed, tended to change, to some extent, his opinion about animals as machines, and in 1649 he shifted from his dogmatic denial of animals' power of thought in the direction of the more moderate view that it could not be proven that animals could think.[94] He now admitted that animals may have sensations and that these may give them something akin to consciousness. He was not saying that animals were unconscious, merely that they were without thought. Sensations and feelings, *i.e.*, passions, in so far as they were dependent upon bodily organs, do occur, but they come about mechanically. Moreover, he granted instinct to animals. In comparing animals to clocks, as in the return of the swallows in the spring and the flying order of cranes, he spoke of their performing these activities by instinct, that is to say, by force of nature.[95] He does not further elaborate. Aside from these changes in details, he never wavered in his conviction that animal behavior was to be explained mechanistically.

The body of a man, as distinguished from his mind, is composed of matter and has the common characteristics of all matter. The body is extension in space and is capable of movement.[96] Fundamentally, Descartes' mechanistic principle stated that all natural phenomena could be reduced eventually to local motion. Action by physical contact was a special instance. Hence, the behavior of the bodies of men was determined by mechanistic laws, that is the law of the movement of bodies in space, and was to be studied in the light of this fact.

From the point of view of movement, the human body is a machine having more parts, to be sure, but not more alive, than any man-made *automata*. [97] By an *automata* he meant a machine which moves itself. [98] If we had made an *automata* with the outward form of a monkey and with organs resembling that of a monkey, we could not tell it from an animal. [99] If a similar machine were made in the likeness of man, however, we could detect that it was a machine because the machine would not speak appropriate to the particular stiuation (even though a machine could be made to say words), and, moreover, we would soon discover "he" did not act from knowledge. These two criteria are also those by which we know man from the brutes. Since even the deaf and dumb are able to invent signs and since very little reason would be required to learn to talk, brutes have no reason at all.[100] Moreover, the same example demonstrates that man is more than body.

Descartes was especially intrigued by the flow of water in fountains, which he compared to the flow of vital spirits.[101] Some of the fountains in royal gardens of his time were so arranged as to perform certain activities when someone stepped on their hidden pedals. Once set into motion, a sea monster would squirt water, or Neptune would appear to threaten the passerby with his trident. Tunnel rides in amusement parks or some of the props used in the more elaborate historical and adventure parks popularized by the late Walt Disney would seem to be appropriate modern illustrations. In a description of the body of man as a machine, Descartes wrote of the actions of clocks, artificial fountains, mills, and similar machines as duplicating its behavior.[102] He then asked the reader to compare these forms of motion with the functions of the body, such as digestion, heart action, respiration, sleeping, sensory experiencing, common sense; imagination; retention by imprinting, the appetites, and the internal movements of the members. He concluded that these functions, which are forms of motion, follow naturally from the arrangement of the component parts, and that all that is necessary to set them in motion in the body is the heat of the vital spirits, which is itself in no way different from that of other fires. The body performs functions arising from the presence of vital heat and is thus similar to animals in the functions it exhibits.[103]

He held that the greater part of muscular action of the human body does not depend upon the mind at all.[104] Beating of the heart, digestion, respiration, and even walking and singing are performed without the mind attending them. A man in falling, who thrusts out his hands to break his fall, does so merely because the sight penetrating the brain drives the animal spirits into the nerves in such a way that the motion is carried out. Mind is not involved. Descartes also used as an illustration of our inability to control the enlarging of the pupil by thinking, because nature had not made this connection but instead connected its movement with looking at far or near objects.[105]

We have here something approaching a statement of reflex behavior. Motion followed predictably from stimulation of nerves. There appear to be fixed channels for the behavior repertory. This gave a conception akin to that of reflex behavior. Sometimes, it would seem, Descartes is given too much credit in the area of reflex theory. True, he used the words, *undulatio reflexa*, in describing the absence of voluntary action, but he was referring to the analogy between mechanical and physiological action expressed in resemblance of the reflection of light and the reflux of water to what he considered to be reflex action in the flow of vital spirits.[106] This involved a "rebound" of particles. Moreover, when writing in this fashion, he generally referred to activities having a considerable degree of co-ordination and integration; for example, all animal behavior and walking and talking in man.[107] On both of these counts modern neurology would disagree with Descartes.

Before considering how Descartes handled the problem of the interaction of mind and body, it is worthwhile to pause and consider both the state of knowledge of physiology of his time and some of his work in physiological psychology. It will be remembered that Descartes came after Vesalius and was familiar with the contemporary work of Harvey. Descartes himself demonstrated through using the excised eye of a bull that an inverted image is actually formed by the lens in the retina at the back of the eye.[108] He also found that sensations of hearing vary in harshness or softness according to the force with which the ear is struck and the harmony or discord of sound depends upon agitations or vibrations of the air. He studied the functioning of muscles and knew that they worked in opposing pairs. He knew something about the anatomy of the brain and argued that, since the construction of the brain differs from man to man, we have individual difference among men in mental activities.[109] Nerves, as such, were known, but the nature of the neural impulse was not. His physiological equivalent for the neural impulse was still the vital spirits. Vital spirits were a kind of rarified blood or subtle wind,[110] and the nervous system had a series of valves, as one might have with water pipes, which allowed their passage. The motor force of the nerves themselves arises in the brain.[111] Despite his limited knowledge, Descartes gave us the first systematic attempt at a physiological psychology since Theophrastus.[112]

Man, to Descartes, was a mind united with a body.[113] The mind and body interacted, so his position came to be called *interactionism,* to distinguish it from another form of dualism of mind and body, referred to as parallelism, to be discussed later. Mind and body interact, each affecting the other. The interaction of mind and brain is merely a more specific instance of this interaction. The mind sometimes acts independently of the brain (as illustrated by innate ideas), sometimes in interaction with it.[114] Thought, originating in the mind, may have consequences, such as movement. These movements are not thought, but activities of the body.[115] In other instances the mind is present in what today might be called a sensory-motor process. In this instance, mind affects the machinery at the critical point of transmission from sensory to motor channels.[116] In both kinds of mental activity—thought as such affecting the body, and sensorially derived functioning of the mind, in turn affecting the body—mind does not do so directly but by directing the vital spirits that pass from the heart through the brain to the muscles.[117]

Although each movement seems to be joined by nature to a particular thought, it may be directed "by habit" which he illustrated by the fact that sounds are understood as words.[118] Those naturally joined can also be separated. This separation comes about from custom. Custom does not require long usage for the separation to be effected and may even be acquired by a solitary action as when something very foul just once in our food causes us to be unable to eat that food thereafter. And the same separation by custom may be noticed in brutes since a setter may be trained to stand still on hearing a gun, instead of fleeing, which he does naturally.

A bodily locus for interactions of mind and body is necessary. Descartes found it deep within the recesses of the brain.[119] The point of contact between mind and body is the pineal gland, actually a vestigial organ of no functional significance. As the mind is unitary, a unitary structure was needed. The pineal gland was chosen by Descartes in part because it was the only organ in the brain that was single, that is to say, not divided into a right and a left half. Moreover, it was adapted for ready accessibility to all parts of the body because of its strategic location.

Movement of the vital spirits in the nerves produces an impression on the pineal gland as a seal might on wax, and from this impression the mind produces a sensation. In effect, then, a quantity of motion becomes a mental quality. The reverse also occurs; the mind makes an impression on the pineal gland but in a way never made clear. At any rate, the mind affects the flow of animal spirits by changing their course in the direction of this or that muscle. To Descartes, there was still a complete dualism; the pineal gland was merely the point of contact.

The soul is united with the body which it uses as an instrument.[120] The pineal gland was not the container or seat of the mind or soul; it was associated with the body, and the soul was not confined within the pineal gland at all. In order to have sensations and appetites the mind must be united with the body.[121] It is not merely lodged as would be a pilot in a vessel, but united with it, in fact, intermingled with it,[122] as a consequence of which pain, hunger, and the like are felt. If there was but lodgement one would not feel pain, but only perceive it as something external, as when a sailor knows that his ship is damaged but does not himself feel pain.

Important for understanding the interaction of body and mind, as Descartes conceived it, were what he called, "the passions."[123] The term, passion, is used by Descartes much more broadly than it might be imagined from its connotation today. When the motions from the vital spirits of the body have effects on the perceptions, feelings, and emotions of the mind, he spoke of the passions.[124] Passions, from the perspective of the mind, are experiences taking place in the mind. This, then, is their mental aspect. On the other hand, the affective aspects or feelings or actions are in the body.[125] Although sometimes the movements of the passions are accompanied by thought in man, they need not be so accompanied because they can arise in spite of his intentions.[126] This is additional evidence that they are of the body.

These psychological experiences need activity of the brain prior to that of the mind. The psychological phenomena that depend, not upon the *activity* of the mind initiated by the mind, but rather upon its *passivity*, upon its being affected from outside the mind, are the passions. The passions include not only feelings and emotions, but perceptual effects as well. It is true that Descartes also used a narrower definition of passion when he called them feelings or emotions that are brought about by the spirits. The definition would bring passions closer to the present day meaning of affective states.[127] In general, however, to Descartes, feeling and emotion are distinguished from the other passions because they arise from considerable agitation of the animal spirits but are *not* referred to objects outside the body.[128] The movements of the spirits nearly always creates an "agitation" which, until it dies down, remains in our thoughts.[129]

Since the passions are received from outside the mind and are not willed to appear, this differentiates them from the will. The function of a passion is to excite the will to action, although the passions should remain under the will's control.[130] The conflict is not between lower and higher levels of the soul, as it was with Plato, but between two sets of tendencies, one arising from the will, an aspect of the unitary mind, and the other from the action of the vital spirits on the passions.[131] In other words, the passions arise from the mind's opposition to bodily impulses. Without a body related to a mind, there would be no passions. It is the effect of body on mind which produces passions.

A comparison of emotion in man and animal is enlightening. A sheep fleeing from the wolf is not afraid since he is an *automata*, but he behaves in a way which we interpret as terror. This is because we are afraid when our body is in the same condition. In the same setting as that of the sheep, our body goes through the mechanical actions, but, since we have a mind, we experience passion due to the motions of the body.

Descartes' account, it may be noted, anticipates to some slight degree the James-Lange theory of emotions in that primacy is given to the physiological processes prior to the mental experience, as in that well-known example that we are afraid because we run. One should hasten to add that this emphasis on physiological conditions and the assertion of the passivity of the soul are hardly new as material in earlier chapters demonstrate. Descartes' account did have the virtue of being read by the psychologists to come, and he thus transmitted and added to a more ancient tradition.

Descartes discussed six primary passions.[132] These are wonder, love, hatred, desire, joy, and sadness. All other passions, and there are many, are derivatives or combinations of these primary passions. From wonder, an intellectual passion, are derived esteem, contempt, generosity, pride, humility, veneration and disdain. All of the other primary passions are forms of desire in a broad sense since they incite to action. Passions of desire (in the narrower sense) arouse hope, fear, jealousy, confidence, courage and cowardice. Joy and sadness are the vehicles for his advancing theory of pleasure and pain, since the latter are predecessors of these passions serving to produce them since joy is agreeableness and sadness disagreeableness. Joy and sadness, too, are related to secondary passions, specifically derision, envy, anger, shame, regret and joyfulness.

The work of Descartes was a catalyst for many later prominent trends in psychology. A summarization of Descartes' psychological views may be given in a setting of later developments that they have influenced. Especially important were the reactions to his dualism of body and mind and to his emphasis on the cognitive phase of the human mind. There were also reactions against his inclusion of the body of man in the mechanistic world and against his exclusion of the mind of man from the mechanistic world.

THE CARTESIAN REACTION TO DUALISM

Descartes' formulation of a basic dualism—that there is a real world and an equally real thinking self from which it is separate and immune—was a view that was to be influential for the centuries since his time, even though the later formulations that were proposed to handle this dualism might be very different from Descartes' original view. His dualism of body and mind, with the former subject to mechanical laws and the latter exercising free will, was to become the common sense viewpoint of many millions of people who have never heard his name.

One of the first problems arising from his dualism that his immediate successors and followers, the so-called Cartesians, became concerned with was his treatment of interaction. Descartes had formulated what he considered to be a complete dualism—an entire separation of mind and body. His followers were anxious to support this basic point, but his formulation allowed certain difficulties to become apparent. He had defined his two substances of body and mind in such a fashion as to make interaction impossible but, nevertheless, he promptly added interaction. He had asserted that a quantity of motion became a mental quality but he had not explained how this could happen. How could two substances, body and mind, utterly different by definition, with one extended and the other unextended, actually interact? The pineal gland is, after all, a bodily organ in space; how could it interact with an immaterial mind? This last was a problem never completely solved by Descartes, even to his own satisfaction.

Some of the Cartesians who stressed the spiritual element in his teaching, such as Arnold Geulincx[133] (1625–1669) and Nicolas de Malebranche[134] (1638–1715) solved the problem by denying that there could be contact. They held that all causal action originated with God, who, while neither body nor mind, embraced both in his infinite being. With interaction denied, the problem now shifted to explaining the appearance of interaction when actually none existed. Why, for example, if I "will" (a mental act) my arm to move, does it appear to mc that the arm does so (a physical act)? This was the problem they faced. Both explained the appearance of interaction by arguing that instead of event A causing B, what actually happens is that A furnished the occasion for God to produce B. They differed on how God acted in these circumstances: according to Geulincx, through acting upon the body which then acted upon the mind, and, according to Malebranche, directly upon the mind without intervention of body, as an analogy to what makes it seem as if there was interaction, Geulincx advanced the theory of the "two clocks." In effect, he said, "Imagine two clocks that keep perfect time and that, while looking at one, you hear the other strike." You would think that the first caused the second to strike. This, he went on, is what happens with the mind and the body. They are so perfectly tuned that events in one realm keep time with the other. On an occasion, such as in willing movements, though it is purely physical laws which cause movement and the will does not really act on the body, the will seems to cause the movement. While denying *reality* to interaction he was accounting for the *appearance* of interaction. This view came to be called "occasionalism" because either a mental or physical event became the occasion for Divine intervention: it was a form of dualistic parallelism, so-called because, while admitting the two realms of the mental and physical, it denied they interacted, but insisted instead that they functioned in parallel.

Other attempts at solving the Cartesian mind-body problem were made by Benedict Spinoza and Gottfried Leibniz. Although profoundly influenced by Descartes, both are too important and too original to be referred to as Cartesians.

BENEDICT SPINOZA [135]

Benedict Baruch Spinoza (1632–1677) lived out his life as a lens grinder in Amsterdam. He was relatively obscure and uninfluential during his lifetime with his most important work, the *Ethics*, [136] only published posthumously.

This work reflects his central aim: he wished to establish a way of life that was ethically correct and satisfying. Psychology, in this context, was a necessary stept toward ethics.

Methodologically, Spinoza was both rationalistic and deductive. Sharing Descartes' enthusiasm for a geometric ideal, Spinoza began with self-evident axioms from which to deduce the nature of reality. He presented his views in geometrical form, that is, each new point was derived from preceding points. His conception of science admirably reflects his rationalistic method. The order of natural objects and the order of knowledge of them are coextensive; *"the order and connection of ideas is the same as the order and connection of things."* [137]

Spinoza's views are firmly rooted in his conception of God. [138] God is infinite, the only substance. Thought and extension are but attributes of God. To think of "things" i.e., the objects of the world as we know them, is incorrect; instead of things they are modes of substance, nothing more than modifications of the one substance which is God. A body is an abstraction, a finite way of regarding the infinite substance which is God. The human mind, it is specified, is no more than an aspect of the mind of God. [139]

Man, a unitary individual, has the modes or forms of attributes of body (extension) and mind (thought). [140] Instead of mind and body being separate substances, as they were to Descartes, they are one to Spinoza; that is to say, they are two aspects of the same reality. Neither body nor mind is an autonomous entity; man has modes of the attributes of both extension and thought. This was a form of parallelism—monistic parallelism. Every bodily event coexists with, and is coordinate to, a mental event. Body and mind correlate, but they do not cause one another any more than the convex side of a glass causes the concave. Apparent interaction arises from ignorance on our part and shows only the conincidence of actions, a matter of appearance, not a reflection of reality. [141] In this connection Spinoza stated clearly that it follows that body cannot determine the mind to think nor can mind determine the body to motion or rest.

Unlike Descartes, to Spinoza the mind is an automaton, a term he explicitly applied to it.[142] Mind as well as body, is to be studied deterministically. Spinoza was perhaps the first modern thinker to view the world, including man, from a strictly deterministic standpoint. Both mind and body are of equal status, and both are subject to natural law. [143] Spinoza saw clearly that his deterministic view of man required that there be laws of nature applicable to man. For example, he mentioned remembering by similarity and contiguity as illustrative of the laws necessary for us to seek.[144]

Time and again he tells us that the will is not free. [145] The mind has no free will, it is determined by a cause which in turn is determined by another cause, and so on.

Although something of a digression, it may be of interest to consider the apparent dilemma that Spinoza seemed to have brought upon himself. How can man be ethically influenced, which is after all his main theme, if there is strict determinism? Throughout his works there is the answer that man's nature may be improved by improving understanding and by following ethical principles which may be learned. The ignorant man is determined from without while the wise man can act in line with greater knowledge of nature. Acting in the light of necessity is man's highest freedom, [146] and freedom is one with necessity.

In contrast to Descartes' view of the mind as primarily cognitive, Spinoza emphasized the conative or drive aspect of mental life. Central to Spinoza's psychology is his concept of *conatus,* something similar to what we would call an impulse toward self-preservation. [147] The striving for self-preservation is desire when conscious of itself, it is appetite when it is not.[148] In another place he also spoke of man being led more by "blind desire" than by "reason."[149]

When unconscious desire is coupled with his emphasis on conation in general and his acceptance of determinism, it is hardly surprising that he is seen as anticipating Freud.[150] Although this may be of some incidental interest, it must be pointed out that Spinoza's thinking was arrived at from a perspective vastly different from that of Freud; and the latter, although he was familiar with the works of Spinoza, [151] shows no evidence of direct influence.

It has been argued by Bidney[152] that Spinoza was the first modern to present psychology as the science of the laws of the mind. While it is agreed that a science of psychology would not have been entirely an alien conception to Spinoza, it is also possible to argue that his interest in psychology was too peripheral, and his influence on later developments in psychology of too little moment, for this claim to receive much support.

GOTTFRIED W. LEIBNIZ [153]

Gottfried Wilhelm Leibniz (1646–1716), one of the inventors of calculus, was also a philosopher, scientist, historian, diplomat, logician and lawyer, and a leading intellectual force in Europe after his death. Among his many other concerns, he investigated the issue of body-mind relationships.

Leibniz' unique contribution on the nature of the mind is to be found in the theory of the "monad," his term for the individual units of all substances. He held that the world is an infinite number of monads.[154] Each monad, as a unit, is unextended. Extension had been rejected by Leibniz as an attribute of substance, and, consequently, this left the monads—all monads—having as their essential attribute, that of mind. Each monad is a psychic entity. The reality of matter had been denied in denying extension of substance, and for it substituted an infinity of monads. Although mental, each of the monads has some of the properties of a physical point, and, when collected into an aggregate, they create what Leibniz called an extension.[155] The tree and the stones of everyday life, although appearing to the senses as objects, are actually aggregates of monads in themselves not phenomenal. Thus, Leibniz satisfied the need for an explanation of at least the appearance of extension in the world.

Each monad acts independently, but is created by God to act in pre-established harmony with other monads.[156] The monads may appear to interact, but they do not. This takes the place of the untenable position that they influence one another.[157] There is no causality between monads. Most significant for our present discussion, there is none between the mind monad and the body monads. Non-interaction of body and mind is but a special case of his parallelism of monads. Mind and body follow their own laws and yet show perfect agreement, giving the impression of interaction. But instead there is a parallelism. The situation is similar to the interplay of the instruments of a symphony orchestra, in which each player follows the score and yet gives the impression of one instrument responding to another. In a similar manner

God had composed the score which was then played out in pre-established harmony.

Leibniz' conception of parallelism, of course stripped of the trappings of monads, was a forerunner of the doctrine of psychophysical parallelism that was to be so important to Wundt and others. (See page 262.) All units of the world are endowed with life and motion and, hence, have something akin to consciousness. Even lifeless matter is only relatively unconscious; it has the least possible degree of consciousness.[158] Living organisms are composed of monads with varying degrees of consciousness.

Mental events, that is to say, the activity of monads, have degrees of clarity ranging from the totally unclear to the most definitely conscious or clearly grasped.[159] To Leibniz, this was more a matter of focal and peripheral attention than it was consciousness as we would use the term.[160] Nevertheless, in view of the closeness of meaning, it was later seen to be a conception of the continuum of consciousness-unconsciousness. At one extreme there are mental events of which we are totally unconscious, while at the other are those which are cleary grasped or, to use the technical term, apperceived.

The degree of consciousness is a relative matter.[161] The supposedly unconscious has the possibility of becoming conscious. There are lower degrees of consciousness, *petites perceptions* to use Leibniz' term. These *petites perceptions,* when they are actualized, are "apperceived." Thus hearing the roar of the surf is apperception, because it is the sum of all the drops of water of which we would not be conscious if we heard them one by one. The sound of a single drop is unconscious perception; sum up many drops at once and there is apperception.

THE PHENOMENOLOGICAL APPROACH

As a consequence of the emphasis upon the cognitive part of the human mind by Descartes and those that followed after, two points of view—the phenomenological and the mechanistic—were to emerge. Descartes' *Meditations,* Husserl[162] asserts, is the prototype of reflection in which the philosopher turns within himself as the source of immediate experience.

The phenomenological approach, about which Husserl was talking, sees the mind as most appropriately studied through the analysis of immediate experience, with the mind separate from the body. The mechanistic approach deals with causal relations, rather than description, and consequently must pay attention to bodily functions so that psychological processes may be brought to natural law. It would appear that Descartes is chiefly responsible for the clear separation of these two views of psychology, although Leibniz and, to a lesser degree, Spinoza as well as others had a share in it. A phenomenological psychology hereafter was to exist side by side with a mechanistic psychology. Ever since Descartes,[163] we have had to face the mind-body problem, i.e., how to render an adequate account of the relation of mental experiences to the corresponding neurophysiological processes. In modern times there has been a division of labor between philosophy with its concern for its logical and epistemological components and psychology, more specifically, psychophysiology, with the talk of relating the phenomenal patterns with the processes on the organism.

The method of Descartes was rationalistic, and his psychological views were primarily intellectualistic. Both of these trends worked together to help produce the phenomenological approach. Through reason one could know truth. The passions for example originated in bodily perturbation and in a sense did hardly more than disturb the mind. The criticism sometimes made that Descartes treated the passions in too intellectual a fashion could be made more precise by saying that, since passions by definition included the intellectual, he left no room anywhere in his position for anything that could be called *purely* affective or irrational or even very much that could be called motivational. Psychology, to Descartes, was almost exclusively cognitive.

A major influence of Descartes, then, was in the direction of an intellectualism with a bias in the direction of cognitive over conative processes.[164] This helped to start a trend which persisted until the end of the nineteenth century when biological findings and conceptions redirected interests toward conative matters. In this regard, Spinoza, whose emphasis was upon the conative, was a voice not to be heard for some time to come.

Descartes never seemed to suggest that the mind, in sharp distinction from the body, could be understood by use of quantitative techniques but only by the process of meditation. In the whole world of nature Descartes was rigidly deterministic with one exception—the mind. Mental events, too, were to be seen as determinate in the phenomenological approach which was beginning to emerge. Spinoza supplied the deterministic correction, while Leibniz presented the argument that activity is the essential of consciousness.

THE MECHANISTIC APPROACH

Descartes had advanced his theory of animals as automata in order to make for a greater cleavage between man and brute in support of religious convictions. But others saw that to admit this argument had value was uncomfortably close to admitting the old foundations for religious belief were, to some extent, inadequate. A vast controversy on the religious implications of his position resulted, extending over many years and many books.

More relevant to psychology is the reaction against his view that man's mind had to be excluded from the mechanical sphere. Many of those who came after Descartes were so convinced of his view that mechanical action accounted for the actions of animals and the body of man that they disagreed with his carefully made distinction between human mind and human body and held that human psychology too was to be accounted for on mechanical grounds. This was very simply done by considering not only animals but also man as automata. This interpretation, abhorrent to Descartes though it would have been, unwittingly made him the father of the modern mechanistic approach to human nature. This is what happened in the eighteenth century. [165] This "correction" was promulgated by several scholars.

La Mettrie (1709–1751), the most influential of those who would render Cartesian views consistently mechanistic, published *Man a Machine* [166] in 1748. He regarded his thesis, given in its very title, as a natural extension of Descartes' teaching that animals are machines. [167] He arrived at his point of view not merely through reading, but from observation, including self-observation. During a severe illness he had noted that his bodily infirmity was associated with a mental disturbance. After recovering, he proceeded assiduously to collect psychological and medical evidence that supported his materialistic thesis which he published in his *Man a Machine.* His theoretical view was that matter was endowed not only with the attribute of motion, but also with that of consciousness. Body, to him, was the only human reality.

It should not be imagined that even the more limited dualistic mechanistic view of animal and human bodily function went without challenge. A reaction against mechanism came about from within physiology itself. Georg Ernst Stahl [168] (1666–1734) took the position that the chemical activities within the living organism are essentially different from those reactions in the laboratory and in non-living matter. The soul permeates the entire organism and controls all functional manifestation. The soul is a force—a living force. The very fact that the body is alive, in his eyes, proved his point. We have in the work of Stahl the beginnings of modern vitalism, a less mystical form to which such eminent men of the nineteenth century as Johannes Müller and Hans Driesch subscribed.

REFERENCES*

1. Good general sources concerning the relevant aspects of the Renaissance are the volumes by E. Cassirer *et. al.*, (eds.), *The Renaissance Philosophy of Man.* (Chicago: University of Chicago Press, 1948); G. Sarton, *Six Wings: Men of Science in the Renaissance.* (Bloomington: Indiana University Press, 1957); and H. R. Hall, *The Scientific Revolution: 1500–1800; the Formation of the Modern Scientific Attitude.* (Boston: Beacon, 1956)

2. PETRARCH, On His Own Ignorance and that of Many Others. (Translated by H. Nachod). In E. Cassirer, *et al.* (eds.), *op. cit.*, pp. 47–133. (1368)

3. *Ibid.*, p. 108.

4. J. H. RANDALL, *The Making of the Modern Mind.* (rev. cd.) Boston: Macmillan, 1940.

5. P. O. KRISTELLER, The Platonic Academy of Florence, *Rennaiss. News*, 1961, 14, 147–159.

6. M. FICINO, Five Questions Concerning the Mind. (Translated by J. L. Barroughs.) In E. Cassirer, *et al.* (eds.), *op. cit.*, pp. 185–214. (1476)

7. J. D. BERNAL, *Science in History.* Vol. 1, New York: Cameron, 1954.

8. R. M. BLAKE, C. J. Ducasse and E. K. Madden, *Theories of Scientific Method: the Renaissance Through the Nineteenth Century.* Seattle: University of Washington Press, 1960.

9. R. McKEON, Aristotelianism in Western Christianity. In J. T. McNeill *et al.*, (eds.), *Environmental Factors in Christian History.* Chicago: University of Chicago Press, 1939, pp. 206–231.

10. P. POMPONAZZI, On the Immortality of the Soul. E. Cassirer, *et al.*, (eds.), *op. cit.*, pp. 257–384. (1516)

11. N. MACHIAVELLI, The Prince. (Translated by W. K. Marriott) In R. M. Hutchins, (ed.), *Great Books of the Western World.* (Vol. 23) Chicago: Encyclopaedia Britannica, 1952, pp. 1–37. (1513)

12. Major references are J. L. Vives, *On Education.* (Translated by F. Watson) (Cambridge: Cambridge University Press, 1913) (*c.*1521–1532); J. L. Vives, *Opera Omnia.* (Farnham-Surrey: Dawson, 1965) (*c.*1520–1540); *Tradado del alma.* (Span. trans. by Jose Antanon of *De Anima et Vita*) (Buenos Aires: España Calyse, S. A., 1942 (1538); and F. Watson, The Father of Modern Psychology, *Psychol. Rev.*, 1915, 22, 333–353.

13. PARACELSUS (Theophrastus von Hohenheim), The Diseases that Deprive Man of His Reason. In H. Sigerist (ed.), *Four Treatises.* (Baltimore: Johns Hopkins University Press, 1941, pp. 127–212. (*c.*1512); Paracelsus, *Sämmtliche Werke.* (4 vols.) (Modern German Translation by B. Aschner) Jena: Fischer, 1926–1932. (*c.*1526–1541)

* See page 16 for description of reference style.

14. Two major secondary sources are C. S. Sherrington, *The Endeavors of Jean Fernel.* (Cambridge: Cambridge University Press, 1946) and C. S. Sherrington, *Man on His Nature.* (2nd ed.) (Garden City: Doubleday, 1951)

15. P. Melanchthon. *Commentarius de Anima.* In C. G. Bretschneider (ed.), *Opera Omnia* (Vol. 13) Halle: Schwetschke, 1834–1840. (1540)

16. Huarte y Navarro, Juan de Dios. *Examen de Ingenios: or, The Tryal of Wits. Discovering the great Difference of Wits among Men, and what Sort of Learning suits best with each Genius.* (Translated by Mr. Bellamy) London: Richard Sare, at Grays-Inn-Gate in Holborn, 1698. (1575)

17. M. E. de Montaigne, The Essays. In R. M. Hutchins, (ed.), *op. cit.*, Vol. 25, pp. 3–543. (1580–1592)

18. R. Goeckel, *Psychologia—Hoc est de Hominis Perfectione.* Cited in G. Zilboorg, & G. W. Henry, *A History of Medical Psychology.* New York: Norton, 1941, p. 178. (1590)

19. Vesalius, *De humani corporis fabrica.* Basel: Oporinus, 1543; Vesalius, *The Epitome.* (Translated by L. R. Lind) New York: Macmillan, 1949. (1543)

20. N. Copernicus, On the Revolution of the Heavenly Spheres. (Translated by C. G. Wallis) In R. M. Hutchins, (ed.), *op. cit.*, Vol. 16, pp. 505–838. (1543)

21. Recently it has come to be argued that more continuity existed between medieval and seventeenth century science than had previously been thought. The seventeenth century science was a culmination of cooperative efforts of generations of scientists, particularly at the School of Padua as J. H. Randall, Jr. demonstrates in *The School of Padua and the Emergence of Modern Science.* (Padova: Editrice Atenore, 1961)

22. L. Thorndike, Newness and Novelty in Seventeenth Century Science and Medicine. *J. Hist. Ideas*, 1951, 12, 584–598.

23. E. A. Burtt, *The Metaphysical Foundations of Modern Physical Science.* Garden City: Doubleday, 1932.

24. E. W. Strong, *Procedures and Metaphysics.* Berkeley: University of California Press, 1936.

25. *Ibid.*

26. Galileo, Dialogues Concerning the Two New Sciences. (Translated by H. Crew & A. de Salvio) In R. M. Hutchins, (ed.), *op. cit.*, Vol. 28, pp. 129–260. (1638)

27. G. Galileo, Il Saggiatore. Quoted in Joan W. Reeves, *Body and Mind in Western Thought.* London: Penguin, 1958, pp. 106–107. (1623)

28. F. Bacon, Novum Organum. In R. M. Hutchins, (ed.), *op. cit.*, Vol. 30, pp. 105–195. (1620)

29. F. Bacon, Advancement of Learning. *Ibid.*, pp. 1–104. (1605)

30. F. Bacon, *New Atlantis. Ibid.*, pp. 199–214. (1614–1617)

31. *Novum Organum, Advancement of Learning, esp.* Second Book.

32. *Advancement of Learning,* Second Book, XVII, 4.

33. *Ibid.*, Second Book, VIII, 2.

34. *Advancement of Learning,* Second Book, VII, 1: *Novum Organum,* First Book, Aphorisms, 71, 95, 98–106.

35. *Novum Organum,* First Book, Aphorisms, 39–68.

36. *Ibid.*, Aphorism 1.

37. R. DESCARTES, *Discourse on the Method of Rightly Conducting the Reason.* (Translated by Elizabeth S. Haldane and G. R. T. Ross) In R. M. Hutchins (ed.), *op. cit.*, Vol. 31, pp. 41–67. (1637)

38. *Ibid.*, VI.

39. SHERRINGTON, *Man on His Nature, op. cit.*, Chap. 4.

40. J. KEPLER, Ad Vitellionem paralipomena, quibus astronomiae pars optica traditur. (Frankfurt) Chap. 5. (Translated by A. C. Crombie.) In I. B. Cohen & R. Taton, (eds.) *Mélanges Alexandre Koyré; L'Aventure de la science.* Paris: Hermann, 1964. (1604) (Herrnstein & Boring Excerpt No. 23)

41. W. HARVEY, An Anatomical Disquisition on the Motion of the Heart and Blood in Animals. (Translated by R. Willis) In R. M. Hutchins, (ed.), *op. cit.*, Vol. 28, pp. 265–304. (1628)

42. *Ibid.*, Chap. 8, p. 285.

43. HALL, *The Scientific Revolution, op. cit.*

44. *Discourse on Method,* I, p. 44.

45. *The Discourse on the Method of Rightly Conducting the Reason (op. cit.)* gives an autobiographical statement of some of the events of his life, while A. G. A. Balz, *Descartes and the Modern Mind* (New Haven: Yale University Press, 1952) and S. V. Keeling, *Descartes* (London: Oxford University Press, 1934) contain good secondary accounts.

46. *Discourse on Method,* I, p. 42.

47. *Ibid.*, p. 43.

48. R. DESCARTES, Rules for the Direction of the Mind. (Translated by Elizabeth S. Haldane, & G. R. T. Ross) In R. M. Hutchins (ed.), *op. cit.*, Vol. 31, pp. 1–40, (1629)

49. R. DESCARTES, Treatise on Man. In R. M. Eaton (ed.), *Selections.* New York: Scribners, 1927, pp. 350–354. (1662) (Part given in another translation in Herrnstein & Boring Excerpt No. 57)

50. *Discourse on Method.*

51. R. DESCARTES, Dioptric. In N. K. Smith (Translated) *Descarte's Philosophical Writings.* London: Macmillan, 1952, pp. 167–179. (1637) (Also in another translation in Herrnstein & Boring Excerpt No. 27)

52. R. DESCARTES, Meditations on First Philosophy. (Translated by Elizabeth S. Haldane and G. R. T. Ross) In R. M. Hutchins (ed.), *op. cit.*, Vol. 31, pp. 69–293. (1641)

53. *Ibid.*, p. 60.

54. R. Descartes, Passions of the Soul. *In Essential Works of Descartes.* (Translated by L. Bair) New York: Bantam, 1961, pp. 108–210. (1649)

55. Keeling, *op. cit.*

56. *Rules,* I–II.

57. *Discourse,* II.

58. *Rules.*

59. *Discourse,* II.

60. A good critique is available in Keeling (*op. cit.*).

61. *Discourse,* I.

62. *Rules,* IX.

63. *Ibid.,* VIII.

64. *Ibid.,* VIII, XII, XIII; *Meditations,* I, VI, *Second Objection, Fifth Objection; Passions,* Part II, 3.

65. *Discourse,* esp., IV.

66. *Ibid.,* pp. 51–52. Quoted by permission.

67. *Meditations,* II.

68. *Ibid.,* p. 79.

69. W. T. Jones, *A History of Western Philosophy.* New York: Harcourt Brace, 1952.

70. *Meditations,* VI.

71. *Meditations,* IV.

72. *Ibid.,* II.

73. *Ibid.,* IV, VI.

74. *Ibid.,* VI.

75. *Ibid.,* Arguments, IV.

76. *Ibid.,* Reply to Fifth Set of Objections.

77. *Ibid.,* Preface to the Reader.

78. *Ibid.,* IV.

79. R. Descartes, Principles of Philosophy. (Translated by Elizabeth S. Haldane & G. R. T. Ross) In *Philosophical Works.* (Vol. 1) Cambridge: Cambridge University Press, 1911, pp. 203–302. (1644) Part I, 53.

80. *Rules,* XLI.

81. *Discourse,* III, V.

82. *Ibid.*

83. *Meditations,* VI.

84. *Ibid.,* II.

85. *Ibid.,* Arguments, Definition I.

86. *Principles,* Part I, XLII.

87. *Ibid.*, I.

88. *Meditations*, IV; *Passions*, XXXV.

89. *Principles*, Part I, XXXVII.

90. *Discourse*, V, VI; *Meditations*, Reply to Fifth Set of Objections.

91. *Rules*, XII.

92. *Meditations*, Reply to Fifth Set of Objections.

93. *Ibid.*, Reply to Fourth Set of Objections, X, first part.

94. R. DESCARTES, Letter to Henry More. In R. M. Eaton (ed.), *Selections. op. cit.*, pp. 358–360.

95. *Treatise on Man.*

96. *Meditations*, Arguments, Definition VII.

97. *Discourse*, V.

98. *Passions*, VI.

99. *Discourse*, V.

100. *Letter to Henry More.*

101. *Treatise on Man*, Part II.

102. *Ibid.*

103. *Discourse*, V.

104. *Meditations*, Reply to Fourth Set of Objections.

105. *Passions*, XLIV.

106. *Ibid.*, XXXVI.

107. *Meditations*, Reply to Fourth Set of Objections.

108. *Dioptric.* (Herrnstein & Boring Excerpt No. 27)

109. *Passions*, XXXIX.

110. *Ibid.*, VII.

111. *Rules*, XII.

112. For a discussion of how he conceived the mechanism of human action, see Herrnstein & Boring (Excerpt No. 57).

113. *Treatise on Man; Meditations*, Reply to Fourth Set of Objections; *Passions, op. cit.*, XXXIV. (Herrnstein & Boring Excerpts No. 44, 103)

114. *Meditations*, Reply to Fifth Set of Objections.

115. *Ibid.*, Argument, Definition 1.

116. R. S. PETERS, (ed.), *Brett's History of Psychology*. London: Allen & Unwin, 1953, p. 351.

117. *Meditations*, Reply to Fourth Set of Objections.

118. *Passions*, LX.

119. *Ibid.*, XXXI–XXXIV.

120. *Meditations*, Reply to Fifth Set of Objections.

121.   *Discourse*, III.

122.   *Meditations*, VI.

123.   *Passions.*

124.   *Ibid.*, XXVII.

125.   *Ibid.*, II.

126.   R. DESCARTES, Letter to Marquis of Newcastle. In R. M. Eaton (ed.), *Selections, op. cit.*, pp. 355–357.

127.   *Passions*, XXVII.

128.   *Ibid.*, XXVIII.

129.   *Ibid.*, XLVI.

130.   *Ibid.*, XLVII.

131.   *Ibid.*

132.   *Ibid.*, LXIX–XCVII.

133.   GEULINCX, Ethica. In J. P. N. Land (ed.), *Opera philosophica.* (Vol. 3) The Hague: Nijhoff, 1892. (1675)

134.   N. DE MALEBRANCHE, *De la recherche de la vérité où l'on traite de la nature de l'esprit de l'homme et de l'usage qu'il en doit faire pour éviter l'erreur dans les sciences.* (Ed. by F. Bouillier) Paris: Garnier, 1879–1880, (1674–1675); N. de Malebranche, *Dialogues on Metaphysics and Religion.* (Translated by M. Ginsburg) New York: Macmillan, 1923. (1688)

135.   Primary sources are mentioned later. Good secondary sources on Spinoza are those of H. A. Wolfson, *The Philosophy of Spinoza.* (2 vols. in one) (New York: Meridian, 1934); R. McKeon, *The Philosophy of Spinoza: the Unity of his Thought.* (New York: Longmans, Green, 1928); G. H. R. Parkinson, *Spinoza's Theory of Knowledge.* (Oxford: Clarendon Press, 1954)

136.   B. SPINOZA, Ethics. (Translated by W. H. White, Revised by A. H. Stirling) In R. M. Hutchins (ed.), *op. cit.*, Vol. 31, pp. 355–463. (1677)

137.   *Ibid.*, Part II, prop. 7, p. 375.

138.   *Ethics*, Part I.

139.   *Ibid.*, Part II, prop. 11.

140.   *Ibid.*, Part II.

141.   *Ibid.*, Part III, prop. 2.

142.   B. SPINOZA, Treatise on the Correction of the Understanding. (Translated by A. Boyle) In E. Rhys, (ed.), *Spinoza's Ethics and de intellectus Emendatione.* New York: Dutton, 1910, pp. 228–263. (1677)

143.   *Ethics*, Part III, Preface.

144.   B. SPINOZA, A Theologico-Political Treatise. In R. H. M. Elwes, (ed.), *Chief Works*, (Vol. 1) London: Bell, 1909, pp. 3–278. (1670) IV.

145.   *Ethics*, Part I, props. 17, 28, 36, appendix, Part II, props. 1, 48–49.

146.   *Theologico-Political Treatise, op. cit.*, Chap. II, Sec. 11.

147. *Ethics,* Part III, props. 4–8.

148. *Ibid.,* Part III, prop. 8.

149. B. Spinoza, Political Treatise. In R. H. M. Elwes (ed.), *Chief Works.* Vol. 1, *op. cit.,* pp. 280–387. (1677)

150. W. Bernard, Freud and Spinoza. *Psychiatry,* 1946, 9, 99–108.

151. *Ibid.*

152. D. Bidney, *The Psychology and Ethics of Spinoza; a Study in the History and Logic of Ideas.* New Haven: Yale University Press, 1940.

153. Good secondary sources include B. Russell, *A Critical Exposition of the Philosophy of Leibniz.* (rev. ed.) (London: Allen & Unwin, 1937), and H. W. Carr, *Leibniz.* (New York: Dover, 1929.)

154. G. W. Leibniz, The Principles of Nature and Grace, Based on Reason. In P. P. Wiener (ed.), *Selections.* New York: Scribner's, 1951, pp. 522–533. (1714)

155. G. W. Leibniz, The Monadology. In P. P. Wiener (ed.), *op. cit.,* pp. 533–552. (1714)

156. G. W. Leibniz, New Essays on the Human Understanding. In P. P. Wiener (ed.), *op. cit.,* pp. 367–480. (1704) Preface.

157. *Monadology,* 61.

158. G. W. Leibniz, Considerations on the Principle of Life and on Plastic Natures by the Author of the Preestablished Harmony. In P. P. Wiener (ed.), *op. cit.,* pp. 190–199. (1705)

159. *New Essays,* Preface.

160. *Principles of Nature and Grace,* 4, 16.

161. *New Essays,* Preface.

162. E. Husserl, *Cartesian Meditations: an Introduction to Phenomenology.* The Hague: Nijhoff, 1964. (1931)

163. H. Feigl, Mind-body *not* a Pseudo Problem. In S. Hook (ed.), *Dimensions of Mind.* New York: New York University Press, 1960, pp. 24–36.

164. Peters, *Brett's Psychology, op. cit.,* p. 348.

165. L. C. Rosenfield, *From Beast-Machine to Man-Machine: Animal Soul in French Letters from Descartes to La Mettrie.* New York: Oxford University Press, 1941.

166. J. O. de la Mettrie, *Man a Machine.* (Translated by G. C. Bussey and Mary W. Calkins) La Salle, Ill.: Open Court, 1912. (1748) (Herrnstein & Boring Excerpt No. 58)

167. *Ibid.,* p. 72.

168. G. E. Stahl, *Theoria Medica Vera.* Halle: Orphonotrophei, 1707–1708.

CHAPTER 8

LOCKE AND BERKELEY:

BRITISH EMPIRICISM AND ASSOCIATIONISM

I N CONSIDERING Spinoza and Leibniz we have moved on into the latter half of the seventeenth century. Meanwhile important events were taking place in Great Britain, for this was the age of the founding of the Royal Society and a general increase in interest in science, of the Newtonian synthesis, and of Locke's struggle to find the limits of human knowledge by the study of human nature.

The Royal Society[1] was chartered in 1662, although informal meetings on the "Invisible College" had been taking place as early as 1645. The doctrines of Francis Bacon were the central force, binding together the founders, although almost without entirely realizing it, they turned more to the experimental method of Kepler and Galileo. Their meetings were not confined to reading papers since public demonstrations of experiments, ranging far and wide as to content, were carried out. The Society also served to create favorable public opinion and its journal, *Philosophical Transactions*, fulfilled the need for a publication source.

Isaac Newton (1642–1727) elected a Fellow of the Royal Society in 1671 and its President in 1703, an office he held to his death, gradually assumed the dominant position not only over the Society but over British science in general. His two major publications were the *Optics*,[2] primarily concerned with the composition of matter as shown by experiment, and *The Mathematical Principles of Natural Philosophy*,[3] concerned with quantity of matter in terms of mathematics. His work most directly related to psychology was that in sensory specification in vision for which he specified seven principle hues[4] and offered justification for a color circle of hue and saturation[5] which is paradigmatic for all later color diagrams.

It was during the same period that John Locke's friend, William Molyneux[6] (1656–1698) gave the definitive answer to the question of the inverted retinal image. The eye is but an instrument, not in itself seeing; it is the mind which sees.

The appeal to rationalism was an intellectual rallying call to the men of the seventeenth and eighteenth centuries. Rationalism, however, was a term used loosely and with several meanings. During these centuries reason was the means for combatting the dogmatism and authoritarianism of the past. In their faith in cool objectivity, impartiality, and intellectualization, Locke and some of the others of the British empiricists were, in this broad sense, rationalists. Others, Hobbes and Hume included, shared considerably less in this tendency to glorify reason.

The major point of agreement uniting the British associationists was their empiricism, which stood in contrast to still another facet of the rationalistic view. Rationalism also meant starting with the assumptions of some metaphysical system and then deducing rationally the place of the human mind in that system. Rationalism as a means of certainty had characterized Descartes, Spinoza, and Leibniz. In contradiction, English empiricists relied on what could be learned from sense experience and tended to be skeptical of achieving absolute certainty in any field. They wanted to find a more "down to earth" philosophy, in contrast to what they considered to be the "speculative" character of the philosophy of the continent. They accepted the Baconian proposition that scientists must start from observations that are collected carefully and from which only cautious generalizations are made. The generalizations to which they turned will be found to center on the laws of association, the ways in which mental events are connected. The great psychologists of this British empirical and associationist tradition are Locke and Berkeley, but chronologically preceding their work was that of Hobbes.

THOMAS HOBBES

Just before the period under consideration lived Thomas Hobbes (1588–1679), a contemporary and acquaintance of Descartes, and the first of the British empiricists. Despite this, he lived long enough *not* to be elected to the Royal Society, an omission that will become intelligible. Hobbes followed the careers of tutor and minor diplomat which resulted in considerable traveling on the continent. For a short time he served as Bacon's secretary-translator.

He was an implacable foe of supernatural and religious beliefs. His favorite tactic was to assert his orthodoxy and then slip in a devastating criticism. Of course, one must accept divine relevation, he asserted piously, and, then almost as an afterthought, added that such an assertion is valid provided one has experienced it personally, for otherwise it is but a belief.[7] It is small wonder that he incurred the wrath of the orthodox majority.

Hobbes is best known as a political philosopher but is relevant to us because psychology formed the foundation for his work in this field. For present purposes, his *Leviathan*,[8] so named because he saw the microcosm of man writ large in the macrocosm of the state, and his shorter work, significantly named *Human Nature*[9] are the most important.

Hobbes considered psychology a field to be investigated preliminary to an attempt to understand the state and government.[10] Consequently his interest in conduct was specifically in social conduct. He held a somewhat cynical and jaundiced view of human nature. Men, he held, originally lived in a state of mutual warfare and it was only enlightened selfishness that permitted cooperation. Without government ". . . the life of man [is] solitary, poor, nasty, brutish, and short."[11] On the basis of self-interest and fear of attack, men agreed to live under government. This doctrine that self-interest is the basis of conduct came later to be referred to as "psychological hedonism."

Influenced by Galileo's conception of motion, Hobbes held that everything that happens is matter in motion; mental activities are motions of the nervous system arising as reactions to motions in the external world.[12] Thinking is, in reality, nothing more than movement excited in the brain.[13] Motions account not only for cognitive processes but also for action and emotion. Everything in nature is material. Thinking implies a thinking thing, just as walking implies a walking thing; in both instances this thing is the body. Consequently, he rejected Cartesian interactionistic dualism in favor of a materialistic monism. Blithely disregarding the difficulties and inconsistencies, Hobbes conceived of sensation, thought, and consciousness as due to the motion of atoms in the brain. He offered no explanation of how the connection between atomic motion and mental processes, two apparently quite different types of activity, came about.

According to Hobbes, the content of mind arises from sense experience, not from innate ideas,[14] thus marking him an empiricist. All complex experience is derived from simple experience, and all simple experience is derived from sensation. In other words, cognitive powers of the mind are derived from the senses and the senses alone. Cognitions are merely corruptions of the original sense elements. For example, imagination and memory are "decaying" conceptions in that they are slowly fading sensations.[15]

Contrary to the common belief, Hobbes argued that all of the qualities of our experience, such as color, are not inherent in the object.[16] He insisted that in all instances "the subject of their *inherence* is not the *object*, but the *sentient*."[17] Psychological experiences, in other words, are subjective and are not counterparts of the objective stimuli which gave rise to them. He goes so far as to call psychological experiences "apparitions" but proceeds to add that they come about as the result of the objects working on the brain.

The notion of association he did little more than partially outline, leaving its development and extension to others. The processes of association or, as he referred to them, "the trains of thought," are of two sorts.[18] There are those that are unguided and without design. In addition, there are those that are regulated and orderly, as when one thought introduces the one that follows or when design or desire regulate thought. This distinction contains a rather clear differentiation between what later was to be called free and controlled association. Moreover, he was showing that coherence (or contiguity, as it would be called today) is one of the bases of sequences of association. Desire and habit serve as agents of selection. More or less incidentally, in the quite different context of the necessity of impressing people with knowledge of the laws, he suggested periodic repetition as a means of making sure they remembered them.[19] Frequency as a factor in learning was thus acknowledged.

Hobbes stressed the influence of the passions and desires, which are motions arising from within man.[20] The basis of human action is "a perpetual and restless desire for power after power."[21] Hobbes distinguished between the appetites and aversions with which one is born and those that are acquired from experience.[22] Although he devotes a chapter to the passions, it is unsystematically presented and digressive. A fair number of passions are mentioned, but in no sense can it be seen as an exhaustive statement. He does make it clear that passions may sway reason.[23] As a consequence, passions are regarded as infirmities of man.[24] The passions serve to sustain and direct thought. Deliberation is simply a choice from among appetites and aversions.[25] Pleasure, pain, pride, and fear are prime determiners of conduct.

Notwithstanding the incompleteness and the obvious vagueness of his views and despite his lack of direct influence upon his successors, he was prophetic of an emerging empirical, monistic, materialistic conception of mind. Many later developments followed along lines he had marked out. Man is an integral part of the natural world, not just his body as Descartes believed, but his mental life as well. He held out the hope of a science of human physics that was to be worked out in more detail by Hume in the next century.

JOHN LOCKE

John Locke (1632–1704), an older contemporary of Leibniz and Newton, lived most of his life in the seventeenth century but belonged in spirit to their eighteenth century. Although anticipated in a few particulars by Hobbes, English empiricism was launched by John Locke. He thus became the founder of psychology as the empirical science of the mind.

Life and Works of Locke[26]

In January, 1649, John Locke was a seventeen-year-old scholar at Westminster School. Close to the Abbey and the School was Whitehall Palace Yard. Here on January 30, Charles I, King by Divine Right, was executed as a traitor to the Commonwealth. For some years both before and after the execution, which he may have witnessed, young John had lived in the midst of the Great Rebellion that was so crucial to English history. Small wonder, then, that he and more than one of his fellow students of this severely studious school, who were within sound of the tumultuous doings outside its walls, were moved in later years to concern themselves with matters of government.

John had been born in Pensford, a village near Bristol, in 1632, ten years before the outbreak of Civil War. His father, a small landowner and lawyer by profession, was a captain in a volunteer regiment under the Long Parliament. The unsettled conditions of the times reduced the already modest family fortunes considerably, but through the influence of his father's colonel, John was sent to Westminster School in 1646. After remaining at Westminster six years, John was granted a junior studentship at Christ Church, Oxford in 1652. Although the standards of scholarship recently had been raised under the firm hand of John Owen, the Puritan dean, and despite the fact that the teachers professed Protestantism, much of what was taught was still scholastic in content and temper. In later years Locke was more than once to complain of the sterility and boredom of the teachings to which he was subjected. He did find some relief in the study of geometry. Despite his distaste for what it had to offer, Locke remained on at Oxford after taking his bachelor's degree in 1656. He took a master's degree and then had academic appointments successively in Greek, rhetoric, and moral philosophy.

Some of his time was free for academic interests other than those called for by his appointments and, among other writers, he read Descartes with critical interest and respect. Seemingly, he was little influenced by Hobbes, although to some extent they moved in the same circles. The founding of the Royal Society at Oxford, of which he became a member, led him to some studies and demonstrations in chemistry and meteorology. He also began the study of medicine, although he never took a degree. At Oxford he took an interest in political questions, particularly the relation of church and state and the importance and desirability of religious toleration. In the meantime, he had lost all, or nearly all, of the Puritan leanings of his family, and, in the face of Cromwell's dwindling power linked with his repressive measures, he saw more hope of religious and political liberty under Charles than under the government of the Rump Parliament. When Charles II was crowned in 1660, Locke welcomed the change in government, and for some years had no reason to regret it.

In 1667 he left Oxford for the political world of London. He had made the acquaintance of Lord Ashley, afterwards the Earl of Shaftesbury, and, on going to London, took up residence with him as his confidential secretary, tutor to his son, personal physician, and, as time progressed, his trusted confidante and friend. In 1669 it was in his capacity as confidential secretary that he was charged with helping to draft a constitution for the colony of Carolina. He managed to have embodied in it some of his permissive views concerning religious toleration.

Shaftesbury became involved in a plot against Charles II and in 1681 fled to Holland where he died early the following year. Although apparently not a party to the plot, Locke, too, was suspected and he also sought refuge in Holland. Meanwhile, during these years he continued working on the *Essay*. It appears probable that he was involved to some degree in the planning of the bloodless Revolution of 1688 which crowned William of Orange as King of England. At any rate, he returned to England in 1689 on the same ship that carried Princess Mary, wife of William of Orange. Shortly afterward, he was offered several ambassadorships but took instead a post that offered considerable leisure, that of the Commissioner of Appeals.

Up to the time of his return to England in 1689 at the age of fifty-six, Locke had published little of importance. In the next few years a whole series of works appeared. There was his *A Letter Concerning Toleration*[27] published in English the year of his return; *Two Treatises on Government* and *An Essay Concerning Human Understanding*[28] appearing the year following; and works on economics, education, and Christianity between then and 1695. *An Essay*

Concerning Human Understanding was rewritten and enlarged to include a chapter on association of ideas in the fourth edition of 1700.

In his pleas for religious toleration, Locke[29] went beyond most of the liberal individuals of his time. He would extend toleration to all outside the Church with the exception of atheists, Catholics because of their allegiance to a foreign power, and those who would use religion as a pretext to put forward social or political views at variance with the best interests of the community.

For psychology, interest in his work centers on *An Essay Concerning Human Understanding*.[30] Aside from the posthumously published, *The Conduct of the Understanding*,[31] essentially all of his psychological views are contained in this one work. The *Essay* was conceived and the resolution to write it formed as Locke tells us in the "Epistle to the Reader," in the following fashion:

> . . . I should tell thee, that five or six friends meeting at my chamber, and discoursing on a subject very remote from this, found themselves quickly at a stand, by the difficulties that rose on every side. After we had awhile puzzled ourselves, without coming any nearer a resolution of those doubts which perplexed us, it came into my thoughts that we took a wrong course; and that before we set ourselves upon inquiries of that nature, it was necessary to examine our own abilities, and see what *objects* our understandings were, or were not, fitted to deal with. This I proposed to the company, who all readily assented; and thereupon it was agreed that this should be our first inquiry.[32]

This work of Locke's was the first large scale attempt to examine critically the certainty and adequacy of human knowledge. It is divided into four books. Basic to his psychological views are the first two of these books concerned with the origin and nature of ideas. More peripheral are the last two books which consider words, knowledge, and probability. Because of his writing, fame, both in the form of support and of attack, came to Locke in England and on the continent. He became the acknowledged voice of philosophical and governmental liberalism. He wrote on many issues in a fashion that gained him wide support. Consequently, he was much more influential than Hobbes, the cynic and malcontent. Shortly after Locke's death, Voltaire (1694–1778), who developed an unbounded admiration for Locke, placing him on the same exalted plane as Newton, did much to spread a favorable opinion of his views on the continent, especially in France.

In 1691 Locke's health, never good, prompted him to leave London for the country at Oakes Manor in Essex. Later, however, he accepted still another governmental assignment, this time on the Board of Trade, which merely entailed visits to London, but in 1700 he resigned. On October 28, 1704, Locke died at the age of seventy-two and was buried in the parish church at High Laver.

Psychological Views

In proposing, as Locke did in the quotation given earlier, that the examination of our ability to understand ourselves is basic to later investigation in other fields, including the sciences, he was making psychology fundamental. In the introduction to the *Essay*[33] he disavowed specifically any intention to be concerned with the physical aspects of understanding. In a similar vein he went on to indicate that such speculative matters, as what the essence of understanding may be, were also to be disregarded. Understanding, as such, was taken for granted, and the inquiry was to be carried on in order to see how far understanding could take him and where it would fail him so that he would be more cautious thereafter in meddling in matters beyond comprehension. He proposed to carry out this task by the method of introspection—an inquiry within himself concerning the data supplied by sensation and reflection.

In order to carry out his intent of looking into the origin, certainty, and extent of human knowledge, Locke proposed a psychological inquiry into the ideas, ". . . which a man observes, and is conscious to himself he has in his mind; and the ways whereby the understanding comes to be furnished with them." [34] "Ideas" were defined very broadly; in fact, as anything about which the mind can be employed in thinking. An idea, then, denoted any sort of experience.

Locke[35] plunged immediately into his task by arguing that there are no innate ideas, thereby adhering to an Aristotelian position and taking issue with Plato. Although he did not mention Descartes by name, probably his attack was directed against him, despite the fact that Descartes held a moderate position involving acceptance of potential innate ideas that are actualized by experience, rather than the extreme position that Locke attacked. Such ideas as, "what is, is," or, "it is impossible for the same thing to be and not to be," are, Locke said, not imprinted upon the mind. We are not born with these or any moral, theological, logical or mathematical principles. Despite his disagreement with the position, Locke could understand how the false opinion of the existence of innate ideas could have arisen. When a man once grasped some general proposition which he could not thereafter doubt, he was inclined to think this now self-evident proposition must have been innate.[36] Locke believed that both the intellectually lazy and the dogmatically minded who recognized that by having propositions that could not be questioned they could ask others to accept them without question, tried to foster the existence of innate ideas. In his crisp way of putting the matter, such acceptance stops the inquiry of the doubtful.[37] In this stand against innate ideas, Locke probably also was prompted by the fact that all sorts of prejudices could easily masquerade as "innate ideas," which, to him, would be nothing more than a disguised form of tyranny.

The argument for innate ideas from the sheer existence of commonly agreed-upon, universally accepted ideas is given short shrift by his argument that universality does not demand innateness if some other way can be found to account for the presence of these ideas. If ideas be universal, he asks, how is it that children and idiots do not have them? Moreover, he points out that children can reason long before they appreciate the truth of such maxims as were earlier used as illustrative. From whence then do generally agreed-upon ideas come? Locke set himself the task of proving that all knowledge is derived from experience.

He utilized the phenomena of habit to explain the apparent innateness of what are mistaken to be first and unquestionable principles.[38] What a child is told and retold by nurses or others, he accepts. When an adult, as a consequence of being unable to remember a time when he did not accept these principles, he believes he must have held them all along.

Ideas come from sense impressions in the form of "particular" ideas. The mind, "the yet empty cabinet"[39] (referred to thusly because of what he considered to be the false analogy of the well-stocked cabinet filled with innate ideas), is furnished with ideas by experience. Sensing takes place when the impression from the sense organs is transmitted to the mind. These sensations are simple ideas. In receiving simple ideas, the mind is essentially passive; it must sense when it senses and cannot refuse impressions or blot them out.[40]

Sensible qualities are simple ideas; that is, they are not divisible into different ideas.[41] Some simple ideas are admitted through one sense, while others depend upon combinations of the senses, such as ideas of space and extension, rest and motion.

What we know through the senses is not immediately known but, rather, is known through the intervention of ideas.[42] Knowledge is real only to the extent that there is conformity between our ideas and the reality of objects. With simple ideas, there is at least a rough correspondence since these ideas are the product of things outside ourselves operating on the mind. He added that all our ideas are not exactly identical to the images and do not exactly resemble the object.[43]

Sensible qualities are of two kinds, the original or primary qualities of solidity, substance, figure, and mobility which are inseparable qualities of the objects no matter how they may change in other ways, and the secondary qualities, such as color, sounds, and tastes, which have no reality in the objects themselves but do have the capacity to produce sensations in the observer.[44] The secondary qualities exist only as modes of the primary qualities. Illustrative is the failure of objects to have color in the dark. For the existence of secondary qualities Locke had other cogent illustrations, such as the influence of jaundice on perception, the change in vision on wearing blue spectacles, and the like. However, the most famous illustration utilized by Locke was the experiment of the three basins of water: if, after placing one hand in a basin of cold water and the other in a basin of hot water, the hands are now placed together in a basin of tepid water, one hand will feel it as warm, while the other will feel it as cold. To Locke, this proved the phenomenal or subjective character of perception. The objective nature of the cause and the subjective character of the effect in consciousness had been established. Although using this and other illustrations to drive home his point about secondary qualities, Locke was no idealist. The tepid water was real enough, as were whiteness and bitterness and other secondary qualities.

This external reality lying behind the ideas we have, the existence of which Locke was convinced, was the crucial issue on which his successors were to seize. How, they were to ask, if we are aware only of ideas for primary and secondary qualities alike, and only these ideas, can we know that there is such a reality? (See page 193.)

Sensations are supplemented by reflection which we carry on with our minds.[45] Together, ideas of sensation and ideas of reflection make up all ideas. These two, the only sources of ideas, are those with which mind deals, together making up all mental activity. There is this operation of the mind itself, in addition to the operation of sensations upon the mind. Reflection gives rise to ideas, but these are ideas based on those already supplied from sensory experience. Ideas of reflection could not be innate by definition, since they use the materials of sensation. The operations collectively called reflection are perceiving, thinking, doubting, believing, reasoning, knowing, and willing.

Reflection comes later than sensation. Children reflect only after time spent in examining their "floating visions."[46] Locke had some crude conception of development since he wrote, as experience increases, the mind has more to think about. Perception is the simplest level of reflection.[47] Children first have ideas of hunger and of warmth which exemplify perceptions. Even animals have perceptions. Perceptive reflection is the first step toward knowledge. Remembering is also present in children. When the same ideas again recur, without the operation of the object of the original sensation, then we have remembering. The other ways in which reflection functions are more appropriately mentioned after introducing another facet of Locke's psychological views, that of complex ideas.

Simple ideas are received passively but the mind can actively make ideas by putting them together in combinations.[48] Complex ideas are derived from simple ideas of sensation and of reflection.[49] Simple ideas from both sources are combined. All ideas, even the most abstruse, remote, and abstract, arise from these two sources.[50] From repeating and joining together ideas from sense or from speech come all ideas.

It is now appropriate to return to the question of reflection in order to consider those particular operations of the mind which involve complex as well as simple ideas. The mind contemplates both simple and complex ideas, discerns similarities and differences, compares and distinguishes them, and composes them in new arrangements. The process culminates when the mind begins to treat them as abstractions and to use these ideas to form general ideas.

How Locke viewed abstract ideas deserves special consideration since his successor, Berkeley, offered a very important critique of them. Locke argued that we join together ideas derived directly from sense or from reflection to form abstract ideas by considering some attributes common to several particular ideas and ignoring those aspects in which they differ. A number of objects, such as a sail, a bone, and a bowl of milk, can give us an idea of whiteness when we ignore the differences among the objects and concentrate on the similarity among them.

Complex ideas have their origins in the thoughts of men more than in the reality of things. Ideas are of utmost diversity as Locke himself illustrates by placing in the same list whiteness, hardness, thinking, motion, man, elephant, army and drunkenness.[51] Complex ideas may be analyzed into simpler ones. Systematically analyzed complex ideas, considered in some detail by Locke, include substance; relation, including cause and effect; identity and diversity, including personal identity; and proportion. Now that complex ideas had been discussed, Locke proceeded to consider such issues as clarity and obscurity, distinctions and confusions among them, reality and fantasy, adequacy and inadequacy, and truth and falsity of ideas.[52]

Feelings play only a secondary role in Locke's treatment of psychology. Pain and pleasure are simple ideas accompanying both sensation and reflection.[53] From the feelings, the passions are derived. The passions are modes or manifestations of pleasure and pain and include love, hatred, desire, joy, sorrow, hope, and anger. Basically, the passions are derivatives of good and evil in that they are such by reference to pleasure and pain to which they give rise. Each passion is related by Locke to good and evil. Desire, for example, is the thought of some attainable good, while envy is the uneasiness we experience when some one obtains a good before we do.

It is seen that pleasure and pain are defined by the ideas one has. Locke's common sense views, deriving complex emotions from a base of simple pleasures and pains, was to have considerable effect on psychological theories throughout the eighteenth century.

The fame which Locke has received for coining the phrase, "the association of ideas," is undeserved to some extent. His chapter bearing this title was interpolated in 1700 in the fourth edition of the *Essay*.[54] His system of psychology had been fully developed without recourse to association of ideas. It is, therefore, fitting and proper that this topic be treated as an appendix to the rest of his thinking.

Before considering what he meant by the association of ideas, it is worthwhile to examine the way in which he treated related issues in earlier editions so it can be seen what advance was made by his later formulation. Earlier he had held that ideas are fixed in memory by attention and repetition, but above all, by pleasure and pain.[55] "Hurts" and "advantages" to the body are taken notice of because of pleasure and pain. Reflection, as we have seen, is a means by which one combines a number of simple simultaneous experiences into a compound but single experience. He thus anticipated a more precise formulation of what later was to be called simultaneous association. He had likewise referred, as mentioned before, to the origin of complex ideas, even the most abstract, as caused by the repeating and joining together of simple ideas.[56] The changeableness of habits, as brought about by reflection, practice, application, and custom, is used by Locke to explain how we can change the agreeableness or disagreeableness of things.[57] The topic of the nature of habit and association, then, had not been completely neglected by Locke.

Aside from the title itself, the phrase, association of ideas, is used but once in this relatively short interpolated chapter.[58] He makes no reference either to Aristotle or to Hobbes and does not in any way refer to "laws of association." He approaches the topic by pointing out that there is something unreasonable in all men since, while each of us can readily perceive flaws in the reasoning of others, he is blinded to even those much greater inadequacies in himself. How did this come about? It is because of wrong connection of ideas that have come about by chance or by custom in a particular individual. An example he gives is that of teaching children that goblins have more to do with darkness than with light and, as a consequence, finding that they are unable thereafter to separate the idea of darkness from the idea of goblins, so that now the dark brings with it these frightful ideas. A not inconsiderable proportion of the chapter is taken up with instances of this theme of wrong associations. However, he does offer an instance of more neutral tying together of ideas, that of a musician, who if he once begins a tune, will be able to continue to play without further care or attention. In no way, however, does he show that he regards this as any more than another, and similar illustration. It would seem that Locke used association to explain errors of understanding, while those who came after him were to use it to explain understanding itself.

Influence

The influence Locke had upon later developments in psychology was varied and profound. A characterization of some of his views will be given in a series of summary statements:

1. Locke, in making understanding central to his work, organized the higher mental processes into a field of psychology broader in nature than anything that could be investigated by physiological methods alone.

2. Locke was the first psychologist of the modern age to use the introspective method carefully, steadily, and thoroughly. Others since Augustine and Aquinas might have appealed to introspection, but theirs was more a hasty glance followed by relatively dogmatic statements. Consequently, the more cautious Locke did much to set the limits of a psychology which, although still relatively speculative, could later be separated completely from philosophy.

3. He denied the innateness of ideas and substituted his notion of mind as a white paper on which experience writes, a *tabula rasa* as Aristotle had called it. This was not a unique idea with Locke, but those who came after him made the notion which they had learned from him the central dominating point of psychology, thus he may be said to have launched British empiricism.

4. He identified ideas as items of knowledge, which some psychologists today would call "meanings." He conceived of ideas as elements and of the complex ideas of the mind as capable of *analysis* into units. This conception was to prove important in the vogue for atomism that took place in the nineteenth and twentieth centuries, epitomized in the views of Wundt and Titchener.

5. To meet the difficulty of accounting for the higher intellectual processes, Locke postulated reflection as coordinate with sensation in the formation of experiences. In solving this problem he made his position a not entirely empirical one. In a sense, he substituted a native power of function of reflection for innate ideas that he had discarded. He made a concession to nativism which Hobbes had held was needless. Locke's concept of reflection was somewhat vague, and out of this very vagueness came a spur to others to find a means of extension of his association principle to account for complex and derivative ideas.

6. In continuing the distinction between primary and secondary qualities and presenting them so graphically, Locke, although not the originator, did much to draw attention to this distinction.

7. In a manner reminiscent of Aquinas, Locke referred to reflection as an internal sense. Locke made a distinction between being aware of an idea (reflection) and merely having an idea in itself. The question of how the mind obtains knowledge of its own operations was thus solved; reflections were ideas about ideas, as it were, reflections on the manner of their occurrence. Act psychologists of the nineteenth century made this distinction an important part of their approach in that they distinguished between act or function on the one hand and content on the other. With Locke, some of them stressed that there are two materials of mind.

8. In originating and illustrating the phrase, "association of ideas," Locke made explicit the possibility of working out the interconnections and sequences of ideas as expressive of experiences. A reduction of the entire mental life to association would soon follow. Association will be found to be one of the principal themes pervading psychology in an open or disguised form to this very day.

GEORGE BERKELEY

George Berkeley, a deeply religious man, was disturbed by the skeptical attitudes engendered by the materialistic emphasis that he believed was threatening to dominate the intellectual life of his time. The guiding theme of Berkeley's writing was defense of religion by the refutation of skepticism. Berkeley realized the danger posed to religion by the new materialistic Newtonian science. It was not science that he wished to banish, but rather the belief in the primordial character of matter which made it possible for impious persons to deride immaterial substance, to consider the soul corruptible, and even to deny providence.[59] He held that spiritual and intellectual confusion arose from the belief in something called matter, independent of mind. To Berkeley, this belief was a chimera.[60] Pursuing his theme he asked, "What sort of world does this science of matter in motion depict?" He concluded that it is the world as revealed by the senses. In an effort to combat the source of danger to religion, he turned to inquiry into our mental life.

Life and Works of Berkeley[61]

George Berkeley (1685–1753) was born in Ireland and educated at Trinity College, Dublin. By the time he arrived at his college, it included in its teachings the works of Descartes, Hobbes, Locke, and Newton. His academic progress was swift; he entered at fifteen, took his bachelor's degree at twenty, completed his master's degree and became a junior fellow at twenty-two, and received ordination as a deacon of the Anglican Church at twenty-four. At the same age, in the year 1709, he published the first account of his psychological-philosophical views in *An Essay Towards a New Theory of Vision.*[62] A year later he gave a more rounded statement in *A Treatise Concerning the Principles of Human Knowledge.*[63] In one sense his life after the age of twenty-five is an anticlimax, since these two works are vastly more important than anything else he ever wrote. Nevertheless, he had a full life—teaching at Trinity; further writing; visiting the London of Swift, Addison, and Steele, where he captivated society by his charm; traveling on the continent; and endeavoring to further educational and missionary enterprises in the American colonies. In connection with these benevolent efforts, he settled with some others for nearly three years at Newport, Rhode Island. When his hopes for support from governmental grants were not realized, he returned to London, leaving his house, farm, and library to Yale University. In fairness it must be added that on later occasions he also donated books to Harvard. For the last eighteen years of his life, Berkeley was Bishop of Cloyne in County Cork, Ireland.

Philosophical Position

The major arguments for Berkeley's philosophical position were psychological in nature. Before presenting them, a statement of this philosophical position is necessary, although the evidence is reserved for the section of the chapter which follows. To appreciate the full impact of his philosophical views, the psychological arguments are essential.

It is convenient to refer to Berkeley's philosophical position as "mentalism," a name given to it in later years because he had insisted that the mental aspects of life are paramount.[64] Berkeley stressed mental phenomena, but he did not deny the existence of a world of physical things. Others who came after him could and did make this specific denial. Their position, in distinction from his "mentalism," came to be called, "subjective idealism," with which his view is sometimes confused.

To elucidate what is meant by mentalism, consider the nature of an object. An object, psychologically speaking, Berkeley said, is a collection, a sum of sensations which experience has given us together, and consequently habit makes it impossible to disassociate them in our minds. The world is the sum total of our sensations. To illustrate:

Take away the sensations of softness, moisture, redness, tartness, and you take away the cherry. Since it is not a being distinct from these sensations; a cherry, I say, is nothing but a congeries of sensible impressions or ideas perceived by various senses; which ideas are united into one thing (or have one name given them) by the mind;— because they are observed to attend each other.[65]

Thus mentalism is the theory that a collection of impressions and ideas makes up our experiences.

Berkeley was insisting on the primacy of consciousness. He declined to accept anyone else's perception, "so long as I myself am conscious of no such thing."[66] Only that of which a man is conscious is important. Man's knowledge of other men is known only through ideas excited in him.[67]

Berkeley argued for direct observation of phenomena. These phenomena are real enough; their *esse* is *percipi*.[68] Perception is the reality. This is his definition of reality, *i.e.*, appearances are real.[69] This position classes him as akin to what we would today call a phenomenologist.[70] That perceived objects do not exist independently of perception is almost as classic a formulation of the phenomenologist's position as we have. This last qualifying phrase is necessary because, of course, he escaped the position since the Infinite Perceiver assured him of the presence of objects. Anticipating much of Mach's analysis of Newtonian assumptions, Berkeley found no justification for Newton's conceptions of absolute space and time and argued that all motion was relative to the observer.[71] Not only matter but Newtonian motion, time, and space he declared to be unknowable.

Berkeley did not, however, deny the reality of matter merely because man's own prowess allows him to be certain only of mental events. It follows from his position on this issue that the unity of mental life cannot be explained by reference to the physical world. Berkeley raises some questions in this connection. The smell and the color of the rose are not "out there" to be experienced together. How then are they experienced together? Similarly two people report the same sequence of events, but Berkeley could not appeal in explanation to the "stimulus objects," as we would call them. How can this come about? Futhermore, what makes a unity of the collection of experiences which belong to an individual mind? In answer, Berkeley concluded that which holds together experiences of this sort is the soul, a logically necessary, although unobservable, substratum to our experience. Moreover, there must be an active cause for the successive experience of the "Works of Nature." This Berkeley found in God.[72] There was a persistence of physical objects guaranteed by the "Permanent Perceiver," God. This phase of his thinking is captured neatly in the famous limerick and reply to it by Ronald Knox:[73]

There was a young man who said, "God
Must think it exceedingly odd
    If he finds that this tree
    Continues to be
When there's no one about in the Quad."

Dear Sir:
    Your astonishment's odd:
I am always about in the Quad.
    And that's why the tree
    Will continue to be,
    Since observed by
        Yours faithfully,
        God.

His views on these matters created a sensation, not only in scholarly circles, but throughout literate society. To the man of common sense what he had advanced was a paradox. Johnson, when he was challenged by Boswell to refute Berkeley, gave a stone a mighty kick, and replied, "I refute it *thus.*" As is sometimes the way of the world, this "refutation" which, of course, is irrelevant to the issue at hand, is perhaps better known than the doctrine which it was intended to demolish.

Psychological Views

In the very first section of the *Principles*[74] Berkeley presented a short statement of the elements of his system of psychology. He asserted that the objects of human knowledge could be reduced to ideas imprinted on the senses, perceptions obtained by attending to the passions and operations of the mind, and ideas formed by the help of memory and imagination. These, to Berkeley, are the aspects of mental life. Knowing the objects of knowledge, or perceiving them and exercising such operations as willing, imagining, or remembering them, Berkeley called mind, spirit, soul, or "myself." This mind is not one of these ideas but something distinct from them.

It will be remembered that Hobbes had denied that psychological quali-ties actually are inherent in the object. (See page 179.) Hobbes did not see that his argument could be carried to the point that external reality could be held as unknown and unknowable. Berkeley asked if our psychological experiences are inherent not in the object but within ourselves, *how do we know the reality of the objects of the world?*[75] Our experiences are within ourselves, not derived from the object, and, consequently, we cannot know with certainty through this means whether or not there is actually any-thing "out there." For Locke, this was not the case. It will be remembered that Locke followed Galileo in making a distinction between primary and secondary qualities, the former inhering in objects, the latter being mere manifestations of our ideas. (See page 185.) But if we know everything, as Locke said, through ideas Berkeley[76] wanted to know how he could know through this means that some qualities inhere in objects while others do not? How could Locke know from experience, and from experience alone, what was not derived from experience? Locke had asserted something which he could not have experienced. The same arguments that were cogent in respect to secondary qualities, Berkeley argued, apply to primary qualities. Berkeley concluded that this Locke could not know on the basis of experience, his only source of data for experience. Berkeley insisted that all ideas were similar to what Locke had called secondary qualities. Primary as well as secondary qualities are merely sensations—or ideas, as Berkeley calls them, and an idea exists in the mind perceiving it.[77] In one bold stroke Berkeley reduced primary qualities to secondary qualities. We never know anything but our experiences. So far as this argument of Berkeley's is concerned, the world is a plausible but unproved hypothesis. Moreover, he held that it is an hypothesis that can never be proven by scientific means. Particular sensation exists, for which we may hypothesize a world, but we can not prove it. We know only our own experience. The outcome was to invert Locke's proposition that ideas entered into the mind by means of the senses from outside, to the query of how it is we can ever obtain a belief in the existence of an external world since all we know are the ideas of which the mind is constituted.

In spite of his divergences from Hobbes and Locke, Berkeley was still an empiricist.[78] Although he disagreed with them on the nature of the "outer" and "inner" worlds, he still agreed that the truth could be established by verification through direct experience, derived from the senses. It is sometimes said he denied the evidence of the senses. On the contrary, he accepted their evidence but considered himself forced to find the existence of the world behind subjective phenomena on other grounds. It will also be seen in a moment that his theory of space perception is uncompromisingly empiricist in nature.

The crucial role of experience is brought out clearly in his handling of the relation among sensory experiences. Ideas are classified by the separate sense departments. Hence, vision, touch, smell, taste, and hearing are five classes of sense ideas with which we are born. Unlike others before him, Berkeley did not appeal to a "common sense" as a means whereby the experience from the various sense classes are intermingled. Moreover, Berkeley insisted that ideas within each sense department are "distinct," that is to say, separate and non-overlapping. The smell of the rose and the color of the rose are distinct sensations, not innately intermingled in any way. The ideas to which they give rise are distinct, one from another. There is no idea common to both, and, yet, somehow they manage to be combined. It is evident that Berkeley had to find a combinatory factor. He found it in experience. It is only loose speaking when we refer to both *seeing* and *hearing* a coach, as if they were a single experience. One says that one "hears" a coach half a mile away. Strictly speaking one hears only a certain *sound* which suggests a coach. The sound itself is no distance at all. Seeing is exactly analogous—I say, I see a coach in the distance, but what is seen serves merely to suggest a coach at that distance. It, nevertheless, can be inferred to be the same coach because the ideas have been observed to go constantly together and are spoken of as one and the same thing. What one visualizes and what one hears are different things; but they are now united by experience, so it becomes natural to treat them as one experience.

Locke had already expressed doubt whether a man born blind, who had his sight for the first time in later life, would be able to distinguish by vision a cube from a triangle although both were known to him by touch. Berkeley[79] unequivocally agreed. The blind man now having sight would have to have new experiences, wherein sight-touch would be associated, just as a man born blind would have no idea of distance by means of vision and would have need of experience before being able to see. In this and in his explicit discussion of association he made the point that ideas are associated when they are connected in experience.

His classification of the principles of association, although he did not use the term itself, was more inclusive than Locke's.[80] In fact, he neatly summarized the nature of simultaneous association in the very first paragraph of the *Principles*.[81] He stated that complex ideas are formed because the ideas of sight (light and color), touch (hardness and softness), smell (odor), and so on accompany each other and come to be marked by one name. As an illustration, a certain color, taste, smell, figure, and consistence which have been observed to go together, we call, *apple*. Elsewhere he writes:

> Men combine together several ideas apprehended by diverse senses or by the same sense at different times or in different circumstances, but observed, however, to have some connection in nature either with respect to coexistence or succession; all which they refer to one name and consider one thing.[82]

Contiguity of sensation is the basis of simultaneous association of ideas. He also specified successive association and distinguished among association by similarity, causality, and coexistence.[83]

Since ideas arise from within separate sense departments, it is not surprising that Berkeley denied the existence of abstract ideas.[84] If a reality, an abstract idea would involve material derived from several sense departments or might even require the adherents of the reality of abstract ideas to deny altogether that sensory content is present. Ideas, for Berkeley, are restricted to perceptions and images—and these come from sense and are always particular. Under these circumstances, Berkeley could not admit that abstractions were images to be presented to the mind.

Berkeley did not disagree with Locke about the existence of what loosely can be called "abstract" ideas. He agreed that we can form general ideas that stand for a whole group of phenomena. However, we can form no new ideas from common content since there is no common content. We merely have words to denote this common element, but we, strictly speaking, have no ideas of it. We can have words to connote such common features of perceived objects, but we cannot have new ideas of a strictly abstract content. One can emphasize the triangularity of a figure without attending to its other qualities, but Berkeley could not, try as he might, frame a definite idea of a triangle abstractly without any of these qualities.[85]

Mental processes, he held, are always particular.[86] A general idea is just as particular as the idea of any single object. The idea becomes general by standing for or representing all other particular ideas of the same sort, and, thus, we have a generalized meaning.

Chronologically, Berkeley's first written presentation of his psychological thinking was titled "An Essay Toward A New Theory of Vision."[87] It is psychology's first monograph and is regarded as the culmination of his work. Accordingly, it will serve to integrate what has been said before as well as to bring us back to his attack upon materialism.

Berkeley embarked upon his famous analysis of the problem of distance perception because of an objection to immaterialism which might be stated as follows: We actually do see things at a distance from ourselves, and consequently they exist independent of the mind. Common man thinks external objects can be seen and that direction and distance, as such, can be seen. "Out there" is a road, and beyond the road there is a tree, and in the far distance there is a range of hills. Objects seem spread out before him in a way that makes him rebel against a contention that he has no knowledge of space from direct perception of it. Locke had offered a modification of his common-sense view by saying that perception occurred only mediately or indirectly by means of images or resemblance. But these images were still images of external things. To be consistent Berkeley had to go further and deny these external things if his espousal of the immateriality of the external world was to be supported. He did this by an analysis of perception.

Berkeley[88] argued that the various properties of depth perception—shape, magnitude, distance, and the relative situation of objects—are not perceived directly by the eye but are learned after visual sensations have been associated with sensations of "touch" (in which he included movement in space, as in reaching and walking). Berkeley goes on to say that pictures cast upon the retina are flat and give no suggestion of the distances of objects from the eye. Nor does the degree of convergence of the eyes (as visual receivers) give us a clue as to distance. Earlier workers had made much of the importance of visual angles in explaining visual convergence.[89] On the basis of introspective evidence, he argued that neither he nor anyone else is conscious of calculating the angle at which the eyes are converging. Even if this effect of convergence is present, there is nothing in the visual experience, as such, that would give the person a reason for associating a sensation of less convergence with more distant objects and *vice versa*. Berkeley does not deny the phenomena of convergence. Quite the contrary, he depends upon it, but it is *movement* of the eyes, not the visual experience of the shift of angles, which aids in perception of distance through convergence. When looking at an object, we "alter the disposition" of the eyes as it approaches or recedes.[90] This is accompanied by a sensation which brings to mind the idea of greater or lesser distance. This, in turn, was learned from experience with situations where objects producing this particular sensation were found to be associated with a given distance. He goes on in a similar vein to elucidate other phenomena involved in the perception of distance. To explain the visual perception of magnitude, he appealed to sensations arising from convergence, to accommodation (straining of eyes in focusing), and to the blurring which occurs when the focus is poor.

One part of his argument merits special attention. It will be noted that Berkeley objected to the discussion of visual angles as an aspect of *seeing.* Much of the work on vision after Newton had been concerned with such matters. Berkeley's analysis of depth perception avoided a confusion prevalent then and still occurring today—the confusion between the psychology of vision and geometrical optics.[91] He was not opposed to the physical sciences, including this subdivision; he was opposed to the confusion of these two areas.[92] Speaking generally, space is not perceived as such, rather it "is suggested to the mind by the mediation of some other idea which is itself perceived in the act of seeing."[93]

In this work on visual perception he did not appeal to association, as such, but to what he called uniting in experience. It is evident that it was association that he meant. To Berkeley, distance perception was not a "given," immediately experienced, but something mediate which had to be learned. Berkeley held that he had demonstrated that sight and touch as expressed in movement have nothing intrinsically in common; "customary connexion" leads them to a common result. Space is not known directly but through this "connexion." This is essentially an introspectionistic theory of visual perception of distance.

Berkeley's theory of space perception is a definite contribution to psychology since he demonstrated that distance or depth is not a sensation but an additional aspect of visual data. An apparently simple experience was reduced by him to the more primitive psychological experiences on which it was based. By stating that our perceptions of distance and magnitude are capable of reduction into simpler elements, he served to encourage those who came after him to attempt to analyse other experiences into elements. Berkeley made clear that the problem of knowledge is not a philosophical problem alone but a distinctively psychological one as well.

David Hume

David Hume[94] (1711–1776) was born in Scotland and educated at Edinburgh. As a youth he gave his family some cause for misgivings about his future since his mother said of him that he was "a fine, good-natured crater but uncommon weak-minded." Probably she was wrong about his intelligence since he later became Undersecretary of State. After several false starts he found his field in philosophy. However, he was never satisfied that his writings in this area received the acclaim that should have been given them. Indeed, the reception of A Treatise of Human Nature,[95] published anonymously before he was thirty, although it sold fairly well, fell so far below his high expectations that he was led to exclaim that it "fell dead-born from the press." Later he recast the first part of the Treatise as what was later to be called An Enquiry Concerning Human Understanding[96] which, during his life time, had little more impact than its predecessor. However, he enjoyed wide-spread popularity from other writings, particularly a history of England. He also served in various governmental posts. He was frustrated, however, in his attempts to secure a professorship because unorthodox religious convictions and the scepticism his views engendered made him suspect.

In introducing his Enquiry, Hume defined his investigation as that of moral philosophy or the science of human nature.[97] For Hume, man was a natural object in a world of nature to be studied by the methods of natural science. The moral subjects, in contrast to the physical subjects, included ethics, politics, criticism, and logic conceived as the art of reasoning.[98] He did not use the word psychology. To anticipate his theme, this new psychological science was to show that some things previously taken to be inalienable features of the universe were actually characteristics of one's own psychological make-up projected onto the world.

Hume argued that we can do more than merely describe the operations of the mental life; we can find the principles upon which these operations are based.[99] Astronomers, he goes on to say, have patiently studied the motion, order, and magnitude of the stars until finally a "philosopher" (Newton) arose who determined the laws and the forces by which they are directed. Can we not, given equal capacity and caution, do the same with mental life? He answered in the affirmative because he thought that he had found the law which corresponded to the law of gravitation in the physical world—the law of association of ideas. Association of ideas is the universal principle of human nature.

Mental contents, Hume[100] held, are of two sorts—the impressions arising from sensing, feeling, and willing which are vivid and strong, and the ideas (images and thoughts as we might call them) which are less clear and fainter copies of impressions. He specifically refused to assign any ultimate cause to impressions. Doubts as to their being any source of external object is probably what he wished to avoid discussing; at any rate impressions are the given elements from which all else starts. Ideas are derived from impressions. As he put it, we must learn from experience that fire burns and that water is wet.

Memory and imagination, to Hume, are not faculties but names for the two different ways in which ideas work.[101] Memory is distinguished from imagination by its greater clarity and vivacity and by the fact that the order of memories repeats the succession of the original impressions. Imagination is neither as clear nor does it follow the order of the impression, but it is relatively free in the course its reconstructions may take. Imagination may be compounded by transposition, augmentation, or diminution; but it still is dependent upon material afforded by experience.[102]

The three principles or laws of association are resemblance (similarity), contiguity in place or time, and causality.[103] To use some of his illustrations, a picture leads our thoughts to the original (resemblance), the mention of one apartment in a building leads to mention of others (contiguity), and if we think of a wound, we can scarcely avoid consideration of the pain which follows (causality).

As Hume's thinking developed, he seems to have become aware that causality was not on the same level of classification as the other two forms of association, and, without eliminating it from the list of the three principles, he reduced it to a special case of the other two. The relation of causality, he concluded, is not an ultimate law of the association of ideas but rests upon the two primary relations of similarity and space-time contiguity. An object follows another, and we come to expect it to happen again.[104]

All reasoning about factual matters, Hume said, seems to be founded on the relation of cause and effect.[105] What is the origin of our notion of cause? A billiard ball moves and knocks against another billiard ball which also then begins to move. Hume held that, despite this sequence, there is nothing in the motion of the first ball to suggest the necessity of movement of the second. No intuition reveals the power whereby one object produces another. All we comprehend is one phenomenon following another. The senses do not supply the ideas of a necessary connection. Can it, perhaps, be due to reflection?[106] Consider, he says, the motion of our bodies when following the command of our will. Throughout the succession of events we are completely conscious, but can we tell how this operation was effected? Hume held that we could not, and considered that it must forever escape our most diligent inquiry. Reflection does not supply the answer. We know that the command of the will is followed by the action, that is all. We observe the succession of two phenomena—nothing more.

The mind can not find the effect in the supposed cause, no matter how acute the scrutiny since the effect is totally different from the cause.[107] Frequent and invariable sequences make us assume erroneously that the effect must occur because the cause has occurred. Actually, there is no necessary relation of phenomena as is ordinarily implied by the concept of causality. Adam could not tell from the transparency and the fluidity of water that immersion would suffocate him.[108] Instead, we know from experience that similar objects are conjoined with similar ones. Hence, we can formulate another definition of cause and speak of it as an "object followed by another, and whose appearance always conveys the thought to that other."[109] Cause, to Hume, is recurrent concomittance. Thus the relation of causality is reduced to similarity and succession. Causality was not a law of thought, but a habit of mind originating in experience and the association of ideas. Causal experience is nothing more than customary expectation. The consciousness of determination, which pervades our view of causality, is false. Objectively considered, causality is regularity of contiguous sequence. The necessity of cause-effect exists only in the mind, not in objects.[110] He is sometimes misinterpreted as denying causation. He was not: he was shifting the locus of causality from the external world to the mind in keeping with his theme mentioned earlier.

Hume held that the principle of connection between our ideas is habit.[111] Habit is the universal law of mind. Not only our external perceptions, but all of our experiences are explained by habit. As it has been put, "Empiricism becomes associationism."[112] When two objects or two events are found constantly joined together, we infer one from the other. For example, flame and heat, snow and cold have in the past been conjoined, and presentation of one or another part of these pairs will lead the mind to expect the other part. For this to take place one experience is not sufficient; several experiences are necessary to establish a habit.

The soul was reduced by Hume to impressions and association of impressions. In introspective examination, Hume stated he always came upon particular impressions[113] and never more than impressions. That which is termed the mind is essentially nothing more than a bundle of sensations.[114] This definition was to have a long history, culminating in the structuralism of Wundt and Titchener.

There has been a clear cut progression of thought from Locke through Berkeley to Hume. Locke had held that experience arose directly or basically from sense impression, but he had accepted the existence of objects similar to, but not identical with, our ideas. Berkeley had denied the existence of objects as far as their knowableness was concerned but had held that soul or mind was necessary to make experiences cohere or hold together. Hume had taken the obvious next step of questioning the existence of mind, leaving it nothing except a collection of impressions from which all else starts.

Hume's clear recognition of the importance of association and his formulation of the laws of association were crucial. Locke had never even considered using association as an explanation of mind and its functioning, but had relegated it to an explanation for abnormal connection between ideas. We must credit to Hume the position which held that compounds of impressions and ideas give us more intricate mental phenomena, a conception to which later psychologists owe a great deal.

The significance of what Hume called his "very curious discovery,"[115]— that our knowledge of causation resulted from habitual sequences of preceptions of events—was not fully appreciated during his life time. Nevertheless, his position became one with which future generations had to deal. Kant's reaction is especially noteworthy. (See page 220.)

David Hartley

David Hartley (1705–1759) is more important for his systematization of what had gone before than for originality. Clarity and comprehensiveness, rather than subtlety, marked his account of association contained in his *Observations on Man*,[116] first published in 1749. The indifference of Locke, the idealism of Berkeley, and the scepticism of Hume had exempted them from any need to pay attention to the physiological relationships to mental processes. It was Hartley's work that restored the body and its functioning as the physical basis for mental interconnections. Unable to become a minister because of doctrinal scruples, Hartley had become a medical practitioner as might be anticipated from the very first sentence of his introduction to *Observations:* "Man Consists of Two Parts, Body and Mind."[117] He was a contemporary of Hume but began writing and publishing in a minor way on these psychological matters before the appearance of the latter's *Treatise.* He was most influenced by Locke and Newton, although he acknowledged the influence of one John Gay, a clergyman, whose writings had called his attention to associationism.

The portion of his *Observations* which is of psychological interest was followed by ethical and theological considerations. In passing it might be noted that the transition from the psychological to the social and religious sphere is prepared for by taking the position that if we know how associations are formed, this gives us the power to see to it that good ones are cherished and that sinful ones are rooted out.[118]

Besides intrinsic merit, events conspired to keep alive the psychological portions while the rest has been forgotten. In 1775 Joseph Priestly[119] arranged re-publication of the portion devoted to psychology, but without either the physiology or the theology. In 1791, fifty years after original publication, Hartley's son issued another arrangement[120] that was finally widely recognized as a clear statement of psychology as associational.

As said before, man consists of two parts, mind and body.[121] Both must be studied because body and mind must be related.[122] In the arrangement of the material in the 1791 edition, thereafter most widely used, the mental and bodily spheres are presented by Hartley in consecutive propositional form, one proposition dealing with the former and the following one with the latter. Thus, one proposition states that sensations, often repeated, leave certain vestiges which may be called simple ideas.[123] The companion proposition holds that sensory vibrations, being often repeated, leave in the brain a disposition for repetition of similiar but minute vibrations.[124] Often the pairs of propositions are identical in statement except that the psychological term is replaced by a physiological one.

The doctrine of vibration suggested by Newton's account of motion, Hartley tells us, is his starting point.[125] Newton had spoken of physical impulses as vibratory. Hartley held that external physical vibrations set in motion the white medullary substance of the brain with which sensations are intimately associated.[126] Changes in the former entailed corresponding changes in the latter. Hartley took pains to insist that the nerves are solid, and not tubes, necessitating his postulation that vibrations transmitted movement from one part of the body to another.

Although not entirely clear on the issue he apparently held that the cerebral vibrations and the ideas perform in parallel. One is not the cause of the other. Rather, they show consistent correspondence. Events in one are correlated perfectly with events in the other. As a consequence, Hartley's view may be interpreted as a simple form of what is called psychophysical parallelism.[127]

With Locke, Hartley agreed that the mind at birth is a blank.[128] Simple sensations supply all states of consciousness. Sensations are internal states of the mind arising from impressions made by external objects; all other internal states are ideas.

Hartley's law of association, the law of the growth of sensation and ideas, is that of contiguity, both synchronous (simultaneous) and successive.[129] The passage from sensation to idea or from idea to idea occurs because of associative contiguity. One is able to induce the other provided the latter has occurred in the past frequently in conjunction with the former. The recurrence of one induces a repetition of the other. By the law of contiguity, Hartley explained memory, emotion, reasoning and voluntary and involuntary action. One or two illustrations might be given. When sensory vibrations subside, they leave their trace in fainter vibrations, the "vibratiuncles." Like Hobbes' "decaying sense," they are the sources of memory and imagination (seeing a tree and remembering a tree are two sets of vibrations differing only in intensity). Vibrations are aroused by means of association. This is to say, when two sensations occur, either simultaneously or successively, they become connected so that when one is re-excited later, the vibrations extend to the other, and we have an idea of that other. Associations are strengthened when vibration is greater. The association, under these circumstances, will be "cemented" sooner and stronger than is the case when the vibrations are less powerful.

Since association is both simultaneous and successive, it becomes for Hartley the basis for mental compounds or "clusters and combinations," as he calls them.[130] Simple ideas mix to form compounds just as letters coalesce into syllables and words. However, if the number of simple ideas in a particular compound are very great, they may not be discernible in the complex because each single idea is overpowered by the sum of all the rest.

Hartley also broadened the conception of association to include motor activities—a movement may recall an idea; an idea may recall a movement. Ideas associated with movements form the basis for voluntary action. Muscular movements repeated in this same sequence become associated into automatic habits. His discussion of voluntary and involuntary action[131] attempted to relate the two in that association by contiguity explained both how automatic movements came under voluntary control and how voluntary movements became automatic.

The special senses are discussed by Hartley in detail in a manner that brought out the dual roles of vibration and association.[132] Color, excited by an object, is a vibration of the other which extends to the eye. In the eye the external vibration is changed to a backward and forward vibration of the nerve which extends to the brain, the seat of intelligence.

Hartley[133] proceeded to apply the twin doctrines of vibration and association to a considerable number of other topics, ranging over sexual desires, respiration, words and association ideas, passions or affections, memory, imagination. In so doing, he can be said at least to be reasonably consistent.[134] He closes the volume devoted to psychological matters with a defense of determinism, although still maintaining that there was a difference between involuntary and voluntary motions. He argued that stating that A and its contrary, a, can follow from similar previous circumstances, is the same as affirming that they occur without cause. If this were the case, he goes on, the foundations of all abstract reasoning would be destroyed.

Hartley was the first to explain all forms of mental life on the basis of association in a manner which made it possible to assume a mechanistic base. Associationism as a system of psychology had been formulated. For those who came after him, especially for James Mill (see page 206), the nature and implications of association had been outlined. Association, because it is simultaneous (as well as successive), was still another step toward that mental atomism which was to come.

Hartley's specific physiological propositions may be of little value today, but his point that body and mind cooperate to function conjointly has become an integral part of much of modern psychological thinking. What was still lacking was anything approaching a detailed understanding of the functioning of the nervous system. His was still very much an imaginary nervous system.

THE SCOTTISH SCHOOL

Thomas Reid (1710–1792), Dugald Stewart (1753–1828) and Thomas Brown (1778–1820) were all professors at Scottish Universities which led to their distinctive doctrines being referred to as those of the Scottish School.[135] It was more persistent than original or profound. Its basic doctrine held that associationism, especially as promulgated by the sceptic, Hume, had degraded the nature of man and its proponents wished to restore man to a dignity that would conform with Christian dogma. To this end they either rejected or modified associationism. Physiological explanations of behavior, especially Hartley's, they likewise rejected as derogatory to human dignity.

Scepticism, however, menaced man in another way; it destroyed the guarantee of the existence of outside objects. Berkeley, although far from a sceptic, had contributed too, by inverting the Lockean solution and insisting that all there is initially is conscious experience and that the problem then becomes that of how the mind creates objects. The general answer of the Scottish School was that objects are restored by appeal to "common sense," which is self-evident and open to all men, as opposed to the subtleties (or sophistries) of the empiricists. Common sense is a vague term, but its employment in argument showed a significant shift from the position taken up in earlier centuries, when authority was the defense offered for religious orthodoxy. The new orthodoxy, the Scottish School, by contrast, answered the empiricists with the empirical defense of common sense. They also answered with more specific arguments this problem of objective reference. Reid[136] conceived that the existence of external objects is divinely implanted. In the course of this argument, he utilized the distinction between sensation as the raw data of experience and perception as involving reference to an object. Brown,[137] whose particular formulation of associative principles is given a little later, used association to show that Reid's distinction, which had been couched in terms of sensation and perception as *powers*, could be interpreted as being due instead respectively to sensitive and associative powers. This rendered unnecessary considering perception as a distinct power but equally well accounted for how we know objects.

Reid's faculty psychology[138] is much like Wolff's. (See page 218.) Stewart[139] largely echoed this position, but Brown,[140] more original, broke from the tradition. Reid and Stewart opposed Hume's scepticism and his view of causality, while Brown came near enough to the Humean view of causality to set a problem in deciding whether or not he belongs in the Scottish School.[141]

In spite of themselves they kept associationism alive. Brown, in particular, drew closer to his associationist predecessors by proposing so-called secondary laws of "suggestion." [142] (He avoided the term "association" as implying mere sequence). Mind was more than a combination of elements. Quite apart from association, there was in it the unity of an operating, controlling self. The different kinds of possible union, the primary laws of suggestion, were resemblance, contrast, and nearness in time and space. The secondary laws of suggestion were duration, liveliness, frequency, recency, degrees of coexistence with other suggestions, constitutional differences of mind or of temperament, differing circumstances of the moment, state of health or efficiency of the body, and prior habits. These modified the primary laws according to prevailing conditions and explained why under specified conditions a particular suggestion appeared rather than another—why, at this particular time and place, the thought of "cold" brought forth "dark" rather than "hot;" why "butterfly," which resembles both "bird" and "moth," produces sometimes "bird," sometimes "moth." Until nearly a century later, when the experimental attack upon problems of learning began, this insight lay fallow.

Brown also distinguished simple and relative suggestion.[143] The latter occurs when we experience a state of feeling of relation as distinguished from simple connections. These feelings include resemblance, difference, and proportion. Thus we have the experience that this house is bigger than that one, this particular class of objects has the relation of subordinate to superordinate, there is an equality of the square of the hypotenuse of a right angle to the square of the two other sides, an incongruity between the shallowness of a posturing player and the drama of heroic proportions in which he appears. Thus Brown recognized a capacity to grasp relations of varying complexity, complementary to learning simple association. This was a contribution of some originality, anticipating the day when combination of simple mental elements would be recognized as insufficient to account for learning and perception.

Brown[144] spoke also of a mental chemistry but used it in precisely the opposite fashion of what the term would usually mean today—the mental analysis of mental elements in isolation. Rather, Brown meant the appearance of a psychological combination which is not present in the elements—the taste of lemonade is a blend, not a sum of sweet and sour. This conception was to be sharpened by John Stuart Mill just a little later. (See page 207.)

The Mills

James Mill (1773–1836) and his son, John Stuart Mill (1806–1873) have been labelled "Utilitarian philosopher" and "Philosopher" respectively.[145] Both are remembered as social theorists, economists, and leaders of the Utilitarians. John later emancipated himself considerably from Utilitarian teachings and also achieved eminence in the fields of logic and the philosophy of science. In their Utilitarianism they followed their friend, Jeremy Bentham (1748–1832). The Utilitarian creed, as Bentham described it, exalted the principle of Utility, summarized in the words "the greatest good for the greatest number,"[146] which held that people are ruled by self-interest, usefulness to self, and that social, political, and legal action ought to lead to the acquisition of pleasure and the avoidance of pain.[147]

James Mill began his career by being licensed to preach in the Church of Scotland, but "abandoned theology after his acquaintance with Bentham."[148] He lived by high-grade and wide-ranging journalism until 1819 when he entered the home service of the East India Company. He is best remembered for his *History of India* (1818), an immense and influential volume. He ended his career as "Examiner" (*i.e.*, Head) of the Company's office.

James Mill's psychology appears most completely in the *Analysis of the Phenomena of the Human Mind*.[149] It is associationism, closer to Hartley and Hume than to Brown.[150] It simplifies associationism, allowing for only two classes of mental elements, sensations, and, when these are removed, ideas. All association (even by similarity) can be reduced to contiguity alone.[151] Mill slightly tempered this extreme view by admitting two subdivisions of contiguity: it may be successive or synchronous. Thus the .words of a poem are associated successively, in time; the objects in a room synchronously, in space.

Mill applied a similar reductive procedure to the causes of variation of strength in association and accepted only frequency and vividness. Differences in strength of associations are explained by these two classes alone. Strength comprised permanence, certainty and assurance, or "correctness," spontaneity, and ease of formation, or "facility."

Association has one side-function; it served to bind experiences together. A complex state of association holds within it all of the original elements. The complex phenomena of the mind are formed out of simple ideas and sensations as elements. The ideas of any object are the fusion of the ideas of the components, nothing more. Thus, the complex ideas of wall are made up of ideas of brick, mortar, position, and quantity. Complex ideas of plank, wall, and nail, united with ideas of position and quantity compose an idea of floor. Similarly, glass, wood, and the like give window, a complex idea. The even more complex idea of house comes from these ideas united. Mill then works through furniture and merchandise to the most complex idea of all, that of "everything" made up of these and all other ideas.

James Mill felt no need of any unifying organization of the total idea. Synthesis was not necessary. Experiences sometimes appear to be simple, but indissoluble association really explains this. Psychological analysis shows that behind "simple" experiences a welter of elementary associations will always be found. Compounding, he held, was an absurdity. As Boring says, the whole is less, as well as more than the sum of its parts.[152] This conception Mill never grasped.

For Mill, association is neither power nor cause. It is a passive process; mind has no creative function. Sensations occur in a certain way, and are reproduced mechanically as ideas in that same order, one following the other. This brought association to its logical, mechanistic climax.

John Stuart Mill was a celebrated child prodigy. According to Cox and her associates his I.Q. in youth was 190, the highest they obtained in their careful reconstruction of the intelligence quotients of many eminent men.[153] He was educated at home by his father, on a plan devised by the latter and Bentham. At three he learned Greek; at eight he read Herodotus and Plato in the original. He had no boyhood friends, never learned to play, and was dominated by his father. This father-domination contributed to the mental crisis of John's early manhood, and helped to delay the publication of *Logic*[154] until 1843. Then he was thirty-seven, young in years, old in thought, and affected by his relationship with Harriet Taylor, whom he married after the death of her husband. After his *Logic*, his works were considerably influenced by her. His output was voluminous, and included philosophy, economics, political science, and psychology. His account of logical induction and deduction, and especially his clear explanation of the methods of agreement, difference, concomitant variation and residues (the 'Canons') are classic in scientific method, though not original with him.[155]

John Stuart Mill's psychology appears mainly in the 1869 edition of his father's *Analysis*.[156] Besides editing along with Alexander Bain and others, he contributed notes. As shown in his *Logic*,[157] he emancipated himself from atomistic associationism, stressed activity in mind (i.e., it was more than the vehicle for adding new experiences), asserted that combination of mental elements gave rise to something new and not present in the original. In the compound, the parts disappear and new properties emerge which bear little or no resemblance to their constituent elements. The whole is more than the sum of the parts, *i.e.*, what Wundt was to call "creative synthesis" had appeared. (See page 276.) This was also to become a central problem for the Gestalt school. (See page 441.)

John Stuart[158] also contributed to the continuing problem of the existence of external objects by holding that the mind is aware of matter in that it has the capability of a permanent possibility of sensation which is all that is necessary in order to say one believes in matter. John Stuart contributed also the suggestion of ethology to be a science of human character, and formulated views on what we may call social psychology (in the *Logic*). Unfortunately both of these had no great influence.

John Stuart Mill was a gentler, more human, and less "dry" character than his father. His life was easier in that the career in the India House, which James began late in life, John entered upon as a young man. (He became Examiner, too.) His married life, though brief, was happy, by contrast with his father's prolonged connubial asperity. Of the two John is the greater in the history of thought, but as a psychologist is of less moment.

ALEXANDER BAIN

Alexander Bain (1818–1903) was born, lived and worked for most of his life in Aberdeen, Scotland. There he had his brief schooling (until his twelfth year), was trained as a weaver like his father, continued his education through night school and reading, entered Marischal College in 1836, where he was assistant to the Professor of Moral Philosophy. As a student he wrote for the *Westminster Review,* and began a life long friendship with John Stuart Mill, whose *Logic* he helped to revise. From this contact in London came about his appointment as Assistant Secretary to the (London) Metropolitan Sanitary Commission, after a brief period of teaching in Glasgow.[159]

Bain's major work covers two volumes, *The Senses and the Intellect* (1855)[160] and *The Emotions and the Will* (1859).[161] These remained standard, as revised, for nearly half a century. Bain's thoroughness appears in his coverage of previous literature, exhaustive for the British and more comprehensive than usual for the Continental. His argumentation is close if not brilliant, his illustrations apposite and at times homely. This text was the first to link psychology to physiology (up-to-date physiology), in particular the reflex, though Bain juxtaposes rather than fuses the two fields. He treated habit and instinct fully, and belief more pragmatically than did others of his time. His analysis of the origin and development of volition is searching.

This publication was probably the turning point in Bain's life. His radicalism (including a flirtation with Positivism), and refusal to become a Church member had, it is said, helped to render abortive his applications for University Chairs.[162] But, in 1860, he was at last appointed Professor of Logic and Rhetoric at the University of Aberdeen. There he remained as Professor until 1880, and in various honorary offices until his death in 1903.

His later writings (barring revisions of his major text) scarcely concern us. They relate mostly to the other areas (rhetoric, grammar, education, administration) to which he contributed. It is as a psychologist that he is mainly remembered, being the only man in his day recorded as such.[163]

Bain's *Mind and Body,*[164] *A Manual of Mental and Moral Science,*[165] and *On the Study of Character,*[166] all belong to his professorial years. The first contains a fine discussion of his solution to the mind-body problem in which it is seen as forming a unity, observed either objectively as matter or subjectively as mind. The second was a condensation and up-dating of the main work. The last was a pioneer work on personality, with a specially apposite critique of phrenology. Bain was also the founder and the original proprietor of the journal, *Mind,* which first appeared in January, 1876. This was the first journal of philosophical psychology: it remains a leading one. The time was not yet ripe for an experimental journal. This is why Wundt's journal, though seven years junior to *Mind,* is considered the first journal of modern psychology.

Argument has run high as to Bain's position. Is he the last of the old psychologists or the first of the new? He was new in his stress on physiology, and his broadening and reworking of associationism to make it serve as the basis of a psychology assimilated to that discipline. Yet he was old in his cautious parallelism, despite his forward-looking view of mind and body as a "double-faced unit." His views on social psychology and individual differences were more modern than is usually realized.[167] Yet he did not assimilate evolutionism as, say, Spencer did, though he gave great weight to Darwin's work, *e.g.,* on emotional expression in animals as illustrating the physical side of anger.[168] He also modified an edition of *The Emotion and the Will* to include a chapter on evolution as related to the emotions,[169] but he thought "the history of the highest races does not fall in with evolution."[170] This meant man from the Greeks onwards: Bain's view of evolution in relation to man was circumscribed. The main forward-looking aspects remain: Bain's psychology rests upon a genuine, thorough, and up-to-date physiology, not a mythical physiology like Hartley's, who created his to fit the psychological facts as he saw them.[171] Bain's *Autobiography* shows the care he took to read, visit with, and understand major physiologists and anatomists, in order to distinguish fact from conjecture.[172] For instance, his analysis of hunger[173] shows how he applied knowledge of those sorts to securing accuracy, precision, and detailed appraisal in this area. (Perhaps Bain's dyspepsia also motivated him.) Yet he still regarded conscious data as primary and he was no reductionist. He regarded the place of psychological experiment as limited.

Bain's modification of associationism has similar Janus-like qualities. According to Cardno,[174] his cardinal statement in all four editions of *The Senses and the Intellect* is as follows. "Actions, sensations or states of feeling, occurring together or in close succession, tend to grow together or cohere in such a way that when any one of them is afterwards presented to the mind, the others are apt to be brought up. . . ."[175] This cohesion embraced contiguity as the law of association proper. Similarity was considered to be the second principle of association. Bain's major innovation was somewhat more adroitly to assimilate what, when discussing Mill, had been called "mental chemistry." Following Brown, Mill had introduced the principle into associationism, but in his system it had no more than the position of an attached foreign body.

Constructive association or imagination, as Bain called the principle, was seen as supplemental to association by contiguity and by similarity. "By means of Association the mind has the power to form *new* combinations or aggregates

different from any that have been presented to it in the course of experience."[176] The mind makes different combinations out of the materials given.
Although it was not so considered by Bain, constructive association can also
be interpreted as forsaking sole reliance upon association. This is not the only
instance of use of non-associationistic factors by Bain. In detail, Bain is often
forward-looking. Thus, in constructive association-making, new combinations
required something other than associations to account for novelty. Moreover,
infants possess reflexes and instincts and differences in acuteness. True, there
are no innate ideas, but there are innate behaviors prior to education. Heredity
was accepted as operative by Bain. Yet Bain's adherence to association as such
a general principle, and with the vocabulary he uses, is conservative. He
represents a culmination rather than a radical initiation. The nature of the
culmination is indicated by the fact that Bain can be suitably discussed here,
but Herbert Spencer, two years younger, only after considering Darwin. After
Bain, association would still live on but not under its old banner. If the
present-day interests of the philosopher in psychology be disregarded as not
being in the main stream of the history of psychology, then Bain was the last
philosopher-psychologist in Great Britain. Probably the evaluation that his
psychology is full of 'seminal ideas' which he failed to develop is as near as
we can come to a one-sentence appraisal.[177]

REFERENCES[*]

1. An excellent authoritative source for the early history of the Royal Society is
    that of Dorothy Stimson, *Scientists and Amateurs, a History of the Royal
    Society*. (New York: Schuman, 1948).

2. I. NEWTON, *Opticks*. London: Smith & Walford, 1704.

3. I. NEWTON, The Mathematical Principles of Natural Philosophy. In R. M.
    Hutchins. (ed.), *Great Books of the Western World*. (Vol. 34) Chicago:
    Encyclopaedia Britannica, 1952, pp. 1–372. (1687)

4. I. NEWTON, An Hypothesis Explaining the Properties of Light Discoursed in
    My Several Papers. In T. Birch, *History of the Royal Society of London* (Vol.
    3). London: Millar 1757, pp. 262–263. (1675) (Herrnstein & Boring Excerpt
    No. 2)

5. *Opticks, op. cit.*, Book 1, part 2, props. 5–6. (Herrnstein & Boring Excerpt
    No. 3)

6. W. MOLYNEUX, *Dioptrica Nova: A Treatise of Dioptrics*. London. (1692)
    (Herrnstein & Boring Excerpt No. 24)

[*] See page 16 for description of reference style.

7. T. Hobbes, Leviathan. (Edited by Nelle Fuller) In R. M. Hutchins (ed.), *op. cit.*, Vol. 23, pp. 49–283. (1651) Part 1, Chap. 26.

8. *Ibid.*

9. T. Hobbes, Human Nature. (Edited by W. Molesworth) In R. S. Peters (ed.), *Body, Man and Citizen.* New York: Collier, 1962, pp. 182–244. (1650)

10. *Ibid.*, Chap. 1, Conclusion; *Leviathan,* Introduction.

11. *Ibid.*, Part I, Chap. 13, p. 85.

12. *Ibid.*, Part I, Chap. 2.

13. *Ibid.*, Part I, Chap. 2, 7.

14. *Ibid.*, Part I, Chap. 1, 2, 7.

15. *Leviathan,* Part 1, Chap. 2.

16. *Human Nature,* Chap. 2, Sec. 4.

17. *Ibid.*, p. 185.

18. *Leviathan,* Part 1, Chap. 3. (Herrnstein & Boring Excerpt No. 66)

19. *Ibid.*, Part II, Chap. 30.

20. *Ibid.*, Part I, Chap. 6.

21. *Ibid.*, Part I, Chap. 11, p. 76.

22. *Ibid.*, Part I, Chap. 6.

23. *Ibid.*, Part I, Chap. 5, Part II, Chap. 19.

24. *Ibid.*, Part II, Chap. 27.

25. *Human Nature,* Chap. 12.

26. An excellent account, not only of his life but also of his views on philosophy, psychology, ethics, education, and politics is to be found in R. I. Aaron, *John Locke.* (2nd ed.) (Oxford: Clarendon Press, 1955)

27. J. Locke, A Letter Concerning Toleration. (Translated by W. Popple) In R. M. Hutchins (ed.), *op. cit.*, Vol. 35, pp. 1–22. (1689)

28. J. Locke, An Essay Concerning Human Understanding. (6th ed.) (Collated and annotated by A. C. Frazer) *Ibid.*, pp. 85–395. (1690)

29. *Letter Concerning Toleration.*

30. *Essay.*

31. J. Locke, *The Conduct of the Understanding.* New York: Alden 1883. (1706)

32. *Essay,* Epistle to the Reader, p. 87.

33. *Ibid.*, Introduction, 2.

34. *Ibid.*, Introduction 3, p. 94.

35. *Ibid.*, Book I, Chap. I.

36. *Ibid.*, Book I, Chap. I, Sec. 25.

37. *Ibid.*, Book I, Chap. IV, Sec. 24.

38. *Ibid.*, Book I, Chap. II, Sec. 22.

39. *Ibid.*, Book I, Chap. I, Sec. 15, p. 98.

40. *Ibid.*, Book II, Chap. I, Sec. 25.

41. *Ibid.*, Book II, Chap. II, Sec. 1.

42. *Ibid.*, Book IV, Chap. IV.

43. *Ibid.*, Book II, Chap. II.

44. *Ibid.*, Book II, Chap. VIII. (Herrnstein & Boring Excerpt No. 5)

45. *Ibid.*, Book II, Chap. I, Secs. 1–4. (Herrnstein & Boring Excerpt No. 104)

46. *Ibid.*, Book II, Chap. VIII, Sec. 8.

47. *Ibid.*, Book II, Chap. IX, Sec. 1.

48. *Ibid.*, Book II, Chap. XXII, Sec. 2.

49. *Ibid.*, Book II, Chap. XIII.

50. *Ibid.*, Book II, Chap. XII, Sec. 8.

51. *Ibid.*, Book II, Chap. I, Sec. 1.

52. *Ibid.*, Book II, Chap. XXIX-XLII.

53. *Ibid.*, Book II, Chap. XX.

54. *Ibid.*, Book II, Chap. XXXIII. (Herrnstein & Boring Excerpt No. 67)

55. *Ibid.*, Book II, Chap. X, Sec. 3.

56. *Ibid.*, Book II, Chap. XII, Sec. 8.

57. *Ibid.*, Book II, Chap. XXI, Sec. 71.

58. *Ibid.*, Book II, Chap. XXXIII.

59. G. BERKELEY, A Treatise Concerning the Principles of Human Knowledge. In R. M. Hutchins, (ed.), *op. cit.*, Vol. 35, pp. 404–444. (1710) Sec. 93.

60. *Ibid.*, Sec. 87.

61. The definitive statement of his life and works is that by A. A. Luce, *The Life of George Berkeley, Bishop of Cloyne.* (London: Nelson, 1949).

62. G. BERKELEY, An Essay Towards a New Theory of Vision. In A. A. Luce & T. E. Jessop (eds.), *Works.* (Vol. 1) London: Nelson, 1949, pp. 159–239. (1709)

63. *Principles.*

64. R. A. TSANOFF, *The Great Philosophers.* New York: Harper, 1953, p. 365.

65. G. BERKELEY, Three Dialogues Between Hylas and Philonus. In A. A. Luce & T. E. Jessop (eds.), *op. cit.*, Vol. 2, pp. 171–263. (1713) Third Dialogue, p. 249.

66. *New Theory*, 12, p. 173.

67. *Principles*, Sec. 145.

68. *Ibid.*, Sec. 3, p. 413.

69. *Ibid.*, Sec. 35.

70. G. A. FERGUSON, A Note on George Berkeley. *Canad. J. Psychol.*, 1953, 7, 156–158.

71. *Principles*, Secs. 12, 98, 117.

72. *Principles*, Secs. 146–147.

73. R. KNOX, quoted in B. Russell, *A History of Western Philosophy*. New York: Simon & Schuster, 1945, p. 648.

74. *Principles*, Sec. 1.

75. *Ibid.*, Secs. 10, 14–15.

76. *Ibid.*, Secs. 9–15.

77. *Ibid.*, Sec. 1.

78. *E.g., Principles*, Sec. 30.

79. *New Theory*, 41–42, 50.

80. Another summarization of his way of conceiving the connection among ideas is given in G. Berkeley, The Theory of Vision Vindicated and Explained. In A. A. Luce, & T. E. Jessop (eds.) *op. cit.*, Vol. 1, pp. 251–276. (1733) (Herrnstein & Boring Excerpt No. 68)

81. *Principles*, Sec. 1.

82. *Dialogues*, Third Dialogue.

83. H. C. WARREN, *A History of Association Psychology*. New York: Scribner's 1921, p. 245.

84. *Principles*, Introd., Secs. 6–25.

85. *Ibid.*, Introd., Sec. 13.

86. *Ibid.*, Introd., Sec. 10.

87. *New Theory*, (Herrnstein & Boring Excerpts No. 28, 36.)

88. *Ibid.*, 16–28, 52–87, 111–112, 121–159.

89. *Ibid.*, 2–15.

90. *Ibid.*, 17, p. 175.

91. *Ibid.*, 14–24.

92. *Ibid.*

93. *Ibid.*, 12, p. 173.

94. F. C. MOSSNER, *The Life of David Hume*. London: Nelson, 1954.

95. D. HUME, *A Treatise of Human Nature*. (2 vols.) (ed. by A. D. Lindsay) London: Dent, 1911. (1739–1740)

96. D. HUME, An Enquiry Concerning Human Understanding. (Edited by L. A. Selby-Bigge) In R. M. Hutchins (ed.), *op. cit.*, Vol. 35, pp. 449–509. (1748)

97. *Ibid.*, Div. 1, p. 451.

98. *Treatise*, Preface.

99. *Enquiry*, 9.

100. *Ibid.*, 12. (Herrnstein & Boring Excerpt No. 69 involves another edition of Div. 11–17)

101. HUME, *Treatise*, Book I, Part I, Sec. III.

102. Hume, *Enquiry,* Div. 13.

103. *Ibid.,* Div. 19.

104. *Ibid.,* Div. 59.

105. *Ibid.,* Div. 24–25.

106. *Ibid.,* Div. 48–57.

107. *Ibid.,* Div. 24.

108. *Ibid.,* Div. 23.

109. *Ibid.,* Div. 60.

110. *Treatise,* Book I, Part III, Sec. XIV.

111. *Ibid.,* 36.

112. P. Janet & G. Seailles, *A History of the Problems of Philosophy.* Part 1, *Psychology.* New York: Macmillan, 1902, p. 369.

113. *Treatise,* Book I, Part IV, Sec. VI.

114. *Ibid.,* Book I, Part IV, Sec. IV.

115. D. Hume, An Abstract of a Treatise of Human Nature. In A. Flew (ed.), *David Hume: On Human Nature and the Understanding.* New York: Collier, 1962, pp. 287–302. (1740) p. 294.

116. D. Hartley, *Observations on Man, his Frame, his Duty and his Expectations.* (2 vols.) London: Richardson, 1749. (Scholars' Facsimiles and Reprints, 1966)

117. *Ibid.,* Introduction, p. III.

118. *Ibid.,* Sec. II, Prop. 14.

119. J. Priestley, *Hartley's Theory of the Human Mind, on the Principles of Association of Ideas with Essays Relating to the Subject of it.* London: Johnson, 1775. (1749)

120. D. Hartley, *Observations on Man.* (6th rev. ed.) (3 vols.) London: Tegg, 1834. (1791)

121. *Ibid.,* Part 1, Introduction.

122. *Ibid.,* Chap. I.

123. *Ibid.,* Chap. I, Sec. I, Prop. VIII.

124. *Ibid.,* Chap. I, Sec. I, Prop. XIX.

125. *Ibid.,* Chap. I.

126. *Ibid.,* Chap. I, Sec. I. Prop. II.

127. There is good evidence (*cf., e.g.,* Peters, *op. cit.,* pp. 423–424) that Hartley was at heart an occasionalist but this point was not appreciated by those whose work he inspired.

128. *Observations,* Part I, Introduction.

129. *Observations,* 1749, Vol. 1, Chap. I, Sec. 2, Prop. 9, 10, 12. (Herrnstein & Boring Excerpt No. 70)

130. *Ibid.*, p. 73.

131. *Ibid.*, Vol. 1, Chap. I, Sec. 3, Prop. 18, 21. (Herrnstein & Boring Excerpt No. 59)

132. *Ibid.*, Vol. 1, Chap. II, Sec. 1–5

133. *Ibid.*, Vol. 1, Chap. II, Sec. 6–7, Chap. III.

134. *Ibid.*, Conclusion.

135. S. A. GRAVE, *The Scottish Philosophy of Common Sense.* Oxford: Clarendon Press, 1960.

136. T. REID, *Essays on the Intellectual Powers of Man.* London: Macmillan, 1941, Essay 2, Chaps. 5, 16. (1785) (Herrnstein & Boring Excerpt No. 37)

137. T. BROWN, *Lectures on the Philosophy of the Human Mind.* Boston: Hallowell, 1828, Vol. II, Lec. 25. (1820) (Herrnstein & Boring Excerpt No. 38)

138. REID, *Essays, op. cit.*

139. D. STEWART, *Elements of the Philosophy of the Human Mind.* (3 vols.) London: Teggs, 1867. (1793–1817)

140. BROWN, *Lectures, op. cit.*

141. F. COPLESTONE, *A History of Philosophy.* (Vol. 5) London: Burns, Oates 1929, pp. 383–385.

142. BROWN, *Lectures, op. cit.* (Herrnstein & Boring Excerpt No. 71)

143. *Ibid.*

144. *Ibid.*

145. *Concise Dictionary of National Biography. Part 1, From the Beginnings to 1900.* London: Oxford University Press, 1961, pp. 875–876.

146. J. BENTHAM, *Works.* (Edited by J. Bowring) Edinburgh: Tait, 1838–1843, Vol. 10, p. 142.

147. J. BENTHAM, *Theory of Legislation.* Oxford: Clarendon Press, 1914. (1789)

148. *Concise Dictionary, op. cit.*, p. 875.

149. J. MILL, *Analysis of the Phenomena of the Human Mind.* London: Longmans & Dyer, 1829.

150. WARREN, *Association, op. cit.*

151. MILL, *Analysis, op. cit.* (Herrnstein & Boring Excerpt No. 72)

152. E. G. BORING, *Sensation and Perception in the History of Experimental Psychology.* New York: Appleton-Century, 1942, p. 9.

153. CATHERINE M. COX, *et al., Genetic Studies of Genius. Vol. II, Regarding Mental Traits of Three Hundred Geniuses.* Stanford: Stanford University Press, 1926.

154. J. S. MILL, *A System of Logic, Ratiocinative and Inductive, Being a Connected View of the Principles of Evidence, and the Methods of Scientific Investigation.* (6th ed.) New York: Harper, 1874. (1843)

155. R. M. Blake, C. J. Ducasse, & E. H. Madden, *Theories of Scientific Method: the Renaissance through the Nineteenth Century.* Seattle: University of Washington Press, 1960, pp. 218–232.

156. J. Mill, *Analysis of the Phenomena of the Human Mind.* (New edition with notes, illustrative and critical, by A. Bain, A. Findlater, & G. Grote. Edited with additional notes by J. S. Mill.) New York: Longmans, Green, Reader & Tyler, 1869.

157. J. S. Mill, *Logic, op. cit.*

158. J. S. Mill, *An Examination of Sir William Hamilton's Philosophy.* London: 1865. (Herrnstein & Boring Excerpt No. 39)

159. A. Bain, *Autobiography.* London: Longmans, Green, 1904.

160. A. Bain, *The Senses and the Intellect.* London: Parker, 1855.

161. A. Bain, *The Emotions and the Will.* London: Parker, 1859.

162. Bain, *Autobiography,* p. 174, 196.

163. J. A. Cardno, Victorian Psychology: a Biographical Approach. *J. Hist. Behav. Sci.,* 1965, 1, 165–177.

164. A. Bain, *Mind and Body.* London: King, 1873. (Herrnstein & Boring Excerpt No. 108)

165. A. Bain, *A Manual of Mental and Moral Science.* London: Longmans, Green, 1875. (1869)

166. A. Bain, *On the Study of Character, Including an Estimate of Phrenology.* London: Parke, 1861.

167. J. A. Cardno, Bain and Individual Differences, *Abeerdeen Univ. Rev.,* 1963, 40, 124–132; J. A. Cardno, Bain as a Social Psychologist, *Austral. J. Psychol.,* 1955, 8, 66–75.

168. A. Bain, *The Emotions and the Will.* (3rd ed.) New York: Appleton, 1875. (1859)

169. *Ibid.,* Preface.

170. *Ibid.,* p. xiii.

171. J. A. Cardno, Bain and Physiological Psychology, *Austral. J. Psychol.,* 1955, 7, 108–120.

172. Bain, *Autobiography.*

173. J. A. Cardno, Bain, Lewes, and Hunger, *Psychol. Rep.,* 1956, 2, 267–278.

174. *Ibid.*

175. A. Bain, *The Senses and the Intellect.* (3rd ed.) London: Longmans, Green, 1868, p. 327.

176. *Ibid.,* Intellect, Chap. 4, Sec. 1, p. 570.

177. L. S. Hearnshaw, *A Short History of British Psychology: 1840–1940.* New York: Barnes & Noble, 1964, p. 13.

CHAPTER 9

KANT AND HERBART:

CONTINENTAL PHILOSOPHICAL PSYCHOLOGY

AS ATTENTION is focused on a period proximate to the present day, it becomes less necessary and more impracticable to say anything about the general scientific and cultural heritage of the times. With the increased complexity, the sheer amount of relevant knowledge, and the increase in the number of those making contributions to psychology, the background for the great psychologists has to be presented in increasingly narrow perspective. The pace has now quickened with various more or less simultaneous developments taking place that cannot be discussed together because they belong in different patterns of intellectual development.

The previous chapter carried British associationism through the work of Alexander Bain whose principal works first appeared in 1855 and 1859. In order to discuss continental philosophical psychology, which is to culminate in the work of Kant and Herbart, a return is now made to 1732, the date of publication of Wolff's *Empirical Psychology.*

WOLFF AND FACULTY PSYCHOLOGY

Implicitly or explicitly, a doctrine of faculties has often been met in earlier views of psychology. The soul was conceived as carrying on its functions, such as knowing, remembering, feeling, and willing, by making use of corresponding faculties. The first important proponent of eighteenth-century German faculty psychology was Christian von Wolff (1679–1754), a Professor at Halle for most of his academic life. To place him in temporal perspective, he was most influenced by Leibniz, his older contemporary. His view is representative of the several versions of faculty psychology prevailing on the continent in the period from the middle of the eighteenth century through most of the nineteenth century. In no sense is he to be numbered among the greatest of psychologists. In addition, his influence upon Kant is still another reason for him to deserve a brief statement.

Wolff's *Empirical Psychology*[1] made its appearance in 1732, followed two years later by his *Rational Psychology*.[2] He saw the tasks of these two psychologies as interrelated. Rational psychology deduced from metaphysical conceptions and from the experience of the soul's activities; empirical psychology was concerned with man, the composite of body and soul. This way of formulating the distinction between rational and empirical had methodological implication through emphasis, since in his view rational psychology depended more on reason and less on experience and empirical psychology more on experience than reason. Still his was primarily a contentual distinction. Soul was the concern of rational psychology; man (soul and matter) was the concern of empirical psychology. Both psychologies used both methods but in varying degrees. Following similar thinking on the part of Leibniz, Wolff held that rational psychology gave clear and distinct ideas, while empirical psychology yielded only obscure, confused ideas of things. Rational psychology depended upon reason; empirical psychology upon sensation. At one extreme were the confused ideas of sensation, and, proceeding through several steps of degrees of clarity, at the other extreme were the clear ideas of reason. In short, mental activities consisted of degrees of reason or degrees of clarity of ideas.

The major theme of his empirical psychology was that, while the soul is unitary[3] and lacks parts,[4] it has different powers and faculties. According to Wolff, faculties are "potencies of action" which are expressed in powers.[5] The major dual classification of groups of faculties are knowing on the one hand and feeling and desire on the other.[6] Knowing is further subdivided into perception, memory, understanding, and reason. To take memory as an example, if asked why something is remembered, Wolff would reply that it is because one has a faculty of memory. Unfortunately to ascribe a mental activity to a faculty served to explain it, making further analysis unnecessary. It was not apparent then, as it was to become later, that the doctrine of faculties was self-defeating and circular.

Wolff's distinction between empirical and rational psychology, although deviating from the usual, since it was not primarily a methodological one, was prophetic of changes to come. It clarified the existence of two psychologies, even though Wolff derogated empirical psychology and defined it so as to make it subordinate to rational psychology. As the influence of Locke and the other British associationists began to be felt in succeeding generations, the relative emphases of the two psychologies began to shift in favor of the empirical.

Kant and Transcendental Mental Activity

Immanuel Kant, (1724–1804), never more than sixty miles from his birth place in East Prussia, lived a wholly uneventful external life while serving as a professor of philosophy at the University of Königsberg. In fact, most of the stories his chroniclers tell concern nothing more than interruptions to his bachelor routines—the consternation of his neighbors when one day he didn't take his accustomed walk at the usual precise hour (a lapse accounted for by his becoming enthralled with Rousseau's *Emile*), or the crisis brought about by fast-growing poplars which obscured his view of a church steeple at which it was his habit to gaze while meditating (a problem solved by the owner of the trees who obligingly cut the tops), or, when fame came to him, the trouble he had to go to in order to avoid sightseers (which led to his changing the restaurant for his noonday meal). Without much loss one can pass on to his views of psychology.

The influence of Kant upon continental thought proved to be enormous. Although not without opposition (his successors, in fact, setting out immediately to "correct" his views), he dominated philosophical thinking for more than a generation. His gigantic shadow could not be ignored. His successors had to come to terms with him in one way or another. His work most relevant to psychology, *Critique of Pure Reason*,[7] appeared first in 1781. This publication was followed in 1788 by his *Critique of Practical Reason*[8] and in 1790 by his *Critique of Judgment*.[9] The very titles of these, his three most important works, show that they must bear some relation to psychology. However, to say that his inquiry was related to psychology is by no means the same as saying his approach was psychological in nature. On the contrary he repeatedly insisted it was not. His philosophical task was conceived to be the question of the validity of knowledge, in contrast to psychology which was seen as the empirical search for laws of mental functioning. His strictly psychological views, less important for their impact than the previous works, is contained in his *Anthropology*,[10] only partially translated into English. Although he had taught a course with the title for many years, beginning as early as 1772, it was not until 1798 that he prepared the lectures for publication.[11] His contributions of greater moment to psychology came from his critical philosophy, not from his psychology.

Kant held that all knowledge begins with experience, but does not necessarily arise out of experience.[12] What he meant by this apparent paradox is a major theme in this account.

In his earlier years Kant did little more than critically elaborate Wolff's rationalist and faculty doctrines. Reading Hume, as has so often been said, he was roused from his dogmatic slumbers. As indicated in Chapter 8, for Hume causality was neither self-evident nor capable of logical demonstration. Kant, convinced by his argument, realized that this same lack of certainty must be true of all other principles fundamental to philosophy and science. There are two alternatives: either to accept Hume's skepticism or to find *a priori* principles that are free of the defect Hume had found. General laws inductively proved from the data of experience can be possible only if rational principles, independently established, can be derived which are *a priori* and true before experience.[13] The alternative of skepticism, Kant, as a rationalist, could not accept, so his task became to establish that synthetic *a priori* principles are possible, despite Hume's cogent objection. He, therefore, set for himself the task of demonstrating the existence of these rationalistic principles.

In agreement with Hume, Kant held that all known objects are phenomena of consciousness and not realities independent of the mind. But for Kant empiricism is not enough. The known object is not a mere bundle of sensations, for knowledge of it includes "unsensational" characteristics or manifestations of *a priori* principles. That is to say, in addition to sense data, phenomena would not be possible without the mind, which is inherently capable of ordering phenomena.

Kant insisted that the scientist and the philosopher approached nature with certain implicit principles which underlie experience, and Kant saw his task to be that of finding and making explicit these principles. He proceeded to derive them from careful inquiry into the logical forms of judgment that we make about the world.

These various transcendental principles, or "categories," as Kant[14] called them, are activities of the mind and *a priori* in that they are independent of sense experience, are universal and are necessary. Consider the argument expressed in the following statement: *Events follow other events according to rules. Every event has a cause. Nature, itself, is a system of causal relations.* These statements were accepted then, as now, as valid, although they are of such a nature as to be impossible of experiential verification. They are *a priori* because they are conditions for the possibility of experience, *i.e.*, without causality and the other categories one would have no way for ordering experiences into a phenomenal world of objects. One of his principles or categories, then, was causality. This particular illustration was chosen since it also served to answer Hume. We cannot know causality from experience, but we do know it *a priori*.[15] Other of the twelve categories of understanding of Kant include unity, reality, totality, existence or nonexistence, community or reciprocity.[16]

Kant reinforced the argument based upon his categories of understanding with that of intuitive forms of sensibility which are also held to be prior to experience. Space and time are intuitively knowable, *a priori*.[17] Kant held that consciousness of time and extension in space are certainly real and not data of the bodily senses. All objects of pure perception are located in space and time, without which objects would not be perceptible. We go on from them to perception of *content* through experience. They are the forms of intuition as distinguished from the contents of experience. The forms of sensibility of space and time join the transcendental principles and, together with them, become the means of structuring and understanding the world.

With space being *a priori*, Kant was a forerunner of what was to emerge as the nativistic theories of space.[18] Although it had definite ties with the past Cartesian notions of innate ideas, it was not the same. Man is not born with ideas but with principles of ordering which provide the conditions for the possibility of experience.

Before dealing with the mind, the more general problem of Kant's view of mathematics and science must be mentioned. Kant was very much concerned with scientific problems. The profound impression science had made upon him is strikingly demonstrated by Kant's emphasis upon space and time and causality. To him, mathematics is the source of scientific knowledge. This follows because much of mathematics represents *a priori*, absolute, non-empirical judgments, requiring no further proof. He believed, indeed considered he had proved, that an empirical inquiry is as scientific as it contains mathematics.[19] Science, to Kant, is exact, quantitative, and mathematical.

Kant dealt specifically with the problem of the mind.[20] The great rationalists, Descartes, Leibniz, and Spinoza, although differing among themselves, had sought to know mind through mind. Kant attacked what he considered to be their fallacious belief that mind is a substance *i.e.*, that it is "some thing." Without attempting to state his argument, suffice it to say he demonstrated to his satisfaction that mind is unsubstantial in that it is a purely formal unity. Rejection of mind as substance had direct implications for psychology as a science. It followed that mental processes cannot be measured, since they have only the dimension of time, not space.[21] If it has but the one dimension of time, psychology as an experimental science is impossible, because there is no other variable with which to relate temporal events.

This did not mean that Kant rejected the concept of the mind. Rather, as a formal unity he lifted it to the pinnacle of his system, since he held mind to be the means whereby the categories and concepts are known. The mind, without being spatial, orders perceptual phenomena through the innate principles of time and space and supplies us with the categories which make it possible to understand experience, to make incoming sensations meaningful. In a manner reminiscent of Plato, the mind is an active agency which composed the raw material of the world into an order of conceptualized phenomena. Kant was, however, no idealist, since the mind does not create the world; there are "things in themselves" with independent existences, but not knowable.

"Apperception" was Kant's philosophical term for the process of assimilating and interpreting new experiences by which the mind gave them meaning. There was unity in every act of perception. In recognizing an object we can find the bits and patches that are elements of the associationists, for example, the hearing elements and the seeing elements of the coach of Berkeley; but these elements are meaningfully organized *a priori*, not through association: The mind has acted to form a unitary experience, to create an object within a meaningful context. There is an active mind which organized the experience with the help of space and time and the Kantian categories. Kant viewed mind as active apperception. For example, apperception was emphasized as a process by which new experiences were taken hold of and brought into relation with other elements in the mind. This was not passive impression, but rather an active grasping. This ordering of experience in accordance with the categories or forms through apperception is a philosophical analysis, not a psychological one.

"Things in themselves," the causes of things, are unknowable. Locke and Hume are right, Kant agreed, in saying that knowledge comes from sensory perception; but this is perception not of things as they really are, but only as they appear to us (phenomena). Thus, Kant was fostering a phenomenal view. We perceive phenomena, not as they are, but the way our mind makes us see them. The mind selects, according to the structures arising from the categories, from the welter of impinging sensations and imposes upon them the unity inherent in the principles.

It is not surprising that faculty psychology which was simultaneously rationalistic, relatively free from appeal to empiricism, and tending to lend itself easily to the support of religious views, proved congenial to Kant. The categories, from this perspective, are forms of the mind. Kant classified mental faculties into cognitive (knowing), feeling, and desire and the subdivision of the cognitive faculty into understanding, judgment, and reason.[22] His *Anthropology*[23] also had three parts roughly comparable to the more or less similar divisions of his three *Critiques* (*Pure Reason, Judgment* and *Practical Reason*) which also lent support to the three-fold classification of mental powers.

Kantian thinking and writing occurred before the emergence of psychology as an experimental science. The immediate effect of his philosophical pronouncements about mind and the impossibility of experiment was to block advance in the move of psychology toward becoming an experimental science. In larger perspective and as a more delayed influence, he helped to create a desire to make psychology both experimental and mathematical. Such was his prestige that never again could it be forgotten that science was mathematical.

Kant also helped to keep subjectivism alive in that he stressed the importance of mental phenomena, as such. He helped to direct psychology toward phenomenalism in holding that events are appearances. Moreover, his view that his ultimate principles lie outside the context of experience made Kant the great champion of nativism in that human beings have innate "given" ways of knowing that are true but not dependent upon experience. This stress on unity of organization with its nativistic base was to have many later effects upon German psychology down to this very day.

HERBART AND EXPERIENCE, METAPHYSICS AND MATHEMATICS

Johann Friedrich Herbart (1776–1841) was a professor at Göttingen and at Königsberg, where he filled the chair vacated by Kant. Earlier, while a tutor in Switzerland, he had made the acquaintance of Pestalozzi, the educator, who directed his attention to pedagogical problems which thereafter formed a supplement to already established philosophical and psychological interests. An account of his psychology is contained in the *Lehrbuch zur Psychologie*,[24] appearing in 1816, and in his more extensive *Psychologie als Wissenschaft, neu gergründet auf Erfahrung Metaphysik und Mathematik*,[25] which appeared in 1824 and 1825. The full title of this, his major book, gives the clue to the nature of his psychology; it is a science based upon experience, metaphysics, and mathematics. These three strands will become obvious in the account that follows.

Herbart's metaphysical starting point for psychology was his concept of being.[26] His general conception of the universe was that of independent elements called *reals*. To some extent he was following Leibniz, but, unlike Leibniz, he did not regard reals as all sharing in the common characteristic of consciousness. Moreover, Herbart's mechanical interaction, discussed in a moment, is the antithesis of Leibniz's conception of pre-established harmony. Despite his dependence upon metaphysics, he was led by his particular definition of being to define psychology as the "mechanics of the mind." However, in keeping with the trend of the times to minimize the mind in favor of an emphasis upon consciousness, he proceeds to explain mental states as an interaction of ideas. The mind is the stage on which the vastly more important players, the ideas, carry on their parts.

Mechanics, once introduced as the basis of psychology, was conceived of as dealing with statics and dynamics in a way similar to that in which these branches of mechanics were then regarded in the physical sciences. Herbart held that experimentation in psychology is impossible.[27] To remain a science, psychology must, at least, be mathematical. He therefore prepared a series of equations which dealt with psychological matters. For example, in dealing with how much of an idea is suppressed, he postulated that σ equals the suppressed portion of the ideas in time (indicated by t), and S is the aggregate amount suppressed. Then $\sigma = S (1 - e^{-t})$. He carried on no actual measurements. The mathematical values he assigned in any given equation were always some guess based on rational plausibility, and his mathematical formulations served only as illustrations.

Herbart's system of psychology concerned elementary bits of experiences, sensations in our terminology, which combined to form ideas. Ideas, he held, are the *real* contents of the mind. To this extent he followed the British associationists. However, the mechanics of Newton and the theory of ideas as activity of Leibniz supplied for him the means of making a substantial modification of British associationism—the conceiving of ideas to be forces. According to British associationism, ideas combined in what he conceived to be entirely too passive a fashion. Herbart argued that associations are in reality much more complicated, digressive, and diversive than they had described them to be.[28] The associationists had assumed, implicitly or otherwise, only the attraction of ideas without particular attention to the nature of the force involved.

Herbart postulated both attraction and repulsion of ideas, particularly when ideas clash. Ideas become forces when they resist one another.[29] Some ideas do not resist one another, and for these associations a conventional explanation is sufficient. These are the ideas that are neither opposed nor contrasted with one another as a tone and a color which unhindered form a complex.[30]

But there are other ideas which contrast, such as red and yellow, which may become blended or fused but never form a complex. Sometimes ideas are so resistive as not to form even loosely affiliated complexes. One idea may be so much a hindrance to another that the second is not even available in consciousness.[31] This hindered idea, although not in consciousness, still exists. Inhibited though these ideas may be, they remained existent as tendencies. When the forces opposing the ideas are changed—when there is a change in the apperceptive mass—then the idea that has previously been kept out of consciousness, returns.

This entering into consciousness requires the conceptionalization of a threshold of consciousness. That is to say, the readily verified subjective phenomena of thinking of something which was not in consciousness a moment before, required, in the opinion of Herbart, that there must be a level below which an idea is unconscious and which must raise above that level to become conscious. He also used this conception of threshold to explain sleep. If only a few active ideas are present, we have dreaming; if all active ideas are driven below the threshold, we have the unconsciousness that is deep sleep.[32]

Herbart pointed out that since an idea, once created, is never lost, this makes very remarkable a comparison of the paltriness of those ideas of which a person is conscious at any given moment with the multitude of ideas he may have potentially at his disposal. The explanation for this poverty of ideas present in consciousness, as contrasted to the wealth of tendencies available, lies in the threshold of consciousness. Besides those few grasped at a given moment, a person can, by quick transition, bring in other ideas in complex relations and modify them.[33]

Some ideas move into consciousness relatively readily, others do not. Submerged ideas move above the threshold to the full focus of attention if they are consonant with the apperceptive mass or dominant system of ideas, a conception derived from Leibniz. An idea that comes into consciousness combines with the extant ideas to the extent that is congruent with those already in consciousness. There is a unity of consciousness—attention, as one might call it—so that one cannot attend to two ideas at once except in so far as they will unite into a single complex idea. When one idea is at the focus of the consciousness, it forces incongruous ideas into the background or out of consciousness altogether. Combined ideas form wholes and a combination of related ideas form an apperceptive mass, into which relevant ideas are welcomed but irrelevant ones are excluded.

Ideas are active and may struggle with one another for a place in consciousness; Herbart's concept of threshold and its corollary that there are both conscious and unconscious mental processes are distinct advances over earlier views as was his account of how ideas held from consciousness could reappear.

Herbart gave psychology the beginning of a theory of inhibition, or inter-ference in learning, which was to reappear in many guises and in theories in times to come extending from Pavlov's "conditioned reflex" to Freud's "repression." However, his contribution in this area should not be overesti-mated. Darwinism, medical psychology, and psychiatry contributed much more than did Herbart to the understanding of the dynamics of unconscious proc-esses.

The concept of psychology as a science had begun to take form with Herbart's claim that it was mathematical, but use of the experimental method, basic to the science, had yet to be worked out. Despite the sterility of Herbart's calculus of the mind, it was to encourage Fechner, who proceeded to combine the Herbartian emphasis upon mathematics with Weber's use of experiment.

Herbart did much to make clear that psychology was crucial for educa-tional theory and practice where his theory of apperception had the most direct and influential application. Since it is on the background of previous experience that a new idea was assimilated in the apperceptive mass, it follows that if information is to be acquired as easily and as rapidly as possible, then in teaching one should introduce new material by building upon the apper-ceptive mass of already familiar ideas. This reasoning eventually led educators to adopt the practice of planning lessons so that the pupil passed from already familiar to closely related, unfamiliar elements. Herbart's work[34] was also influential in exposing the shallowness and sterility of a faculty psychology which was so prevalent during this time.

LOTZE AND NATIVISM AND EMPIRICISM

In 1844, Rudolf Hermann Lotze (1817–1881) succeeded Herbart to the chair at Göttingen. Also primarily a philosopher, he is nevertheless important in the history of experimental psychology for two reasons. In 1852, he published *Medicinische Psychologie*.[35] The mind, he held, is inherently capable of arrang-ing its content spatially. So far, this is nativistic and Kantian. However, his theory of local signs is meant to account for perception of space which is definitely empiricistic in nature. Each tactual or visual sensation has a char-acteristic distinctive sign of its physical locus in bi-dimensional (not tri-dimen-sional) visual and tactual space. By experience one learns to perceive space by these local and non-spatial signs. Spatial order is built up in experience. The other reason for his importance is more incidental. His students in-cluded G. E. Müller (see page 290) and Carl Stumpf; and unlike the other philosopher-psychologists of his time he gave psychology his enthusiastic support.

Significance

In the eighteenth and early nineteenth centuries the philosophically rooted views of Wolff, Kant, and Herbart helped to prepare the way for a psychology separate from philosophy. Wolff espoused the separation of empirical and rational psychology. Kant made a sharp, often-emphasized distinction between a philosophical theory of knowledge and an empirical psychology. Herbart considered that psychology should be based upon mathematics and experience as well as metaphysics. The first two philosophers just mentioned each showed to his own satisfaction that psychology was halting, limited, and relatively unimportant, (Lotze, on the contrary, was an enthusiastic supporter), nevertheless all of them proceeded to make distinctions which helped psychology to emerge as a separate science, once answers to their arguments could be found. Psychophysics and physiology, fields in which the next developments in psychology took place, helped to supply the answers.

REFERENCES *

1. C. von Wolff, *Psychologia empirica*. Frankfurt: Rengeriana, 1732.

2. C. von Wolff, *Psychologia rationalis*. Frankfurt: Rengeriana, 1734.

3. C. von Wolff, Rational Psychology. (Sec. between 48–67) (Translated by E. K. Rand) In B. Rand (ed.), *The Classical Psychologists*, New York: Houghton Mifflin, 1912, pp. 229–231. (1734)

4. *Ibid.*, Sec. 57.

5. *Ibid.*, Sec. 54.

6. W. B. Pillsbury, *The History of Psychology*. New York: Norton, 1929, pp. 110–111.

7. I. Kant, The Critique of Pure Reason. (Translated by J. M. D. Meiklejohn) In R. M. Hutchins (ed.), *Great Books of the Western World*. (Vol. 42) Chicago: Encyclopaedia Britannica, 1952, pp. 1–252. (1781)

8. I. Kant, The Critique of Practical Reason. (Translated by T. K. Abbott) *Ibid.*, pp. 291–361. (1788)

9. I. Kant, The Critique of Judgment. (Translated by J. C. Meredith) *Ibid.*, pp. 461–613. (1790)

10. I. Kant, *Anthropology*. (Partial Translation by A. E. Kroeger) *J. Speculative Phil.* 1875–1882, 9–11, 13–16. (1798)

11. I. Kant, *The Classification of Mental Disorders*. (Translated & Edited by C. T. Sullivan) Doylestone: Doylestone Foundation, 1964. (1798)

* See page 16 for description of reference style.

12. *Pure Reason.*

13. *Ibid.*

14. *Ibid.*

15. *Ibid.* (Herrnstein & Boring Excerpt No. 105)

16. *Ibid.*

17. *Ibid.*

18. *Ibid.* (Herrnstein & Boring Excerpt No. 30)

19. I. Kant, *Metaphysische anfangsgründe der naturwissenschaft.* Riga: Hartknoch, 1766, Preface.

20. *E.g., Pure Reason.*

21. *Metaphysische Anfangsgründe.*

22. *Judgment,* Introd. IX.

23. *Anthropology.*

24. J. F. Herbart, *Lehrbuch der Psychologie.* Königsberg: Unzer, 1816.

25. J. F. Herbart, *Psychologie als Wissenschaft neu gegründet auf Erfahrung, Metaphysik und Mathematik.* (2 vols.) Königsberg: 1824–1825.

26. *Ibid.,* Chap. 2.

27. J. F. Herbart, *A Text-book in Psychology.* (2nd Rev. ed.), (Translated by M. K. Smith) New York: Appleton, 1891, Sec. 4. (1834)

28. *Ibid.,* Sec. 72.

29. *Ibid.,* Sec. 10.

30. *Ibid.,* Sec. 22.

31. *Ibid.,* Sec. 11.

32. *Ibid.,* Sec. 50.

33. *Ibid.,* Sec. 127.

34. *Ibid.,* Sec. 9, 53–125.

35. R. H. Lotze, *Medizinische Psychologie, oder Physiologie der Seele.* Leipzig: Weidmann, 1852, Book II, Chap. 4, Sec. 281. (Herrnstein & Boring Excerpt No. 31)

CHAPTER 10

FECHNER:

PSYCHOPHYSICS

ENGROSSED in philosophical and mystical interests, Fechner devoted several periods of his long life to speculation and investigation of what to him was the most fundamental problem of life—psychophysics or the scientific investigation of the functional relations of dependency between body and mind.[1] We shall find in his work a marked contrast between the "dry-as-dust" psychophysical studies, as rigorously scientific as anything that had as yet emerged in psychology, and his burning enthusiasm to grapple with the very nature of the man.

LIFE AND CAREERS OF FECHNER[2]

Gustav Theodor Fechner was born in a small village in the Wendish country of southeastern Germany in 1801. His father, a preacher of the Lutheran faith, died when Gustav was but five years old, but not before he had given his precocious son a grounding in Latin. After attending a *gymnasium,* Fechner matriculated at the University of Leipzig in 1817. This association with the University was to last for seventy years. He took his degree in medicine in 1822, but he decided against going into practice.

Even in his youth there were some glimmerings of humanistic interests. Under the pseudonym of Dr. Mises, he turned the weapon of satire upon a variety of views with which he disagreed. The first of these satirical pieces, appearing in 1821, even before graduation, was directed against the then current medical fad for the use of iodine—*Proof that Man Is Made of Iodine.* For a period of twenty-five years thereafter, occasional satirical pieces from his pen would appear. In Germany, earlier in the century, there had been a resurgence of interest in materialism. To Fechner, materialism was a shallow theory devoid of any truth. Several of these satires were devoted to an attack on the view that the universe is inert matter, the "night view," as he called it, and to a defense of the position that the universe can be regarded from the point of view of consciousness, the "day view."

This anti-mechanist position was to be a constant point in what otherwise appeared to be a series of shifts of interest. Throughout his life Fechner moved from one field to another, although in a larger sense these moves formed an integrated whole. The nature of this unity should become apparent as we move through these careers. According to Boring,[3] in the productive years between 1817, when he started medical school, and 1887, when he died, Fechner was successively a physiologist, a physicist, a psychophysicist, an experimental estheticist, again a psychophysicist, and throughout most of the later years, a philosopher. Following his aim steadfastly through these careers, he happened to found psychophysics which in turn had so much to do with the founding of experimental psychology.

After graduation he began his second career by studying physics. In 1824, after a period without official appointment, he started to lecture on this subject and to conduct laboratory investigations in electricity. In 1833, he married. In 1834, he was made a professor of physics when but thirty-three years of age. His future in academic work in physics at this time seemed secure and predictable.

During these years sheer economic necessity had led him into translating various French scientific works which served to add to his scientific knowledge; however, some of his means of adding to his income took the form of hack work, such as editing and writing a considerable share of an encyclopedia of household knowledge in eight volumes. He broke under the strain of the tremendous amount of work he carried and became, in the language of the day, a "nervous invalid." In general it could be characterized as a neurotic depression with pronounced hypochondriacal features.

In the winter of 1839–40 an eye disorder, involving considerable pain, developed, and he resigned his chair in physics. Fechner had studied after-images by staring into the sun, which undoubtedly aggravated the condition, if it did not bring it on. Years of suffering followed. His eyes were so hyper-sensitive to light that he could not leave the house without bandaging them, and for the rest of his life he had to curtail his reading. Sometimes for weeks on end he could not eat but eventually found that fruit, strongly spiced raw ham, and wine could be tolerated. He could not talk for long periods and thought of suicide. Some slight improvement occurred late in 1843, but it was thought there was no chance of his regaining his health. In 1844, he received a small pension from the university, thus establishing officially his position as an invalid. However, hardly one of his remaining forty-four years went by without some serious contribution from his pen. There is no doubt that he really suffered, so it would be unfair, as well as inaccurate, to apply to him that grand phrase, "he enjoyed poor health." Nevertheless a defensive component in his illness was undoubtedly present, but speculation is fruitless as to whether this was a secondary gain to an organic disorder or was of primarily psychogenic origin.

His inability to use his eyes meant many hours spent in speculation. This reinforced his speculative turn of mind which came to the fore as soon as he was able to resume working. He now entered the third phase of his career as a psychophysicist with philosophical leanings. It is in connection with psychophysics that we reach the reason for his inclusion among the great psychologists. Reserving details for later systematic and methodological discussion, suffice it to say that he became interested to the point of obsession in demonstrating that mind and body are aspects of a unity.[4] Since matter (body) is not to be denied any more than is consciousness (mind), the two must be reconciled and made as one. His fundamental conception was this—the difference between mind and body, the dualism that some find, to Fechner was nothing more than a difference in point of view concerning the psychophysical entity. The mind is related to the body as the inside of a circle is related to the outside. This made his view a double aspect theory—mind and body are but two aspects of a fundamental unity. Since the two aspects are identical, the view is also referred to as the "identity hypothesis."

The solution, he tells us,[5] came with dramatic suddenness on the morning of October 22, 1850. In bed, "before getting up," he realized that the law of the connection between body and mind is to be found in a statement of the quantitative relation between mental sensation and bodily stimulus, not in simple proportion, but such that increases in the former correspond to proportional changes in the latter.

Ten years later in 1860, when he was fifty-nine years of age, his *Elemente der Psychophysik* appeared. For this book, Fechner ranks among the great psychologists. Here he discussed the functional relations of mind and body and reported investigations of his own and others on the various senses—sight, sound, and the cutaneous and muscular senses.

Some conception of Fechner's intent to measure psychological functions can be gained by turning directly to the next of his undertakings, the study of experimental esthetics, which is another field he founded. Fechner had had a long standing and deep interest in art. His first paper in this new career appeared in 1865, and had to do with the "golden section," the most esthetically pleasing relation of length to breadth in an object. Here again, Fechner applied his exact method to a global goal. He rebelled against the attempt to develop an esthetics "from above down" by formulating abstract principles of beauty from which to judge the concrete object, in the manner of the Romanticists. Instead, he believed one must start with simple figures. In order to find out what linear proportions the artist had used, he measured endlessly and patiently the dimensions of pictures, cards, books, snuff boxes, writing paper, windows, in fact, any object that was purported to have esthetic appeal. Thus, he sought to develop an experimental esthetics "from below."

Fechner also became very much involved in a *cause célèbre* of his day concerning the authenticity of two paintings of the Madonna, each attributed to Holbein. Although very similar, they differed in detail, and the authenticity of each was in dispute. Fechner inclined to the opinion that both were authentic. There was also a dispute over which was the more beautiful. Taking advantage of an exhibition in which both of them were exhibited together, he launched what may be the first public opinion poll. He made arrangements for the public to be invited to record comments in a book placed alongside the paintings. Sparseness of returns and a disproportionate number from art critics, who had already formed opinions, made this particular venture a failure.

His major book on esthetics, *Vorschule der Aesthetik,*[6] appeared in 1876. Its appearance also served to close his participation in esthetics. Experimental psychology in the person of Wundt, now also at Leipzig, and the intense interest of many others, protagonists as well as antagonists, would not leave him in peace to pursue his still strong philosophical interests. He was drawn back to a second career in psychophysics which lasted until his death in 1887. In this, his last year, he wrote a paper so well summarizing psychophysical research as to draw from Wundt the comment that it was the clearest extant summary.

THE AIM OF FECHNER

The careers through which Fechner moved through during his lifetime did not reflect a change in fundamental interest. His guiding aim was a search for an answer to an all consuming question—the nature of the relation between the spiritual and material worlds. He sought a unified conception of body and soul which, while based upon mystical speculation, had a scientific basis.

Post-Kantian philosophers had promulgated "the philosophy of nature" which was romantic, transcendentalist, and vitalistic. A characteristic tenet was that spiritual influences express themselves through physical symbols. This belief fired the imagination of Fechner and became an important aspect of what, in a somewhat over-simplified fashion, can be referred to as the mystical strain in his nature. And yet the vague symbolism with which the philosophers of nature pontificated could not escape criticism from that other aspect of his personality, the scientific. From Herbart he had obtained both the conception of psychology as a science and the value of mathematics in this pursuit. However, he could neither go along with Herbart's metaphysics nor accept his denial of experiment to psychology. Fechner struggled with both the mystical and scientific sides of his nature, feeling it necessary to unify them. This union finds no favor among psychologists today, but it must, nevertheless, be explored as the background against which Fechner's psychological contributions were to be made.

In the spirit of Plotinus, his ancestor of seventeen centuries before, Fechner saw the world as a system of souls appearing to each other as bodies. His mystical strain was reflected in the very title of one of his works, *Zend-Avesta or the Things of Heaven and the Hereafter.*[7] In this book, Fechner endowed all things with personal souls. The world is made up of external manifestations, bodies which are correlated with internal animate realities, the souls. This is panpsychism, a theory of the world which endows plants as well as animals with some rudimentary kind of soul. Its relation to primitive animism is direct and obvious. But Fechner was no simple throwback to primitive times. He argued these and related problems with verve, subtlety, and enthusiasm.

Consonant with the two major influences that affected him, Fechner sought precise confirmation of a metaphysical cosmic speculation. His was a nature that asked for a relation between a poetical and speculative world-view, to be demonstrated by means of precise measurement. He made the mystical aspect his goal, and the scientific aspect his method. And, actually it was the philosophical, even mystical views which led to the first precise measurements in psychology.

The starting point for measurement of physical stimulus and mental sensation he found in the research of Weber, who was also working at Leipzig. He specifically disclaimed having in mind Weber's work when this idea occurred to him, although it is reasonably certain he knew of it before this date. At any rate, shortly thereafter he made Weber's work the basis of his subsequent investigation. It becomes necessary to stop to consider the influence of Weber upon his thinking and research.

THE INFLUENCE OF WEBER[8]

Ernst Heinrich Weber (1795–1878) had been appointed *Dozent* in physiology at the University of Leipzig in 1817, the same year Fechner arrived as a medical student. The next year he was appointed Professor of Anatomy, and later in his career was made Professor of Physiology. For many years Weber and Fechner moved in the same academic circles and lived in the same community.

As a physiologist, Weber was particularly interested in touch and in the muscle sense,[9] hitherto relatively neglected research fields. At first Weber's research interests will appear to be a far cry from Fechner's lofty aim. The research, as Weber saw it, concerned the muscle sense. In investigating the part played by the muscle sense in relation to touch, he wished to find out what was the smallest difference between weights, the so-called "just noticeable difference," that his subjects could discriminate. Their task was simple. On each trial they lifted two weights, one a standard weight, the other a comparison weight; and they reported which one felt heavier. On subsequent trials the same or different comparison and standard weights were used. Large differences between the weights were obvious to all subjects and were reported as differences, but small differences in weight resulted in the subjects' reporting that the two weights were the same. When Weber studied the results of many trials and several standard weights in relation to the weights just noticeably different, he found that for each standard weight there was a relation between the sheer heaviness of the weight being compared to the perception of their differences. This finding was expressed in the form of a ratio of one-fortieth to each of the standards. Suppose he had used standard weights of twenty, forty and eighty ounces (actually, lighter weights in units of half-ounces were used). He found that a weight of forty ounces usually could be judged as different if there was one ounce difference in the comparison weight but that usually no difference was perceived when the difference was less than this amount. This gave a ratio of one-fortieth. This same ratio was found when the standard weight was cut in half to twenty ounces or doubled to eighty ounces. It needed only one-half ounce difference at twenty ounces (one-fortieth of twenty ounces), while two ounces were required at eighty ounces (one-fortieth of eighty ounces) for a just noticeable difference to be perceived.

Next Weber asked, suppose instead of being lifted, the weights were allowed merely to rest upon the skin; what would the ratio now be? When comparison weights were allowed to rest on the skin a ratio was found, but now it was one-thirtieth instead of one-fortieth. In other words, one-thirtieth of the standard weight must be added to that of comparison weight if a difference just noticeable to the subject was to be detected. Since smaller differences in weight could be discriminated when the weights were actively lifted (one-fortieth) compared to when they were passively resting on the skin (one-thirtieth), he concluded that this difference demonstrated the influence of the muscle sense upon discrimination as compared to the lower degree of discrimination when touch alone was operative. Adding the muscle sense to touch increased accuracy of discrimination. Weber also tested capacity to discriminate length of lines and marshalled evidence on differences in the pitch of tones and found other constant ratios.

Weber generalized that for each of the senses there is a constant fraction for which a difference is just noticeable. He admitted that this ratio does not hold without exception for extremes of tone. It was later established, irrespective of the mode of sensory stimulation, that this ratio does not hold at the extremes of any range of stimulus, and, in general, that it is only approximately true.

Weber's second major contribution was the experimental determination of the accuracy of two-point discrimination of the skin.[10] This is to say, Weber established the distance apart that two points must be in order for them to be felt on the skin as two. With vision eliminated, a subject would be instructed to report whether he felt one or two points touching the skin. Using a drawing compass, Weber then stimulated the skin either with one or with two points simultaneously at varying pre-established distances apart. When the two points were a relatively small distance apart, a subject would report a clear and sharply defined "one"; at relatively great distances, he would report "two points"; and when in the region in between these two extremes he would report, "uncertainty and blurriness." There was a threshold at which two points could just be discriminated. He showed that this "two-point threshold," as it came to be called, varied according to the part of the body stimulated. On the finger tips the subject would report discriminating two points as two when they were but .220 cm. apart, but for the same discrimination on the small of the back the points had to be 4.06 cm. apart or nine times greater. His explanation of this difference in sensitivity from one part of the body to another rested upon his hypothesis of "sensory circles," i.e., there are regions of the skin in which doubleness is not perceived because immediately adjacent tactile nerve fibers are stimulated. For doubleness to be sensed, at least one unstimulated fiber must lie between those stimulated. Regions with large thresholds would thus have touch fibers relatively sparse; the points stimulated had to be further apart in order to skip an adjacent fiber.

Although peripheral to the problem of psychophysical measurement, it should be mentioned in passing that since the sensory circles were a matter of distribution of sensory nerve fibers, his findings could be interpreted as lending support to a nativistic theory of space perception.

More generally, it can be seen that Weber's studies are experiments in the strict sense of the term. Varying the intensity of weights and the length of lines and the distance apart of two points on the skin, under the control of the experimenter, allowed the experimenter to study their differential effect upon the perceptual experience of the subject. These experiments stimulated considerable subsequent research and helped to lead to the establishment of experimental psychology as a separate discipline in its own right.

PSYCHOPHYSICS

Weber held that when one distinguishes between objects, it is not the difference between them that is perceived, "but the ratio of this difference to the magnitude of the things compared."[11] He made it clear that the magnitude of stimuli just noticeably different from each other can be stated as a ratio between the intensities and that this ratio is independent of the particular intensities used. It was Fechner who grasped the implications of Weber's statement for his psychophysical problem and proceeded to develop them.

Fechner[12] believed that Weber's results meant that one could measure sensation as well as the sensory stimulus and state the relation between the two in the form of an equation. After years of repeating and extending Weber's research, he formulated Weber's ratio in the form of an equation. This formulation may be stated as follows: $\Delta R/R = K$; where ΔR is the just noticeable stimulus increment, K is a constant, and R is the standard stimulus magnitude. In other words, a stimulus increment when divided by the magnitude of the standard stimulus gives a constant value. This, strictly speaking, is Weber's law, although Fechner in a burst of too great gratitude, gave Weber's name to the final result of several steps further on in his thinking. Hereafter, this equation with which Fechner started will be referred to as "Weber's law" while the final equation will be called "Fechner's law."

Instead of working it through mathematically as did Fechner,[13] let us try to get the general relation clear. As one proceeds arithmetically by steps of one in the scale of sensation aspect—so Fechner's law asserts—one multiplies the value of the stimulus magnitude by a constant ratio. Stimuli of twenty, forty, and eighty ounces should give equal steps of sensation. A long and complicated argument was offered by Fechner about measuring sensations indirectly from direct measurement of the stimulus, but, instead of carrying through, we shall move to discussion of direct measurement that is based on the assumption that just noticeable differences are equal. Fechner reasoned that it can be assumed that just noticeable differences, j.n.d.'s, as they came to be called, are equal through the range of the sense quality, that these j.n.d.'s are thus equal increments and measure sensation. Being equal they can be added up to make magnitudes. There remained only the question of finding a zero point from which to start so that we can know when we are dealing with "one," "two," and so on, the number of units above zero as the j.n.d.'s are cumulated up the scale. This zero point Fechner took as the threshold stimulus, that value of the stimulus at which the sensation is just ready to appear. This value is zero in his scale. The j.n.d. appearing thereafter is one, the next j.n.d. is two, and so on.

Increase of subjective intensity of a sensation varies directly with the increase of strength of stimulus, although not proportionally because the psychic increases arithmetically by a constant difference when the physical increases geometrically by a constant multiple. When one series increases arithmetically while the other series increases geometrically, we are dealing with a logarithmic relation. This was demonstrated by the mathematical manipulation of Weber's law, a process by which Fechner emerged with the equation $S = K \log R$ in which S is the sensation's magnitude, K is a constant, and R is the stimulus' magnitude. A sensation equals a constant multiplied by the logarithm of the stimulus. This is Fechner's law. Sensation has been measured, and the identity hypothesis, so Fechner thought, has been demonstrated. He had found his proof of his identity hypothesis in a table of logarithms!

To summarize Fechner's research and the researches of those who have followed Fechner, we may say that the experiments indicate that Fechner's law holds approximately for the middle range of stimulus intensity but not with either small or very large intensities. Visual brightness has a ratio of about one-hundredth, lifting weights one-fortieth, and tone one-tenth. For instance, in visual brightness the ratio just given means that for a change in illumination to be perceived the total illumination must be increased by one-hundredth of its amount.

Fechner established what he considered to be the absolute stimulus threshold or limen, the value of which the subject's sensing of the stimulus is just ready to appear, as that value of stimulus which marks the limit of a sensory continuum. Anyone familiar with the fact that vibrations are heard as sound in the range between from about sixteen vibrations per second, the lowest audible tone, to about 20,000 vibrations per second, the highest audible tone, and knowing that there are vibration rates both higher and lower not heard as sound, is aware of the existence of thresholds. (The dog whistle of vibrations beyond 20,000, unheard by humans, shows that dogs have a higher tonal threshold than humans.) Subject to qualifications to be given later, one can speak of sixteen and 20,000 vibrations per second as the stimulus thresholds of hearing. Lower stimulus thresholds were established by Fechner and others for weights, brightness, and many other sensory intensities. No upper thresholds could be established since these were intensities capable of limitless increase.

Now that the so-called absolute threshold is familiar, it can be seen that when j.n.d.'s were under discussion we were dealing with something else that can be called the *differential* threshold. Fechner believed the differential limen to be the least amount of change in a stimulus necessary to produce a sensed difference. Changes below this limen, he held, are not sensed as different. The addition before the change was below the differential threshold, the amount necessary to produce just the perceived difference is the differential limen. The differential threshold resembles the just noticeable difference enough to be frequently confused with it. Speaking more accurately than did Fechner, the differential threshold is a statement of the statistical quantity for the point between what is sensed as not different *and* the just noticeable difference. It is a statistical value representative of the point where the sensation is just as often not sensed as it is sensed.

In the course of his research, Fechner developed one and systematized two others of the three fundamental methods of psychophysics. These three were the method of limits, the method of average error, and the constant method. The method of average error that Fechner developed, along with his brother-in-law, is the most fundamental and will be used as an illustration. The subject, himself, adjusts a variable stimulus so as to fulfill the instructions given him, say, to make one line equal to the length of a standard line. Before him he sees a length of line, the standard. Another line is to be adjusted by him to be as close to the standard in length as he can make it. No matter how closely he approximates the line, however, an error, large or small, will be made. Sometimes he makes the line too long, sometimes too short, but always he makes some error. After many trials on his part, the average of his errors is found, the so-called average error.

After publication of the *Elemente* in 1860, interest was immediate, intense, and widespread. Many others, seeing the value of his work, proceeded to carry out similar experiments. Various controversies and objections raged. One criticism directed against his work, the so-called quantity objection, is that we are not aware introspectively that sensations have magnitude. James,[14] the phrase maker, said in substance that our feeling of pink is not a portion of scarlet. Another argument centered on the question of whether Fechner was really measuring sensation, since he had assumed the equality of j.n.d.'s. From the vantage point of today it can be said that Fechner erred methodologically in the direction of treating psychophysical findings without full consideration of the various sources of complication present in the individual and in the conditions of the experiment.[15] As a matter of fact, sixteen and 20,000 vibrations a second as stimulus thresholds for hearing are not constant limits for all people. Fechner was wrong; there are no absolute thresholds. Precise thresholds change from one individual to another and from one condition to another. Auditory sensitivity varies widely because of differences in native acuity, or changes occurring in the ear due to injury or the ageing process; while conditions, such as the state of the background noise-level or the precision of the sound source delivering the particular pitch, are also known to effect the results.

SIGNIFICANCE OF WEBER AND FECHNER

Since Weber's work preceded Fechner, it is plausible to ask why is not Weber stressed and Fechner merely treated as someone who later, more or less independently, worked in the same area? Precedence is given to Fechner because he is an "event-making" man, while Weber was merely an "eventful" man in the felicitous terminology that Hook[16] applied in similar circumstances. Weber, as a physiologist, carried on some research on a problem which interested him. It was a different problem, to be sure, from that occupying most of his fellow physiologists, but neither he nor they saw it as different in spirit. He did not realize that he had hit upon something that would profoundly effect future developments in psychology. But he had, and, therefore, in this sense, he was an "eventful" man. At a propitious time he worked on research that was to give him a prominent place in the history of psychology. But its larger significance escaped him. Fechner, in distinction from Weber, was an event-making man. He saw what others, including Weber, had not seen—the implications and consequences of psychophysics. Fechner's insight that October morning about measuring sensations and relating them to measures of their stimuli was independent of Weber's researches. It was related to this prior work on magnitude of stimuli and was recognized by Fechner as supplying a method, but the insight had to occur before recognition of the relevance of the method. Weber took the first step along a fork in the road, but did not realize he was walking a different road; Fechner realized the road was there, looked down that road, and in this way created it.

Ironically enough, with all the excitement his findings engendered, little attention was paid to Fechner's goal for psychophysics. His attempt to found a philosophy upon exact science was a failure, but his work was fruitful for the advancement of psychology as a science.

Sensory psychology was put upon a quantitative basis with the introduction of Fechnerian psychophysics. No less a person than Wilhelm Wundt[17] said of him that his was the "first conquest" in the field of experimental psychology. In all fairness it must be admitted that not all psychologists have held such a high opinion of the work of Fechner. William James,[18] for example, some thirty years after the appearance of Fechner's major work, concluded that the yield of psychophysics in psychological outcome was precisely "nothing," and that his findings were "dreadful." He went on to point out that Fechner's successors, laboring mightily, could topple over every one of his findings, but invariably they ended up by praising him for his contribution to the scientific methodology of psychology. Indeed it is true that his conclusions have not stood the strain of later criticism; nevertheless his methods are still not only serviceable and useful, but actually fundamental in sensory measurement.

REFERENCES*

1. G. T. FECHNER, *Elemente der Psychophysik* (2 vols.) Leipzig: Breitkopf & Härtel, 1860.

2. The major source for the details of Fechner's life was G. S. Hall, *Founders of Modern Psychology* (New York: Appleton, 1912) but the organization of the material about his life and his careers owes much to the presentation of E. G. Boring, *A History of Experimental Psychology*, (2nd ed.) (New York: Appleton-Century-Crofts, 1950), pp. 275–283.

3. *Ibid.*, p. 283.

4. G. T. FECHNER, *Elements of Psychophysics*, (Vol. 1) (Translated by H. E. Adler; ed. by E. G. Boring and D. Howes) New York: Holt, Rinehart and Winston, 1966, Chap. 1. (Herrnstein & Boring Excerpt No. 107)

5. *Elemente*, Vol. 2, p. 554.

6. G. T. FECHNER, *Vorschule der Aesthetik.* Leipzig: Breitkopf & Härtel, 1876.

7. G. T. FECHNER, *Zend-Avesta, On the Things of Heaven and the Hereafter.* Leipzig: Voss, 1851.

8. Lest the emphasis placed upon Weber and Fechner give a false impression about initiating research in the field, one aspect, that of threshold measurement, had not waited for their work. P. P. Bouguer, *Traité d'optique sur la gradation de la lumière.* (Paris: Guerin & Delatour, 1760) (Herrnstein & Boring Excerpt No. 15) had already measured the differential threshold for brightness and C. É. J. Delezenne, Sur les valuers numériques des notes de la gamme, (*Recueil*

*See page 16 for description of reference style.

des travaus de la Société des Sciences, de l'Agriculture et des Arts de Lille, 1827, pp. 4–6) (Herrnstein & Boring Excerpt No. 16) had studied the differential threshold for pitch.

9. E. II. WEBER, Der Tastsinn und das Gemeingefühl. In R. Wagner (ed.), *Handwörterbuch der Physiologie* (Vol. 3) Braunschweig: Vieweg, 1846, pp. 481–588 (Herrnstein & Boring Excerpt No. 10); E. H. Weber, *De pulsu, resorptione, auditu et tactu: annotationes anatomicae et physiologicae*. Leipzig: Koehler, 1834. (Herrnstein & Boring Excerpt No. 17)

10. E. H. WEBER, Ueber den Raumsinn und die Empfindungskreise in der Haut und im Auge. *Berichte der königlich-sächsischen Gesellschaft der Wissenschaften zu Leipzig mathematisch-physische Classe 4*, 1852, 87–105. (Herrnstein & Boring Excerpt No. 32)

11. *De pulsu*, p. 172.

12. G. T. FECHNER, Elements of Psychophysics. (Translated by H. S. Langfeld) In B. Rand (ed.), *The Classical Psychologists*. Boston: Houghton Mifflin, 1912, pp. 562–572. (Herrnstein & Boring Excerpt No. 18)

13. The mathematical derivation involves calculus. Those interested in tracing it through mathematically are referred to Boring, *History, op. cit.*, pp. 287–289.

14. W. JAMES, The Principles of Psychology. In R. M. Hutchins (ed.), *Great Books of the Western World*. (Vol. 53) Chicago: Encyclopaedia Britannica, 1952, p. 356. (1890)

15. *E.g.*, R. S. WOODWORTH, *Experimental Psychology*. New York: Holt, 1938, Chap. 18.

16. S. HOOK, *The Hero in History*, New York: Day, 1943, pp. 181–183.

17. W. WUNDT, Zur Erinnerung an Gustav Theodor Fechner: Worte gesprochen an seinem sarge am 21. Nov. 1887, *Philosoph. Stud.*, 1888, 4, 471–478.

18. JAMES, *Principles, op. cit.*, pp. 356–359.

CHAPTER 11

HELMHOLTZ:
NEURAL PHYSIOLOGY

O NE of the sources from which experimental psychology was to emerge was experimental physiology, the study of the functioning of the organ systems of the body. It is customary to say that general physiology became a separate discipline with the appointment of Johannes Müller to the first professorship of physiology in 1833 at the University of Berlin. Here between 1834 and 1840 Müller compiled his *Handbuch der Physiologie des Menchen,*[1] a systematic organization of comparative anatomy, chemistry, and physics, as related to general physiology. More pertinent to psychology at this time, however, was the study of the nervous system by physiologists. In this field the giant among pioneer neural physiologists was Hermann von Helmholtz. But, as always, the way was prepared by other men.

Physiology before Helmholtz

During the later half of the seventeenth century and the eighteenth century, physiology assumed many of its modern characteristics, going beyond the hypothetical physiology of Hartley and LaMettrie. Robert Whytt[2] (1714–1766), for example, in summarizing in 1751 the physiology of the reflex, formulated the beginnings of many modern concepts. According to him, the "fundamental" experiment on the nature and existence of the reflex had been performed about 1730 by Stephen Hales, who, utilizing the already known fact that a decapitated frog responded to pinching by withdrawing the legs, found that it failed to continue to do so when the spinal cord was destroyed. Whytt, himself, repeated and extended this experiment, in the course of which he introduced the terms "stimulus," and "response" while Unzer (1727-1799) in 1771 utilized the word, "reflex," to distinguish between this kind of action and that carried on volitionally.

The first half of the nineteenth century yielded a variety of developments firmly establishing physiology as a science. Simultaneous with these was the rise of phrenology, which, scientific blind alley though it may have been, served to bring attention to the mind and its relation to the brain.

The Bell-Magendie Law

During the years 1811-1822 Charles Bell[3] (1774-1842) in Great Britain and François Magendie[4] (1783-1855) in France, working independently, performed the research which distinguished between the sensory and motor nerves. In a general way this distinction had been known to Galen, and others had from time to time rediscovered it. Prior to the work in question, however, the distinction had been lost sight of and the nerves were conceived as if all of them more or less indiscriminately carried on both motor and sensory functions. A controversy developed over the priority of the work of Bell and Magendie.[5] Bell published first, but it is not entirely clear that his original paper reported what he later claimed for it; while Magendie, when he published eleven years after Bell, stated the matter with unequivocal clarity. The important thing, after all, is that through their work a clearcut research distinction had been made.

Magendie established the distinction between motor and sensory nerves by cutting the nerve roots at the spinal cord and studying the functions that were lost. He found that it is through the posterior (dorsal) roots of the spinal cord that sensory fibers enter, while the anterior (ventral) roots are the route through which the motor fibers leave the spinal cord. For instance, when Magendie cut an anterior root, he found a complete paralysis, which was not present when the posterior root was cut. Since movement was prevented by this cutting, it must have been the anterior root that had to do the movement.

One effect of this work was to separate clearly neural physiology into the study of sensory and of motor functions or, to use more obviously psychological terminology, to establish a distinction between that of sensation and of movement. This distinction between sensory and motor nerves, according to what in time came to be called the Bell-Magendie law, is still fundamental today in bringing order into the study of physiology and psychology.

Gall and Phrenology

At about the same time as Bell and Magendie made their important contributions, the long-lived craze of phrenology was rampant. Franz Joseph Gall (1758–1828), first in Vienna and then in Paris, was working on the physiological localization of the functions of the brain. However, his research more and more turned to what came to be called phrenology to which he devoted the rest of his life.[6] While still a boy, Gall had been impressed by what he thought to be a relationship between prominent mental characteristics of his schoolmates and the shape of their skulls. As an anatomist, years later, when he embarked on mapping out the location of the centers for various functions on the surface of the cerebrum, the cerebral cortex, he tried to verify this impression. He reasoned that if a region of the cortex was well developed there would be a characteristic bump or protrusion of the skull at this point, or a comparable hollow if underdeveloped. Gall collected instances of what appeared to be over- or underdevelopment of areas of the brain as reflected in the shape of the skull and formed an impression of their possessors' striking characteristics. He did this by seeking out instances where he thought he might find them. Among pickpockets from the prisons he found the bump of acquisitiveness. Later he extended his search among friends and public figures. He also sought out persons who seemed to show a same trait to a striking degree and received permission to search their skulls for bumps and hollows. Once he found some sort of correspondence between one, two or a few individuals in the possession of the certain characteristic and their bumps or hollows, he named it, and assumed that when the bump was found thereafter the characteristic would be prominent.

From a modern perspective one is struck by the glaring inadequacy of the method that Gall used. Today, any college sophomore in psychology would be able to tell him that his research called for taking an "unselected" sample of the population, measuring all of their bumps, and without knowledge of these measurements, estimating their standing on the psychological characteristics with which Gall was concerned, and then comparing the two streams of data for the degree and nature of the relationship that they showed.

Nevertheless, it was not long before Gall's teaching excited popular attention, and soon he had disciples and practitioners, including Johann Kaspar Spurzheim, (1776–1832) who did much thereafter to extend the list of characteristics and to spread the phrenological doctrine.

When this mapping was completed, each characteristic had a definite place of localization in an area of the cerebral cortex. Thus, with the aid of a chart, the phrenologist could then examine the subject's skull and from what he found plot the individual's strength and weaknesses in abilities and personality.

Phrenology was a faculty psychology to end all faculty psychologies with a formulation by Spurzheim[7] of thirty-seven characteristics or faculties. He divided them into affective and intellectual faculties and further subdivided these two classes into propensities and sentiments, and perceptive and reflective faculties. Some of the affective faculties were destructiveness, amativeness, self-esteem and benevolence, while the intellectual capacities included calculation, order, and causality. As in all faculty psychologies, the major task was naming and estimating the strength of the function which, once done, made further analysis superfluous. Thus, it served as a block to further inquiry.

Phrenology was never generally accepted by scientists even while it was still possible to hold this as a plausible hypothesis. It was opposed by such familiar figures as Charles Bell and Thomas Brown in Great Britain and Flourens in France. Spurzheim was most active in spreading phrenological views in England and in the United States. His visit to the United States in 1832 produced considerable interest among physicians practicing in the mental hospitals.[8] Rather than necessarily accepting his views *en toto*, psychiatrists found that phrenology offered them general guidance in their thinking about the abnormal functioning of the mind as it depends upon the condition of specific areas of the brain. To this extent phrenology was not entirely without value, and its appeal continued, despite the scientific opposition, and lasted even into the present century. To this very day, popular magazines are devoted to it, and the display of phrenological charts with their neat squares superimposed on an outline of the head still occurs at the booths of fortune tellers at amusement parks and fairs.

Phrenology did serve the function of making the man in the street aware that he had a brain. Even more important, it stimulated scientists to take up research on the brain and established, once and for all, that the brain was the organ of the mind.

Flourens and Localization of Function in the Cerebrum

One of Gall's sharpest critics was Pierre Flourens (1794–1867), who was also engaged in investigating the function of various parts of the brain. His research led him to the conclusion that removal of the cerebrum, while leaving the reflexes intact, abolishes thought and volition.[9] Moreover, he concluded that the cerebrum, as a whole, not limited portions of it, is responsible for all thought and volition. Other functions he localized in the other major parts of the brain, the cerebellum, and the medulla oblongata, for example, but each part functioned as a whole. This theory was, of course, directed against phrenology since the phrenologists localized each of their thirty-seven faculties in definite parts of the cerebrum. For years thereafter, Flourens' view of the cerebrum functioning as a whole prevailed, if anything, strengthened by being in opposition to the phrenologists.

It was not until 1861 that Broca[10] showed that the loss of speech was due to a lesion centering in the third convolution of the left frontal lobe. This was the first successful challenge to Flourens' doctrine of the unity of the cerebrum, since Broca had found a localization of function within a specific area of the cerebral cortex. That speech was too complicated a mechanism to be confined to one specific region, as later research showed, does not detract from his first demonstration of specific localization. Direct electrical stimulation of the brain followed in 1870, first demonstrated by Fritsch and Hetzig,[11] and leading to the establishment of a series of motor centers and seeming to establish what was then accepted as fact that there were a variety of brain centers. Needless to say, the other functions isolated, bear no resemblance to those of the phrenologist.

Müller and the Specific Energy of Nerves

In 1833 Johannes Müller (1801–1858) was named to the just-created chair of physiology at Berlin. Previously it had been combined with that of anatomy. His appointment signaled the recognition of physiology as an independent sphere of science. His major work, *Handbuch der Physiologie des Menchen*,[12] which appeared between 1834–1840, systematized and exhaustively summarized the knowledge of physiology of his time in a primarily inductive fashion of which Bacon would have approved. This work served to place general physiology upon a scientific footing. In it, he brought comparative chemistry and physics to bear upon physiological problems. Müller may be said to have done for general physiology what Helmholtz in the next generation was to do for neural physiology.

The most direct contribution of Müller to psychology was his doctrine of the specific energy of nerves.[13] He arrived at the conclusion that each sensory nerve, however stimulated, gives rise to only one type of sensory process, and no other.[14] The sensation that is experienced is due, not to the nature of the stimulus, but to the sense organ, nerve or brain center that is stimulated. For example, the optic nerve always responds by the sensation of light whether it is stimulated in the usual fashion or it is pinched, heated, irritated by acid or shocked by electric current. (An easily verified every-day illustration is that of pressing with the thumb against the closed eye, and by so doing, producing a flood of light). Müller was saying that every sensory nerve responds in its own characteristic way, no matter how stimulated. To paraphrase a statement of James,[15] if we were to interchange surgically the optic and auditory nerves, we would hear the lightning and see the thunder. Müller, a Kantian, saw his doctrine as offering unequivocal support for nativism since what is more innate than the nervous system itself? In a moment, however, we shall find Helmholtz using the same doctrine to support empiricism.

Where does the specificity arise? Müller considered seriously two possibilities, either that it was in the nerves themselves or in the centers in the brain where the nerves terminate. Both views seemed to him to be defensible, but he decided in favor of the specific energies being in the nerves themselves. In view of Flourens' researches bringing discredit upon the doctrine of cortical localization, this conclusion is hardly surprising. Müller's version of specific energies was consequently not brought into question by the arguments concerning brain localization. Nowadays, with increased knowledge, we would place the specificity in the brain, not in the nerves.

It is agreed today that "specific energy" is the basic principle governing the physiology of the special senses. To place Müller's doctrine in its broadest perspective is to say that we are not aware of objects directly but only through some form of intermediary, in this case, the sense organs and nerves. For example, Müller[16] used his doctrine of specific nerve energies to answer that old problem, encountered so often before, of how whatever the eye received could represent the object. In addition to the inverted image problem, he dealt with the question of the size of an object, especially large objects being so represented. His answer to both problems was that all the mind perceives is the state of the nerves leading to the brain. This principle of knowing only through an intermediary was understood since Herophilus and the British associationist had, in their various interpretations, made much of the fact. Müller's research however, placed it upon a scientifically solid footing in a way that still prevails.

Donders and Reaction Time

The speed of reaction had been a research problem ever since the end of the eighteenth century when the Astronomer Royal at Greenwich dismissed his assistant who was apparently making errors in observing the time at which stars crossed the meridian.[17] A moment's reflection can show that this is a very serious matter because astronomical findings were calibrated by this observation.

A few years later, Bessel, an astronomer at Helmholtz's own University of Königsberg, came upon an account of the incident, and realized that the unlucky assistant might not be unique and that astronomers in general might differ in accuracy of their observation of the times of stellar events. When structured this way, other astronomers agreed with Bessel and the "personal equation," as it came to be called, became a matter of intense and widespread interest among them. A variety of methods of comparison of the personal equation of one astronomer to another came into use. That is, relative personal equations were established—astronomer A was shown to be one-tenth of a second slower than B, but two-tenths of a second faster than C in carrying out his stellar observations. A constant correction, the personal equation of B − A = .10 second could then be used in collating their astronomical observations.

After the discovery of electric currents and electromagnets, these relative personal equations became absolute measures through the invention and perfection of the chronograph and chronoscope. The chronograph was an instrument which, by pressing a key, a mark is placed upon a drum which also has constant marks placed upon it by a tuning fork vibrating 500 times a second. It measured the time accurately to less than a tenth of a second. Technical advances continued rapidly. By 1862 an instrument, the Hipp Chronoscope, was being used to measure the personal equation to a thousandth of a second. The measurements these instruments supplied could be now stated in absolute terms—A took 300 milliseconds while B took 200 milliseconds to respond.

The absolute personal equation of the astronomer, when adapted to physiological tasks, came to be called reaction time. Donders,[18] a Dutch physiologist, a contemporary of Helmholtz, became interested, and in 1868 extended its study by going beyond simple reaction time or the reaction to a predetermined stimulus by a given predetermined response. For example, a reaction already agreed on, pressing a key, would be made when a light went on. The elapsed time was simple reaction time. Donders asked whether, if this reaction was made more complicated, could not the increased time taken to react be attributed to that which was added to complicate the reaction? He performed experiments to study so-called discrimination and choice reaction times.

Simple reaction time had called for subjects to respond to stimulus A with response a. For discrimination time, Donders presented several stimuli, A, B, C, D in irregular order but his subjects were instructed to respond only to A, not to the others. Consequently, they had to discriminate A from all of the other stimuli before responding with a. In his new discrimination reaction, A was to be made to a red light, but he was to *withhold* his reaction if a green light, B, or a yellow light, C, was flashed. As he predicted, his subjects took longer to make the discrimination reaction than they did to make the simple reaction. Subtracting simple reaction time from the discrimination reaction time gave him the discrimination time. This was called the subtractive procedure. Choice was even more complicated: subjects responded to A with a, B with b, C with c, and so on. This gave a still longer reaction time; the choice time was the total time minus the discrimination and simple reaction times. From the measures, Donders obtained three reaction times—simple, discrimination, and choice. The very time taken by mental events had been brought to heel and measured. Thus, the temporal study of various mental functions—"mental chronometry," as it was called—was launched to be followed up by Wundt and others later.

HERMANN VON HELMHOLTZ

The existence of compartmentalized knowledge is a limitation that most scientists, including psychologists, suffer gladly, human capabilities being what they are. They find one thing quite enough to do. The great abilities of Hermann von Helmholtz permitted him to disregard the convenient but artificial boundaries that had been set up between the sciences.

By what resembled a process of natural growth, Helmholtz was led by his research interests through physics, as a co-formulator of law of the conservation of energy; neural physiology, including the measurement of the rate of the neural impulse; optics, extending from the invention of the ophthalmoscope to the theory of color vision associated with his name; acoustics, extending from Oriental music to the theory of resonance as the basis for hearing; and other important, but less relevant work, in hydrodynamics, electrodynamics, and meteorological physics. In all, he wrote more than 200 papers and books, a high proportion of which made definite important contributions to science.

Helmholtz conceived of psychology as a separate discipline, but as one allied to metaphysics insofar as it ascertained the laws and nature of the products of the mind.[19] He made an exception of the psychology of the senses because of its close alliance with physiology. Consequently, he had no hesitation in discussing psychological issues pertinent to his interests.

Helmholtz was empirical in the tradition of Locke and Hartley. With admirable brevity he states his major argument against nativism. It is not that it is disprovable; it is simply non-parsimonious.[20] In spite of his strong empiricitic tendencies, he was also influenced to some extent by Kant. For example, he accepted the law of causality as *a priori* and transcendental and not demonstrable from anything else.[21] Causality was not a law of nature but a regulative principle which guides the scientist in comprehending phenomena. How he related his empirical position to space perception is considered later. (See page 256.)

Life and General Scientific Endeavors of Helmholtz

Hermann Ludwig Ferdinand von Helmholtz[22] was born in Potsdam, Germany, in 1821. His father taught in the *Gymnasium* of that city, and, because of his son's delicate health, at first tutored him at home; at the age of nine the boy entered the *Gymnasium*, proceeding so rapidly as to graduate at seventeen. Lacking the financial means to study physics, an already formed major interest, Helmholtz continued his studies at the Medico-Chirurgical Friedrich-Wilhelm Institute in Berlin where no tuition was charged those promising to serve as surgeons in the army upon graduating. Although Helmholtz was never a student at the University of Berlin, Johannes Müller, its Professor of Physiology, was the teacher that had the most profound effect upon him during these student days. Students under Müller, who became his friends, included DuBois-Reymond, Virchow, and Brücke. They all admired Müller immensely, but he was of an older generation and, although he had helped to win physiology away from the philosophy of nature, still held to the prevailing vitalistic theory of biological activity. This his students could not accept. The spirit of their attitude is caught in a solemn oath that Brücke and DuBois Reymond imposed upon themselves during their student days, pledging to prove and expound the principle that "No other forces than common physical chemical ones are active within the organism."[23] Such was the temper of these young scientists, all under thirty, which Helmholtz shared.

Shortly after graduation in 1842 Helmholtz became an army surgeon at Potsdam. While carrying on his duties with the military, he continued his studies in physics and mathematics, and wrote and published several papers. Already his tremendous energy, which never left him, was becoming evident.

In 1847, less than five years after his graduation, Helmholtz, a twenty-six-year-old army surgeon, read before the Physical Society of Berlin his classic paper on the indestructibility of energy, giving mathematical formulation to the law of conservation. A few years earlier in 1842, Julius Mayer (1814–1878) had published a theoretical paper on the topic, along with the method for calculating the dynamical equivalent of heat. J. P. Joule, almost immediately after Mayer, published the experiments of several years which he had conducted and which led to a theory substantially similar to Mayer's. Controversy about priority sprang up. Helmholtz freely acknowledged their priority. All of these men deserve credit, Mayer more for the theoretical formulation, Helmholtz more for its mathematical statement, and Joule more for its research verification. It is worthy of remark that this paper by Helmholtz was in the spirit of that oath taken by his friends a few years before, since the theory of the conservation of energy is simultaneously a denial of the existence of biological vital force and the substitution for it of the physical and chemical analysis of energy transformation.

After serving in the army for five years and after a short stint as instructor in anatomy at a Berlin art school, Helmholtz was called to Königsberg as Associate Professor of Physiology. Since he had a reasonably secure position, he married. He then turned to what proved to be his second major contribution, the measurement of the speed of the neural impulse, a topic to which we shall return presently.

During these years he also worked in physiological optics. In 1851 he invented the ophthalmoscope, which was a concave mirror with a small hole in the middle through which the observer looked as he reflected light into the eye of the patient. Once conceived, this relatively simple device to look into the eye itself was of enormous value in research and medical practice.

In 1856 the first volume of the *Handbuch der physiologischen Optik* appeared, with the last of its three volumes to appear ten years later; and then issued as a unit in 1867.[24] Nearly sixty years later in 1924–25 it[25] was translated into English, not just as a classic, but as an indispensable tool for the serious student of vision

In 1855 Helmholtz went to Bonn as Professor of Anatomy and Physiology. While still at Königsberg he had become interested in acoustics. During his three years at Bonn, his first major research on hearing was carried out. In 1858, during the period in which he centered his attention on acoustical problems, he moved to an even more important position in the German university system, the Professorship of Physiology at Heidelberg, a chair he occupied until 1871. If anything, his already tremendous productivity increased during this period. In addition to the research on audition relevant to this particular account, he showed a remarkable ability to come to grips with important and crucial problems in hydrodynamics and electrodynamics. He ranged over many areas. The titles of some of his papers between 1858 and 1871 were on such topics as after-images, color blindness, the Arabian-Persian musical scale, relation between the natural sciences and the totality of sciences, the form of the horopter, the movements of the human eye, the regulation of ice, the axioms of geometry, and hay fever. His acoustical researches culminated on the appearance of *On the Sensations of Tone* in 1863.[26] Just as did his book on vision, this new book summarized not only his investigations, but sifted, summarized, and systematized the entire available literature. During this period, honors were showered on him, invitations to lecture, calls from foreign countries, and the Prorektorship of the University of Heidelberg among them.

In 1870, when Helmholtz was fifty years of age, the chair in physics at the University of Berlin became vacant and he was asked to set his own conditions of acceptance. He asked for and received a salary of 4,000 thalers (a huge sum for that day), a promise of a new institute of physics, its director-ship and living quarters in that institute. Until arriving at Berlin in 1871, Helmholtz had been somewhat cramped for space and limited as to apparatus. In 1887 he was made the first director of the new Physics-Technical Institute at Charlottenberg, near Berlin, while still retaining his professorship.

Such were his interests in espousing empiricism that during the period extending from 1866–1894, he published five papers on geometrical axioms with the intention of showing, contrary to Kant, that they, too, are products of experience. He did his job so well that his discussion of non-Euclidian space made those who came after him cite his work as evidence for a (non-experiential) fourth dimension.

A bizarre consequence of this work was the support some contemporaries thought it gave to spiritualism. The American medium, Slade, had been performing such feats as seeming to remove objects from sealed boxes. From this a fuzzy explanation in terms of the fourth dimension became popular. It was argued that Slade's feats were capable of performance because he worked in the "fourth dimension" where it would be as easy to remove an object from a sealed box as it was in the world of three dimensions to lift an object out of a square. Such ran the argument which various scholarly figures in Germany hotly and acrimoniously debated. In the course of this Helmholtz was blamed for creating a scientific scandal. Such was the passion aroused that one professor was dismissed from Berlin because of his accusations against Helmholtz.

Although he continued his interests in physiological problems, revised his books on hearing and vision, and made that spirited defense of empiricism mentioned earlier, his researches during these years tended to center on problems of physics less close to present interests. For example, he helped to direct his pupil, Hertz, to the problems which made a crucial contribution to the founding of wireless telegraphy and radio.

He developed popular and elaborate lecture demonstrations and continued to give scientific lectures designed to be of popular nature of which a total of four different collections appeared in print. In 1877 academic freedom was the basis of one of his popular lectures in which the "admirable" state of German universities, where, having thrown off the yoke of the Church, its professors taught unhindered, was contrasted with the lowly backwardness of British universities which had not made these advances.

In 1893 Helmholtz came to the United States for the first and only time to attend the Chicago World's Fair as a delegate from Germany. While returning, he had a severe fall down the ship's stairs from which he never fully recovered. He died from a cerebral hemorrhage in September 1894.

The Speed of the Neural Impulse

As expressed by J. Müller,[27] the scientific opinion prevailing before the research of Helmholtz was either that the speed of the neural impulse was instantaneous or at least so fast as to be incapable of measurement. Estimates of speeds many times the velocity of light had been secured by assuming that the rate of flow of "animal spirits" would be similar for vessels of the same size and that speed varied inversely with the diameter of the conductor. Since the diameters of nerve fibers were very, very minute, indications of tremendous speeds were obtained. The method used by Helmholtz,[28] which would have been entirely inadequate had the previous estimates been true, was to take a motor nerve and attached muscle from a frog's leg, the so-called nerve-muscle preparation, and arrange it so that both the moment of stimulation and the resultant movement would be recorded on a drum revolving at a known speed. Helmholtz measured the time between stimulation and the muscle twitch for different lengths of nerve. The difference in time interval between stimulation of the nerve near the muscle and its recorded reaction and that for stimulation far from the muscle gave him the time taken for passage. Since he knew the distance between the points of stimulation, he could now calculate its speed per second. Helmholtz found the speed to be the very modest one of about ninety feet per second.

The Bell-Magendie law, which distinguished between sensory and motor nerves, made it unsafe for him to leave the problem measured with motor nerves alone, so he now turned to sensory-motor nerves to find out whether their speed was similar or different. He also turned to human subjects. When stimulated on the toe and on the thigh, a man can respond with his hand. The difference in the time between stimulation and reaction over differing lengths traversed in the two instances gave Helmholtz his measure of speed of reaction—something between fifty and 100 feet per second, but variability from trial to trial and subject to subject was so great that he did not follow up the original study. The individual differences, later to become so important in themselves, were, for Helmholtz, nothing more than an indication of inadequate control, as indeed they turned out to be. Nevertheless these two phases of the study gave him rough measures of the speed of sensory and motor neural impulses. In general, later, more accurate research has demonstrated that the neural impulse varies enormously. The speeds, Helmholtz found, proved to be too slow. Nevertheless it was Helmholtz who carried out the pioneer study.

The fact that the nervous impulse is not instantaneous but takes appreciable amounts of time signified that mental events were definitely limited by the properties of the body and that an analysis of bodily motion was relevant to psychological phenomena. Mental events that seem instantaneous may actually be temporal events. As Boring so aptly phrases it, ". . . it brought the soul to time. . . ."[29]

This was the first "reaction-time" study as it came to be called. However, Helmholtz was interested only in the sheer speed of the neural impulse, and it was the work of Donders published some fifteen years later (already described) which showed a grasp of the psychological significance of the problem.

Vision

While integrating the previously available research in the field of visual physiology, Helmholtz also did an enormous amount of original and important work which is presented in his *Handbuch der physiologischen Optik*.[30] The three volumes have been characterized respectively as physiological, sensory, and perceptual accounts of vision.[31] Some of his own specific research studies show a similar affinity to psychological problems.

He measured the optical constants of the eye, demonstrated how the eye accommodates for different distances, and developed and supported by research a theory of visual space. Most important of all was his theory of color vision.

As early as 1802, Thomas Young (1773–1829) had published a theory of color vision in which he postulated that the retina is equipped with three kinds of color sensitive points.[32] These three primary colors, working cooperatively, were said to furnish the range of experienced colors. The derivation of all colors from a limited number of colors was not new, as we know from Newton. (See page 177.) Going beyond Newton, Young's contribution was the suggestion of a physiological basis of three kinds of "particles on the retina," (receptors) each kind acting independently. This suggestion lay fallow until Helmholtz espoused the theory, to be known thereafter as the Young-Helmholtz theory of color vision.

In Helmholtz's theory three sets of fibers in the retina are said to give rise respectively to sensations of red, green, and violet.[33] There are supposed to be three kinds of photo-chemically decomposible substances in the end organs, each with different degrees of sensitiveness to different parts of the visible spectrum. With disintegration of these substances, neural excitation occurs. The three kinds of excitation act differently on the brain only because, while playing the part of connecting wires, they are united to different functioning parts of the brain. Using these particulars of receptor and cerebral localization, Helmholtz then proceeded to suggest how they could be used to explain various psychological visual experiences. On stimulation of the red and green fibers together, yellow results. Other combinations produce other colors. When all three kinds of organs are stimulated in the right proportion, white results. Negative after-images on looking at a white surface, after colored stimulation, arise because after one of the organs have been thoroughly fatigued by use, we see with the unfatigued organs alone. Color blindness (red-green blindness) could result from lack of either red or green organs, or both. An objection to the theory that arose from critics was that yellow, postulated as arising from stimulation of red and green organs, should not be seen by color-blind individuals, whereas actually they can see yellow. In spite of criticism, modification, elaboration, and correction, the Young-Helmholtz theory is still taken very seriously today.

Helmholtz[34] held that this color theory is a particular application of Müller's general law of the specific energy of nerves, with "three nerve systems." Müller himself had applied the principle of the specific energy of nerves to the differentiation of one sense from another, but not to the separate qualities within a single sense, such as sweet and sour or red and green. Helmholtz was applying the rule within a single sense modality. If we speak of Müller's theory as one of specific *nerve* energies, then Helmholtz was advancing a theory of specific *fiber* energies.[35] Although Helmholtz did much to advance this theory of fiber energies, he had been anticipated by several other investigators, including Thomas Young himself who, by advancing his theory of specificity for different color qualities, anticipated Müller's more general doctrine. Despite his citing Müller, the theory of Helmholtz turned out to be more a doctrine of the specific energies of *cortical areas* than it did of nerves. As we know, the cortical area alternative had been raised, but not accepted by Müller. In the location of specificity, later research was to support Helmholtz and not Müller.

Space Perception

In interpreting space perception, Helmholtz was also an empiricist. Here he saw as his opponent, Ewald Hering,[36] who held that every point on the retina was innately capable of perceiving height, breadth, and depth. In part, Helmholtz defended an empirical position by use of Müller's doctrine of specific energies.[37] Helmholtz held that the various sense organs and nerves each have characteristic qualities, which are not, in themselves, meaningful, being bare sense impression. At this point experience enters, for recurring association gives them meaning.[38] The doctrine of specific nerve energies interpreted by Müller as a defense of Kantian nativism was now being interpreted by Helmholtz as a defense of empiricism.

Helmholtz also stressed the importance of the empirical process of unconscious inference in space perception.[39] Perception of space, he said, is not inherent; instead we "infer" space from past experience, but without awareness that this process of inference is going on. Certain small cues constitute a sign that the object is to be found at a certain distance. Without noticing the sign itself, we infer how far away the object is. To use only one example—in gazing at an object twenty feet away there are intervening objects at various closer distances that are actually seen as double, but without our noticing it. (This can be verified by anyone who takes the trouble. Look across the room while holding a pen first, a few inches from the nose, and then at arm's length, while still looking across the room. The doubleness of the pen will be evident in both instances but greatest when close up.) Closer objects are seen, while looking at the far object, with varying degrees of doubleness. A specific degree of doubleness is unconsciously interpreted, without noticing the doubleness at a certain distance to the object. This is what Helmholtz meant by "unconscious inference."

Audition

In the field of hearing Helmholtz made many contributions.[40] Among them were his clarification of the role of timbre to round out the major harmonic components and his theory of how hearing is mediated by the ear and the relation of this theory to the doctrine of specific energy of nerves. Each of these must be examined in more detail.

That pitch depends primarily on frequency of sound waves and intensity upon the amplitude of the waves had been understood and explained in Müller's *Handbuch;* as yet timbre had no similar explanation. The *fact* of timbre, that is to say, that there are qualitative differences between tones other than pitch was, of course, well known. Anyone hearing the same note being played by different instruments cannot escape realizing the existence of something which makes them sound different despite their identity of pitch. Helmholtz explained this experience of timbre by the presence, in addition to the fundamental pitch, of so-called overtones or vibration rates more rapid than the fundamental tone which fixes the pitch.[41] Most vibrating bodies, vibrate not only as wholes, but simultaneously as parts. It is these partial vibrations which give rise to timbre. The shape of waves making up a tone from a musical instrument, if visualized, would show the main wave being the same as that for all other instruments and giving the fundamental pitch when playing that note, but with the part waves unique to this particular instrument, giving rise to the timbre. The more similar the tone of two instruments, the more similar the characterizing overtones were found to be. Here again, Helmholtz was not content merely to advance a theory; he conclusively demonstrated his contention by building a series of tuning forks and resonators which permitted systematically varying the intensity of the overtones accompanying a fundamental tone. From these he produced synthetically the characteristic timbre of various instruments.

His theory of hearing evolved over the years, and this is not the place to trace these modifications. His theory was essentially a theory of pitch; he assumed that intensity was more or less explained by varying degrees of excitation of the fibers.

Helmholtz marshalled evidence that a portion of the inner ear responded to an auditory wave stimulus by resonance, vibrating in tune with the frequency of the sound wave. The ear behaved similarly in the same way as striking a note on one tuning fork will set in vibration an unstruck tuning fork. This is the phenomena called resonance.

After discarding the organs of Alfonso Corti as the basis of differential tuning, he finally reached the conclusion that the basilar membrane with its many hair cells in the cochlea of the inner ear is the resolving organ of hearing. This basilar membrane is trapezoidal in shape (narrow at one end and increasing gradually in width). The hairs on its narrower end he thought to be tuned to high pitches; the hairs on the wider portion to the low pitches. Pitch, then, transmitted to the brain after analysis by resonance on the basilar membrane, is dependent upon place of stimulation. The differential action of a portion of the basilar membrane is the means whereby the pitch of the heard sound is determined.

The resonance theory gave rise to many alternative theories.[42] The most formidable competition to the resonance theory has come from the frequency theory in which the basilar membrane is said to vibrate as a whole, thus, giving rise to nerve impulses which preserve, unchanged, the frequency of the stimulus so that the brain, itself, not the basilar membrane, becomes the place where auditory analysis into different pitches takes place. Today each theory is seen as explaining some, but not all, of the evidence. It is clear that the old theories are too simple. Resolution of the present discrepancies is a task for future research.

The doctrine of specific nerve energies was regarded by Helmholtz as an important established fact. It was natural for him to apply it to hearing. Differences of quality *ipso facto* thus meant that there are differences in the conduction sensory fibers. Research since Helmholtz's day has demonstrated the existence of anywhere between 1500 and 11,000 distinguishable pitches.[43] This means that Helmholtz had been arguing there was somewhere between these number of specific energies in hearing alone! This bold step could hardly avoid being noticed, and the issue of the specific energies in hearing became a prominent one for research in all of the sense modalities.

Helmholtz as a Great Scientist

Helmholtz was deeply devoted to an empirical approach to science and yet had a broad philosophical outlook and possessed curiosity and originality. He had the skill to carry a problem through from its conception, the construction of the necessary apparatus, and the execution of the research design. He was cautious in the interpretation of the results, yet he possessed great synthesizing ability in coordination of his findings with discovery in other related fields. Although it is perhaps out of fashion to say so, Helmholtz was one of the great scientists of modern times.

REFERENCES[*]

1. J. Müller, *Handbuch der Physiologie des Menschen.* (3 vols.) Coblenz: Hölscher, 1834–40.

2. R. Whytt, *An Essay on the Vital and Other Involuntary Motions of Animals.* Edinburgh: Hamilton, Balfour & Neill, 1751. (Herrnstein & Boring Excerpt No. 60)

3. C. Bell, *Idea of a New Anatomy of the Brain: Submitted for the Observation of His Friends.* London: Strahan & Preston, 1811. (Herrnstein & Boring Excerpts No. 6, 8)

[*] See page 16 for description of reference style.

4. F. Magendie, Expériences sur les fonctions des racines des nerfs rachidiens, *J. Physiol. Expér. Pathol.*, 1822, 2, 276–279; Expériences sur les fonctions des racines des nerfs qui naissent de la moëlle epinière, *J. physiol. expér. pathol.*, 1822, 2, 366–371. (Herrnstein & Boring Excerpt No. 7)

5. L. Carmichael, Sir Charles Bell: A Contribution to the History of Physiological Psychology, *Psychol. Rev.*, 1926, 33, 188–217; J. M. D. Olmsted, *François Magendie, Pioneer in Experimental Physiology and Scientific Medicine in Nineteenth Century France.* New York: Schuman, 1944.

6. F. J. Gall, Sur les fonctions du cerveau et sur celles de chacune de ses parties. (Vols. 4, 6) In W. Lewis (Trans.) *Gall's works.* Boston: Marsh, Capon & Lyon, 1835. (1825) (Herrnstein & Boring Excerpt No. 45)

7. G. Spurzhiem, *Phrenology or the Doctrine of the Human Mind.* Philadelphia: Lippincott, 1825.

8. E. T. Carlson, The Influence of Phrenology on Early American Psychiatric Thought, *Amer. J. Psychiat.*, 1958, 115, 535–538.

9. M. J. P. Flourens, *Recherches expérimentales sur less propriétés et les fonctions du système nerveux dans les animaux vertébrés.* Paris: Crevot, 1824. (Herrnstein & Boring Excerpt No. 46)

10. P. Broca, Remarques sur le siège de la faculté du langage articulé, suivies d'une observation d'aphémie (parte de la parole), *Bull. Soc. Anat.*, 1861, 6, 330–357. (Herrnstein & Boring Excerpt No. 47)

11. G. Fritsch & E. Hitzig, Ueber die elcktrische Erregbarkeit des Grosshirns, *Arch. Anat. Physiol.*, 1870, 300–332. (Herrnstein & Boring Excerpt No. 48)

12. Müller, *op. cit.* (Herrnstein & Boring Excerpt No. 9)

13. Charles Bell had anticipated Müller to some extent in a privately printed paper and many others had implied the doctrine, but it was Müller whose authoritative publication made it an accepted and acceptable principle.

14. J. Müller, *Elements of Physiology.* (Translated by W. Baly) London: Taylor, 1837–1842. (1833–1840)

15. W. James, *Psychology: Briefer Course.* New York: Holt, 1892, p. 12.

16. J. Müller, *Zur vergleichenden Physiologie des Gesichtssinnes.* Leipzig: Cnobloch, 1826, pp. 55–66. (Herrnstein & Boring Excerpt No. 25)

17. E. G. Boring, *A History of Experimental Psychology.* (2nd ed.) New York: Appleton-Century-Crofts, 1950, pp. 134–142.

18. F. C. Donders, Die Schnelligkeit psychischer Processe, *Arch. Anat. Physiol.*, 1868, 657–681. (1862)

19. H. L. F. Helmholtz, *Treatise on Physiological Optics.* (3 vols.) (ed. by J. P. C. Southall) Rochester, N. Y.: Optical Society of America, 1925. (1856–1866)

20. *Ibid.*

21. V. F. Lenzen, Helmholtz's Theory of Knowledge. In M. F. A. Montague (ed.), *Studies and Essays in the History of Science and Learning. Offered in homage*

to George Sarton on the Occasion of His Sixtieth Birthday, 31 August, 1944. New York: Schuman, 1946, pp. 299–320.

22. The major source of details about his life was H. Margenau, Introduction. In H. L. F. Helmholtz, *On the Sensations of Tone.* (New York: Dover, 1954) This was supplemented by H. Gruber & Valmai Gruber, Hermann von Helmholtz: Nineteenth Century Polymorph. (*Sci. Mon., N. Y.,* 1956, 83, pp. 92–99)

23. Quoted in Boring, *History, op. cit.,* p. 708.

24. H. L. F. HELMHOLTZ, *Handbuch der physiologischen Optik.* Leipzig: Voss, 1867. (1856–1866)

25. *Treatise.*

26. H. L. F. HELMHOLTZ, *On the Sensations of Tone.* (Translated by A. J. Ellis) New York: Dover, 1954. (1863)

27. MÜLLER, *Elements, op. cit.*

28. H. L. F. HELMHOLTZ, On the Rate of Transmission of the Nerve Impulse, *Ber. könig. preuss. Akad. Wiss. Berlin,* 1850, 14–15. Reprinted in W. Dennis, (ed.), *Readings in the History of Psychology,* New York: Appleton-Century-Crofts, 1948, pp. 197–198.

29. BORING, *op. cit.,* p. 42.

30. *Optik.*

31. BORING, *op. cit.*

32. T. YOUNG, On the Theory of Light and Colours, *Phil. Trans. Royal Soc.,* 1802, 92, 18–21. (Herrnstein & Boring Excerpt No. 4)

33. *Treatise,* Vol. 2, Sec. 20. (Herrnstein & Boring Excerpt No. 11)

34. *Ibid.*

35. BORING, *op. cit.*

36. E. HERING, *Beiträge zur Physiologie: Zur Lehre vom Ortsinn der Netzhaut.* Leipzig: Engelmann, 1861–1864. (Herrnstein & Boring Excerpt No. 33)

37. *Treatise.*

38. *Ibid.,* Vol. 3, Sec. 26. (Herrnstein & Boring Excerpt No. 34)

39. *Ibid.,* (Herrnstein & Boring Excerpt No. 40)

40. *Sensations of Tone.*

41. *Ibid.,* Chap. 6. (Herrnstein & Boring Excerpt No. 12)

42. R. S. WOODWORTH, *Experimental Psychology.* New York: Holt, 1938, pp. 535–537.

43. E. G. BORING, *Sensation and Perception in the History of Experimental Psychology.* New York: Appleton-Century-Crofts, 1942, pp. 341–342.

CHAPTER 12

WUNDT:

INTROSPECTION AND EXPERIMENT

WILHELM WUNDT is the first man who can be called a psychologist without qualifying the statement by reference to another perhaps stronger interest. In his self-image he was a psychologist even more than he was a philosopher. This subjective criterion of a psychologist will be found to be supported by a crude but adequate summary of his life's work. Although he wrote four major books in philosophy running to perhaps twenty-one editions, in psychology he published six books which appeared in about thirty-six editions.

In founding the modern science of psychology, Wilhelm Wundt was fully aware of what he was doing. In his preface to the first edition of his *Principles of Physiological Psychology*, dated 1874, he begins with the impressive statement that the work was presented in order to "mark out a new domain of science."[1] He also states flatly that, as a science, psychology cannot be based upon metaphysical assumptions of any sort.

To Wundt, the use of the experimental method, whenever possible, was mandatory. Moreover, he sharpened and made more exact and exacting the age-old method of introspection. Prior familiarity with how Wundt interpreted introspection and experiment will help to clarify the events of his life and the experiments conducted in his laboratory.

THE MEANING OF INTROSPECTION AND EXPERIMENT

Since Wundt referred explicitly to physiological psychology in his title, just what he meant needs clarification. Essentially he held that the already available physiological methods were to be used for psychological study whenever they appeared appropriate; although there was no *a priori* way of determining when these should be employed. This particular contention owes much to Helmholtz's view of the nature of physiological psychology. To Wundt, then, use of physiological methods depended upon relevance to the problem in question.

Despite Wundt's calling the new science "physiological psychology" he insisted the psychic and the physiological process are separate and parallel.[2] As causality in natural science is a closed system, the phenomena that are studied by natural science cannot affect the mind or be affected by it. Outer experience (physics) and inner experience (psychology) again differ in the point of view from which the experience is observed. The former is mediate, the latter is immediate. Conscious phenomena, therefore, are observable without reference to the body in which they occur, and "physiological psychology" does not imply an attempt to explain the phenomena of the psychical by examining the physical life. In short, mind-body interaction was rejected and instead, Wundt was a dualist of the psychophysical parallelistic variety.

When psychology investigated the relation between the processes of the physical and the mental life, it was called psycho-physics. On this subject Wundt[3] explicitly acknowledged he followed Fechner, but denied Fechner's hope that the psychophysical methods could be used for metaphysical purposes. Metaphysical implications, he admitted, may later emerge from experimental research but only as an end result of research.

Although using the psychophysical methods for many problems, Wundt disagreed with Fechner on what was being measured.[4] Wundt held that to put the matter correctly one must state that two sensations are of equal intensity or one sensation is just noticeably different from another sensation. Wundt was seeking to study, not the relation of the body and mind, but, instead, the relation between sensation on the one hand and the process of psychological judgment on the other. A purely psychological interpretation with no appeal to the relation of stimulus and sensation resulted. To Wundt, data obtained from psychological study were illustrative of a law of psychological relativity. Sensations differ to a degree which make possible judgments of their relative magnitude.

Wundt firmly established the method of introspection as psychology's characteristic task. The use of introspection, in itself, was not new as even a fragmentary review will show. Socrates had made an appeal to introspection, and Plotinus and Augustine had sharpened this method. Descartes and the British empiricists were agreed on its use. Despite this agreement, a significant difference separated them. Descartes' method of introspection has been characterized earlier as contemplative meditation upon problems that interested him. (See page 166.) Intuitive self-evidence sought about cognition or the passions, both highly complex states, were Descarte's favorite topics. The English empiricists shifted introspective interests from the area of the higher mental processes to that of sensation. The reduction by Hume of soul or mind to a bundle of sensations and his doctrine that images are faint copies of sensations are illustrative of this shift. Wundt continued this tendency toward simplicity by further refining the conscious elements and by combining the introspective process with experiment.

Wundt recognized that conscious contents are fleeting and in continual flux;[5] he therefore laid down explicit rules for proper use of the introspective method:[6] (1) The observer, if at all possible, must be in a position to determine when the process is to be introduced. (2) He must be in a state of "strained attention." (3) The observation must be capable of being repeated several times. (4) The conditions of the experiment must be such as to be capable of variation through introduction or elimination of certain stimuli and through the variation of strength and quality of the stimuli. The first rule is necessary so that the observer is not caught off guard but is set for the task. According to Wundt's arrangement for introspection, the observer knew when to expect the introduction of the stimulus and was ready to observe the state of consciousness. He was, therefore, capable of isolating the mental processes of that moment. As for the second rule, the observer must be conscious of every nuance of that which is presented. Repetition, the third rule, allows for the uncovering of omissions and distortions of earlier trials. The fourth rule makes it possible to study the effect of variation, i.e., the effect of the change resulting from addition or subtraction of various aspects of stimulating conditions as shown in variations of the experience. This last rule takes us to his conception of an experiment.

Insofar as physiological psychology draws upon experiment, Wundt held we can refer to experimental psychology.[7] It is perhaps from John Stuart Mill that he derived his conception of psychology as a science of observation and experiment.[8] But Mill only talked about experiments; Wundt carried them out. Wundt[9] asserted that in psychology pure self-observation is insufficient. It is only when additional recourse to experiment is made that exact quantitative results are possible. The essence of an experiment is to vary the conditions of a stimulus situation and then observe the changes in the experience of the observer. In advocating experimental control of conditions of introspection, Wundt was taking a giant step.

Herbart had urged using mathematics in the study of psychological problems, although he had denied the possibility of using experiment. Kant had not only denied the possibility of experiment in psychology, but also held that the use of mathematics itself was impossible. He had held that the only dimension of consciousness was time and that with one dimension one could not carry out experiments, and, consequently, psychical processes are indeterminate.[10] Since practically all German philosophers of his time were either Kantians or Herbartians, it is to Wundt's credit that he overcame this formidable intellectual block and saw that both mathematics and experiment could be applied in psychology.

Wundt agreed that Kant was correct concerning the uni-dimensional nature of consciousness when we confine ourselves to internal experience. But when we turn to *external* stimuli, not only are units of measurement supplied, but also one more dimension that Kant had omitted is added, namely, intensity.[11] With the dimensions of quality and intensity, experiment became possible. Every simple sensation has a qualitative determinant, such as blue, warm, or sweet.[12] Qualities are not divisible into simpler units. As for Herbart, as we have seen, he recognized that these classes of variables were present, but had not appreciated how they could be turned to experimental use.

Armed with intensity and quality as the two classes of variables, Wundt was prepared for the experimental study of psychological phenomena. In sound, for example, intensity, it is true, is never separable from some quality of pitch, but it is possible to change either the intensity alone (loud-soft), or the pitch alone (high-low), while maintaining the other unchanged. Moreover, we may use two notes and consequently change the quality of the sound so that it is different from that of either note alone. Intensity and quality became subjects for scientific study. On these premises Wundt was able to launch the experimental study of psychology.

LIFE AND RESEARCH OF WUNDT[13]

Wilhelm was born at the village of Neckarau near Heidelberg in Baden on August 16, 1832, the son of a Lutheran pastor. He was a solitary child, never close to his parents, played little, and absorbed himself in study. Even as a young child he stayed in the home of a Lutheran vicar who was his tutor. He had formed so strong an attachment to this tutor, presumably at first his father's assistant, that when the vicar was transferred, he was unconsolable until allowed to board with him and to continue under his tutelage. At thirteen he entered the gymnasium, where he also boarded and was ready for the university at nineteen.

His medical studies took him to Tübingen, Heidelberg, and Berlin. It has been hazarded that Wundt went into medicine without any special call, but in part it was because he wanted to continue away from home! There is some doubt whether he ever intended to practice medicine. As with many others before and after him, the study of medicine was the means of entering into a scientific career which even at this age he seems to have had in mind. He did some work at the Institute of Johannes Müller in physiology, and a year or two later he shifted to physiology as an academic field.

In 1857 he was appointed *Dozent* at Heidelberg and began to lecture in physiology. His first announced course in physiology attracted four students! Between 1858 and 1864 he served as assistant to Helmholtz, who had just arrived from Bonn. Relations with the taciturn Helmholtz were non-existent, according to Titchener. In 1864 Wundt was appointed assistant professor. Somewhat surprisingly, in 1866 he was chosen to represent Heidelberg in the Baden Chamber, but he soon resigned. There was a delay of academic advance until 1874 when he was called to Zürich to the chair of Inductive Philosophy. This, it should be noted, is only an apparent shift in field. In academic circles he had come to be viewed as a promising man for appointment to a post in philosophy. After all, psychology was formally still a branch of philosophy.

During these years, Wundt was very active in physiology. In 1858 he published a study of muscular movement and elasticity during action[14] in which he reported investigating the effect of constant galvanic current and mechanical thermal and chemical stimuli upon muscles. Not only was he working in this field, but a conception of psychology as a distinct science was beginning to emerge. Between 1858 and 1862 various sections of his *Beiträge zur Theorie der Sinneswahrnehmung*[15] appeared. This volume so much anticipated later developments in his thinking that Titchener, one of his greatest students, has argued that it outlined the program of his entire life.

In the introduction of this work Wundt stressed the primacy of method as a means of scientific advance. He also cited apparatus advances, such as the laryngoscope and the ophthalmoscope, as a means of ushering in whole series of discoveries. Psychology, he goes on, has not yet felt the impulse of the new empirical method being used all around it. It has asked metaphysical questions first, such as the essence of the soul, its origin, and its destination. These are questions appropriate to where psychology may end, but not to where it should start. It must take experiences, and the simplest of these experiences at that, for its point of departure. He seems to be saying, psychology should first crawl before it can walk. In that which follows, he marshals evidence primarily from vision and secondarily from touch. One may recognize in this work his struggle to utilize physiological methodology in dealing with psychological problems.

From 1867 onward, he gave a course at Heidelberg entitled, "physiological psychology." This date establishes the formal offering of an academic course of this nature. As he "worked up" his lecture notes over the next few years, a new book, by general agreement his most important book, began to take form. This was his *Grundzüge der physiologischen Psychologie*.[16] The first half was published in 1873 and the second in 1874. It was destined to go through six editions, the last in 1911, and swell in size to three large volumes. (It was characteristic of most of his books that new, amplified, and revised editions would appear from time to time.) The *Grundzüge* changed in detail, sometimes very important detail, but it is remarkable how the expansion and change did not require major shifts in his systematic views. It is the one indispensible source for an account of his system of psychology. Wundt entered on the last, longest, and most important phase of his career in 1875. In that year he became Professor of Philosophy at Leipzig. Here he lived and worked for forty-five years.

At the University of Leipzig in 1875, Wundt established one of the first two experimental laboratories of psychology in the world.[17] For many years it has been customary to consider 1879 as the founding year for the first experimental laboratory in the world on the mistaken belief that it was in this year that Wundt's Leipzig Laboratory was given formal recognition by university authorities. Formal recognition to a course in "experimental psychology" did not come from the university until the winter of 1883, as did an appropriation for the laboratory, while an "Institute for Experimental Psychology" as such, was not listed by university authorities until 1894. In this connection 1879 is notable only for appearance of the first student to do publishable psychological research with Wundt, which may be the reason for saying that it was "founded" in that year. Actually, before Wundt's arrival in October, 1875, the Royal Ministry had set aside a room to be used by Wundt for his own experimental work and for demonstrations connected with his *Psychologische Übungen* or "Psychological Practicum." A good case can be made for the establishment of the first laboratory in psychology in this year of 1875—or rather of the two first laboratories—since William James also equipped a small laboratory in the same year. (See page 349.) Even this brief account brings out both the subjectivity of deciding upon and the gradualness of the "founding" of this important psychological agency.[18] Nevertheless, if psychology must have a date to celebrate its coming into full-fledged scientific status, this is perhaps the best choice.

In 1881, Wundt began to publish a journal, *Philosophische Studien*, containing reports of experimental studies beginning to flow from his laboratory. This was the first journal devoted as much to psychology as to philosophy. Lest the title be puzzling, it should be indicated that Wundt thought philosophy should be psychological. He did not support attempts to have psychology a separate department from that of philosophy. Moreover, between 1880 and 1901 he published four books in philosophy—a logic, an ethics, a systematic philosophy, and an introduction to the field.

One of the results of the founding of the laboratory and the spreading fame of Wundt was the migration of students to Leipzig to study with him and to work in the laboratory. There gathered around him would-be psychologists using introspection and experiment to derive the laws of the human mind. In this way Wundt became the leader of a "school" of psychology. These students were united in their systematic views as well as sharing a common purpose. Instead of each of them working alone, with their labors eventuating in books, the laboratory atmosphere resulted in specific research studies appearing as articles in journals. Wundt would then synthesize the results of the various studies in the successive editions of the *Grundzüge*.

The sheer availability of co-workers was important. Since the "experimenter" could hardly be the "observer" at one and the same time, the experimenter of one study was available as a subject for another. Lest this point be dismissed as trivial, it is pertinent to indicate that "introspection" as practiced in Wundt's laboratory was not a skill acquired without a period of rigorous apprenticeship. To get at the elements of experience required arduous training. Moreover, even if non-student assistants could be trained as subjects, the nature of the tasks to which they were put, to be illustrated in a moment, would have demanded payment. One does not embark upon introspection as a lark! In later days when simple report, not introspection, was all that was needed, the problem was solved by American ingenuity through the use of a captive population of college students.

The work of the Leipzig Laboratory may illustrate what a major segment of experimental psychology was like before and at the turn of the century. About one hundred experimental studies appeared in the *Philosophische Studien* during its twenty-odd years, almost all of them carried out either in the laboratory or conducted by Wundt's students soon after they left Leipzig. Consequently, the research bore very heavily the impress of Wundt's aims, since typically he assigned the problem on which a particular student was to work.

Boring's summarizing classification will be utilized to sketch the research coming from Wundt's laboratory.[19] In quick overview the studies may be classed as those in sensation and perception, reaction, attention, feeling, and association. About one-half of the researches concerned problems in sensation and perception, particularly in vision. Papers on the psychophysics of color, peripheral vision, color contrast, negative afterimages, visual contrast, and color blindness are typical of these concerned with visual sensation; visual size and optical illusions are characteristic of those on visual perception. Auditory sensation was investigated by psychophysical methods, and beats and combination tones also were studied. An attack was carried on with the problem of time perception by studying the ability of subjects to reproduce intervals of varying lengths in the comparison of "filled" times (time occupied with mental work or sensory stimulation) and unfilled time. Tactual sensation came in for investigation through the problems of the two-point threshold, using the already familiar methods of Weber and Fechner.

About one-sixth of the time and effort of the workers in the laboratory was given to the reaction experiment. The subtractive procedure of Donders was used, (see page 248) although his times for choice and discrimination was replaced by a more complicated classification of times for volition, perception, apperception, cognition, association, and judgment.

Hopes ran high in the Leipzig Laboratory for a chronometry of the mind, since, by the additive and subtractive procedures, it appeared entirely feasible to work out the times necessary for each of these processes to take place. However, these hopes were dashed, for, as Boring notes, the times for a separate process was neither constant from person to person nor from study to study, ". . . and later introspection showed that in a more complicated reaction the entire conscious pattern is changed and that the alteration is not merely the insertion of another link on a chain."[20] Oswald Külpe[21] was the one who delivered the most telling blow against the view that the elements are additive. He showed that changing the task does not merely add another unit; instead, it alters the whole process. Külpe interpreted Lange's results as showing that the subject's predisposition or attitude alters the perceptual-reactive process. Previously Lange's classical research study[22] had established characteristic differences in speed between some subjects who attend to the stimulus as compared to other subjects who attend to the response, in favor of the greater speed of the latter. This did much to solve the problem of the personal equation. Those who attend to the response react more quickly than those who must shift attention from stimulus to the reaction to be made.

As interest in the reaction experiment waned, studies first of attention and then of feeling came to take its place, each including about one-tenth of the laboratory's studies. Lange's study, just mentioned, helped to create the interest in attention. To Wundt, attention was that clear perception of a narrow region of the content of consciousness. An example of this is the word or words we are reading on this page relative to the rest of the page, as well as the adjoining page and much of the surrounding environment of the room. Whatever is in the focus of attention becomes distinct and is separated from the rest of the field. Research in the area of attention was performed by means of the complication experiment, *i.e.*, the range of attention and fluctuation of attention were studied. Following the lead of Jacobs, Cattell[23] was responsible for carrying out the classic study of attention span (meaning that which can be taken in at a glance) finding that four, five or six units (lines, letters or words) could be apprehended in an exposure which was of too short duration to allow a "movement" of attention.

Studies of feeling, the work of the laboratory in the 1890's, involved the use of the method of expression through which feelings and correlated changes of pulse, breathing, muscular strength, and the like were studied. The method of paired comparisons was also developed. This method requires the subject to compare each particular stimulus with every other stimulus being used in terms of the subjective feeling aroused. Suppose the task was to judge the pleasingness of a variety of colored paper patches: patch A is compared to B, C, D, E, F, then patch B is compared to A, C, D, E, F, and so on. On each trial the observer was to say which was most pleasing of each pair A or B, A or C, and so on.

Studies of association make up another one-tenth of the total output of the laboratory during these years. Under Wundt's direction much was done to refine the method. Galton, it will be found in a subsequent chapter, (see page 308) although using single words as stimuli, had often allowed his responses to take the form of a connected narrative description of the images. Wundt required each response to be a *single* word which not only made classification of responses easier to handle, but also the time relations involved to be more susceptible to precise measurement. More exact instruments of measurement such as the lip key and the chronoscope, which measures time in thousandths of seconds, were used. The major categories of association derived by Wundt's students were two in number, "inner" and "outer." Inner associations are those showing intrinsic connections between the words, as in lion-animal, spear-shield, cow-milk, and white-black. Outer associations are those in which there are other purely extrinsic or "accidental" associations, as in curve-accident, or book-concept, or in speech-habit associations, such as fur-fly, or crash-helmet. Cattell was chiefly responsible for discovering the importance of control in association. Instruction to give reactions which bore a definite relation to the stimulus word—an opposite, or a subordinate, or the like—made for quicker reactions than did free association in which there was freedom to choose any word that one wished. Thus giving the response "dark" to the stimulus word "light" when one had been told in advance to give the opposite of the stimulus word resulted in a more rapid reaction than when no control on the associations to be given was exercised. It would appear that when there are many possible responses more or less equally associated with the stimulus word, then there is a process of interference which delays the reaction. An everyday example is the interference met by one who speaks more than one foreign language in arriving at the correct word, especially if the languages themselves are similar, as in Spanish and French. Emil Kraepelin,[24] the great psychiatrist who had studied under Wundt, extended the experimental use of association to problems in pscyhopathology. He found that under experimentally induced fatigue, alcoholic intoxication, and similar states there is an increase in super- ficial, extrinsic, or "outer" associations dependent upon habit, an increase at the expense of "inner" associations which depend upon meaning. The former resemble the associations of some psychotic patients, particularly the manics.

It becomes apparent from the survey of the research from his laboratory that Wundt did not occupy himself with developing new kinds of experiments; the methods he used are already generally familiar to the reader from the account of psychology *before* Wundt. Studies of the psychology and physiology of the senses owe much to the work which went before, particularly to Helmholtz. Reaction time studies again owe something, not only to Helmholtz, but also to Donders, while the association study can be attributed to Galton. Even the study of feeling, where Wundt was at his most original in a the- oretical fashion, was dependent upon extension of Fechner's method of impression to that of paired comparisons and in studies of expression to the utilization of already existing methods of study of pulse, breathing, and the like. Even for attention there had been antecedent studies, although no occa- sion to discuss them had arisen. Wundt wished further to reduce to quantita- tive terms the research areas already extant. His view of the scope of experi- mental psychology consequently was a narrow one, practically confined to the five topics into which the research from his laboratory was classified.

Wundt began sponsoring doctoral dissertations as early as 1875.[25] By 1919 the total had reached an impressive 186 of which 70 were on philosophical topics and 116 on psychological problems. Not all of the men whom he sponsored were destined to become leading psychologists. Struck by the number of unfamiliar names, one psychologist[26] tried to trace them down and the astonishing number of 86 could not be found. A not inconsiderable number of the students were apparently content, after receiving the precious title of "*Herr Doktor,*" to sink back into the oblivion of the *gymnasium.*

His students came to him from all over Europe and from the United States. Many were American. The first of these was G. Stanley Hall, fresh from his studies at Harvard. This roving ambassador of American psychology-to-be "dropped in" for a time in the first year of the existence of the new laboratory and studied with Wundt. Although ambivalent as he was toward Wundt, he is careful to state that most of his time was spent with Ludwig, the physiologist.[27] But his story is best told in a later chapter. James McKeen Cattell, Wundt's first *bona fide* American student, studied at Leipzig on two occasions. It was on his second sojourn in 1885 that Cattell made his pronouncement to Herr Professor that he needed an assistant and that he, Cattell, was that assistant. He, too, will be considered later. Among other American students of Wundt's were Edward W. Scripture, later director of the Yale Psychological Laboratory and a student of hearing; Edward A. Pace, for many years head of the Department of Psychology at Catholic University and the leading voice in interpreting the "new psychology" to Catholics; Lightner Witmer, the founder of the first psychological clinic at the University of Pennsylvania, and Charles H. Judd, the pioneer educational psychologist at the University of Chicago. Even this short list shows something of the breadth of activity that these Americans managed to show on their return to the United States after the severely rigorous "pure" training they received. Born in England where there was no suitable post for an experimental psychologist such as he, Edward Bradford Titchener, another of Wundt's students, came to America to direct the psychological work at Cornell University. Among this group he was the most unswervingly faithful to the program of his teacher. The best known continental psychologists who worked in the Leipzig Laboratory, besides Külpe, already mentioned, were Hugo Münsterberg, Alfred Lehmann, Ernst Meumann, Theodore Lipps, and Felix Krueger.

According to Titchener,[28] Wundt was a quiet, unassuming, pleasant person whose life followed a totally regulated pattern. He worked on his current book or article in the morning, then had a consultation hour. In the afternoon he paid a formal visit to the laboratory, following this with a walk during which he cast his lecture into rough form, then the delivery of the lecture without notes, and a second informal return to the laboratory. He was a very popular lecturer, apparently simplifying his material somewhat to suit his audience. As Hall[29] puts it, Wundt's style of writing is as lusterless as lead— but as solid. To perhaps a surprising extent, concerts and interests in current affairs occupied many of his evenings. He was a man of simple tastes, who avoided public functions and virtually never travelled.

It is not surprising that from this background would emerge the serious hard-working, hard-driving writer of so many books in so many editions that no single person would be so humorless as to read every work in every edition. If he did try to do so, what would he face? Assuming the figures which had been calculated by Boring[30] with tongue in cheek as to his productivity of 53,735 pages (averaging out to 2.2 pages per day for every day from 1853 to 1920) as a base, the consumer-reader, reading at the rate of sixty pages per day, would need nearly two-and-a-half years to go through the entire output.

In 1902, only twenty-eight years after the preface to the first edition of the *Principles* in which he had expressed his intent of presenting a new science, he could say in the fifth edition that the material now was pouring in from all sides.[31] No longer was there any doubt as to the legitimacy of his endeavors. Instead, divergent trends within the field itself were becoming a cause of concern to him. European psychology was beginning to have centers of influence other than Wundt and Leipzig. The climate of the times was producing other psychologists independent of Wundt who had drawn on their common cultural heritage and arrived at an experimental psychology by the end of the century. Some of them will be considered in the next chapter. At the moment concern is with Wundt's reaction to work which deviated from his own.

He was unalterably opposed to the application of psychology.[32] When Meumann, a gifted pupil, turned to educational psychology, Wundt treated it as if this were desertion in the face of the enemy. Kraepelin, another student who applied psychology to psychiatry and was advised by Wundt to leave psychology for psychiatry,[33] came off somewhat better. Work outside of that of his own students came in for even more severe criticism. He was especially critical of the work of the so-called Würzburg School. After securing the immediate response to stimulation, the workers at Würzburg went on to question their subjects about all that went on in their minds. Wundt considered this nothing more than a blatant violation of the rules of introspection.

Despite the admission that child (and animal) psychology were supplementary branches[34] of the field, he rejected categorically the beginning of child psychology in the work of Preyer and Baldwin. Their work was not psychology since the conditions of study could not be controlled adequately.[35] Lest this last stricture cause raised eyebrows, it should be emphasized this evaluation occurs about the turn of the century and concerned the work of the men just mentioned. There is no indication, however, that he changed his view in later years. In his laboratory, no work with animals was conducted.

He was also very critical of French psychology, claiming that the work done in that country was reduced to studies of suggestion and hypnotism.[36] Somewhat petulantly he argued that one cannot give the name, "experimental psychology" to each and every operation that brings about a change in consciousness. Those studies lack exact introspection, so they are not true psychological experiments.

The idea of a social psychology was part of the *Zeitgeist*.[37] Steinthal and Lazarus had published the first issue of their journal devoted to the topic in 1859–1860. At first social psychology was seen by Wundt as only an auxiliary science. It was not until 1893 that he was convinced that social psychology deserved to be considered a coordinate branch along with experimental psychology. Experiment is not feasible when more complex problems than those of perception and memory are considered. Beyond this point, experiment fails us and we must have recourse to folk psychology. In making this division of labor, Wundt was also saying that the higher mental processes, incapable of direct experimental attack, should, perforce, be studied through the chief products of common mental life, that is to say, studied through language, myth, and custom.[38] Language, for example, he held to be the major key to understanding thought. In order to consider the problems of the higher mental processes, he began writing the *Völkerpsychologie*[39] (*Folk Psychology*) the first volume appearing in 1900 with nine more volumes between then and 1920.

Folk psychology was conceived to be the investigation of the various, still existing stages of mental development in mankind.[40] In this sense it can and has been called "genetic" psychology. To Wundt, mankind shows development through a series of successive levels with primitive man as the lowest grade of culture, moving on to the totemic age, thence to the age of heroes and gods, and, finally, the age in which we are now living, that of the advance toward humanity. Folk psychology is differentiated from ethnology by Wundt because the latter is concerned primarily with the external cultures and only in a very incidental fashion with the psychological characteristics that are at the core of folk psychology.

As if according to plan, Wundt wrote his psychological reminiscences, *Erlebtes und Erkanntes*[41] in 1920. Shortly afterward, he died near Leipzig on August 31, two weeks after his eighty-eighth birthday.

SOME SYSTEMATIC VIEWS

Wundt's claim to greatness rests much more upon what has been said of him earlier than it does upon his systematic views of psychology. His system amounted primarily to a classificatory scheme, and, as Boring[42] observes, this itself was not capable of direct or indirect experimental proof or disproof. Wundt was constantly revising his position on various issues from one edition of his books to the next as new evidence appeared. It would be impossible to do justice to these changes in a short space, so only his mature theoretical guide lines, as established in the fifth edition of the *Principles*, published in 1902,[43] and in the second edition of his *Introduction*,[44] published in German in 1911 and in English in 1912, will be examined unless otherwise specified. The effort to offer a rather tightly compressed account of his schema for psychology is rendered easier by his dependence upon already familiar formulations.

To Wundt, psychology is the science that investigates the facts of consciousness. Mind is a process, and yet it has elements, a somewhat confusing ambiguous view of the matter. Consciousness supplies us the total of its immediate experience. The more specific immediate experiences involved, to name only the most important, are sensations, feelings, ideas, volitions and apperceptions. None of these is given in an uncompounded state; they must be abstracted from the compound by introspective analysis. In fact, all of our experiences are complex and must be analysed introspectively.

The elements of the mind, or the basic states of consciousness, are sensations and feelings. When abstracted by introspection, pure sensations are found to possess only intensity and quality and are without spatial or temporal aspects. Sensations are objective in the sense that they have reference to "external" things. Experiences directly aroused by external stimuli often were referred to by earlier systematists as sensations while those dependent upon internal conditions were called ideas. Wundt held this to be an error. The sources for touch and organic sensations of our body are just as much part of our outer world as are stimulation from external objects. Hence, these sensations, too, were "external."

Feelings that accompany sensations are the subjective complements referring to states of consciousness itself. Sensations and feelings are simultaneous aspects of immediate experience. Sometimes the aspect of feeling is apparently negligible, but it is always present. If intensity be increased, it becomes apparent in, say, a light increased in intensity to the point it becomes dazzling. Wundt, nevertheless, considered feeling an experience that was distinct from that other conscious element, sensation.

Feelings cannot be described in terms of pleasantness–unpleasantness alone, as Wundt had held earlier. Two additional dimensions—tension-relaxation and excitement-depression—must also be used to account for the range of the experiences of feeling. Wundt had found that a given feeling experience shows three dimensions but in different combinations, say pleasant, tense, and excited in one case or unpleasant, relaxed, and depressed in another. Feeling experience is not a matter of simultaneity alone. The dimensions in the experience change through time: tickling at first might move along the dimension of pleasantness; but then tension and excitement would become apparent, and unpleasantness would come to predominate over pleasantness.

This tri-dimensional theory of feeling, as it was called, stimulated a tremendous amount of research both in his own and rival laboratories, but the theory was not borne out by post-Wundtian research. However, the results of these studies were found to be applicable in other situations. It is in this way that psychology, having become an experimental science, advances. A theory may stand or fall; the experiments persist, either interpreted as isolated facts or worked into a modified or different system when they are congruent with it.

When sensation and feeling are combined, they form ideas and perceptions. To Wundt, the term, "idea," included within its scope such "complexes" as both "memory images" and "perceptions."[45] Ideas, including both sensations and feelings in composite, are representative of objects either in perception or in memory.

Wundt, chronologically following Mill, made use of association. However, it was but one of the principles of combination.[46] He would prefer to limit it to successive association, such as learning, since he considered simultaneous compounds to be so much more tightly knit as to require a different principle of combination. This was fusion, such as that which occurs in tones in the musical chord or in illusions.

Consciousness shows various degrees of apperception, of contexts, and of connections—the unification of the conscious contents. Children may run together words in something they recite without understanding what it is they are saying. Adults may parrot a difficult concept but not understand what is meant by what they are saying. To bring about unification requires apperception, a combination of a complex into a unity. This doctrine of apperception is already familiar, but Wundt stressed its cognitive aspects more than did his predecessors. To define it more fully, clearness of comprehension of conscious content, occurring by combining of sensory experiences with pre-existing ideas and accompanied by feelings, gives apperception. Feeling enters into the process and the particular quality of the experience of the feeling of a compound is dependent upon apperception. Easy, smooth flowing reactions give rise to pleasure, conflictual ones to pain.

Wundt made a distinction between the whole range of consciousness and the so-called fixation point of apperception. Only processes in the fixation point of apperception are apperceived. This does not mean that apperception cannot range over the complex of ideas, referred to as the apperceptive mass, but at a given moment the matter in the fixation of apperception is a selection from this mass. When apperceptions refer to any given content, Wundt says they are customarily called "states of attention."[47] Wundt preferred to discuss the phenomena in terms of apperception, possibly to bring out its active character in contradistinction to states of attention as a more passive process, but knew, of course, that others could and did discuss this problem in terms of attention, a rather more familiar way of handling the issue.

Combinations of feelings along with ideational processes give the emotions. In some emotions, such as joy and delight, pleasure predominates; in others, such as anger and fear, displeasure is the stronger.

Closely related to the emotions are the volitional processes. To Wundt, volitions, instead of being ideational, are primarily affective. The feelings were the "determining factors" of volition. Sometimes feelings are not so strong as to produce volition, but volition is not operative unless they are present. Volition culminates in an action as when the angry person strikes the object of his anger. Without the striking it would have been an emotion alone.

In dealing with volition Wundt was considering action as differentiated from reception. The distinction between sensory and motor nerves arising from the work of the physiologists carried over into Wundt's psychology at this point. Sensations are the psychological phenomena associated with the former, movements, called reflexes, are the psychological phenomena associated with the latter. There was a natural coherence between a sensation and a movement which was modified through experience.

That the mind was reducible to elements and the fashion in which its elements cohere is obviously a heritage from the empiricist-associationist tradition. But Wundt went beyond this level; the experiences we have are more than the sum of their parts—there is a creative synthesis of immediate experience (the principle of mental chemistry in Thomas Brown). Once the systematic analysis into elements had been accomplished, their manner of synthesis could be carried-out. It was as if the elements once accounted for went a long way toward explaining the total reality. There was still something left over, a fact which Wundt recognized but did not work out fully. Seeing a landscape did *not* add up to thirteen specified visual sensations of variant hues and the accompanying feelings of mild excitement, high pleasure, and low tension, meaningfully perceived. That which remained, however, did not interest him very much. Although synthesis, as differentiated from analysis, was relatively neglected by Wundt, that he did make it part of his formal system and thereby called attention to it, was to have later important repercussions.

OVERVIEW

Wundt was the first modern psychologist—he conceived of experimental psychology as a science. He founded the first laboratory, and he edited the first journal. In addition to these pioneering efforts, Wundt was the great synthesizer of research findings, both of the work that preceded him and of that carried on by his students. Wundt's *forte* was not luminous ideas lighting upon the dark corners or giving us a new dazzling perspective on the old picture. Rather, he worked over a thousand details, cleaning here, repairing there, filling a crack here, so that psychology leaving his hands was an improved, more coherent picture, but still a familiar one.

The areas of investigation worked out by Wundt—sensation and perception, reaction, attention, feeling, association—were such as to become firmly fixed as the very chapters in the textbooks that were to come, making this work a not inconsiderable portion of psychology. And yet there were other areas of psychology where his treatment was either nonexistent or, at best, woefully inadequate. The problem areas of learning (as differentiated from association), motivation, emotion, intelligence, thought, and personality were to be systematically brought within psychology by men who had other points of view.

Whatever one may think of the narrowness of Wundt's conception of psychology, it must be admitted that the course he chose to follow had the effect of solidifying an independent field of psychology. If he had struck out on uncharted paths it is quite conceivable that psychology as a separate discipline would not have been forthcoming until later. It does not detract from his achievement to add that much of the history of psychology following Wundt consisted of rebelling against the limitations he had placed upon the field. In fact, forward movement is most sure when it has something to push against.

REFERENCES [*]

1. W. WUNDT, *Principles of Physiological Psychology*. (5th German ed.) (Vol. 1, translated by E. B. Titchener) New York: Macmillan, 1904, Author's Preface to First Edition. (1874)

2. W. WUNDT, *Lectures on Human and Animal Psychology*. (2nd German ed.) (Translated by J. E. Creighton & E. B. Titchener) New York: Macmillan, 1894, pp. 440–450. (1892); W. Wundt, *An Introduction to Psychology*. (2nd

[*] See page 16 for description of reference style.

ed.) (Translated by R. Pintner) New York: Macmillan, 1912, Chap. 5. (1911); W. Wundt, *Grundriss der Psychologie.* Leipzig: Engelmann, 1896, Section 1, para. 2 (Herrnstein & Boring Excerpt No. 109)

3. *Introduction, op. cit.*

4. G. MURPHY, *Historical Introduction to Modern Psychology.* (rev. ed.) New York: Harcourt Brace, 1949, pp. 155–156.

5. *Principles,* Introd.

6. W. WUNDT, *Kleine Schriften,* (Band 2.) Leipzig: Engelmann, 1911.

7. *Principles,* Introd.

8. E. B. TITCHENER, Wilhelm Wundt, *Amer. J. Psychol.,* 1921, 32, 161–178.

9. *Principles,* Introd.

10. *Ibid.*

11. *Ibid.*

12. W. WUNDT, *Outlines of Psychology.* (7th German ed.) (Translated by C. H. Judd) Leipzig: Engelmann, 1907. (1896)

13. Some of the facts of his life and research as reported here were derived from Titchener, *op. cit.,* while other sources, unless otherwise specified, are: G. S. Hall, *Founders of Modern Psychology,* (New York: Appleton, 1912) Chap. 10, and Wundt's own psychological reminiscences, *Erlebtes und Erkanntes* (Stuttgart: Kröner, 1920).

14. W. WUNDT, *Die Lehre von der Muskelbewegung.* Braunschweig: Vierweg, 1858.

15. W. WUNDT, *Beiträge zur Theorie der Sinneswahrnehmung.* Leipzig: Winter, 1862.

16. W. WUNDT, *Grundzüge der physiologischen Psychologie.* Leipzig: Engelmann, 1873–1874.

17. R. S. HARPER, The First Psychological Laboratory, *Isis.* 1950, 41, 158–161.

18. E. G. BORING, On the Subjectivity of Important Historical Dates: Leipzig, 1879, *J. Hist. Behav. Sci.,* 1965, 1, 5–9.

19. E. G. BORING, *A History of Experimental Psychology.* (2nd ed.) New York: Appleton-Century-Crofts, 1950, pp. 340–344.

20. *Ibid.,* 342.

21. O. KÜLPE, *Outlines of Psychology,* (Translated by E. B. Titchener) New York: Macmillan, 1909.

22. L. LANGE, Neue Experimente über den Vorgang der einfachen Reaktion auf Sinneseindrücke, *Phil. Stud.,* 1888, 4, 479–510.

23. J. M. CATTELL, The Time it Takes to See and Name Objects, *Mind,* 1886, 11, 63–65. [Reprinted W. Dennis, (ed.), *Readings in the History of Psychology.* New York: Appleton-Century-Crofts, 1948, pp. 326–328].

24. E. KRAEPELIN, Der psychologische Versuch in der Psychiatrie, *Psychol. Arb.,* Leipzig, 1895, 1, 1–91.

25. M. A. TINKER, Wundt's Doctorate Students and Their Theses (1875–1920), *Amer. J. Psychol.*, 1932, 44, 630–637.

26. S. W. FERNBERGER, Wundt's Doctorate Students, *Psychol. Bull.*, 1933, 30, 80–83.

27. HALL, *op. cit.*

28. TITCHENER, *op. cit.*

29. HALL, *op. cit.*

30. BORING, *History, op. cit.*, p. 345.

31. *Principles.*

32. W. WUNDT, Ueber rein und angewandte Psychologie, *Psychol. Stud.*, 1910, 5, 1–47.

33. HALL, *op. cit.*

34. *Principles.*

35. H. EBER, Zur Kritik der Kinderpsychologie, mit Rucksicht auf nuere Arbeiten, *Phil. Stud.* 1896, 11, 586–588.

36. *Principles.*

37. TITCHENER, *op. cit.*

38. *Ibid.*

39. W. WUNDT, *Volkerpsychologie.* (10 vols.) Leipzig: Engelmann, 1900–1920.

40. W. WUNDT, *Elements of Folk Psychology: Outlines of a Psychological History of the Development of Mankind.* London: Allen, 1916, pp. 4ff. (1912)

41. *Erlebtes.*

42. BORING, *History, op. cit.*, p. 328.

43. *Principles.*

44. *Introduction.*

45. *Ibid.*, p. 45.

46. W. WUNDT, *Outlines of Psychology.* (Translated by C. H. Judd) New York: Macmillan, 1897. (1896) (Herrnstein & Boring Excerpt No. 76)

47. *Principles.* p. 316.

CHAPTER 13

BRENTANO AND EBBINGHAUS:

WUNDT'S CONTEMPORARIES AND SUCCESSORS

D ESPITE the dominance that Wilhelm Wundt exercised upon German psychology, there were some psychologists outside of his orbit. Of Wundt's contemporaries and successors there are four who merit special attention: Franz Brentano, who advanced a view that psychology is properly concerned with acts rather than contents; Hermann Ebbinghaus, who became the first psychologist systematically to study memory and learning; G. E. Müller, who carefully followed up and expanded the work of his predecessors on psychophysics, color vision, and memory; and Oswald Külpe, Wundt's erstwhile assistant, who became the leader of the group of psychologists that came to be called the "Würzburg School," the school that attempted to broaden the use of introspection to include the study of the higher mental processes.

FRANZ BRENTANO

In 1874, the year that saw the complete publication of the crucial first edition of Wundt's *Grundzüge*, another significant but markedly different book appeared. This was the *Psychology from an Empirical Standpoint*, written by the Catholic priest, Franz Brentano. While Wundt had drawn his inspiration from practically contemporaneous work, Brentano reached back far into the past to the work of Aristotle, from him to Aquinas, and thence to Locke and to Mill. An account of Brentano's life will help to understand his book's significance.

Life of Brentano[1]

A nephew of the German Romantic poet, Clemens Brentano, Franz was born in Marienburg on the Rhine in 1838. When he was very young, his family moved to Bavaria. He lost his father early, and his mother, a devout Catholic, encouraged his early inclination toward a vocation in the clerical life. He first studied at Berlin where he was thoroughly trained by F. A. Trendelenburg in the works of Aristotle. This training was decisive in all that he did afterward, for his psychological and philosophical thinking bore the impress of Aristotle. In 1856 he moved on to Munich where he worked under Ignatius Dollinger, the famous church historian. He also studied philosophy and theology at Munich and later at Tübingen, where he took his degree in 1862. He then entered the priesthood in 1864. Two years later he became *Dozent* in philosophy at Würzburg. For the next few years he busied himself with lecturing and writing papers on the philosophy of Aristotle and the history of science within the Church.

During the sixties a controversy of considerable moment within the Catholic Church concerned the infallibility of the Pope. Ignatius Dollinger, Brentano's former teacher, was a leader of the group within the Church which opposed the doctrine of papal infallibility. Brentano, too, had strong convictions about this proposed dogma and wrote and published a memoir in its refutation on the basis of which he became something of a leader among the dissident clerics. Then, in 1870 the Vatican Council accepted papal infallibility, making it dogma. Brentano was now faced with that age-old decision, to acquiesce or to become a heretic. In his preface to a posthumously published work,[2] he emphasized that this dilemma was but the last of a series of his doubts about being able to reconcile faith and reason. Before the meeting of the Vatican Council took place, he had doubted papal infallibility without other matters beclouding the issue. After the Council's decision, he still found it untenable, and so, in 1873, he resigned his professorship to which he had been appointed as a priest. He thereafter put off clerical duties and garb. Unlike many of the other priests who left the Church at this time, he did not join another church, such as the so-called "Old Catholic Church," which was sponsored by Dollinger. Nor did Protestantism appeal to him. He remained to his death a devout Christian of simple faith, but without church affiliation.[3]

During the period that followed, without either university or clerical duties to interfere, he produced the book, *Psychology from an Empirical Standpoint.*[4] It was planned as the first of two volumes, the second of which was never completed. In 1874 he was appointed, as a layman, Professor at the University of Vienna, a post he held until 1880.

It was in that year a second major crisis arose. He wished to marry a Catholic, which was impossible for a former priest under Austrian law. He once again resigned his professorship, took citizenship in Saxony, and married. He then immediately returned to the University of Vienna, not as a professor, but as a lecturer.

Over these years his lectures were very popular. The hall was always crowded, and informal smaller discussions were usual; his students often followed him home.[5] Among his students, first at Würzburg and then at Vienna, were such diverse persons as Carl Stumpf, the assiduous student of the psychology of sound; Edmund Husserl, the philosopher of phenomonology; Christian von Ehrenfels, the originator of the concept of form quality and founder of the Austrian school of the philosophy of values; Thomas Masaryk, the founder of the Czechoslovakian Republic; and Sigmund Freud, the originator of psychoanalysis. The influence of Brentano upon Freud is still a moot question. He may have been more influenced by Brentano than is generally recognized.[6]

Brentano's students testified to their devotion to him; Stumpf and Husserl were especially glowing in this respect.[7] It is generally agreed that Brentano expressed himself most completely orally rather than in his relatively few publications, and that he is to be judged more through the contributions of his students than his own efforts. He, himself, apparently believed his contribution was more through oral exchange than through the written word.

In 1894 his wife died, and his own health became poor. An eye disorder threatened his sight. In that year he resigned for the last time, never to hold an academic post again. After his resignation he devoted the remainder of his life to study, occasional writing, and informal conversational teaching among his friends and admirers. In 1895–6 he settled in Florence.

During the years in Vienna he had published hardly any psychological works. Shortly before he left, he did write some papers on visual illusions. In 1907 a small but significant book on sense psychology[8] appeared, and in 1911 he published *Von der Klassifikation der psychischen Phänomene,*[9] his nearest approximation to the missing second volume of the *Psychologie* of thirty-seven years before. After Italy entered the war, Brentano, a pacifist, moved to Zürich, where he died in 1917.

Act Psychology

For Brentano there was no essential difference between philosophy and psychology.[10] In this regard he was returning to the work of Locke where psychology was basic to philosophy. Psychology became the means of rescuing philosophy from the morass into which it had slumped under Kant, whom he considered a mystic to be classed with Plotinus. John Stuart Mill also influenced his thinking in regard to psychology as basic to other fields.

Even the title of his book is firmly rooted in the past because the monopoly on "empirical" that the associationist had established for the meaning of derivation from sense experience was minimized, and a return to the Greek meaning was made. By empirical, Brentano intended to emphasize activity. As Brett put it, ". . . it was 'empirical' in the sense that it was based on the claim that it reached a pure experience and analysed it." [11]

Titchener[12] considered that Brentano's use of "empirical" was meant to draw attention to the fact that he used a consistent and reasoned account of mind, which is essentially argumentative in nature, rather than being descriptive, which Titchener considered Wundt's psychology (and his own) to be. Carmichael,[13] on analyzing this argument, reached the conclusion that a more apt term to describe Brentano's approach would be to call it, "rational." It would be easy to agree with this position, since Brentano's approach was essentially logical. He presented arguments and offered proofs. Observation rather than experiment was his primary tool. He did not reject experiment, as such, although in discussing experiments where he disagreed with the results, he tended to try to destroy them by argument, not by carrying out or suggesting research. In his studies of illusions, it was characteristic that his method of exposition was to suggest to the reader that he, too, see for himself. He would reproduce the illusions, and on this test by the reader he was content to rest his case.[14] His writing also gave the impression that, once developed, his system was permanently fixed.[15]

As a first approximation, before turning directly to the way Brentano stated his system of psychology, let us try to relate his thinking to Aristotle. It may be remembered that Aristotle (see page 56) had taught that sensation received the form of object, as distinguished from nutrition which took in the material itself from the object. We eat the nutritive object, the fig; we sense its form without assimilating the matter. In sensing there is assimilation of form, not merely passively but actively in that sensing actualizes the quality of the object. When we pass beyond sensing to knowing (see page 64)—

from color or magnitude to asking *what* is color or magnitude—these universals are actualized by knowing, and knowing as actualized is identical with the form.

Brentano was moved by a similar spirit; he wished to find a way of relating the person, the experiencer, to the environment. He insisted that a distinction must be made between the experience as structure and the experience as a way of acting.[16] The quality "blue" and the sensing of blue and different. This latter process is the true subject matter of psychology. Going back to Aristotle for something similar to his psychology, it might even be said that psychology is concerned with the experiences the mind carries out when it actualizes blue. The blueness, as such, is merely passive, something akin to the unmoved mover of Aristotle. Looking at blue is a way of experientially doing. Without going into further details or tracing the development through the thinking of Aquinas, it may be noted that it was in the spirit of these and other considerations that Brentano derived a psychology of the act. This is to say that he stressed activity of the mind at the expense of the content of the mind. Psychology is concerned with the act, not the content.

This does not mean that content disappears, nor does it mean that the content with which it deals is always "real." We refer our ideating to objects whether they do or do not exist. We may ideate blue of the sky or the skin sheen of the unicorn even though in the two cases their epistemological status is different. Nevertheless, they may be the objects in our thinking. Nor is the content of a psychical phenomenon always physical; it may be another psychical act. The act has become the content or object of another act.

On seeing a color, the color, itself, is not mental; it is the act of seeing which is mental. The color itself belongs to physics. Psychical phenomena *relate* to content, but they are not that content. Nevertheless, to see, some thing must be seen. It "inexists" in the seeing. Act psychology constitutes an intentionalism, since mind is represented as comprising mental acts which by intention are directed upon some object. Seeing, hearing, and so on are mental acts which must have some object like blue which they "intend." In Brentano's terminology seeing "intends" the blue which "inexists" within the act of seeing, being the "immanent" object of the seeing. "I see blue," is the act of the mental datum, and the blue is this commonest object of the act.

We can define psychical phenomena, says Brentano, by saying that they are phenomena which intentionally contain an object in themselves.[17] Mind points to something outside itself, called by Brentano, "intentionality." When we see something, two things take place—first comes the *act* of seeing, and then comes the seen object or content of seeing. The objects are not part of the act. The object intentionally inexists with the act (not actually existing, hence "inexisting," but present by implication). Mental acts refer to something outside themselves. An act has an object which it intends or is directed upon.

The source of all psychological experience is inner perception. Each of us has an inner perception which supplies the psychological phenomena. Calling them psychic phenomena or subsuming them under soul makes no difference. If we do, the soul *is* its acts. In this connection it can be seen that Brentano is neatly disposing of physiology. Psychology cannot be reduced to physiology, since its field is the act.

Psychic phenomena consisted of acts of three kinds—ideating, judging, and feeling. Quite consistently, Brentano arrived at his classification of function by an examination of the various types of a relationship of a subject to an object.[18] The first and ubiquitous relationship is that of having an idea of an object—real, imaginary, past, present, future, and even negative. Hence, there is *ideating*. But in addition the sheer diversity of kinds of objects ideated make possible an affirmation or denial of the object. Hence, there is *judging*. Moreover, one may take attitudes toward these objects which may be expressed as running the gamut from love (attraction) to hate (repulsion). Hence there is *feeling*. In a larger sense loving-hating is the motivating source of psychic life. In ideating, something is ideated; in judging, something is judged; in feeling, something is felt. Every act refers to an object or content which inexists within it, no matter the kind of act.

Despite the ancient sources of Brentano's system of act psychology, it came as a revolt against established ways of thinking, especially those sponsored by Wundt. As a contemporary of Wundt, Brentano's system gained stature and point as being clearly in opposition to Wundt's psychology of content. Wundt saw mind in terms of static elements. He had admitted apperception to his system, but more or less as a reluctant after-thought and not as an integral and primary conceptual tool. Hence, the lines were drawn for a distinction between a psychology of content and a psychology of act, each to have its devoted followers.

HERMANN EBBINGHAUS[19]

In about 1876 a student of philosophy and psychology, browsing at a book stall in Paris, chanced upon a second-hand copy of Fechner's *Elements*. The mathematical approach to psychological problems that it contained came as a revelation to young Hermann Ebbinghaus. From his reading of this book arose his greatest intellectual feat—a conviction that the strictly scientific measurement that Fechner had carried through with psychophysics could also be applied to the higher mental processes. Wundt's recently published *Princi-*

ples contained his contention of the impossibility of experimentally studying the higher mental processes. Ebbinghaus was probably familiar with this volume.[20] If so, it merely served as a challenge to him, not a deterrent.

Hermann Ebbinghaus had been born in Barman, near Bonn, in 1850, the son of a merchant. He had studied history and philology at Bonn and then had moved, first to Halle and thence to Berlin, in the meantime shifting his interests to philosophy. After serving in the army during the Franco-Prussian War, he returned to Bonn for his doctorate in philosophy, writing his dissertation on Hartmann's philosophy of the unconscious. This was in 1873. Then followed seven years of independent study, first in Berlin, where he followed the then not unusual practice of the philosopher in studying the sciences. After 1875, he spent three years in England and France in private study and tutoring. It was during these years that he chanced to discover Fechner's book.

Without a teacher, a university environment, or a laboratory and, indeed, without any inspiration except the general climate of the times, Ebbinghaus plunged into the study of learning and memory, subjects heretofore untouched by measurement and research. Working alone, he saw clearly the difficulties standing in his way, devised the necessary methods and materials and, using himself as the only subject, carried through the research, which was to eventuate in his monograph, *Über das Gedächtnis*.[21]

He perceived that his self-appointed task required careful preparation and planning. He saw that he could not take over Fechner's psychophysical methods as they stood, because they would be entirely too slow and cumbersome. Rather, he used a method that was in the spirit of Fechner.

Associationists, particularly Brown and Mill, had attached importance to the principle of frequency as a condition of recall. Frequency of repetition of material or number of trials until learning was complete was seen by Ebbinghaus as the essential condition for associations to be formed. He would use the number of repetitions to serve as his measure of learning. Not only was there to be repetition of the same material to the point where it was wholly learned; there must also be repetition of the task, each time with similar but not identical materials, until he could be confident of the accuracy of his findings. In order for variable errors from trial to trial to be cancelled out, Ebbinghaus would use the same procedure again and again, as did Fechner, varying only the particular content to be learned, and then he would find an average measure. In deference to the experiment, he went so far as to regulate his habits, following the same rigorous pattern day after day and learning the materials always at the same time of the day.

He was familiar with the fact that some pieces of poetry or prose can be learned much more easily than others. Associations already formed with such materials facilitate learning. Recognizing that differences due to acquaintance with the material to be learned must be eliminated, Ebbinghaus needed homogeneous, equally unfamiliar material for the many learning sessions that he was planning. Thus, although he used poetry and prose to some extent, the majority of his studies were carried out with new materials of his own invention, the nonsense syllables. Two consonants with a vowel between, as in *nuz*, *lef* and *bun*, formed these syllables. All possible combinations of German consonants and vowels were prepared by him, and each one was put on a separate card. This gave him a reservoir of 2,300 nonsense syllables from which to draw at random to form lists to be learned.

The following specific procedure is representative of what he did. Cards for the twelve syllables on a particular list would be read through by him at a uniform rate of two-fifths of a second (controlled by the ticking of a watch). When the reading of the list was completed, there was a pause of fifteen seconds, which he used for recording the trial. Again and again he would read through the cards until he believed he could repeat them without mistake. At this point he would try to recite them without looking at the cards. If he failed, no matter how few the mistakes, he would record the errors; and then he would read them again. This procedure he continued until he could give the complete list of nonsense syllables from memory without error. Then the list was considered learned. That was the method of "complete mastery," as it came to be called. He now passed on to other lists of syllables. After a given lapse of time, an hour, a day, or a week, whatever his schedule called for, he would return to the originally learned list, and ascertain the number of repetitions now necessary to relearn it again for complete mastery. There would be a saving in the sense that relearning did not take so many readings as originally. This came to be called the "savings method." Thus if sixteen readings were at first necessary to reach the complete mastery of one correct run-through, and relearning the material twenty-four hours later took only eight readings, then the savings was eight-sixteenths or 50 per cent, a measure of what had been remembered for twenty-four hours.

The very first relearning trial also gave him another measure of memory. When the time came to test this first memory of a given list of nonsense syllables, he would find out how many of the syllables he still knew before learning them again. The number still known divided by the total learned was this measure of memory. Suppose twelve syllables were originally learned. At the first relearning trial, say a day later, he remembered four of the nonsense syllables. That meant that four-twelfths or 33 per cent was retained.

From these experiments came the well-known Ebbinghaus curve of forgetting. One of the conditions he studied experimentally was the effect of varying lengths of the time since learning the lists of nonsense syllables. The material turned out to be forgotten very rapidly in the first few hours and then more and more slowly thereafter. When the results were plotted on a chart, they formed a curve that went down very sharply at first, then gradually leveled off. If the material was "overlearned" (that is to say, if Ebbinghaus went beyond bare learning by repeating the material to the point of several correct series in the original learning, instead of one) the material was forgotten more slowly. Under these circumstances the plot of the curve would now show a more gradual drop and even after considerable lapse of time would show more retention of the material than the learning to merely one correct repetition. Later research confirmed these findings.[22] After carefully verifying these and many other findings by repetition, Ebbinghaus finally published his monograph in 1885.

In 1880, while still carrying on his research in memory, he became *Dozent* at Berlin, and a year after his research appeared, in 1886, he was advanced to a rank equivalent to that of assistant professor. During this period he founded the Berlin psychological laboratory, but it was small and not well supported.

Ebbinghaus left the field for others to develop. In 1890, in collaboration with Arthur König, he founded the *Zeitschrift für Psychologie und Physiologie der Sinnesorgane,* a journal that was badly needed to represent psychology outside the sphere of Wundt's *Studien.* It is plausible to believe[23] relative lack of publication was the reason behind his failure to be advanced in academic rank at Berlin to a full professorship. At any rate, in 1894, when Carl Stumpf came from Munich to Berlin as professor, Ebbinghaus moved to a lesser post in the hierarchy of German universities at Breslau where he founded another laboratory.

Here he made his second major contribution, which, although not at the level of eminence of his studies of learning, deserves mention. The school officials of the city of Breslau called upon him to help in solving a problem of fatigue in school children, *i.e.,* to find the time of the continuous five-hour school day at which the child was least efficient. Accordingly, he devised three tests to be given in a few minutes before each class period.[24] The first and second were rapid addition and multiplication and a test of memory for digits. The third, the "completion method," which was original with Ebbinghaus, was destined to have pronounced usefulness in the intelligence tests to come. Ebbinghaus argued that mental ability demands, among other capacities, the ability to combine verbal material into a significant whole. Essentially, the test consists of omitting words (or portions of words) from sentences in a story and asking the subjects to restore the appropriate words or syllables. An example in the spirit of the original ones used is "Big things are heav____ than_____things" with the missing syllable and word to be supplied by the child.

When the students were grouped by scholastic standing into good, average, or poor, the results from the completion test proved markedly superior in discriminating among the groups when compared with the results from the other two tests. Ebbinghaus argued that this measure showed the great importance of a combining function in intelligence. The fatigue problem, the impetus for the study, it might be added, was largely lost sight of, with the question still left open so far as the report went.

Alfred Binet,[25] the pioneer in the development of intelligence tests, acknowledged that the success of the Ebbinghaus Completion Test had encouraged him in his conviction that he should use complex tasks to measure intelligence, rather than simpler ones, such as tapping rate or reaction time, hitherto used with little success.

Ebbinghaus wrote two very successful books. His general text *Die Gründzüge der Psychologie*[26] was published in complete form in 1902, and a shorter sketch, *Abriss der Psychologie*[27] was issued in 1908. They became a tremendous success, in their sprightliness and lucidity of style, resembling the *Psychology* of James. In fact, demands for repeated revisions interfered with their author's other activities.

The first sentence of the *Abriss* was that often quoted, beguiling half truth, "Psychology has a long past, but only a short history."[28] Ebbinghaus was acutely aware that experimental psychology had just begun. He had seen its beginnings in the work of Fechner, Helmholtz, and Wundt, all carried out not more than fifty years before the time at which he wrote and most of it practically contemporaneous with his own work. Present perspective, removed in time from these pioneering days, makes it possible to see that pre-experimental contributions were also necessary and that they, too, formed an essential part of the history of psychology. Experimental psychology, as we know it, had had but a short history, psychology a very, very long one.

In 1905 Ebbinghaus left Breslau for Halle. Generally in good health, he contracted pneumonia and died suddenly in 1909 at fifty-nine years of age.

Ebbinghaus published relatively little, although what he did publish was important. Moreover, he made no systematic contributions. In fact, he cannot be said to have had a system. Nevertheless, he made an important contribution. Before Ebbinghaus, the associationists had speculated on how associations were established. Ebbinghaus started by forming these associations experimentally and then testing their resistance by later recall. At first it might be thought that what he did was but a small contribution compared to all the sweeping claims of his predecessors. In the perspective of modern research, these earlier claims are seen as grandiose, rather than great. True, they took in much more territory than did Ebbinghaus. They might be compared to monarchs who added to a statement of their holdings, "and the lands beyond the seas," without occupying these lands. Ebbinghaus not only occupied the territory, he tilled the soil. Finding a way to do research on memory, important and highly original though it may be, is not his major claim to be mentioned in a history of the great psychologists. Rather, it is his determination to control factors so as to eliminate sources of error and to quantify his results as precisely as possible. He did such careful work in his studies of memory that they are quoted to this very day in contemporary textbooks side by side with later studies, not as of historical interest, but as valid and accurate research findings.

GEORGE ELIAS MÜLLER

George Elias Müller (1850–1934), a student of Herman Lotze, was a physiologist and philosopher with psychological interests. That Müller was not a student of Wundt's meant that, free of immediate proximity to this overpowering figure, he was able to develop an independent program. In a sense he was a rival of Wundt. Müller became Professor at Göttingen in 1881, succeeding Lotze, and held that post for forty years until 1921. Over the years he attracted a number of students, the more prominent of which were Oswald Külpe, E. R. Jaensch, David Katz, and Edgar Rubin.

Müller undertook extensive criticism and extension of Fechner's work in psychophysics in his *Zur Grundlegung der Psychophysik*[29] published in 1878 and in *Die Gesichtspunkte und die Tatsachen der psycho-physischen Methodik*[30] in 1904. In particular he demonstrated that the fluctuations of the threshold in the same person from day to day are not due to error but are real fluctuations in sensitivity itself. He laid down what he considered to be the fundamental psychophysical axioms of the relations between perception and neural excitation as expressed in a parallelistic fashion. (See page 262.) While he also spent many years on problems of color, it is research in learning for which he is most noteworthy.

He was among the first psychologists to work in the research field of learning and memory opened up by Ebbinghaus. He carefully verified and extended Ebbinghaus' findings, which had taken the objective approach exclusively.[31] He had, for example, found how many trials it took for him to learn or relearn, but he had not recorded introspections about his mental processes while the learning was going on. Müller doubted that Ebbinghaus' account of learning, which made it appear to be a mechanical and automatic process, was correct as it stood. Accordingly, he added introspective report while applying the methods of Ebbinghaus and found that, instead of their learning mechanically, the subjects are very active, using groupings and rhythms, finding meanings even in nonsense materials, and, in general, consciously organizing the material. He believed that this activity not only shows that learning is not mechanical, but also that it requires the combination of introspective and objective methods. He concluded that association by contiguity is not enough to account for learning. An active search for relations is also taking place. A "preparatory set" (*Anlage*) influences the memory processes. Müller demonstrated that judgment involves not only the expected images, sensations, and feelings, but also mental events incapable of thus being classified. For example, readiness, hesitation, and doubt seem to be present, a class of mental phenomena usually called "conscious attitudes." These findings anticipated work that followed very shortly from the Würzburg Laboratory under Oswald Külpe.

Müller also worked through many other learning problems and made methodological improvements and increased the precision of the equipment used in its study. It was he, along with a collaborator, Friedrich Schumann,[32] who introduced the familiar revolving drum for uniform presentation of nonsense syllables used since that time in various adaptations for countless studies of memory and learning. This is a small matter, perhaps, but, since it increases objectivity and precision, is not unworthy of mention.

Oswald Külpe and the Würzburg School[33]

Oswald Külpe (1862–1915) already has been encountered as a student and assistant to Wundt. After studying with C. E. Müller at Göttingen, he had received his degree at Leipzig and had remained on as *Dozent* and assistant in the laboratory.

His book[34] published in 1893 and translated in 1895 as *Outlines of Psychology*,[35] significantly bears the subtitle, *based upon the results of experimental investigation*. He wrote clearly and attractively, but he was still under the shadow of Wundt. Only one aspect of his distinctive views made its appearance. This was his telling criticism of the subtractive procedure on reaction time.

In 1894, Külpe became Professor at Würzburg where by 1896 he had founded a laboratory with the aid of private funds. Its progress was such that in a few years it could be referred to as the outstanding laboratory in Germany after Leipzig. Charming and friendly, Külpe attracted many students and visitors, including several Americans, among them—J. R. Angell of Chicago, R. M. Ogden of Cornell, W. L. Bryan of Indiana, and W. B. Pillsbury of Cornell and Michigan.

Külpe's distinctive work in psychology arose from his conviction, contrary to Wundt's, that the thought processes can be studied experimentally. Most of the Würzburg studies were not themselves performed by Külpe; but he was the professor, with all that this meant in a German university of that day, and frequently he served as a subject in the experiments of his students. There was enough integration for it to be correct to speak of this collective effort as the work of the Würzburg School.

"Systematic experimental introspection," to Külpe and the members of his school, meant performance of some complex task, such as that involved in thinking or remembering or judging, about which they afterward rendered a retrospective report of their experiences during the original operation. It was systematic in the sense that the whole experience was described methodically, time-period by time-period, thus fractionating it. This procedure contrasted vividly with the description of immediate experience demanded by Wundt. To use the Würzburg version of introspection, one must think, memorize, or judge, and then turn around and examine how he thought, memorized, or judged. That to which he was to attend was not specified in advance, as it was with Wundtian introspection, so the subject at Würzburg did not know beforehand exactly what he was to observe.

Closely identified with the Würzburg School is the conception of what came to be called in English, "imageless thought"—the representation of meanings in thinking which did not seem to be carried by specific images. Watt, Bühler, and others, in the course of their controlled introspections supplied many instances of how, while thinking of a definite problem or reaching a conclusion, they did so without their being aware of having any specific mental content of the sort previously identified. Another feature of this work was the emphasis on the influence of the task itself to which the subjects are set.

A capsule description of two characteristic experiments is in order. Marbe,[36] in a study of judgment of weights, found that while sensations and images were present as usual, their presence told nothing about how the subjects made their judgments. The subjects just judged a weight as heavier or as lighter, usually being right, but simply did not know how they did it, in the sense that the sensations and images they reported did not describe the process of how they reached their judgment.

Watt[37] studied association in a variety of ways. For example, his subjects were faced with finding a subordinate or superordinate for the word *bird*. They reacted correctly, but often without being conscious that they intended to. It would seem that the conscious work had been done earlier, not after the stimulus was presented, but before when the instructions were understood. Once understood, it would seem that the subject thereafter gave the response to the stimulus without conscious effort. To account for such findings, Watt emphasized the concept of task (*Aufgabe*). The subjects did not think of the task as, say, of searching for the superordinate of *bird* and arriving at *animal;* they just thought "animal." The conscious phenomena he obtained in the introspection corresponded closely to the volitional variable previously spoken of in connection with Külpe's early work. Although terms similar in nature are used now more or less indiscriminately for any potentiality in consciousness, for Watt, task meant the purpose, or conscious task, that precedes a later unconscious course of events. The conscious task (*Aufgabe*) brings about an unconscious set (*Einstellung*) in the subject.

Watt (and Ach) in research related to the study of association held that the organism had a set, or, to use Ach's term for it, a "determining tendency" to react in the way the given instruction called for. If, in advance of exposure to material, one has decided to subtract, seeing a "6" and a "4," produces the response "2," not "10," which a determining tendency to add would have produced to the same visual stimuli. Once the task has been accepted and the set has been adopted, the actual performance runs off with remarkably little conscious content to be found during it. These determining tendencies, not present consciously during performance, seemed important in volitional activities. The Würzburgers were suggesting that predispositions outside of consciousness act to control consciousness.

This work on thought elements was negative in the sense that the studies stressed their finding of something which lacked sensory content. It was not until the work of Karl Bühler in 1907 and 1908 that a new element in consciousness was announced.[38] His method of conducting introspections was even freer than that of systematic experimental introspection. He used very complicated problems, far removed from those of simple addition or subtraction but such that always they were to be answered first with a "yes" or "no." After answering affirmatively or negatively, the subject gave the fullest possible account of the experiences by which he reached his decision, with questions interjected from time to time by the experimenter. Illustrative are: "Was the theorem of Pythagoras known in the Middle Ages?" "Can we with our thought comprehend the nature of thought?" or, my favorite, "The smaller the woman's foot, the larger the bill for shoes?"[39] The subjects (including Külpe) in their introspections used such terms as "awareness of a consciousness that," but more frequently simply referred to them as "thoughts." Thought was the new element that Bühler claimed must be accepted if his results were to make any sense. He went on to describe three types of thoughts—consciousness of rule, consciousness of relation, and intention. The first type of thinking was used by his subjects most often in solving mathematical, logical, or grammatical problems. The second occurred when several parts of a thought required a relation to be established as consequence or opposition, and the third took place when a problem was seen over-all and an outcome was to be reached.

It must be emphasized that, while opposed to the Wundtian position concerning the sensory nature of certain kinds of conscious experience, Külpe and the others were still seeking to find new elements in thought. They were still analytical in their approach.

Their use of analytical methods did not render their interpretations acceptable to the Wundtian psychologists of content who considered what they were doing as a caricature of psychology. The reports of their introspections, particularly those of Bühler, drew vigorous opposition, especially from Wundt,[40] who offered scathing criticism, calling their procedures "mock" experiments and arguing that what they called experimental introspection was neither experimental nor introspective. Recollection of what Wundt meant by these operations will show the logical rigor of his criticism, even though one may regret he could not permit a broadening of the older meaning to encompass the work of the Würzburg School.

Of course, a distinction such as that between the warring views of the Würzburg School and Wundt is never as clean-cut as enthusiasts would like to believe. Wundt had spoken of apperception, even though he can hardly be said to have stressed it. From the perspective of today, it can be seen that the views of the Würzburgers and Wundt were not incompatible. After all, the conscious attitudes or preparatory sets of G. E. Müller had been demonstrated without creating a furor or outright rejection within the ranks of the psychologists of content. In fact, as a student of Müller as well as Wundt, Külpe had probably been influenced by him. But the temperaments of the critics of the Würzburg School would not permit a reconciliation.

Külpe, for his part, both then and later, showed his high admiration and regard for Wundt. Müller also attacked Külpe's methods and results, as did Titchener, a friend and companion from Külpe's Leipzig days. For both Külpe preserved the highest regard. But the issue had been forced, and a rival school was consequently established.

Külpe's own interpretation of the work from his laboratory is rather hard to specify. He wrote very little on the matter, and his contemplated description of the psychology of the thought processes was never completed.

Külpe's fifteen years at Würzburg are his most important for the history of psychology. It was not that he lost interest later, for at Bonn, where he went next, he founded a laboratory; and, in 1913, when he moved to Munich, he saw to it that the laboratory allocated to his predecessor was suitably equipped. It was rather that his continuing interests in philosophical problems, particularly in esthetics, which in no way did he conceive as antagonistic to his interests in psychological issues, came to the fore. He sought to prove that the actualities of conscious experience required that there be independent objects for them to have any significance. He never completed the statement of his later views. His student Karl Bühler, published posthumously his *Vorlesungen über Psychologie*[41] in 1920. What he had covered in the *Grundriss* in 1893 constituted in this new work the content of psychology; the contribution of the Würzburg School was what he called *function*.

The psychological implications of these views led him to a position much closer to that of Brentano. By now Külpe conceived of psychology as including *both* content and act (although he called the latter, function) and it is to be regretted he did not live long enough to work out fully his own synthesis. To Külpe[42] content and function both are facts of mental life because they can be demonstrated to be different. They are separable in experience: in dreams there is content but little function; in "barely" noticing something there is function with little content. They are independently variable: content changes without function when one perceives objects one after the other; function changes when one object is first perceived, then recognized, and then judged. They possess characteristic differences: contents are analyzable in consciousness, observable in introspection, and relatively stable; functions are not analyzable in consciousness (analysis alters the function), observable in retrospection only, and relatively unstable. They obey different laws; the laws of content are association, fusion, contrast, and a relation to stimulus and sense organ; function includes the effects of the laws of determining tendency. Külpe was actively engaged in this combined psychological and epistemological enterprise on his death in 1915.

The work of the Würzburg School was prophetic of developments of a holistic view as it was to be differentiated from the elementalist view of Wundt. Indeed, the Gestalt psychologists who were to come later owe a debt to Külpe for attempting to deal both with act and content.

The results of the Würzburg School were interpreted as they relate to thought as such, which was their own emphasis. But two other aspects of their thinking are significant today. First, there was the emphasis they gave to volition or motivation as we would call it. Task, set, determining tendency, to use their key words, have a motivational connotation today. Motivation was treated by them as a variable affecting the results of thinking, a topic that is very much a part of the modern scene in psychology. The relatively simple kinds of association of the British and of Wundt were not enough to explain the variations in volition that they found from one experiment to the next. Second, it seemed as if behavior depended not only upon the elements present in the subject's consciousness but also upon the way he adjusted to the experiment, even though he was not aware of their operation in conscious analysis. These directive tendencies were not present directly in consciousness. They were often unconscious in nature. Unconscious determinants of behavior were being demonstrated.

Members of the Würzburg School were working at the same time as Freud, but they did not have his ruthless radicalism to cut through to the bold conclusion that many of the experiences with which they were dealing were unconscious. Instead, they treated these impalpable phenomena with which they were struggling as being a consequence of some vague conscious element. Freud was a greater man than Külpe.

Külpe and the Würzburg School bring to a close the account of German psychology during the second half of the nineteenth century as well as the beginnings of the breakdown of the national boundaries through Wundt's students from the United States. Before considering still later developments, it is necessary to return to England to the time just after the Mills and Bain in the middle of the nineteenth century.

REFERENCES[*]

1. O. Kraus, *Franz Brentano, zur Kenntnis seines Lebens und seiner Lehre*. Munich: Beck, 1919; M. Puglisi, Franz Brentano: a Biographical Sketch, *Amer. J. Psychol.*, 1924, 35, 414–419.

2. F. Brentano, *Die Lehre Jesu und ihre bleibende Bedeutung*. Leipzig: Meiner, 1922.

3. *Ibid.*

4. F. Brentano, *Psychologie vom empirischen Standpunkte*. Leipzig: Meiner, 1874.

5. J. R. Barclay, Franz Brentano and Sigmund Freud, *J. Existentialism*, 1964, 5, 1–36.

6. This fascinating issue has a number of ramifications. Some of the references are J. Barclay, *op. cit.;* P. Merlan, Brentano and Freud, *J. Hist. Ideas*, 1945, 6, 375–377, and *ibid.*, Brentano and Freud—a Sequel., *J. Hist. Ideas*, 1949, 10, 451. John C. Brentano (Professor of Physics Emeritus, Northwestern University) the son of Franz, who has been devoting his retirement years to his father's works, assures me in personal conversation that Freud was relatively uninfluenced by his father and that, so far as his father was concerned, he broke not only with Freud but also with Breuer as a result of the publicity arising from the case of Frl. Anna O. This implies a closer

[*] See page 16 for description of reference style.

relationship between Brentano and Freud than E. Jones (*The Life and Works of Sigmund Freud*, Vol. 1, New York: Basic Books, 1953), dean of the biographers of Freud, would admit.

7. KRAUS, *op. cit.*

8. F. BRENTANO, *Untersuchungen zur Sinnespsychologie.* Leipzig: Duncker & Humblot, 1907.

9. F. BRENTANO, *Von der Klassifikation der psychischen Phänomene.* Leipzig: Duncker & Humblot, 1911.

10. G. S. BRETT, Associationism and "Act" Psychology. In C. Murchison (ed.), *Psychologies of 1930.* Worcester: Clark University Press, 1930, pp. 39–55.

11. *Ibid.*, p. 48.

12. E. B. TITCHENER, *Systematic Psychology: Prolegomena.* New York: Macmillan, 1929.

13. L. CARMICHAEL, What is Empirical Psychology? *Amer. J. Psychol.*, 1926, 37, 521–527.

14. E. G. BORING, *History of Experimental Psychology.* (2nd ed.) New York: Appleton-Century-Crofts, 1950.

15. TITCHENER, *op. cit.*

16. *Psychologie*, Bk. II, Chap. 1, Sec. 9 (Herrnstein & Boring Excerpt No. 112)

17. *Ibid.*, Chap. 1.

18. *Von der Klassifikation.*

19. D. SHAKOW, Hermann Ebbinghaus, *Amer. J. Psychol.*, 1930, 42, 505–518; R. S. Woodworth, Hermann Ebbinghaus, *J. Phil.*, 1909, 6, 253–256.

20. BORING, *op. cit.*

21. H. Ebbinghaus, *Ueber das Gedachtnis.* Leipzig: Duncker & Humblot, 1885. (Herrnstein & Boring Excerpt No. 95)

22. R. S. WOODWORTH, *Experimental Psychology,* New York: Holt, 1938.

23. BORING, *op. cit.*

24. H. EBBINGHAUS, Ueber eine neue Methode zur Prüfung geistiger Fähigkeiten und ihre Anwendung bei Schulkinder, *Zsch. für Psychol.*, 1897, 13, 401–439. (Herrnstein & Boring Excerpt No. 82)

25. A. BINET, Description d'un objet, *Année Psychol.*, 1897, 3, 296–332.

26. H. EBBINGHAUS, *Die Grundzüge der Psychologie.* Leipzig: Veit, 1897–1908.

27. H. EBBINGHAUS, *Abriss der Psychologie.* Leipzig: Veit, 1908.

28. *Ibid.*, p. 1.

29. G. E. MÜLLER, *Zur Grundlegung der Psychophysik.* Berlin: Grüben, 1878.

30. G. E. MÜLLER, *Die Gesichtspunkte und die Tatsachen der psycho-physischen Methodik.* Strassburg: Bergmann, 1903.

31. G. E. MÜLLER, and A. Pilzecker, *Experimentelle Beiträge zur Lehre vom Gedächtniss.* Leipzig: Barth, 1900.

32. G. E. MÜLLER, & F. SCHUMANN, Experimentelle Beiträge sur Untersuchungen en des Gedachtnisses, *Zsch. Psychol.*, 1893, 6, 81–190, 257–339.

33. R. M. OGDEN, Oswald Külpe and the Wurzburg School. *Amer. J. Psychol.*, 1951, 64, 4–19.

34. O. KÜLPE, *Grundiss der Psychologie.* Leipzig: Engelmann, 1893.

35. O. KÜLPE, *Outlines of Psychology: Based Upon the Results of Experimental Investigation.* (Translated by E. B. Titchener) New York: Macmillan, 1895.

36. K. MARBE, *Experimentell-psychologische Untersuchungen über das Urteil, eine Einleitung in die Logik.* Leipzig: Engelmann, 1901.

37. H. J. WATT, Experimentelle Beitrage zur einer Theorie des Denkens, *Arch. ges. Psychol.*, 1905, 4, 289–436.

38. K. BÜHLER, Tatsächen und probleme zu einer Psychologie der Denkvorgänge, *Arch. ges. Psychol.*, 1907, 9, 297–305; 1908, 12, 1–3, 24–92.

39. K. BÜHLER, Quoted in G. Humphrey, *Thinking: an Introduction to its Experimental Psychology.* New York: Wiley, 1951, p. 56.

40. W. WUNDT, Kritisch Nachlese zur Ausfragemethode, *Arch. ges. Psychol.*, 1908, 11, 445–459.

41. O. KÜLPE, *Vorlesungen über Psychologie.* (Posthumously ed. by K. Bühler) Leipzig: Hirzel, 1920.

42. BORING, *op. cit.*, pp. 451–452.

CHAPTER 14

GALTON:

EVOLUTION AND INDIVIDUAL DIFFERENCES

A FAITH in the timelessness of nature was still accepted by a great majority of men, learned and unlearned alike, in the first half of the nineteenth century. There was, however, a substantial minority who had some conception of an evolutionary process. The fundamental idea of evolution, that living things do change with time, was not new, having been a part of the intellectual history of man since Anaximandros, a contemporary of Thales. In the centuries before Darwin, the philosophers and scientists of the Enlightenment, Locke, Hume, and Diderot, for example, had spoken of only small gradations separating plants, animals, and men, as well as of generation and transformation. Philosophers, such as Kant and Hegel, had written of development in a fashion not incompatible with evolution. Lyell had introduced evolution into geological theory; Erasmus Darwin, the grandfather of Charles, had written on evolution, and, in 1809, the very year of Charles Darwin's birth, Lamarck[1] had published a work on his theory that the great variety of animal species was to be explained by the inheritance of acquired characters, such as may be brought about by change in the environment or through the use or disuse of a part of the body. Herbert Spencer, moreover, was championing an evolutionary point of view prior to Darwin's publication in 1859 of *The Origin of Species*. Nevertheless, it was the work of Darwin which created a veritable scientific revolution which demanded an intellectual reorganization in the thinking of mankind. After 1859 no well-informed thinker, not blinded by preconceptions, religious or otherwise, could ignore the fact that for all biological phenomena, a genetic, as well as a cross-sectional view of their nature was imperative.

DARWIN AND EVOLUTION

The theory of evolution advanced by Charles Darwin[2] (1809–1882) is too well known to require more than a reminder of its most salient features. Darwin demonstrated that living matter is in a plastic rather than a fixed, immutable form and that the spontaneous variability which each species demonstrate is inheritible. There is a struggle for survival, and the forms that survive are the ones that have made the successful adaptations to those inexorable difficulties that they have had to face. The exigencies of the struggle for existence under natural conditions accomplish what every animal breeder who practices artificial selection knows—that certain strains are perpetuated by breeding. Only those forms fittest for their particular environment survived this process of natural selection, the rest died out. Man was no exception to this process. He, too, is the result of this struggle.

Darwin believed that the variations that were perpetuated were always slight. Through later research on the mutation of genes, it is now known that the variations are often abrupt and of considerable magnitude. But this later finding does not detract from Darwin's theory concerning the process of evolution. He demonstrated the process and the range of the reasons for it, but not its genetic mechanism.

No summary can give more than a hint of the overwhelming mass of data which Darwin had collected. Much miscellaneous biological information, hitherto unrelated, was organized by Darwin in such a fashion that his theory and conclusions appeared irresistible to those persons who did not find in it anything antagonistic to their deep laid convictions. As Thomas Huxley[3] said of himself, "How extremely stupid not to have thought of that." And he was not alone. There were many who saw in Darwin's evidence a means of organizing and understanding a great mass of otherwise puzzling data.

In relating the Darwinian evolutionary doctrine to religious orthodoxy, fertile sources of controversy appear. Theological disagreement was inevitable, as were arguments from all others who saw man as separated by an impassible gulf from the "brutes." Moreover, there were those who saw in Darwin's work contradictory scientific evidence. The stormy controversy which broke out was one from which Darwin himself held aloof—his temperament was such that speaking sharply to some one made him unable to sleep. He found, however, able champions, the greatest of which was Thomas H. Huxley. The protest and acrimony died hard, stretching from 1860 in the debate of Huxley and Bishop Wilberforce of Oxford to the Scopes trial with the antagonists, William Jennings Bryan and Clarence Darrow in 1925.

Darwin's second major report on evolution, *The Descent of Man*,[4] appeared in 1871. It was written primarily to present the evidence that the conclusions of the *Origin* had applied to man, a position he had held all along, but which had not been understood by some contemporaries. Moreover, in the *Origin* he had not tried to apply his conclusions to a species taken singly. Now he marshalled the evidence for the evolution of man from some lower form, along with evidence about his subsidiary theme of sexual selection.

Darwin made more specific contributions to psychology. He kept a diary of his infant son, which he began in 1840 but did not publish until 1877.[5] Along with similar work by Preyer, this record was one of the sources for the beginnings of modern child psychology.

Darwin also studied emotional expression in animals and man. Sir Charles Bell, the anatomist already familiar because of his differentiation of function in sensory and motor nerves, had held that facial movements used in the expression of emotions are primarily expressive, that is to say, their function is to express emotions.[6] Darwin upheld the alternative theory, that facial movements are originally practical, as when an angry dog bares his teeth in action preparatory to biting.[7] Expressive functions, Darwin believed, may be derived subsequently from practical functions. To present his argument, he developed three principles of emotional expression, and he gave illustrations. The first, the principle of serviceable associated habits, was that many expressive movements in emotion are vestiges of originally practical movements. A sneer was seen as a remnant of a response to a malodorous substance, clenching the fists as a vestige of preparation for combat, and startle as a remainder of a larger flight reaction. The second, the principle of antithesis, was that opposite impulses tend to show opposed movements. When a cat shows affection by arching her back, drawing up on her paws, arching her tail, and pointing her ears, these are all movements the opposite of which she would make when about to attack or defend herself. Antithesis is to be found in laughter, which requires expiration of breath, while sobbing, the opposite, requires inspiration. The third principle has to do with the direct action of the nervous system. There is the overflow into motor channels that we call "trembling." These expressive characteristics were acquired from prior practical functions. They then could be inherited. This assumption, of course, was more in line with Lamarckian inheritance of acquired characters than what is often considered to be Darwinian evolutionary theory. However, he is quite explicit in stating directly that these were originally voluntary movements which turned into reflex actions through continued habits, which are then inherited.

Something should now be said about Darwin's more general and less direct influences upon the field of psychology. Among the more important of these were his emphasis upon drives to action, his making clear the possibility of an animal psychology, and his illustrating the fruitfulness of attention to individual differences.

The study of lower animals was shown by Darwin to demand consideration of their drives to action. Study seemed always to lead to an examination of the causes of their activity. Often even their more complicated activities appeared to be free of the influence of learning. To these activities the term instincts had already been applied. An important chapter of the *Origin* had been devoted to the topic of instincts, in which Darwin compared and contrasted instinct with habit and showed that instincts are not perfect. There was available to Darwin a variety of accounts of the instincts of animals, particularly domesticated animals, for example, the shepherd's dogs' tendency to hunt hares, the brooding of hens, and cell-making of bees. These behaviors can best be understood as inherited. Darwin's evidence showed that, if the animals did not have the proper instincts, they did not survive. Evolutionary theory forced a recognition of the essentiality of understanding the drives to action of both man and beast. The continuance of an instinct approach in psychology was assured.

In effect, Darwin had demonstrated that all animals were related, and that they all faced the common problem of adjustment and survival. In *The Descent of Man,* he emphasized the similarity of reasoning in man to what appeared to be similar processes in the lower animals. More specifically, he attempted to show that many of man's mental capacities had rudimentary prototypes among lower animals. He also appealed to accounts of primitive man, as for example, their susceptability to praise and blame. If the human body evolved from lower animals, does it not also follow that the human mind developed from more primitive minds? If all animals are related, does it not follow that there will be similarities in behavior and mentality among animals? It was on the basis of such questions as these that the comparative viewpoint in psychology came into being. Psychology was made ready to return to the wisdom of Aristotle, to be concerned with all living things, not with man alone. After Darwin, comparative psychology came to be recognized as a branch of psychology.

Darwin found significant and interesting individual differences in physical forms between animal species and, to some extent, within species. This discovery was to lead to the study of individual and racial psychological differences.

Great as was Darwin's work, he was not a great psychologist. Rather, as was the case with Galileo and with Newton before him, his service was to reorganize the scientific view and to stimulate others in other sciences, psychology included. It was, however, Darwin's work which stimulated an interest in these psychological problems. The vehicle for the almost entirely new aspect of psychology, the field of individual differences, was Francis Galton.

FRANCIS GALTON

Francis Galton was the pioneer who brought about a union between psychological methods of measurement and the theory of evolution, a union that came about because Galton's studies and observations initiated considerable interest in the study of individual differences among men.

Life[8]

Francis Galton, a cousin of Charles Darwin, was born near Birmingham in 1822. His large family possessed considerable wealth and had among its members clergymen, physicians, military officers, M.P.'s, and landed gentry. This background afforded Galton connections with a large number of important persons in England at the height of the British Empire. In his autobiography,[9] Galton studs his pages with mention of names either in terms of indices of their progression through life or about their family connections. For instance, he refers to "Sir Joseph (then Mr.) Hooker", to "Henry Fitzmaurice Hallam . . . the younger son of the historian Henry Hallam . . . and brother to Arthur Hallam . . . , the subject of Tennyson's In Memoriam," and even to his wife as the daughter of the "Dean of Peterborough, previously headmaster of Harrow . . . and before his appointment, the Senior Wrangler at Cambridge. . . ." In his day, "the establishment" may have referred to the relation of church and state, but its modern meaning was very much in evidence. It is not denying his great gifts to say that a way of life surrounded him, a way that could lead him to a conviction that eminence runs in families. True, others, before and after, merely accepted this state of affairs, but Galton had the genius to see the obvious.

Following his own and his family's wishes, in 1838 he began as an apprentice to study medicine in Birmingham General Hospital. He rolled pills, made up medicines, attended rounds, and participated in first aid in the accident room.

Boldly curious as he was always to be, he decided to find out for himself the effects of the different medicines. Commencing with those under the letter A in the pharmacopoeia he began taking small doses of each, one after the other. He had reached nearly the end of the letter C when stopped by the effects of croton oil, notorious as an extremely powerful purgative.

After completing a period of experience at this Hospital, he continued some of his medical training at King's College, London. In 1840 Galton changed his plans and enrolled in Trinity College, Cambridge, for the usual university program. Although deficient in the classics, he had managed to keep up in mathematics, the field in which he specialized. He had occasion to wonder at one form of narrowness of the academic horizon of Cambridge of that time—faculty and the students alike showed no interest at all in what he had learned about biology from his medical education. After a severe mental breakdown had interrupted his studies, he took his degree without working for honors.

In 1845–46, he travelled in the Sudan, and in 1850 he explored Damaraland and the Ovampo country in Southwest Africa. On his return he published accounts of his travels. The novelty and the danger of these trips is manifest when we note that the second trip was taken more than twenty years before the meeting of Stanley and Livingston.

In 1854, the Royal Geographical Society awarded him one of their two annual gold medals for exploring the then unknown country of central Southwest Africa. Subsequently, he was elected a Fellow of the Royal Society on the same grounds.

A spirit of adventure seemed to come over him from time to time, and even later in life these moods occurred. He tells in his autobiography that one way he came to know John Tyndall, the physicist, was to go on climbing expeditions with him, where he would give in to Tyndall's claim that it is easy to find difficult (*i.e.*, dangerous) places to climb, even in England.

In 1853 he married. Again he was immersed in a large and distinguished family, since his wife, besides her three sisters, had four brothers, all noted for scholastic or administrative ability. Travelling annually to the continent, visiting at one or another of the houses of his friends, and living in London occupied some of his time. Exploration had become a topic of wide-spread interest, so he devoted his attention to the preparation of a book—*The Art of Travel*, a practical guide for the explorer. He also gave lectures on the art of camp life to soldiers in training for the Crimean War. For several years he tried the life of a country gentlemen, riding to hounds and, in season, shooting in Scotland, meanwhile managing his estate, adding the not too incongruous touch to this particular picture by experimenting with electricity.

He then turned to the serious study of meteorology. The book that summarizes his findings is said[10] to be the first serious attempt to chart the weather on an extensive scale and to contain the first establishment of the existence of anti-cyclones. His health gave him much concern, especially since a not infrequent reaction to his ill health was the tremendous difficulty in carrying through intellectual activities. Severe bouts of fever also would come unexpectedly.

Mental Inheritance

It was during the early sixties that Galton was stirred by his cousin's *Origin of Species* to study anthropology and heredity, an interest which resulted in the founding of the field of eugenics. Galton wished to encourage the productivity of the fit while restricting the birth rate of the unfit. To do so, he undertook to demonstrate that human heredity is important and relevant. He wished to study the inherited transmissible qualities of men and hoped that this knowledge would be used for the welfare of mankind. His first publication in this area was a magazine article on hereditary talent and character in 1865.

In 1869, just ten years after the *Origin*, the first edition of *Hereditary Genius* appeared.[11] The range of human mental power from the highest to the lowest was held to be enormous. Galton not only marshalled evidence about superior persons but also referred briefly to the mentally retarded and mentioned in passing the work of Seguin with idiots and imbeciles. Once variability in ability is accepted we come to the major issue: Is ability related to heredity?

He specifically acknowledged in his preface to *Hereditary Genius* that on considering his contemporaries at school and in later life he was surprised to find how frequently ability seemed to go by descent. Most of his book is occupied with reporting a large quantity of biographical data about eminent men. Since, in a later edition,[12] he expressed regret at having used the word, "genius," when he really meant mental ability of high order, we shall use the term, "eminent" hereafter. Galton hypothesized that there was not only a general tendency for eminence to run in certain families, but also that there are specific forms of eminence in the sciences, in the arts, in jurisprudence, and in similar fields.

Galton selected the eminent men by the use of biographical sources and then found the number of eminent relations they had. The proportion of eminent relatives that he located much exceeded that to be expected by chance. There were 977 eminent men in his main sample, each judged as being so outstanding as to be one man in 4,000. By chance the group would have had only one prominent relative. Instead they had 332 close relatives about as eminent as themselves. Although upheld later in a general way, his specific results are subject to many forms of serious criticism.[13] In his own day, his results were taken as unequivocal evidence for the biological inheritance of mental ability. It has become evident since that his demonstration of eminence running in families can be interpreted as due, in part at the very least, to similarity of education, socio-economic status, and proximity to other eminent (and influential) men.

Galton did not entirely overlook the influence of the environment. In fact, for this reason he later made the first psychologically oriented research study of twins in which he endeavored to separate the influence of heredity and environment. He found that in physical characteristics, at least, twins had much more in common with each other than did other non-twin children of the same parents.

His essential thesis in all of this was that mental characteristics are inherited in the same fashion and at the same rate as are physical characteristics. He converted his cousin to this view that intellectual ability is inherited, since Charles Darwin explicitly stated in a letter of 1869 to him that on reading *Hereditary Genius,* he had been "made a convert since previously he had believed that excepting fools, men did not differ much in intellect, only in zeal and hard work. . . ."[14]

Statistics and Correlation

Before Galton became interested in statistics, Quetelet[15] (1796–1874), the Belgian astronomer, had obtained the chest measurements of a large number of Scottish soldiers and the heights of French conscripts and found, in effect, that these two sets of measures not only showed the same shape of distribution when plotted on a graph, but also that they both followed the same shape of distribution as did plots of runs of luck at a gaming table, and the spread of shot around a target. Graphically speaking, each of these measures when plotted formed a curve which resembles many other common measures with a peak in the center of the distribution, while on each side the scores fall off symmetrically in such a fashion as to make the curve. Laplace and Gauss before him had applied mathematical principles to data on human errors; Quetelet extended their normal law of error to measures other than errors. It was Quetelet's work with which Galton first became familiar. What Quetelet had demonstrated was that human variation in physique follows the same statistical laws as do certain other living and non-living phenomena.

Inspired by Quetelet, Galton took the next step by extending the findings to a psychological characteristic. He found that marks given on carefully administered and lengthy university honors examinations followed the same distribution as did the biological measures studied by Quetelet.[16] Galton saw these results not only as interesting in themselves but also as justifying the application of statistics to psychological measures.

He went further and developed one of the most important of all statistical measures, the correlation. In 1888 he gave a report[17] that described for the first time what he called "co-relations," as well as the working-out of several of the basic procedures. He presented by means of graphs the fundamental properties of the correlation coefficient, as we now term it, and even developed a formula for its calculation although it was soon superseded. Galton applied his method to variations in bodily measurements, showing that, for example, stature and head length, and head length and head breadth, were correlated. For instance, tall stature and long head length go together, as do short stature and short head length, and also the various dimensions between. As stature increases, head length tends also to increase.

It was with Galton's encouragement and aid that his student Karl Pearson later improved on his work and gave rise to the present mathematical formula for its calculation, the so-called Pearson product-moment coefficient of correlation. This formula worked out by Pearson allowed one to calculate the precise numerical degree of relationship. The values that are to be found range between nearly perfect correlations through zero to nearly perfect inverse correlations.[18] The latter occurs when an increase in one score is accompanied by decrease in the other measure. The correlation was to prove an exceedingly useful tool because it made it possible to state results of research in quantitative terms, such as, .30 or .61, instead of qualitatively as in, "some, but not a great deal of relationship." This formula is now applied regularly, not just in psychology alone, but in all fields where statistics are used.

Galton's Versatility

For a time after writing *Hereditary Genius,* Galton was absorbed in collecting measures of physical characteristics—height, circumference of head, and so on. According to Pearson,[19] it was in the middle seventies that he came to the conclusion that static, anthropometric measures like those just mentioned were not so fruitful to understanding diversity among individuals as are psychometric or psychological measures which get at how individuals *function.* Thus, Galton moved from physical anthropology to psychology.

His psychological contributions are contained in his *Inquiries into Human Faculty and its Development,*[20] appearing in 1883 and based upon work which had occupied him for at least the previous seven years. This collection of studies is of striking originality. However it includes no attempt to unify its contents beyond the theme stated in its title and certain implicit general methodological guide lines which can be inferred—human beings vary enormously, man is a biologically rooted organism that evolved, empiricism is the road to knowledge, observations may be quantified and statistics applied to the results.

The appearance of this book gives us an opportunity to pause and specify some of Galton's diverse contributions as they appeared in the *Inquiries* and later, reserving for a more detailed discussion his major contributions to psychology. In this work, we find articles on spectacles for divers, the breeding of rabbits, gregariousness in cattle, a statistical analysis of the efficacy of prayer, visualized movement, composite portraitures, color blindness, outfitting an anthropometric laboratory, the Australian marriage system, dice for statistical experiments, arithmetic by smell, and the speed of trotting horses.

Galton tells how, as a means of studying the diversity of association,[21] he walked along Pall Mall, a distance of about 450 yards. He found that he had developed numerous associations with nearly 300 objects. A few days later he repeated the walk and again was struck with the variety of ideas that welled up, although somewhat chastened by the realization that there was considerable repetition of those associations shown on the first occasion. He compares these associations to a procession of players, who, having once marched across the stage, went round by the back to come on again, giving the impression of a larger group than there really was.

On another occasion he tried to work himself into the state of mind of the insane. He hit upon the plan of consciously trying to invest everything human, animal, and inanimate he met on a walk with the attributes of a spy. By the end of the morning stroll, every horse seemed to be watching him either directly or, what was just as suspicious, they were disguising their espionage by elaborately paying no attention! Hours had to pass before this state of mind wore off, and later he discovered it was all too easy to reinstate.[22]

On still another occasion he wished to gain some appreciation of the feeling that a savage might have for his idol, so he selected the drawing of Punch, the traditional cover of that magazine, and pretended with all the fervor that he possessed that it was something with divine attributes, having the power to reward or to punish.[23] He was so successful in empathizing with his role that for a long time after the experience he retained for this picture a feeling that a barbarian might have for his idol.

For Galton nothing was too trivial to be counted. He used an audience's yawns and fidgets, per unit of time, as a measure of boredom. He familiarized himself with the ways of wild animals by visiting zoos. It is here he put to good use his invention, the Galton whistle, which gave pitches beyond the audibility of human ears, but not that of various animals.

Three of his contributions to psychology deserve more detailed consideration: his work on mental imagery, on association, and on mental tests. As Galton saw them, these problems involved not only the evolutionary principle but the already familiar older and associationistic and sensationistic traditions.

Mental Imagery [24]

Galton became interested in the problem of visual mental imagery because he thought demonstrations of its presence in varying degrees might help to establish an essential difference in the mental operations of different men. After some preliminary inquiries, he constructed a questionnaire which he had completed both by students and by men from the various professions. It contained specifications for various situations for which they were to try to elicit images. The most famous of these was the request to call up from memory the scene of their breakfast table that morning. His subjects were to say whether the image they had was dim or clear, the objects well or ill defined, the colors natural or absent, the extent of contents of the field of view, the steadiness of maintenance of the mental picture, and the like.

To his astonishment, many men of science whom he had first questioned about mental images, protested they did not know what he was talking about. They strenuously denied having any imagery. They resembled in this respect color blind persons who did not know of their disability. He accounted for this relative absence of mental imagery in scientists by their habits of highly abstract lines of thinking, considering that, if they ever possessed such imagery, they must have lost it through disuse. At the more general levels of society, and among women, boys, and girls, imagery of a clear, well defined, distinct sort was present. In fact, when Galton feigned disbelief at the answers of these particular people, they were just as surprised by his inability to accept such obvious facts as were the scientists by his claim that such images existed. With more returns available, although similar differences persisted, he found numerous exceptions. Some scientists did have vivid imagery; some persons in the general population lacked imagery.

Not infrequently, it is said of Galton that he found distinct imagery types. His preliminary finding about the absence of imagery in scientists may have helped to bring about this belief. As a matter of fact, although he had spoken of types in his summarization, Galton stressed that there was a gradation of clarity of imagery from distinct to faint. It was other workers after him who popularized the notion of imagery types as if this had been his major finding. Careful later work demonstrated that Galton was right, and those who came later were wrong in that imagery falls, not into types, but is more or less normally distributed in the population with the great majority having some, but not a great deal, of imagery.

Association[25]

Another problem of even more systematic importance in psychology with which Galton concerned himself was that of association. One phase of his work, the finding of diversity of association, but with repetition, has already been described. This form of study of the free play of his own associations he did not find particularly fruitful. Much more important was his work on the reaction time necessary to produce associations. Words with which to associate, each written on a separate slip, were exposed to his view one at a time. When he had given two associations to each word, he recorded the time taken from a watch. This gave him an association reaction time. He followed the same procedure for each word in turn. Many of his associations were single words, but on some occasions the response took the form of a mental image which to be recorded had to be described in some detail and with many words. He wished to find the probable origin of these associative reactions. Presently it became evident that a large number of the associations came from experiences in childhood and adolescence; in fact about 40 per cent came from this period, about 45 per cent from manhood, and only 15 per cent from the immediate past. This was one of the first demonstrations by research of the importance of childhood experience upon subsequent adult thinking.

Mental Tests[26]

In addition to being the first to study scientifically through estimates of the abilities of eminent men, Galton was also the first to develop certain specific mental tests. In fact he may be said to have invented mental tests (although not the term itself, for it came later). The first phase of his interest in tests was shown in his efforts to develop measures of intelligence based upon sensory capacity, an undertaking that rested on the supposition that discrimination would be highest among the ablest individuals. He offered various anecdotes on the sensory obtuseness of idiots and imbeciles. Galton was using highly contrasting groups, the able on the one hand, the idiots-imbeciles on the other, to bring out sensory differences between them. He devised a set of weights for lifting and suggested other measures in the sensory area. Characteristically, he did not collect a great deal of data, but he was clearly implying that intelligence can be measured and that sensory ability is correlated with intelligence. Not only this test of weight discrimination, but also his measures of association can be seen as mental tests.

As early as 1882[27] Galton established a small laboratory in London where, for payment of a fee, a person could take a battery of tests—physical measurements, reaction time measurements, and tests of sensory acuity. Each client was given the results, and another copy was kept by the laboratory. Thus Galton, in addition to inventing mental tests, started the world's first mental testing center and in the process became the first psychological practitioner. He had, however, no intention of trying to do more than break even financially and did not succeed even in that.

One of Galton's works published in 1884,[28] brings out very clearly his interest in the measurement of personality. After suggesting somewhat over-optimistically that intellectual performance had been already "adequately" measured and, more correctly, that temperament and character had been neglected, he offered a variety of suggestions for the measurement of these latter attributes by the cardiograph, the sphygmograph, and blood pressure apparatus employed to test the effect of small emotional shocks. Among a variety of other suggestions, there is one that bears quoting:

> The poetical metaphors of ordinary language suggest many possibilities of measurement. Thus when two persons have an "inclination" to one another, they visibly incline or slope together when sitting side by side, as at a dinner table, and they then throw the stress of their weights on the near legs of their chairs. It does not require much ingenuity to arrange a pressure gauge with an index and dial to indicate changes in stress, but it is difficult to devise an arrangement, that shall fulfill the threefold condition of being effective, not attracting notice and being applicable to ordinary furniture. I made some rude experiments, but being busy with other matters, have not carried them on, as I had hoped.[29]

The article makes it evident that he was striving to develop an inventory of human abilities as broadly as possible. If the word "personality" had had the meaning it does today, he surely would have used it.

Only a few other details about Galton's life need recounting. He was knighted in 1909 and died at Haslemere in 1911. In his will he left funds for the support of a laboratory for the study of eugenics. Such, then, was the varied career of Francis Galton.

Evaluation

The measurement of individual differences in psychology, it is correct to say, was launched by Galton. Consider the work on the continent at this time. Helmholtz had given up the measurement of reaction time because the times varied so much from trial to trial. Wundt was not interested in Cattell's self-imposed problem of individual differences in reaction time. Galton had the insight to see individual differences, not as a nuisance to be eliminated but as something profoundly important to be investigated for their own sake. He also forged the link between an evolutionary and developmental outlook and psychology. He was the originator of the mental tests. He made the first extensive use of the questionnaire for psychological research. For these reasons, Galton is included among the great psychologists.

Galton continued the individualistic spirit of English nineteenth-century science. He never had a specialty but ranged broadly over a wide number of fields. He was not a eugenicist, an anthropologist, or even a psychologist; he was Galton. Like Boyle and Darwin, he never held academic position. The brute fact was that Oxford and Cambridge were only beginning to awaken to the continental scientific spirit. They were far from ready to welcome so young an upstart as psychology, far down in the prestige order of the sciences. In Galton's case, it is fortunate that he was not confined within the mould of a professorship, where specialization would have been demanded; yet the advantages of the University were also denied him. There was little of the follow-through in his work that a university setting might well have encouraged. His work—although he had Karl Pearson as a faithful follower, and an American, James McKeen Cattell acknowledged Galton's profound influence upon him—did not attract students, as did Wundt's in Germany. There was no group of enthusiastic followers to carry on his work in psychology and to clean up details and generally bring order to his thinking although in this regard his work in eugenics and biometrics fared somewhat better.

HERBERT SPENCER[30]

Herbert Spencer (1820–1903) was born in Derby, the son of a schoolmaster. Although tutored by his father, he was otherwise practically self-taught. As a young man he worked as a surveyor and a railroad engineer. He then secured an appointment as a junior editor of the journal, *The Economist,* and was launched upon his career as a writer, which was to be his means of livelihood thereafter. At this time Spencer contributed numerous articles to the *Westminster Review,* articles which sketched aspects of what was later to emerge as his philosophical doctrines. He became a friend of many of the leading scientific figures of his age, Huxley, Darwin, and others.

Spencer preceded Darwin in his public espousal of evolution. It was about 1840 that he read Lyell's *Principles of Geology,* whose arguments against Lamarck's theory of the inheritance of acquired characters had the effect of leading him to accept Lamarck's position. As early as 1852 he had definitely disassociated himself from a belief in the immutability of species. He developed an evolutionist doctrine in the years immediately preceding the publication of Darwin's *Origin of Species,* but his publications attracted relatively little attention at that time.[31] Before Darwin, Spencer's views were primarily based on philosophical, geological, and anthropological arguments and very little in the way of biological data. When Darwin produced his theory and precipitated a movement, Spencer associated himself with it.[32] Once reinforced by the genius of Darwin, Spencer was caught up in the great new trend, though he preserved his independence and remained very much his own man. Darwin had supplied the detailed proof while being very careful not to generalize beyond his data; in his turn, Spencer supplied a universal application, drawing out the implications of the theory so as to extend it over the range of human knowledge and endeavor.

Spencer did this through his *Synthetic Philosophy,* which was a comprehensive system in which he attempted to apply the master concept of evolution to all human knowledge. After failing to secure a state subsidy, he sent out to prospective subscribers a syllabus for his *Synthetic Philosophy,* eventually to encompass ten volumes, and secured enough money to go ahead with its preparation. Once started on the undertaking, he never wavered, working doggedly towards its completion despite frequent ill health and very little money.

Successive parts of *The System of Synthetic Philosophy* appeared over the period of years from 1862 to 1893. It opened with the *First Principles*[33] and proceeded through *The Principles of Biology,*[34] *The Principles of Psychology,*[35] (the second edition), *The Principles of Sociology,*[36] and *The Principles of Ethics.*[37] He continued writing and reviewing through a long productive life and died in 1903.

The main outline of his position is rather easy to present in short compass. The nature of reality is unknowable. All philosophy and science are concerned only with sensible experience. The sciences work in more restricted areas, while philosophy serves to unify their concepts. The ultimate law of development, which runs through all things, is based upon the principle of the conservation of energy, and the task is to specify how this energy is transformed.

There is a unity to all the sciences, and the unity exists in evolution. All existence *is* evolution. Development of men and the stars involves differentiation followed by integration. Everything proceeds from homogeneity toward heterogeneity. "Evolution," he said in that famous rolling Victorian sentence, "is an integration of matter and concomitant dissipation of motion; during which the matter passes from an indefinite, incoherent homogeneity to a definite coherent heterogeneity. . . ."[38] The physical sciences he dismissed after a very general discussion, leaving himself free thereafter to concentrate on the sciences of man. Biologically, life is an adjustment of internal relations to external conditions. As for psychology itself, consciousness accompanies increased correspondence and better adjustment. With increased complexity of structure, there is increased differentiation in consciousness.

It was John Hughlings Jackson (1835–1911) who provided the physiological interpretation for his evolutionary views. As his ardent disciple, he worked out a view that would make the nervous system subject to an evolutionary hierarchy.[39] In this conception the opposite of evolution, dissolution, to use as he did, Spencer's term, accounted for nervous disease in which higher levels were attacked first and only then proceeded to lower levels. This hierarchical view naturally led to less emphasis, if not outright rejection, of exact localization of function in favor of the position that higher and lower levels were involved according to the complexity of function.

Spencer gave considerable attention to association, the elements of which he referred to as "feelings," and "relations between feelings."[40] A feeling is a portion of consciousness with a perceivable individuality and is not further reducible into elements. A relation between feelings on the other hand occupies no appreciable part of consciousness. Take away the feeling units, and the relations, too, disappear. But feelings and relations between feelings still must be kept separate for reasons that later discussion will show.

"Feelings" include emotions and sensations, the former centrally initiated, the latter peripherally initiated. Spencer also makes a distinction between these real or primary feelings and the "ideal" feelings, (*i.e.*, remembered sensations or emotions or ideas of sensations and emotions) on the basis of the greater vividness of the former and the relative faintness of the latter.

Feelings of relation include those of difference, coexistence, and sequence.[41] The feeling of difference is illustrative. This feeling occurs when we pass from one conscious state to another, as when we are aroused from a train of thought on reading this material by the call to supper. The passage from one state to another creates a momentary slight "shock" because of the difference between the temporally adjacent states. Similarly, there are relations of coexistence and of sequence in our continuing conscious experience.

Feelings of relation, being a "given" of consciousness, helps to reduce the burden upon the working of association.[42] These feelings of relations were the result of association itself to Spencer's predecessors. James Mill, as we have seen, burdened the mind with an impossible number of associations. As we also know, John Stuart Mill and Bain both struggled with this problem, not too successfully. By postulating feelings of relation, Spencer helped to get around this difficulty. The affinity of the "relations" to the solutions of the problem which the Würzburg School suggested is apparent.

As to the mechanism of association itself, Spencer stressed similarity, but since associations are built up by experience, he could not dispense with the principle of contiguity entirely; he, therefore, mentioned, as additional conditions of association, vividness and repetition.[43]

Aside from his postulation of feelings of relation, Spencer's position here differs only slightly from the earlier individual versions of associationism. This account, however, is but a pale preliminary to the over-all originality of his discussion of other psychological topics.

After a lengthy physiological introduction, Spencer considers the relation of psychology to biology. In the classification of the sciences, psychology appears as a division of biology. Physiological processes are correlated with psychological processes. Adjustment of interactions to outer conditions is a persistent theme that Spencer stressed.[44] The life of every organism is a series of adjustments to the environment. Just as in biology, the environment must always be considered in dealing with psychological phenomena. In fact, the environment must be considered just much as the "correlated phenomena of the organism."[45] For example, as they were for Hartley, pleasure and pain are adjustive.[46] If animals find poisonous foods enjoyable, they die. "Survival of the fittest,"[47] (Spencer's phrase, not Darwin's) brings inclinations into harmony with environmental conditions.

As might have been gathered from the discussion of feelings of relation, Spencer emphasized the constant flow of consciousness. There had been some conception of a stream of consciousness in Bain, but Spencer developed the idea much more fully. Interruptions in this flow of consciousness were expressed by feelings of relational difference; coexistence and sequence stressed its continuity.

According to Spencer there are two separable aggregates of consciousness, objective (vivid) and subjective (faint). He meant that the former has to do with consciousness of what we today would call the present environment, whereas the latter is our thoughts of situations not physically present. States of consciousness arising from the objective world will show cohesion and continuity, provided we are physically passive. To change this state, we must change ourselves.

At the seashore it is still the sand, the sea, and the pier of which we are aware, despite our sitting through the sunlight of day to the dusk of night with all the changes of experience that this entails. There is no break in the consciousness throughout. By contrast, subjective states, characteristically less vivid, are easily changed. As we sit at the beach, the sight of a book in the hand of a passerby or a sea gull crossing our line of vision may start a new subjective state of consciousness, totally breaking off our reverie, say, about some past triumph. Nevertheless, the objective state of consciousness remains through the subjective shifts.

In discussing consciousness in general, he states that changes of a particular sort do occur. Without change, consciousness is impossible. But this is not simply random change. It is orderly change. There is an organization to these changes.[48] Changes would pass as images do across a mirror, unless there was assimilation, the work of intelligence.[49] So change (differentiation) and assimilation (integration) continually take place. Intelligence is this process of assimilation of impressions.[50]

Spencer emphasized much more *what* intelligence does than what it *is*.[51] Intelligence is the means of bringing about that adjustment of internal to external relations,[52] which previously had been called the definition of life. Intelligence establishes this correspondence to the best of its ability, using its feeling of relation and other activities, such as instinct, perception, conception, memory, will, and the like. In fact, only feelings as such are omitted, since they are not a constituent of intelligence but only its raw materials. Intelligence is to be judged by its remoteness from reflex action.[53] He specified the dimensions in which intelligence and reflex differ as relative simplicity, poverty, and rigidity of the latter. When there are limitations of intelligence in an individual, abstract conception becomes impossible.

Mind and intelligence are specifically distinguished by Spencer. Intelligence involves the relational aspect of mind, but this in turn demands the presence of the feelings with which they are related. Intellect consists of various degrees of flexibility in form of the relations of the mind.[54] Assimilation of a relation to its past kindred is the means of intelligence of operation.[55] Intelligence increases progressively throughout the scale of the animal kingdom.[56] Within the individual, growth of intelligence is shown in three ways: increase in *accuracy* with which inner tendencies are proportioned to outer persistences, increase in *number* of cases of equal difficulty, and increase in *complexity* of coherent states of consciousness answering to coherent complexities in the environment.[57] This is a definition of intelligence of astonishing complexity and subtlety, considering the relatively primitive state of understanding of the nature and function of intelligence current at the time.

We now come to the crucial issue, the means by which Spencer made association an evolutionary doctrine. He held that often-repeated associations develop a hereditary tendency so that the offspring are more likely to inherit a tendency that their forebears had learned.[58] This is cumulative effect in successive generations. To put it succinctly, there is an inheritance of acquired associations.

This supposition that habits acquired by the individual can be transmitted by means of heredity is, of course, dependent upon the reality of the transmission of acquired characters. Later research in genetics has not demonstrated such transmission.

Despite this difficulty, the old quarrel between the empiricists and nativists was in some measure resolved by Spencer's theory. As Boring writes:

Finally we must note that evolutionary psychology played into the hands of nativism and against geneticism. It is almost paradoxical that such should have been the case. Locke's empiricism led to associationism, and the genetic view of perception, for example, was the natural result. In fact, this view was as often called empiristic as genetic. Nativism, the opponent theory, seemed to go back through Kant to the innate ideas of Descartes', the very view that Locke brought empiricism to combat. Spencer's theory was essentially a resolution of the two views, although, because of the failure of science generally to accept the doctrine of the inheritance of acquired characters, his synthesis lacks the importance that it would otherwise have. Spencer simply substituted phylogenetic origin for ontogenetic origin in many cases. What is empiristically derived in the race may nevertheless be native in the individual, he might have said.[59]

The *tabula rosa* was banished. The individual, it is true, does not inherit experiences, but does inherit certain organic capacities which make for different experiences for later members of the species.

For a variety of reasons given in this and earlier chapters, association as we have followed it through the centuries is no longer the same doctrine. This is signalized by the use hereafter of different conceptual terms—historically derived from associationism, to be sure, but deserving of a new terminology to accompany the new outlook.

There remains only Spencer's interpretation of pleasantness–unpleasantness. In the various species of animals there is a correlation between the pleasant and the beneficial and the unpleasant and harmful, as noted earlier. That which is pleasant, the organism maintains, and this association is inherited; on the other hand, that which is painful is abandoned. Spencer was saying that there was a selection of pleasant acts which are useful, and abandonment of unpleasant acts which are harmful. A version of what came later to be called the law of effect was being advocated by him. That rewards and punishments are instigators of behavior was, in later generations, to become a central theme of psychology.

Other philosopher-psychologists than Spencer were profoundly influenced by evolutionary thinking. One of these was James Ward (1843–1925) who wrote the account of psychology for the ninth edition (1885) of the *Encyclopaedia*

Britannica and later revised it for the eleventh edition.[60] He is chiefly remembered today for this article which had a remarkable influence on succeeding generations of British psychologists. His was a combination of phenomenology and evolutionary doctrine. In a manner akin to Brentano he objected to conceiving the mind as passive. Instead, the mind was active in its judging and perceiving. Mental processes rather than being Wundtian building blocks, evolved from an undifferentiated state in the direction of greater and greater differentiation. Mental elements, instead of existing from time immemorial, went through a process of emerging from out of more undifferentiated mental states. There was not combination and recombination of elementary units; instead, there was growth and differentiation where none was before.

Morgan and Comparative Psychology

In the early nineteenth century, there had been some interest in animal behavior. The concern centered primarily on the question of instinct as contrasted with reason. Meanwhile, biologists and physiologists were becoming interested in the sense organs and the motor activities of various kinds of animals.

With the advent of Darwinism, research with animals accelerated rapidly. It took as its major problem the relation of forms of behavior to the phylogenetic scale of animals, particularly as expressed in the similarity and difference between man and the lower animals.

In the earliest phase, and still for some time to come, the task was conceived as investigation of mind. G. S. Romanes[61] saw his task as involving observed behavior, right enough, but to do so in order to draw inference about the animals subjective status. This he did on the theoretical premise that the degree of differences between man and animal depended upon the degree of evolutionary separation between them. He concluded from the evidence he collected that in varying degrees animals do possess the mental characteristics of man. In its earliest phase the question at issue was still seen as the contrast between instinct and reason. Naturally on the side of diminishing the gulf between man and animal, evolutionists stressed finding evidence of "reason" in animals. Their major tool at first was to collect anecdotes about animals, that is to say, the accounts of casual observations of remarkable feats of animals upon which they chanced or had ferreted out by questioning farmers, animal breeders, zoo keepers, and their like. Most often the anecdotes unearthed involved behavior on the part of some animal which seemed to show that the particular behavior involved doing something that could not be accounted for by instinct, such as a dog's lifting a gate latch without known previous training. Would not this seem to be because the dog had reasoned that he could get out, if he did what he had seen his master do, and accordingly did so?

This particular instance of the dog and the opening of the latch serves admirably to introduce one of the first crude but effective experiments which C. Lloyd Morgan, (1852–1936) reported.[62] Morgan considered precisely this behavior of a dog lifting a latch. He agreed that it was not due to instinct but asked could not this behavior be explained otherwise than by assuming that the dog had reasoned out a relation of the means employed to the end obtained. Morgan answered that there could be; he had been fortunate enough to have observed what had happened in his own dog in precisely this instance. He agreed that the person observing the behavior *after* the process was fixed could not be blamed for assuming that it was reasoning which brought about the solution. The surety, smoothness, and celerity with which the dog performed the necessary toss of the catch and, then, immediately bolted off down the road seemed to indicate reasoning. What had actually happened? Before the dog could lift the latch with his muzzle Morgan had observed that he would run up and down, sticking his head through the vertical bars at various points, sometimes near the catch, sometimes farther away. He wanted to get out, and in his excitement behaved restlessly. To quote Morgan from this point on:

At length it so happened that he put out his head beneath the latch, which, as I have said, is at a convenient height for his doing so, being about a foot above the level of the wall. The latch was thus lifted. He withdrew his head and began to look elsewhere, when he noticed that the gate was swinging open, and out he bolted. After that, whenever I took him out, instead of opening the gate for him, I waited until he lifted the latch. Gradually he went, after less frequent poking of his head in the wrong place, to the one opening from which the latch could be lifted. But it was nearly three weeks, during which I took him out about a dozen times, before he went at once and without hesitation to the right place and put his head without any ineffectual fumbling beneath the latch. Why did he take so long? I think partly because there was so little connection between gazing out into the road and getting out into the road. He did not, at first at any rate, seem to do the former in order to effect the latter. The relation between means and end did not appear to take form in his mind, even subconsciously as means to the end. And I take it that he never had the faintest notion of how or why looking out just there came to mean walking forth into the road.[63]

In addition to such findings, Morgan carried comparative psychology farther by criticizing vigorously the anecdotal work that went on before him, and he supplied more rigorously interpreted instances of observations than his predecessors. As a means of increasing rigor, he formulated a famous inter-pretive dictum as a guide for the psychologist.[64] This was a version of the law of parsimony, first encountered centuries before. His phrasing, which has come to be called Lloyd Morgan's canon, was that in no case should animal activity be interpreted in terms of higher psychological processes, if it is interpretable in terms of processes standing lower in the scale of psychological evolution.

The work of Morgan was representative of that of a small but increasing number of persons who were founding the field of comparative psychology. In fact, research studies had been performed even before those of Morgan. Spalding[65] had been among the first. He took young swallows from the moment of hatching, confined them in cages away from other birds, and released them at an age when normally they would be able to fly. He found that they soon "learned" to fly, despite never having observed the flight of other birds.

In the United States, simultaneously with Morgan, E. L. Thorndike was carrying on his studies with the added controls of laboratory equipment. His pioneer studies on learning in cats, chicks, dogs, and monkeys began to appear in 1898.[66] However, major discussion is reserved for later. (See page 414.)

LATER DEVELOPMENTS

Accounts of mental development by psychologists, largely due to the pioneering work of Darwin and Galton, began to appear in increasing numbers at the end of the nineteenth and the beginning of the twentieth centuries, particularly in England and the United States. More specifically, studies of mental development in the race and in the individual, studies in child psy-chology, and studies in animal psychology increased in number and quality.

The evolutionary biological influence upon psychology served as a corrective to the earlier almost exclusively cognitive psychology, but it did not change psychology overnight. Evolutionary thinking modified many psychological foci of interest in the direction of placing many of the old problems of sensation-perception and association in different perspectives. It introduced more func-tional issues, such as those of intelligence as a process and of adaptation to the environment. The old problem of instinct *versus* reason was now banished, and the new question of the relative influence of instinct and learning coming to take its place. However, psychology remained predominately introspective, with mind still the central problem until the twentieth century was well under way.

Emphasis upon adaptability of man to his environment and, indeed, upon behavior as such, as one of the considerations for psychology will be seen as important sources of inspiration for the functional and behavioristic approaches of the twentieth century. Meanwhile in France other developments were taking place.

REFERENCES[*]

1. J. B. LAMARCK, *Zoological Philosophy: an Exposition with Regard to the Natural History of Animals.* (Translated by. H. Elliot.) London: Macmillan. 1914. (1809)

2. C. DARWIN, The Origin of Species by Means of Natural Selection. (2nd ed.) In R. M. Hutchins (ed.), *Great Books of the Western World.* (Vol. 49) Chicago: Encyclopaedia Britannica, 1952, pp. 1–251. (1859)

3. L. HUXLEY, (ed.), *Life and Letters of T. H. Huxley.* (2 vols.), New York: Appleton, 1900, Vol. 1, p. 183.

4. C. DARWIN, *The Descent of Man and Selection in Relation to Sex.* New York: Appleton, 1871.

5. C. DARWIN, A Biographical Sketch of an Infant, *Mind,* 1877, 2, 285–294.

6. C. BELL, *Anatomy and Philosophy of Expression.* London: Longmanns, Hurst, Rees, & Orme, 1806.

7. C. DARWIN, *The Expression of the Emotions in Man and Animals.* London: Murray, 1873. (1872)

8. K. PEARSON, *The Life, Letters and Labors of Francis Galton.* London: University of Cambridge Press, 1914–1924; F. Galton, *Memories of My Life.* London: Methuen, 1908.

9. *Ibid.*

10. GALTON, SIR FRANCIS, In *Encyclopaedia Britannica,* Chicago: 1955, Vol. 9, p. 989.

11. F. GALTON, *Hereditary Genius.* London: Macmillan, 1869. (Herrnstein & Boring Excerpt No. 78)

12. F. GALTON, *Hereditary Genius.* London: Macmillan, 1892, Prefatory chapter.

13. PEARSON, *Life, op. cit.,* Vol. 2.

14. *Ibid.* Vol. 1, p. 6.

15. A. QUETELET, *Physique sociale.* (Vol. 2) Brussels: Marquardt, 1869.

16. PEARSON, *Life, op. cit.,* Vol. 2.

17. F. GALTON, Co-relations and Their Measurement, chiefly from anthropometric data, *Proc. Roy. Soc.,* London, 1888, 15, 135–145.

18. K. PEARSON, Regression, Heredity and Panmixia, *Phil. Trans.,* 1896, 187A, 253–318.

19. PEARSON, *Life, op. cit.,* Vol. 2.

* See page 16 for description of reference style.

20. F. GALTON, *Inquiries into Human Faculty and its Development.* London: Macmillan, 1883. (Herrnstein & Boring Excerpt No. 79)

21. F. GALTON, *Inquiries into Human Faculty and its Development.* (2nd ed.) New York: Dutton, 1907.

22. *Memories.*

23. *Ibid.*

24. *Inquiries.* (2nd ed.)

25. *Ibid.*

26. *Ibid.*

27. F. GALTON, Psychometric Experiments, *Brain.* 1879, 2, 149–162.

28. F. GALTON, Measurement of Character, *Fortnightly Rev.,* 1884, 36, 179–185.

29. *Ibid.,* p. 184.

30. Sources for the details of the life of Herbert Spencer are very meager, a result of his almost complete neglect during the last 50 years or so. To be sure there is his *An Autobiography* (2 vols., New York: Appleton, 1904) but it is more a reworking of a diary then it is a full-fledged autobiography. Other details had to be sought in secondary sources, such as E. Nordenskiold. *The History of Biology* (New York: Knopf, 1928) and W. C. Dampier, *A History of Science: and its Relations with Philosophy and Religion* (4th ed., Cambridge: Cambridge University Press, 1949)

31. DAMPIER, *History, op. cit.*

32. NORDENSKIOLD, *History, op. cit.*

33. H. SPENCER, *First Principles.* London: Williams & Norgate, 1862.

34. H. SPENCER, *The Principles of Biology.* New York: Appleton, 1872.

35. H. SPENCER, *The Principles of Psychology.* (2nd ed.), London: Williams & Norgate, 1870–1872. (1855)

36. H. SPENCER, *The Principles of Ethics.* New York: Appleton, 1879–1893.

37. H. SPENCER, *The Principles of Sociology.* New York: Appleton, 1876–1879.

38. H. SPENCER, *First Principles.* (6th ed.) London: Williams & Norgate, 1908, p. 321. (1862)

39. J. HUGHLINGS JACKSON, *The Croonian Lectures on the Evolution and Dissolution of the Nervous System.* London: 1884, pp. 3–5. (Herrnstein & Boring Excerpt No. 49)

40. *Psychology.* (2nd ed.) pp. 64ff.

41. *Ibid.,* Sec. 89.

42. E. G. BORING, *History of Experimental Psychology.* (2nd ed.) New York: Appleton-Century-Crofts, 1950, pp. 241–243.

43. *Ibid.*

44. *Psychology.* (2nd ed.), Sec. 57.

45. *Ibid.,* Sec. 54.

46. *Ibid.*, Sec. 125.

47. *E.g., Biology*, III, Chap. 12.

48. *Psychology*, (2nd ed.), Sec. 49.

49. *Ibid.*, Sec. 382.

50. *Ibid.*, Sec. 475g.

51. C. E. SPEARMAN, *Psychology Down the Ages*. London: Macmillan, 1937.

52. *Psychology*, (2nd ed.) Sec. 203.

53. *Ibid.*, Sec. 486.

54. *Ibid.*, Sec. 76.

55. *Ibid.*, Sec. 120.

56. *Ibid.*, Sec. 177–181.

57. *Ibid.*, Sec. 188.

58. H. SPENCER, *The Principles of Psychology*. London: Smith & Elder, 1855, Part 4, Sec. 173–174, pp. 179–180. (Herrnstein & Boring Excerpt No. 74)

59. BORING, *op. cit.*, pp. 243–244. Reprinted by permission.

60. J. WARD, Psychology, *Encyclopaedia Britannica*. (9th ed.) New York: Encyclopaedia Britannica, 1886. (Vol. 20) (1885) (Herrnstein & Boring Excerpt No. 113)

61. G. J. ROMANES, *Animal Intelligence*. London: Appleton, 1882. (Herrnstein & Boring Excerpt No. 87)

62. C. L. MORGAN, *An Introduction to Comparative Psychology*. (2nd ed.) New York: Scribner's 1904.

63. *Ibid.*, p. 293.

64. *Ibid.*, e.g., pp. 53, 292. (Herrnstein & Boring Excerpt No. 88)

65. D. SPALDING, Instinct and Acquisition, *Nature*, 1875, 12, 507–508.

66. E. L. THORNDIKE, Animal Intelligence: an Experimental Study of the Associative Processes in Animals, *Psychol. Rev. Mon. Suppl.*, 1898, 2, No. 4.

CHAPTER 15

BINET:

FRENCH PSYCHOLOGY
IN THE NINETEENTH CENTURY

$\mathbf{F}$ROM the beginning of the nineteenth century, France had a tradition that centered on psychopathological problems. Pierre Janet, one of their leading psychologists toward the end of the century, was to attest to the fact that what was most characteristic of France was the development of "pathological" psychology.[1] Even when they had their degrees in philosophy or in one of the sciences, psychologists still were apt to be influenced by this tradition. There seemed to be two distinguishable groups of psychologists in France at the time—the physician-psychologist interested in abnormal mental phenomena and in their treatment and the academic-medical psychologist who paid some attention to the more conventional aspect of psychology, including its teaching, but who also was drawn into consideration of the same phenomena which interested his medical confreres. Charcot and Bernheim are representative of the former group, whereas Ribot and Janet are representative of the latter. Binet, as befits the greatest French psychologist of his time, shared in this tradition but also created one of his own.

Just before the beginning of the nineteenth century, France became the first country to begin to develop adequate care for the insane and the feeble-minded. One of its leading physicians at the turn of the century was Philippe Pinel (1745–1826).[2] In 1792, he had been appointed superintendent of the asylum at Bicêtre. In the wake of the Revolution came his own particular application of the "Rights of Man" to the miserable patients in his charge who had been kept in chains and treated as wild beasts, even to the point of being on exhibit to those who paid a small fee. After a personal plea before the Revolutionary Convention, Pinel was permitted to dispense with the chains. He treated his patients humanely and placed them under the care of reasonably competent physicians. His book[3] on mental diseases was a potent plea for more humanitarian treatment of the insane. Instead of accepting the then current view of their being wicked people in the grip of demoniacal possession, Pinel was convinced that brain dysfunction may be related to severe psychological disorders. True, he knew too little to advance very far, but the conviction was there. Pinel was succeeded in his work by Jean Etienne Esquirol (1772–1840), who worked assiduously at establishing properly run asylums. He also wrote a monumental work on mental diseases, one more rational and descriptive than the barren speculations of most of his predecessors.[4]

Jean Itard (1775–1838), a contemporary of Pinel and Esquirol, was the pioneer in the systematic study of mental deficiency.[5] A teacher of the deaf, he was consulted about the "wild boy of Aveyron" in 1798. The year before in a woods in the Department of Aveyron, a so-called wild boy had been found by hunters. He was brought to Itard to see if he could be trained to live in civilization, a topic of more than usual interest because of prevalence of theories of the "noble savage." Itard worked long and arduously but could not in any way restore the child to normality. The boy through much effort learned a few habits more in keeping with his new environment, but was still unable to take care of himself. Finally it dawned on Itard that the boy was an idiot or an imbecile. He abandoned further work with the child as hopeless since he shared in the common belief that idiots or imbeciles were but brutes incapable of any sort of training. However, his assistant, Edouard Seguin (1812–1880), continued to work with the boy after Itard had given up because he appreciated that the gains made, slight though they were, made the child both happier and better adjusted to society. Afterward, Seguin devoted his career to attempts to train feebleminded children and eventually was put in charge of a school for the feebleminded. This was the first institution of its kind and marks the beginning of training schools for the mentally retarded.

Another source in France making for a medical psychology was an interest in hypnotic phenomena. The history of phenomena of what came to be called hypnotism is at least as old as temple medicine in ancient Greece. Its modern phase begins with the work of Franz Anton Mesmer (1734–1815).[6] After attracting considerable notoriety in Vienna through use of his so-called animal magnetism, in treating all sorts of patients he was ordered to leave the city.

He settled in Paris during the 1780's, where his remarkable cures, especially of what we would now call hysterical patients, made him well known. He thought of animal magnetism as an invisible fluid whose magnetic power he communicated through his hands by making passes over the bodies of his patients, after which he gave them assurances of their cure from the ailment from which they suffered. Physicians called Mesmer an imposter, and the first of several commissions was appointed by the French government to investigate his powers. It included among its members, Benjamin Franklin. The general conclusions of this and later commissions was that Mesmer effected many cures, but was mistaken in attributing to animal magnetism what was actually due to some as yet unknown physiological cause. Whatever else may have been taking place, magnetism as known in physics had nothing to do with these phenomena. The reports, generally unfavorable, were widely disseminated. As a consequence of this unfavorable publicity, Mesmer lost his practice and returned to private life.

For some time after the French Revolution, mesmerism, as it was by then called, led a checkered career, kept alive by a few who used it with little or no understanding of what they were doing. Meanwhile, it was derided as quackery by most physicians.

It was James Braid (c.1795–1860) in England, who named the phenomena, "hypnotism."[7] He considered that in hypnotism some sort of change took place in the nervous system as the result of psychological instigation. Braid[8] described hypnotism as induced sleep and considered hypnosis nothing more than a convenient and quick means of throwing the nervous system into a state useful for the treatment of certain disorders. He showed that hypnotism could be produced by focusing the eyes on an inanimate object, a procedure which helped to remove it from the realm of the uncanny. His lack of exaggeration, his caution, and his modest admission of lack of understanding impressed other medical men. The fact that he first expressed his interest in the topic by publicly attacking the mesmerists probably served to provide him with a respectability that the earlier workers lacked. His work became known in France in the middle of the nineteenth century through a Dr. Azam, a surgeon of Bordeaux. Azam saw its advantage in surgical operations and proceeded to use it in this way. He was followed by others. However, hypnosis came into national prominence only with the work of Charcot.

JEAN CHARCOT[9]

Jean-Martin Charcot (1825–1893), a physician, was appointed Professor of Pathological Anatomy at the University of Paris in 1860. Two years later, he was appointed a senior physician to the Salpêtrière, a hospital for mental disorders, where he established a neurological clinic. He is often referred to as the father of neurology because of his ability to relate clinical signs present in the functioning of his patients to the normal and morbid anatomy of the nervous system, a correlation which is precisely the basis of neurology today. He carried on important studies of such diseases as multiple sclerosis and spinal paralysis and worked with problems of the localization of lesions in the brain and spinal cord. He was also famous as a teacher, for he was skilled in communicating his knowledge of diagnosis and of anatomy to his pupils through case conferences. His fame was international, and students came to him from all over Europe. In 1885–1886 Sigmund Freud worked under Charcot, learning enough from him to refer to him later as "my master."[10] (See page 463.)

Charcot was already a well-established teacher and research man when he acquired his interest in hypnosis. Charles Richet (1850–1935) in 1875 had judged the phenomena of hypnosis to be undoubtedly genuine. Accepting this statement of a respected colleague, Charcot launched into a period of intense clinical investigation and made his case conferences famous by demonstrating the many phenomena which can be induced by hypnosis. He began to center his attention on patients showing symptoms of hysteria.

What are some of the symptoms of hysteria? Somnambulism (sleep walking), fugues (running away without awareness of so doing), multiple personalities, convulsive attacks are all included whenever organic causes can be ruled out, as are also contractures, paralyses, vomiting, deafness, blindness, loss of speech, and anaesthesia (loss of sensitivity) of parts of the body.[11] To add to the complexity the symptoms change even from day to day, for one day a patient may complain of vomiting, and the next day of headache. Mesmer and the other mesmerists must have treated a large number of individuals who later would have been in this category. Moreover, hysteria is the great simulator of other diseases, such as tumors, intestinal obstructions, lesions of the bones and muscles, as well as organically based blindness and deafness.

Charcot soon compared the phenomena of hypnosis to artificial hysteria. The patients of Salpêtrière, whom he found to be amenable to hypnosis and especially to very deep phases of hypnosis, were those already diagnosed as hysterics. Moreover, he soon discovered that the symptoms of the hysteric patient could be modified by hypnosis; thus hypnosis came to be the preferred method of treatment for this category of patients. He thus moved against established medical opinion which still regarded hypnosis as somewhere between a theatrical stunt and sheer charlatanism.

At Salpêtrière under Charcot's leadership it was believed that the hypnotic phenomena arose from hysteria in that only a person with an hysterical make-up could be brought to hypnotic sleep. Based on studying various degrees of the depth of hypnosis, Charcot [12] asserted the existence of three main progressive stages in the depth of hypnosis: lethargy (drowsiness), catalepsy (isolated suggestions can be accepted and acted upon, since there is no interference by other ideas), and somnambulism (ability to carry out complicated activities with no recollection afterward).

His interest in producing deep hypnosis arose from his desire to be absolutely certain of being able to distinguish between true hysteria and simulation of these conditions. Hysteria and malingering are not easy to differentiate, and Charcot was satisfied only with placing his patients under deep hypnosis in order to be sure that faking was eliminated.

Meanwhile another approach to hypnosis was being developed in Nancy by Liébeault and Bernheim.

LIÉBEAULT AND BERNHEIM[13]

A country doctor, Ambroise-Auguste Liébeault (1823–1904) had been using hypnosis in his practice without fee with all peasants who would agree to its use, whereas for other forms of treatment they had to pay. Peasants knowing a bargain when they see one, flocked to him. It was not until he happened to treat a former patient of the neurologist, Hyppolyte Bernheim (1840–1919), that his work received the attention that would place it ultimately in the history of psychology and medicine. This patient, who suffered from sciatica, had not responded to Bernheim's treatment, but he did to Liébeault's hypnosis. The already well-known Bernheim was impressed and became a pupil of Liébeault in 1882. He was destined, it is said,[14] to hypnotize 10,000 persons during his remaining years of clinical activities.

Together, Liébeault and Bernheim founded the clinic at Nancy, which was presently to rival Paris as one of the two centers in France for work in hypnotism. These workers, seeing no essential difference between spontaneous and induced sleep,[15] used the suggestion of sleep as the basis for the production of hypnosis. Essentially, the method of treatment of the Nancy school was based upon suggestion. To them, suggestion meant that under hypnosis new attitudes and beliefs were accepted by the patient uncritically, and he would then behave in accordance with these new ideas. During hypnosis, these two doctors would tell their patients, they would feel well or their symptoms would disappear. In a fair number of instances, the effect was not, as might have been expected, merely temporary but appeared to be permanent.

The clinics of Nancy and Paris were ideological rivals. At Nancy it was taught that hypnosis, at least in the mild form which it was customarily used there, could be induced in nearly all subjects and that it was essentially a passive-receptive state brought about by suggestion. On the other hand, Charcot regarded hypnosis as a pathological state of the organism. At Nancy they challenged the identification of hypnosis with hysteria, arguing that the very stages that Charcot found were the result of specific suggestions. Later events have tended to support Bernheim and Liébeault rather than Charcot.

Workers at Nancy and at Salpêtrière, far apart as they might have thought themselves at the time, were both laboring with similar groups of patients—the neurotics. No longer was interest in abnormal mental phenomena to be confined to wards of the mental hospitals. These men had isolated the neuroses from other mental diseases and in doing so had discovered them.

Théodule Ribot

Théodule Ribot (1839–1916) had perhaps the greatest breadth of interests and certainly was the most well read of the French psychologists of his time. He served as the psychological educator of his countrymen. In 1870[16] and 1879[17] he published books which interpreted English associationism and German experimentalism to his countrymen. In general, French psychologists tended to be skeptical about the value of the German experimental psychology and to make only sparing use of associationism. As a medical psychologist in the French tradition, Ribot also systematically explored what was known about the pathological aspects of affective life, and he wrote books about the diseases of the will, memory, and personality, regarding these abnormalities as products of faulty brain functioning. In discussing diseases of personality and in his presentation of cases, Ribot stressed dissociation, the splitting of the bonds of consciousness. He also reintroduced evolutionary thinking into French psychology. In 1875 he founded and edited the *Revue Philosophique*, which was to publish a fair amount of psychological material.

Ribot was appointed Professor of Experimental Psychology in 1889 at the College of France. He was not, however, an experimental psychologist in the sense of having a laboratory. In his strategic position he was to have as students many of the next generation of the academically oriented French psychologists.

Pierre Janet[18]

Pierre Janet (1859–1947) studied philosophy and psychology in the Faculty of Letters and then went on to the Faculty of Medicine at the University of Paris. Before completing his medical training, he accepted a teaching post in philosophy at a *Lycée* outside of Paris. At this time he was only twenty-two years of age. Eager to advance his career, he became interested in a patient named Léonie, already known to the medical profession for exhibiting both hypnotic and clairvoyant phenomena. After making a careful study of this intriguing combination, he reported that it seemed possible that she could be hypnotized from a distance. Through this case study Janet came into contact with Charcot.

Shortly afterward Janet returned to Paris to study again in both the Faculties of Letters and Medicine, and in 1889 he received his doctorate in letters with a thesis on psychology of automatic activities.[19] The following year he was invited by Charcot to become director of the psychological laboratory of Salpêtrière, where he tried to bring some order and system into the classification of hysteria and tried to relate these, in turn, to the conceptions of academic psychology. This study[20] became his thesis for his doctorate in medicine, a degree he received in 1892. After teaching at the Sorbonne from 1895 to 1902, Janet succeeded Ribot in the chair in the College of France which he held until his retirement. He visited the United States in 1906 to lecture at Harvard University Medical School. The lectures were published in English as *The Major Symptoms of Hysteria,*[21] the book for which he is best known in the United States. During all these years, in addition to carrying out his academic duties, he was also a busy practicing physician, specializing in mental diseases. He died in 1947.

Janet himself clearly differentiated his work from that carried on at Salpêtrière. The work under Charcot was primarily neurological so that paralyses, contractures, and disturbances of the senses were emphasized. Janet, on the contrary, saw hysteria as a *mental* disease, consisting chiefly in an exaggeration of suggestibility; and, therefore, he emphasized mental phenomena—particularly impairments of memory and the presence of fixed ideas. This appeal to fixed ideas was based on the fact that, somehow, these patients fastened onto the idea that they were paralysed or had lost sensitivity. These symptoms were not readily resolved and, hence, were referred to as "fixed" ideas. Thus Janet was closer to Bernheim in his interpretation than to Charcot, for both Janet and Bernheim saw many of the phenomena of hypnosis and of hysteria as products of suggestion. This resemblance becomes evident when one stops to consider that the behavioral phenomena are similar; for the only difference seems to be that under hypnosis, since we know how the behavioral phenomena were instilled, we know their origin, whereas in hysteria we do not.

Psychic energy and its diminution or depletion was a guiding concept of Janet.[22] Feelings of pressure experienced by the patient and consequent feelings of effort served to indicate this diminution of functioning quite apart from behaviors considered as symptomatic of this energy. Janet held that we do not know the nature of the energy, but we can study its manifestations. Individuals differ in quantity of energy available to them from both hereditary and environmental origins.[23] The environmental sources which Janet cited as responsible for lessened energy included fatigue, malnutrition, disease, pernicious experience, and inadequate education. Neuroses are fundamentally due to conditions of low mental tension—an inability to mobilize enough energy to meet the exigencies of life. There was a weakness in these patients. Illustrative of how weakness came to be postulated is the frequent triviality of the precipitating situation. At the age of twenty a man found himself near a heavy object as it fell from a window, breaking glass with the sound like that of a gun shot. The man became dumb for two months, and twenty-six years later the slightest unexpected noise would still strike him dumb for several months at a time.[24] An even more famous case was observed in Boston,[25] where a young lady, upon being kissed unexpectedly, developed symptoms which kept Morton Prince, an American psychologist, busy for years.

Personality to Janet was a matter of integration. Within the normal individual, this integration of tendencies and ideas is relatively stable; in the hysterical individual this unity is lacking, and, in extreme cases, a lack of integration may extend to the point of splitting of the personality into alternating personalities, most often two, but sometimes more. In these extreme cases a failure of conscious control had taken place. There is, said Janet, a narrowing of the field of consciousness open to the individual. In the contraction of consciousness, the hysterical symptoms are carried on without the individual being consciously aware of them. A rhythmic movement of the arm evokes in the patient no sense that he is doing it; he looks at it as something alien. The arm is carrying out the movement without his volition. The paralyzed leg is an alien "stump," as some of his patients called it, attached to the body, but not part of the person. If double personalities develop, the primary personality may not be aware of the thoughts, feelings, and experiences of the secondary personality. When a fugue occurs, a person may travel, eat in restaurants, answer questions, and generally behave in a fashion that attracts no attention, yet he will, on "awakening," not know where he is, how he got there, or what he did in the interval of, perhaps, weeks or even months, during which he lived in the fugue state.

Janet considered that the dissociative split of consciousness came about because of some mental or physical shock. Often he found that the history of the patient showed either a long maintained or a continued series of conflicts. Essentially, then, hysteria is a contraction of consciousness due to exhaustion of the higher functions.[26] Over all, the dynamic factor is *conversion symbolism,* the "driving back" of that which is unacceptable in consciousness. The patient tries to get rid of thoughts which are painful or in opposition to moral feelings; he struggles to drive them out of consciousness. When he succeeds in making these experiences unconscious, his symptoms develop with the contraction of consciousness. As a result of clinical investigation, Janet came close to a conception of unconsciousness as a dynamic process. He had spoken of "automatic" activities as early as 1889 in his doctoral thesis and had discussed the "unconscious," but impartial critics see in his usage hardly more than a figure of speech.

As for treatment itself, Janet found that under hypnosis these "forgotten," experiences can often be recalled to the patient and that the symptoms, the origin of which was unknown, could be traced back to their source and, after hypnotic suggestions, would even disappear (although other symptoms might turn up to take their place).

As might be anticipated, these views created a strained relationship with Sigmund Freud, whose formulations in a similar fashion are discussed later. (See Chapter 20.) Freud saw Janet as working in a similar area but at a superficial level. In turn, Janet claimed that psychoanalysis originated from his and Charcot's work.[27] Moreover, as an eclectic in psychotherapy he considered psychoanalysis to be one among many forms of treatment. Specifically, it served to bring about dissociation of traumatic memories.

ALFRED BINET

In the early fall of 1904, the Minister of Public Instruction appointed a committee to recommend what should be done about the education of subnormal children in the schools of Paris. The decision to place them in special schools necessitated the development of some means of their identification. It was to this task, a call which he himself had invited, that Alfred Binet, then a man of forty-seven, turned his talents and experience by constructing the first intelligence scale.[28] To appreciate properly the nature of his contribution, it is necessary to say something about the years of preparation for the task and the status of psychological testing at that time.

Life of Binet[29]

Alfred Binet was born in Nice in 1857. He was educated at Paris in law, a subject in which he received his degree in 1878; but his interests in the sciences and in medicine came to the fore, and he abandoned the law to plunge into their study. While still a law student, he had been attracted to the

Salpêtrière where Charcot was the center of attention, and Binet's predilection for psychological problems became evident to him, particularly in respect to that burning question of the day, hypnotism. Binet took a degree in the natural sciences in 1890 and a doctorate in science in 1894 with a thesis on the nervous system of insects. While still working on his degree, Binet had written a book on hypnosis with Féré,[30] giving a detailed account of its history. This book appeared in 1886. He had studied hypnosis using such devices as the dyna-mometer to measure strength of grip and the pneumograph for the recording of breathing rate. A few experiments were reported; these measures were taken in the normal and in the hypnotic state and under the effect of various sug-gestions and compared. Another book[31] by Binet, also appearing in 1886, was concerned with reasoning. The volume was prophetic of his life-long interest in higher mental processes. However, in its writing, he depended for his sources on a general theory of association, upon some incidental findings with hypnosis, and upon his knowledge of logic, rather than upon research data. Meanwhile, events were making him a psychologist, perhaps partly because of these books.

Beaunais, professor of physiology on the Faculty of Medicine at Nancy, became the first director of the psychological laboratory in the Sorbonne, which was founded in 1889.[32] Although in the Sorbonne, the laboratory was administratively not part of the Faculty of Letters but of the Ecole Pratique des Hautes Etudes. Ribot, who had previously been in charge of the course in experimental psychology but without a laboratory, moved from the Sor-bonne the same year to the chair of experimental and comparative psychol-ogy at the College of France. Binet, who was associated with Beaunais during these years, was asked in 1892 to be adjunct director. On the retirement of Beaunais in 1894 because of ill health, Binet became director of the laboratory, a post he held to his death in 1911 at the age of fifty-four.

Some of Binet's early work stressed the abnormal, since he wrote a book on *The Alterations of the Personality*[33] in 1892 and one on *Suggestibility*[34] in 1900. In the same period, he carried on studies in tactile sensibility and optical illusions in a fashion similar to that of his German contemporaries. Then, or later, he studied handwriting, using blind analysis to increase his objectivity; he investigated the thinking of chess players; and he carried on a series of studies of suggestion. Within the tradition of medical psychology, it was these studies of suggestibility for which Binet was best known.

In collaboration with Beaunais and with Victor Henri as his assistant, he had established in 1895 what was to become the leading French psychological journal, *L'Année psychologique*.

About 1900 Binet began to study thinking by the use of introspection. His previous book on reasoning had been written without the hindrance of research

data. Now in his new work, published in 1902,[35] he depended for data upon
the reports of the thinking of his two daughters, then of high school age.

As was the case in his studies of intelligence later, he failed to be impressed
by the necessity of working with minute elements of psychic life and believed
that psychological problems of thinking may be attacked globally. (In fact,
it was only in keeping with contemporary usage that this may be called a
study of thinking. Actually, Binet referred to it as a study of "intelligence.")
He asked his daughters to solve problems and then to report to him the steps
they took to reach a solution. Often the girls specifically denied the presence
of images. In general, these results anticipated and supported the research
of the Würzburg School. Like those at Würzburg, Binet found much thinking
that could not be reduced to sensory or ideational elements.

Although the girls were similar in their thinking in regards to matters so
far described, it also happened that the two girls differed strikingly in their
particular ways of thinking and in their personality, differences to which their
father's account devotes considerable attention. Undoubtedly, this study had
something to do with strengthening Binet's interest in individual differences.

Aside from a somewhat greater interest in laboratory research than was
characteristic of his fellow Frenchmen and the writing of a textbook of
experimental psychology,[36] Binet's career with its interest in abnormal phenomena was quite in keeping with the tradition of psychology in his country.
However, busy as all this work kept him, his claim to greatness rests primarily
upon his contribution to an understanding of the nature of intelligence.

Measurement of Intelligence

In 1905 Binet[37] urged that it was necessary to establish an accurate diagnosis
of intelligence if the recommendation of the committee concerning placement
of feebleminded children in special schools was to be carried out adequately.

He was sharply critical of medical diagnosis of this condition. Previously,
diagnosis of mental deficiency was considered as analogous to diagnosis of
physical disease. It is not surprising that errors occurred, since no one invariable
sign of mental deficiency was known, then or later. For this purpose, Binet
drew attention in copious detail to the errors that physicians had made in
diagnosis by showing how the same child could carry different diagnoses as
he was evaluated by different physicians, even just a few days apart. It was
thus that the work of the Parisian committee precipitated the development
of the Binet Scale and centered Binet's interest upon the problem of the
diagnosis of the feebleminded. It did not create his interest in the problem
of intelligence.

For many years before the establishment of the Paris committee of 1904, Binet had had an interest in the measurement of intelligence and individual differences. Ever since about 1887, his principle source of subjects for study had been the school children in and around Paris upon whom he had tried out various tests.[38]

With his long-time collaborator and assistant, Victor Henri, Binet published seven papers on individual differences. The crucial paper on tests appeared in 1896.[39] First Binet and Henri reviewed the literature which was already quite extensive. Without confining discussion to the specific tests they reviewed, it will suffice to say that presumably they were familiar with the work of Galton and perhaps also with the contribution of Ebbinghaus on the completion test to be published in 1897. There was also available to them a considerable literature on elementary sensory, perceptual, and motor measures. Narrow phases of mental activity, such as sensory acuity, reaction time, attention span, speed of movement, and the like had been studied during preceding years. Binet and Henri pointed out that too-limited and too-specialized abilities were being utilized for a measurement of so complex a matter as intelligence. Moreover, when such a problem as the relation of memory to intelligence was to be studied, it would be necessary to examine various kinds of memory, rather than to be content with studying one kind alone. Several variations of memory must be tapped. Binet and Henri proposed that visual memory of a geometrical design, memory of a sentence, memory of musical notes, memory of color, and memory of digits should all be included as tests of intelligence. Recognition of the differences in endowments among individuals indicated the need for tests covering a wide scope. They urged for this purpose tests, not of elementary functions but of the higher mental processes. Among the ten mental processes they proposed to study were (1) *memory*, as already noted; (2) *images*, measured by recalling twelve randomly selected letters exposed to view long enough for two readings at a "natural" rate; and (3) *attention*, divided into duration (reproduction of the length of a line of a given length shown only once) and scope (the ability to count the total number of strokes of two metronomes set for slightly different speeds with gradual increase of the speeds on successive trials until the subject's limit is reached). The other tests were for measurements of imagination, comprehension, suggestibility, esthetic appreciation, moral sentiments, strength of will, and motor skill.

During the years between 1897 and 1905 Binet and his collaborators had busied themselves with developing new tests, particularly for the higher mental processes. Théodore Simon, a new collaborator, also collected anthropometric measurements.

In 1905 the first intelligence scale appeared as the joint effort of Binet and Simon.[40] It consisted of a long series of tests they had given to what was for this time, a rather large sample of children. Their guiding concept in its construction was that of a *scale*—a series of tests of increasing difficulty starting with the lowest intellectual level and extending to that of the average level.

The scale was avowedly a test to be applied rather than just a means of research, for they encouraged others to use their instrument for the measurement of intelligence. They urged prospective testers to secure training from them, stressed the need for uniformity of administration, and warned against permitting coaching of the children tested.

In 1908 they revised and improved the scale.[41] The tests were arranged, not merely by level of difficulty but according to the age from three to twelve at which presumably normal children could pass them successfully. If on the tryout of a test, being evaluated for possible inclusion, it was found that all or nearly all of the children six years old failed, the item was obviously too hard for that age; whereas if practically all eight-year-olds passed it, it was too easy. The only possibility remaining would be to place it at the seven-year level. This particular test would then have been placed at the seven-year level provided it met the general criterion for placement of a test. The rule was that if 60 to 90 per cent of the children at a given age passed a particular test, it was to be considered standard for that age and included in the scale. Thus the first *age scale* was launched. In this way, it came about that children of all levels of intelligence were brought into the focus of attention, and the feebleminded were left merely as a deviant from the normal. A shift away from the relatively specific problem of the detection of feeblemindedness to the more general problem of the measurement of intelligence at all levels had taken place.

Tabulated below are the tests at both ends of the scale grouped according to the age at which the "majority" of children succeeded on them:

Age 3 Years

1. Points to nose, eyes, mouth.
2. Repeats sentences of six syllables.
3. Repeats two digits.
4. Enumerates objects in a picture.
5. Gives family name.

Age 4 Years

1. Knows sex.
2. Names certain familiar objects shown to him; *key, pocketknife*, and a *penny*.

3. Repeats three digits.
4. Indicates which is the longer of two lines five and six cm. in length.

Age 11 Years

1. Points out absurdities in contradictory statements.
2. Sentence construction as in test 3 for age 10 years. Hardly one fourth pass the test at 10 years, while all do at 11 years of age.
3. Names sixty words in three minutes.
4. Defines abstract terms—*charity, justice, kindness.*
5. Puts words, arranged in a random order, into a sentence.

Age 12 Years

1. Repeats seven digits.
2. Finds in one minute three rimes for a given word—*obedience.*
3. Repeats a sentence of twenty-six syllables.
4. Answers problem questions—a common-sense test.
5. Gives interpretation of pictures.

Age 13 Years

1. Draws the design that would be made by cutting a triangular piece from the once-folded edge of a quarto-folded paper.
2. Rearranges in imagination the relationship of two triangles and draws the results as they would appear.
3. Give differences between pairs of abstract terms, as *pride* and *pretension.*[42]

By means of the 1908 scale one could find the mental age of the child, irrespective of his actual chronological age. If he passed the tests of eleven years, but not those of twelve years, he had a mental age of eleven years. However, very few children were so obliging as to pass all tests at one level and fail all of them at the next, so inherent difficulties of scoring existed which were not cleared up until the next and last revision.

Binet and Simon applied the scale to feebleminded children and on the basis of their results, they set limits for three degrees of feeblemindedness as follows: idiot, two years mental age or below; imbeciles, between two and seven years; and morons, above seven years. They recognized that the classification lacked prognostic value, since they were dealing with absolute limits.[43] That is to say, their definitions did not take into account the actual or chronological age of the child. Hence, as the child with the passage of years could continue to grow mentally (although more slowly than the average child), he might pass from an idiot to an imbecile to a moron.

Sometime later this problem was solved by William Stern[44] (1871–1938), a German psychologist, who suggested as a solution of this problem the use of an Intelligence Quotient or I.Q., to be found by dividing a subject's mental age (M.A.) by his actual or chronological age (C.A.). Since the resulting I.Q. is a ratio, it did away with the difficulty of M.A.'s as an absolute measure being used to define degrees of intelligence, including feeblemindedness. Using the I.Q., a child C.A. four with a M.A. of two would have an I.Q. of 50 (2/4) as would a child eight with a mental age of four (4/8). (The use of a decimal result is eliminated by multiplying by 100.) The I.Q. was adopted by Terman in the United States in his 1916 *Stanford Revision of the Binet Scales* for which he provided a classification of degrees of intelligence in terms of I.Q., not M.A. Mental age as an absolute measure was still useful; it was supplemented by the I.Q., which placed the individual's intelligence relative to his age.

Considerable interest was shown in the United States in utilizing the 1908 version of the Binet-Simon Scale.[45] However, one early significant study in Belgium was performed by Decroly and Degand.[46] They tested a group of boys and girls in a private school in Brussels, to find that, on the average, their subjects were one and a half years in advance of the expected standards or norms published by Binet. After a certain amount of understandable confusion, it was realized that what had been found was the effect of superior social class, since the Belgian children were the sons and daughters of professional men, while Binet's Parisian children on which the norms were based, were from poorer sections of the city. This finding opened up the whole problem of the relation of intelligence to social class.

In 1911, the year of Binet's death, the last of his revisions appeared.[47] He had profited from the research done with the test, restandardized the placement of tests, added some new tests, and discarded others, particularly because they were too dependent upon school information. He also took care of the difficulties of scoring the 1908 revision by making each test at each year worth a certain fraction of a year of mental age, expressed as months of mental age, so that all the tests passed, irrespective of the years at which they were placed, could be added together to get the mental age.

Binet had not attempted to analyse intelligence into parts and then devise tests based upon this analysis, but, rather, he used the combined efforts of a series of promising complex tasks selected as generally relevant to intelligence. Naturally, he had devoted some thought to the nature of intelligence. Throughout the years he offered, withdrew, and amended a whole series of definitions. We have already seen that he considered intelligence to be related to judgment. Probably the most characteristic definition and certainly the definition most commonly associated with his name is that intelligence is a combination of capacities to make adaptations to attain a desired end, to maintain a mental set, and to be self-critical.[48]

Evaluation

Speaking generally, Binet advanced objective measurement in psychology. His work and that of others, with his or similar instruments, demonstrated the superiority of objective measurement over clinical diagnosis carried on without such an instrument. The Binet Scales and the later instruments derived from them were quickly demonstrated to be of practical value in educational, social, and medical settings. He also contributed to the more theoretical aspects of psychology by developing a concept of intelligence as a combination of cognitive abilities, and, in the process of doing so, he distinguished intelligence from the specific sensory and motor abilities with which it had earlier been confused by Galton and others.

One criterion of the greatness of a psychologist is the fruitfulness of his contribution in leading to other research. In this regard Binet stands very high. Probably more psychological research studies have been stimulated by his work than by that of any other psychologist.

OVERVIEW

The French psychopathologists saw their patients as *people*—sick individuals in need of care. They saw them as individuals and were interested in them as people as well as what they could learn about them. An impersonal attitude, natural to study of the generalized human mind, was in the process of being supplemented by an interest in the welfare of the individual. Janet[49] made this explicit in a paper describing his way of investigating the individual's unique characteristics. Binet worked in a similar spirit. He saw children as individuals, extending from his own daughters to those tested for the sake of establishing the norms of his scale. After all, an intelligence test-score is that of an individual and represents something about a person. Binet and his associates were applying a clinical method by studying their patients not only so as to understand them but also in order to help them. The French psychologists of the nineteenth and early twentieth centuries advanced the understanding of the clinical method in psychology to a point where Freud and the others could carry through the next stage.

REFERENCES°

1. P. Janet, *The Major Symptoms of Hysteria*. (2nd ed.) New York: Macmillan, 1920.

2. J. C. Flugel, *A Hundred Years of Psychology: 1833–1933*. New York: Macmillan, 1933.

3. P. Pinel, *Traité médico-philosophique sur l'aliénation mentale*. Paris: Richard, Caille & Revier, 1801.

4. J. E. Esquirol, *Des maladies mentales*. Paris: Bailliere, 1838.

5. R. Pintner, *Intelligence Testing: Methods and Results*. New York: Holt, 1923.

6. J. Ehrenwald, (ed.), *From Medicine Man to Freud*. New York: Dell, 1956.

7. *Ibid.*

8. J. Braid, *Neurypnology; or, the Rationale of Nervous Sleep; Considered in Relation with Animal Magnetism*. London: Churchill, 1843. (Reprinted, 1899)

9. G. Guillain, *J.-M. Charcot 1825–1893: His Life—His Work*. (Translated by P. Bailey) New York: Hoeber, 1960.

10. S. Freud, The History of Psychoanalytic Method. In A. A. Brill (ed.), *The Basic Writings of Sigmund Freud*. New York: Random, 1938, p. 943. (1912)

11. Janet, *Major Symptoms*.

12. J.-M. Charcot, *Clinical Lectures on Diseases of the Nervous System*. (Vol. 3) (Translated by T. Savill) London: New Sydenham Society, 1889.

13. G. Zilboorg & G. W. Henry, *A History of Medical Psychology*. New York: Norton, 1941, pp. 357–378.

14. Ehrenwald, *op. cit.*

15. A. A. Liébeault, *Du sommeil et des états analogues, considerérés surtout au point de vue de l'action de la morale sur le physique*. Paris: Masson, 1866.

16. T. A. Ribot, *English Psychology*. London: King, 1873. (1870)

17. T. A. Ribot, *German Psychology of To-day*. New York: Scribner's, 1886. (1879)

18. P. Janet, Pierre Janet, In C. Murchison (ed.), *History of Psychology of Autobiography*. (Vol. 1) Worcester: Clark University Press, 1930, pp. 123–133; W. S. Taylor, Pierre Janet, 1859–1947, *Amer. J. Psychol.*, 1947, 60, 637–645.

19. P. Janet, *L'automatisme psychologique*. Paris: Alcan, 1889.

20. P. Janet, *L'état mental des hysteriques*. Paris: Rueff, 1892.

21. P. Janet, *The Major Symptoms of Hysteria*. New York: Macmillan, 1907.

22. P. Janet, *L'analyse psychologique*, (Psychology analysis.), (In English), In C. Murchison (ed.), *Psychologies of 1930*. Worcester: Clark University Press, 1930, pp. 369–373.

23. Taylor, *op. cit.*

° See page 16 for description of reference style.

24. *Major Symptoms.*

25. M. Prince, *The Dissociation of a Personality.* New York: Longmans, Green, 1905.

26. *Major Symptoms.*

27. P. Janet, *Psychological Healing: a Historical and Clinical Study.* (2 Vols.) (Translated by E. & C. Paul) London: Allen & Unwin, 1925.

28. A. Binet & T. Simon, Sur la nécessité d'établir un diagnostic scientific des états inférieurs de l'intelligence, *Année Psychol.*, 1905, 11, 163–190. (Partial translation in W. Dennis (ed.), *Readings in the History of Psychology.* New York: Appleton-Century-Crofts, 1948, pp. 407–411)

29. T. Simon, Alfred Binet, *Année Psychol.*, 1912, 18, 1–14.

30. A. Binet & C. Féré, *La magnetisme animal,* Paris: Alcan, 1886.

31. A. Binet, *La psychologie du raissonement.* Paris: Alcan, 1886.

32. Personal communication from P. Fraisse to E. G. Boring, February 5, 1962, through the kindness of the latter. There has been some confusion about who had priority in founding the first laboratory in France. Presumably this is attributable to the fact that three independent institutions of higher education all were involved in the events of 1889. Ribot moved to the College of France from the Sorbonne, or the College of Letters of the University of Paris. The same year a laboratory was placed in the Sorbonne under the direction of Beaunais in association with Binet, although it was administered by L'Ecole Pratique des Hautes Etudes, still a third educational Institution.

33. A. Binet, *Les altérations de la personalité.* Paris: Alcan, 1892.

34. A. Binet, *La suggestibilité.* Paris: Schleicher, 1900.

35. A. Binet, *L'étude expérimentale de l'intelligence.* Paris: Schleicher, 1903.

36. A. Binet, *Introduction á la psychologie expérimentale.* Paris: Alcan, 1894.

37. Binet & Simon, *Sur la necessité.*

38. A. Binet & N. Vaschide, La psychologie en l'école primaire, *Année Psychol.* 1898, 4, 1–14.

39. A. Binet & V. Henri, La psychologie individuelle, *Année Psychol.*, 1896, 2, 411–465. (Herrnstein & Boring Excerpt No. 81)

40. A. Binet & T. Simon, Methodes nouvelle pour le diagnostic du niveau intellectual des anormaux, *Année Psychol.*, 1905, 11, 191–244.

41. A. Binet & T. Simon, La développement de l'intelligence chex les infants, *Année Psychol.*, 1908, 14, 1–94.

42. J. Peterson, *Early Conceptions and Tests of Intelligence.* New York: World Book, 1925.

43. Binet & Simon, *La développement.*

44. W. Stern, *Die psychologische Methoden der Intelligenz-prüfung.* Leipzig: Barth, 1912, Chap. 2. Translated by G. W. Whipple as *The Psychological Method of Testing Intelligence.* Baltimore: Warwick & York, 1914, Chap. 2. (Herrnstein & Boring Excerpt No. 86)

45. Peterson, *op. cit.*

46. O. Decroly & J. Degand, Le mesure de l'intelligence chez des en fants normaux d'apres les tests de Binet et Simon: nouvelle contribution critique, *Archives de Psychol.,* 1910, 9, 81–108.

47. A. Binet & T. Simon, *A Method of Measuring the Development of the Intelligence of Young Children.* (Translated by Clara H. Town.) Chicago: Chicago Medical Book, 1915. (1911)

48. Peterson, *op. cit.*

49. Janet, *L'analyse psychologique.*

CHAPTER 16

JAMES:

THE BEGINNINGS OF
PSYCHOLOGY
IN THE UNITED STATES

IN THE United States before the 1880's there were two major psychological traditions—phrenology and Scottish psychology.[1] Despite its errors, phrenology in its way was objective in that it depended upon measurements. Moreover, it had a practical aim in view. It flourished outside the schools as illustrated by its previously mentioned appeal to medical men (see page 245), while business men and reformers of all persuasions also found it met their needs. If the interest of the latter seems incongruous, it should be remembered that phrenology was a doctrine upholding the changeability of human nature. Hence, phrenology was a minor theme in various activities directed toward other ends: temperance, anti-tobacco and birth control—to name three where the element of control of human nature is self-evident. The works of Gall and Spurzheim were popular in America where they inspired the numerous publications of the Fowler Brothers.[2]

Scottish psychology had been the heir to the associationistic tradition. It was primarily introspective and still a non-experimental branch of philosophy. Just as was the case with its Scottish forebears, in the United States it was used as a defense of revealed religion. James McCosh, President of Princeton University, 1870 to 1892, and Noah Porter, President of Yale University, were two of its most prominent exponents. This combination of teaching the subject and occupying the presidency of the college was not unusual. Textbooks were written to review the European literature, and there was a certain amount of original work which the new psychology to come so far overshadowed as to reduce it to almost complete oblivion. An attempt is being made to review and to restore this work to the main stream of historical scholarship.[3]

Between 1880 and 1895, psychology in the United States was transformed in a dramatic and sweeping fashion.[4] By 1895 there were twenty-four psychology laboratories, three journals, and a flourishing scientific society, many of whose members were full-time psychologists. The new psychology had made its appearance, yet in 1880, only fifteen years before, none of this had existed.

The antecedents for these changes were to be found in the system of higher education that prevailed at the beginning of this period and the reaction in the United States to the German university system.

Higher Education in the United States

Before the Civil War, one-curriculum colleges prevailed with their emphasis upon Latin, Greek, mathematics, and philosophy. What little instruction existed in the physical sciences was offered without laboratory work of any kind.[5]

At that time educational theory was based upon a faculty psychology. This phase of the Scottish psychology served as a justification for the method of mental discipline. The faculties of the students were to be exercised by those subjects which, to use the words of Jeremiah Day, President of Yale in the early decades of the century, are "best calculated to teach the art of fixing the attention, directing the train of thought, analyzing a subject proposed for investigation, following with accurate discrimination the course of argument; balancing nicely the evidence presented to the judgment; awakening, elevating, and controlling the imagination; arranging, with skill, the treasures which memory gathers; rousing and guiding the power of genius. . . ."[6]

Scientific work was carried on almost entirely outside the colleges in a manner reminiscent of England, but without the saving grace of the well-to-do amateur. The establishment of scientific schools, beginning with those at Rensselaer, Yale, and Harvard, helped to break this exclusion, although they were isolated from the colleges. The medical schools also began to contribute, although they did not do a great deal to encourage research. Much of what was done was carried out without the support of universities. Enrollments actually declined as colleges became more and more out of touch with the times, while the number of students going abroad to Germany and Austria for graduate study increased.[7] In 1880 there were about as many graduate students abroad as there were in all of the United States.

As we have seen, the German universities were dominated by the idea of research, and the teacher had considerable amount of freedom to work on problems of his choice and, within the limits of his field, to choose to teach what he wished. There was also the complementary freedom of the student to study what and when he chose. Above all, the German universities were the scientific centers of the world, due to the effectiveness of their research.

Educators reacted vigorously to the example of the German universities. After the Civil War, a strong movement sprang up to extend the scope and improve the quality of university education. To mention only three college presidents from among the leaders, Eliot of Harvard, (despite an anti-research bias), White of Cornell, and Gilman of Johns Hopkins were all influenced by the German university system in the changes they introduced at their respective institutions. As a result, these three schools figure prominently in the account that follows. In addition, Clark University, whose first president was G. Stanley Hall, was avowedly modeled on European graduate schools. Stanford University and the University of Chicago were also to come into prominence as examples of the new trend. Meanwhile a gradual reform and reorganization of the so-called graduate schools already in operation was taking place at such universities as Harvard, Yale, and Princeton. These older schools had suffered loss of students, a lowered prestige, and the services of some of their abler professors to the new graduate schools; so they, too, incorporated the German university pattern into their graduate schools.

Reform took place through the introduction of the elective system to replace the fixed curriculum. This resulted in an increase not only in the number of courses but also in the number of departments offering them, such as the modern languages, the social sciences, and psychology. Most important of all was the establishment of graduate schools to take the place of the fifth year in residence which, heretofore, had led to the M.A. degree based on an extension of college work. Johns Hopkins, opening its doors in 1876, as a graduate school, was the leader in this field, with an independent research project required of each student.

In these changes psychology occupied a favored and strategic position. It was one of the "new" subjects introduced into colleges and universities from the German system. Whereas psychology was still located in the departments of philosophy in German universities, the introduction of the subject in schools in the United States often meant the creation of an independent department. It also supplied a weapon to attack faculty psychology. No matter what the differences of opinion among the first American psychologists, they were united in their opposition to faculty psychology. Moreover, the economic and social conditions prevailing under the pioneer spirit made application of psychology almost a foregone conclusion.

As Albrecht[8] reminds us, these years were years of preparation to become a science, rather than years necessarily marking scientific advances themselves. Consequently, in what follows it is not only the research articles on scientific problems that will be of concern, but also psychology as a social institution and the men who helped to make it.

WILLIAM JAMES[9]

Suitably muted as befits the field, an academician's moment of truth comes when he hears the citation read during the awarding of an honorary degree. The moment for William James was to come at the Harvard commencement of 1903. We do not know his reaction to the award itself, but more accessible is what happened *before* this moment. According to his son, Henry, he went about for days, half in jest, half in earnest, dreading to hear President Eliot pronounce him "psychologist."[10] He was not a psychologist, he insisted, but a philosopher.

In spite of himself, William James was the first of the new psychologists in the United States. Not only on occasion did he deny that he was a psychologist; he even denied that there was a new psychology. To add to these paradoxes, he was not primarily a founder, certainly not an adherent, and not even an experimentalist. He founded no system of psychology and lacked disciples. There were to be no Jamesians as there were Wundtians. He drew the inspiration for his position concerning psychology, not from one man or one movement, but from a combination of sources in such fashion as to be self-initiated. He knew of the developments in German experimental psychology, and he assimilated some aspects, rejected others, but was guided by none of them. He showed similar independent selectivity about British associationism and French psychopathology. In spite of all of this, William James was the first great psychologist in the United States.

Life and Interests

Just before the beginning of the nineteenth century, the founder of the James family in America, William's grandfather, came from Ireland. Beginning with a meager capital, he amassed a fortune through business ventures and investments. Among his thirteen children by three wives was Henry, senior, the father of William and Henry James. Independently wealthy, their father never worked in the accepted sense of the term. Instead he devoted his time to religious questions in which he struggled to give utterance to his deep but unorthodox beliefs. He was especially influenced by Swedenborg and found his mission in life in writing a series of books, essays, and pamphlets, which made, however, so little impression upon others that William Dean Howells was to say of him that, "He had written a book about the 'Secret of Swedenborg' and had *kept it*."[11] Nevertheless, wherever Henry went in his ceaseless travels, he had distinguised friends. Ralph Waldo Emerson in particular impressed him, although in later life he found Emerson lacking in intellectual coherence and showing too blithe a dismissal of the reality of evil.

William was born in New York City, in January 1842. His brother Henry was also born in New York City, fourteen months later. Their father devoted himself enthusiastically to their education, alternating between rushing them off to Europe because of his conviction of the "narrowness" of American schools and then bringing them home because of an equally strong feeling that his children should be with their own kind. Extensive travel and sporadic schooling in the United States, England, France, Switzerland, and Germany followed for William and Henry and their younger brothers and sisters. They studied with tutors and in various kinds of schools, learning even more from the galleries, museums, and theatres of the cities they visited. Unlike the rigors that faced John Stuart Mill in having his education supervised by his father, they had a delightful, although unsettling time with their kindly, enthusiastic father.

As befitting their very different personalities, Henry and William later flatly disagreed on the value of their schooling. William regretted its lack of discipline and drill which he believed interfered with his developing an ability for orderly rigorous thinking; Henry found it invaluable in stirring the free play of curiosity. Although there was but a year's difference in age between the two, William, then and later, was the "big brother." He took the lead, responding more quickly and with much greater assurance than did Henry. In later years William vigorously criticized his brother's writing with no complaint or impatience being shown by Henry. Finally, Henry calmly declared his independence which, in everything but name, had been his all along.

There was a very deep affection between the brothers, although in many respects they were utterly unlike. Henry, who became a naturalized British subject late in life, reflected at least the stereotype of the formal and reserved Englishmen, as expatriates have been known to do, while William, despite his cosmopolitan experiences, was still something of the breezy American. H. G. Wells[12] tells a story which illustrates neatly the brothers differences in this regard: In later years when the brothers were famous, Wells came to visit them while they were in England and found Henry very upset. Henry appealed to Wells to tell his brother what *is* and *is not* done. It seems that William had happened upon a small inn whose garden was separated only by a high wall from that of a house at which G. K. Chesterton, the British writer, was staying. With American directness William had placed the gardener's ladder against the wall, climbed up, and peeped over. And Henry had caught him at it!

Following the advice of his father who insisted that a hasty decision would be wrong and "narrowing," William took years to decide upon the work for which he was most fitted. He tried painting for six months at the studio of William Morris Hunt in Newport, Rhode Island, but realized his lack of promise to be an outstanding painter.

In the autumn of 1861, at the age of nineteen, William enrolled at the Lawrence Scientific School of Harvard University; by now his choice of future career had been narrowed down to the sciences and philosophy. Despite his interest in chemistry on which he first concentrated, William's teachers observed an impatience which drove him away from accurate, painstaking laboratory determination, prophetic of his distaste for such work throughout his life. He soon left chemistry for physiology, anatomy, and biology and enrolled in the medical school, despite the already formed conviction that the practice of medicine held no attraction.

In 1865 he went with Louis Agassiz to the Amazon as a trial of a possible career in biology, but he soon found that he hated collecting. On his return he resumed his medical studies, interrupting them again to go abroad for two years, because he felt that he did not have the stamina to continue the arduous work. Indecision about a career was now complicated by a neurotic depression with insomnia, eye trouble, digestive disorders, very severe back pain, and other symptoms which lasted for nearly five years. There was even some preoccupation with thoughts of suicide, but he managed to put them aside, even being able to write home to his father in a carefully restrained fashion that "thoughts of the pistol, the dagger, and the bowl began to usurp an unduly large part of my attention; and I began to think that some change . . . was necessary."[13] During this trip abroad in a letter to a friend he mentioned that he considered the time had come for psychology to begin to be a science and that he had decided to do some work in it.[14] He also mentioned plans to go to Heidelberg to work with Helmholtz and Wundt, but, whatever the reason, he merely was to catch a glimpse of them and no more. His knowledge of their work attests to his general alertness to contemporary developments in psychology. This visit was in 1868, only eight years after Fechner's *Elements* had appeared.

He returned to the United States to take his medical degree in 1869. It was "obvious" to William, to his friends, and his family that he could not practice, and, since his back pain precluded standing for long hours, laboratory work, too, was out of the question. He resolved that summer to continue to work in "psychological subjects." [15]

A philosophical crisis preceded the beginning of a partial recovery from his various ills. Feeling lost and alone, and, indeed on occasion becoming panic stricken in a world he saw as filled with evil, William read the evolutionary philosophy of Renouvier's *Second Essay* which persuaded him of the existence of the freedom of the will, that spontaneity is available to him who makes it so. James resolved that his ". . . first act of free will shall be to believe in free will." [16] This apparently delivered him from the clutches of the strict determinism of Mill, Spencer, and Bain and opened up the way to his becoming a philosophical psychologist.

In 1872 he received an offer from President Eloit to teach physiology at Harvard, which he accepted. By this time a gradual recovery of his health was taking place. Despite the lure of more general philosophical issues, after the first year he felt he should continue but postponed a decision and finally decided to take a year off to be with his brother in Italy. He then returned and resumed teaching.

In 1875 James gave his first course in psychology on the relation between physiology and psychology, thus moving closer to his now established goal. James never had instruction in psychology. As he put it, the first lecture he ever heard, he gave himself.

It was in 1875 (the same year as Wundt) that William James established the other of the two first psychological laboratories in the world. [17] In retrospect James, himself, was not sure whether it was 1874, 1875 or 1876, but the new evidence found by Harper in the references cited above demonstrate it to have been 1875. One especially compelling item he cites is the report of the Harvard Treasurer of that year which cites an appropriation to James of $300, for use in physiology. Other evidence, including the nature of his 1875 course mentioned earlier, shows that it was equipment for physiological psychology. Therefore, it would seem a laboratory in psychology was found at Harvard in 1875 by James. It was located in Lawrence Hall. In 1876 James was advanced to Assistant Professor of Physiology. G. Stanley Hall, about whom we shall be hearing presently, arrived as a student in that same year, taking his degree in 1878.

The year 1878 was notable for two events. First, James married Alice Gibbens, a Boston school teacher. She shared his interests and watched over him with untiring devotion. She, and marriage itself, introduced a certain greater amount of organization into his life than had been present before. However, with his sensitivities and nervous temperament, it is hardly surprising that the five children which were born over the next several years occasionally got on his nerves. Moreover, the financial strain of a growing family led James to write a considerable number of popular articles and to give many lectures for the sake of the financial return they brought. The second event of 1878 was his signing of a contract with the publisher, Henry Holt, for a volume on psychology. At the time he apologized to his publisher that he would have to take two years in which to write it. Actually he took twelve!

In 1880 he was made assistant professor of philosophy, a department where psychology more properly belonged. He was admitted to the department but "not without opposition."[18] The thought of a "physiologist" teaching psychology infuriated some members of the department, who were quite content with the accustomed Scottish variety. Despite the lack of a major work, he was advanced to professor of philosophy in 1885, and in 1889 his title was changed to professor of psychology.

During the years he was working on the *Principles*, he traveled abroad, further delaying his writing. In 1882 a leave of absence from Harvard allowed him to go to Europe, where he made important professional contacts, thereby acquiring a recognized name on the continent. James began many friendships with psychologists and philosophers which strengthened over the years.

The closest of friends that he made, then and later, among European psychologists were James Sully, James Ward, Theodore Flournoy, and Carl Stumpf. It is perhaps significant that none of them was hardly more than mentioned in the earlier chapters on European psychology. The senior European psychologists with whom we are familiar did not appeal to him. Herbert Spencer, despite his debt to him, was an "ignoramus";[19] Wundt ". . . the finished example of how much *mere* education can do for a man";[20] and G. E. Müller was "brutal" (a comment made in connection with a highly critical review of a work by Münsterberg)[21] Fechner was viewed ambivalently, seen both as a source of inspiration and as a kindred spirit because of his philosophical views[22] but also as a source of irritation, because the upshot of his careful work in psychophysics was "just *nothing*."[23] It is true that he assessed Hermann Ebbinghaus as "one of their best men."[24] These comments by James, it must be emphasized, with one exception, were made in personal correspondence. In his writings he gave their work careful attention, even though he made it clear that he did not necessarily accept their views except some of Spencer's. He did not reject the findings of experimental psychology *in toto*. After all, a goodly number of pages of his *Principles*[25] was taken up with this work (even though it was relegated to fine print).

His book was growing in connection with his classroom teaching. In the classroom, as in his writing and in conversation with friends, James was charming and without obvious order of presentation. He was vivacious, so full of humor that one of his students interrupted him one day by the remark, "To be serious for a moment . . ." [26] His picturesque language and vivid appropriate imagery were such that his students remembered them years afterward, while the more methodical lectures of others had long since vanished from memory. For all of his delight in the insight of the moment, he did not shirk thinking through thoroughly and laboriously whatever he wrote and said; he would painstakingly present details and scrupulously examine counter-arguments. Writing did not come easy to him, and he worked the material over and over again. His infinite pains, however, were rewarded with a clarity unexcelled in the literature of psychology.

Since university administrators expect frequent publication from professors, he arranged for various chapters or sections of chapters of his forthcoming book to be published as articles. This was the case with his famous formulation of emotion, which was in print in 1884, a year before a very similar view of the Danish physiologist, Lange.

In 1890 *The Principles of Psychology* [27] finally appeared. The delay and prior publication of parts of it had built up keen anticipation among psychologists. As in all of his writings, even when he was not original, an old theme was given new life by its brilliance of formulation. The reviews hailed it as a very important contribution, and it was a pronounced success. An observation made some years ago is still true; it is read by people who have no obligation to do so. [28] The criticisms offered tended to center around its "unsystematic" or "impressionistic" character. To call the *Principles* unsystematic does not mean that it is disorganized. Sometimes, in fact, it would appear that what people meant by this charge is that James did not follow the conventional ordering of topics. James believed that the proper starting point is experience as immediately given and as it flows in perception. Hence, he did not start with sensations, as others had done before and after him, since those were not the way in which we experience. Its contents will be considered later.

Two years after the *Principles*, James published the *Briefer Course*, [29] a condensation explicitly planned to serve as a textbook, and to make him and the publisher money. [30] For many years "Jimmy," as the book became known to distinguish it from its parent, was used as a textbook, since it eliminated many of the digressions of the portlier "James."

Laboratory work was more of a symbol and never a habit with James, despite the rooms used for equipment when he was in the department of physiology and his mention of spending two hours a day in his psycho-physics laboratory which he started in 1885.[31] Both in the *Principles* and in other writings James took a pessimistic, disparaging view of experimental or laboratory psychology. In 1849 he commented that here in the United States we are overstocked with laboratories.[32] In the *Principles* James offered the opinion that the results of laboratory investigation were not yet commensurate with the labor involved; while, in another well-known passage, he remarked that the experimental introspective method "could hardly have arisen in a country where natives could be *bored.*[33] Elsewhere he said that ". . . brass-instrument and algebraic-formula psychology fills me with horror."[34] In view of such an attitude, it is not surprising that he did not contribute experimental results of any importance except a study of transfer of training, discussed later.

James recognized that laboratory work was desirable for psychology, but he wanted to be relieved of its responsibility. In 1890 he succeeded in raising $4,000 for a psychology laboratory.[35] Having already been impressed by the work of Hugo Münsterberg (1863–1916), a German, then at the University of Freiburg, James arranged for his being made the director of the new Harvard laboratory, a post that Münsterberg occupied beginning in 1892. It should be mentioned that Münsterberg never fulfilled James' hopes to acquire for Harvard a leader in experimental psychology. The first few years went well with a certain amount of material coming from the laboratory. After that, Münsterberg scattered his efforts among a variety of fields—psychotherapy, legal psychology, and industrial psychology among others—while paying relatively little attention to the laboratory.

In 1895, G. Stanley Hall, by then a rival psychologist and President of Clark University, stirred up controversy about priority of laboratory founding in the United States with his claim for founding the first laboratory at Johns Hopkins in 1883, along with a sweeping statement about other laboratories being organized by his Hopkins and Clark students. James, as a loyal Harvard man, issued a claim for priority for his work of 1875.[36] In part, Hall was moved to this claim by an understandable confusion about what constitutes the organization of a laboratory. Is it when research is performed using equipment by the professor? Is it when it is performed by his students? Is it when the university gives space or equipment? Or is it when the university formally proclaimed it supports a psychology laboratory? Based, as it was, on this last and rather incidental criteria, it would seem as if Hall was wrong in this claim of priority.

The number of psychologists trained by James was surprisingly small. Moreover, even fewer doctoral dissertations in psychology were completed under the sponsorship of James. Hall had worked with him in 1876–1878. From about 1890 onward he had some students who became psychologists, including James

R. Angell, Mary W. Calkins, William Healy, Edward L. Thorndike, and Robert S. Woodworth. The number may have been small, but later they were all to achieve considerable prominence.

James grew up in an atmosphere of liberalism where such topics as abolition, homeopathy, and women's rights were freely and eagerly discussed. More often than not they were championed rather than condemned. When this is coupled with his father's devotion to the teachings of Swedenborg which formed part of his son's experience, it is no wonder that James expressed a kindred interest in spiritualism. He found mediumship, clairvoyance, and automatic writing something to be approached with an open mind. He approached it in the same spirit in which he came to the defense of mental healers when they were under the attack of the medical profession. In 1882–1883 James met the Englishmen who were the founders of the new *Society for Psychical Research*, and, when their friendships ripened, their cause became his. He was an eager student, attending many seances, carrying on an extensive correspondence, and publishing his findings. As usual, *facts* were what he wanted. He was interested not only in the problem of survival after death but also in psychic phenomena as forming a continuity with those of hypnotism, hysteria, and multiple personality. Did he accept the existence of a residue of reality after charlatanry, suggestion and abnormal psychology had been eliminated? In speaking of Mrs. Piper, the medium, whom he most thoroughly investigated, his final report contained these words:

It is enough to indicate these various possibilities, which a serious student of this part of nature has to weigh together, and between which his decision must fall. His vote will always be cast (if it ever be cast) by the sense of the dramatic probabilities of nature which the sum total of his experience has begotten in him. *I myself feel as if an external will to communicate were probably there*, that is, I find myself doubting, in consequence of my whole acquaintance with that sphere of phenomena, that Mrs. Piper's dream-life, even equipped with "telepathic" powers, accounts for all the results found. But if asked whether the will to communicate be Hodgson's, [her spirit control] or be some mere spirit-counterfeit of Hodgson, I remain uncertain and await more facts, facts which may not point clearly to a conclusion for fifty or a hundred years. [37]

In the 1890's James came to be recognized as America's leading philosopher. As a philosopher it was his work on pragmatism and radical empiricism which were his major contributions. Years before he had read and admired Charles S. Peirce. The work of Peirce, however, had been virtually ignored. James wrote so persuasively on this topic in 1907 in *Pragmatism*[38] and in 1909 in *The Meaning of Truth*[39] that it became an important philosophical doctrine. The central theme of pragmatism is that the value of ideas must be tested by their consequences in action. Contrary to what people generally supposed, beliefs do not work because they are true, but rather they are true because the "work." This usage of "work" was open to various criticisms in terms of ambiguity which were not long in coming. Despite these merited criticisms, pragmatism was a popular success.

James advanced the pragmatic view as one resolving the dilemmas created by the perennial clash between rationalism with its eternal principles and empiricism with its immutable facts. Rationalists, he went on, are "tender-minded," "intellectualistic," "idealistic," "optimistic," "religious," "free willed," "monistic," and "dogmatical." Empiricists, in contrast, are "tough minded," "sensationalists," "naturalistic," "pessimistic," "irreligious," "fatal-istic," "pluralistic," and "skeptical."[40] His doctrine of radical empiricism was first published in 1904 in an article, the purpose of which was to deny that the subject-object relation is fundamental in consciousness.[41] Thereafter he elaborated it in many articles and books. In respect to the subject-object relation, James held that the distinction between one kind of occurrence, "knowing," and another entity, the object or "known," is false. In the view which he was rejecting, mind or soul, the knower, was seen as in sharp contrast to the object known which might take the form of a material object or another mind. This dualism of subject and object James rejected in favor of a monism in which the world is neither mind nor matter.

Empiricism needs radical revision, he believed, because earlier empiricists had accepted heretofore, the dualism of knower and known and accepted consciousness as one thing and the object as another thing. Empiricism is correct, James said, in that we learn only from experience, but that from which we learn is "pure experience," the one primal substance in which consciousness is *not* a thing but a relation or a process. Similarly the known is a relation. Both the knower and the known are relations within pure experience.

In 1898 James overtaxed his heart during a climb in the Adirondacks, and the following summer, out for a short walk, he lost his way and again strained his heart. The consequences affected his health to the extent that two years of comparative idleness in Europe were necessary.

In 1899 James published *Talks to Teachers*,[42] which grew out of public lectures given to teachers in 1892 and afterwards. He helped to bring psychology into the classroom by stressing applications to everyday problems. He stressed the individual rather than the social goals of education.[43] He had received, some years before, an invitation to prepare and deliver the Gifford Lectures at Edinburgh, which he gave in 1901–1902. These lectures formed his book, *Varieties of Religious Experience*.[44] He contended that he spoke as a psychologist and, in so doing, made considerable use of personal documents that recounted religious experiences and paid particular attention to the pathological strain evident in many of them. He insisted, however, that the presence of psychopathological traits in these persons did not vitiate the reality or value of their religious experiences. In fact, he challenged the use of mental stability as a criterion of social value. There is, he said, a type of religious experience of shallow healthy-mindedness which has the defect of denying real anguish. In contrast, there is the religion of the "sick soul."[45] Despite the revulsion that arises in the healthy-minded, James argued that this recognizes the existence of a wider scale of experience. This kind of person recognizes evil and passes into a state of agony, but in this process eventually he may conquer despair, resulting in his feeling a justifiable optimism in which the world, good *and* evil, is seen as unified.

After the Gifford Lectures James resolved to forego the "popular lecture style" and do something serious and systematic, but he never managed to keep his resolution. The nearest approach to a formal exposition of his philosophy is the unfinished, posthumously published, *Some Problems of Philosophy*,[46] which, following his directions when he realized it would not be finished, had as its subtitle, *a beginning of an introduction to philosophy*. After talking for years about retiring from his professorship, he finally did so in 1907.

In 1909 G. Stanley Hall, as President of Clark University, invited Sigmund Freud as one among many distinguished figures to a celebration in Worcester. James attended, and, naturally, he met Freud. James was, of course, already familiar with the fact of the existence of a mental life of which the individual is not fully aware. Earlier, he had praised F. W. H. Myer's view of extra-marginal consciousness as the most important advance since he began the study of psychology.[47] That there are some mental events outside of awareness was, to James, a very intriguing fact, since it seemed such an unexpected peculiarity of human nature. There is, however, a tremendous gulf between Myer's subliminal consciousness and Freud's unconscious. Myer and the others of similar interests were looking for subconscious feats, while Freud searched for unconscious motives. In keeping with his openmindedness and desire to give everyone a hearing, James hoped that Freud would push his ideas to their utmost limit, although he added in the next breath, that Freud impressed him as a man with fixed ideas and that he could make nothing of his dream symbolism.[48]

For the sake of his health, James went to Europe in the spring of 1910. He did not, however, slow down his pace sufficiently to reap any benefit. Despairing of any relief he turned homeward to die two days after his return, late in August, 1910, at his country home near Mount Chocorua, New Hampshire.

Selected Psychological Views [49]

It would be false to James to try to present his thinking about psychological matters in a fashion which would reflect an overall systematic point of view. He avoided the outward appearance of system quite deliberately because he believed that to do so would result in an artificial premature schematization. As Perry [50] remarked, James was an explorer, not a map maker. Only some of the more important and characteristic psychological views can be given. To show the charm and vividness of his style, liberal use is made of quotations.

The starting point for psychology is that which is immediately given—the stream of consciousness. Earlier psychologists, James said, had thought of consciousness in terms of discrete elements; *e.g.*, of ideas and sensations. These elements, he goes on, were then treated as the building blocks for more complicated levels of organization in which they were joined together. James could not accept the elements presumed by others to be that of which the mind is composed. Moreover, the analytical method that they used seemed to him to be unwarranted, since experience is what it is and not groups of elements teased out of this matrix by introspection. These elements of his predecessors, far from being experienced directly, are the products of a sophisticated discrimination, often arduous in nature.

What is experienced is a flow of consciousness without its being chopped up into bits. Consciousness is not a mosaic of separate bits and pieces but a flowing, unbroken continuous affair without cracks or joints. Things shade and merge in space and in time. Consciousness is a stream. This continuity is one of the five major characteristics James attributes to consciousness. To be sure, relative differences exist. There are more stable substantive states of consciousness, which are the most obvious and the usual source of study by psychologists. Also very much present, although apt to be neglected, are the vague, fleeting, intangible, unstable, transitive states, such as the feeling of "and" and "but," resembling in some respects Spencer's "feeling of relation." These transitive or relational states help to give consciousness a streamlike continuity. James offers a vivid illustration of what he means by the substantive and relational state:

Like a bird's life, it seems to be made of an alternation of flights and perchings. The rhythm of language expresses this, where every thought is expressed in a sentence, and every sentence closed by a period. The resting-places are usually occupied by sensorial imagination of some sort, whose peculiarity is that they can be held before the mind for an indefinite time, and contemplated without changing; the places of flight are filled with thoughts of relations, static or dynamic, that for the most part obtain between the matters contemplated in the periods of comparative rest. *Let us call the resting-places the "substantive parts," and the places of flight the "transitive parts," of the stream of thought.*[51]

He then goes on to say:

There is not a conjunction or a preposition, and hardly and adverbial phrase, syntactic form, or inflection of voice, in human speech, that does not express some shading or other of relation which we at some moment actually feel to exist between the larger objects of our thought.[52]

In a similar vein James discusses feelings of tendency, expectation, and intent which are also of the more elusive variety. James admits that there may be consciously experienced interruptions in this continuity of the stream of consciousness as in sleep, but on waking there is no trouble in reaching back and making connection with the stream of consciousness that was one's own.

Its personal nature is another major characteristic of consciousness. Consciousness "tends to appear" as a part of a personal consciousness. It is not merely *a* thought; it is *my* thought. There is a personal self which separates by a wide gulf one's consciousness from that of others. The qualifying expression "tends to appear" a few sentences before, was applied to this characteristic of the stream of consciousness because James was well aware of the phenomena, such as multiple personalities, automatic writing, and posthypnotic suggestion, which seemed to show the presence of secondary personalities.

Still another characteristic, James finds, is that consciousness is a state of constant change. He held that we can never have twice the same thought or conscious state. True, we may think more than once of the same object, say in hearing the same note or seeing the same color, but each time we do so we experience it differently (even though not aware of doing so) because of intervening experiences. This is most obvious on occasions which are separated by relatively long periods of time, when we wonder, as it might be expressed, "what we could have seen" in a given person, book, or idea. It may be convenient to formulate the matter as if ideas were simple and unchanging, but, to put it in James' own words, "A permanently existing 'idea' or 'Vorstellung' which makes its appearance before the footlights of consciousness at periodical intervals is as mythological an entity as the Jack of Spades."[53]

Consciousness also has the characteristic of dealing with objects independent of itself. Many earlier psychologists had confused these objects of thought with the thoughts themselves. It was a version of the psychologist's fallacy which they were committing. In its most general form, this fallacy is confusion of his individual standpoint with that of the mental fact with which he is concerned. In this particular instance James wrote:

> *Another variety of the psychologist's fallacy is the assumption that the mental state studied must be conscious of itself as the psychologist is conscious of it.* The mental state is aware of itself only from within; it grasps what we call its own content, and nothing more. The psychologist, on the contrary is aware of it from without, and knows its relations with all sorts of other things. What the thought sees is only its own object; what the psychologist sees is the thought's object, plus the thought itself, plus possibly all the rest of the world. We must be very careful therefore, in discussing a state of mind from the psychologist's point of view, to avoid foisting into its own ken matters that are only there for ours. We must avoid substituting what we know the consciousness *is*, for what it is a consciousness *of*, and counting its outward, and so to speak physical, relations with other facts of the world, in among the objects of which we set it down as aware. Crude as such a confusion of standpoints seems to be when abstractly stated, it is nevertheless a snare into which no psychologist has kept himself at all times from falling, and which forms almost the entire stock-in-trade of certain schools. We cannot be too watchful against its subtly corrupting influence. [54]

In committing this fallacy we start to describe the object, not the thought, as in the following:

> If, for example, the thought be "the pack of cards is on the table," we say, "Well, isn't it a thought of the pack of cards? Isn't it of the cards as included in the pack? Isn't it of the table? And of the legs of the table as well? The table has legs—how can you think the table without virtually thinking its legs? Hasn't our thoughts then, all these parts—one part for the pack and another for the table? And within the pack-part a part for each card, as within the table-part a part of each leg? And isn't each of these parts an idea? And can our thought, then, be anything but an assemblage or pack of ideas, each answering to some element of what it knows?"
>
> Now not one of these assumptions is true. The thought taken as an example is, in the first place, not of "a pack of cards." It is of "the-pack-of-cards-is-on-the-table," an entirely different subjective phenomenon, whose Object implies the pack, and every one of the cards in it, but whose conscious constitution bears very little resemblance to that of the thought of the pack *per se*. What a thought *is*, and what it may be developed into, or explained to stand for, and be equivalent to, are two things, not one. [55]

Each thought is a unity, just as a soap bubble is a unity. Touch a bubble, and the bubble disappears. So, too, does a thought. Each thought is a unity —once gone it cannot be brought back again.

Consciousness also has the characteristic of being selective. There is always rejecting, accepting, uniting, and keeping apart of objects and parts of objects. One cannot direct attention over everything impartially. Monotonous, regular progression as in the ticking of a clock are broken up into rhythms, now one, now another; dots scattered on a surface are grouped in a pattern, and then regrouped in another different pattern. One's very sense organs in their threshold limitations are selective instruments. Even more important, is selection from those things open to one's sense organs only a small portion of those available. Helmholtz had reported research on blind spots, after-images, double images, marginal changes of color, and movement of accommodation—studies of visual sensations of which the ordinary run of mankind are simply not even aware they exist. Even from a separate object as when a tabletop is "seen" as square, when, from any of our usual particular perspectives, the image falling on the retina is not that of a square; we see grass as green in bright sunlight and the same shade of green at dusk although the colors are very different. Speaking generally, James contends, the members of the human race agree more or less on what to notice or not to notice from among the welter of those available.

One matter which we all examine and then come up each with our own answer is the nature of "me" and "not me." The consciousness of self, to James, is not an abstract, but a living, breathing thing. As aspects of the "empirical" self or "me," he distinguished among the material self, the social self, and the spiritual self.

The material self embraces not only one's body but also one's clothes and possessions. In an extended sense, the material self includes the immediate family, the home, and worldly possessions. They, too, arouse the same feelings as the narrower material self, although in varying degrees. When they flourish, we too flourish; when we diminish, they too diminish.

The social self is, more properly, spoken of as social selves, since a person has a different social self for every individual who has some sort of image of him. Fortunately, however, the social selves tent to fall into classes to the extent that there are different groups of persons about whose opinion the person cares enough to show a different "side" of himself—a family self, a club self, an employer self, a friend's self, a lover self. James reminds us that even in everyday speech there is this discrimination among selves—"as a soldier I condemn him, as a father I pity him."

The spiritual self is more intimate than the other two, more subjective in the sense that it is a person's personal impression of his skills or faculties, say, his feeling toward his ability to argue, his inflexible determination his purity of conscience, his conscientiousness, and his feelings of guilt.

James finds this self in activity, in a person's ways of preparing to meet a situation. Some persons would consider them a manifestation of the action of a soul; others would argue that this contention is but a fiction. As for James, the activity in the "spiritual" self, so-called, was such that he actually found nothing spiritual, but rather, some sort of obscure body process generally localized within the head. Attending, accepting, negating, making an effort seemed, to James, to involve these head movements. The self, in this instance, is present in these activities but is not the same as these activities. When making an effort to remember, James felt as if there was a pulling in of the periphery, a withdrawal from the world, a rolling upward and outward of the eyes, the exact opposite of fixating. He hastened to add that he is not saying this is all the spiritual self is for other persons. All he can do is speak for himself. Taken together the material self, the social self, and the spiritual self form the empirical self.

Within this heterogeneous self, seeds of conflict are going to be sown. There often is a conflict of these different aspects of their different selves: one is often confronted with the necessity of accepting one self and forsaking the rest. Here are the inimitable words of James:

> Not that I would not, if I could, be both handsome and fat and well dressed, and a great athlete, and make a million a year, be a wit, a *bon-vivant,* and a lady-killer, as well as a philosopher, a philanthropist, statesman, warrior, and African explorer, as well as a "tone-poet" and saint. But the thing is simply impossible. The millionaire's work would run counter to the saint's; the *bon-vivant* and the philanthropist would trip each other up; the philosopher and the lady-killer could not well keep house in the same tenement of clay. Such different characters may conceivably at the outset of life be alike *possible* to a man. But to make any one of them actual, the rest must more or less be suppressed. So the seeker of his truest, strongest, deepest self must review the list carefully, and pick out the one on which to stake his salvation. All other selves thereupon become unreal, but the fortunes of this self are real. Its failures are real failures, its triumphs real triumphs, carrying shame and gladness with them. [56]

Failures in connection with activities germane to potentially available, but non-selected selves, find no place in our self-esteem. A poet may be complacent about his ignorance of automobile mechanics, while to a self-made man the lack of a college education may even be a source of pride. In neither instance is that which is lacking a source of self-feeling. The lack of knowledge of auto mechanics or the lack of a college education are not, to use James' term, part of their pretensions to success. Our pretensions on what we do consider part of the self, compared to successes in these particular areas, decide our self-esteem. In other words, our self-esteem is a ratio of our successes divided by our pretensions to success.

Over and above the empirical self with all of its selves is the Pure Ego, the self or principle of personal identity. Here the problem is the self as thinker, not as an object of thought. The problem at hand is whether or not one must go beyond what has already been discussed to account for personal identity. To James, there is no evidence of absolute oneness, even though introspectively there seems to be a center of one's existence which remains steadfast throughout the shifts of experience. This steadfastness James explained by appeal to the transitive states, the consciousness of relation of the stream of consciousness. They give the needed continuity without appeal to something behind experience. This led James to compare the hypothesis of an immortal soul or transcendental principle of unity, with the associationist solution which would be to deny there is a principle, and hypothesize that all there is is a stream of passing thoughts. The upshot of the analysis was the conclusion that, for psychology, with its task of describing what can be studied within the field of direct experience, it is unnecessary to take a stand. To introduce a "knower" beyond that which has already been described is to proceed beyond psychology into metaphysics.

James insisted, as did Spencer before him, that the mind did more than passively adapt to the external environment.[57] The mind has a spontaneity, a selectivity of its own. Consciousness in the mind is causative; it intervenes in cause-effect sequences. As for the reality of the intervention of consciousness as causative, he advanced the argument that this is demonstrated by our more intense awareness of the functioning of consciousness when obstacles are encountered. When there are no obstacles and things run smoothly, consciousness tends to lapse; and habit takes over. Consciousness, moreover, shows interest or attention. It is volitional as well as sensory. It selects and dwells upon some aspect of the experience to which it is open and rejects others. What is selected becomes vital and real; what is rejected becomes unimportant and unreal. Mind is an instrument drawing from the world whatever interests it. Persons differ in that they introspect identical situations in different ways according to their interests. This selectivity of consciousness, presumably due to the action of selective natural evolution, runs as a theme through the chapters of the *Principles* devoted to attention, conception, and discrimination and comparison, and is most explicitly stated in Chapter 5 when he argues against man being conceived as an automaton.

Habit is treated by James as a matter of functioning of the nervous system. The argument shows his strong physiological bent. Habits are due to increased plasticity of neural matter which serves to make it easier for repeated actions to be carried out, while, at the same time, lessening the need for attention to the activity in question. Moreover, habit has enormous social implications.

James' account of habit is the most famous chapter in the book. It even received separate publication many years later. The sheer grace of his writing makes quotation imperative.

Habit is thus the enormous fly-wheel of society, its most precious conservative agent. It alone is what keeps us all within the bounds of ordinance, and saves the children of fortune from the envious uprisings of the poor. It alone prevents the hardest and most repulsive walks of life from being deserted by those brought up to tread therein. It keeps the fisherman and the deck-hand at sea through the winter; it holds the miner in his darkness, and nails the countryman to his log-cabin and his lonely farm through all the months of snow; it protects us from invasion by the natives of the desert and the frozen zone. It dooms us all to fight out the battle of life upon the lines of our nurture or our early choice, and to make the best of a pursuit that disagrees, because there is no other for which we are fitted, and it is too late to begin again. It keeps different social strata from mixing. Already at the age of twenty-five you see the professional mannerism settling down on the young commercial traveller, on the young doctor, on the young minister, on the young counsellor-at-law. You see the little lines of cleavage running through the character, the tricks of thought, the prejudices, the ways of the "shop," in a word, from which the man can by-and-by no more escape than his coat-sleeve can suddenly fall into a new set of folds. On the whole, it is best he should not escape. It is well for the world that in most of us, by the age of thirty, the character has set like plaster, and will never soften again.[58]

Later he wrote:

Could the young but realize how soon they will become mere walking bundles of habits, they would give more heed to their conduct while in the plastic state. We are spinning our own fates, good or evil, and never to be undone. Every smallest stroke of virtue or of vice leaves its never so little scar. The drunken Rip Van Winkle, in Jefferson's play, excuses himself for every fresh dereliction by saying, "I won't count this time!" Well! he may not count it, and a kind Heaven may not count it; but it is being counted none the less. Down among his nerve-cells and fibres the molecules are counting it, registering and storing it up to be used against him when the next temptation comes. Nothing we ever do is, in strict scientific literalness, wiped out. Of course, this has its good side as well as its bad one. As we become permanent drunkards by so many separate drinks, so we become saints in the moral, and authorities and experts in the practical and scientific spheres, by so many separate acts and hours of work. Let no youth have any anxiety about the upshot of his education, whatever the line of it may be. If he keeps faithfully busy each hour of the working-day, he may safely leave the final result to itself. He can with perfect certainty count on waking up some fine morning, to find himself one of the competent ones of his generation, in whatever pursuit he may have singled out.[59]

Although James rejected the fundamental presupposition of associationism, namely its atomism or elementarism, he did not reject association itself, despite denial that it was a matter of simple couplings. He insisted that what is associated is not ideas, but objects. Earlier psychologists had confused the objects of thought with the thoughts themselves—the psychologist's error. The basis of association is through brain processes. Association is a merging of physiological processes in the nervous system, not in discrete bits.

Contiguity is a way of expressing the basic law of association—objects "experienced together tend to become associated,"[60] but he preferred, in keeping with his stress on physiology, to formulate it as the law of neural habit: "When two elementary brain-processes have been active together or in immediate succession, one of them, on reoccurring, tends to propagate its excitement into the other."[61] James was writing on this topic before the acceptance of the neurone theory, and consequently he did little more about its physiological basis than to speak vaguely of irradiation of energy over the cortex without making clear the mechanism of spread or connection. James[62] saw associationism as further restricted because the mind in keeping with, or as an aspect of, its spontaneity (see page 361) possesses an innate capacity to perceive relations and categories evolved in the process of rational selection. This was in contradistinction to Spencer's inherited associations. (See page 316.)

In the course of writing the chapter on memory in the *Principles,* James became intrigued with verifying an opinion he had expressed to the effect that, after memorizing material, one did not develop a better retentive power in general but, instead, became more efficient merely with the particular kind of material on which one practiced. This contention contradicted the view of the faculty psychologists who said that if you cultivate any phase of memory you have a better memory for everything. He decided to try to find out whether a certain amount of daily training in memorizing poetry would shorten the time necessary to learn an "entirely different kind of poetry."[63] This, the first experiment on transfer of training, he carried out first on himself and then on a few of his students. He obtained results more or less in favor of his view in that his subjects did not tend to do better on a second kind of material after learning a certain kind of poetry. More carefully controlled studies by others which followed, especially those of Thorndike and Woodworth,[64] demonstrated unequivocally that the doctrine of formal discipline of faculty psychology was false. They found that amount of transfer of improvement depended mainly upon the degree of community of the tasks. Transfer effects are far from general, and, for the most part, have been found to be confined to closely related activities, thus disproving the faculty psychology point of view.

James would have had us reverse the usual way of thinking about the emotions. The customary view holds that perception gives rise to the emotion which, in turn, brings about bodily expression. "No," said James, the bodily expression follows directly the perception of the emotion provoking events. The feeling engendered *is* the emotion.

Common-sense says, we lose our fortune, are sorry and weep; we meet a bear, are frightened and run; we are insulted by a rival, are angry and strike. The hypothesis here to be defended says that this order of sequence is incorrect, that the one mental state is not immediately induced by the other, that the bodily manifestations must first be interposed between, and that the more rational statement is that we feel sorry because we cry, angry because we strike, afraid because we tremble, and not that we cry, strike, or tremble, because we are sorry, angry, or fearful, as the case may be. [65]

For evidence he appealed to introspection; if all experiences of bodily symptoms, such as the heart beat, the tensions in the muscles and so on, are abstracted, there is nothing left to the emotion. Without knowledge of the work of James, almost simultaneously Lange, [66] studying specifically the circulatory system, reached the conclusion that feelings of vascular change were the essentials of emotion.

Evidence has been brought to bear against the so-called James-Lange theory in later research which was almost immediately stimulated by their work. James' felicitous expression could and did lead to misunderstanding. When he said, ". . . we feel sorry because we cry, . . . afraid because we tremble," he disregards the fact that we can be sorry without crying and afraid without trembling. This does not alter the fact that some bodily process precedes and is the sensory source of the emotion, which is, after all, the essence of his theory. No one denies that emotions have physical causes, but modern research shows that they are caused by processes in the thalamic region of the brain, mediated through the autonomic nervous system. Nevertheless, James' theory did much to stimulate the research which established the organic basis of emotion.

James endowed the human organism with a generous number of instincts, more, in fact, than those of the lower animals. He drew upon observations of children by Preyer, an embryologist and a pioneer child psychologist, for the beginnings of his catalogue and then extended it considerably. He listed sucking, biting, crying, locomotion, and vocalization among the human instincts. They were the more specific forms of instinct, reflexlike in character, which stood in contrast to the broad generalizations sometimes offered as instincts, as when postulating an instinct of self-preservation. This is not meant to imply that James did not list instincts more complicated than those just mentioned, since he went on to include imitation, emulation, pugnacity, hunting, fear, acquisitiveness, play, curiosity, shyness, cleanliness, modesty, love, and jealousy.

The dictates of instincts are followed by us, James said, because at the time of their operation doing so seems the natural and the appropriate thing to do. Every instinct is an impulse to action of some sort but they are not always blind or invariable. The sheer possession of many and contrary instincts means that with slight alterations of conditions, now this, then another impulse may be in the ascendant. Pugnacity and timidity, bashfulness and vanity, sociability and pugnacity are paired antithetical instincts which create conditions which make for variability in behavior since they mutually conflict with one another, and at a given moment only one or the other can be manifested. An additional factor making for non-uniformity of expression of instincts is that instincts may be inhibited by habits.

After the work of James, preparing catalogues of instincts became a popular pastime of psychologists, and considerable ingenuity was exercised in getting a logically consistent classification with the goal of completeness in mind. In today's perspective we consider this a self-defeating form of armchair theorizing because the concept of instinct lends itself to an explanation of behavior akin to that of faculty psychology—we fight because we have a fighting instinct. But in the time of James, appeal to instinct in the human species was a way of calling attention to man's biological heritage, a view which then needed defense. Man as an organism in a world of nature was being defended by an appeal to instinct.

Psychologist or Philosopher?

James' opinion of himself as a psychologist and philosopher demands examination. One must be careful to distinguish this more general opinion from that negative one already expressed concerning the value of laboratory work.

Philosophy and psychology were freely intermingled by James in the study of perception, thought, will, the self, religion, experience, and association. When, as he often did, he introduced philosophy into his psychology, he recognized it for philosophy and was apt to make this clear to the reader. He also seemed to be given to yearning to be that which he was not. He was an empiricist, a pluralist, a pragmatist, and an individualist, but, when set for the moment on any of these, he yearned for rationalism, monism, intellectualism, or socialism. No important intellectual problem to James was of such a nature that it could be settled, once and for all. Even against his strongest intellectual antipathies the door was not slammed shut; a crack was left standing open, so if he wished he might later slip through.

Was he a psychologist or a philosopher or both? James, himself, did not change, he directed his interest to a different aspect of an over-all interest. He was aware of these shifts, as when in the *Principles* he speaks of staking his all on being a psychologist, with the significant qualification, "for the time."[67] Nevertheless, he always treated psychology philosophically and philosophy psychologically. It would seem as if he was always both but that one or the other would predominate at a given time, at which point he would castigate his subordinate interest. He was a *psychologist*-philosopher when he worked on his *Principles* and when he said of philosophy, "What a curse philosophy would be if we couldn't forget all about it." He was a *philosopher*-psychologist when he called psychology a, "nasty little subject."[68] or, with his usual fine inconsistency, when, after completing the *Principles*, he wrote his publisher that writing it proved there was no science of psychology at all and, secondly, that he, James, was "incapable."[69] He was a *philosopher*-psychologist when he was given the honorary degree at Harvard.

One may ask if this was what he thought of the new psychology, why did he bother with it? First, he was most interested in its possibilities for the future and not for its past accomplishments.[70] In this context the *Principles* is a critical survey which would help to give psychology a future. In regard to this he took a definite strategical position. In writing to Stumpf in 1892 he expressed this conviction as follows: "A psychologist's merit seems to me in the *present* condition of that science to consist much less in the *definitiveness* of his conclusions than in his suggestiveness and fertility."[71] Second, he grew away from it, or, as it is perhaps more preferable to put it, his interests in philosophy were strengthened.

James helped to give psychology an indigenous vitality and freedom from the narrowing influences of an exclusively laboratory approach and served to broaden the field to include the whole wealth of human experience. James exercised his great talents as a psychologist and philosopher to separate the two fields. He united these fields in his own person, but he did not wish to continue to have psychology bound to philosophical assumptions. Instead, he wanted to liberate psychology, using philosophy as one of his tools. This liberation did not extend to the point that he wanted psychology to have a separate department of its own. He was quite content with having psychology remain in the philosophy department.

And yet there is the other side of the coin. His very receptivity, enthusiasm, and complexity made for contradiction and confusion. It was the other Alice, his sister, who perhaps summed up William James and his work most acutely. He had told her that his Chocorua summer house had fourteen doors all opening outward. She commented, "His brain isn't limited to fourteen, perhaps unfortunately."[72]

The thinking of James contained many paradoxes, as Gordon Allport[73] has neatly and succinctly demonstrated. These paradoxes were such as to be productive of thinking in the generations that followed. Precisely because they

36. J. M. CATTELL, Early Psychological Laboratories, *Science*, 1928, 67, 543–548.

37. W. JAMES, Report on Mrs. Piper's Hodgson-Control, *Proc. Amer. Soc. Psyhical. Res.* 1909, 3, 470–589.

38. W. JAMES, *Pragmatism: a New Name for Some Old Ways of Thinking*. New York: Longmans, Green, 1907.

39. W. JAMES, *The Meaning of Truth: a Sequel to "Pragmatism."* New York: Longmans, Green, 1909.

40. *Pragmatism*, p. 22.

41. W. JAMES, Does Consciousness Exist? *J. Phil. Psychol., Sci. Meth.*, 1904, 1, 477–491.

42. W. JAMES, *Talks to Teachers on Psychology: and to Students on Some of Life's Ideals*. New York: Holt, 1899.

43. M. CURTI, *The Social Ideas of American Educators*. New York: Scribner's, 1935.

44. W. JAMES, *The Varieties of Religious Experience*. New York: Longmans, Green, 1902.

45. *Ibid.*, Lec. V, VI.

46. W. JAMES, *Some Problems in Philosophy: a Beginning of an Introduction to Philosophy*. New York: Longmans, Green, 1911.

47. *Varieties*, p. 233.

48. PERRY, *op. cit.*

49. *Principles*.

50. PERRY, *op. cit.*

51. *Principles*, p. 158.

52. *Ibid.*, p. 159.

53. *Ibid.*, p. 153.

54. *Ibid.*, p. 129.

55. *Ibid.*, pp. 180–181.

56. *Ibid.*, pp. 199–200.

57. *Ibid.*, pp. 84–94. (Herrnstein & Boring Excerpt No. 91)

58. *Ibid.*, p. 79.

59. *Ibid.*, p. 83.

60. *Ibid.*, p. 367.

61. *Ibid.*, p. 370.

62. *Ibid.*, pp. 851–865. (Herrnstein & Boring Excerpt No. 75)

63. *Ibid.*, p. 436.

64. E. L. THORNDIKE & R. S. WOODWORTH, The Influence of Improvement in One Mental Function Upon the Efficiency of Other Functions, *Psychol. Rev.*, 1901, 8, 247–261; 384–395; 553–564. (Herrnstein & Boring Excerpt No. 100)

65. *Ibid.*, p. 743.

66. C. G. LANGE & W. JAMES, *The Emotions.* (ed. by K. Dunlap) Baltimore: Williams & Wilkins, 1922.

67. *Principles,* p. 200.

68. H. JAMES, *op. cit.*, 2, p. 2.

69. *Ibid.*, p. 48.

70. E. G. BORING, Human Nature vs. Sensation: William James and the Psychology of the Present, *Amer. J. Psychol.*, 1942, 55, 310–327.

71. PERRY, *op. cit.*, 2, p. 180.

72. *Ibid.*, I, p. 411.

73. G. W. ALLPORT, The Productive Paradoxes of William James, *Psychol. Rev.*, 1943, 50, 95–120.

CHAPTER 17

HALL, CATTELL, AND TITCHENER:

PIONEERS IN PSYCHOLOGY IN THE UNITED STATES

Wᴵᴸᴸᴵᴬᴹ JAMES was the first American psychologist, but the growth of psychology before and after the turn of the century was not the work of one man alone. James had worthy younger contemporaries in G. Stanley Hall, James McKeen Cattell, and Edward Bradford Titchener, as well as that group of psychologists who founded functional psychology.

G. STANLEY HALL

G. Stanley Hall was much more important in his role as the first organizer and administrator in American psychology than for his contribution to psychological research or theory. But these functions, too, must have its pioneer, and his effect on psychology in the United States must be considered.

Life of Hall[1]

Granville Stanley Hall was born of Puritan ancestry in 1844 at Ashfield, a rural hamlet in Massachusetts. The Halls were substantial, hardworking, pious farmers. His parents were unusual only in the extent of their education. His mother had attended the Albany Female Seminary, then one of the very few institutions in the East for higher education of women; and his father had saved his money from some years of farm labor to return to school. Both parents then taught school for several years. Hall's boyhood was spent on the farm, working hard out-of-doors, except in the winter, when the long evenings were filled with reading aloud by his mother.

After doing well in the local rural school, Hall "kept school" for a while and, on the whole, enjoyed it. His mother had always wanted him to go to college, and they finally convinced his father. Hall, himself, was more than willing. A year's work in a seminary prepared him for Williams, where he enrolled in 1863. It was not until after the Civil War that Hall discovered his father had bribed a physician into certifying him "exempt" from military service.

At Williams, Hall studied with Mark Hopkins and found interests in diversified fields—associationism, the Scottish school, John Stuart Mill, and the theory of evolution. Without too much in the way of a "call," he prepared for the ministry. Consequently, on graduation in 1867, he enrolled in the Union Theological Seminary in New York City. During his year in New York, he explored the city with zest, roaming the streets, visiting police courts, attending churches of all denominations. He joined a discussion club interested in the study of positivism, visited the theater for plays and musicals, tutored young ladies from the "elite" of New York, visited a phrenologist, and, generally, had an exciting year. He was not noted for his religious orthodoxy. After preaching his trial sermon before the faculty and students, he went to the office of the president for criticism. Instead of discussing his sermon, the president knelt and prayed that Hall would be shown the errors of his ways!

One member of the faculty, a foreign-trained scholar who tutored him in philosophy, advised him to seek foreign study. Through the intercession of Henry Ward Beecher, the famous preacher, he received a loan of $500 for this purpose.

In the early summer of 1868 Hall sailed for Europe and made his way to Bonn. After a period studying theology and philosophy there, he moved on to Berlin, where he not only continued with theological and philosophical studies, particularly Aristotle, but also worked under DuBois-Reymond in physiology, studied physics, and attended a clinic for mental diseases as well as satisfying a very wide array of other interests. Beer gardens, theaters, and some lighthearted romantic episodes helped to round out his German education.

It was not until 1871 that he returned home, heavily in debt and without a degree. He expected to take up an appointment at a midwestern university but its administration cancelled the appointment, fearing that his proposal to teach the history of philosophy would be unsettling. Through a friend he received an appointment as a tutor to the five children of Jesse Seligman, the banker. He remained over a year with the family, in New York City and at their country places.

Antioch College, a "western outpost" of Unitarianism, in Ohio, had need of someone to teach English literature. To this post Hall was appointed. Later he shifted to French and German language and literature and, finally, to philosophy. As was not unusual in small colleges he had many extra-curricular duties—serving as librarian, leading the choir, and taking his turn at preaching. In his second and third year he managed to spend most of his time teaching philosophical subjects. He read the first volume of Wundt's *Physiological Psychology* immediately after its publication and decided to return to Germany to study psychology. In the spring of 1876 he started out but got only as far as Cambridge, Massachusetts. Here he was met with an offer of an instructorship in English at Harvard. He took it, hoping for a chance to transfer to philosophy and psychology. His work in required sophomore English was monotonous and time-consuming, but he found time to work with H. P. Bowditch at the Harvard Medical School and to carry out in his laboratory a study on "The Muscular Perception of Space," which he presented as a thesis for the doctorate in philosophy at Harvard in 1878. He also did work with James, whom he got to know quite well. Hall received his degree in psychology upon recommendation of the Department of Philosophy. After his degree he immediately left for Europe.

Hall first studied at Berlin doing a considerable amount of work in physiology. In his second year he moved on to Leipzig to become Wundt's first American student. Despite the enthusiasm with which he had looked forward to working with Wundt, the reality does not seem to have been to his liking. Hall attended Wundt's lectures and served as a subject in experiments but seemed to have performed no research of his own in the laboratory. Instead he undertook a considerable amount of work in physiology, particularly in the physiology of muscles, and then he went on to Berlin to work with Helmholtz, only to find him immersed in work in physics. Nevertheless, he wrote James that he was disappointed in Wundt and got much more out of Hemholtz.[2] Travel to educational centers followed, since he had decided that the way to make a living was to apply psychology to education, although when he returned to the United States, he was without a job or any prospects of one.

Meanwhile he had married a girl whom he had known from his days at Antioch and whom he had met again in Berlin, where she had been studying art. They took a small flat in a suburb of Boston in September, 1880. Things appeared bleak until a good fairy in the unlikely guise of President Eliot appeared at their house with the request that Hall give a series of Saturday talks on education in Boston under the auspices of Harvard University. These talks, which were well attended, brought him considerable favorable publicity.

Upon the strength of reports of his Saturday morning lectures, President Gilman of Johns Hopkins University asked Hall to Baltimore for a series of public lectures. In 1882 Hall arrived at Johns Hopkins, a school already celebrated for the beginning in 1876 of its bold experiment in higher education on the German plan. President Gilman had been having trouble finding just the right philosopher for his school, one that would be both "modern" and a scientist, yet not such as to offend orthodox religious sensibility. For a while there was considerable academic "in-fighting" involving Hall and the two other part-time appointments in a department for which one professorship was planned. Both the other contestants, Charles S. Peirce and George Morris, were very eminent men in philosophy. Hall was a scientist, which Gilman wanted, but the scales tipped more in his favor due to his accommodating attitude toward religious orthodoxy. Hall, as one might imagine, wanted nothing more than to dissociate psychology from religion, but he held no animosity toward his former field. He remained discreetly silent. In 1884 he was appointed professor of psychology and pedagogics, thus settling the matter.

After his professorial appointment Hall immediately took steps to separate his work from that in philosophy, for example, arranging it so that the Metaphysics Club, which had flourished before his time, died for lack of appropriate material for presentation.

In 1883 while still a lecturer, Hall set up laboratory equipment in a private house adjacent to the campus.[3] The next year he was given rooms on the campus. Hall's laboratory at Johns Hopkins, opening in 1884, is often said to be the first formally accepted psychological laboratory in the United States, but the claim is obscured somewhat because the university did not officially list it as a laboratory[4] and its equipment was treated as private property; Hall later took it with him to Clark University. A rather plausible case[5] has been made that the laboratory at the University of Wisconsin, under Jastrow, founded in 1888, was the first laboratory in the United States that received formal recognition from university authorities; yet Cattell speaks of founding a laboratory in 1887 at the University of Pennsylvania.[6] Jastrow, himself, acknowledged the priority of Cattell.[7] James' laboratory of 1875 was without formal recognition, but the university did supply space and funds. (See page 349.) James, then is entitled to be considered to have organized the first psychological laboratory in the United States.

Among Hall's students were James McKeen Cattell, John Dewey, Joseph Jastrow, William H. Burnham, and Edmund C. Sanford—all destined to be prominent psychologists. However, Cattell and Dewey were only incidentally his students. Cattell was at Hopkins when Hall arrived and left shortly thereafter for Leipzig. Dewey's degree, although taken during Hall's professorship, was for work done under Morris. However, Dewey did work in the laboratory and appreciated the significance of the "new psychology." The first Ph.D. in psychology at Hopkins went to Joseph Jastrow. Hall's own degree at Harvard had been awarded in psychology but this was in one sense an afterthought decided by the Philosophy Department apparently only at the time of completion of the work. Jastrow had enrolled for a degree in psychology, so his was the first Ph.D. in psychology in the United States.

Besides the laboratories of Johns Hopkins, Harvard, Pennsylvania, and Wisconsin, research laboratories were soon started at Columbia, Clark, Cornell, Indiana, Brown, Stanford, Yale, and Chicago. As mentioned before, at least twenty-four laboratories were founded before 1894, although some were small affairs designed only for undergraduate instruction. This was an impressive number, bringing out clearly the rapid spread of the new psychology.

In 1887, while still at Hopkins, Hall established the *American Journal of Psychology*. Its founding was entirely unexpected, although Hall had hoped to found a journal some day. A total stranger walked into his office, suggested he found a journal, and, then and there, gave him a check for $500. Later, it turned out that his benefactor had confused experimental psychology with psychical research and cancelled his subscription in the second year of its publication. This mistake is by no means as foolish as it sounds. The designation, "committee on experimental psychology" was used by psychical research organizations as the name for their investigatory bodies.

By then, Hall was preparing to leave Hopkins for the presidency of the soon-to-be-established Clark University in Worcester, Massachusetts. A wealthy merchant, Jonas Gilman Clark, had decided to endow an institution of higher learning in his home town. Before the school actually opened its doors, Hall had high aspirations for it, higher than could be realized later. He embarked on a tour of the European educational centers. Hall's letters[8] from Europe addressed to Clark are filled with the ideas suggested to him by these encounters, discussion of the chance of persuading a distinguished scholar to come to Worcester, and the like. He planned to make Clark University a graduate scientific institute, modeled after the German universities

and surpassing Johns Hopkins. Research was to be its task; education a necessary accompaniment. Clark University, founded in 1889, began with a faculty
organized into a small number of departments with no pretense of covering
the remaining fields.

Hall was soon to find that Mr. Clark had ideas different from his own about
the nature of the school he was endowing. Naturally reticent, Clark could
not or would not commit himself on money matters, and the amount of money
advanced was much smaller than Hall had been led to expect. Instead of
confiding his troubles to the faculty, Hall chose to keep silent at the time,
so he was blamed by them for the tight budget, but years later he was to
say his strongest motive for publishing his autobiography, the *Life and Confessions of a Psychologist*,[9] was his desire to tell the full story of Clark
University.

By 1892 faculty dissatisfaction had reached the point where resignations
of a majority of the faculty were imminent. Unknown to Hall at the time,
the situation was aggravated by the appearance of President Harper of the
newly-founded University of Chicago, who desperately needed to build a
faculty to fulfill plans to utilize the Rockefeller millions. A faculty raid
of monumental proportions took place, with Harper offering to double salaries.
Three Clark men were made department heads of chemistry, physics, and
biology at Chicago. At the end of the expedition Harper even offered an
appointment to Hall, who, on hearing from him what he had done, told him
he thought, "his act comparable to that of a housekeeper who would steal
in at the back door to engage servants at a higher price."[10]

Clark University continued its work, although with a vastly reduced staff.
Those faculty members who remained were intensely loyal. Of the twelve
men who started the academic year of 1892, there were no resignations for
twenty-one years thereafter! Some other money came in, and Hall and the
Clark faculty adjusted to this economic level. Finally, near the turn of the
century, the bulk of the Clark estate came to the university, divided between
the library, the graduate school, and a new undergraduate institution which
Hall had opposed but Mr. Clark had long advocated. The terms of his will
stipulated that Hall was to have no connection with the college as such;
although he continued as head of the graduate school.

Fortunately for psychology, President Hall had also made himself Professor
of Psychology and continued to teach in the graduate school all during these
years and afterward. He also had brought along Edmund C. Sanford from
Baltimore to head the laboratory. William H. Burnham, another Hopkins
student, was put in charge of pedagogics, which in this setting meant educational psychology and mental hygiene. Adolph Meyer, later the leading psy-

chiatrist of his time, who was then at Worcester State Hospital, also gave lectures.

Hall's last publication within the conventional limits of experimental psychology (on touch sensitivity) occurred in 1887. His own work thereafter was non-experimental in nature, but this limitation does not indicate his attitude toward the field and his faith in the advantage of scientific rigor. He unequivocally and eloquently defended laboratory work. Moreover, his students saw him as the leader of the forces which would make psychology a science. True, there are many indications that the laboratory was too far removed from life to meet his own personal interests. Also, he was occasionally impatient with the slow plodding of the laboratory. Nevertheless, experimental psychology was still his vision of psychology, even though he saw that it was for others to carry on the work.

His own teaching struck sparks in all directions. He was at his best in his weekly seminar, held at his home, where students and faculty presented papers. L. M. Terman, who originated the Stanford-Binet Scales of Intelligence and became the leading student of intelligence in the United States for some decades, expressed a representative opinion. "For me, Clark University meant briefly three things: freedom to work as I pleased, unlimited library facilities, and Hall's Monday evening seminar." [11] Hall was the great graduate teacher of American psychology. By 1893 eleven of the fourteen Ph.D. degrees from American universities had been given by him; by 1898 this had increased to thirty awarded out of fifty-four.[12]

It was Hall's idea to institute the first scientific organization of psychologists, the American Psychological Association, which was founded in July 1892.[13] He issued the invitations, arranged for it to be held in Worcester, and in general dominated the meeting. Almost as a matter of course, he was elected the first president. It was at this first meeting that the scientific character of the organization was established firmly. Through the haze of the years it is impossible to determine who was present, but it seems as if ten to eighteen psychologists were there.[14] James was in Switzerland, but was included in the twenty-six charter members who received invitations. The first annual meeting was held later the same year. From these small beginnings has come an organization now having a membership of 25,000. After considerable controversy over the years, it has broadened its functions so as to be concerned with the application of psychology and the advancement of its professional status as well as with maintaining its original scientific goal.

A guiding intellectual theme for Hall was evolutionary theory, which had fascinated him since his student days at Williams. Hall's thinking concerning a whole host of psychological topics was guided by the conviction that the normal growth of the mind is to be seen as a series of evolutionary stages. Pursuing this aim, he turned to the psychological study of the child through the use of questionnaires, a procedure he had learned in Germany. In fact, in 1881, before leaving Boston for Baltimore, Hall had had a chance at research in the Boston school system. In this study, entitled "The Contents of Children's Minds," [15] and in subsequent studies, he unearthed a considerable body of miscellaneous information about children's thinking on a variety of subjects. By the end of 1915 at least, 194 questionnaires had been developed and applied by Hall and his students. The topics included anger, dolls, crying, the early sense of self, fears, foods, religious experience, death, conventionality, mathematics, superstitions, dreams, and, of course, many more.

Although in present perspective these studies are seen to be naïve and poorly executed, they created great public enthusiasm and led to the founding of the so-called child-study movement. Large numbers of parents and teachers turned to the task of applying and interpreting questionnaires. All over the world they uncritically and dogmatically stated their superficial excursions into child development. The sentimentality and general wooliness of the movement led to a reaction against it, both within psychology and from various sections of the public, and in a few more years it disappeared. Nonetheless, the concept of psychological development had been firmly established through this work. The child-study movement served to bring home forcefully the importance of the empirical study of the child, while through its very excessess it made for an increased critical evaluation of research.[16]

In 1893, Hall, at his own expense, had founded the *Pedagogical Seminary* (now the *Journal of Genetic Psychology*), to which he and his students contributed a large share of the articles. This journal was the chief outlet for research in child study, as well as that in educational psychology.

It was in his huge work entitled *Adolescence*[17] in 1904 that Hall stated most completely his particular recapitulation theory of development. He offered the conjecture that in his individual development, the child repeats the life history of the race. For instance, the level of the primitive man is repeated when the child plays at cowboys and Indians.

Hall continued his interest in religion, expressed in speculation and research on the psychology of religion. During the latter years of the last century, he offered a course in the psychology of Christianity and encouraged studies in this area by his students. In 1917 he published his own major contribution, *Jesus, the Christ, in the Light of Psychology*.[18] To view Christ as the title implies did not sit well with his former brethren of the cloth.

Hall had been one of the first Americans to become interested in psychoanalysis. The twentieth anniversary of Clark University in 1909 was celebrated with a series of conferences, including the famous visit of Freud and Jung to the United States at Hall's invitation. This invitation was a courageous step in view of the suspicion and dislike which Hall knew to be associated with the whole psychoanalytic movement.

He also showed his interest in psychoanalysis through teaching of the subject. A report of his teachings for the academic year 1916 included this description of a course he offered:

> Much stress is laid upon the score or two of so-called mechanisms of the Freudian school, its history and development, and epitomes of the works of the chief representatives, along with an account of the two divergent groups of workers represented by Jung and Adler. The work was correlated to some extent with matter derived from the history of marriage and of the family, and the history of monogamy. The view taken by these lectures is that the methods of psychoanalysis open up, as nothing has yet done, the more or less unconscious domains of the psyche, and enable us to explain some hitherto insoluble problems and far more yet of the emotional or affective life of man. The chief trend of this course, however, is to show that many of the mechanisms apply not only to ordinary life, but to all the other great emotions besides love, so that not so much the psychology of sex as that of the deeper nature of man is considered.[19]

This last sentence captured his attitude. He was an eclectic, cheerfully borrowing from Freud what he saw as useful and equally without malice accepting work which was contradictory to his teachings.[20] He could admire Freud, but wanted to go beyond the "psychology of sex." As his letters show, he could never understand why Freud was so intolerant of eclectic borrowing.[21] Freud, of course, saw this behavior as unforgivably inconsistent. Hall maintained his interest in psychoanalysis throughout his life. In the last conversation that Cattell had with him, Hall expressed himself as puzzled why academic psychology so vehemently rejected psychoanalysis.[22]

In another perspective this advocacy of a hearing for psychoanalysis was but one of Hall's contributions to what later was to emerge as clinical psychology. Even before arriving at Clark, Hall had been interested in abnormal psychology, having taken his students to Bayview Hospital for the Insane for demonstrations, and for a time he had even functioned as its superintendent. The presence of Adolph Meyer, as a lecturer in abnormal psychology, at Clark University has already been mentioned. Although commonplace in France, in the United States the teaching of psychopathology to psychologists was most unusual. It was Hall's student, H. H. Goddard, who did the pioneer important work on feeblemindedness, and another student, L. M. Terman, with his Stanford-Binet, who supplied the indispensible tool for the measurement of intelligence. Arnold Gesell, still another student, was responsible for tremendous amount of painstaking research on the physical and mental growth of children. Moreover, Hall lent his encouragement to this kind of work by giving it access to publication sources in his journals.

After resigning the presidency of Clark in 1920, Hall continued writing, including his autobiography. Characteristically enough, he became interested in the problems of aging and published a volume on *Senescence*[23] in 1922. In 1924, four years after his retirement he died at his home in Worcester, Massachusetts, just a few months after being elected president of the American Psychological Association for a second time. With his death, a romantic and heroic era closed.[24]

Overview

Some clues as to Hall's stature can be gleaned from the opinions of a large sample of psychologists who were solicited in connection with a commemorative statement about him.[25] Despite the veil of adulation that clouds such ceremonies, it is clear that he was primarily a source of stimulation for others, opening up for them areas of study and research. As Titchener[26] put it at about the same time, "He sought to inspire and I tried to train," but they shared the goal of research; their difference, therefore, was in the means, not in the end sought. A psychologist[27] who worked with Hall at Clark spoke of Hall's conviction that psychology should not set limits for itself and of his desire, "to build the top of the mountain first." This psychologist pointed out that he, himself, would have them start at the bottom.

G. Stanley Hall was versatile and broad in his interest, a pioneer in many areas of psychological endeavor. A considerable number of the psychologists polled considered him to be *the* pioneer in studies of childhood, adolescence, senescence, and human genetics. Of these, the stimulation he gave child psychology is most important. In a sense Hall made a gospel of childhood. He lifted the child to a new plane of importance, focusing on a child as a child, to study him for his own sake.

Hall remained throughout his life intensely agile in his thinking with boundless enthusiasm and with many and contradictory views on everything. He was a founder so intent on his pioneering that he almost always moved immediately on to his next adventure, leaving for others the task of tidying up. He himself wondered if his life had not been a series of fads or crazes.[28] He said that Wundt would rather have been commonplace than brilliantly wrong.[29] One suspects that Hall would have reversed the statement for himself.

James McKeen Cattell[30]

In the course of an after-dinner speech, James McKeen Cattell once told the story of his boyhood visit to a phrenologist. After due inspection of the bumps of his head, the phrenologist proceeded to reel off characteristics that were laudatory with one distinguished exception—he suffered from a deficiency in will power! The eruption of laughter from his friends that greeted this remark seemed to surprise Cattell.[31] In point of fact, many of Cattell's major characteristics centered around this salient trait. Dogged determination, unflagging energy, and resistance to domination by those having what he considered to be undeserved authority seemed to have characterized this American psychologist and scientific statesman.

James McKeen Cattell, met before as Wundt's self-appointed first assistant and as a student at Johns Hopkins, was born in 1860 in Easton, Pennsylvania, where his father was professor of classics and later president of Lafayette College. Here, in 1880 Cattell took his bachelor's degree. His undergraduate interests had been primarily in literature, but they changed so that he followed the then usual custom of graduate study abroad and went to Göttingen and to Leipzig to study philosophy. Naturally he studied under Wundt. After a paper in philosophy had won him a fellowship at Johns Hopkins for the years, 1882–1883, he returned to the United States, just at the time Hall was starting his laboratory. In the laboratory Cattell started research on the time taken for different mental activities. This research reinforced his desire to become a psychologist, so he returned to Leipzig the following year. It was on his return to Leipzig that he announced to Wundt he was to be his assistant.

Indications of his independence and firm convictions appeared early. Contrary to the usual custom of being assigned a problem by Wundt, Cattell worked on his own problems in reaction time. He also became convinced that the introspective efforts directed toward fractionation of the reaction time into perception, choice, and the like, then current gospel in Wundt's laboratory, was something which he could not carry out and, indeed, he doubted whether others could do so. The situation reached the point that he did some of his experiments at his lodging rather than in the laboratory, since Wundt would not permit subjects in his laboratory who could not profit from introspection.[32] Although somewhat strained, relations never reached a breaking point. Wundt and Cattell did agree on the value of the study of reaction time. In Cattell's eyes it was a valuable tool for the study of the time necessary for mental operation, especially, for investigation of individual differences.

As early as 1885,[33] Cattell published a paper on the exposure time necessary before perception of colors, letters, and words. It concluded with a discussion of what he called a matter of "special interest," the "individual differences" he had obtained. Cattell worked prodigiously during the Leipzig years of 1883 to 1886 publishing nine research papers before the following year was out. Studies on the influences of stimulus intensity upon reaction time (1885), the time of word perception (1886), and the association time for various categories (1887) were typical subjects of his research.

After taking his degree at Leipzig in 1886, Cattell divided the next two years between the United States and England. On one side of the Atlantic he taught at Bryn Mawr College and at the University of Pennsylvania and on the other worked in Galton's laboratory in London and lectured at Cambridge.

Cattell found in Galton a kindred spirit—"the greatest man whom I have known."[34] Contrary to the opinion sometimes expressed, his interest in individual differences, as we have seen, had made themselves apparent before his contact with Galton. In fact, his research concerned with individual differences was begun in America *before* he went to Leipzig and, consequently, before working with Galton. From the tone of his writings, the most specific reason for his interest in variability is the climate of the times in the United States.

In 1888, Cattell was appointed professor of psychology at the University of Pennsylvania. This was the first professorship in *psychology,* not just in the United States but anywhere in the world. Psychologists before him had been appointed in the department of philosophy. With the appointment of Cattell, the field of psychology had the recognition of its independence from the older discipline. Thereafter, the practice of naming professors of psychology spread rapidly, and before the beginning of the twentieth century there was a considerable number. Cattell founded a laboratory at Pennsylvania in 1887, although it was not until 1889 that an adequate laboratory was opened.[35] While not the first in the country, it did have the distinction of being the first to serve to introduce the undergraduate student to the methods of experimental psychology.

In 1891 Cattell moved to Columbia University as professor of psychology and administrative head of the department and, at first, with the additional task of administering the work of anthropology.[36] His rapid rise on the American psychological scene is shown by a professorship at the University of Pennsylvania at twenty-eight, the chairmanship of the department of Columbia University at thirty-one, the presidency of the American Psychological Association at thirty-five, and the first psychologist to be elected to the National Academy of Sciences at forty.

Meanwhile, Cattell continued to be active in research. In a paper published in 1890 in *Mind*, the British journal, he coined the term, "mental tests," [37] in describing a series of tests administered to students at the University of Pennsylvania. As distinguished from Binet's later more complex tasks, these involved more elementary operations. The basic tests of this series were dynamometer pressure, rate of movement, sensation areas by means of the two-point threshold, just noticeable differences in weight, reaction time for sound, time for naming colors, bisection of a line, judgment of times, and memory span for letters.

At Columbia, Cattell continued his testing program with a substantially similar battery of tests. After collecting data from several entering classes, an analysis of the results was made by Wissler in 1901.[38] Correlations of the individual test scores with academic class standings were found to be inconclusively low, as were the intercorrelations among the scores of the tests themselves. In sharp contrast, academic grades in the various subjects and overall academic standing were substantially correlated with one another. Results with specific sensory-motor tests, likewise showing negligible correlations with other measures, also emerged from Titchener's laboratory at Cornell.[39] It began to appear that the then available psychological tests were relatively useless as predicators of ability. Further exploration along the lines suggested by these studies tended to dwindle. Knowledge of Binet's results, which were later to dominate, had yet to show themselves in the university setting.

In the spirit of the earlier work of Galton, but with vastly improved methodology, Cattell also carried on studies of the nature and origin of scientific ability, using the method of the order of merit. This method is applicable to any set of stimuli which is capable of being ranked according to some criterion, such as the relative brightness of shades of gray, the problem he first investigated.[40] It could be and soon was applied to such problems as the relative appeals of pictures or of colors. A number of judges would be asked to arrange the items to be evaluated in a rank order, the first in order of merit ranked first, and so on. The average ranking for each item is then calculated and a final rank order obtained.

This method was applied by Cattell to the relative eminence of American psychologists in 1903.[41] For obvious reasons, the actual names associated with specific ranks were not published immediately. It was not until 1929 that the order of names was released. Rank number one went to William James, while the next five ranks went to Cattell, Hugo Münsterberg, G. Stanley Hall, J. Mark Baldwin, and Edward Bradford Titchener. In present perspective two of these men do not rank as among the great psychologists. It will be instructive to pause and examine their careers.

Hugo Münsterberg has been met before as James' rather unfortunate choice to head the laboratory at Harvard. It is probable that his present lack of influence can be attributed to the fact that he turned to arguing the case for the application of psychology to fields which did not yet have a research basis from which to operate.[42] A glorification of matters German immediately preceding World War I resulted in personal unpopularity and public disfavor.

James Mark Baldwin (1861–1934), whose most productive period was a ten year stay at Princeton, was an "international" psychologist, teaching not only in the United States but also in Mexico and finally in Paris, where he died. Theoretically rather than experimentally oriented, he vigorously pursued the theme of the importance of evolutionary doctrine for psychology, including the importance of the study of the child.[43] In cooperation with others, he edited a huge *Dictionary of Philosophy and Psychology*.[44] His departure from the American scene as early as 1909 had something to do with his relative lack of influence.

In further developing the method of order of merit, Cattell asked men acknowledged to be competent in each of the various scientific fields to rate their colleagues in order. Those emerging at the top of the lists for each science were given a star in the *Biographical Directory of American Men of Science*, a source book which emerged from this work. Through the seventh edition the starred men were asked to select the new men for the directory, a technique not followed in subsequent editions. To this very day, this directory in its successive editions is a basic reference book, comparable to a specialized *Who's Who*. Although originating in a purely scientific study, its practical value has been considerable.

After experiencing financial difficulties, *Science*, a weekly journal, had been acquired in 1895 by Cattell from Alexander Graham Bell. In its publication, Cattell sought and secured the help of leading scientists throughout the country. After overcoming the financial difficulties, *Science* became the leading general scientific publication in the United States and in 1900 it was made the official organ of the American Association for the Advancement of Science.

Cattell and other American psychologists, including James,[45] had decided that the *American Journal of Psychology* was functioning primarily as a house organ for the staff of Clark University and some of their associates. Accordingly, in 1894 in collaboration with J. Mark Baldwin, Cattell founded a rival journal, the *Psychological Review*. In his hands this journal grew into an entire series of journals. Editing a weekly and managing journals takes time, and Cattell's personal research productivity began to drop off.

Robert S. Woodworth and Edward L. Thorndike had joined him at Columbia very soon after his arrival and were associated with him for many years. The separation of the psychologists at the College and Graduate School from those at Teacher's College, where Thorndike did his work and where Cattell did some of his teaching, fortunately did not yet exist. It was only later that 120th Street, separating Teacher's College from the main campus, became "the widest street in the world."

During the years Cattell was at Columbia, more psychologists-to-be studied at Columbia University than at any other institution in the United States. They are active in the contemporary period and, hence, beyond scope of the present chapter. By and large, Cattell gave his students freedom to advance on their own, and, while he remained available for guidance, he stressed independent work.

He insisted on a similar independence for himself, arguing that a professor's time, if spent within his areas of competence, should not necessarily be devoted solely to the university and to its students. He established his home on a hilltop near Garrison, forty miles from New York, coming to the university only on certain days each week. Later he equipped a laboratory and an editorial office in his home. To some extent this served to free him from the interruptions of university life.

Relations with the University administration became strained. Moreover, he believed that many decisions which were being left to university administrators were properly matters for faculty decision. He not only raised his voice in pursuit of the aim of faculty participation, he also helped to found the American Association of University Professors. During the years of World War I, Cattell wrote a letter to members of Congress protesting the sending of conscientious objectors to combat duty. This unpopular and personally disadvantageous position was one from which he could not in good conscience desist, so he stood by his position. The President and the trustees judged his action to be treason and on this ground dismissed him from the University. Cattell, in turn, sued for libel, and the case was settled by his receiving a large annuity.

Many of Cattell's most important activities thereafter continued to be, in the best sense of the word, promotional in character. His numerous presidential addresses often concerned growth and the present status of psychology.[46] He also served as a spokesman of psychology to the other sciences in the United

States, as his editorships show. He did not hesitate to criticize and to advise in print the universities, the philanthropic agencies, the Carnegie Institution, and the National Academy of Sciences. He vigorously defended the growth of applied psychology, and psychology as a profession. As early as 1904, he predicted that there would eventually be a profession of psychology as well as a science.[47] In a similar spirit he organized the Psychological Corporation in 1921 in order to promote the application of psychology.[48] This corporation has grown considerably, while using its profits to support other research, and it still continues to play an important role in professional psychology at the present time. Cattell remained active as an editor and senior citizen scientist until his death in 1944.

Cattell epitomizes a major movement of American psychology. Never given to theoretical writing, he remained in research for some years of his life, thereafter maintaining a respect for and an ability to criticize research. His interest in individual differences was instrumental in his working for psychology as a profession as well as a science. His bent toward administration and editing placed him among that small group of men who gave the beginnings of psychology in the United States its characteristic flavor.

Edward Bradford Titchener

During the second decade of this century at Cornell University, an academic ceremony took place each day that the Professor of Psychology lectured on introductory psychology. Shortly before the class hour the Professor inspected the demonstrational material which had been laid out; the staff and assistants gathered in his office adjoining the lecture room; the professor donned his Oxford master's gown, "which gives me the right to be dogmatic"; the staff filed through one door to take front row seats; the Professor emerged through another door directly onto the lecture platform. The lecture began.

Such was the grand manner in which lectures were offered by Wundt's most faithful pupil, Edward Bradford Titchener. Trenchant and powerful lectures, they were often the forum for pronouncements about his system of psychology, and to Titchener's audience of staff, graduate students, and sophomore college students, Titchener's system *was* psychology.

After Wundt's American students returned home they almost always significantly modified his views according to their particular temperament or social environment. This was not the case with Titchener. Titchener held to the tradition of Wundt, both in teaching and writing; although he developed and modified specific details. His contribution to Wundt's theory was systematic explicitness in which he surpassed his prolific and erudite master.

Life of Titchener[49]

Titchener was born in 1867 in the old Roman town of Chichester, England. Titchener's father died shortly after his marriage, leaving young Titchener with little monetary security. At fourteen Titchener went to Malvern College, a new but already recognized public school. He continued his studies at Oxford, where he concentrated upon philosophy and the classics for four years. In his fifth year he became a research assistant to Burdon-Sanderson, the physiologist, for whom he was to hold a lasting admiration.

Dissatisfaction with what he called the "logical constructions of the English school,"[50] was instrumental in drawing Titchener to Leipzig. As he was later to evaluate it, he heard about psychology at Oxford; he studied it at Leipzig.[51] Upon arrival he found himself in an active, enthusiastic group of young future psychologists, among them a half-dozen from the United States. Meumann, mentioned earlier, was his room-mate, and Külpe was *Dozent*. Titchener actually saw very little of Wundt who was thirty-five years his senior and who had already adopted his characteristically aloof pattern. Despite this lack of a personal relationship and only a two-year stay at Leipzig, Wundt made a life-long impression.

After receiving his degree from Leipzig in 1892, Titchener returned to Oxford, where for a few months he served as an extension lecturer in biology. To stay on at Oxford would have been his ambition, but Oxford was not ready for psychology. In any event, he had agreed to accept a position at Cornell University replacing a friend from Leipzig, Frank Angell, who was leaving for Stanford University.

So in 1892 Titchener arrived in Ithaca, New York, to the raw and new (and muddy) campus of Cornell University. He was assistant professor of psychology, but, more important, he was in charge of the laboratory that his friend Angell had founded the year before.

For the next few years, Titchener was busy organizing the laboratory, buying and building equipment, carrying out research, and writing articles (sixty-two between 1893 and 1900) and gradually attracting more and more students. At first he cooperated personally with every study in his laboratory, but discontinued this arduous practice[52] in later years. His research then came almost entirely through his students; he, himself, published nothing from the laboratory under his own name alone. His own published research consequently gives no indication of his productivity; it was through his direction of student investigations that the base for his systematic statements was developed. Under his direction fifty-eight doctorates and many minor studies were conducted.

Of the forty-six studies published in the first thirty volumes of the *American Journal of Psychology,* fifteen were on sensation, eight on perception, six each on memory and attention, and the rest scattered in related fields.

What could be more natural than to translate the Master? This he proceeded to do for several of Wundt's works. With one project of this kind Titchener found it hard to keep up with him. Years before, while still in England, Titchener had finished translating the third edition of the *Principles of Physiological Psychology* only to find that the indefatigable Wundt had written the fourth edition. Titchener, therefore, started over again, translating completely this new edition—only to find the prolific Wundt now had his fifth edition ready. This time Titchener translated but six of the twenty-two chapters, and, taking no chances, went to press. The rest of the book was never put into English. Titchener also translated works of Külpe, his friend from Germany who had not yet strayed from the true path of Wundtian exactitude into the luxurious, but overgrown jungle of imageless thought. Moreover, before the new century was six years old, Titchener had, on his own, written his *Outline of Psychology* (1896), his *Primer of Psychology* (1898), and the four important volumes of his *Experimental Psychology* (1901–1905).

His *Experimental Psychology*[53] bears the significant and relevant subtitle, *A Manual of Laboratory Practice,* designed to be used in "drill" courses for training in the method of psychology. It is divided into four parts, two instructor's manuals and two student's manuals, one of each devoted to qualitative experiments—sensations, affective qualities, attention, action, perception and association of ideas—and another of each devoted to quantitative experiments—thresholds for pressure, tone and sound, Weber's law, the various psychophysical methods, the reaction study of simple discrimination, cognition and choice times, and the reproduction of a time interval. Qualitative experiments, as he saw them, were essentially descriptions of conscious experiences by means of introspection, in which questions of "what" or "how" are asked; quantitative experiments assume that the mental process as such is already familiar from prior examination, and the task is to gather a long series of rather simple observations which are then expressed through mathematical shorthand in which questions of "how much" are asked. These volumes are probably the most erudite and encyclopedic works on psychology written in English.

As a younger man Titchener had close friends from his student days whom he cherished through the years. Throughout his life he always had a small group of psychologist friends with whom he kept up a voluminous correspondence. One psychologist[54] had a collection of 212 letters addressed to him from Titchener. (They are now in the Cornell archives.)

At first Titchener entered into social life at Cornell, but as he grew older, he withdrew more and more from the usual social and university contacts. He had been a living legend to some members of the faculty of Cornell, who, although they had heard of him for years, had never met him. Punctilious and somehow formidable, he gave deference where he thought it due and expected in turn to receive it from those he thought owed it to him.

His relation with psychologists outside of his own group also showed a tendency toward withdrawal. The American Psychological Association to which he was elected by the charter members in 1892, did not claim him for long. He resigned almost immediately in response to the Association's refusal to support a measure that Titchener considered to be a matter of professional ethics. Moreover, the Association's membership as a whole was by no means as rigorously scientific as Titchener's standards demanded. In 1897 he was host to a meeting of the Association, but he was still not a member. He did later rejoin only to resign at a later date, meanwhile refusing to attend any meetings. When the Association meeting was held in Ithaca in 1925, Titchener held "open house," for those who cared to come to see him at his home.

Beginning in 1904, Titchener organized his own group, the "Experimental-ists." [55] It was not an organization in the strict sense; annual meetings were arranged by the host, the director of the laboratory where the group was to meet. Needless to say, Titchener dominated the meetings, selecting those to be invited and the topics to be included. To this very day, this group, now somewhat more formally organized, carries on as a worthy representative of experimental psychology of the purest variety.

The *American Journal of Psychology*, for which Titchener became an associate editor in 1895, served something of the same function for him as did the *Philosophische Studien* for Wundt. However, it was not until 1921 when he moved up to become sole editor that it could begin to be employed as his own journal and, therefore, could serve as a platform similar to Wundt's. Titchener held firmly to his conviction that Cornell graduates in psychology formed a group, unified by their shared psychological orientations and there-fore differentiated from the rest of the psychological world. He was staunch in defending his opinions against outside disagreements, yet flexible under self-criticism. In these and other respects he resembled Wundt.

Toward the close of the first decade of the century Titchener prepared the *Textbook of Psychology*.[56] A systematic work in relatively brief compass, this gives what is still the most comprehensive account of his psychology available. After publication of the *Textbook*, Titchener began to prepare an extended statement of his systematic views. This work he found impossible to complete, although its appearance was expected for many years. A part of this work was published as articles in the *American Journal of Psychology,* and republished posthumously as a book.[57]

During the fifteen years preceding his death in 1927 his productivity showed neither the scope nor the depth of his earlier work. This is sometimes attributed to the cerebral tumor from which he suffered, but there is some evidence that the tumor did not originate until shortly before his death.

In his later years Titchener developed an intense interest in numismatics, especially in Mohammedan coins, even going so far as to learn Arabic in order to read the inscriptions, but one may question why a man heretofore so wrapped up in psychology found it necessary to turn to a hobby at all. Perhaps he had known honorary degrees and the trappings of academic success too early. Perhaps the decline had something to do with geography; Titchener never really became a part of the American scene, and he never considered giving up his English citizenship. Hence, he was ineligible for election to the National Academy of Sciences, and, as a psychologist in the "colonies," he never received his F.R.S.

Did his loss of interest in psychology, perhaps, have something to do with the changing face of psychology? Here, the record becomes obscure, and what follows must be seen as a personal interpretation, not necessarily shared by those who knew him personally and perhaps understood him better. As a younger man in a magnificent sort of simplicity, he had seen his particular views as that of psychology, while other points of view, admirable perhaps though they might be, were simply not psychology. In later life, except at Cornell and two or three student-manned laboratory outposts at other universities, psychology as a whole was moving steadily away from him. Did Titchener refuse to face this tragedy of seeing psychology, his psychology, changing irrevocably? We cannot be certain, but this might have made him unable or unwilling to continue with what should have been his most important work.

The Point of View of Psychology

Titchener[58] started with the view that all scientists are concerned with a subject matter in some phase of human experience; all knowledge is based on human experience. While biologists deal with living forms and chemists investigate elements, the psychologist also studies experience, but from the special point of view of the experiencing person. Perception, especially the perceptual illusion, is illustrative. For instance, if one sees a stick part in and part out of water, it appears bent. The experience as given, therefore, is that the stick is bent, even though applying a straight edge to it would disprove this. Even "white" as experienced is a mixture of colored lights, none of which is white. Yet as a datum in consciousness, white is simple in nature. Neither the physical stick nor the multitude of lights are the concern of psychology; the experience, as such, is its province. The psychologist's interest is in the process of experiencing these phenomena.

In the study of experiencing, to confuse the mental process and the object is to commit the "stimulus error." [59] To describe the object in common-sense terms of everyday language, instead of reporting the conscious content of the experience, is to commit this error. An "orange" is not an orange so far as introspective report is concerned, but the hues, brightnesses, and spatial characteristics of that stimulus object. Nor should a subject say he is afraid, for this is merely an interpretation; he must describe the conscious content if he is to avoid the stimulus error.

For Titchener,[60] mind is the sum total of human experiences considered as dependent upon a nervous system. Mind and consciousness are essentially the same, but the latter involves mental processes occurring *now,* rather than the sum-total. Human or mental experiences are always processes. According to Titchener the most striking fact about these is change. Nothing is stable; everything is in flux, a mosaic in motion.

It is perhaps appropriate to examine at this point what Titchener considered to be outside the field of psychology. Needless to say, Titchener shared Wundt's distaste for the applied aspects of psychology. Moreover, behavior is not the concern of a psychology of consciousness. If experience is the sole concern of psychology, then performance (behavior) is irrelevant. Behavior is worthy of study—as a branch of biology, not as psychology. Titchener objected to what he called, "the penny-in-the-slot sort of science," in which consciousness is said to be "inferred" when it was always there waiting to be interrogated.[61] Objective study is always inferential; experience and its study set the pattern. Logically, behaviorism, the point of view which would see study of behavior as paramount, is irrelevant to psychology. Nevertheless, psychology will obtain information concerning bodily mechanisms from the study of behavior, examining this biological information in the light of psychology.[62]

Titchener's dictum concerning unconscious phenomena was simply that consciousness includes only present mental processes. The unconscious consists of not present processes. Thus Titchener was not concerned with what lies below the surface of consciousness. In fact, he was definite in disparaging psychology as seen by James. Titchener spoke of James' *Psychology* as "theory of knowledge" and not psychology at all![63]

Introspection as the Method of Psychology[64]

All science depends upon observation. Psychological science depends upon observation of conscious experience or, to put it more succinctly, upon introspection. For introspective purposes to "look-within" consciousness, to Titchener, was the having of clear experiences regarded as dependent upon the experiencing individual.

Sometimes this may involve hardly more than simple inspection. Consider the following illustration: In front of a subject are two color wheels (motors so arranged to spin paper discs rapidly). On one wheel is a violet disc, on the other both a blue and a red disc, so interlocked that, when the wheel is standing still one sees portions of both the blue disc and the red disc. They are adjustable, so that an increase of either portion is possible. When spun, the second wheel will give a blue-red, that is, a shade of violet. The task of the subject is to adjust as exactly as he can the red and the blue portions until the resulting violet matches the violet of the first disc. The introspection is essentially inspectional; he merely reports when the two discs match.

Another illustration may be drawn from the already familiar two-point threshold. When the stimulus separation is very small the perception is that of a single pressure, which is reported as "one." When the stimulus separation is great, there is a report of two pressures. Intermediate between these two and the experience of pressure resembles that of a pattern of a dumbbell *i.e.*, two pressure points which are joined by a narrower band of pressure. The naïve subject would report, "two" because he knows that one round point could not give that particular stretched-out pattern. But in so doing he commits the "stimulus error." He has lapsed from the psychological point of view to *infer* what the stimulus must be. The sophisticated introspectionists would report "one," because he perceives a unitary pattern.

The material for introspection often may be more complex, say, a word called out to the subject who is to report the effect it produces on consciousness. Sometimes conditions get complicated, as in a long drawn out observation in which the introspection is delayed until the experience has run its course. Even a short temporal exposure may require a very long description. In both instances the introspector has to use retrospection. Often when he finds he cannot maintain an introspective attitude throughout the course of a complicated experience, he can have the experience repeated as many times as desired, removing the danger of missing some aspect of it.

The Tasks of Psychology[65]

The problems of the psychologist are "what," "how," and "why." The task of analysis is to answer the question of "what." Consciousness is directly observable. It is composed of simple describable units, and the analytical task of the psychologist is to break it down into its simplest components. The task of "how" is the task of synthesis. The psychologist does this by placing the elements found in the previous analysis in various combinations to arrive at the laws of their combination. For example, sensations of tone will blend, but they give an imperfect fusion, as in a major chord, whereas sensations of color fuse perfectly as when the spectrum mixes to give a simple white. The question of "why" gave Titchener more difficulty. One mental process cannot cause another. As evidence Titchener cited that an experience may be due to present stimuli to which he has never before been exposed. He rejected neural processes as the cause of mental processes, since the theory conflicted with his already postulated psychophysical parallelism. Titchener solved the problem to his satisfaction by arguing that, while the nervous system does not cause mental phenomena, it may be used to explain them. By introducing the "map" that the nervous system makes, it is possible to systematize our introspective data. The parallel processes in the nervous system explain the mental processes as a map explains the terrain.

Structuralism

Description of Titchener's system of psychology is sometimes oversimplified. He was a structuralist, critics said, meaning that the static elements of experience were his concern, as contrasted with functional study of the process of experience which had been espoused by James and others. This is simply not true. There is no doubt he utilized functional material; and the findings of psychophysics, which formed one major segment in his system, are readily viewed as depending upon the functions of discrimination and estimation. Unequivocally, he accepted the existence of a functional aspect of psychology.

Titchener held that his systematic view of psychology was that of psychology with no qualification whatsoever. Titchener did formulate the so-called structural position in an article published in 1898.[66] In investigating mental structure, he noted, a very large proportion of experimental psychology corresponds to morphology in biology. "Descriptive" psychology, concerned with function on the other hand, corresponds to physiology in biology. In his opinion, psychology's study of structure must precede study of function. He pointed out in justification that, while considerable agreement has been reached concerning the postulates of a stuctural psychology (*e.g.*, among Wundt, Külpe, Ebbing-haus, and, of course, Titchener), this is not the case with those he considered functionalists, such as Brentano, James, and Stout, who disagree among them-selves. Functional study, he concluded, is neither as accurate nor as scien-tifically final as is structural investigation, and a swing toward a functionally oriented psychology would be regrettable, since there is so much work yet to be done on structure.

Titchener's view has sometimes been referred to as existential psychology, since experiences are studied by him as existences, *i.e.*, as facts deserving of study for their own sake.[67] For example, content as lacking verbal meaning, as in the nonsense syllables of Ebbinghaus, present themselves to the experi-encing person as existential. A word of caution is necessary. The present-day popular meaning of existentialism has no more relation to that applied to Titchener's psychology than, for example, would the existentialism of Thomas Aquinas.

From the standpoint of those who applied the terms "structural" or "existential," his was a school of psychology. As for himself, it was simply psychology.

Views on Some Psychological Problems

Elementary mental processes to Titchener consisted of sensations, images, and affections.[68] This is to say in each of these three categories there are irreducible experiences which are incapable of analysis into anything simpler, similar in this respect to so-called chemical elements. As a youthful effort,[69] he even calculated the number of sensory elements, finding that the eye supplied somewhat less than 33,000, the ear less than 12,000 and all the rest about 18. Each of these qualities was a distinct conscious element, blended in various ways to form perceptions and ideas. Sensations are the elements of perception; images are the elements of ideas; and affections are the elements of emotions. In practice, Titchener stressed study of sensations, minimized that of ideas, and placed that of affections somewhere between.

The Wundtian attributes of quality and intensity were expanded by Titche-ner by adding duration, clearness, and (sometimes) extensity.[70] Duration is self-explanatory. Clearness was introduced as an attribute to lend systematic clarity to the place of attention in psychological experience. Clearness allows a particular place to a sensation in consciousness; clear sensations are dominant and outstanding; less clear are subordinate and undistinguished. Clear sensa-tions are those to which we attend; attention and sensory clearness are identical. By making attention into an attribute, Titchener eliminated the need to appeal to a "power" of attention while at the same time giving it a systematic place within his system.

Titchener later postulated that these attributes might be the datum of observation, while sensation was only a systematic classificatory device almost without existential reality.[71] Attributes, once they become the object of direct study, were the "systematic concepts" that stood up under observation.

After examining the imageless-thought controversy, Titchener saw no reason to change his basic assumption concerning the primacy of sensation, images, and feelings.[72] In thinking there may be obscure, fleeting, or faint aspects of the experience, but these are still imaginal or sensory elements. Conscious attitudes, to Titchener, were no more than complex integrations of sensory components, improperly analyzed by the Würzburg group and others. Even if later these proved to be non-sensory meaning elements, they would be the concern of logic, not of psychology.

Meaning as conscious representation comes about from combining primary elements in a manner reminiscent of Berkeley. Perceptions, to put it simply, are sensations (and images) with meaning, and this meaning is defined by Titchener as context. Sensations, therefore, are the core of perceptions to which images contribute as well to the context.

In order to be systematically rigorous and parsimonious, Titchener did not wish to introduce perception as still another mental element.[73] Sensation and attention, as a pattern of clarity, account for some of the phenomena of perception, but there remains an unexplained aspect. Meaning is that something which we expect to be accounted for by perception; perceptions are meaningful, we say, when we perceive an apple, a friend, or a sentence in a book. To Titchener,[74] meaning shows itself in context—one mental process is the meaning of another, if it is the other's context. In its simplest form it takes at least two sensations (or images), then, to make a meaning, one serving as core, the other as context. Illustrative would be seeing a strange face (core) and having a visual image of the name come to one (context). Hence one knows what it means (perception). By some process of accretion, presumably associative, meanings as composed of sensory or imaginal contexts accrue to an initial sensory or imaginal core. Thus, context gives meaning in the framing of new perceptions and ideas. Titchener does note an important exception: habitual meanings can occur without conscious context, which means they may be carried unconsciously. In this acceptance of unconscious context Titchener went beyond Berkeley in his theory of meaning. In addition, then, to perception having as its core a sensation, to which the context is other sensations and images, an important addition is the unconscious context. All three make up the context.

Feeling or affection received special attention from his students in the Cornell Laboratory. On the basis of introspective studies carried on in his laboratory, Titchener dissented from Wundt's tridimensional theory.[75] He denied to feeling the dimensions of tension-relaxation and of excitement-depression, since he found these to be "muscular attitudes." This left to feeling the traditional dimension of pleasantness-unpleasantness.

At one time Titchener held that feeling was a conscious element, distinct from sensation. Work from his laboratory during the last years of Titchener's life tended to show that this view must be modified.[76] Under introspection, feelings turn out to be modes of pressure. Pleasantness is a bright pressure; unpleasantness is a dull pressure. Affective experience from every sense department may take on an increment of bright or dull pressure. For pleasant experiences, terms such as "liveliness," "brightness," "airy" were used by the introspectors, while unpleasant experiences were identified as "dull," "heavy," and "hard." Direct appeal to pressure, as such, was very evident among all the observers. Thus feeling was related to touch. This study, appearing in 1924, was made too late to be incorporated into Titchener's own systematic publications.

Overview

The biography of Titchener, published the year of his death by Boring,[77] closes with the statement that a century may have to pass before it is possible to assess Titchener's place in the history of psychology. From the present perspective of only some thirty-five years later, the approach to psychology through introspection seems to have closed with Titchener's death. Not that content of consciousness as a source of psychological data disappeared. Verbal report and free association are still with us, but a unified, unsupplemented appeal to introspection and nought beside has disappeared. That we have progressed beyond Titchener's views anyone with a sense of history would acknowledge, but this inevitable lesson does not detract from the contribution they made.

Instead of setting the pattern for psychology, as Wundt and Titchener thought they had, their work has proved to be but a stage of its history, barely surviving Titchener's death. In fact, the remarkable aspect is the speed with which the change took place. By 1930 students of Titchener[78] were arguing that the homogeneity among psychologists is much greater than the differences and that a reconciliation among the warring schools was actually taking place, except for a few diehards.

The transfer of Wundtian, German psychology as a unitary social institution was a failure. A sociologist of today would have predicted it, reminding us that transfer from one culture is relative and selective, not wholesale. But Titchener's attempt was a magnificent failure!

FUNCTIONAL PSYCHOLOGY

As the name implies, functional psychology was concerned with the mind as it functions or is used. Emphasis on use lent itself readily to the practical and to the struggle to get ahead. Even before its meaning is elaborated, it is easy to anticipate why the temper of the times in the United States would be receptive to this approach to psychology. This congeniality to practical applications of psychology mark a separation of the functionalists from the structuralists. The latter were impatient with such efforts, for, in fact, to see functional psychology characterized in terms of use constituted to them a criticism. The functionalists, however, not only tended to welcome application of psychology by others but also to engage in it themselves. The lives of some of the functionalists stand witness to this. John Dewey became a leading educator, and J. R. Angell became President of Yale University and, on his retirement, an executive of a radio corporation. Lest this lead to a misunderstanding, let it be noted that functionalists were still very much interested in psychology as a science. Here they showed a partiality for research on learning, perception, and similar processes and were especially receptive to animal psychology, physiological psychology, and differential psychology.

Functional psychology has many forebears. In the modern era it was James who was singled out by Titchener as a typical functionalist in his 1898 article contrasting functionalism and structuralism.[79] As we have seen, James was too many-sided an individual to be pinned down by a label. Only in contrasting his views with those of Titchener does it become possible to do so. As a matter of fact, James had anticipated Titchener by differentiating between a structural and a functional position as early as 1884.[80] He attached no great importance to it, since in 1890 in his *Principles* he banished it to a footnote.[81]

In what sense was James a functionalist? In the *Principles*[82] James assimilated psychology to biology and treated thinking as an instrument in the struggle for life. Mental processes were conceived of as activities. Mind was not an entity, but a functional activity of the organism. The biological survival value of mind was stressed in that if consciousness had no value it would not have survived. James saw consciousness as useful because it intervened in the cause-effect sequence, resulting in a spontaneity and productivity of the mind. This particular view was accepted and elaborated by John Dewey in his appeal to consciousness as part of the adjustive equipment of the organism, and

Angell[83] used James' already familiar argument about consciousness not being present when it has no utility value.

Even earlier, Darwin had helped to prepare the way for functionalism through his emphasis on adaptation, on activities, and on individual differences. Galton and Spencer continued this tradition, each in his own way, the first emphasizing individual differences and the second adaptation. Showing its evolutionary heritage, functionalism saw psychology as the study of the adaptation of the organism to its environment. In the United States there were already familiar kindred spirits, such as James McKeen Cattell and Robert S. Woodworth at Columbia, James Mark Baldwin and, in some ways, G. Stanley Hall. However, none of these psychologists were identified with functionalism as a separate and distinct school of psychology.

In this narrower sense, John Dewey (1859–1952) was the first functional psychologist.[84] After appointment in 1884 to the Department of Philosophy of the University of Michigan, following the usual custom, he taught psychology as well as philosophy, and, indeed, he published in 1886[85] a not uninfluential text in psychology (with the philosophical presuppositions characteristic of his time). His period as a force in psychology, however, coincided with his stay at the University of Chicago during the years 1894 to 1904. When he left Chicago for Columbia University, he no longer worked directly in the field, although he did utilize psychology in the larger educational and philosophical perspectives which thereafter concerned him.

It was Dewey's paper of 1896 on the reflex arc concept which served to introduce the school of functionalism.[86] As James before him had attacked psychological atomism through demonstrating that simple ideas have no existential reality in the stream of consciousness, Dewey found the same doctrine of elementarism lurking in the reflex arc. He was searching for a unifying concept for mental life, and he considered the reflex arc, recently borrowed from physiology, as a likely possibility. Despite its promise, detailed analysis led him to reject it for this purpose because of its "patchwork" qualities.[87]

As Dewey saw it, a child's withdrawal of his finger from the flame, often given as the classical example of the reflex arc, does not tell the whole story of what is happening. After an experience of this sort, the visual perception of the flame, heretofore inviting to the child, is now permanently altered. The stimulus and the response of the burn-withdrawal reflex does not end with the withdrawal. It now serves as the stimulus for another situation which belongs to the same act, instead of being a new occurrence. Every reaction, Dewey argued, is a circuit—adjustment is more than a response to a stimulus, it is a realignment within one's environment. The unitary act completes a circle from sensation through movement to a new sensation that arises out of that movement. Sensation as an "existence" and motion as a response do not account for the psychological facts which form, not an arc, but a circuit. Reflexes, as well as other forms of behavior, Dewey urged, should not be treated as artificial constructs by the abstraction of their sensory and motor phases. It is their significance for adaptation which is crucial. In this way Dewey was making a plea for function as the basis of psychological study.

Without deliberate intention, the functional view point became crystallized as a school. In some measure this came about through answering attacks made by their critics. When Titchener christened functionalism by contrasting it with structuralism, James Rowland Angell (1869–1949), a former student of James and Dewey's younger associate at the University of Chicago, accepted the challenge, and in a paper and a book attempted to present the functional point of view. The University of Chicago was, hereafter, to be the major source from which functional psychologists were to come. It should be emphasized, however, that the Chicago functionalists argued that the heritage of functionalism was of such a broad nature that it was, properly speaking, not a school at all, and they expressly stated that it should not be identified with psychology as taught at Chicago. Despite this disclaimer, most psychologists outside of the spokesmen for functional psychology and their students, were inclined to consider the Chicago psychologists as being sufficiently different from other psychologists and sufficiently similar among themselves in their thinking to be classed as adherents to a particular school.

In 1906 Angell's presidential address to the American Psychological Association was "The Province of Functional Psychology." [88] He brought together three conceptions of function which he considered acceptable to functional psychologists. (1) Functionalism is concerned with mental operations, the "how" and "why" of consciousness, as contrasted to the "what" of the psychology of mental elements. (2) Mind is a means of mediating between the needs of the organism and the environment. Consciousness, in the spirit of the emergency theory of James, is utilitarian, since it serves some end. Because consciousness helps to solve problems, an interest in the applied fields of psychology flows naturally from an interest in it. (3) Functional psychology is a psychophysical psychology which demands that the mind-body relationship be significant for psychology. The functional psychologist is interested in studying mental processes as a means of adjustment, which, in turn, implies that the epiphenomenalistic solution, which holds mental activity to be nothing more than a useless by-product, is incompatible with functionalism. Other than this, no special psychophysical position is necessary. This article clearly spelled out the functionalist position, and in this sense was more important than

Dewey's paper, which, though it showed a functionalist spirit in dealing with a particular psychological issue, did not explicate the conceptions of a functional psychology.

Angell also wrote a textbook in 1904[89] concerned with both the structure and the function of human consciousness, as its subtitle attests. However, functional solutions were sufficiently emphasized to make clear what he meant by functional psychology. He still saw the introspective study of consciousness as the major method, but added the objective observation of the individual's actions as a supplemental method. Thus the study of behavior was explicitly accepted as being a method of psychology.

Harvey A. Carr (1873–1954) had studied at Chicago with Angell. When Angell left, he took over as head of the department from 1906 to 1938, during which time he continued the Chicago functionalist tradition.[90] He wrote a text[91] and a book on space perception,[92] both from the functionalist's point of view. During Carr's years at Chicago about 150 psychologists received their Ph.D.'s, whose later careers showed the influence of the functionalist spirit.

Carr[93] helped to clarify the meaning of "functional," over which there had been considerable controversy. A charge has been made[94] that "function" had been used inconsistently by the functional psychologists. It was argued that sometimes what was meant by functional were the mental activities, such as seeing, hearing, perceiving, and the like; while at other times functional served to indicate use or service for some end, as when speaking of the function of a word. The functionalists, it was said, would apply the word function to an activity, such as breathing or digestion, and then later use the word to denote the utility of an activity as when it is said that oxidation of the blood is a function of breathing. This made it possible to speak of a function of an activity, or, in other words, of a function of a function, which critics of functionalism saw as an absurd confusion. In replying to this charge, Carr insisted that there is really no discrepancy because in the use of both meanings at a higher level of interpretation the two are actually the same. The common identity of the two meanings—process and end—is the mathematical meaning of "function," as in the expression $y = f(x)$; *i.e.*, "y" is a function of "x." When a mathematician says y is a function of x, he is merely saying there is a contingent relation without specifying the precise nature of that relation. Functional psychologists use the term the same way, whether they speak of process or end, act or structure, cause or effect. A contingent relation and a functional relation, then, are synonymous. In this, Carr came very close to contemporary usage. The use of cause and effect, which Carr specifically mentioned as one of these functional relations, later lead to statements that psychology is the study of functional or contingent relations between antecedent psychological events and their consequents. It would be possible to find a considerable number of contemporary psychologists who would subscribe to this definition.

Clear-cut self-conscious allegiance to their school of thought did not characterize the functionalists as it did the structuralists. As has already been mentioned, Columbia University in the person of James McKeen Cattell was sympathetic to a functionalist point of view without being narrowly identified with it. In the next generation, he was ably seconded by Robert Sessions Woodworth, whose position also was more eclectic—in 1918 he saw psychology as embracing both the older tradition of introspection and the newer one of behavior.[95] By 1930, Carr[96] said he dared not list functionalists by name lest some he considered to fall within its scope be "rudely shocked." It is probable that a large number of psychologists of the first three decades of the century who thought of themselves simply as "psychologists" (with the exception of the Titchenerians) were closest in spirit to functionalism. This, however, was a functionalism much more slanted to the side on the study of behavior than Woodworth intended, because the latter half of these three decades saw the appearance of Behaviorism as the next chapter will discuss.

REFERENCES [*]

1. L. N. WILSON, Biographical Sketch, Granville Stanley Hill, Feb. 1, 1844–April 24, 1924. *Publ. Clark Univ. Library*, 1925, 7, 3–33; G. S. Hall, *Life and Confessions of a Psychologist*. New York: Appleton, 1923.

2. H. JAMES, (ed.), The *Letters of William James*. (2 vols.) Boston: Atlantic Monthly, 1920, II, pp. 17–18.

3. J. M. CATTELL, The Founding of the Association and of the Hopkins and Clark Laboratories, *Psychol. Rev.*, 1943, 50, 61–64.

4. F. M. ALBRECHT, The New Psychology in America: 1880–1895. Unpublished Ph.D. dissertation, Johns Hopkins, 1960.

5. *Ibid.*

6. CATTELL, *op. cit.*

7. J. JASTROW, American Psychology in the '80's and '90's, *Psychol. Rev.*, 1943, 50, 65–67.

8. N. O. RUSH, (ed.) *Letters of G. Stanley Hall to Jonas Gilman Clark*. Worcester: Clark University Library, 1948.

9. *Life and Confessions.*

10. *Ibid.*, p. 296.

[*] See page 16 for description of reference style.

11. L. M. TERMAN, Trails to Psychology. In C. Murchison (ed.), *A History of Psychology in Autobiography.* (Vol. 2) Worcester: Clark University Press, 1932, 297–332.

12. R. S. HARPER, Tables of American Doctorates in Psychology, *Amer. J. Psychol.,* 1949, 62, 579–587.

13. W. DENNIS, & E. G. BORING, The Founding of APA. *Amer. Psychologist,* 1952, 7, 95–97.

14. *Ibid.*

15. G. S. HALL, Contents of Children's Minds, *Princeton Rev.,* 1883, 11, 272–294.

16. DOROTHY E. BRADBURY, The Contribution of the Child Study Movement to Child Psychology, *Psychol. Bull.,* 1937, 34, 21–38.

17. G. S. HALL, *Adolescence: its Psychology and its Relations to Physiology, Anthropology, Sociology, Sex, Crime, Religion and Education.* New York: Appleton, 1904.

18. G. S. HALL, *Jesus, the Christ, in the Light of Psychology* (2 vols.) New York: Doubleday, 1917.

19. G. S. HALL, Department of Psychology, *Publ. Clark Univ. Libr.,* 1917, 5, No. 2, 35.

20. J. C. BURNHAM, Sigmund Freud and G. Stanley Hall: Exchange of Letters, *Psychoanal. Quart.,* 1960, 29, 307–316.

21. *Ibid.*

22. CATTELL, *The Founding of the Association, op. cit.*

23. G. S. HALL, *Senescence: the Last Half of Life.* New York: Appleton, 1922.

24. CATTELL, *op. cit.*

25. E. D. STARBUCK, G. Stanley Hall as a Psychologist, *Psychol. Rev.,* 1925, 32, 103–120.

26. E. B. TITCHENER, Letters in Memory of G. Stanley Hall. In Granville Stanley Hall, Feb. 1, 1844–April 24, 1924, *Publ. Clark Univ. Library,* 1925, 7, No. 6, 1–92.

27. STARBUCK, *op. cit.,* p. 117.

28. M. L. REYMERT, Letters in Memory of G. Stanley Hall. In Granville Stanley Hall, Feb. 1, 1844–April 24, 1924, *Publ. Clark Univ. Library,* 1925, 7, No. 6, 81–84; G. S. Hall, *Founders of Modern Psychology.* New York: Appleton, 1912.

29. *Ibid.*

30. R. S. WOODWORTH, James McKeen Cattell, 1860–1944, *Psychol. Rev.,* 1944, 51, 201–209; W. B. Pillsbury, James McKeen Cattell, 1860–1944, *Nat. Acad. Sci. Biogr. Mem.,* 1947, 25 (1). 16.

31. R. S. WOODWORTH, James McKeen Cattell—in Memoriam: Some Personal Characteristics, *Science,* 1944, 99, 160–161.

32. J. M. CATTELL, Psychology in America, *Scient. Mo.,* 1930, 30, 114–126.

33. J. M. CATTELL, The Inertia of the Eye and Brain, *Brain*, 1885, 8, 295–312.

34. CATTELL, *Psychology in America, op. cit.*, p. 116.

35. CATTELL, *Founding, op. cit.*

36. C. WISSLER, The Contribution of James McKeen Cattell to American Anthropology, *Science*, 1944, 99, 232–233.

37. J. M. CATTELL, Mental Tests and Measurements, *Mind*, 1890, 15, 373–381. (Herrnstein & Boring Excerpt No. 80)

38. C. WISSLER, The Correlation of Mental and Physical Tests, *Psychol. Rev. Monogr. Suppl.*, 1901, 3, No. 6. (Herrnstein & Boring Excerpt No. 84)

39. STELLA E. SHARP, Individual Psychology: a Study in Psychological Method, *Amer. J. Psychol.*, 1899, 10, 329–391. (Herrnstein & Boring Excerpt No. 83)

40. J. M. CATTELL, The Time of Perception as a Measure of Differences in Intensity, *Philos. Stud.*, 1902, 19, 63–68.

41. S. S. VISHER, *Scientists Starred 1903–1943 in "American Men of Science."* Baltimore: Johns Hopkins Press, 1947, 141–143.

42. H. MUNSTERBERG, *Psychology and Life.* Boston: Houghton, Mifflin, 1899; H. Munsterberg, *Psychotherapy.* New York: Moffat Yard, 1909.

43. J. M. BALDWIN, *Mental Development in the Child and the Race.* New York: Macmillan, 1895. (Herrnstein & Boring Except No. 92)

44. J. M. BALDWIN, (ed.), *Dictionary of Philosophy and Psychology.* (new ed.) (3 vols.) New York: Macmillan, 1901.

45. PERRY, *op. cit.*, Vol. 2.

46. A. T. POFFENBERGER, (ed.), *James McKeen Cattell: Man of Science.* (Vol. 1) *Psychological Research.* (Vol. 2) *Addresses and Formal Papers.* Lancaster: Science Press, 1947

47. J. M. CATTELL, The Conceptions and Methods of Psychology, *Pop. Sci. Mo.*, 1904, 46, 176–186. (Reprinted, in part, Retrospect: Psychology as a Profession, *J. Consult. Psychol.*, 1937, 1, 1–3)

48. POFFENBERGER, *op. cit.*, 1, p. 498.

49. E. G. BORING, Edward Bradford Titchener, 1867–1927, *Amer. J. Psychol.*, 1927, 38, 489–506.

50. E. B. TITCHENER, *Experimental Psychology: a Manual of Laboratory Practice.* (4 vols.) New York: Macmillan, 1901–1905, Vol. I, Part. II, p. VII.

51. W. B. PILLSBURY, The Psychology of Edward Bradford Titchener, *Phil. Rev.*, 1928, 37, 95–108.

52. *Ibid.*

53. *Experimental Psychology, op. cit.*

54. E. G. BORING, *Personal Correspondence*, 1960.

55. E. G. BORING, Titchener's Experimentalists, *J. Hist. Behav. Sci.*, 1967, 3, 315–325.

56. E. B. TITCHENER, A *Textbook of Psychology*. New York: Macmillan, 1910.

57. E. B. TITCHENER, *Systematic Psychology: Prolegomena*. New York: Macmillan, 1929.

58. *Textbook*, pp. 2 ff. (Herrnstein & Boring Excerpt No. 111)

59. *Ibid.*, pp. 202f.

60. *Ibid.*, pp. 9 ff.

61. E. B. TITCHENER, The Problems of Experimental Psychology, *Amer. J. Psychol.*, 1905, 16, 220–224.

62. E. B. TITCHENER, On Psychology as the Behaviorist Views it, *Proc. Amer. Phil. Soc.*, 1914, 53, 1–17.

63. BORING, *Edward Bradford Titchener. op. cit.*

64. *Textbook*, pp. 19 ff. (Herrnstein & Boring Excerpt No. 111)

65. *Ibid.*, pp. 36 ff.

66. E. B. TITCHENER, The Postulates of a Structural Psychology, *Phil. Rev.*, 1898, 7, 449–465.

67. E. G. BORING, Titchener and the Existential, *Amer. J. Psychol.*, 1937, 50, 470–483; E. B. Titchener, *Lectures on the Experimental Psychology of Thought Processes*. New York: Macmillan, 1909.

68. *Textbook*, p. 48.

69. E. B. TITCHENER, *An Outline of Psychology*. New York: Macmillan, 1896, pp. 74–75. (Herrnstein & Boring Excerpt No. 14)

70. E. B. TITCHENER, *Lectures on the Elementary Psychology of Feeling and Attention*. New York: Macmillan, 1908, pp. 4 ff.

71. BORING, *Titchener and the Existential.*

72. *Thought Processes.*

73. *Textbook*, pp. 135–136.

74. *Ibid.*, pp. 367–371. (Herrnstein & Boring Excerpt No. 41)

75. *Ibid.*, pp. 225–264.

76. J. P. NAFE, An Experimental Study of the Affective Qualities, *Amer. J. Psychol.*, 1924, 35, 507–544.

77. BORING, *Edward Bradford Titchener, op. cit.*

78. E. G. BORING, Psychology for Eclectics. In C. Murchison (ed.), *Psychologies of 1930*. Worcester: Clark University Press, 1930, 115–127; J. P. Nafe, Structural Psychology. In C. Murchison (ed.), *Psychologies of 1930*. Worcester: Clark University Press, 1930, 128–140.

79. *Postulates of a Structural Psychology.*

80. W. JAMES, On Some Omissions of Introspective Psychology, *Mind*, 1884, 9, 1–26.

81. JAMES, *Principles, op. cit.*, pp. 311–312.

82. JAMES, *Principles, op. cit.*, Vol. 1, 5, pp. 6–8. (Herrnstein & Boring Excerpts No. 91, 114)

83. J. R. ANGELL, *Psychology, an Introductory Study of the Structure and Function of Human Consciousness.* New York: Holt, 1904.

84. E. G. BORING, John Dewey: 1859–1952, *Amer. J. Psychol.*, 1953, 66, 145–147.

85. J. DEWEY, *Psychology.* New York: Harper, 1886.

86. DEWEY, The Reflex Arc Concept in Psychology, *Psychol. Rev.*, 1896, 3, 357–370. (Herrnstein & Boring Excerpt No. 64)

87. *Ibid.*, p. 358.

88. J. R. ANGELL, The Province of Functional Psychology, *Psychol. Rev.*, 1907, 14, 61–91. (Herrnstein & Boring Excerpt No. 93)

89. ANGELL, *Psychology.*

90. HELEN L. KOCH, Harvey A. Carr: 1873–1954, *Psychol. Rev.*, 1955, 62, 81–82; W. B. Pillsbury, Harvey A. Carr: 1873–1954, *Amer. J. Psychol.*, 1955, 68, 149–151.

91. H. A. CARR, *Psychology: a Study of Mental Activity.* New York: Longmans, Green, 1925.

92. H. A. CARR, *An Introduction to Space Perception.* New York: Longmans, Green, 1935.

93. H. A. CARR, Functionalism. In C. Murchison (ed.), *Psychologies of 1930.* Worcester: Clark University Press, 1930, 59–78.

94. C. A. RUCKMICK, The Use of the Term *Function* in English Textbooks of Psychology, *Amer. J. Psychol.*, 1913, 24, 99–123.

95. R. S. WOODWORTH, *Dynamic Psychology.* New York: Columbia University Press, 1918, pp. 34–36. (Herrnstein & Boring Excerpt No. 115)

96. CARR, Functionalism, in *Psychologies of 1930.*

CHAPTER 18

WATSON:
BEHAVIORISM

IN 1913 an article appeared in an American psychological journal which was the manifesto of a new psychology. Written by a thirty-five year old psychologist, John Broadus Watson, it opens with these sentences:

Psychology as the behaviorist views it is a purely objective experimental branch of natural science. Its theoretical goal is the prediction and control of behavior. Introspection forms no essential part of its methods, nor is the scientific value of its data dependent upon the readiness with which they lend themselves to interpretation in terms of consciousness.[1]

So begins the first statement of the goal and the object of attack of Behaviorism.

This was more than a declaration of independence, it was an announcement of the intent of Behaviorism to occupy the entire field of psychology. It was not enough that the study of behavior be lifted to dignity equal with that of consciousness. Behavior was hereafter to be the only method of psychology, and its study was to be the definition of psychology. Psychology had failed in its fifty years as an experimental study, in Watson's view, to establish itself as a science. To reach its rightful place, it must discard consciousness. To quote further: "The time seems to have come when psychology must discard all references to consciousness; when it need no longer delude itself into thinking that it is making of mental states the object of observation."[2]

Anything smacking of the mental was anathema to Watson. It was as if to him the mental was outside this rational world of ours, dwelling in the dark with the other ghosts and goblins. His conception of the earlier work in psychology was simple and clear; the introspectionists assumed the soul or its substitute (consciousness) to exist and then proceeded to study this airy nothing by introspection.

As a method, Watson saw introspection as notoriously unreliable as exemplified in the quarrel between the Leipzig and the Würzburg schools over imageless thought. As he saw it, almost all psychology before him was tarred with the same mentalistic brush and therefore, unscientific. He specifically mentioned that his "quarrel" was not only with the structural psychology of Titchener but with functional psychology as well, since it, too, used mentalistic terms and emphases. He did agree that a functional emphasis upon biological significance was laudable, but the so-called functionalists still failed to be scientific because they had slipped into an interactionistic position in which mental states were seen by them as playing some part in the adjustment of the individual. This is nothing more than a relic of philosophy, Watson argued, and the whole issue should and can be ignored by focusing on behavior to the exclusion of all else. Behaviorism, he claimed, is the only consistent functionalism. The study of functional capacities expressed in behavior are relatively easily and directly determined; references to conscious states in functional terms are not only uncertain, but also trivial and unreal.

One may assume, Watson said, the presence or absence of consciousness as one wishes; it does not affect the problems of behavior one iota.[3] A man has something which, if one wishes, may be called consciousness—a psychologist as a human being, may have this something. So, too, may a physicist as a human being. However, that which the psychologist shares with the physicist in this regard is no more part of his field of research than it is that of a physicist.

In 1913 Watson stood alone. Before his last major publication[4] (in its original edition in 1924, eleven years later, and in its revised edition in 1930, seventeen years later), his view had swept through psychology in the United States leaving it in many respects a new field.

PAVLOV AND RUSSIAN PHYSIOLOGY

Emphasis upon behavioral study had preceded Watson. One generation earlier there had been the work of two Russian physiologists, Ivan P. Pavlov and Vladimir M. Bekhterev. In turn, it was a publication by Ivan M. Sechenov, the "Reflexes of the Brain,"[5] which Pavlov acknowledged as the single most important theoretical inspiration for his work on conditioning.[6]

Sechenov[7]

It is generally agreed that Ivan M. Sechenov (1829–1905) founded Russian physiology. After early training in Russia and studying abroad with Claude Bernard, DuBois Reymond, Johannes Müller, and Hermann von Helmholtz, he returned to teach physiology at the Saint Petersburg Military Medical Academy and various other places, spending his last years as professor of physiology at Moscow University.

Early in Sechenov's career, he carried on experimental investigations of the inhibition of reflex movements by the cerebral cortex. This inspired him to begin work to show that there was a physiological basis for psychical processes. Thereafter, he labored with the problem of demonstrating that the psyche, instead of being independent of the body, is a function of the brain and central nervous system and, therefore, is a physiological problem.

His thesis was that psychical activity can be explained by reflex activity. With his physiological orientation he tended to emphasize the receptor and motor (muscular) phases of the reflex psychical processes. All psychical processes are expressed in motor activity of one sort or another.

A few of his characteristic teachings might be mentioned. Sechenov identified reflexes as innate or learned. Learning, itself, was a process of association. It is implied that contiguity is the most important principle, but learning is not the primary subject of investigation. Thinking, Sechenov held, was an inhibited reflex. In thinking there is the receptive phase of the reflex, its transmission, but the end of the reflex, expressed in movement, is absent. In all of this, as Pavlov[8] remarked, Sechenov was developing a theoretical outline. It was Pavlov who took the giant step of submitting his contentions to experimental study.

Pavlov[9]

Ivan Petrovich Pavlov, the son of a village priest, was born in Russia in 1849, and received his early education in a local seminary. In 1870 he entered the University of St. Petersburg in the natural history section with animal physiology as his specialty. After obtaining his degree in 1875, he enrolled as an advanced student in the medical school, not with any thought of a career as a practicing physician but as further preparation for a research post in physiology. His academic success was such that on completion of his thesis, he won a scholarship to Germany where he worked with prominent physiologists for two years. Nevertheless, it was not until the age of forty-one, in 1890, that he was made professor of pharmacology (later physiology) at the St. Petersburg Military Medical Academy and head of the physiology department of the Institute of Experimental Medicine. For many years he devoted his research attention to the processes of digestion. In fact, half of his career was devoted to work on digestion, for which he received the Nobel Prize in 1904. Only after the age of fifty did he study what became known as conditioning, which study covered a span of another thirty years.

The specific impetus for the study of conditioning was a phase of his work on the digestive glands. Using the dog as the experimental animal, Pavlov's general method was a surgical arrangement so that digestive secretions flowed to the surface of the body for collection and measurement. One aspect of his work was on the functioning of saliva in digestion. By operation, a salivary duct could be diverted so that the saliva stimulated by meat in the mouth of the dog flowed through a fistula to the outside of the body where it was collected. Prior to 1900 and before working with the conditioned response, he had noticed that a dog secreted saliva before the meat was given him. Further observation showed this occurred not only when the dog saw the meat, but even on hearing the footsteps of the attendant.

The secretory reflex with the innate response of salivation to ingested food had now become "conditioned," to the sight of the food or the sound of the footsteps of the attendant. Pavlov realized that this happened because this sight or sound had been so often associated with ingestion of food. This is association by frequency of contiguity, as it would be called in associationistic terms. The term, "conditioned reflex," was first applied to this phenomenon in 1901.[10]

Should he follow up this new lead into an area which many physiologists would view with disdain, since it was psychic in nature? Some leading physiologists, in point of fact, on hearing of his dilemma, advised him against embarking on the work. On the other hand, he had the example of Sechenov before him. After a long struggle with himself, he resolved to go ahead and to make it a physiological problem by maintaining the role of the external observer with no consideration of introspective findings.[11] This was in 1900–1901.

He absorbed himself in his new task. The basic procedures, with the exception of the selection of the stimulus to bring on salivary flow, had already been standardized through his work on digestion. His already extensive laboratory resources were directed to this new problem. When the Soviet government came to power, his research faculties were expanded. An increasing number of associates and assistants joined him. This collaborative effort was an example of coordination of research involving more researchers and extending over more years than anything since Wundt. Over the years, some two hundred collaborators worked with him on problems in conditioning.[12]

The basic model for Pavlov's work was the presentation of two kinds of stimuli, one, "appropriate," biologically "adequate," or "unconditioned;" the other, "psychic," "conditioned," or "learned."[13] Each reflex has an appropriate (unconditioned) stimulus which brings it on. If the patellar tendon is struck, the knee jerks; if food is placed on the tongue, saliva flows; if the finger is pricked, it is jerked back. In his studies, Pavlov tended to depend upon the food powder leading to the salivary response, although other forms were also used. When a response such as salivation becomes attached to a stimulus that formerly did not arouse it, it is said to be conditioned.

Practically any stimulus, Pavlov found, can act as a conditioning stimulus to produce a conditioned response. The salivation to the sight of the food or the sound of the footsteps of the attendant are stimuli for conditioned responses. Sight of food or the sound of footsteps had come to serve as signals, and they now brought about a response formerly elicited by food in contact with the tongue.

Pavlov originally referred to "psychic reflexes," that is, reflexes aroused not by the adequate stimulus of meat in contact with the tongue but by some other form of stimulation which had been presented along with the meat. He almost immediately dropped this term, in favor of "conditioned" responses. Over the years, Pavlov preferred to use as conditioned stimuli, the sound of a tuning fork, a bell, and a light flash. These were the stimuli which acquired a new reaction, namely a flow of saliva.

A specific instance might be given: A hungry dog would be led into the experimental room and placed in a restraining harness (to which he was already accustomed). After a few minutes a metronome would tick for thirty seconds, and then food powder would be mechanically introduced into the dog's mouth. Saliva would begin to flow. Every fifteen minutes the same sequence—thirty seconds ticking, then food introduced—would follow. Before many repetitions, saliva would begin to flow while the metronome was ticking and *before* the food was introduced. A conditioned response had been established. A previously inadequate stimulus (inadequate, that is, to produce saliva) would now produce a response formerly elicited only by the adequate stimulus of food powder.

In addition to the study of their formation, conditioned responses were open to all sorts of other quantitative manipulation. Among other phenomena studied by Pavlov are what have been called extinction, reinforcement, spontaneous recovery, generalization and discrimination, and higher order conditioning.[14] "Extinction" has been studied in the following fashion: after the conditioned response has been formed, the stimulus, say the bell, is continued on the trials that follow, but the natural or adequate stimulus of meat powder is no longer introduced. This results in the conditioned stimulus losing its capacity to elicit the conditioned response. When the adequate stimulus for the conditioned response is not given, it is said to be non-reinforced. Generally speaking, repetition without reinforcement through the meat powder results in a decrease of amount of salivation from trial to trial until it ceases, that is, shows extinction. A conditioned response extinguishes, unless periodically reinforced. Extinction, however, may not be permanent. After a rest, the application of the conditioned stimulus may again produce a flow of saliva. This is an instance of so-called, spontaneous recovery.

Pavlov and his collaborators also conducted experiments on generalization and discrimination. When a stimulus different from the one to which conditioning has already been developed is introduced and, nevertheless, produces the conditioned response, generalization has occurred. A "spread" or generalization has taken place. Suppose a sound of a particular pitch has been used to begin to form a conditioned response. Now a sound of somewhat lower or higher pitch is substituted. The conditioned secretion occurs as it did to the original pitch. This is generalization. However, with continued training, the conditioned reflex acquires a certain degree of specificity, that is, it can no longer be elicited by stimuli which differ too greatly from the training stimulus. This is discrimination. This degree of discrimination is obtained without particular effort. However, the procedure used, which consists of merely continuing to present the same stimuli while occasionally interposing stimuli of different pitch to see if it will elicit the response, still leaves a relatively wide band of pitch differences which the dog will treat as the same by salivating when they are presented.

The degree of generalization remaining can be cut still further by training of a specific kind. The task now is to test the limits of the dog's discriminability, that is, to refine still further his discrimination to the point where, despite an actual difference in pitch, no difference can be detected from the dog's behavior. This training in discrimination is done by differential reinforcement; one pitch serves to lead to food, another slightly different pitch does not lead to food. Say, food is not presented to the dog after a pitch of 825 vibrations per second, but it is presented to a pitch of 812 vibrations. The dog, after repeated trials, will discriminate between the two pitches by salivating to the latter and not to the former. The pitches selected for illustration are the limits of discrimination for this particular dog, because trying to train him to a pitch difference less than that of thirteen vibrations per second (825 minus 812) led to failure to learn. In this connection, Pavlov discovered that some dogs, pushed beyond their limits of discrimination, break down, lose whatever discriminatory ability they have already gained, and become agitated. This opened up still another facet of research, that of the study of experimental neuroses, in which a dog was found to show a variety of forms of abnormal behavior by being driven beyond his capacities.

An already established conditioned response may be treated as if it were an unconditioned one in order to bring about still further or so-called higher-order conditioning. Suppose a dog has been conditioned to the sound of the tuning fork vibrating at a certain rate paired with the meat powder so that it evokes salivation. The sound of the tuning fork (without the meat powder) is now paired with a sight of a black square, which prior to the experiment produced no secretory response. After paired stimulation of sound and square, the black square will now produce salivation. (Of course, if this were kept up too long, without reinforcement, extinction would occur.) This is second order conditioning. Pavlov also found it possible to go on to third order conditioning but not beyond it.

Pavlov considered conditioning a cortical, not a subcortical affair, as is the case with a reflex. As his findings accumulated, Pavlov worked through a theory of cortical excitation and inhibition to account for his results in purely physiological terms. Although his method was seized on avidly, his theory has received little attention outside of the USSR; so no attempt is made to present details.

It will be remembered that following Sechenov, Pavlov saw this work as a problem in physiology, not psychology. He never wavered in his view. It colored his attitude toward what the world called psychology. It can only be described as one of pessimistic skepticism. He believed psychology never could be an independent science and its position to be "completely hopeless."[15] Moreover, in his own work he believed he had completely excluded it.[16] Thus, Pavlov wished everyone in his laboratory to use physiological terms exclusively; a worker was fined if he used psychological terminology.[17]

Pavlov's attitude toward the Soviet regime is a complicated one and defies adequate summarization in a sentence or two. For many years he was outspokenly blunt and critical, once even being called in by the secret police.[18] On the other hand, he received generous government support for his research, and there is no suggestion of any pressure being put upon him to carry on work along lines selected by the government. His work was always of his own choosing. Pressure on those who came after him is a different matter.

In 1935 Pavlov gave voice to a changed attitude. In a speech before the Fifteenth International Congress of Physiologists, he spoke of the very favorable position that science occupied in his country and, as an experimenter, saw his country as an experimenter of an "incomparably higher category."[19]

Babkin, a co-worker, who left the USSR for Canada, believes his change of heart came about due not only to the support of science that the USSR gave but also to the fact that he was very much alive to the threat of Hitler, having expressed forebodings on several occasions before this date.

He died in 1936.

Bekhterev[20]

Something must also be said about the physiologist, V. M. Bekhterev (1857–1927), a countryman, a contemporary, and a rival of Pavlov in the opening years of the century. Independently of Pavlov, he also became interested in the study of conditioning. He, too, worked at the St. Petersburg Military Medical Academy, where he was graduated. After study abroad and holding a chair in psychiatry at the University of Kazan, he returned to a chair in mental and nervous disorder at the Military Medical Academy where he later had his own research institute. Bekhterev studied conditioning or, as he called it, associative reflexes, through the study of muscular or motor responses.

By motor responses, Bekhterev meant such processes as retracting the finger from an electric shock. The associative reflexes were not the result of any mental process, but they remained reflexes. He became convinced that more complex behaviors could be explained in a similar manner. Habits were seen as the compounding of motor reflexes, and even the thought processes were essentially activities of the speech musculature.

He expressed his convictions in a book, *Objective Psychology*, which appeared in Russian in 1907, was translated into German and French in 1913, and into English in 1932, with the title *General Principles of Human Reflexology*.[21] The change of title reflected the shift of name for his point of view. At first he had called his work *Objective Psychology* but later preferred *Reflexology*. It was a plea for a psychology based upon the tools and concepts of physiology with no appeal to subjective processes. Psychology expressed in study of states of consciousness was simply ignored. Objective study would be sufficient for a complete account of man's behavior.

Thorndike, Behavioral Studies, and Functionalism

Another of the sources from which Behaviorism was to come was animal psychology as studied in the United States. There were also currents in psychology in the United States contemporaneous with Watson that had their influence upon him, despite his expressed opposition to their views. This was the case with Edward L. Thorndike and Jacques Loeb.

Edward Lee Thorndike[22] has already been mentioned as a student of James and as one of the psychologists at Columbia University with Cattell. While at Harvard, he had started research with chickens and, lacking more suitable quarters, took advantage of James' generosity and used the basement of his home as his laboratory. When offered a fellowship at Columbia by Cattell, he took it and continued his work with chickens, "the most educated" pair accompanying him in a basket from Cambridge to New York.

Along with two other psychologists at Clark University, Thorndike deserves credit for introducing the modern laboratory type of experiment into animal psychology. Pavlov himself acknowledged that the researches in 1898 of E. L. Thorndike were the first experiments in this general research area but stated that when he began is own work he was unfamiliar with them.[23]

Thorndike's study of the behavior of kittens in a puzzle box is classic.[24] A series of these boxes, open-slatted affairs, each had a different "combination" which, when learned, allowed the hungry kitten to escape from the box and to secure food placed outside the box. The learning tasks for a kitten involved strings to pull, buttons to turn, and levers to press. At first, the kitten's behavior showed excessive activity, clawing all over the box and trying to squeeze through the bars. In this struggle the kitten happened to claw the string or button, and the door opened. In other words, the kitten carried on very actively and randomly until the successful act was hit upon. On repeated trials, gradually the erroneous, unsuccessful acts were dropped, one by one. Ultimately, when the kitten was placed in the puzzle box, he would immediately claw the button or string or whatever and escape from the box.

This process of learning Thorndike came to call trial and error learning. As the trials succeeded one another, both the number of errors and the time taken to escape decreased. The learning as expressed in decrease of errors and time was gradual. He interpreted the results to mean that practice stamped in correct responses and stamped out incorrect ones.

As a result of his studies, Thorndike[25] formulated two fundamental laws of learning: (1) the "law of effect" in which it is stated that any act in a given situation producing satisfaction becomes associated with that situation, so that when the situation recurs that act is also more likely to recur, and (2) the law of exercise in two complementary parts, the laws of use and of disuse. The law of use, says in substance, that there is a strengthening of connections with practice; the law of disuse that there is a weakening of connections when practice is discontinued. Research he conducted[26] many years later convinced him that sheer repetition was unimportant and that reward was much more effective than punishment. The law of exercise is a direct descendant of the old law of association, not association of ideas, to be sure, but rather a connection of stimulus and response. The law of effect is of more dubious parentage, but it is at least partially related to the pleasure-pain or hedonistic principle. However, here again, an objective cast has been given in that its functioning has been inferred from behavior. Thorndike did not hold that psychology could dispense with consciousness, but he did hope that much of psychology could be objectified.

Thorndike was not alone in performing pioneer objective research studies with animals in the United States. Robert M. Yerkes[27] (1876–1956), under Thorndike's influence, went down the phyletic scale to study learning and intelligence in the turtle in a setting more a maze than a puzzle box. A Clark University student, Willard S. Small[28] (1870–1943) using a miniature of the Hampton Court maze with rats was one whose study of learning firmly established both the maze as a method and the rat as an experimental animal.

Jacques Loeb (1859–1924), the physiologist, and one of Watson's teachers, must have had some influence on his student, although Watson makes little mention of him (and that disparagingly), presumably because of Loeb's failure to reject completely an appeal to the psychic processes. Loeb had revolted against anthropomorphism and sentimentality in interpreting animal activity, but he did not reject consciousness, which he thought to be associative memory or the capacity of the animal to learn from experience.[29] Loeb had announced his theory of tropisms in 1890 and thereafter embarked on mechanistically oriented studies of simple organisms and plants. The classical or narrower theory of tropism would have it that their behavior is nothing more than a forced movement of a physical-chemical nature. In more general fashion, the theory of tropism has to do with the orientation of the organism in a field of force. According to this view, recourse to such terms as sensation or pleasure is not necessary.

Although Watson rejected functionalism as a school, he was at the University of Chicago during its formative years; and its emphasis upon activity became part of his heritage. From his point of view he had just as much a quarrel with functionalism as with structuralism. From the present perspective his disagreement with the functionalists was on comparatively trivial grounds —they refused to give up mental processes which they insisted were an integral part of psychology. From his point of view they wished merely to study the biological significance of conscious processes rather than analyze conscious states as did the structuralists,[30] and he found the distinction "unintelligible."[31] In this connection, a case can be made that a good bit of functionalism's conservatism was no more than lip service to the old tradition of psychology as the science of the mind.[32] Much as Watson was to claim he rejected functionalism, a fundamental similarity still existed in that he, too, stressed function and demanded a larger scope of application for psychology.

During these years there were also more general trends operative with which Watson presumably was familiar. For example, Cattell in 1904 was so far removed from introspective emphasis that he could write that most of the research done in his laboratory "is nearly as independent of introspection as work in physics or in zoology."[33] Cattell cited studies in which no introspective report was asked; for example, studies of reaction time, accuracy of perception, color preference, fatigue, animal, and child behavior studies. At about the same time certain psychologists were even defining psychology as the study of behavior, as witness McDougall in 1905[34] and again in 1923[35] and Pillsbury[36] in 1911. Neither one, however, would exclude introspective data from the field of psychology. This was the step taken most effectively by John B. Watson. Others, working on the same climate of opinion, but independently of Watson, also presented general behavioristic statements, excluding mind and consciousness from psychology. There was Max Meyer (1873–1907) whose book, first published in 1921, bore the apt title, *The Psychology of the Other-One.*[37] Four years later, Albert P. Weiss (1879–1931), who dedicated his book to Meyer, published *A Theoretical Basis of Human Behavior.*[38] These were both statements that in many ways were more erudite and sophisticated than Watson's. But neither one had anywhere near Watson's impact upon psychology.

LIFE OF WATSON[39]

John Broadus Watson was born on a farm near Greenville, South Carolina, in 1878. At first he attended rural schools; but, when he was twelve, the family moved into Greenville, so that Watson went to its public schools. According to his own account, he was lazy and insubordinate, never making more than passing grades. Nevertheless, at the age of sixteen, as a sub-freshmen, he entered Furman University in his hometown. Its prescribed curriculum of Latin, Greek, mathematics, and philosophy (including psychology) was more characteristic of the college in the United States prior to the eighties, than in his own day, except that Watson had some work in chemistry. Here he remained through 1900, leaving with a master's degree.

Being more interested in philosophy than in psychology, and knowing of the fame of John Dewey, Watson enrolled as a graduate student at the University of Chicago. He found Dewey "incomprehensible" and almost immediately lost enthusiasm for philosophy. He continued a minor in the subject, however, taking a considerable number of courses; but, as he commented, somehow, philosophy did not take hold. In these years the Department of Philosophy included the courses in psychology, and it was James R. Angell, the functionalist, who awakened his interest in psychology as a career. A second minor, one in neurology, eventuated from his work in the neurological laboratory of H. H. Donaldson, where he made the acquaintance of the white rat. He also took biology and physiology under Jacques Loeb, who wanted him to do his dissertation with him. Angell and Donaldson did not consider Loeb quite "safe," so he worked with the two of them instead. His doctoral dissertation used both neurological and behavioral techniques in the study of the correlation of the behavior and the growth of medullation in the central nervous system in the white rat. It was to Angell and Donaldson that he dedicated his first book. These two, along with Loeb, were, in his opinion, his most influential teachers.

In the fall of 1903, his degree year, he had a breakdown, with anxiety attacks, inability to sleep without the light on, and comparable symptoms. After a few weeks of enforced rest, he was back to work. In retrospect he saw his breakdown as a valuable experience because it taught him his own limits.

Watson had worked his way through graduate school as rat caretaker, assistant janitor, and fraternity house waiter. On receiving his degree he was offered an assistantship to work with Angell. This he did for a year and then was made instructor. As others before him have done, he promptly married.

While he taught the usual kind of Jamesian psychology in the classroom at Chicago, his major interest was in the studies he was conducting in the animal laboratory he had constructed in the basement. It was familiarity with Lloyd Morgan's work which first stimulated his researches in animal psychology and then, even more directly, the work of Thorndike.[40] At this time he was not aware of the work of either Pavlov or Bekhterev. Watson was a hard worker, producing a considerable number of studies with the white rat, the monkey, and the tern before he left Chicago in 1908.

That year, as he was to become an assistant professor, Johns Hopkins University in Baltimore, however, offered him a full professorship in experimental and comparative psychology and the directorship of the laboratory as well. The advance in rank, a substantial increase in salary, and freedom to vary his teaching from the traditional pattern left him with no choice but to go to Baltimore. During the ensuing period between 1908 and 1920 while at Johns Hopkins University, Watson did his most important work in psychology. Founding an animal laboratory at Johns Hopkins had been one of his first considerations. Several years of research, organization, and writing followed.

In 1913, there appeared the article which was the manifesto of Behaviorism. Before it saw print, there had been several preliminary steps. Actually, Watson said, it was in 1903 that he first broached a behavioristic psychology, presumably in conversation with a colleague at the University of Chicago.[41] He goes on to say that he was told it might work with animals, but not with humans. Public expression of his views first occurred in 1908 at a colloquium at Yale University. Four years later, in 1912 at Columbia at the invitation of Cattell, Watson gave a series of lectures which included the contents of the crucial article.

In 1914, in his book, *Behavior: An Introduction to Comparative Psychology*,[42] he marshalled the available evidence to demonstrate the right of animal psychology to be considered a major specialty. This was an important consideration for Watson. Indeed he admitted in his earliest statement of Behaviorism[43] that part of his motivation for a new psychology was embarrassment about the skepticism he met concerning the value and relevance of animal research to psychology. Animal research contributed very little of value to psychology as long as it was considered to be a study of human experience. What Watson wished to combat is represented by the attitude held by Titchener. In allowing for an animal psychology, Titchener[44] had had to appeal somewhat lamely to an analogy. Since an animal shows movements similar to those of a man in similar circumstances, it is possible to reconstruct the animal's consciousness as essentially similar to that of man under these same circumstances. The observations are then very cautiously to be interpreted in terms of human consciousness.

The attention actually paid to this translation into mentalistic turns was not necessarily more than perfunctory, but it was done. Even Watson's first publication bore the subtitle, "the psychical development of the white rat." To this attitude he began to object strenuously. Watson went so far as to call interpreting animal behavior in terms of the information it gives about conscious states, "absurd." [45]

Behavior[46] brought out forcefully the advantages of using animals as sources for psychological material. Animals, as subjects, offer the advantage of achieving much more complete control of the experimental conditions. Careful control of environmental conditions, such as rest, diet, activity, living conditions, even extending over its entire previous life span, is quite feasible. Known hereditary strains of rats can be studied. Moreover, it is possible to follow procedures too drastic to use with humans.

The manifesto of 1913 lacked a major positive characteristic of Watsonian Behaviorism—emphasis upon the conditioned response as the methodological tool *par excellence*. Watson had found the German and French translations of Bekhterev and was familiar with the salivary conditioned response studies of Pavlov. So rapidly did he assimilate this material into his approach that he used the theme of the place in psychology of the conditioned reflex (with particular emphasis upon the value of Bekhterev's motor reflex) for his presidential address before the American Psychological Association in 1915.[47] At this time he was still under forty years of age.

In 1918, Watson extended his researches to young children through the facilities of the Phipps Clinic in Baltimore. Very little experimental work on human infants had been conducted prior to that of Watson and his co-workers. Baby biographies had been maintained, questionnaires used, and tests developed, but the deliberate manipulative introduction of forms of stimulation demanded by experimental study had hardly been attempted.

Setting aside conditioning for later discussion, Watson's methods of studying hand preference merit mention as illustrating the other research techniques he used.[48] It is well known that the great majority of adults are right handed. Whether or not this was an instinctive response was the question Watson set out to answer with a variety of techniques applied to young infants. He measured the anatomical structure of the arm; the time that the infant would hang suspended from a bar by right and by left hand; and the total amount of work done with each hand by an infant measured by attaching "work adders" (wheels which turn in one direction when there is movement) attached to both hands in such fashion that when the child slashed about with his hands the wheel revolved, pulling up the cord to which a small weight was attached. After reaching toward an object was established in the infant's behavior repertoire, he noted the particular hand extended to secure a peppermint stick. The over-all evidence tended to show little or no favoring of the right hand over the left hand. He, therefore, concluded that right-handedness was not instinctive but a matter of social pressure, taking the form of conditioning.

Psychology from the Standpoint of a Behaviorist,[49] Watson's second major and definitive book appeared in 1919, was revised in 1924, and revised again in 1929. Essentially it was his attempt to extend the methods and principles of animal psychology into the human sphere. The value of conditioning as a method of study was extolled.

In 1920, Watson's academic career came to an abrupt end. Divorce proceedings had been instituted, which brought extensive sensationalized publicity, so much so, in fact, that he was asked to resign from the faculty of Johns Hopkins. In the same year, he married Rosalie Raynor, with whom he had carried on a research collaboration in the study of infants. Although he knew nothing of the world of business, he made contacts which in 1921 resulted in his affiliation with the New York City advertising agency of J. Walter

Thompson. To learn something of the business world, Watson made a house-to-house canvas to find what rubber boots were being worn, sold coffee, clerked in Macy's, and went through every department of the advertising agency. He must have been successful, for he was advanced to vice-president in 1924. He remained with this company until 1936 when he went with William Esty and Company.

He continued contact with psychology by writing popular articles for McCall's, Harper's, and Collier's magazines. His book, *Psychological Care of the Infant and Child,*[50] published in 1928, was meant for general reading. It was almost inevitable that he would write this book. He had a deep-seated enthusiasm for the practical value of psychology in controlling behavior and his environmentalist position demanded that infancy be seen as an extremely important formative period, for good or for ill. Illustrative of its contents is his raising the question of whether or not children should live in individual homes or even know their own parents, since it was these parents who were the major source for faulty conditioning. The avoidance of creating fears by adverse conditioning, the dangers of too much stroking beyond that socially necessary, and the pernicious effect of the hampering of movements are illustrative of the advice he would give parents. In the terminology of a later time, Watson very strongly aligned himself with the regulatory rather than the permissive school of child rearing.

In articles and books he carried on polemics for Behaviorism, including a famous extended argument[51] with William McDougall (1871–1938). McDougall was a British psychologist who had come to the United States to Harvard University in 1920 and from there went on to Duke University. While still in England, he had made notable contributions, particularly in social psychology, but, almost from the moment he arrived in the United States, he found himself engaged in a series of controversies. Although unfortunate, the reason is not hard to understand. He was an unyielding supporter of unpopular causes—freedom of the will, psychic research, the inheritance of acquired characters, and Nordic superiority among others. It was still other opinions contrary to those of the majority of psychologists that brought him into conflict with Watson. McDougall is best known through his vigorous espousal of an instinct theory of considerable scope and complexity and his fervent opposition to a mechanistic interpretation of the behavior and expe-rience of man. To anticipate a more systematic later discussion, Watson issued a sweeping denial of the existence of any instincts in man whatsoever and became an enthusiastic, rather naïve mechanist. On these issues the battle was joined. After it was over, it left neither man changed; each remained satisfied with his essential correctness. Later events have given Watson rather the best of the argument.

While in New York City, Watson secured a grant for research on the human infant, and the work was carried out by a research associate. For a time, he lectured at the New School for Social Research. These lectures are the basis for his book, *Behaviorism,*[52] a statement of his view in a form suitable for general, popular reading. In retrospect Watson conceded that the book was too hastily prepared. The revision of this book in 1930 marked his complete departure from psychology. After that date Watson occupied himself exclusively with work in the business world until his retirement in 1946. He died in 1958.

CHARACTERISTIC INTERPRETATIONS OF PSYCHOLOGICAL PROBLEMS

In his zeal to remake psychology, Watson attempted to apply the Behavioristic approach to a large variety of psychological problems. Characteristic are his interpretations of instinct, emotion, thinking, learning and conditioning, and personality. In their study he was guided by the concept of stimulus-response and would limit their study to certain psychological methods considered acceptable for research.

Behaviorism and Stimulus-Response[53]

Psychology is concerned with the behavior of the whole organism. Physiology, its closest neighbor among the other sciences, is concerned with the functioning of the parts of the body, the organ systems, circulation, digestion, and the like. To reduce behavior to its simplest terms, it is found that the acts of human behavior always involve a stimulus which brings about a particular response. The stimulus is provided by something either in the environment external to the body or by movements of the muscles or glandular secretions. The response follows upon the incidence of the stimulus. If these assumptions are accepted, it follows that the task of psychology is to study the laws of behavior, such that, when given the stimulus, one may learn to predict the response, or, given the response, one may isolate the effective stimulus. In terms of a formula, psychology was the science of S-R, where S refers to stimulus and R refers to response. If the stimuli are of a complex character, it is appropriate to speak of the stimulus situation, which is ultimately resolvable into its component parts. Actually, except in the rarest of instances, we are dealing with situations, not an isolated stimulus. Likewise, responses involve not only the simple responses that are also studied in physiology, such as the knee jerk or eye blink, but also more complex responses, to which the term "act" may be applied. Usually, what is meant by action is that the organism responds by some movement in space as in walking, talking, fighting, or eating. Nevertheless, these actions reduce to two forms— motor and glandular responses. Responses may be overt, that is, observable; or they may be explicit or non-overt, that is, non-observable or implicit. A man may show responses while standing apparently immobile; precise measurement would nevertheless show that muscular and glandular changes were taking place.

Responses, besides being either implicit or overt, are either learned or unlearned. Specification of the extent and nature of both the unlearned and learned responses is necessary. So too is the discovery of the laws of acquisition of the latter responses.

Stimulus-response units are, by an extension of their meaning in physiology, called reflexes. They are not to be analysed by a psychologist as minutely as by the physiologist. Watson did devote attention to the structures which made behavior possible, but he said he left to the physiologist a detailed analysis and the intricate task of unraveling whatever organization there was to take place within the central nervous system. Brain processes, as such, did not particularly interest him, because of the inaccessability of the brain, that "mystery box," as he called it. [54] Moreover, the brain had been used by earlier psychologists to store away that which they could not explain in mentalistic terms. Behavior is of the whole body, not of the nervous system alone, but of the muscles and glands as well. Watson's interest was in larger segments of behavior; what an individual would do in a given situation, for example, with which hand the infant would reach for the peppermint stick, or what his response would be to a loud noise.

Psychological Methods [55]

Naturally only objective methods are open to the Behaviorist. Watson explicitedly states that methods used by the psychologists are: (1) observation, with and without the aid of instruments; (2) the conditioned reflex methods, both secretory and motor; (3) testing; and (4) the verbal report method. Observation is, of course, fundamental and the basis for all other methods. How Watson would use it has been illustrated in his studies of handedness. The conditioned-reflex method is described in a later section. The test methods include use both of those instruments already extant and new ones to be developed, but with their results treated as behavior samples to ascertain general level of behavior and special abilities. Incidentally, intelligence as measured by tests is nothing more than the capability to form new habits.

The verbal report method merits special attention. Speech reactions are observable and, hence, open to use by Behaviorists. They cannot be ignored any more than any other motor reaction. An illustration would be the study of the response to warm and cold for a given skin area. The observer is told to tell when the warm cylinder is applied and when the cold cylinder is applied. He responds with the words, "cold" or "warm," as the case may be. "Sensation," as such, is rejected by Watson because we cannot observe a sensation of another person, but we can observe their verbal report. This response is overt and is recorded as the results of the experiment, just as if conditioning trials had been used. However, verbal report is a relatively inexact method, which should be discarded as soon as possible. However, for some problems it is the only one available.

Some would say this admission of verbal report into Behavioristic psychology by Watson simultaneously with the rejection of sensation is nothing more than verbal quibbling. Sensation as experience is not acceptable, but an auditory response heard as a word is permissible. Whether recourse to verbal report was anything more than banishing introspection by the front door, to allow it to return by the back, was hotly debated by Watson's contemporaries. It is evident that he was particularly vulnerable to this criticism. In defense of Watson, although he does not say so explicitly, it is evident he would rule out unverifiable verbal reports as in imageless thoughts, but he did not qualify his statements carefully enough in this regard. He indicated that he would severely limit the use of verbal report but failed to specify how he would do so.

Instinct

Watson's views about instincts passed through three stages. He started from a more or less conventional acceptance and ended with a sweeping denial of their existence in humans. In his 1914 book[56] on animal psychology, he devoted a considerable number of pages to discussing instinct, noting it, however, to be a much abused word. Nevertheless, he used it, characterizing it as a series of joined reflexes which unfold as heredity dictates. By 1919, in his *Psychology from the Standpoint of a Behaviorist*,[57] he argued that unlearned behavior can be seen only in young infants because this behavior is quickly overlain by habits. His position at this time was that, if we study infants, we can tease out the processes by which the complex learned behavior patterns, loosely called instincts, have developed.

In his *Behaviorism*[58] of 1925 he rejected flatly the concept of instinct for man. As evidence for his denial of instinct, he offers a catalogue of the reflex behavior repertoire of the human infant, such as sneezing, crying, voiding, smiling, turning the head, arm movements, feeding responses, crawling, walking, and handedness. Due to slight structural differences among infants, there are equally slight but significant differences in how these reflexes are performed. Given the individual differences and the presence of rapid habit formation, we have the basis for what has erroneously been called inherited characteristics.

In showing how habit formation works, consider handedness which Watson had studied by the methods outlined earlier. Watson suggests that a dominance present at birth might be due to long maintained intrauterine position which makes it essentially a habit either of right or of left handedness learned before birth. Most infants show no hand dominance at birth; as he had demonstrated, they use both hands interchangeably. Watson argued that social pressure steps in to establish handedness, through such means as training to shake hands, to wave "bye-bye," and to eat in the customary fashion. Handedness is not an instinct; it is a socially conditioned response.

Not only did Watson claim there were no instincts, he went further and said there were no inherited capacities, temperaments, or talents. In so doing, Watson was taking an extreme environmentalist position. Such was his zeal for plasticity of human nature that he wrote as follows:

> Give me a dozen healthy infants, well-formed, and my own specified world to bring them up in and I'll guarantee to take any one at random and train him to become any type of specialist I might select—doctor, lawyer, artist, merchant-chief and, yes, even beggar-man and thief, regardless of his talents, penchants, tendencies, abilities, vocations, and race of his ancestors. [59]

Actually, this extreme environmentalism does not logically rest upon the Behavioristic tenets of emphasis upon objective methodology and the rejection of introspection. Although Watson's stand on instincts was part of his system, it did not follow it was an integral part of Behaviorism. One could be a Behaviorist and still reject his interpretation of environmental effect.

Emotion[60]

It almost goes without saying that emotions are not matters of experienced states to Watson but bodily reactions to specific stimuli. The presence of danger as a stimulus causes visceral body changes and overt responses. For Watson, there is no appeal to the perception of danger or to the sensory experiences from the internal organs. Nevertheless, emotion involves implicit behavior in these visceral changes, but these changes are, to some extent overt or visible, in the behavior such as that found in his study of infants reported in a moment. It is these visceral responses of involuntary muscles and glands which distinguish emotions from other bodily reactions.

Watson was just as emphatic in denying the inheritance of complicated emotional patterns as he was about the inheritance of instincts. He gathered his evidence of the stimuli and the responses in emotion from children observed over long periods of time, some from birth, living in hospitals or in homes that were often visited.

One of the tests of fear he used was a measurement of the reactions to animals introduced into the laboratory room with the infants, one at a time. A friendly, purring cat and a rabbit always produced reaching-out and touching by these infants. Dogs and white rats, while not producing as much in the way of positive responses, provoked no fear. Watson considered these results to be conclusive evidence that the alleged hereditary or instinctive fear responses to furry objects was false.

His most famous study was the search for the stimuli which produced emotional responses. Consonant with his methodological tenets he not only paid attention to the stimuli, but he also described objectively the responses which the stimuli brought forth. He stimulated each infant in a considerable variety of ways and narrowed down those eliciting emotional responses to a very small number. Watson believed he had found evidence for only three emotions in infants—fear, rage, and love. Fear was produced only by a loud noise (made by striking a steel bar with a hammer) and loss of support (carried out by allowing the child to drop a few inches, or by jerking his blanket). Other situations, such as the presence of furry objects mentioned earlier or the dark or a snake or the thousand and one things of which children were supposedly afraid simply did not at this young age produce fear responses. Watson described the responses of fear as involving startle, a catching of breath followed by rapid breathing, changes in skin color, hand clutching, puckering of lips and crying, and, if the child was old enough, crawling, walking, or running away.

The only stimulus for rage that Watson found from a wide variety of stimuli was hampering or restricting the infant's movements in one fashion or another, such as holding his head firmly or restraining his movements. The behavior exhibited in response to this stimulus was described as stiffening of the body, holding the breath, and slashing movements of arms and legs.

Love, not as fully investigated as the other two emotions because of the restrictions of convention, was found to be produced by stroking of the skin, by gentle rocking and by patting. Smiling, cooing, and gurgling were the responses to this form of stimulation.

These were the only unlearned emotional responses which Watson could find, although more cautiously than he is often pictured, he said that the presence of others must be left in doubt. All of the other emotional reactions, he concluded, have, to some extent, a component of learning, largely acquired through conditioning during early childhood. Just as the child acquires his motor skills, walking, skating, or typing, he acquires his fears, his loves, and his hates.

Watson's findings on emotions stimulated considerable research interest in the emotional development of children, including many studies which attempted to refute his contentions. A considerable amount of evidence has been collected which fails to confirm the existence of the specific emotional responses advanced by Watson. In 1927, Sherman,[61] for example, asked observers to judge the emotion being displayed by infants under various conditions. When the stimulating conditions, such as dropping or restraint were available to them, the judgments they offered followed the Watsonian classification fairly well. For example, seeing the infant lose his support, they labeled the response, "fear." But, in the second phase of the study, when they were kept in ignorance of what precisely were the particular stimulations being applied, seeing only the responses, there turned out to be little correspondence in the names that they gave the emotions with those called for by Watson's theory. A final telling blow to Watson's contentions was delivered when they viewed motion picture film so spliced that the stimulus they saw and the emotional reaction that followed were not related. They tended to label the emotion in terms of what they inferred to have been the stimulating condition. This is to say, seeing the infant restrained, with the emotion shown by the infant response, unknown to them, being actually produced by a "fear" stimulus, it was judged to be anger. Contemporary interpretation would have it that rather than there being clear-cut emotional responses in infants, as claimed by Watson, there is a mass of random movements to any strong stimuli out of which individual emotions emerge as the child grows older.

Thinking [62]

To Watson, the most important kind of implicit sensory-motor behavior occurs when the person stands stock still and, after a lapse of time, comes forth with a solution to some problem, the solution being expressed verbally or by some movement of the body, arms, or legs. The implicit behavior prior to the overt action, of course, would be thinking. To Watson, committed as he was to behavior as his datum, this implicit behavior was genuine and relevant. Thinking, he said, is nothing more than subvocal talking or muscular habits learned in overt speech which become inaudible as we grow up. After learning to talk by conditioning, thought is nothing more "than talking to ourselves."[63] A bodily response is a word substitute. A man thinks, that is, makes implicit verbal reactions which do not differ in spirit from the overt movements made by a rat in running a maze. Thinking, to be sure, is more implicit and more economical of time and effort, but this is a difference only of degree. Attach recording devices to the larynx of the thinker, and we get movement that thus becomes explicit. Moreover, in a young child, who is in the process of learning a language, these quantitative differences in amount of movement are even less great. Often children, and occasionally adults, think aloud. The child will say what he is going to do and then do it. Under the influence of social pressure (conditioning), he learns to give up clear articulation for whispering and finally reaches the stage of inaudible or implicit speech, characteristics of the adult. The one source of evidence, of course, which Watson could not use is the most obvious—that introspectively sometimes we are aware that we do talk to ourselves while thinking. However, he could hardly bolster Behaviorism by an appeal to introspection![64]

Thought is not merely behavior of the larynx or subvocal talking; it involves the whole body as in gesturing, frowning, or nodding, or by the carrying out of any movement which stands for an object or a situation. Watson suggested observing a deaf mute's fingers. During his thinking, muscular movements of the fingers will be found, just as there were movements from the larynx of normal persons. Failure to always get positive results from this method Watson attributed to the lack of delicacy of the instruments available. As a matter of fact, use of improved methods has demonstrated that thinking does involve these peripheral muscular factors, but that central or brain processes have also been shown to be present by later research. The judgment of later generations of psychologists is that Watson's theory of thinking as subvocal speech is too schematic and over-simplified.

Learning and Conditioning

Watson's views of learning showed progressive change and expansion. In his 1913 article[65] he conceived of Behaviorism as using stimulus-response and habit formation but made no mention of conditioning. By 1916 in his Presidential Address[66] he enthusiastically endorsed conditioning. In his *Behavior*[67] of 1919 the available research on discriminatory maze and puzzle-box learning was described in detail. He called Thorndike's law of effect "highly figurative." [68] Evidently, he saw conscious feeling lurking somewhere in this way of formulating the animal's responses. Watson would have substituted for the influence of effect that of recency and of frequency. Maze learning and problem solving were to be explained as being due to recency and frequency, Watson held, because the successful act, over a series of trials, was most frequent and, by its position within a trial, was also the one that occurred most recently. He argued that, after all, the animal takes the correct path at least once every trial, while particular blind alleys are skipped in a given trial; and the successful path occurs, by definition, as the last and, therefore, is the most recent.

After 1916, Watson emphasized the importance of conditioning. The conditioned reflex became the heir of associationism. He expressed it in contiguous conditioning or a continuation of stimuli accompanying a movement, so that, when this combination recurred, it tended to be followed by that same movement. Watson emphasized repetition while he rejected effect and, consequently, failed to recognize the importance of reinforcement, a key problem in later conditioning theory.

Watson's application of conditioning principles to learning in general and to thinking and emotion in particular, now becomes relevant. Habits are nothing more than complex conditioned responses, such as those involved in playing tennis, soleing shoes, or maternal reactions to children. [69] These habits are integrations of conditioned responses around an activity build up from the available behavior repertoire, starting with innate movements. Movements combine by conditioning into complex acts. Language habits are merely a special case in that to some extent they become implicit.

Conditioning is the basis of speech, and speech is the basis of thinking. This bald summary shows why conditioning is important in thinking. Shortly after birth the infant shows vocalization which, after conditioning, are the spoken words. The vocalizations of the infant, the "da-das" and the like, are attached to father, and through further conditioning it becomes, "daddy." With stronger verbal habits, the child no longer has to say the word, *i.e.*, give the conditioned response of, "father," which had been selectively conditioned from the more primitive, "daddy." Thinking it alone, may now suffice. Other words and thoughts develop in a similar fashion. Subvocal speech, or thinking, has been developed through conditioning.

The child's fears and other emotional reactions beyond those given to the unlearned responses are brought about by conditioning. Watson and Rosalie Rayner proceeded to demonstrate this contention by building up a conditioned

are only a sampling of the habit systems which constitute the personality. In another person, another classification of habit systems would be used, although some of those that are listed are of a general character applicable to anyone. Since the cross-section is taken at a point in time, later or earlier cross-sections would show differences because habits are changeable; and no individual's personality remains the same throughout life.

In this changeability of personality lies the opportunity to use it for the betterment of mankind. Behaviorism, Watson believed, should stimulate adults to change themselves and especially to be prepared to bring up their children in a scientific way. Will not, they, "in turn bring up their children in a still more scientific way, until the world finally becomes a place fit for human habitation?" [73]

OVERVIEW[74]

Watson's career as a psychologist hardly lasted two decades, and yet his effect upon psychology has been pronounced. As even the brief review of earlier work has shown, he did not originate the objective approach to psychology. What he did was to give it a direction by making it a cause and by stressing its value in such a single-hearted, massive fashion that he could not be ignored. For many psychologists he was a breath of fresh air, clearing away the musty accumulation of the centuries.

His pronounced influence also originated from a source he would have denied—he was a functionalist, not in the superficial sense of accepting conscious experience within the ken of psychology, but in the much more salient sense of emphasis upon the adaptiveness of psychological activity. In this way he moved *with*, not against, the other dominant aspect of the psychological scene.

Quite apart from the nature of his claims, his appeal was enhanced by characteristics he manifested—the youthful optimism, the tough mindedness, and a trenchant, self-confident style of writing—all of which contributed to his great effect upon psychology. Each new problem, say, emotion and instinct, when first broached, would be introduced by a sweeping denial of the value of earlier work. As he saw it, the "great mass" of literature on emotion lacked a central scientific viewpoint; James' evidence for his theory of emotion became nothing more than "a bit of introspecting," while McDougall's list of emotions was dismissed because no "objective" methods were used to derive them. He would then make a new start.

By the same token, these characteristics repelled others, or at least moved them to ridicule and satire. As a case in point, his conditioning studies, such as that of Albert B., convinced him that practical control of infant behavior (and by implication that of the adult) was possible. No doubt moved by high social motives in his comments on social control through conditioning they left him, however, open to satire. The satirization of the social use of conditioning and other aspects of Behaviorism in Aldous Huxley's *Brave New World* comes to mind in this connection.

Limitation of discussion to Watson's own research interests and of what he stressed in describing Behaviorism gives a limited impression of what he admitted within its precincts. Accepted as objective were those methods concerned with reaction time and business psychology.[75] Personality was to be studied by intelligence, achievement, and motor tests; personality questionnaires; and interview techniques. Moreover, he explicitedly denied that applied psychology is of lesser dignity than pure psychology. Workers in the areas of application, since they were accepted as enjoying full stature in psychology, could perhaps enjoy, with a touch of glee, his vigorous attack on their more academic colleagues. For all of these reasons, Watson affected psychology profoundly.

Some of the consequences that followed will be examined when contemporary psychology in the United States is considered.

REFERENCES *

1. J. B. WATSON, Psychology as a Behaviorist Views It, *Psychol. Rev.*, 1913, 20, 158–177. (Herrnstein & Boring Excerpt No. 94)

2. *Ibid.*

3. *Ibid.*

4. J. B. WATSON, *Behaviorism.* (2nd ed.) New York: Norton, 1930.

5. I. M. SECHENOV, Refleksy golovnogo mozga. (Translated as Reflexes of the Brain, by A. A. Subkov.) In I. M. Sechenov, *Selected Works.* Moscow & Leningrad, Gozmedizdat, 1935, pp. 264–322. (1863) (Herrnstein & Boring Excerpt No. 63)

6. I. P. PAVLOV, *Selected Works.* (edited by K. S. Kostoyants) (Translated by S. Belsky) Moscow: Foreign Languages Publishing House, 1955. (1873–1936)

7. SECHENOV, *op. cit.*

8. *Selected Works.*

9. I. P. PAVLOV, Autobiography. In *Selected Works,* pp. 41–44. (Undated); B. P. Babkin, *Pavlov, a Biography.* Chicago: University of Chicago Press, 1949.

10. I. P. PAVLOV, *Lectures on Conditioned Reflexes.* (3rd ed.) (Translated by W. H. Gantt) New York: International, 1928. (1904)

* See page 16 for description of reference style.

11. *Ibid.*

12. I. P. FROLOV, *Pavlov and His School.* London: Kegan Paul, Trench, Trubner, 1937.

13. *Lectures,* pp. 76–80. (Herrnstein & Boring Excerpt No. 101)

14. *Ibid.; Selected Works.*

15. *Lectures,* p. 219.

16. *Ibid.*

17. Frolov, *op. cit.*

18. BABKIN, *op. cit.*

19. *Ibid.,* p. 162.

20. A. L. SCHNIERMANN, Bekhterev's Reflexological School. In C. Murchison, (Ed.), *Psychologies of 1930.* Worcester: Clark University Press, 1930, 221–242.

21. V. M. BEKHTEREV, *General Principles of Human Reflexology.* (Translated 4th Russian ed.) New York: International, 1932. (1907)

22. E. L. THORNDIKE, Edward Lee Thorndike. In C. Murchison (ed.) *A History of Psychology in Autobiography.* (Vol. 3) Worcester: Clark University Press, 1936, 263–270.

23. *Conditioned Responses.*

24. E. L. THORNDIKE, Animal Intelligence: an Experimental Study of the Associative Processes in Animals, *Psychol. Rev. Monogr. Suppl.* 2, No. 4. (Herrnstein & Boring Excerpt No. 97)

25. E. L. THORNDIKE, *The Elements of Psychology.* New York: Seiler, 1905, p. 203.

26. E. L. THORNDIKE, *The Fundamentals of Learning.* New York: Teachers College, 1932; E. L. Thorndike, *The Psychology of Wants, Interests, and Attitudes.* New York: Appleton, 1935.

27. Ř. M. YERKES, The Formation of Habits in the Turtle. *Pop. Sci. Mo.* 1901, 58, 519–525. (Herrnstein & Boring Excerpt No. 98)

28. W. S. SMALL, Experimental Study of the Mental Processes of the Rat, II. *Amer. J. Psychol.,* 1901, 12, 206–232. (Herrnstein & Boring Excerpt No. 99)

29. J. LOEB, *Einleitung in die vergleichende Gehirnphysiologie und vergleichende Psychologie mit besonderer Berücksichtigung dir wirbellosen Thiere.* Leipzig, Barth, 1899. (Eng. trans. 1900) (Herrnstein & Boring Excerpt No. 89)

30. Behavior, p. 8.

31. *Ibid.*

32. G. BERGMANN, The Contribution of John B. Watson, *Psychol. Rev.,* 1956, 63, 265–276.

33. J. M. CATTELL, The Conception and Methods of Psychology. *Pop. Sci. Mo.,* 1904, 66, 175–186.

34. W. McDOUGALL, *Physiological Psychology.* New York: Macmillan, 1905.

35. W. McDOUGALL. *Outline of Psychology.* New York: Scribner's, 1923. (Herrnstein & Boring Excerpt No. 116)

36. W. B. Pillsbury, *The Essentials of Psychology.* New York: Macmillan, 1911.

37. M. F. Meyer, *Psychology of the Other-one: an Introductory Text-book of Psychology.* (2nd ed., rev.) Columbus: Missouri Book, 1922. (1921)

38. A. P. Weiss, *A Theoretical Basis of Human Behavior.* Columbus: Adams, 1925.

39. J. B. Watson, John B. Watson. In C. Murchison (ed.) *A History of Psychology in Autobiography.* (Vol. 3) Worcester: Clark University Press, 1936, 271–281; R. S. Woodworth, John Broadus Watson: 1878–1958, *Amer. J. Psychol.,* 1959, 72, 301–310.

40. J. B. Watson, *Psychology from the Standpoint of a Behaviorist.* (3rd ed. rev.) Philadelphia: Lippincott, 1929, preface.

41. *Ibid.*

42. J. B. Watson, *Behavior: an Introduction to Comparative Psychology.* New York: Holt, 1914.

43. *Psychology as a Behaviorist Views It. op. cit.*

44. E. B. Titchener, *A Textbook of Psychology.* New York: Macmillan, 1909.

45. *Behavior,* p. 3.

46. *Ibid.*

47. J. B. Watson, The Place of the Conditioned-Reflex in Psychology, *Psychol. Rev.,* 1916, 23, 89–117.

48. *Behaviorism.*

49. J. B. Watson, *Psychology from the Standpoint of a Behaviorist.* Philadelphia: Lippincott, 1919.

50. J. B. Watson, *Psychological Care of Infant and Child.* New York: Norton, 1928.

51. J. B. Watson & W. McDougall, *The Battle of Behaviorism.* New York: Norton, 1929.

52. *Behaviorism.*

53. *Ibid.; Psychology,* 1929.

54. *Behaviorism,* p. 49.

55. *Psychology,* 1929.

56. *Behavior.*

57. *Psychology,* 1919.

58. *Behaviorism.*

59. *Ibid.,* p. 104.

60. *Ibid.*

61. M. Sherman, The Differentiation of Emotional Responses in Infants, *J. Comp. Psychol.,* 1927, 7, 265–284, 335–351.

62. *Behaviorism; Psychology,* 1929.

63. *Ibid.,* p. 238.

64. Margaret F. Washburn, Introspection as an Objective Method, *Psychol. Rev.,* 1922, 29, 89–112.

65. *Psychology as a Behaviorist Views It.*

66. *Place of Conditioned-Reflex.*

67. *Behavior.*

68. *Ibid.*, 256.

69. *Behaviorism.*

70. J. B. WATSON & ROSALIE RAYNER, Conditioned Emotional Reactions, *J. Exp. Psychol.* 1920, 3, pp. 1–14.

71. *Behaviorism.*

72. *Ibid.*

73. *Ibid.*, p. 304.

74. The best over-all evaluation of the contribution of John B. Watson to psychology in my judgment is that of Bergman (*op. cit.*)

75. *Psychology*, 1929.

CHAPTER 19

WERTHEIMER:

GESTALT PSYCHOLOGY

IN 1910 a psychologist, Max Wertheimer by name, was traveling by train from Vienna to the Rhineland on his vacation.[1] During this journey an idea came to him for a research study which was to found Gestalt psychology. Gone were his plans for a vacation. At Frankfurt, the next major stop, he left the train, bought a toy stroboscope, and took it to his hotel room to verify, in a preliminary way, the "insight" that had just come to him. The stroboscope, it should be explained, is a device allowing successive still pictures to be exposed at a constant rate of speed so that movement is perceived. Before the advent of motion pictures, which itself is a later development of the same principle, stroboscopes were relatively common as children's toys. However, Wertheimer did not have to use the stroboscope in his formal experiment; the University of Frankfurt placed at his disposal a tachistoscope. This is a device for regulating the length of time a visual stimulus, such as a nonsense syllable, or figure drawing, is exposed. It may also be used to present successive stimuli, separated by short, precisely regulated intervals of time.

What was this epoch making experiment? It was a problem in the perception of apparent motion, that is, the perception of movement when actually no movement had taken place.[2] Two lines were exposed in two different places on the face of the tachistoscope. Each exposure lasted a very short time and was separated from the next exposure by varying lengths of time. If there

436

was too long a time between the exposures, the subject would see the lines successively. If the time was too short, he would see the lines simultaneously. However, if the time interval between the exposures was at an optimal length, the subject saw, not two lines successively or simultaneously, but *one* line *move* from one place to another. The experience is that of a single line which visibly moved, despite the fact that actually there are two successively exposed stationary lines separated by an interval of time. Variations, such as exposing a vertical line followed by a horizontal line, for which the observer saw a line swinging around through ninety degrees, gave the same result—an impression of motion lines. This apparent movement Wertheimer called *phi phenomenon*. Sometimes an observer reported movement alone, with no line being seen to move. Movement without the lines being experienced at all, he called "pure phi."[3] Although the name was new, the phenomenon itself had been known for many years. This seemingly trivial verification of what was known was to launch another new movement in psychology. It is the interpretation extending far beyond its ostensible subject, not the results, as such, that is important.

Wundt's view of psychology will serve as an illustration of what Wertheimer and others were to attempt to combat through this and similar studies. To Wundt, there were various psychological dimensions available for compounding—quality, intensity, pleasantness-unpleasantness, tension-relaxation, and excitement-depression. When these are compounded by association, ideas and perceptions are formed. That these compounds had characteristics as a whole, not readily explained by the parts, Wundt had been aware. Somewhat lamely, Wundt's solution depended upon creative synthesis in the spirit of John Stuart Mill's mental chemistry. Wertheimer's study arose from dissatisfaction with this elementaristic, associationistic position of Wundt and others, which had left many characteristics of percepts unexplained by their supposedly ultimate components.

ANTECEDENTS OF GESTALT PSYCHOLOGY

Some of the perplexities of configuration had already been elucidated and explanations had been attempted before Wertheimer appeared in Frankfurt. Ernst Mach in his book, *The Analysis of Sensations*,[4] originally published in 1886, showed that changes in spatial orientation, such as first viewing a square from one of its sides and then shifting to a corner; or first learning a series of sounds at one tempo and then hearing them at a faster or slower tempo did not bring about in either instance a radical change in the experience of the over-all configuration. Despite wide variation in viewing conditions, a table remains a table, no matter how viewed. Look at a table from one corner with the edge of the table at eye level. Although the retinal image is a complex quadrilateral, you see a rectangle oriented obliquely in space. Mach went on to speak of sensations of space-form and sensations of time-form, meaning that these two forms were kinds of experience in themselves. The circle may change size or color without changing its space-form of circularity.

In Austria, Christian von Ehrenfels,[5] about twenty years before Wertheimer's study, had noted that in the visual field certain visual characteristics, such as roundness, angularity, and slenderness are ignored when we deal with sensations. Their occurrence seems to be due to something beyond single sensations. If individual stimuli are changed in the same proportion, these particular characteristics of slenderness, angularity, and roundness are still present as before. Among other phenomena which he also considered was the effect of transposing a melody. A melody made up of one series of notes is still heard as the same melody when heard in a different set of notes. A melody played in different keys is still recognizable as the same. That aspect of perception given by the transposition of melodies and proportionate changes in roundness, angularity, and slenderness, von Ehrenfels called *Gestaltqualität* or form quality. These perceptions were based on something more than the sum of the individual lines, something over and above the tones. The form quality, however, was treated by von Ehrenfels as still another element (although not a sensation) in a summative fashion, so that, if there were nine notes and a *Gestaltqualität*, there were ten elements—nine sensory and one non-sensory.[6] A variant explanatory principle that was also offered, spoke of "relations between elements" as accounting for the phenomenon. Ehrenfels and the Austrian School of *Gestaltqualität* which developed at Graz held that form qualities were constructed out of the sensory data and, since the elements were the ultimate facts of consciousness, continued an old tradition, rather than began a new one.

Other relevant work by individuals outside what was to become the Gestalt tradition was going on more or less simultaneously with that of Wertheimer. Friedrich Schumann, met before as G. E. Müller's assistant and collaborator in the invention of the memory drum, and who was Wertheimer's host in Frankfurt, had already found in studies of visual shape and size perception that analysis into sensory elements was of no help in explaining the results.[7]

The arguments of William James[8] helped in this revolt against elementarism. James had held that elementarism fails to account for the simplest facts of experience. For example, our field of vision is ordered and extended. We see unitary objects of definite extension, form, and size, not a bundle of sensations.

Gestalt psychology was influenced by the continuing phenomenological trend. From the days of Goethe and Purkinje and their observations of color in the early nineteenth century, a phenomenological strand of development had continued to hover close to the main stream of psychology, although not accepted by the dominant tradition. Since phenomenology involved the study of immediate experience, its conclusions were seen as following directly from the experience. For example, in Hering's studies of color and space what he did essentially was to demonstrate the presence of some color phenomena or visual perception without feeling the need, from his point of view, to go beyond this demonstration. Many of the illustrations of Gestalt psychology will be found to take this phenomenological form. However, the Gestalt psychologists were sufficiently imbued with other trends to proceed to experiment and measurement.

Edgar Rubin,[9] a Danish phenomenologist, contemporary with Wertheimer, emphasized a distinction between the figure, the substantial appearance of objects, and the ground, the general homogeneous environment in which the object was placed. Perception, he argued, is selective. Not all stimuli are perceived with the same clarity and distinctness. Those perceived with greater clarity form the figure, while the remainder give the ground. The house against the sky, the word or picture on the white page, the recognized face against the rest of the faces in the photograph, have this relation of figure and ground.

Wertheimer went beyond his predecessors in that he submitted these convictions to experimental study of a crucial kind. From these experiments, Wertheimer was to see a new way of understanding these perplexing phenomena and to integrate the results with a new way of looking at psychological phenomena.

EARLY YEARS OF MAX WERTHEIMER[10]

Max Wertheimer had been born in Prague in 1880 where his father directed and taught in a commercial school. After attending a local gymnasium, he studied law at the University for two and a half years but then shifted to the study of philosophy while still at Prague. Among others, he attended the lectures of von Ehrenfels whose work had led to the theory of *Gestaltqualität*. He continued work at Berlin in philosophy and psychology, where he studied under Schumann, mentioned earlier, and Carl Stumpf, the friend of William James and a specialist in the psychology of music. He then went on to Würzburg, where he received his degree in 1904 *summa cum laude* under

Külpe, during the period the Würzburg School was carrying on the revolt, not against elementarism as such but against the constraints Wundt would put upon the elements with which psychology was concerned.

An early research interest, in keeping with Wertheimer's interest in the law, had been in the association experiment as used for the detection of guilty knowledge on which he had published in 1905 [11] and in later years. The years 1904 to 1910, before his arrival in Frankfurt, are not well documented, although some of his activities in Prague, Vienna, and Berlin concerned psychological matters.

FRANKFURT, PHI PHENOMENON, KÖHLER, AND KOFFKA

On arrival in Frankfurt in 1910, after trying out his hypothesis with the toy stroboscope, Wertheimer sought out his old teacher Schumann, who had just arrived at the University of Frankfurt. It was he who placed a tachistoscope at his disposal. His first subject was Wolfgang Köhler (1887–1967) and his second, Kurt Koffka (1886–1941). These two men were destined to be junior only to Wertheimer in their pioneering contributions to Gestalt psychology in the years to come. Koffka and Köhler had taken their degrees at Berlin in 1908 and 1909 respectively and were the new assistants in the Psychological Institute at Frankfurt.[12] They had also already done some research in psychology, Köhler on hearing and Koffka on imagery and thought. What first united these three was their discontent with Wundtian elementarism. As good subjects should be, Köhler and Koffka had been kept ignorant of the purpose of the experiment until after its completion. Sometime in 1911, Wertheimer called them in to explain the experiment.[13] From then on their lives and work were intricately interwoven.

Wertheimer's paper on the "Experimental Studies of the Perception of Movement" [14] appeared in 1912. This single study stimulated over a hundred papers on apparent movement in the next thirty years.[15] By and large, Wertheimer's findings were substantiated. Reverberations from his study were to extend into other psychological fields, particulary memory, thinking, and action.

Several explanations of apparent movement were already current.[16] The traditional view of discrete elements would have it that each stimulus gives rise to its own sensation and, on the basis of past experience, our perceptions of them are integrated. To be more specific, Wundt attributed apparent movement to the kinesthetic sensations produced by the movement of the eyes.[17] Wundt's explanation was neatly ruled out by Wertheimer's arranging the experimental setting with suitable pairs of lines as to require two simultaneous movements in *opposite* directions. Phi phenomenon still occurred. Since the eyes could hardly move in both directions at the same time, Wundt's explanation fell to the ground.

The Nature of Phi Phenomenon and Gestalt

Wertheimer argued that the apparent movement generated in his experiment had no counterpart in the sensory elements. Local sensory stimulation cannot be responsible for the actually perceived phenomenon. It is this fact which he could not fit into existing theories of perception. Hence a general re-evaluation of the basic nature of perception seemed necessary to him.

Whatever it was that Wertheimer explained to Köhler and Koffka in 1911 about his experiment on phi phenomenon, it was not the full blown Gestalt theory.[18] That what was said seemed to them to be a challenge to the established order, there is no doubt. Wertheimer did know by then that the *Gestaltqualität* interpretation was not sufficient, and said so in the paper, but a more complete statement had to await later work. To explain Gestalt theory in a preliminary way, there are two papers devoted to theoretical statements which were published by Wertheimer in 1922[19] and 1925.[20]

In the phi phenomenon, Wertheimer wrote, the subjects were perceiving a whole, or Gestalt, not the isolated elements. Von Ehrenfels and the members of the Graz School had been on the right track, Wertheimer said, in raising an important problem; but, by depending upon a summation principle, they had been wrong.[21] What takes place in each part depends upon the whole. This is true of all perceptual experience. In our perception of objects there are characteristics that cannot be attributed to a single sensation. This Gestalt or whole is a "given" of perception, not something unstructured. The Gestalt is, in itself, primary and inherent in the process of sensory reception. With James, Wertheimer agreed that what the elementarists had found were the secondary products of analysis. What was important was not the mosaic but a dynamic field in which the parts are interacting through the receptive process. Perception shows a totality, a whole, a configuration, an articulated structure; and it is the task of psychology to account for it, not by explaining it away but by exploring its characteristics as a structure itself. Gestalt psychology restored the "thing-language," as Brunswik[22] phrased it many years later, to its place in the psychology of immediate experience. For psychology to advance, requires "a procedure 'from above,' *not* 'from below upward' "[23], understanding of whole properties must precede consideration of the significance of the "parts." A Gestalt is primary to the parts, not merely its sum. It now becomes relevant to quote Wertheimer's formal definition of Gestalt: "There are wholes, the behavior of which is not determined by that of their individual elements, but where the part-processes are themselves determined by the intrinsic nature of the whole." [24]

Sometimes the words "configuration," "structure," and "whole" are used as English translations for Gestalt, but the untranslated term is preferable, since none of these words capture its complete meaning. Two meanings of Gestalt in German must be specified. On one hand, that is Gestalt as object. A Gestalt is an object which has shape, an entity in itself which has form, as a chair or table. On the other hand, Gestalt is the property of things as in squareness or triangularity. Gestalt, then, is both the object and the form characteristics of that object.

The emphasis upon wholes has sometimes led to a misunderstanding about the Gestalt theorists' precise attitude toward parts in the psychological field and toward the process of analysis. The Gestalt position does not demand, for example, that the *entire* visual field be organized into a *single* pattern. One has to do no more than use his eyes to see it is not. There are aggregates *within* this field that are *Gestalten*. The Gestalt psychologists do use analysis; they object to analysis into sensational elements which have no existence as bits of experience, but not to analysis as such. If there is analysis into *genuine* parts, then this is more than permissible; it is demanded.

Analysis is exemplified in the various laws of *Gestalten*. Each law, in one sense, is a statement of analysis, as for example, the distinction made between figure and ground. The parts, however, are derived from their meaningfulness in the total context, not from sensory elements. Attitudinal analysis is also possible. An observer may, by adopting a particular attitude, select some part of the Gestalt and suppress others. This happens in reversible perspective, as when one sees a line drawing of an illusion capable of being seen two ways, permitting one to switch from one view to the other. This is a kind of analysis in which there is a change in the organization of the field, so that the impression one receives is different in one way of perceiving it from another.

GESTALT AS A PSYCHOLOGY OF PROTEST

There was to develop not only a Gestalt theory, but also a Gestalt movement with these three men zealously propagandizing for the Gestalt point of view, a task to which they dedicated much of their efforts in the years to come. In furthering this aim, however, Köhler and Koffka were much more ready than Wertheimer to systematize their thinking and put it into print.

Coming into being in Germany at the same time as Behaviorism was making its appearance in the United States, Gestalt psychology was likewise a psychology of protest.[25] Unlike the Behaviorists, Gestalt psychologists did not question the existentiality of consciousness, but rather they doubted the reality of the elements of which other psychologists said consciousness was constituted. Wertheimer summarized these mistaken beliefs in terms of the "bundle hypothesis" and the "association hypothesis."[26] Sensory elements do not form a bundle and association does not serve as a means of binding together, because there is not a summative relationship as the psychologists whom they were attacking claimed. Gestalt psychology was very much a revolution against the established order in psychology. In its early years, the exposing of the inadequacies of the entrenched position in psychology was almost as important to them as their positive contributions. They aspired to nothing less than a complete revision of psychology, but from the figure down, rather than from the ground up.

Wertheimer and the Principles of Organization

Wertheimer lectured at Frankfurt from 1912 on, where he was *Dozent,* as he did later at Berlin, where he went in 1916. He became an "Assistant Professor" in Berlin in 1922, and Professor at Frankfurt in 1929 where he returned to take Schumann's old chair. Relevant publications from Wertheimer were slow in coming. During the war years, Wertheimer collaborated on research in the development of binaural listening devices for use in submarines and harbor defense installations which were not particularly relevant to Gestalt psychology.

The influence of Wertheimer on the thinking of other psychologists was considerable although, as Newman[27] remarks, hard to evaluate. It was primarily from his lectures and his inimitable conversations that his students including Kurt Lewin, learned about Gestalt psychology. At Berlin and Frankfurt, colleagues and students carried on research theses on a variety of studies.

Much of what was contained in Wertheimer's lectures during these years did not see print until after the war. A paper on creative thinking which appeared in 1920[28] anticipated in some respects (as did a paper on thinking appearing as early as 1912) his major work in this field, which was not to appear for more than twenty years.

In 1923, an important paper on perceptual grouping appeared which requires detailed consideration.[29] In this paper Wertheimer attempted to show that a person perceives objects just as directly as he saw motion in the study of the phi phenomenon, not as clusters of sensations but as unified wholes. The principles of organization of *Gestalten* that Wertheimer formulated had specific reference to perception, *i.e.,* having to do with how *Gestalten* were organized. He preferred to use simple visual phenomena, such as dots, lines, or figures made of a few lines or simple auditory stimuli, individual musical notes, for example, so as not to be charged with confusing the issue by inclusion of common objects whose sheer meaningfulness would suggest organization. He presented various principles, some of which follow. There is the principle of proximity—parts close together are perceived together, as in tap-tap, pause, tap-tap, pause, tap-tap. The two taps together will be heard as belonging together rather than the last tap before the pause being perceived as related to the first tap after it. Things close together in time tend to be grouped together. To use another illustration, this time concerning space, dots relatively close together are readily seen as a group. Second, there is a principle of similarity. Imagine a soft tone represented thus . while ! represents a loud tone. Then in . . . ! ! . . . ! ! . . . the three soft tones are heard together, as are the two loud tones, and so on. With effort we can hear some other arrangement as . . . ! ! . . . ! ! . . . , but this cannot be long maintained. It should be noted that this visual representation of auditory stimuli functions in much the same fashion as the auditory stimulus it is designed to symbolize. To use another visual illustration, dots of the same shape or color are readily seen as a group, as distinguished from those of another shape or color which will form still another group.

Wertheimer was demonstrating that we respond not to isolated stimuli, but to the nature of the setting in which they were found. A considerable amount of work by others developing these and other laws of form followed. By 1933, Helson[30] was able to isolate 114 separate laws of *Gestalten*.

Certain illustrations in this later work will make more meaningful this problem of the laws of organization of *Gestalten*. A principle was borrowed from the research of Rubin, whose investigations of figure and ground have already been cited. In the present context, the differentiation into figure and ground became a law of Gestalt organization.

Still another principle of organization is that of closure. Closure is the tendency to complete a figure, no matter what the sensory modality. Visual forms are, of course, included. For example, if a figure is drawn with incomplete lines or small gaps (as are many cartoons and sketches) the perceiver completes it, typically disregarding, or not "seeing" its incompleteness. A children's puzzle picture in which the task is to find hidden faces, also illustrates closure. The obvious figures that the artist has drawn completes some pattern, say a country scene with trees and a brook, which we accept. The figure for which one is to search is hidden, say a face, because lines making up the face are incorporated into the country scene which is composed of figures for which closure is easier to make. The same illustration supplies another instance of closure. As one searches, there is tension, a sense of incompleteness; when the face leaps into view, closure has taken place. In the same vein, a favorite conversational illustration of Wertheimer, which he would demonstrate in a restaurant, involved the waiter and the bill. Before being paid, when asked the amount of the bill, the waiter would be able to state it promptly, since the transaction had not been completed. Called over again a minute after it was paid, he would not be able to remember the amount. Before payment there was tension; payment made for closure. This is the completion principle of closure.[31] But there is another aspect of closure that must be distinguished. This is the perceptual principle of closure. Many superficial accounts of closure use a circle made from short, dashed lines as the example, *par excellence*, of completion closure. It is nothing of the kind; it is not seen as an unbroken circle which completion closure calls for. It is seen as a circle made of broken lines—a broken whole rather than a series of unrelated stimulus points. It illustrates what is called perceptual closure. Despite being broken, it still has perceptually the appearance of a circle.

Closure is essentially a special instance of the most general of configurational laws, that of *Prägnanz*, the principle that all experienced fields tend to become as articulated as possible. Besides closure, other factors of proximity, similarity as well as symmetry and regularity are embraced in this Law of *Pragnänz*.[32]

Köhler and the Mentality of Apes

Köhler remained at Frankfurt until 1913 when an opportunity arose to go to the Anthropoid Station on Tenerife in the Canary Islands, where he worked with apes and chickens.[33] Because of the war, he remained there longer than he had intended.

An experiment of Köhler's[34] with chicks, performed during these years, simple in nature though it is, brings out clearly what the Gestalt psychologists were trying to demonstrate. Two shades of gray paper on which grain was scattered were exposed. Hens were trained to take grains from one of these papers, a darker shade of gray than that of the other paper. If they pecked at a grain on the darker paper, they were permitted to swallow it; if they pecked at a grain on the lighter paper, they were driven away. After hundreds of trials, they learned eventually to peck only at grain on the darker paper. So far this is only preliminary to the experiment itself. The crucial series of trials was now inserted. The darker gray paper of the learning trials was used again, but now it was accompanied by a sheet of a *still darker* gray, instead of the original lighter sheet. If the hens pecked on the original gray they were responding to specific brightness, as such; if they pecked at what now was the darker paper, they would be reacting to a total situation or Gestalt, that is, to a relation of lighter-darker. As a rule, the hens pecked at the darker gray, not the particular one on which they had learned to peck. This was a relative response in which "darker of two" was the clue, not the specific gray. The hens reacted, not to a specific element in the learning situation, but to the pattern or Gestalt.

Köhler's work on chimpanzees while at Tenerife appeared as the *Mentality of Apes*, first published in 1917 and later translated into English[35] along with an important paper in 1927.[36] His problem was the investigation of the intelligence of chimpanzees as shown in the solving of problems. The studies of chimpanzees took place in and around their cages and involved such simple props as the bars of the cages serving as a means of blocking direct access, bananas for them to secure, sticks to be used to draw in the bananas from outside of the cage, and boxes on which to climb.

One study involved a stick hidden by Köhler in the framework of the roof of the cage with the chimpanzees watching. The animals were then taken to their living dormitory for the night. The next morning one of the apes, brought back to the cage, found that outside the cage there was a bunch of bananas. He was already familiar with using a stick to draw them in. He looked around, as Köhler put it, as a man would in seeking a tool, but did not find one. After some seconds, his eyes went to the place where the stick had been hidden the night before. Although the stick was not in sight, he immediately climbed up to where it was hidden, brought it down, and used it to draw in the bananas.

Another study involved a banana placed at ceiling level of the cage as well as a box, which if maneuvered properly so it was under the banana, would permit the chimpanzee to jump up from its top to secure the banana. Almost all the chimps solved the problem of moving the box to the correct spot under the banana, climbing up on the box, and jumping to get the banana.

Contrast their behavior with that of a relatively stupid chimpanzee. He had been present many times when the others had learned to use the box as a tool to reach the banana. These other chimpanzees even tried to show him how to use it, but his behavior imitated only parts of their behavior. He would move the box, but, as often as not, away from the food. He would then climb on the box and jump, but not under the banana and, after climbing off the box, would then jump up under the banana. He never formed the Gestalt; for him there were two separate groups, climb-box-jump and jump-under-fruit. He did not relate the parts of the activity to the essential structure of the total situation.

These and similar results were interpreted by Köhler[37] as evidence of insight—the seeing of relations. These *Gestalten* occur in the process of solving problems. There is an activity on their part which is a continuous whole in which everything falls into place. There is continuity, a direction toward a goal, and closure. The insightful solutions they displayed are interpreted as making for closure of the gap in the animal's psychological field. Capacity for perception of relations varied in different animals and thus became an indication of intelligence.

KÖHLER AND PHYSICAL GESTALTEN

In 1920 Köhler left Tenerife for a Germany in the throes of economic and social reconstruction. He managed to secure only temporary academic appointments for a year or so. Formal recognition of Gestalt psychology by the academic world, however, came in 1922 when Köhler was appointed to a chair and the directorship of the laboratory at the University of Berlin. This was a post he occupied until 1935. Presumably in part responsible for this major appointment was the publication of a book the year before, whose translated title is the formidable, *Static and Stationary Physical Gestalts.*[38]

To evaluate its significance, it is necessary to return to Wertheimer's original experiment.[39] Wertheimer postulated brain action as a configural total process to account for phi. These processes must be essentially similar for apparent and for true motion, since they are experienced as identical. If one assumes that wherever there are two identical phenomena, one may also assume that there are corresponding brain processes. If the nervous system was so organized that it consisted of interlocking elements, it simply could not account for phi. There must be some correspondence between the patterning of the psychological experience and the underlying brain process. The nervous system has unitary properties with its parts being included in the larger units or *Gestalten*. Wertheimer suggested that, physiologically speaking, the seen movement was a consequence of a physiological short cut. With precisely the right temporal interval, "physiological cross processes' took place. These were modes of functional interconnection in larger patterns rather than points on the cortex. The physiological processes had whole properties themselves, and they were essentially the same in phi as they were in real motion.

This point of view was generalized by Köhler in his book of 1920.[40] A theory that physical systems possess Gestalt properties was the consequence, and this theory made it possible for Köhler to offer a transition from psychological to physical systems. Both the brain process and the perceived object correspond in that they are *Gestalten*. In relating the mental and physical, Köhler advanced the thesis that the *form* of the mental event is the same as the form of the physical.[41] This is the principle of isomorphism; there is a formal correspondence between the brain processes and the experienced consciousness. This correspondence is not the relation of object to its mirror image; rather it is *topological.* These two, the physical process and experience, are different spatially. There is a formal correspondence but not a literal copy between the experience and the brain pattern. In framing a psychophysical isomorphism he could draw not only on Wertheimer's formulation for perceived movement already cited,[42] but also Hering's anticipation of isomorphism concerning visual phenomena[43] and George E. Müller's use of the principle in formulating what he considered to be fundamental psychophysical axioms.[44] This last brings out that by his statement of isomorphism Köhler was offering his particular solution to the age-old mind-body problem. Isomorphism was his way of integrating the mind with the rest of the world.

Isomorphism, however, was but a phase of a much more ambitious undertaking on the part of Köhler.[45] He was intent on nothing short of demonstrating that biology, chemistry, physics, and even astronomy, were also sciences involving *Gestalten.* It should be mentioned that Köhler had studied physics under Max Planck, whose work in the quantum theory influenced him considerably. Köhler's attempt at model building was a heroic effort, the effect of which is hard to assess. Certainly it was meant to be more than an analogy, and in the contemporary period of psychology Köhler has had success in utilizing it to further psychological investigation.

Koffka and the Growth of the Mind

Koffka had left Frankfurt in 1911 for a long period of service at the University of Giessen (1911–1927), which was interrupted by visits to universities in the United States.[46]

During these years Koffka wrote the *Growth of the Mind,*[47] which was published in English in 1924 and which is based upon a work in German which had appeared three years before. It bore the subtitle, *an Introduction to Child Psychology.* Koffka made use of a developmental concept in his account, stressing what he called the convergence theory.

To place convergence theory in its proper setting, it is necessary to say something more about the phenomenological strain in Gestalt psychology. Phenomenology tended to go hand in glove with more sympathetic acceptance of nativism, as distinguished from empiricism. It has been established that, according to Gestalt theory, one does not need to learn to see structures in the sense that the properties of the psychological field are used to explain the events taking place within that field.

A neglected facet of Wertheimer's demonstration of phi phenomenon should be made explicit.[48] His was a nativistic conception. In modern guise he was continuing the position of Hering as differentiated from Helmholtz, the empiricist. Although without calling himself a nativist, he was taking a nativistic stance—movement is perceived as itself, is immediately seen, is given.

If the controversy over the influence of hereditary *versus* environmental influences be conceived relativistically, Gestalt psychology is more nativistic. And yet, there is also acceptance of the importance of learning in development. A compromise was expressed by Koffka's acceptance of a convergence theory, originally proposed by William Stern, in which every capacity is the result of a collaboration of inner and outer conditions of development. There is a convergence of these inner capacities and outer conditions so that both share in any psychological process.

Koffka submitted the concepts of reflex and of instinct to Gestalt analysis. Consistent with the Gestalt principle of the priority of the whole over the part, he saw reflexes as derived from instincts, rather than the reverse. To illustrate his handling of instinct, Koffka[49] held that one of its most conspicuous characteristics was the tendency of an instinct to require the individual to work toward the attainment of some goal. This working toward a goal, in turn, is directly interpretable as being an instance of bringing about closure in a temporal Gestalt.

Although there had been earlier work by Wertheimer in learning, Koffka's book served to emphasize in a detailed fashion that the learning process is clearly within the sphere of Gestalt psychology. The laws of organization in perception are seen as applicable to learning problems. Köhler's work on chimpanzees illuminates the point. His results were used by Koffka to challenge in a detailed fashion the theory of trial and error learning to the point that insight was offered as a replacement for it as a means of accounting for the learning process. The trial and error hypothesis assumes that in learning a large number of random movements are made, that the correct responses are gradually learned, and that the incorrect ones are eliminated. A variety of explanations are offered as to why this takes place. During the years in question the differentiation between those responses stamped in and those stamped out was attributed to the respective pleasure and pain that accompanied them.

To Koffka, learning is not a gradual mechanical process, but involves the same principles as perceptual *Gestalten*. Koffka rejected trial and error as an explanatory principle for learning and pointed out that the customary puzzle boxes and mazes were apparatuses that forced the animals to learn by trial and error because no other approach was possible under these circumstances. The results of such studies, just as those in sensation, were seen as an artifact of the laboratory procedure. To be sure, an obstacle between the animal and the goal must be provided, but it should be of such a nature as to permit intelligent, insightful behavior, if the animal is capable of it. This was the case with Köhler's procedures. The causative relations were open to the animals' observation, and insight resulted. Insight takes the place of practice or repetition as the crux of learning in the Gestalt description of learning. Practice does have some effect—after the Gestalt has been assimilated, practice makes its execution easier, as is the case when a musician grasps the Gestalt of a composition and with the aid of practice proceeds to play it better.

Gestalt Psychology Comes to the United States

With the rise of Hilter in the early thirties, Gestalt psychology experienced an almost complete transplantation of its leaders to the United States. Gestalt psychology, however, did not entirely disappear from Germany. Its principles were applied in other areas, as in personality theory. It was diluted to some extent by eclecticism; and some of its adherents splintered into smaller groups, each separated from the others by some theoretical difference. Under Hitler, psychology as a whole became a minor subject in the German academic hierarchy.

Before the migration, psychologists in the United States were not unfamiliar with the Gestalt psychologists' work. They had read their publications, and several visits by leading Gestalt psychologists had been made. In 1922, Koffka in the *Psychological Bulletin* wrote for American psychologists the introductory statement of the Gestalt position.[50] He used as the medium for his presentation the study of perception, a field in which he was by now specializing. Although admirable in many respects, his article had the unfortunate effect of creating the misapprehension among psychologists that Gestalt psychology was little more than a theory of perception—a view not entirely dissipated to this very day. Koffka and Köhler made several visits during the twenties and early thirties. Koffka was the first to settle in the United States, in 1927 becoming a professor at Smith College and remained on its faculty until his death in 1941. He worked principally on color vision in relation to perceptual organization. Köhler's book, *Gestalt Psychology*,[51] appeared in 1929. In 1934, he lectured at Harvard, returned to Germany, and in 1935, in view of his open conflict with the Nazi regime, he decided to migrate permanently. He became professor of psychology at Swarthmore College, where he remained until his retirement. Köhler and Koffka between them carried on more of the polemics for Gestalt psychology in the United States than did Wertheimer.

Wertheimer and his family left Germany in 1933 and came to the United

States. In 1934, he became a part of the "University in Exile" of the Graduate School of the New School of Social Research in New York City. This was an affiliation which was to continue until his death in 1943.

Other psychologists more peripherally related to Gestalt psychology also came to the United States. There was Kurt Lewin, who had taken his degree at the University of Berlin after World War I. He arrived in 1933 and went on to do important work related to Gestalt psychology in the contemporary period. There was also Kurt Goldstein, the neurologist, who was affiliated with Gestalt psychology in Germany. When he came to the United States in 1935, Goldstein continued to make use of Gestalt concepts in his clinical work.

The reception of Gestalt psychology in the United States was a mixed one, and it made relatively slow progress. Behaviorism was riding the crest of a wave. The language barrier stood in the way. A philosophical substratum was seen as lurking in the background of Gestalt thinking. The Gestalt critique of introspective elementarism left many American psychologists somewhat baffled. Titchenerian structuralism had passed its peak some years before, and functionalism was asking and answering questions which, in part at least, made them think that the Gestalters were insisting on fighting about a dead issue. Instead of arguing that they were wrong, some American psychologists said that they were correct, but left it at that or added that they were unoriginal.

A new opponent for the Gestalt movement to attack was readily apparent. Behaviorism with its reductionist tendencies became the new target. Gestalt psychology accepted the study of behavior as legitimate, but insisted that the approach to it should be molar, not molecular. Moreover, their isomorphic view was opposed to the point-by-point correspondence of the S-R formula. This controversy was accentuated by the disagreement over the validity of introspection, even though this was not the same sort of introspection as that of Wundt or Titchener. Behavior as composed of reflexes and conditioned responses was considered to be open to the same criticisms that had been made of the brick and mortar psychology of Wundt and Titchener.

American psychologists who were sympathetic to Gestalt theory seldom went so far as to become complete adherents. Rather, seeing it as valuable, they assimilated it more generally into an eclectic pattern where it served as a needed corrective to a more atomistic approach.

Criticism, as a matter of fact, had been published before the arrival of Gestaltists in the United States. Helson,[52] a sympathetic critic, had pin-pointed what was to be a major criticism, then and later. He argued that they had followed the advice of Goethe to a friend on how to solve problems; they had changed the problem into a postulate. The issue of organization in mental life was treated, he said, by Gestalt psychologists, not as a question to be wrestled with, but instead treated as a "given" of nature. This is, of course, close to solving a problem by denying its existence.

The ten years between 1933 and 1943 in the United States were busy ones for Wertheimer, but not as productive in a quantitative way as one might have wished. Burdened as he was with adapting to a new environment and a struggle with a foreign language, Wertheimer suffered increasing exhaustion.[53] He continued trying little experiments in an informal fashion, communicating them to his friends, and at meetings of psychologists, but without recording them in published form.

Wertheimer did not live by psychology alone. He was a man of broad interests in social issues, in logic, and in ethics, areas to which he devoted time and energy. At the New School of Social Research he was a member of a hetero-geneous group of social scientists, which facilitated the spread of his interests beyond psychology. He saw the Gestalt point of view as extending into these areas in order to help us understand the complex problems these fields repre-sented. Wertheimer felt deeply the social issues of his time and wrote elo-quently and incisively on matters such as the meaning of freedom.[54]

One characteristic of the then current work in anthropology caused him considerable distress. This was the doctrine of cultural relativism. He combatted this vigorously. He discussed ethics in a setting of this principle of relativity and pleaded that studies of ethnology, sociology, and cultural history are not enough.[55] The conditions of evaluation themselves need study. This would lead to psychological studies some of which would use Gestalt concepts. Another paper concerned the question of truth.[56] Science and logic have applied the proposition that truth is correspondence to the object, but a difficulty has tended to arise because it is possible to define an object by a part, making this part statement true, but false to the whole. For example, a man who hires another to steal something for him, when asked if he stole, replies, "No,"—he is telling the truth to the question (which is only a part), but he is lying so far as the whole situation is concerned. This error is an instance of a piecemeal view of reality. From this point of departure Wert-heimer goes into logistics, the study of relational networks, in which the Gestalt part-whole problem is considered. This paper serves to lead directly to his remaining major contribution to Gestalt psychology, a posthumously published book on thinking.

WERTHEIMER AND PRODUCTIVE THINKING

This investigation of thinking has been a guiding implicit and explicit interest for many years. In fact, Wertheimer's interest in the problem of thinking goes back to at least 1912, for it was in that same year as his historic paper on perception he first published on this topic. Since Gestalt psychology is sometimes described as if it contributed only to perceptual problems, it is fitting to emphasize that Wertheimer's interest in thinking was contemporaneous with that in perception. His study of thinking culminated in the book, *Productive Thinking*.[57] As Wertheimer interpreted it, the main factor in productive or creative thinking is to grasp the structure of the situation, or the Gestalt. Productive thinking serves as a means to relate the problem at hand, whatever it may be, to the tasks and goals and to the total situation. Analysis goes on, not of parts, but of part-whole relationships.

It would be impossible to capture the full characteristic flavor of Wertheimer's presentation without direct lengthy quotations quite beyond present scope. A summary, no matter how plausible on the surface, is to some extent false to the original. It was characteristic that he gave not a polished presentation leading remorselessly step by step to the solution, but the raw protocol of both productive and unproductive thinking using a great variety of sources of material—geometrical figures, numerical manipulations, physical principles, and social situations. Productive thinking would have its fumbling and false starts, just as would unproductive thinking; but unlike it, there would be a return to the theme without undue delay, showing a sense of direction and an ability to isolate the essential features. In productive thinking, the material given is seen in a new light, and that which was obscure before becomes obvious. Consider Wertheimer's example of the task of computing the sum of the numbers in an arithmetical series presented with numbers in an ascending direction, *i.e.*, $1 + 2 + 3 + 4 + 5 + 6 + 7 + 8 + 9 + 10$. If, instead of laboriously adding, as the structure of the problem presented seems to call for, the individual saw that, from the two ends of the series toward the middle, the terms increase and decrease at the same rate, a new approach would suggest itself. It will be noted that the middle pair are 5 and 6, on one side of which the numbers increase and on the other side decrease by one, giving pairs $4 + 7, 3 + 8, 2 + 9$, and $1 + 10$. Each pair equals 11. There are five pairs of 11 each; therefore, the answer is 55. There is a recentering; a regrouping has taken place so that a new figure-group organization emerges. Instead of perceiving it as a single progressive series $\longrightarrow$ it is seen as two series meeting in the center $\longrightarrow$ $\longleftarrow$. There had been a reorganization of the field. Once the principle or reorganization has been grasped, the recognition of the particular steps necessary for the solution to the problem can then be found.

In productive thinking, habitual methods of using familiar concepts often have to be overcome in order to solve problems in a novel fashion. Especially fascinating in this regard is Wertheimer's account of Einstein's thinking that culminated in the theory of relativity. His account was derived from the many hours that the two spent together in reviewing, decisive step by decisive step, the thinking which Einstein had done in formulating his theory. In this recounting, each step seemed to emerge because it was the one required for the solution. This production had the difficulty of moving against the strong Gestalt which was the traditional Newtonian system of physics. Einstein's general transformation formula was a transformation in another sense; he had to transform at any given stage his thinking against the weight of this well-articulated structure.

The relevance of Gestalt principles to teaching was also shown by Wertheimer; it became the basis for criticism of the emphasis on repetition and routine practice, which had derived its rationale from the associationistic theory of learning. Inculcation of rules and principles by rote memory is rarely productive, Wertheimer held, in that, more often than not, the student's response is a blind repetition of arbitrarily learned materials. This lack of productivity is demonstrated, Wertheimer believed, by the student's inability to solve a variation of the original problem when it is presented to him. When teachers arrange their problems so that the whole is available to the student, insight is more likely to occur.

OVERVIEW

Max Wertheimer saw an old problem in a new way and thereby founded a new approach to psychology. He was joined in this enterprise by two other psychologists, Wolfgang Köhler and Kurt Koffka, but it was he who first saw the problem and was the one to grasp the significance of spontaneous groupings in sensory fields, as Köhler[58] said, and it was he who was the "first founder" as Koffka[59] called him.

Wertheimer never wrote a systematic, complete statement of Gestalt psychology. It is probable that he had no desire to do so, any more than he wished to engage in the endless polemics concerning the value of Gestalt psychology. It was not that he did not care; he did care, but these were tasks for someone of the different temperament. He had a restless, inquiring approach to many aspects of life and psychology, and he was prodigal with his carelessly tossed-off insights. His spontaneity and brilliance made for his productive contribution to psychology. Paradoxically, he was compulsively careful about gathering and analysing data. Only if the data were crystal clear and the experiment unequivocal would he publish his results. This prodigality and brilliance helped his students to learn more from him than did students who had to depend upon the written word for their knowledge of his work.

REFERENCES*

1. E. B. NEWMAN, Max Wertheimer: 1880–1943, *Amer. J. Psychol.*, 1944, 57, 428–435.

2. M. WERTHEIMER, Experimentelle Studien ueber das Sehen von Bewgung, *Zschr. für Psychol.*, 1912, 61, 161–265.

3. *Ibid.*

4. E. MACH, *The Analysis of Sensations.* La Salle, Ill.: Open Court, 1914. (1886)

5. C. v. EHRENFELS, Ueber Gestalt qualitäten, *Vtjsch, wiss. Philos.*, 1890, 14, p. 249. (Translated in *Psychol. Rev.*, 1937, 44, pp. 521–524).

6. M. WERTHEIMER, Ueber Gestaltheorie, *Philos. Zschr. für Forschung u. Aussprache*, 1925, 1, 39–60. (Translated in *Soc. Res.*, 1944, 11, 78–99).

7. E. G. BORING, *Sensation and Perception in the History of Experimental Psychology.* New York: Appleton-Century-Crofts, 1942, pp. 247–248.

8. W. JAMES, The Principles of Psychology. In R. M. Hutchins, (ed.), *Great Books of the Western World.* (Vol. 53) Chicago: Encyclopaedia Britannica, 1952, Chap. 19. (1890)

9. E. RUBIN, *Synsoplevede figurer.* Copenhagen: Gyldendal, 1915.

10. The major source for biographical details is Newman (*op. cit.*).

11. M. WERTHEIMER, Experimentelle Untersuchungen zur Tatbestandsdiagnostik, *Arch. für ges. Psychol.*, 1905, 6, 59–131.

12. C. MURCHISON, (ed.), *The Psychological Register.* (Vol. 2.) Worcester: Clark University Press, 1929.

13. K. KOFFKA, *Principles of Gestalt Psychology.* New York: Harcourt, Brace, 1935.

14. WERTHEIMER, 1912.

15. BORING, *Sensation and Perception, op. cit.*

16. *Ibid.*

17. G. W. HARTMANN, *Gestalt Psychology: a Survey of Facts and Principles.* New York: Ronald, 1935, p. 5.

18. B. PETERMANN, *The Gestalt Theory and the Problem of Configuration.* New York: Harcourt, Brace, 1932.

19. M. WERTHEIMER, Untersuchung en zur Lehre von der Gestalt, *Psychol. Forsch.*, 1922, 1, 47–58. (Abridged translation in W. D. Ellis (ed.), *A Sourcebook of Gestalt Psychology*, New York: Harcourt, Brace, 1938, pp. 12–16.)

20. WERTHEIMER, 1925.

* See page 16 for description of reference style.

21. *Ibid.*

22. E. Brunswik, The Conceptual Framework of Psychology. In O. Neurath, *et al.* (eds.), *International Encyclopedia of Unified Science.* Chicago: University of Chicago Press, 1955, pp. 655–760.

23. Wertheimer, 1922, p. 55.

24. Wertheimer, 1925, p. 43.

25. Newman, *op. cit.*

26. Wertheimer, 1922, p. 49.

27. Newman, *op. cit.*

28. M. Wertheimer, *Über Schlussprozesse im produktiven Denken.* Berlin: De Gruyter, 1920.

29. M. Wertheimer, Untersuchungen zur Lehre von der Gestalt, *Psychol. Forsch.*, 1923, 4, 301–350. [Abridged translation in D. C. Beardsall, & M(ichael) Wertheimer, (eds.), *Readings in Perception.* Princeton: Van Nostrand, 1958, pp. 115–135]. (Herrnstein & Boring Excerpt No. 43)

30. H. Helson, The Fundamental Propositions of Gestalt Psychology, *Psychol. Rev.*, 1933, 40, 13–32.

31. M(ichael) Wertheimer, *Personal Communication.*

32. Koffka, *op. cit.*

33. Murchison, *op. cit.*

34. W. Köhler, Optische Untersuchungen am Schimpasen und am Haushuhn, *Abh. d. Preuss. Akad. d. Wiss.*, 1915, *(phys.-math. Kl.)*, nr. 3.

35. W. Köhler, *The Mentality of Apes.* New York: Harcourt, Brace, 1927.

36. W. Köhler, Intelligence in Apes. In C. Murchison (ed.), *Psychologies of 1925.* (2nd ed.) Worcester: Clark University Press, 1927, pp. 145–161.

37. W. Köhler, Intelligenzprufung an Anthropoiden, *Abhl. preuss. Akad. Wiss. Berlin (Phys.-math. Kl.)*, 1917, Nr. 1. (Herrnstein & Boring Excerpt No. 102)

38. W. Köhler, *Die physischen Gestalten in Ruhe und im stationären Zustand.* Erlangen: Weltkreisverlag, 1920.

39. Wertheimer, 1912, pp. 247–250. (Herrnstein & Boring Excerpt No. 55)

40. Köhler, *Die Physischen Gestalten.*

41. *Ibid.*, pp. 189–193. (Herrnstein and Boring Excerpt No. 56)

42. Wertheimer, 1912.

43. E. Hering, *Zur Lehre vom Lichtsinne.* Vienna: Gerolds Sohn, 1878, pp. 74–80. (1872–1874) (Herrnstein & Boring Excerpt No. 53)

44. G. E. Müller, Zur Psychophysik der Gesichtsempfindungen. *Zschr. für Psychol.*, 1896, 10, 1–82. (Herrnstein & Boring Excerpt No. 54)

45. Köhler, *Die physischen Gestalten.*

46. Murchison, *op. cit.*

47. K. Koffka, *The Growth of the Mind: an Introduction to Child Psychology.* (2nd ed.) London: Routledge & Kegan Paul, 1928. (1921)

48. Wertheimer, 1912. (Herrnstein & Boring Excerpt No. 35)

49. Koffka, *Growth of Mind.*

50. K. Koffka, Perception: an Introduction to the Gestalt-Theorie, *Psychol. Bull.,* 1922, 19, 531–585.

51. W. Köhler, *Gestalt Psychology.* New York: Boni & Liveright, 1929.

52. H. Helson, The Psychology of Gestalt, *Amer. J. Psychol.,* 1925, 36, 342–370.

53. W. Kohler, Max Wertheimer: 1880–1943, *Psychol. Rev.,* 1944, 51, 143–146.

54. M. Wertheimer, A Story of Three Days. In Ruth N. Anshen (ed.), *Freedom: its Meaning.* New York: Harcourt, Brace, 1940, pp. 555–569.

55. M. Wertheimer, Some Problems in the Theory of Ethics, *Soc. Res.,* 1935, 2, 353–367.

56. M. Wertheimer, On Truth, *Soc. Res.,* 1934, 1, p. 135–146.

57. M. Wertheimer, *Productive Thinking.* (enlarged ed.), (ed. by M(ichael) Wertheimer) New York: Harper, 1959.

58. W. Köhler, *Gestalt Psychology.* (2nd ed.) New York: Mentor, 1947, p. 85.

59. Koffka, *Principles,* p. 18.

CHAPTER 20

FREUD:

PSYCHOANALYSIS AND
RELATED VIEWS

WHILE modern psychology was developing in an academic setting, other important contributions were taking place in a quite different situation. Far removed from the psychological laboratory, Sigmund Freud was developing another approach to psychology from the study of personality disturbances as revealed by clinical observation. He was learning that behind the psychology of the conscious and rational person there was another phase of human nature, expressed through the dark, emotion-ridden unconscious motivations of his patients. He used the controls of the clinical method rather than those of traditional experimentation. After a long period of isolation, he gained a few supporters. Among these, were two who went on to develop their own views, which are both important and significantly different from those of Freud. Consequently, after discussing psychoanalysis as expressed through the life, the work, and the theoretical system developed by Sigmund Freud, attention will be devoted to Alfred Adler and his Individual Psychology, and to Carl Gustav Jung and his Analytical Psychology.

THE HERITAGE OF FREUD

In a needless effort to glorify Freud some enthusiastic disciples write as if his genius came into the world unaided by an intellectual-cultural heritage.

They would interpret psychology before Freud as being concerned exclusively with conscious experience, with the world having to wait until Freud discovered the unconscious. Nothing could be further from the truth.[1]

The influence of unconscious psychological phenomena has been a theme throughout the ages, from Plato's sleeping beast through Augustine's limitless room of memory to Aquinas' inability to view the soul apart from awareness of its acts. One can leave aside Descartes, Spinoza, Leibniz, and the others after them who considered unconscious phenomena in some detail and move directly to the nineteenth century. Fechner was the most influential upon Freud in his suggestion of the iceberg analogy of the mind; i.e., that the mind was mostly below the surface where it was moved by powerful hidden currents much more than by the winds of awareness. Fechner also introduced a topographical distinction between sleep and the waking state. Sleep was to be differentiated from the waking state, not only by a difference in intensity of mental function but also through the activities displayed in different stages. There were others of the time just before Freud who seriously considered unconscious psychological phenomena although, perhaps, without any direct influence upon him. Helmholtz utilized unconscious inference. Ebbinghaus wrote his dissertation on Hartmann's philosophy of the unconscious. Even Wundt had to be aware of unconscious phenomena in order to deny them a place in psychology! In varying degrees, those who came before Freud attached significance to unconscious functioning. Some dismissed unconscious psychological phenomena as *curiosa*, to be mentioned and then ignored. Others attached a fair amount of meaningfulness, or even importance, to manifestations of unconscious functioning. Yet, none of them grasped the crucial importance of unconscious motivation and found a way to study it as well. This was a contribution of Freud. It was he who found use for the unconscious, who thought that its exploration might help to explain otherwise inexplicable phenomena, and who saw that thoughts and feelings not in awareness played a role in directing behavior. Moreover, he found a way to study these unconscious processes.

Among familiar aspects of the intellectual atmosphere that Freud absorbed in developing psychoanalysis were the Helmholtzian view of mechanistic determinism, the Darwinian ideas of development, the French psychopathological view of dissociation, and the Galtonian-Wundtian-Kraepelinian view of association. Factors outside of the main psychological tradition were also operative, particularly the writings of Goethe, to which aspects of libido theory are traceable.[2] Freud specifically acknowledged that it was the theories of Darwin and the famous essay on nature by Goethe that influenced his choice of a medical profession.[3] Many of the strands of the past affected his thinking.

His genius lies in utilizing them in the service of a dynamic interpretation of unconscious motivation.

THE DEVELOPMENT OF PSYCHOANALYSIS THROUGH THE LIFE OF FREUD

The sheer wealth of available material[4] about the life of Freud makes it possible to relate rather closely the experiences during his lifetime to the development of his ideas. This is especially pertinent to Freudian conceptions regarding sex, since it is easy to be skeptical concerning the sources of his views, unless it can be shown that they came, not from his own biases and preconceptions but experiences with his patients. Some of his first patients suggested aspects of what was to emerge as the method of free association and helped him to construct some of his major theoretical concepts.

Sigmund Freud was born in 1856 in Freiburg, a town in what is now Czechoslovakia but was then a part of the Austro-Hungarian Empire. His father was a wool merchant, and the family background was that of the lower middle class. When Sigmund was four years of age his family moved to Vienna where he was to live and work for nearly eighty years.

His high intellectual capacity was recognized early, and it soon became established in the family circle that Sigmund was destined to be its scholar. A homely but revealing instance is the fact that his study-bedroom was the only one equipped with an oil lamp; the rooms of other members of the household only had candles. A year earlier than usual he entered the gymnasium, from which he graduated with distinction at the age of seventeen. Reading and studying seemed to have filled the greater part of his life during these years. Then and later, he read widely in many areas. He was very interested in problems of social reform and, perhaps somewhat surprisingly, in military history. He had a considerable gift for languages, knowing in maturity four or five quite thoroughly.

As far as a choice for a career was concerned, the only professions open to a Viennese Jew in the 1870's were law and medicine. Freud turned to medicine, not because of any direct or compelling attraction toward medicine as such, but because he felt that it might give him an opportunity to work in the problems of science which did interest him. As was not too uncommon in his time, he took eight years, several more than necessary, to complete the medical curriculum. His penchant for sampling other fields not directly required for his training delayed his graduation date to 1881.

This penchant for wide study led him to take several non-obligatory courses in philosophy with Franz Brentano. Freud, as a consequence, was thoroughly familiar with Aristotle. The precise relation of this intellectual excursion to his later thinking is still one of the obscure phases of Freud's intellectual development. (See page 282.) Among his other teachers was the German physiologist, Ernst Brücke, met before in connection with the pact sworn against vitalism. (See page 250.) It was from Brücke that Freud learned to see man as a dynamic system following the laws of nature.

During these years, Freud had somewhat vaguely considered following a medical teaching career. Believing that an academic career was not to be open to him, he turned to medical practice. However, Freud had rather neglected the clinical phases of medical training. After graduation, realizing that he would need this experience, he worked in a variety of clinics and hospitals, devoting considerably more time to neurology and speech psychopathology than was customary. He carried on research in a variety of problems. Then and later he was a prodigiously hard worker. It is worthy of note that his very first research endeavor involved sex—in this case an attempt to determine the precise structure of the testes of a species of eel. The results were inconclusive; the future discoverer of the castration complex was unsuccessful in this endeavor.

Freud did a considerable amount of microscopic work in Brücke's physiological institute. It was here that he discovered the analgesic power of cocaine, although he just missed the fame that came to the first physician to apply it in eye operations, which turned out to be by far its most useful application in medicine. Freud also became a very competent neurologist and actually coined the term "agnosia" still used in neurological clinics. Indeed he maintained an interest by a part-time practice in this speciality until almost the end of the century.

He now had even more compelling reason for going into practice; he had met and fallen in love with Martha Bernays. The courtship was a stormy one on his side, Sigmund showing violence, jealousy, and moodiness to a much greater degree than was characteristic of him before or afterwards. It was typical of this courtship that after some fancied slight from a relative of his fiancée, he demanded she no longer see the person in question.

After marriage the home life of the Freuds was conventional and quite in keeping with the middle-class pattern of his time. Despite the wild stories that were to circulate about his sex life, Freud seems to have been faithful to his marital partner. With his tremendously lengthy work hours, he saw relatively little either of his wife or of his children. His wife did not accompany him on his vacations since he had discovered she could not keep up with his rapid travel pace. It seemed never to have occurred to Freud to slow his pace to that of hers! To Freud, the place of women was in the home. In Vienna his social recreations were card games with old cronies and visits to his mother, who lived to an advanced age.

One friendship that had developed during these years was to be very important both for Freud and for psychoanalysis. He had become intimate with Joseph Breuer, a highly successful, sophisticated, urbane practitioner whom Freud admired immensely. Breuer became for Freud, what today we would call in Freudian language, a father figure. Breuer also helped him in a material way, loaning him money and offering him advice both of a practical and of a medical kind. Naturally, this included discussion of the cases which had been seen by Breuer. One of these cases about which Freud heard in 1882 was of crucial significance.

In December, 1880, Breuer began to treat Fraulein Anna O. This girl of twenty-one had developed a whole host of symptoms. She showed a picture of a classical case of hysteria—paralysis of the limbs, anesthesias, disturbances of sight and speech, nausea, and confusion. The illness had first appeared while she was caring for her severely ill father. She was compelled by her own illness to abandon nursing him. The events during her nursing had made a deep impression upon her, yet when she was first seen by Breuer, she could not remember them. Anna got into the habit of relating to Breuer the disagreeable events of the day. This gave her a release of the pent-up emotions, or *catharsis* as it came to be called. She experienced relief through talking about her troubles and on occasion even the disappearance of a particular symptom. For example, during a period when she could not drink water, despite an intense thirst, she related to Breuer that as a girl she had had a period when the same thing had occurred. She now remembered that at the time she had seen a very much disliked dog belonging to a governess who was drinking from a glass. She told this particular story to Breuer in disgust and anger and, afterward, found she could drink water again without trouble and thereafter had no recurrence of this particular difficulty.

She, herself, spoke of her talks with Breuer as the "talking cure" and as "chimney sweeping." Breuer discovered she was relieved of her symptoms if she was placed under hypnosis and was then induced to express verbally her feelings and emotions dominant at the moment. It also turned out that what was unconscious to her, except under hypnosis, was some thought or impulse which was repugnant to her. Symptoms served to replace these thoughts or impulses. When she lived again through the traumatic scenes without inhibition of the feelings she was experiencing, Breuer found that the symptoms in question reduced in severity or even disappeared. Her emotions up to this time could not be expressed in a normal way, so the emotion associated with these events had expressed themselves in symptoms.

In his interest in her, Breuer began to devote more and more of his evenings to working with her. Apparently he saw Anna hours every day for more than a year. He became so engrossed in working with Anna that his wife first became bored and later jealous. All unknowing, Breuer had developed what, in later psychoanalytic perspective, would be called a counter-transference. When finally he realized what was happening, he broke off treating Anna. Anna, herself, had developed a positive transference, that is, she had transferred to his person, as she conceived him to be, the loves and hates which she had felt toward her father. The same evening that Breuer had told Anna of his decision to break off seeing her, he was again called to her home to find her most excited and in the throes of hysterical childbirth which he succeeded in terminating by hypnosis.[5] This incident was too much for Breuer who fled Vienna with his wife to Venice on a second honeymoon. Freud was very interested in this particular case and found it exciting and, unlike Breuer's reaction, in no way threatening.

In 1885, Freud was granted a small stipend to go to France to work under Charcot. Charcot's influence upon Freud as a result of this visit was expressed in theoretical and procedural influences. Heretofore he had held what might be called an organic point of view; after working under Charcot he became much more interested in functional aspects of mental disorder.

A casual incident which occurred about this time is of importance. In the course of an informal conversation one evening, Charcot, in an animated and positive fashion, insisted that the etiology of the difficulties of a particular patient, the wife of an impotent man, had sexual basis.[6] The gist of this incident was repeated for Freud on several occasions with other physicians, but always it was mentioned casually and in passing. Freud, naturally, began to wonder why this lead was not followed up in more systematic and serious fashion in the medical literature. Freud, an intensely ambitious man, who wanted to make a name for himself, chagrined by his failure to be the discoverer of the surgical usefulness of cocaine, remembered this incident and was thereafter on the alert for indication of sexual factors in the etiology of his patients. To this particular lead, his knowledge of Anna O. must also have sensitized him.

Freud also learned from Charcot about his methods, particularly his use of hypnosis in the study of hysteria. Hysteria was a condition not at all well understood. At that time the very symptom picture of hysteria was one that made it faintly unrespectable. It was still interpreted by many physicians as being a confusing mixture of simulation, an overwrought imagination, and a wandering womb. Greek medicine had made hysteria a condition due to this latter organ movement and the very word hysteria comes from the same root as does the term "hysterectomy." With this etiology it was popularly and professionally supposed that hysteria was a condition limited to women. While working with Charcot, Freud had observed instances of male hysteria. On his return to Vienna he insisted on lecturing on this topic. To say the least, his views, especially on the reality of male hysteria, were not well received. He was actually publically challenged to find a case in a male with the symptoms Charcot claimed it would show. Without going into further details it is easy to see why Freud thereafter disliked the members of organized medicine in Vienna, and they, in turn, would regard him as an unconventional medical practitioner.

In his practice he had been using electrotherapy. This is not the same as electric shock therapy as used today; it consisted of the application of a painful electric shock directly to the afflicted organ, such as the arm. (In those cases where it was successful, suggestion was operative as was demonstrated shortly afterward.)

Having found the results of electrotherapy disappointing, Freud turned to hypnosis, a technique still in ill repute. Its use in his practice hardly served to add to his professional standing. His interest in hypnosis-concentration was prompted by its power to bring to the surface forgotten thoughts, an important aspect for the understanding of hysteria, as Breuer and Charcot had demonstrated.

Freud modified hypnosis in the direction of Breuer's cathartic method. This is to say, gradually the production of the hypnotic trance was eliminated by Freud until eventually he arrived at a technique in which he merely had the patient lie on a couch, touched her forehead and told her to start talking. During this time, one of Freud's patients one day threw her arms around him. Unlike Breuer's panic over a display of affection, Freud saw it merely as a matter of considerable scientific interest. He began dimly at first, but with gradually increasing clarity, to realize that somehow or other effective work with the neurotic depended upon a personal relationship between the physician and his patient.

During these years it was his custom to question the patient rapidly and in considerable detail and to interject other comments freely as they occurred to him. One of his patients, Fraulein Elizabeth, sharply reproved him for interrupting her flowing thoughts. He saw the plausability of her reproof and gradually what came to be called the method of free association emerged. Basic to this concept, to be described in a moment, is a thoroughgoing belief in causality—that all matters, dreams, thoughts no matter how trivial and incongruous and inconsequential, actually did have some cause. The value of allowing one's mind to wander had also been discussed by one of his favorite authors, Ludwig Borne. This author had written an essay with the striking title, "The Art of Becoming an Original Writer in Three Days." As quoted by Jones it concludes in the following fashion:

Here follows the practical prescription I promised. Take a few sheets of paper and for three days in succession write down, without any falsification or hypocrisy, everything that comes into your head. Write what you think of yourself, of your women, of the Turkish War, of Goethe, of the Fonk criminal case, of the Last Judgment, of those senior to you in authority—and when the three days are over you will be amazed at what novel and startling thoughts have welled up in you. This is the art of becoming an original writer in three days.[7]

The essence of the method of free association that Freud was to use hereafter consisted of instructing his patients that the basic rule they were to follow was to say whatever came to mind, allowing no selection and no rearrangement whatsoever. This letting one's mind go, akin to day-dreaming aloud, sounds relatively easy to do, but his patients often found it unexpectedly difficult, since there would be blanks or they would, violating the rule, struggle to rearrange the flow of their thoughts. Freud soon realized that these unexpected difficulties were significant in that they were signs that meaningful material about the patient was close to the surface. He became alerted to the fact that when his patients experienced difficulties in associating, something of significance seemed to be occurring. From this finding arose his insistence that they must follow the basic rule, and, when they did so, the analysis was found to progress.

Other aspects of the psychoanalytic method developed during these years. Freud recognized his patients' remarkable unwillingness to disclose painful memories, a behavioral mechanism which he called *resistance.* Freud saw that there was a connection between resistance and repression. Repression causes memory gaps or amnesias. The forces that produced repression also produced resistance.

The following example of free association illustrates a purposeful failure of memory, the Freudian significance of which is discussed a little later. It is atypical only in that it occurred during a conversation, rather than in the course of the analysis of a patient. An acquaintance, in conversation with Freud, had stumbled over a Latin quotation omitting a word, *aliquis.* Knowing of Freud's contentions on this matter, this acquaintance challenged him to find the reason for forgetting the word, to which Freud agreed. He gave the young man the usual instructions about free associations; the young man responded by what he himself considered to be the faintly ridiculous idea of dividing the word into two parts *a liquis.* The gist of the succession of free associations thereafter was as follows: "reliques—liquidation—liquidity—fluid—an article entitled, 'What St. Augustine said Concerning Women,'—St. Januarius and his Blood Miracle." (Freud—"Didn't St. Januarius and St. Augustine have something to do with the calendar?") "Yes, and as for St. Januarius a phial of his blood liquified on the date of a certain holiday, and if it doesn't take place the people get excited. A French general occupying the town once demanded the miracle take place forthwith." Young man hesitates. (Freud—"Why do you hesitate?") "Something too intimate to tell, comes to mind." At this point let us pause and consider the sequence of liquid, liquifying of blood, excitement if it doesn't take place, and the demand that it does take place. Ask yourself what was it that the young man thought at this point that was too intimate to mention? I suspect that some of you at least have recognized that the sequence had to do with the menstrual cycle. As the acquaintance admitted, he was hoping for a miracle since a friend of his had missed her period.

Although Freud altered his method of approach during these years, he did not vary the aims of his procedures. His principle endeavor was to bring to the surface in the patient's consciousness the traumatic event which was the presumed pathological starting point. Even when this point was achieved and the trauma revealed, Freud's thoroughness came to the fore; and he continued back in time beyond this point. The memories that these patients were able to produce inexorably tended to go further and further back into childhood, as if somehow the patients were attracted by this period of life. The importance that Freud attached to childhood will be brought out later in more systematic discussion of the psychoanalytic theory.

He found that a remarkable number of his patients' repressed memories centered on sexual matters. This, of course, was long before the importance of sexual factors in psychoanalysis was to become a matter of common knowledge and, hence, could not be attributed to knowledge on the part of his patients that sexual disclosures were expected of them. After trying the method of direct inquiry into these sexual matters, Freud realized that this impeded treatment. He therefore resumed his passive position in treatment, but maintained an alert vigilance to detect the appearance of sexual material.

His sensitization to matters sexual had already occurred from the hints that he had received from Breuer and Charcot and he was determined to discover something new and dramatic about neuroses. Albeit dimly, he was reaching the conviction that a sexual factor was to be the key to this discovery.

In the late eighties and early nineties, Freud tried to interest Breuer in publishing material on his patient, Anna O., as well as the others whom Freud had by now treated. From Freud's point of view, Breuer was inexplicably reluctant. Eventually, however, they prepared and published in 1895, the *Studies on Hysteria*,[9] from which it has become customary to date the advent of psychoanalysis. It included a joint paper, previously published, and five case histories, among them those of Anna O. and of Elizabeth. Although *Studies on Hysteria* received some reviews, mostly unfavorable, it created little stir. Only 626 copies were sold in the next thirteen years, for which each author received in royalty a sum equivalent to $85.00. Between 1895 and 1897, bitterness developed between the two callaborators creating a breach which was never healed; thereafter, they went their separate ways.

In 1896, Freud gave a paper to a psychiatric and neurological society in Vienna on the etiology of hysteria. In it he referred specifically to his conviction that at the basis of every case of hysteria will be found a premature sexual experience early in childhood. He had become convinced that all of his patients showed something resembling seduction when they were children, most often with the adult seducer being an older relative and often the father. It was this trauma which produced the symptoms. One of the points that convinced him of the validity of his interpretation was the extreme reluctance of his patients to describe in detail that scene and a feeling of unreality which seemed to hover over it. It was as if, unlike other forgotten material, they really did not remember the experience. This convinced him they were not malingering, because they seemed to be protesting that, although they reported the incident and it was the truth, they felt that somehow it could not have happened. A short time after he gave this paper the horrible truth began to dawn on him—these seductions in childhood, in most, but not all instances, had never actually occurred.

A lesser man might have hidden his mistake and tried to forget it. A less clinically acute individual might have "bravely" confessed his error and turned to other more profitable matters. Freud did neither. Instead, he went beyond his mistake and asked the question as to why their fantasies (for these of course were what they were) took the particular form they did. His patients were not lying; they believed their fantasies. Was not the very fact that their fantasies took the form of sexual matters evidence that there was a sexual tinge or basis to their thinking, and was he not, consequently, right in emphasizing the sexual basis of their difficulty even though the situations which they had described had actually never taken place? Despite the temporary setback, this "mistake" was actually later to be seen as an advance. Freud, armed with this new insight, was now ready to explore the whole range of sexuality.

For some time Freud had been developing the conviction that he needed to explore his own personality make-up. It was obvious immediately that the method of free association would be impossible, since he could not assume the attitude of the patient and give uncritically his flow of free associations, while at the same time taking on the role of the analyst alertly listening to the material. In earlier years some of his patients had spontaneously brought to him their dreams as appropriate material for analysis, and he had already done some work with dream interpretation. Consequently, dream interpretation suggested itself to him as a means of self-analysis.

This self-analysis was important to Freud. There is a psychologist, whom it is irrelevant to identify, who endeared himself to the writer when, as a member of a panel of psychologists who were giving their learned (and often ponderous) views of their experiences on being analyzed, advanced as his principal reason for being psychoanalyzed simply that, "he needed it." So, too, did Freud. Quite apart from some of the indications of neurotic difficulties earlier mentioned in passing, there were others; for example, a considerable fear of railroad travel. Incidentally, in later psychoanalytic thinking this often symbolized leaving the security of the mother! His neurosis with its frustrations, insecurities, intensities, impracticalities, uncertainties, and vulnerability to threat, gave way in the course of his self-analysis to that more integrated, assured, persevering person that his disciples were to know.

His own self-analysis and the writing of *The Interpretation of Dreams*,[10] which was finished in the summer of 1899, went hand in hand. This book is by general consensus Freud's most important single work. The procedure that he followed would be to record his dream on waking and then free-associate to the material of the dream. He found that his dreams contained material touched off by events of the day, but which had not been completely worked through to some satisfactory solution. In dreaming, the problem would be taken up again. Dreams represent a disguised effort to bring about a solution. This wishful aspect of the dream he referred to as wish fulfillment. A person dreams of drinking before waking up thirsty. A medical student, wishing to continue to sleep after being called, dreams he is already at the hospital. Dreams thus have meaning, and the deep seated desires could be investigated by dream analysis, even though dream analysis was but an extension of free association in the treatment of patients, not a substitute for it.

Freud drew a distinction between the manifest and the latent content of the dream. The manifest content is the dream as given, taken at its face value, as it were; the latent content is the meaning lying behind this overlay. The task of interpretation is to go from manifest to latent content. This is a complex task, and only some of Freud's dream symbols can be illustrated. Dreams of falling were seen by Freud as circumlocutions for giving way to erotic temptations; dreams of flying signified longing for ability of sexual accomplishment. Certain images in dreams stood for or symbolized objects and desires from the patient's world in a relatively constant fashion. The more common symbols in dreams tended to repeat themselves from patient to patient—money for feces; journey for death; a king for a father; a tree, a steeple, a sword, or a snake for the penis; a box, a book, or a purse for the vagina; or a pair of sisters for the breasts. Common symbols, Freud warned, are not to be inter preted without knowledge of the particular patient's unconscious conflicts since the symbols have usual but not invariable meanings.

In spite of the fact that the book devoted to so-called symptomatic acts was not published until 1904, the subject was of concern to him during these earlier years. This book, *The Psychopathology of Everyday Life*,[11] had as its theme the interference of conscious functioning by unconscious processess. The lengthy illustration already presented on page 465 of the young man who could not remember a crucial word when he worried about the pregnancy of his sweetheart is illustrative. A boy who forgets a date with a girl quickly discovers she is an amateur psychoanalyst, since she will question whether this meant he actually did not wish to keep the date. Freud supplied a wealth of illustrations drawn from many areas to bring out the unconscious significance of common errors: the forgetting of names; mistakes in speech, reading, and writing; forgetting of intentions; "chance" activities; "clumsy" actions; and the like. Such acts, he found, are revelatory of unconscious desires.

The fact that "chance" acts, mannerisms, and slips of the tongue have an unconscious motive behind them opened for Freud another route to the understanding of the patient. Again he had evidence that no act is uncaused. Analysis of actions, along with dream analysis, became subsidiary to free association as the method of psychoanalysis. With these developments we come to the end both of a century and of the formative and, in many ways, the most important period of Freud's life.

In the years 1901 through 1906, Freud began to emerge from the isolation which had heretofore surrounded him. As the period began, he was forty-five years of age, his practice was increasing, and, in 1902, a weekly discussion group was founded in order that those interested might learn his conceptions of "psychoanalysis," a term which during the last few years he had been applying to his approach. Not only were these men young, they were relatively obscure and just at the beginning of their careers. Alfred Adler, to be discussed later, worked with him during these years. A visitor who first came to see him in 1907, Carl Gustav Jung, had already established himself as a promising and potentially very important young psychiatrist in Zurich. Unlike most of the others who lived in Vienna, Jung visited Freud and then returned to his practice in Switzerland. For the next five years they were closely associated, and Freud began to feel that Jung was his spiritual son and the heir to psychoanalysis. It was during these years that Jung suggested to Freud that prospective psychoanalysts should themselves be analyzed, a procedure which Freud adopted and which has been maintained since.[12] Otto Rank joined him in Vienna as a disciple at about the same time, while A. A. Brill, his American translator, and Ernest Jones, his biographer, were both in touch with him in 1908.

Freud during these years published prolifically, including the highly important volume *Three Essays on the Theory of Sexuality*.[13] Just as the interpretation of dreams had marked him as ridiculous in the eyes of many of his contemporaries, this new volume showed him to be prurient as well, since he argued that all children are born with sexual drives. Despite the notoriety that his views were now receiving, other more perceptive individuals showed some appreciation of what he was attempting to do.

The first official recognition of Freud's work on an international scale came in 1909 when, on the invitation from G. Stanley Hall, then president of Clark University in Worcester, Massachusetts, and a prominent psychologist in his own right, he addressed a convocation in celebration of the twentieth anniversary of that university. Although appreciative, he was not too attracted to Hall and spoke of him as having "a touch of king-maker about him," [14] a rather preceptive remark. Many other psychologists were in attendance at these meetings, and Freud met Titchener, Cattell, and James. Jung accompanied him and gave lectures at the celebration. Troubled as Freud was by a bladder infection and affected by the roughness of some aspects of American life, he did not consider the trip an unqualified success and thus maintained his rather uncomplimentary view of the United States. Although the papers which he gave were subsequently published in American psychological periodicals, it probably was somewhat of a blow to him that so far as the public was concerned he received hardly any attention whatsoever. One of the speakers on the same program with Freud was William Stern. In the reports which appeared in the public press, a considerable number of inches of space were devoted to the talk of this worthy psychologist. The account concluded with the remark, "Sigmund Freud of Vienna also spoke."

Two years later, in 1911, came the break with Alfred Adler, one of his earliest associates. Aside from personality differences, the question at issue was whether or not Adler's ideas could be incorporated within psychoanalysis. Adler held that man had a tendency to compensate for a feeling of inferiority. In this and other respects, Adler was focusing upon aspects of behavior which demanded consideration of the social environment. At this time Freud could not see how it could be explained in terms of his theoretical position. Differences of opinion between Adler and Freud were aired through the discussion group which by now was called the Vienna Psychoanalytic Society. Both Freud and Adler eventually came to realize that their differences were irreconcilable, and Adler and some of the other members resigned from the Society. Acrimony seemed to have existed on both sides, expressed by Adler through forming a group of his own under the name, "Society for Free Psychoanalysis." By this title, which was only shortlived, Adler was attempting to interject into the controversy the claim that he was fighting for the freedom of science against the dictatorial methods of Freud. Freud, himself, was relieved rather than anything else by this final break with Adler because, rightly or wrongly, he had come to consider him unreliable and recalcitrant.

This was not the case, however, with the break which came with Carl Jung. In Freud's view, very relevant to the issue over which they ultimately separated was the general religious and moral climate of Switzerland. Jung and other Swiss psychoanalysts had for some time shown a tendency to minimize the theoretical importance of the sexual basis of psychoanalytic theory. They had found when they did so that their relations both with their patients and with the general public improved considerably. In May 1911, Jung told Freud that he regarded "libido" as a term expressing general, not sexual, tension. After a trip to New York, Jung wrote Freud on how successful he had been in making psychoanalysis acceptable by leaving out matters of sex!

On Freud's part, this was not seen merely as a matter of disagreement about the theoretical importance of sex in psychoanalysis, important though this undoubtedly was, but to a great extent his distress arose from a conviction that Jung's reason for minimizing sex was an intellectually dishonest one. Freud believed Jung was catering to popular opinion by omitting the sexual factor. Moreover, then and later, there was some suggestion that Jung believed Freud's Jewish background had something to do with this overemphasis on sex, which hurt Freud deeply.

In 1914, Jung formally severed his connection with Freudian psychoanalysis by resigning his position as President of the International Association of Psychoanalysis. As Freud put it, they took leave of one another without feeling a necessity for further meetings.[15] The break was a difficult one on both sides, but it was inevitable and final. The Jungian side of the story will be taken up later.

In the midst of these and other defections from the ranks of the psychoanalysts, Ernest Jones suggested to Freud that a secret "committee" should be formed to serve to guide the destiny of psychoanalysis. When this idea was broached to Freud, he received it enthusiastically, although he admitted it had a youthful, romantic aspect to it. He experienced considerable relief because he felt that through this committee psychoanalysis would be able to continue under competent guidance. The first meeting of the five-member (later six) committee took place in 1913, and Freud commemorated the meeting by presenting each of them with a ring in which was mounted an ancient Greek itaglio, similar to one Freud had worn for a long time. The committee functioned with considerable efficiency for some years.

The years of the World War I interrupted Freud's work to some extent but brought no personal tragedy or unusual hardships and no limitations except in number of patients, food restrictions, and reduced income.

His own interests were moving into the more theoretical channels of "metapsychology," as he called it. Metapsychology was a term coined by analogy with Aristotelian metaphysics—going beyond psychology. He meant by it the accounting for a mental process in terms of its dynamic significance, topographical features, and economic significance. His aim was to arrive at a general theoretical structure which would guide psychoanalysts in the collecting of clinical data and the organizing of it in a meaningful fashion. These contributions will form a major part of the systematic account of psychoanalysis given later. During his remaining years Freud was occupied with a great variety of writings. He continued to make clinical contributions, but much of his time was taken up by metapsychology and the contribution of psychoanalysis to biology, anthropology, sociology, religion, art, and literature. The standard English edition of his works, beginning with the *Interpretation of Dreams*[16] in 1900 and terminating with the posthumously published *Outline of Psychoanalysis*,[17] fills twenty-four volumes.

The period from 1919 until his death in 1939 are the years when Freud was at the pinnacle of his fame. In the beginning of this period, the immediate post-war years, Europe was in chaos, the International Association of Psychoanalysis and the newly organized publishing house founded in Vienna in 1919 were both in precarious state.

One of his more faithful and hard-working assistants in these administrative ventures was Otto Rank. When younger he had been a protegé of Freud, and had even been made a member of the committee. Under Freud's urging he had taken a non-medical university degree preparatory to further theoretical work in psychoanalysis. He had a special flair for the interpretation of myths, legends, and dreams. Rank's book, *The Trauma of Birth*[18] appeared in 1923. Birth trauma as a source for the creation of anxiety was the theme. At first, Rank saw this conception as falling within the framework of conventional psychoanalysis, but his tendency to reinterpret other Freudian contentions in terms of this as a guiding theme—weaning as anxiety-provoking because it was a separation from the mother, and male sexual urges as a desire to return into the mother's body—was not accepted by the other psychoanalysts. Considerable heated arguments began. Because of his fondness for Rank, Freud tried to reconcile his views with those Rank expressed as well as those of Rank's opponents. The attempt was doomed to failure since Rank saw this as a rejection by Freud. Rank, meanwhile, had developed an increasingly severe emotional disturbance. After making several trips to the United States, he eventually settled here. The break with Freud was final and complete.

In 1923 the first symptom of cancer of the jaw, from which Freud was eventually to die, had developed. A series of operations was necessary and he had to wear a prosthesis so that his voice was thereafter interfered with to such a point that he could hardly be understood. In all, he had thirty-three operations. During these years his daughter, Anna, was his nurse. He had to reduce the number of patients he saw and make arrangements for longer summer vacations. During this period, he had many financial worries, created by the publishing house as well as by the ambivalent attitude of the public toward him. Abuse from the medical profession continued. On the other hand, he became a world figure, acquainted with and, in some instances, close friends with prominent individuals. Among these were Thomas Mann and H. G. Wells.

Meanwhile the International Association was going through a certain amount of controversy. One of the most important sources of contention was the question of the practice of psychoanalysis by individuals without medical training. The American Psychoanalytic Association, which had been formed under medical leadership, was vehemently opposed to so-called lay analysis. Associations in other countries were divided in their opinion but generally favorable to the practice of psychoanalysis by individuals who had the requisite training even though they had no medical degree. Freud wrote in 1926 a book entitled *The Question of Lay Analysis*.[19] In it he unequivocally supported the position that a medical degree was not necessary in order to practice psychoanalysis, a position from which he never wavered.

In the 1930's Hitler came into power. In Berlin as early as May, 1933, the Nazis made a bonfire of Freud's books. By 1934 all Jewish psychoanalysts in Germany who were to escape had done so. Freud's friends had been urging him to leave Vienna, but he insisted stubbornly that he would remain. In March 1938 the Nazis invaded Austria. The Nazis had actually taken over Vienna, and storm troopers had broken into his home before he could be persuaded to leave. The Nazis held him in Vienna until his stock of unsold books could be brought back from Switzerland for public burning. The Nazis were persuaded to release Freud partly through the intervention of W. C. Bullitt, then American Ambassador to France. Freud's arrival in London created a sensation which was given considerable space in the press. During this time he was failing rapidly so far as his physical health was concerned, but he was still very alert mentally. He continued, in fact, to work almost up until the end. He finished his book, *Moses and Monotheism*,[20] in 1938. He died on September 23, 1939.

THEORY OF PERSONALITY

From the work of Freud came a method of research, an approach to psychotherapy, and a theory of personality which was a major aspect of his metapsychology.[21] Further discussion of these first and second contributions is foregone in order to concentrate upon his theory of personality. Any summarization of Freud's metapsychology is apt to give the impression of its being static—a fixed system, frozen into the form in which it is being encountered. This is misleading because, to Freud, it was a loosely integrated group of theories, which evolved through the years with some momentarily important points discarded by the wayside as his thinking progressed. With Freud, as with others, theoretical formulations outlived their usefulness. They are vehicles to be used in part of one's journey but eventually to be given up when no longer cogent. This same evolution continued after Freud. In what follows an attempt is made to give a classic picture of psychoanalysis as Freud saw it. By the same token, it cannot be a complete view of contemporary psychoanalysis. An effort is made to present only the orthodox Freudian position, differentiated from the steadily increasing number of neo-Freudians, who would assimilate Freud into a larger—most typically into a social—framework of non-Freudian origin. These latter developments are part of the contemporary picture beyond the scope of this chapter.

The Dynamics and Structure of Personality

To Freud, personality was essentially a dynamic concept in which mental life was an interplay of reciprocally urging and checking forces.[22] Consequently, it is necessary to examine the nature of these forces and the structures through which the interplay of forces takes place. This is tantamount to saying that there needs to be concern with the dynamics and the structures, or systems, of personality. One form of specification of dynamics is to be seen through examination of Freud's theory of instincts.

In accordance with the deterministic and positivistic philosophy of his era, Freud employed the theory of finite energy as the power behind this reciprocal interplay of forces. He maintained that the physiological energy of the human organism, by virtue of Helmholtz's principle of the conservation of energy, may be transformed into energy for psychological activity. Therefore, psychic energy and its psychological manifestation, instinct, emerge as the basic unit in the dynamics of personality structure. It is a quantum of psychic energy which functions on transformed physiological energy, linking a body's need to a psychological wish. There will be found a number of separate bodily needs, each of which gives rise to erotic wishes. These may be identified by reference to the erogenous zones of mouth, anus, and sex organs as centers for different wishes. When taken together, the instincts are the sum total of psychic energy. An instinct has four functional characteristics: (1) impetus, the motor element in the amount of force which is represents; (2) aim, the satisfaction obtained by abolishing the condition of stimulation; (3) object, that through which the aim can be achieved; and (4) source, the somatic process in a body part from which eventuates a stimulus.[23]

Instinct and energy were appealed to by Freud to place his views on sex on a scientific footing and to describe their interrelationships in a meaningful fashion. This formulation can be dated as shortly after the turn of the century.

About two decades later, Freud faced another problem. The war years forced him to direct his attention to aggressive behavior and the subsidiary problem of understanding it in relation to sex. The theory of the death instinct was the consequence. At this point he held that in representing body demands, the instincts follow two aims, the life instinct and the death instinct.[24] Under these two headings, Freud assumed a multitude of instincts, although he never identified all of them specifically nor derived their total number. The life instinct operates for human survival and racial propagation, including such categories as hunger, sex, and thirst. The form of energy for the manifestations of the life instinct is called *libido*. The death instinct of Freudian theory, impelling one toward death, is analogous to the catabolic, the breaking-down processes of the body, and is, therefore, in opposition to the anabolic or building processes of the life instinct. The death instinct, which has the aim of reducing living things to inorganic matter,[25] is systematically less important and, following Fenichel,[26] will be dispensed with in the account to follow. However, aggression is utilized within the framework of libido theory. Aggression is an innate, independent, instinctual disposition.[27]

Originally Freud conceived of the personality structure in terms of the unconscious, the conscious, and the preconscious (that which is capable of consciousness without special effort). This original focus upon conscious and unconscious phenomena was brought about by Freud's concern with hysteria and hypnosis. In hypnosis, for example, there is a clear distinction between what the subject is aware of in the waking state and what he can report in the hypnotic state. The distinction between consciousness and unconsciousness was sufficient at this point to account for the phenomena theoretically. Later, however, he preferred to use the unconscious in a descriptive fashion as

qualities of experience.[28] In the psychoanalytic hour with the shifting pano-
rama of its free association, terms like conscious and unconscious are too bald
to be used for behavior which is the resultant of interacting, supporting, or
cancelling forces. Identification is difficult when only these resultants are open
to observation. Consequently, in the interest of a greater dynamic emphasis,
Freud modified his conceptual scheme.

The structural components of the personality are the inherent system of
the id and its derivatives, the ego and superego.[29] The ego and superego derive
their energy from the primary psychic energy reservoir of libido in the id.
The libido, consequently, is not only the basic force for personality dynamics
but also the source of organization of the personality structure as well. Each
of these structures must now be examined in detail and attention must be
paid to their interrelationship in the fully developed personality. The course
of the development of the three structures is reserved for presentation in terms
of psychosexual stages.

The id, as such, is unconscious[30] and the oldest of the personality structures.[31]
It contains everything that is inherited, present at birth, or fixed in the
constitution.[32] This includes the source of the instinctual energy, the libido,
which demands discharge.[33]

The libido's expression in the id is through the principle of tension-reduc-
tion—the pleasure principle—by which the id operates. Physiologically, a
tension occurs in a source of bodily need and is then translated into a psychological wish, the aim of which is tension reduction. It obeys the pleasure
principle[34] in the seeking of pleasure and avoidance of pain without any other
consideration, so far as id is concerned, entering to modify or direct it.[35] The
purpose of the id is the satisfaction of needs, irrespective of considerations
of danger or of preservation of life.[36] In the words of the musical comedy
song of some years ago, "It wants what it wants when it wants it." There is
no consideration of decorum, of morals, or of modesty.[37]

The id has no direct relation with the external world.[38] Everything we know
about the id relates to the ego.[39] Since it is unconscious, it can only be known
through the ego which does have the characteristic of being conscious. Consequently while still considering the id it is necessary to deal briefly with this
ego function. The id is known through intrusions in the consciousness of the
ego. Dreams, for example, are an externalization of this internal process[40] in
which the id tendencies are partially released through relaxation of the ego
during sleep. Their examination is one way to gain some dim and frightening
knowledge of id sources.[41] According to Freud, the dreams of even the most
straight-laced person contain amoral elements, illustrative of the functioning
of the id.

The ego includes the conscious portion of the personality structure. The processes of the ego alone are capable of being conscious.[42] More strictly, the ego also includes the preconscious as well, *i.e.*, that which is capable of becoming conscious voluntarily.[43] The ego is determined by the individual's experience.[44]

In contradistinction from the id which is guided by the pleasure principle, the ego follows the reality principle.[45] This is to say, the ego in guiding activities takes into account the external world and its realities. The ego is the organization which is interpolated between sensory and perceptual processes on one hand and motor activity on the other, of which the individual is aware as his "I."[46]

The instincts of the id press for satisfaction; the ego modifies and channels these drives.[47] Since all libido was originally id, the ego arises from a modification of id.[48] Once it does so, the ego serves as an intermediary between the id and the external world. Here its constructive function is to interpose intellectual activity which calculates ways and considers alternatives before allowing the demands of instinct to be accomplished.[49] As an approximation, the ego represents reason, while the id represents the untamed passions; although, of course, when the latter are represented in consciousness, it is also through the ego.[50] If one were to draw upon the previous history of psychology for an illustration, Plato's fable of the charioteer would come to mind. The ego is in control of voluntary movement and is aware of external events.[51] It stores up experiences in memory; it adapts; it learns; it avoids. Thus it has relation both with the id and the external world.

In summary, ego refers to both awareness of self and to the carrying on of executive functions. In following the reality principle, the ego mediates between the imperative pressures from the id, the structures of the superego (described in a moment), and the demands of external reality.

Despite what was just said about ego and consciousness, a portion of the ego is unconscious.[52] This unconscious portion results from repression. Materials once conscious, but unacceptable to the ego, are pushed back into the unconscious.[53] Because of its origin, we call this portion of the ego, the repressed. Repression, in refusing to allow unwelcome impulses to appear in consciousness,[54] is a flight mechanism.[55] That which is repressed has an "upward driving force," that is, an impulse or drive to break through into consciousness.[56] The ego, under the influence of external reality, controls the entrance into consciousness, and, therefore, an interplay or reciprocally checking and urging forces is developed in which libido must be expended. To repress requires a continuous expenditure of effort.[57]

Anxiety, by definition, is something "felt."[58] As an affective state it is experienced by the ego and serves as its danger signal. The id cannot be afraid; it cannot estimate danger as it knows nothing of the external world. There are three kinds of anxiety.[59] When faced by evidence of its weakness, reality anxiety occurs in the face of the dangers from the external world; normal or moral anxiety (guilt) in the face of superego restrictions, and neurotic anxiety in the face of the demands of the id. Anxiety, no matter what its particular form, serves as a signal of danger.[60]

The ego operating through the reality principle is capable of investing energy in an object either inanimate, as in some "favorite" possession, or in some other person. This energy attachment, Freud called cathexis. Cathexis is a sum of psychic energy with which an object is invested.[61] This attachment of energy is analogous to an electric charge.[62] When libido of the ego is invested in an object (including persons) it becomes object-libido.[63] This process of investment is one in which ego-libido is transformed into object-libido.[64] The reverse also takes place, object-libido can return to ego-libido. Moreover, libido is mobile[65] in that it can pass from one object to another.

A form of cathexis is operating within the structure *per se* in the process of ego-id interaction.[66] In its check upon the id, the ego must automatically expend a great amount of energy. This checking force is anti-cathexis and is the principle which maintains the repression.[67]

The so-called ego defense mechanisms need elucidation.[68] Each ego makes use of various characteristic ways of defending itself against feelings of anxiety. Since there are a large number of defense mechanisms, the fact that each individual has a characteristic pattern of them, with some stronger than others, allows for a considerable variety in personality structures. Repression, just described, is one of the major ego defense mechanisms. Not only repression but also fixation, projection, introjection, and others serve in this fashion. Just as in repression, they have the characteristic of demanding the expenditure of libido to keep anxiety from appearing. They maintain "peace and quiet," but in a manner analogous to a garrison keeping an otherwise unruly population in check. At best they maintain a stalemate; at worst they express themselves in the eruptions of neurotic or psychotic symptoms.

An important ego function that does not require this continual expenditure of energy is sublimation. This is the most successful of the various mechanisms in that it allows the discharge of energy to bring about a cessation of impulses without the continued defensive function of the other mechanisms. Sublimations are the socially approved ways of discharging libido without anxiety; they are expressions of libido with aims other than sexual gratification. Illustrations may be drawn from the various stages of psychosexual development. Oral pleasures may be sublimated by pleasures in speaking, and the child may go on to a career as a politician or as a professor. Interest in anal matters may be sublimated by work in the arts or phallic interests in nature study. Many forms of sublimation, however, would not show the obvious relations just sketched. Sublimation, in fact, takes on protean forms with law, order, social progress, interaction, and achievement as areas of manifestation.

The superego is the third of the personality structures. It serves as the vehicle for the conscience.[69] It develops out of the ego, arising as an aftermath of the Oedipus Complex, a facet of development discussed later. It is organized in much the same manner as the ego and deals with the ego as a strict father would toward his child.[70] The tension this engenders is guilt,[71] which was defined earlier as a form of anxiety, moral in nature. The superego serves the special function within the ego of representing the demand for restriction and rejection.[72] Since the superego is a special function within the ego, it follows that repression is also the work of the superego.[73] Although sometimes in conflict in many situations, the superego and ego may function harmoniously; in fact, only when there is a conflict can we distinguish them.[74] When this happens, the superego serves as a pressure upon the ego. It makes the child feel guilty, just as the parents had made him feel guilty. In a more general fashion, the superego expresses the child's moral imperatives, ideals, and the like. It serves to control those sexual and aggressive impulses which, if not controlled, would endanger social stability.

Such, then, are the dynamics and structure of personality as Freud and his followers viewed them.

Stages of Psychosexual Development

Psychoanalytic personality development is conceptualized by Freud[75] as a progression through a series of psychosexual stages. These stages are determined by changes in areas of libidinal localization expressed in changing modes of pleasure findings. They are characterized by differences in object relations, differences in the structural organization of personality, and in the appearance of various behavior mechanisms, i.e., the ego defense mechanisms. Freud's original notion about psychosexual stages was developed to explain the appearance of sexuality in infancy and childhood and the underlying structure of the sexual perversions. One of Freud's senior collaborators, Karl Abraham,[76] had much to do with the theoretical elaboration of the concept of the various psychosexual stages, especially with its extension to explain character structure in the adult on the basis of the child's experiences in the various stages. Freud subsequently accepted this work, so in this sense it is orthodoxly Freudian in nature.

In the progression from birth to adolescence, there are the oral, anal, phallic, and genital psychosexual stages (with the latter two stages separated by the so-called latency period). Although the stages overlap and characteristics of an earlier stage are not entirely absent before the temporal appearance of later stages, erotic pleasure tends to be localized successively in the particular erogenous zones of the body.

The oral stage extends from birth to somewhere in the second year. In the early oral phase the mode of pleasure finding is most concretely expressed in sucking and swallowing and, more figuratively, in incorporating, *i.e.*, symbolically making a part of himself, Sensations of the lips, mouth, tongue, and cheeks are exciting for and by themselves. Freud points to the prevalence of thumbsucking without the reward of food as an illustration of pleasure of and for itself.[77] Sucking is pleasurable and, thus, a manifestation of libido. The infant's general mouth-centeredness is also illustrative. "He puts everything in his mouth," says the mother.

At birth the infant makes no distinction between world and ego. Libidinal energy is entirely narcissistic, *i.e.*, directed upon himself but without awareness that there is a separation of self and world. For example, mother's breast and body are not distinguished from his own body.

The distinction between himself and the environment comes with the diversion of libido from id to ego functions. This distinction comes about, according to Anna Freud,[78] because his needs are not met immediately. If he could always summon up the breast immediately, there would be no occasion to develop any awareness of "self" and "other" from this experience. But his needs are met only after a delay, the mother, by the very nature of things, fails to respond instantaneously. The inevitable delays in ministering to his wants forces a recognition on his part that there is a world "out there" which is not part of "him," and "he" is separate from that world. Thus, self and social awareness develop hand in hand, when the world and ego begin to be distinguished.

The mother is the first object of the infant's libido, *i.e.*, ego libido becomes object libido as invested in the mother. In non-psychoanalytic terminology, the child is beginning to form a positive attachment, learning in an infantile way to "love" his mother. Some id has been transformed while the remainder is not altered.[79] Out of the id, present from birth, there is a beginning of ego expressed in the awareness of the world.

In attempting to control id impulses, the ego supplements the pleasure principle, previously the only regulating principle, with the reality principle, which requires the individual to take into consideration conditions imposed by the outer world.[80] The first signs of the operation of the reality principle in infants may be non-dramatic and hardly noticeable, but they are there. For example, there is the barest beginnings of toleration to a delay in having his needs met, shown by the infant not crying continually when hunger pangs are present. After a signal cry, he may be quiet for a few seconds. As the mother describes it, "Johnny isn't as impatient as he used to be." This toleration is the beginning of reacting in line with the reality principle.

If the mother is gentle and adroit, the infant's little world is pleasant; if the mother is rough and clumsy, the world is "bad," not in any clear-cut thought-out way, but in a "felt," non-verbal fashion. This last observation goes a long way toward accounting for the fact that difficulties of adjustment can occur in homes which in an adult's eyes look ideal. The world of the infant is very small and does not take into account the income of the family, the amount of land surrounding the house, the number of servants, or any other indices so obvious to adult eyes. His world *is* in his interaction with his mother.

Incorporation is important in this oral phase. From incorporation or non-incorporation comes the development of two important personality mechanisms, that is, characteristic ways in which the infant (and later the adult) operates. These mechanisms are introjection and projection. To bring out their nature a quotation from Blum is pertinent here.

The first judgment of the ego is said to be the distinction between edible and nonedible objects: the first acceptance is swallowing; the first rejection is spitting out. Introjection is a derivative of the former, projection of the latter. In the early stage of development of the ego, everything pleasurable is experienced as belonging to the ego (something to be swallowed), while everything painful is experienced as being nonego (something to be spat out). . . .

At this point it might be well to attempt to clarify the terms "introjection," "incorporation," and "identification." Introjection and incorporation are generally used synonymously; some also employ identification in the same way. However, identification usually connotes a type of relationship to objects, in other words, a state rather than a process. Thus, oral introjection is said to be the executive of the "primary identification." By introjecting or incorporating, one achieves a state of identification. Primary identification refers to the first relationship to objects, whereas secondary identification is a later repetition of the earlier one.

Projection starts as a primitive method of getting rid of pain, by attributing unpleasant stimuli to the outside world. It is a sort of reverse introjection—instead of the ego's being perceived as having the object's characteristics, the environment is perceived as having the ego's characteristics. In these early phases of development, the mechanism can function without difficulty. Later it requires a serious impairment of the sense of reality for it to play a major role.[81]

The late-oral or oral-sadistic phase begins at about the age when the eruption of teeth occurs. The modes of pleasure-finding shift. Concretely biting dominates, while devouring and destroying are its more figurative expressions. The situation is intensified by the process of weaning, which usually occurs at this time. The child is in pain and is frustrated, and ambivalence makes its appearance. No longer is there unalloyed positive attachment to the mother. The object relation with the mother, heretofore only loving, is complicated by the appearance of feelings of hatred, so that both positive and negative feelings are present concurrently. How these problems of weaning affect the infant depends in considerable measure upon whether or not weaning is either too abrupt or too early. In either case, trouble of adjustment is to be expected. Anxiety will appear inevitably, but it will be intensified if these sources of frustration are not introduced slowly and gradually. Each child fixates, *i.e.*, invests some libido in oral matters; but the amount is determined by the extent of oral gratification.[82] Undue frustration or too much gratification can produce too great a fixation, possibly resulting in less than optimal adjustment later.

The oral stage ends somewhere in the second year of life, but oral activities continue to be sources of satisfaction, though in varying degrees, from individual to individual.[83] Too great or too little gratification may result in an oral character, one whose oral preoccupations form a disproportionate part of day-to-day interests—excessive eating, drinking, kissing and smoking. Not only will be there be these excessive mouth habits, but there will also be more symbolic manifestations of orality in attitudes of dependence or assurance. An infant overgratified in the oral stage may in adulthood be sanguinely optimistic that everything, *à la* Micawber, will turn out all right. Or lack of gratification may in later life contribute to the formation of a pessimistic individual, passively dependent upon others for his feelings of esteem. Consequences of frustrations arising from the late oral stage are a host of ambivalent adult attitudes, friendly-hostile, aggressive-submissive, and so on, along with a tendency to exaggerate and to swing from one extreme of these attitudes to the other. A tendency toward "biting" remarks is also characteristic.

The area of libidinal localization is shifted to the anal region some time during the second year of life, giving rise to the anal stage. Before examining the phenomena, look for a moment at the situation as the infant might. There is nothing about the odor, texture, or appearance of the feces that are inherently unpleasant. The infant has no innate repulsion. He has created it, and the mother seems to prize it, since she is pleased when he has a movement and concerned when he does not. According to Freudian thinking, defecation is "perceived" by the infant as the giving of a gift. What happens to his gift? The mother flushes it down the toilet! Often he acts out his puzzlement about this strange behavior by toilet play, throwing toys in the toilet, only to retrieve them again.

There are two phases to the anal stage—the expelling and the retaining phase. In other words, pleasure is obtained first from the sheer act of expelling and later from the feeling of a full lower intestine. The more figurative or symbolic expressions of the pleasures of the first phase are expressed in rejecting or destroying, while in the later phase they are expressed in controlling or possessing. Extending over both phases is a sadistic overlay. The use of anal behavior for the purposes of hurting someone else as may be seen in the more symbolic manifestations of pleasure associated with both phases. The infant may take pleasure in using expulsiveness as a means of defying the parents, or he may withhold excretion as a means of defiance. Parents may not necessarily agree with the Freudian interpretation, but they will certainly agree that the toilet training period is typically one of struggle and that the infant seems to be doing just what has been described!

The ego, equipped with self-awareness by the oral stage, extends its prowess in the anal stage away from the passive functions toward actively directing his own behavior according to his changing environment. In short, the ego begins to take on executive functions; it is becoming the doer. The infant no longer must induce others to do for him, but begins to do for himself. He learns to keep clean, to walk, and to talk. With these accomplishments, he can begin to manipulate his environment. In learning to talk, he can let his wants be known more efficiently. Speech is also important in ego development, since through it he learns to handle himself as well as to communicate with others. He now self-communicates. In fact, language is such a wonderful tool that in psychoanalytic thinking it is seen as assuming a magical and symbolic significance to the child. An illustration from children somewhat older than the age under consideration is particularly apt. "Sticks and stones may break my bones, but names may never hurt me!" This chant is learned by children for its reassurance value. They have to be reassured that names will, as a matter of fact, not hurt them. Parents, I am sure, will attest to the fact that on occasion they do have to tell their children at this age that being called a "garbage pail" does not make them one!

Not only is mastery of motility taking place, judgment on the part of the ego is beginning to develop. Partly dependent upon the growth of speech, judgment is shown through reality testing. The infant tries out everything, in the process of which his behavior is such that most mothers would modify the old saying to read—"Fools (and little children) rush in where angels fear to tread." However immature his judgment may be, the child certainly is exercising it.

Difficulties of adjustment experienced during the anal stage also may leave their mark upon the adult personality in the so-called anal character. According to Freud[84] the triad of characteristics that are associated with the anal character are orderliness, parsimoniousness, and obstinacy. In this context orderliness refers to scrupulousness as in keeping everything just so—socks placed away by color, the desk blotter in its precise place, and finickiness about cleanliness. Parsimoniousness refers to "tightness" about money and other matters, such as taciturnity in speech. Obstinacy refers to immobility even to the point of defiance and irritability. Scrooge, the character in Dickens, and his present-day comic strip descendants exemplify the anal character. These characteristics are generalized extensions of earlier compliance with the parents' wishes regarding excretion. "Cleanliness," "tightness," and "unmovableness" will suffice to show the rationale of this extension.

Libidinal interests are shifted to the genital zone at about the end of the third or beginning of the fourth year. Genital interests have been present before this age—erections have occurred and masturbation is not unknown—but the interests are intensified. Part of this intensification is maturational in character in that physical changes are taking place. This is referred to as the phallic stage. Interests center on the sex organs themselves with touching, looking at, and exhibiting genitals, rather than heterosexual behavior, characteristic of the genital stage yet to come. Sexual phantasies appear, and, in general, a high valuation is placed upon the sex organs as such. An important consequence of the phallic stage is that boys become more masculine and girls more feminine. As a result, it will no longer be possible to use "he" generically for both boys and girls. The sexes must now be distinguished, psychoanalytically speaking.

An event of tremendous importance takes place during the years of the phallic stage—the formation and, under normal circumstances, the dissolution of the Oedipus Complex. Hence, it is both logical and convenient to discuss it at this point. However, unless attention is directed to it, a historical inaccuracy would be perpetrated. The theory of the Oedipus Complex arose prior to the theory of psychosexual stages. It was one of Freud's own unique contributions, dating from the period around the turn of the century, not from the later years when the theory of psychosexual stages was formulated.

The high valuation of the sex organs characteristic of the phallic stage is significant for the emergence of the Oedipus Complex which, as might be expected, takes a different course for boys and girls. Its operation in boys will be considered first.

The legend of Oedipus is best known in the trilogy of plays by Sophocles.

The essentials of the plot revolve around Oedipus' killing of his father and marrying of his mother. Freud turned to this legend for the name, Oedipus Complex, to describe the symbolic playing out of this same drama in the life of every boy. By the very nature of things, the boy will fall in love with his mother and direct death wishes toward his father.

With the coming of phallic interests, the boy develops feelings and behavior directed toward the mother which, commensurate with his age and physical state, is sexual in nature. In fumbling childish ways he shows his sexual feelings. These advances his mother rebuffs.[85] The father is also seen as having privileges with the mother from which the boy is barred. For example, when the father is away, he may have the privilege of sleeping in the mother's bed, but when the father returns, this is not permitted. He becomes jealous and strong hostile feelings toward the father develop. But mother-son incest is prohibited in almost all cultures, bringing into play a powerful taboo reinforced by the father's authority over the boy. The boy is a rival to an all-powerful father, and he also has feelings against which all society sets its face. Small wonder, then, that he develops anxiety and fears the loss of love of both his parents. Therefore, anxiety of a massive sort makes its appearance. As if these were not enough, he has a more specific anxiety about his sex organ, on which, it will be remembered, he places a high value. This is castration anxiety, a fear from implied or actual threat to the organ that some parents employ. When the boy learns of the anatomical lack in the girl, this may reinforce his belief in the reality of castration. The cumulative pressures of these anxieties is so great that he represses his desires for the mother, replacing them with tender affection, while his feelings of hostility toward the father are replaced by identification. The Oedipus Complex is "smashed," but its effects are still there. It has not disappeared, but is under control, sometimes shaky in nature, of maintained repression.

In the girl the Oedipus Complex takes a different course, because she, unlike the boy, must give up her original pre-Oedipal object choice of the mother and redirect libido toward the father.[86] Moreover the castration anxiety of the boy is impossible for her since the lack that this implies is already a fact. This lack she notices, and "penis envy" develops. She has fantasies that this castration has happened as a punishment, and she wishes to regain it through the father. This drives her into the Oedipus situation in which the loss may be repaired again in fantasy by having a child through the father. She "loves" the father and, therefore, "hates" the mother, her rival, whom she also blames for her castration. As a means of solving this problem, the girl learns to identify with the mother. The already existing ambivalence toward the mother aids in this displacement to the father. In this way the girl is prepared for the Oedipus shift, the events driving her into it, rather than destroying it, as was the case with the boy. As a consequence of the way it was formed, there is less drive for the girl to overcome it as abruptly as does the boy, and, as a matter of fact, the Oedipal situation remains in effect with the girl for longer periods and is continued more or less indefinitely.

If one asks, not unnaturally, why this stirring drama of both boys and girls is not so clearly remembered as to be a commonplace of our knowledge of our individual past, the answer, psychoanalytically speaking, is simple. We have repressed our knowledge, and so, although it is still operative unconsciously, we cannot consciously recall it.[87]

For both the boy and the girl the aftermath of the Oedipal situation is the formation of the superego.[88] The superego is the heir of the Oedipus complex in that it arises after the complex has been repressed.[89] Parental influence again is paramount.[90] The child identifies with parental views on manners and morals, or rather with these views as idealized and purified. He takes unto himself both their approving and disapproving attitudes and makes them his own. These demands are often exacting, beyond his childish capacities of accomplishment. Consequently, he is plagued with feelings of guilt; he has measured himself with this idealized view and falls short.

In adult life, an individual showing disproportionate effects of the phallic stage would show it through continuing castration anxiety or penis envy. The male phallic character gives the impression of being a devil-may-care, masculine, assured person.[91] Intense vanity, exhibitionism, sensitiveness, and a tendency to maintain the offensive are characteristic. At least fitting the stereotype of the phallic character would be the motorcycle fan, the professional wrestler, and the like. A girl driven by her envy would use her physical charms or other capabilities to overcome the male in any way she can. Actually, both male and female phallic characters are dependent, narcissistic, and unable to have mature heterosexual relationships. Sexual conquests are precisely that, not means of relatedness to other individuals.

With the formation of the superego the last major constituent of the topographical organization of personality has come into being. The interrelationships among id, ego, superego, and the environment are taking on their final form. Earlier in this account, consideration was given to the dynamics and structure of personality. If a strictly developmental sequence of presentation had seemed desirable that discussion could have been interpolated at this point with relatively little modification.

The latency period extends over the years five to ten with no new area of libidinal localization making their appearance. The latency period was originally considered a period of sexual quiescence. However, sexual interests are still very much present, but sublimation and other mechanisms are operative which makes for a relatively quiet period. Social feelings are extended by children of this age to individuals outside of the family circle. To them, the opinion of their peers looms very large.

About the age of ten, the genital stage is introduced by the prepubertal phase preparatory to physical maturity. During the next two or three years or so, there is a sharp increase in sheer amount of libido available. As sketched by Anna Freud, regression occurs; libido is redirected to infantile love objects; Oedipal fantasies reappear; aggressive impulses are intensified; habits of cleanliness may be lost; immodesty and cruelty may be apparent.[92] There are no new elements, but a revival of tendencies from infancy. A general disruption of id, ego, superego relationships occurs. When the id is in the ascendency, means of pregenital gratification predominate; when the ego is the stronger, anxiety results. Criminal attacks that make the headlines of our newspapers, although more often involving a youngster a year or two older, frequently involve what is essentially a failure to hold id impulses in check.

With the arrival of bodily sexual maturity or puberty as such, there tends to be a dropping away of the sloppy and violent behaviors characteristic of the earlier phase and greater refinement and even fussiness may make their appearance. Sexual interests again extend beyond family figures. The boy or girl may behave as if a stranger in his own family with uneasiness over displays of affection. "Crushes" of high intensity, but of short duration and quickly forgotten, may appear, bestowed on persons who are parent substitutes. In general, the disruption of the earlier genital phase gives way to the beginnings of some approximation of the genital character of adulthood.

The normal, genital character of adulthood is characterized by sexual adjustment of a non-neurotic sort with extensive use of sublimation as a constructive means of ego adjustment.[93] Nevertheless, all adults show some effects of the other previous psychosexual stages. Oral, anal, and phallic characters, despite their deviations, are within the normal range of adjustment. In fact, the dividing line between them and the genital character is a matter of degree. In a sense the genital character is an ideal imperfectly achieved by most adults.

It should be obvious that the psychoanalytic theory of psychosexual development places considerable stress on the formative decisiveness of the early years of life. More of the space has been devoted to the first five or six years of life than to the rest of the first fourteen years through adolescence while adulthood has received hardly more than a footnote. This proportion of space is in keeping with psychoanalytic emphasis.[94] Adulthood is an elaboration of the events in infancy and childhood.

OVERVIEW

In considerable measure, psychoanalysis has been seen to emerge from Freud's experience with patients. His was a clinical method of both investigation and verification. Through the free associations, actions, and dream analyses he found an individual interpretive clue which he then related to other presumably congruent findings from the same sources, either from the same or other patients. Consistency of the data, either within a case or from one case to later cases, led to his increased confidence and ultimately to certainty about them. Conspicuous by its absence was the control which would have been given by experiment or by some other method of studying exceptions to his generalizations. His emphasis on sex, extended sex as it were, with ramifications into all areas of human behavior and experience, is at the same time indicative of the emphasis he would place on the instinctual character of man's drives to action, his needs, his tensions demanding reduction. He attached crucial importance to childhood development in which its decisive imprint upon our adult behavior was not only a psychogenetic emphasis, it was also to be played out following a remorseless, biologically genetic pattern. Similarly he placed emphasis upon the dark, primordial forces of the id which had the ego at its mercy.

All of these foci were in varying degree to be questioned, modified or amplified by followers and critics. The use of methods other than the clinical, emphasis on other forms of motivation than the sexual, greater emphasis upon experience after childhood, increased emphasis upon the social at the expense of the instinctual factors, and recognition of a greater autonomy of the conscious control by the ego, all were to come in the period after his death. Psychoanalysis, then, as a means of investigation, as a method of treatment and as a theory of personality continued after Freud. To these themes the book will later return. (See pages 560–562.)

ALFRED ADLER

Although Alfred Adler disagreed with Freud on many issues, he came from a similar tradition since he worked in a clinical setting with disturbed individuals. Consequently, the approach to psychology that emerged from his interaction with his patients shows much closer kinship with that of Freud than it does with anything encountered earlier.

Life and Earlier Views of Adler[95]

Alfred Adler was born in 1870 in a suburb of Vienna, the second son of a relatively well-to-do grain merchant. Although his early years had many attractive features, being spent in the open country, in comfortable circumstances, and with a love of music shared by all of his family, Alfred believed he had an unhappy childhood. The "villain of the piece" was his model eldest brother, whose achievements he never felt he could equal. This brother was his mother's favorite while Alfred was that of his father. Alfred suffered from rickets and was watched over with the greatest solicitude. The running and jumping at which his brother excelled, therefore, caused Alfred unhappiness, and he apparently felt himself to be undersized and ugly. In spite of all this, he was a friendly, outgoing child. Adler reports that his decision to become a physician was made at the age of five when he was recovering from an illness that he learned had been almost fatal. He later interpreted this life goal as a means of ending his childlike distress at the fear of death, expecting more from this choice than it could accomplish. More than one facet of what was to emerge as Adler's psychological views may be found in these memories of childhood.

He attended the University of Vienna, taking his medical degree in 1895. Two years after graduation, he married Raissa Tinofejewna, a wealthy young Russian girl, who had come to Vienna to study. An emancipated, outspoken woman whose greatest interest was in the social betterment of her homeland, her independence of thinking and her liberalism formed a considerable contrast to the domestic ideal of Viennese men of his class. As a biographer remarked, it is easier to believe in equal rights for women than to live with a woman who practices them. That they had their difficult times there is no doubt, but in later years while there occurred no change of their respective fundamental convictions, a mellowness seems to have marked their life together.

Throughout his years in Vienna, the cafe, so much the part of the life of that city, was also part of his life. He met his friends and students there, thoroughly enjoying the informality, the jokes, the wine, the food, and the animated conversation. Adler loved people and was always charming, friendly, and informal. In turn, many individuals from all walks of life were attracted to him. For a time socialistic in his political views, he insisted that his psychological views had nothing to do with politics, as such. His political position, however, was but a specific manifestation of a dedication to social betterment, a purpose upon which he acted all of his life.[96]

Adler was familiar with the *Interpretation of Dreams*, which he believed to be an important contribution to the understanding of human nature. The occasion of his first association with Freud and his precise status in relation to him is a matter of interpretation and uncertainty as an examination of even a portion of the literature demonstrates.[97] To put it bluntly, the Freudians claim he was a disciple who sought and received membership in the Freudian group. The Adlerians see it as a joining forces of equals at the invitation of Freud. At any rate, he became a leading member of the group and was named by Freud as his successor as President of the Vienna Psychoanalytic Society and as co-editor of *Zentralblatt für Psychoanalyse.*

In 1907 Adler published his views on organ inferiority and compensation.[98] As an ophthalmologist and then as a general practitioner, Adler had recognized that disease afflicts inferior organs, a point already well known. In his monograph Adler went on to indicate that this inferiority must be considered as relative to the environment of the person. Disease is a result not only of organ inferiority but also of external demands upon the organ. Moreover, an outcome other than disease may occur to a person with an inferior organ in a particular environment. One outcome may be to overcompensate for this inferiority through that particular organ. History and literature, Adler points out, are filled with instances where an individual's compensation for a weakness of some sort went beyond this level to overcompensation. Demosthenes, the stutterer, who overcame his handicap to become a great orator is illustrative. To draw upon the legends of the United States, the saga of Teddy Roosevelt, the weakling, and his struggle to physical prowess is well known. Another outcome may find the overcompensation expressed through the development of superiority in some other field, as did Nietzsche, who, afflicted with a physical infirmity, took up a pen, instead of a sword, and wrote a philosophy of power.

In 1910, Adler[99] went on to explore more fully the notion of overcompensation. He recognized that organ inferiority led to subjective feelings of inferiority, a concept not used in his earlier paper. Often children who have inferior organs and inadequate development manifest it in weakness and clumsiness (as Adler, himself, showed in childhood) which give rise to feelings of inferiority.

This signalized a shift of emphasis from biology and disease to psychology and the subjective state of the person. For feelings of inferiority, individuals may overcompensate by excessive striving in the area of the felt weakness, in some other area, or, instead of striving in either fashion, may become submissive. More specifically, Adler introduced the concept of masculine protest—the striving to be strong and powerful in compensation for a feeling of being unmanly.

Freud had already defined compensation in terms of inadequate sexual development, leading to a need to compensate for this deficiency. Adler was using it to bring to bear a social emphasis upon sex. Freud adopted the term and used it in relation to castration fear, and penis envy. While Freud used the findings to indicate the omnipresence of sex, Adler used it to point up the individual's interaction with the world, particularly the social world. In women, the masculine protest occurred because in our social world they are made to feel inferior in countless ways. Men, too, show the same protest; in their case it is directed against the assumption that men have to be superior, that they have to live up to this demand despite feelings of inadequacy.[100]

This social emphasis was clearly present as early as 1905.[101] In an account of Freud's *Three Essays on the Theory of Sexuality* for the general public, Adler asked the question, what purpose is served when nature equips the infant with sexuality? His answer was that the passion for satisfaction it engenders forces him to enter relations with the outer world, a very precise foreshadowing of his emphasis on the social aspect of sexuality.

To return to the theme of organ inferiority, as his thinking developed, Adler realized that, irrespective of the presence or absence of organ inferiority, this inferiority feeling of children is a universal fact, since children are small and dependent upon adults. Big, strong people, adults, try to control their every movement. Neurotic tendencies develop when manifestations of this feeling of inferiority are used by children as excuses to prevent them from doing that which they are capable of. When this continues into later life, inferiority feeling becomes the Inferiority Complex. The individual may overcompensate or use inferiority as an excuse to give up striving. Inferiority *per se*, however, is not a sign of abnormality. It is a fact of normal development which occurs when the individual combats his feelings of inferiority by striving to be superior. Aggression then arises, not from felt superiority but from felt inferiority. At this stage of his thinking, Adler said, everyone had a drive toward a superiority in order to overcome feelings of inferiority. As will be seen, this view also changed.

At the time, this work of Adler's was seen by Freud as a contribution to ego psychology and compensation, a valuable, although peripheral clue to the neuroses. The charge that Adler's approach is superficial in that it is an "ego" psychology alone (as differentiated from a psychology of id, superego *and* ego) is still the basic argument of the psychoanalyst against Adlerian psychology. But at the time under discussion, Adler's views were not seen as a separate system. It was only when it was realized that compensation was being made central by Adler, other than peripheral, that there was a parting of the ways.

The two put up with one another for some time. Finally, Adler rebelled against Freud's demand that his publications in Freud's *Journal* be censored by Jung, and won the argument. At this juncture Freud wrote the proprietors of the *Journal* demanding either they withdraw his name or that of Adler's from the title page. Several meetings of the Vienna Psychoanalytic Society were spent in considering Adler's views.[102] Since Freud and several others of those present argued that Adler's views were impossible to reconcile with psychoanalysis, Adler and a group of his followers withdrew. This was when they called themselves, the "Society for Free Psychoanalytic Research," but shortly thereafter they began to refer to their work as "Individual Psychology." Contrary to the frequently expressed opinion, this was not done in order to stress individuality of personality.[103] Nor does it mean that man moves alone, barred from effective relation with his fellows. In fact, this is the diametric opposite of Adler's position because only within a social matrix do the partial processes of the individual achieve meaning.

Adler was later to speak of what he called Freud's mythology of sex, and later he regarded psychoanalysis as founded upon the selfishness of a pampered child and containing within it an attack upon moral law itself. In general, Adler objected to the pan-sexualism of psychoanalysis as expressed in libido theory. Adler also believed, as we have already seen in connection with the "masculine protest," and the sexuality of infants, that the phenomena with which Freud dealt were capable of a non-sexually oriented interpretation. For example, the Oedipus Complex, if it arises at all, comes about from the dependency of the pampered child upon his mother. Sexual feelings exist, to be sure, just as does hunger and thirst, but these biological factors come into psychological prominence only to the extent they come into the striving for superiority. Adler did not deny the reality of unconscious motivation, although he was inclined to stress ego functions to a greater degree than did Freud. He also found dream interpretation useful, although he saw the dream as a vicarious solution of a problem of the individual, a means of planning for the future. The dream had an emotion-producing function, expressed by Adler referring to dreams as the factory of emotions.

In 1911, a German philosopher, Hans Vaihinger, published a book, *The Psychology of "As If,"*[104] that almost immediately influenced Adler's thinking. Vaihinger advanced the idea that man lives by fictional goals which actually have no counterpart in reality. He said that man creates the fiction that the universe is an orderly determined affair, and, by acting as if it were so, even though the universe may really be chaos, in a sense he makes it orderly. We create the fiction of a God when we act as if He existed. Although these goals may be falsifications of experience, we act as if they were real, and, hence, they affect our thinking and behavior.

Adler applied this notion to his more specifically psychological problems,[105] especially the issue of purpose and causality. Freud, it will be recalled, established causality as a fundamental principle and laid great stress upon constitutional factors and childhood experiences as determiners of personality. Adler found in these conceptions of Vaihinger, a means of rebutting this rigid determinism. Man, Adler said, is motivated more by his future expectations than by his past experiences. He behaves as if a goal were that which motivated him. These goals are a part of a teleological design, although they are fictions; they permit the individual to guide his behavior in line with his expectations. The goal toward which a person strives explains his behavior. The goals he "sees" determines what he will do. Not that he is aware of these goals, as a matter of fact he is largely unaware of them—they are goals which he does not understand. The hidden goals are the essential content of unconsciousness.[106] Adler called one aspect of the fictional goal the guiding self-ideal.[107] It was the individual's unifying principles by which he found superiority, an enforcement or the safeguarding of self-esteem. The neurotic tries to enforce self-esteem by being a "real man."

During World War I Adler served as a physician in the Austrian Army. Afterward, through the intercession of a leading Viennese citizen interested in education, he was given the opportunity of organizing child-guidance clinics in the school system of Vienna. His point of view had expanded to the point that it was applicable to teacher-child as well as parent-child relationships and to normal as well as problem children. His influence on teachers, then and later, was very strong. Unlike Freud, he never insisted on long, drawn-out training for practitioners, and many of the more successful and prominent Individual Psychologists have come from the ranks of teachers who combined his teachings with educational practices. It is perhaps appropriate to add that for the rest of his life much of his teaching was carried out through public lectures and institutes to which teachers and anyone else who was interested were invited.

In the nineteen-twenties Adler's fame spread. In Vienna many students and admirers surrounded him, and he spent much time with them. Lecture tours took him to various countries. In 1926, he made his first trip to the United States, where he was warmly received by the teachers who had attended his European conferences. He made several half-year visits thereafter. In 1927 he was appointed lecturer at Columbia University and in 1932, he was made professor of medical psychology at Long Island College of Medicine, a connection which continued until his death.

In 1934, Adler decided to make the United States his permanent home. The following year he founded the *International Journal of Individual Psychology*, which was destined to be only short-lived. Adler embarked in the spring of

1937 on a strenuous lecture tour of Europe, which sometimes called for appearances in two different towns in one day. After completing the continental portion of this tour, he had a fatal heart attack while walking the streets of gray, granite Aberdeen.

Adler was a prolific writer who addressed a large number of books to the general public. Since his writings were based upon his lecture series, they lack the systematic coherence which is to be arrived at only by selection and rearrangement, a task which the Ansbachers have carried out in an admirable fashion.[108]

Systematic Position

Adler's systematic views may be sketched against the setting of his earlier conceptualizations of inferiority feeling, fictional goal, and family situation, but in a larger and somewhat changed perspective.

To Adler, the individual person exists in a context of social relations.[109] Everyone has an innate urge to adapt positively to the social environment that he experiences. This innate capacity for friendly and loving responses, called "Social Interest," is the most important facet of his striving. Instead of all people being driven by inferiority feelings to strive toward superiority, as Adler had earlier urged, his final mature view held that Social Interest was more basic, permitting the normal individual to move toward participation and integration. The neurotic suffers from these feelings of inferiority and has a drive to superiority, but the normal person does not. The normal person, although inferior in the sense that by the very nature of things he must be incomplete, shows a willingness as well as an ability to participate which are basic to Social Interest. There are three major social ties which set for each person three major problems—occupation, social contact with one's fellowmen, and love and marriage. Failure in any or all of these tasks is a failure as a human being. If one failed to adjust to these problems, or if he were to direct his life to escaping these tasks, the individual is potentially neurotic or delinquent. A complete refusal to accept these tasks indicates a psychosis.

In a variety of other ways, Adler emphasized the social factors that are operative in helping to shape the personality. One expression of Adlerian interest in social factors is his emphasis of the importance on the child's position in the family in relation to that of other children.[110] Sibling relationships may lead to certain characteristic experiences of a given child. To mention only some of the more prominent characteristics: The only child who is most often spoiled by the parents, although occasionally hated by them, tends to dominate the mother and father, to be hyperintellectual and overmature for his age, and to show considerable adroitness in getting along with adults. The second born not only dethrones the oldest born, but often ends up dominating him as well as his parents, and often tends to be somewhat more competitive. The youngest child in the family enjoys the doubtful privilege of never being displaced, that is of being "little" and "helpless" forever, and as a consequence, he often learns to get his way by use of stealth and guile.

The characteristic way in which a person's individuality is expressed in its environment is called by Adler "style of life."[111] The individual's life style is an effort to reach his goals. These styles of life are generalized ways of coping with the problems that the individual faces which are unique to each individual. Everyone has a style of life, but no two are alike. The goal of security, of unity, of oneness, is the same, but the routes to it are different. "Acting out of character" is an everyday phrase that shows recognition of the style of life. In every expression of his personality man shows a unity, a consistency, which is his style of life.[112]

A way of identifying the life style that Adler found highly useful was to ask a person to recount his first memories. His own early memory of his illness at five years of age and his decision to become a doctor in order to ward off fear of death is illustrative of what he was seeking to find. Incidentally, he checked this particular conviction by asking a sample of doctors for their first childhood memory and found that they most often reported something involving recovery from a serious illness or a death in the family. Conversely, he asked children in families where there had been a death, what they thought they wanted to do when they grew up—with the answer most often being "doctor" or "nurse."[113]

A faulty style of life may arise from three major sources in childhood experiences—inferiorities, neglect, and pampering. Children with infirmities carry a handicap in that they may consider themselves failures. However, with the aid of understanding parents or by appropriate psychotherapy they may compensate for these inferiorities and actually transform them into strengths. Pampering may produce a child without social feeling who is self-centered and expects society to conform to his wishes, which results in a clash between the child and society. Neglect in childhood may lead to a style of life in which revenge against society is sought. Pampering or neglecting the child usually results in the individual's lacking confidence to meet the demands of life.

Qualification by such expressions as "may" or "usually" have been interjected into this discussion of the sources of a faulty style of life. In addition to parents or psychotherapy, the decision to compensate is dependent upon individual courage quite apart from these external sources. These particular sources may lead to compensation, or they may not, depending upon the child's interpretation of them and his courage in facing them. He may creatively choose to compensate or he may choose to remain a failure. Adler pointed out that man is not merely the creation of the environmental forces to which he is exposed; there is a creative power of the individual.[114] The individual fashions his own unity, he directs his drives, and decides his goals. It is interesting to observe that neglect, pampering, and organic inferiority were all present in Adler's own personality and could have led to inferiority feelings and neuroses, yet they did not. Adler's forms of compensation, both personally to solve these problems and socially to develop his systematic approach, show his own creative solution.

Psychotherapy

A patient comes to the therapist because his life style is incapable of solving his life situation, his particular difficulty being a way of evading the conflicts. The fundamental mistake that a patient makes is to draw false conclusions about the world from his early social relations. The goal of psychotherapy is to cut through this erroneous life style and to suggest a new one.

The patient cannot change his style of life until he gains understanding.[115] He gains that understanding when his Inferiority Complex is traced to its origin in early childhood maladjustments. More specifically, Adler recommended that the following points of departure be used: (1) to study the family constellation; (2) to infer from the earliest childhood recollection some of the aspects of the style of life ideal; and (3) to investigate and interpret dreams so as to see in what particular was guided by his style of life ideal he allowed emotions to interfere with his style of life.

Adler, needless to say, did not follow the techniques of Freudian therapy. He used a face-to-face situation much more conversational in nature than Freud would have countenanced. He was sympathetic and encouraging in attitude, appealing to the patient's social interest, while at the same time trying to aid him to make a solution through his own efforts. Encouragement was by no means an incidental attitudinal matter—its use was an essential aspect of his therapy. Exaggerated inferiority feeling leading to an Inferiority Complex is, in another sense, discouragement arising from maladjustments and deficiencies. Hence, encouragement was important.

There was a characteristic "openness" to his therapy. His clinics with children were conducted before any and all interested individuals who wished to attend—parents, teachers, and, in fact, anyone. Questioning of the child was direct and at the level of a contemporary, although in the simplest of language. On first meeting the child, it was also characteristic of Adler to try to make swift insightful decisions on the child's problem. Seeing a very discouraged child whom he judged had a passionate desire to shine, Adler promptly sat down on a step lower than that of the child. On first seeing a boy with a strong temper, Adler asked what he liked to do and receiving the reply, "Play football;" Adler said, "Its fine barging into the other boys isn't it?" On meeting a child noted for showing off in class, Adler drew himself up on tiptoes as high as he could, and sank slowly back and said, "I am making myself bigger than I am, just as you do, but there are other ways of doing this than by upsetting the class."

Overview

Adler directed his thinking toward the social sciences and away from biology and medicine. The heart of his teaching was social interest, although in a restricted sense, his was a biological theory in that man inherently was a being with social interests. Nevertheless, Adler directed his thinking to exploration of how the social environment influenced the individual's development and personality.

Freud, to be sure, had found the family and society necessary for the viscissitudes of the libido to unfold, but the influence of specific experiences arising in the family or in society can hardly be said to be elaborated. In contradistinction, Adler made the social setting fundamental. Although at first stressing organ inferiority, in time this gave way to emphasis on the attitude that the person adopted toward his defect, and finally eventuated in a view in which positive Social Interest was basic. Adler's influence upon others will be considered in a later chapter.

Carl Gustav Jung

Another former colleague of Freud's, Carl Jung, made contributions of such magnitude and originality as to demand detailed consideration.

Life of Jung

Carl Gustav Jung[116] was born in 1875 in the Swiss village of Kesswil located on Lake Constance, and grew up at Basle, a university town, where he received his early schooling. The family background was scholarly: one grandfather had been a professor of anatomy and internal medicine at Basle, the other a grammarian, and his father a philologist and pastor in the Swiss Reformed Church. Jung's youthful interests were in philosophy and in ancient history.

He would have liked to have become an archaeologist, an early expression of his desire to explore the roots of man's thinking in his historical past.[117] Another current of interest, reflected in his dreams during his student years, led him to the study of the natural sciences. The difficult choice of a profession was limited by the fact that the University of Basle offered no curriculum in archaeology, and Jung was not financially able to study elsewhere. He decided to combine his humanistic and scientific interests in the study of medicine, and he received his medical degree at Basle in 1900. After a year or two of clinical experience, he went on to Paris for a semester to study psychology with Pierre Janet. In 1903, he married Emma Rauschenbach who, over the years, did much collaborative work with him.

Jung's first clinical appointment was to the Psychiatric Clinic of the University of Zurich and its hospital, known as Burgholzi. In 1898, both had come under the leadership of Eugen Bleuler (1857–1939), the best known psychiatrist in Switzerland. Bleuler's particular interest was in the psychopathology of dementia praecox on which in 1911, he was to publish a monumental work. He coined the term "schizophrenia" to signalize the revolutionary reformulation he made. He argued that contrary to the previously held view, so-called dementia praecox was a group of psychiatric reactions, not a single formal disease. Patients so designated were not incurable; mental deterioration did not inevitably occur; and the patients did not lack an affective or feeling life. In 1900, Jung was appointed Bleuler's assistant and in 1905, a lecturer in psychiatry at the University and, at the same time he was advanced to physician of the Clinic, a position he occupied until 1909.

The first publication of Jung in 1902 was a clinical study of an adolescent girl who, in sonambulistic states, performed as a medium.[118] It clearly bore the impress of Janet's teaching, under whom Jung worked the year of its publication.[119]

Beginning in 1903, Jung devoted a considerable amount of attention to experiments in word association.[120] His immediate inspiration for his work was a review by the Swiss psychologist, Claparède. Jung stressed the affective determinants as differentiated from the earlier ones, already familiar from the studies of Galton, Cattell, and others who emphasized cognitive aspects.[121] He investigated the emotional preoccupations of his patients and of normal persons through their responses to a specially prepared list of 100 words. To each of these words subjects were instructed to respond with the first word that came to mind. Typical words were "head," "green," "water," "sing," "dead," and "ship." Time to respond to the word was taken with a stop watch. With some of his subjects a measure of breathing rate was also taken through use of a pneumograph strapped to the chest, while changes in the electroconductivity of the skin caused by sweating were measured by a psychogalvanometer attached to the palm of the hand. If a word produced a long reaction time, an irregularity in breathing, and the onset of sweating, an emotional response connected either with the stimulus word or with the reply seemed indicated. Sometimes matters brought to light by responses are those of which the individual is aware but has chosen to keep secret, as exemplified in this method's later, relatively widespread use in lie and crime detection. Actually, Jung did apply it in precisely this fashion on the occasion of a theft at one of the hospitals. He used as "complex indicators" the names of objects in a stolen purse, such as "key" or "mirror" which to an innocent person would seem quite neutral in content.

To Jung, the use of the method to detect unconscious problems, however, was much more important systematically. In such instances, when the subject responded to a word by showing signs of emotion while showing no knowledge of its significance, *i.e.*, he was unconscious of its meaning, it still served as an emotional indicator. Jung asserted that a "complex" had been touched when this happened.

To Jung, complexes were psychic fragments which have been split off owning to traumatic influences or certain incompatible tendencies. From the association experiments, Jung concluded that complexes interfere with the intentions of the will and disturb the conscious performance; they produce disturbances of memory and blockages in the flow of associations; they appear and disappear according to their own laws; they can temporarily obsess consciousness, or influence speech and action in an unconscious way.[122] It is clear that at this time Jung was dealing with the concept of repression, *i.e.*, the disturbing effect of pain-producing thoughts when they are repressed into the unconscious. He saw how these repressed contents tended to erupt into consciousness, interfering with the normal processes of associative thought.

On reading *The Interpretation of Dreams* soon after its publication, Jung was greatly interested, seeing in it an exposition of the concept of repression from a point of view different from his own, that of its effect in the formation of dreams. In many ways Freud's understanding of the complex agreed with Jung's independent observations. Encouraged to do so by Bleuler, Jung began to apply Freud's theories to his patients at Burgholzi. This resulted in his monograph, *The Psychology of Dementia Praecox*, published in 1907.[123] His application of psychoanalytic principles to the psychotic was highly original. He was led by his clinical findings to compare the contaminated, disintegrated associations of the dementia praecox patient with those of the dream life of the neurotic patient, and he attributed the inadequate and "flat" feeling tone that the former manifested to repression. He applied his own technique of controlled association to these patients and related the two kinds of findings.

In 1906, Freud and Jung began correspondence, and in 1907 Jung made the journey to Vienna to meet Freud; a meeting from which came a strong friendship, based upon mutual liking and respect, which was destined, however, to last but for a few years.

Until 1913, Jung worked closely with Freud, serving as an editor of a yearbook sponsored by Bleuler and Freud and, in 1911, as first president of the International Psychoanalytic Society. Also in 1911 Jung expressed to Freud his doubts about the essentially sexual nature of libido. In 1912, a book, *The Psychology of the Unconscious*,[124] and a series of lectures given at Fordham University entitled, *The Theory of Psychoanalysis*,[125] served to bring their differences about libido into sharp focus. Although Freud broadened his views later, at this time he conceived libido as narrowly sexual in nature. Moreover, sexual trauma, although no longer interpreted according to the seduction hypothesis, was still seen as operative in the patient's fantasies almost to the exclusion of all else. While Jung recognized the importance of early sexual trauma, he did not give this a central position in his theoretical approach. Libido was understood by Jung as psychic energy which was able to communicate itself on different levels of intensity or value to any field of activity: power, hunger, hatred, sexuality, or religion, without ever being itself a specific instinct.[126] Sexuality, then, was but one manifestation. Libido expressed itself in nutrient terms in infancy, in play and social interaction in the years following, and finally took a heterosexual form only after puberty. Jung did not deny there may be a relationship between nutritive and sexual traits. In fact, libido frees itself from the nutritional only with difficulty, and some individuals never do break the association. The libido in its progression from nutritional to sexual zones carries with it the nutritive traits so abundantly demonstrated by Freudian study. Libido, then, included the whole range of drives, being all embracing in nature, closer in spirit to Plato's *Eros* or to Schopenhauer's will to live than to Freud's more restricted meaning. Psychological trauma, instead of being stressed, was seen by Jung merely as a device of the patient to bring his difficulty into focus. The past experiences of the patient were important to Jung primarily in their usefulness in delineating a pattern by means of which the present needs of the patient could be better understood.

Even while Jung and Freud were closely associated, between the years 1909–1913 during which time they traveled together to the United States to lecture in behalf of the psychoanalytic movement, Jung could not fully accept what appeared to him as Freud's "dogmatic" view on sexuality. He noted in his autobiography[127] that he alone logically pursued the two problems which interested Freud most: the problem of "archaic vestiges" and that of sexuality.

Jung saw the value of sexuality and this played an essential part in his psychology, as an expression of psychic wholeness. But his main concern was to investigate, over and above its personal significance and biological function, its spiritual aspect and its meaning in myth and religion. Freud saw Jung's divergence as an attempt to desexualize psychoanalysis and thus to negate his own efforts; consequently a rift developed between the two. In 1914, Jung officially severed his connection with psychoanalysis by resigning the presidency and, a little later, by giving up his membership in the Society. Jung retained his admiration for Freud and, on several later occasions, explicitly acknowledged the importance of his work. Thereafter Jung applied the term, "Analytical Psychology," to his own theories.[128]

Jung first presented his views on extraversion and introversion at the International Psychoanalytic Congress at Munich in 1913,[129] although he had been thinking about these conceptions in his years of practical medical work.[130] He was struck with the fact that among the many individual differences in human psychology, there also existed these "typical" distinctions, and the two types were described in one of his best known works, *Psychological Types*.[131] Those individuals who habitually derive their motivations from inner necessity and are preoccupied with the inner life, Jung called introverts. Those individuals who habitually derive their motivation from external factors, including social relations, he called extraverts. Later, he used these two types to explain the differences between Freud and Adler.[132] An even more personal reason for his interest is admitted. He elaborated his type theory in an attempt to understand better what brought about his own break with Freud. Freud's view was interpreted as that of an extravert, based as it was on a relation with a sexual object, while Adler's view was introvert, since it was based on the subjective side, individual and the will to power. The essential point of the type theory is that it holds the germ of Jung's recognition that every psychological phenomenon contains implicitly the seeds of its opposite, and that for an understanding of man's complete nature it is necessary to discriminate the tendencies which are overtly expressed as well as those which are latent.

To follow this trend of thinking, Jung realized he would have to devote more time to research into the nature of the unconscious. He gave up his university appointment in 1913 in order to work independently without the restrictions of academic tradition. He could then devote his attention to the significance of myths, legends and cultural history for the unconscious life of the individual.[133] This interest became most prominently expressed in his contention that, in addition to the individual unconscious, there is a collective unconscious, which expressed through the individual the deeper images and experiences shared in common by all mankind.

His interest in this problem led him to make field expeditions to study the mental processes of primitive peoples, first in North Africa in 1921, later among the Pueblo Indians of Arizona and New Mexico, and in 1926, in Africa, to study the natives of Kenya. Jung also carried on collaborative work with the aid of specialists in philology, mythology, Chinese philosophy, and poetry. An astonishing array of books was the result. Not only did he study medieval alchemical texts, but he wrote commentaries on Chinese and Tibetan historical documents which had recently become available through translation into German. He also considered modern mystical writings, and reported on the phenomena of occultism.

The results of some of these studies may at first appear puzzling to the modern reader accustomed to a logical exposition of factual material. Consider a book originally appearing in 1944 and published in the English expanded form in 1953, which bears the title, *Psychology and Alchemy*.[134] Its editors for the English edition assure us that it is of such major importance as to rank with *The Psychology of the Unconscious* and *Psychological Types*. Along with the text it contains 270 illustrations drawn from prints, beginning with one depicting "the Creator as Ruler of the threefold and fourfold universe," from a manuscript of 1652 through the allegory of the psychic union of opposites *circa* 1550 and ending with the phoenix as a symbol of resurrection from a manuscript of 1702. The symbols which Jung found in the works of alchemy were seen by him as a projection of psychic contents into matter. The decoding of these symbols, then, served as a parallel or model for understanding the psychic processes through analysis. He noted that some alchemists who were aware of the spiritual aspect of their work stated that "our gold is not the common gold," indicating that their search was more than an attempt to turn base metals into gold. For many of those who worked with it, alchemy was a symbolic way to understand nature—to find the philosopher's stone. Alchemy, to use Jung's term, was an "undercurrent" to the Christianity that rules on the surface.[135] He went on to indicate that alchemy occupied the position to Christianity that the dream did to consciousness. In this framework, alchemical symbolism is discussed in the book by drawing upon material from several hundred dreams.

In another book, Jung argued that the religious impulse is a fundamental instinct in man.[136] Take away his gods, and man will find others, whether it be the deified leaders of the state, or the obsessive charging of such factors as money or work with god-like qualities. Only with the recognition of good and evil within us can we come to a true understanding of self and have a chance for solution of the crises of the present-day world.

In 1933, Jung had resumed academic lecturing when he became professor at the Federal Polytechnical University in Zurich, where he remained until 1942. He gave up this post for reasons of health. In 1944, Jung was named professor of Medical Psychology at Basle, a position especially created for him. He held this appointment only a year or so. On relinquishing this post he also gave up medical practice. In 1948, a Jungian training center, the C. G. Jung Institute, was founded in Zurich, through the initiative and funds of various persons and institutions who wished to further his work. Honorary degrees and other academic and professional honors came to him from all over the world during the decades of the thirties through the fifties. In 1961 he died at his home in Küsnacht, near Zurich.

Systematic Views on Psychology

Jung considered his systematic position to be a growing, changing one, and, therefore, tentative and incomplete.[137] Some of the earlier steps have already been mentioned: how he defined complex, his formulation of libido including its development, his general conception of introversion-extraversion, and his emphasis on the importance of the collective unconscious. These earlier conceptualizations must now be integrated into a larger perspective, involving his mature views on introversion-extraversion, the personal and collective unconscious, the polarities and antitheses, the conscious ego, and the self.

Introversion and extraversion, defined by Jung as attitudes or directions of outlook and interest, are considered collectively in Jungian theory as the direction of libido. In the introvert, there is turning inward of libido toward the self. In the extravert, libido is directed outside the self to objects and relationships to objects. An introvert is reflective, thoughtful and tending to be self-assertive; outside influences meet resistance, expressed by the individual wanting his own way. An extravert adapts quickly to his environment, pays attention to objects; his shyness is minimal.

As Jung is sometimes labeled a "type" theorist, the Jungian concept of the average man needs clarification before proceeding to further ramifications of the theory. In the earlier stage of his theorizing, Jung stated that average men numerically form an even more extensive group than do the introverts and extraverts. Although later he would not make this claim, he then saw such a person as influenced in more or less equal measure from within as from without.[138] Even here, however, the introverted and extraverted attitudes which should be complementary tended to function in opposition. Moreover, Jung warned against a rigid dependence on types, "Every individual is an exception to the rule."[139] Man shows not only conformity but also uniqueness.

Without altering the essential meaning of extraversion and introversion as based on direction of libido, Jung later went on to treat them as superordinate categories to the four functions, which may be thought of as four possible ways of viewing or dealing with any specific situation. The functions were indentified by Jung as thinking, feeling, sensation and intuition. These functions were selected as basic since they are not further reducible, *i.e.*, thinking is different from feeling and cannot be reduced to it, any more than any one of the other functions can be reduced to another. Each of the four functions may be carried on either through an introverted or an extraverted attitude depending upon the direction in which the libido is turned.

A theory of two types had given way to a theory of two classes and four types.[140] Feeling imparts value in the subjective sense of rejection or acceptance. Thinking is conceptual and apperceptive, telling us what a thing is. Sensation transmits a physical stimulus to conscious perception. Intuition transmits perception in an unconscious way (as when having a "hunch"). Sensation and intuition are the perceiving functions, and thinking and feeling carry on the rational or judging functions. To consider thinking as telling us what a thing is causes no particular trouble. However, feeling as a judging function seems, at first glance, to be contradictory. For it to make sense requires an unusual separation—but one demanded in Jungian theory—the separation of feeling from emotion and mood. Mood and emotion are not matters of function, but of sensitiveness, which actually is unsettling of judgment. Feeling, to Jung, has a judging function; it gives a positive or negative value to a thing, and consequently is not an aspect of emotion. Indeed, any function can lead to, but is distinct from, an emotion. Emotion, from Jung's point of view, is the result of being hit in a blind spot, a consequence of the individual being touched in an unconscious, usually "defended" area. It is an affect and may be characterized by a measurable physiological reaction.

Only one of the perceiving functions and only one of the judging functions can be dominant at the same time. Either sensation or intuition and either thinking or feeling can be dominant, but not both, for a person either tends to observe consciously what is going on about him, or he unconsciously perceives the details and responds with an awareness which is a synthesis of what he has "seen" and is experienced by him as an intuitive impression or "hunch." Likewise, either thinking or feeling is dominant, for a person either approaches something with the objectivity that comes from a neutral logical approach or else he weighs it and gives it a subjective value. Since it is already established that either introversion or extraversion can be dominant, but not both, it follows that eight possible combinatory types emerge up to this point. There may be an extravert (1) with intuition and feeling, (2) with intuition and thinking, (3) with sensation and feeling, and (4) with sensation and thinking. The introvert would show the same four combinations among these variables. It may be well to give examples. A person who is an introverted, thinking, intuitive "type," like Jung himself, with the consequent combination of abstraction and hunch, may result in the creative scientist whose brilliant excursions must be checked and elaborated by others plodding behind. On the other hand, intuition and feeling in a setting of extraversion might give a visionary prophet, burning with zeal to lead others but distrustful of logic.

In terms of degree of dominance, one may call an individual an introvert when numerically there are more occasions that this aspect dominates over the extravert. On some occasions he will manifest the unconscious attitude, though sporadically and without finesse, as when an "introvert" in a burst of enthusiasm over something which interests him considerably, say a coin collection, will chatter on and behave as an extravert might, but with no realization that his captive audience is bored.[141] To consider introversion-extraversion alone utilizes only a portion of Jungian theory. One must specify about this person both the presence of one or the other of the perceiving functions and one or the other of the judging functions and then determine the dominance of either the perceiving or thinking function over the other one. Only through this procedure will all of the ramifications of Jungian type theory be employed.

Each person manifests these attitudes and functions in varying degrees but tends to emphasize in one or another of the combinations a habitual attitude and the functions. The harmonious adjustment of attitude and functions is achieved by but few individuals. Usually the predominance emphasized earlier will be found, and one sided, rather than the ideal harmonious development will be found to have taken place.

At a given moment, although mutually exclusive aspects cannot be operative, non-habitual, non-dominant, latent functions nevertheless appear in relation to a given experience.[142] A type, in the sense just discussed, applies to the conscious psyche. A response always implies a choice, and the alternative response not chosen remains unconscious as a potential, rather than an actual, way of dealing with the situation. This is borne out in the analysis of dreams, through which Jung was able to find evidence that a conscious type of introvert with intuition and feeling dominant will unconsciously be extraverted with sensation and thinking dominant. The more the individual consciously develops his natural inclination toward one or the other of attitudes and functions, the greater is the unconscious libidinal charge of its opposite. This contrast between the conscious and unconscious facets of an individual's personality runs as a theme through all that follows. It is Jung's conception of the complementary relationship between conscious and unconscious that now must be examined.

The ego, at the centrum of consciousness, possesses a high degree of continuity and identity, having, as it does, an awareness of "I."[143] It is often regarded by the individual as the center of his personality although, as we shall see, Jung held that this is not the case.

The persona, a term derived from the masks worn in ancient Greek plays, refers to a similar mask figuratively worn by the individual in society, *i.e.*, the expected social role he plays which covers the private personality existing behind this facade. The individual adopts to some extent the characteristics expected in his role—a business man is energetic, an artist otherworldly, and so on. The persona is the outer layer of the personality, serving as mediator between the exterior world and the other aspects of personality, including the ego and the other even deeper unconscious layers.

The unconscious includes both individual factors in the personal unconscious and dispositions inherited from one's ancestors in the collective unconscious.[144] The personal unconscious is derived from several sources. Forgotten experiences may become unconscious; repression occurs in our more or less deliberate withdrawal of attention, and subliminal perception occurs without the individual's awareness leaving traces which are to be found in the unconscious. Instead of education removing the child's natural, animal-like acquisitiveness, aggressiveness, and lustfulness, these tendencies are pushed back into the personal unconscious, where they live on. Even more important than any of these sources for the personal unconscious, is the fact that it serves to reflect one-sided development, the neglected attitudes and functions being active in this area in accordance with the principle of unconscious development of opposites.[145]

The collective unconscious, more or less common to all individuals, is the product of generations past, the deposit of the experiences to which our ancestors have been exposed. It contains the wisdom of the ages in which man's innate potential lies, and which emerges from time to time in the form of "new" ideas and various creative expressions. Jung attached great importance to the collective unconscious; elucidation of its secrets serving to point the way to the individual's future, and to relate that individual to the development of all mankind.

The collective unconscious consists of the sum of the instincts and their correlates, the archetypes.[146] These are archaic vestiges or primitive modes of functioning which carry a charge of energy and which may be manifested through their ability to organize images and ideas.[147] "Archetypes are typical modes of apprehension," says Jung, "and whenever we meet with uniform and regularly recurring modes of apprehension we are dealing with an archetype, no matter whether its mythological character is recognized or not."[148]

The archetypes themselves are unconscious and should not be confused with their conscious representations in images and ideas,[149] since they are but possibilities of ideas.[150] They are the "a priori determinants" of all psychological experiences.[151] Archetypes are inherited with the structure of the brain, of which they represent the psychic, *i.e.*, non-material, aspect.[152] Despite the contrary opinion sometimes expressed, it would seem as if Jung was talking, not about the inheritance of archetypes as acquired characters, but the inheritance of potentialities or predispositions.

These archetypes rooted in man predispose him to react the same way as did his ancestors to experiences common to mankind over all parts of the world, "primitive" and "civilized" alike. Even more important than the sheer frequency of these ever-repeated experiences is their attachment to significant, emotion laden events—births, death, marriages, transitional stages of life, such as adolescence, and awe-inspiring experiences. An example of this last category is the course of the sun and the change from day to night, impressed upon the mind of each man from time immemorial.[153] What is found in the archetypes is not a scientific explanation but an expression in terms of a worldwide analogy. The conglomerate basic tale that Jung found is that of a god-hero born from the sea, who mounts the chariot of the sun; in the west a great mother awaits him by whom he is devoured as evening comes; in the belly of a dragon he travels the midnight sea and, after a combat, he slays the dragon of the night and is born again.

While almost entirely submerged during the waking state of normal adults, archetypal images tended to emerge in dreams, in adult fantasies, in children, in the delusions of the insane in whom the individual ego has been overwhelmed by the collective unconscious, and in myths and fairy stories found throughout the world.

It is from these sources that Jung sought his evidence. For example, among his patients a dream image that had been reported would be isolated, and the patient would be encouraged to elaborate upon it until a more complete image was formed.

His general argument for the reality of the existence of archetypes rests upon finding that highly complex and detailed representations of them, similar down to the smallest detail, may appear in all parts of the world and at different points in time. Also the fact that archetypal images are produced by patients who had no conscious knowledge of their existence or significance attests to their universality. In *Psychology and Alchemy*, for example, Jung argued that he has presented the evidence that demonstrates the existence of the archetypes in man. He finds his evidence in the parallels between dream symbols and the symbols of the medieval alchemist. To lend more concreteness to this contention an illustration of Jung's from another source,[154] first published in 1927, follows: Around 1906 Jung had observed a paranoid patient who had grandiose ideas and active hallucinations. One day Jung saw him gazing at the sun through the window and making a curious movement of his head from side to side. He told Jung he wanted to show him something—if one looks at the sun with eyes half shut one could see the sun's phallus and by moving the head from side to side the sun's phallus would likewise move from side to side. The patient then added this was the origin of the wind. At this time Jung saw it as a bizarre incident and nothing more. In 1910, Jung came across the so-called Paris magic-papyrus of the Mithraic cult of many, many centuries before, which just recently had been deciphered and found it to contain an account of a vision that the sun had a tube by the movement of which one could tell the prevailing wind. Still later, he found that in medieval art, the tube of the sun was depicted as serving as a sort of hose pipe by which *conceptio immaculata* reaches Mary in the form of a dove. These widely scattered incidents, separated by centuries of time and thousands of miles of space, Jung believed, were evidence for the assumption of the working of a collective unconscious.

Jung would not accept the contention that the collective unconscious was a consequence of nothing more than diffusion, a common conception of cultural anthropology, which holds that the scattering of a myth (or any other cultural product for that matter) from a central source occurs by cultural contact with neighboring peoples. Instead, Jung insisted that myth and ritual appeared in similar form the world over because people, no matter where they happen to be, are endowed with certain innate tendencies which result in their thinking in the same way and their symbolization in the same manner. This similarity Jung attributed to the collective unconscious. Archetypal images appear in many forms—as persons, as supernatural figures, as geometrical shapes, as numbers. Behind this diversity of form, the archetypes themselves are limited in number.[155] There is the mother archetype, embodying nourishment, and the father archetype, indicating strength. All pre-existing mothers with their protective nourishing influences combine to form an image, while fathers signify strength and authority. Jung finds the mother archetype in the Chinese *yin;* the father archetype is exhibited in *yang.*[156] Archetypes are not always expressed as something readily recognizable as "mother," but there are many more distant associations as with "earth," the warming hearth, the protecting cave, or even the milk-giving cow. So, too, the "father" is glimpsed in rivers, winds, storms, battles, bulls, and all things that are moving and dynamic.

In contrasting his view with those of Freud and Adler, Jung claimed that his theory was, ". . . based on the principle of opposites, and possibly pluralistic, since it recognizes a multiplicity of relatively autonomous psychic complexes."[157] There is a self-regulative function expressed by these opposites; the libido flows between opposite poles as between the positive and negative poles of an electric circuit.[158]

The psyche or total personality is constructed in terms of complementary opposites. It is already apparent that in his system, Jung recognized several pairs of polarities or opposing forces. When libido flows into introversion, it is withdrawn from extraversion. Similarly, libido directed toward certain functions is withdrawn from the others. The same principle of complementarity holds in the relation of the conscious to the unconscious. Psychic energy is constant, only its distribution is variable.[159] Several other complementary opposites drawn from the theory of the archetypes must be indicated.

The shadow or darker self is unrecognized and disowned; the inferior, animal-like part of the personality is rejected by the ego, but it is, nevertheless, present and active although unconscious. As an archetype, it is Mr. Hyde to our Dr. Jekyll, wanting to do everything which we will not permit ourselves. When the shadow dominates, as it sometimes does, we speak with more truth than we know: "I was not myself." In archetypical collective fashion, the shadow is expressed by the image of a demon or a witch. The man without awareness of his shadow, statistically a very common occurrence, is the man who believes he is actually only that which he knows about himself, and is thereby not a complete individual. He usually projects his shadow, and this becomes evident when he reacts with inappropriate affect to someone who expresses views or values which he consciously rejects. Thus unreasonable predilections against certain types of persons—xenophobia, racial prejudice—may be partially understood as evidence of the projected shadow. Only by recognizing that not all the evil is outside of the individual himself, can a person withdraw the projections and attend to that aspect of the problem which is a part of his own shadow personality.

Jung held that at a psychological level masculine or feminine characteristics are exhibited by the opposite sex. Under certain circumstances, homosexuality may be an extreme manifestation of this condition. The personality structure of the man contains elements of repressed femininity, while the woman is largely unconscious of her masculine tendencies. These contra-sexual elements in the man are referred to as a feminine archetype, the anima; those in the woman as a masculine archetype, the animus.[160] Characteristically, the man experiences unconscious feminine attitudes expressed through the anima, while the woman experiences unconscious masculine attitudes expressed through the animus. A man first makes a relationship with a woman through the projection of his anima; a woman with a man through her animus. However, in both sexes, trouble is to be expected in heterosexual relationships if the archetypal image of the opposite sex is too disparate from the love object upon whom it is projected. Discrepancies between real and ideal must be compromised for adequate adjustment to take place.

The self is to be differentiated from the ego, since the latter is mostly conscious. The self is the central archetype, the archetype of order, and of the totality of the personality.[161] It embraces not only the conscious, but also the unconscious psyche and is therefore a personality which we *also* are. There is little hope of our ever being able to reach even approximate consciousness of the self, since however much we make conscious there will always exist an indeterminate and indeterminable amount of unconscious material which belongs to the totality of the self.[162]

The self as an archetype is expressed in man's striving to reach psychological unity. For a healthy or integrated personality each of the elements must be permitted to reach its fullest development, and differentiation is, therefore, necessary. This developmental process is referred to as individuation, or an urge toward self-realization.[163] It does not call for the self to take the place of the ego; if the ego becomes identified with the self it becomes inflated into a sort of pseudo-superman. If the reverse occurs, and the self becomes all-important with a resultant dimunition of the ego, the individual will have a very low opinion of himself—he may become depressed or even psychotic. Therefore, both ego and self must preserve their intrinsic qualities. The appropriate adjustment occurs when the self acts compensatorily to the ego-consciousness. A continuing dialogue between the two is healthy, not unhealthy, and makes for self-realization. Nevertheless, the self, the midpoint of personality, is the means whereby its various parts are unified. It acts as a balance point thus making for stability and equilibrium.

Psychotherapy

Jung's approach to treatment emerged from his theoretical position. The purpose of psychotherapy is to help the patient become a whole man.[164] It is necessary to aid in releasing the hidden potentialities that are being stifled and to integrate them with the already more active and dominant aspects of the personality. Man's religious striving, too, must be recognized and made a part of the integrated harmony between various polarities and systems, separating him from his self. This last point is especially pertinent with older patients. In a complete orientation of consciousness all the functions should cooperate with one another.[165] Moreover, cooperation, instead of conflict, between the conscious and the unconscious is sought as a goal of therapy. More specifically, it is necessary for the conscious ego to come to terms with the unconscious components of its personality.[166] For example, there must be a realization that the shadow is present and active. In selected cases the therapist interprets the meanings of archetypes, the deep universals, to the patient. Instead of stressing the sexual etiology of the individual with the intent of uncovering the conflicts of childhood, Jung found it more useful to stress analyzing the immediate conflicts in all of their various ramifications.

Overview

Central to Jung's view of development was his emphasis on goals that guide or direct the destiny of man. True, man is determined by the past under the principle of causality, but also he is determined by the future (teleology).[167] Man, then, is guided not only by his individual and racial history but by his aims and aspirations as well. Jung's approach is functionally oriented toward the present and future. In this respect, he stands in contrast to Freudian exclusive dependence upon causality.

REFERENCES*

1. L. L. WHYTE, *The Unconscious Before Freud*. New York: Basic Books, 1960.

2. S. ROSENZWEIG, The Cultural Matrix of the Unconscious, *Amer. Psychologist*, 1956, 11, 561–562.

3. S. FREUD, An Autobiographical Study. In J. Strachey (ed.), *The Standard Edition of the Complete Psychological Works of Sigmund Freud*. (Vol. 20) London: Hogarth, 1959, pp. 7–70. (1925)

4. The standard reference is E. Jones, *The Life and Work of Sigmund Freud*. (3 vols.) (New York: Basic Books, 1953–1957). This is supplemented by Freud's Autobiographical Study, *op. cit.*, and by The History of the Psychoanalytic Movement (*vide* ref. 6), which are specifically cited when used. Otherwise, Jones is the source.

5. ANNA O's real name was Bertha Pappenheim. She never married, was very devout, and went on to a career in social work. She became so distinguished in her field that in 1954, Germany issued a semi-postal stamp in her honor.

6. S. FREUD, The History of the Psychoanalytic Movement. In A. A. Brill (ed.), *The Basic Writings of Sigmund Freud*. New York: Random, 1938, pp. 933–977. (1914)

7. JONES, *op. cit.*, I, p. 246.

* See page 16 for description of reference style.

8. S. FREUD, Psychopathology of Everyday Life. In A. A. Brill (ed.), *The Basic Writings of Sigmund Freud.* New York: Random, 1938, pp. 35–178. (1904)

9. J. BREUER and S. FREUD, *Studies on Hysteria.* London: Hogarth, 1955. (1895)

10. S. FREUD, *The Interpretation of Dreams.* London, Hogarth, 1953. (1900)

11. *Psychopathology of Everyday Life.*

12. M. FORDHAM, *The Objective Psyche.* New York: Humanities, 1960.

13. S. FREUD, *Three Essays on the Theory of Sexuality.* London: Hogarth, 1953. (1905)

14. *Autobiographical Study,* p. 51.

15. *History of Psychoanalytic Movement.*

16. *Interpretation of Dreams.*

17. S. FREUD, *An Outline of Psychoanalysis.* New York: Norton, 1949. (1939)

18. O. RANK. *The Trauma of Birth.* New York: Harcourt, Brace, 1929. (1923)

19. S. FREUD, *The Question of Lay Analysis.* New York: Norton, 1950. (1926)

20. S. FREUD, *Moses and Monotheism.* New York: Knopf, 1939.

21. N. FODOR & F. GAYNOR, *Freud: Dictionary of Psychoanalysis.* New York: Philosophical Library, 1950. This reference is a convenient source to find citations of the definitions of some of the crucial characteristics of psychoanalysis.

22. S. FREUD, Psychogenic Visual Disturbances According to Psychoanalytic Conceptions. In *Collected Papers.* Vol. 2. London: Hogarth, 1924, 105–112. (1910)

23. S. FREUD, Instincts and Their Vicissitudes. In *Collected Papers.* (Vol. 4) London: Hogarth, 1925, pp. 60–83 (1915); S. Freud, *The Ego and the Id.* London: Hogarth, 1947. (1923)

24. S. FREUD, *Beyond the Pleasure Principle.* New York: Boni & Liveright, 1922. (1920)

25. *An Outline.* Chap. 2.

26. O. FENICHEL, *The Psychoanalytic Theory of Neuroses.* New York: Norton, 1945.

27. S. FREUD, *Civilization and its Discontents.* London: Liveright, 1930, Chap. 6. (1929)

28. *An Outline.*

29. *Ibid.*

30. *Question of Lay Analysis,* Chap. 2.

31. *An Outline,* Chap. 1.

32. *Ibid.*

33. S. FREUD, *New Introductory Lectures on Psychoanalysis.* New York: Norton, 1935, Chap. 3. (1932)

34. *An Outline,* Chap. 8.

35. *Beyond the Pleasure Principle.* Chap. 1.

36. *An Outline,* Chap. 2.

37. *New Introductory Lectures,* Lec., 2.

38. *An Outline,* Chap. 8.

39. *Ibid.,* Chap. 2.

40. S. FREUD, Metaphysical Supplement to the Theory of Dreams. In *Collected Papers.* (Vol. 4) London: Hogarth, 1925, 137–151. (1916)

41. *An Outline,* Chap. 5.

42. *Question of Lay Analysis,* Chap. 2.

43. *Moses and Monotheism,* Part III, Sec. 1.

44. *An Outline,* Chap. 1.

45. *Question of Lay Analysis,* Chap. 3.

46. *Ibid.,* Chap. 2.

47. *Ibid.,* Chap. 3.

48. *An Outline,* Chap. 1.

49. *Ibid.,* Chap. 8.

50. *New Introductory Lectures,* Lec. 3.

51. *An Outline,* Chap. 1.

52. *New Introductory Lectures,* Lec. 1.

53. *An Outline,* Chap. 4.

54. S. FREUD, Repression. In *Collected Papers.* (Vol. 4) London: Hogarth, 1925, 84–97. (1915)

55. S. FREUD, *The Problem of Anxiety.* New York: Norton, 1936, Chap. 10. (1926)

56. *New Introductory Lectures,* Lec. 3.

57. *Problem of Anxiety,* Chap. 10.

58. *Ibid.,* Chap. 8.

59. *New Introductory Lectures,* Lec. 3.

60. *An Outline,* Chap. 1.

61. S. FREUD, *Wit and its Relation to the Unconscious.* New York: Moffat, 1916, Chap. 5. (1905)

62. *An Outline,* Chap. 2.

63. *Three Essays.*

64. *New Introductory Lectures,* Lec. 4.

65. *An Outline,* Chap. 2.

66. *Ibid.,* Chap. 6.

67. S. FREUD, The Unconscious. In *Collected Papers.* (Vol. 4) London: Hogarth, 1925, 98–136. (1915)

68. ANNA FREUD, *The Ego and the Mechanisms of Defense.* London: Hogarth, 1937.

69. *An Outline,* Chap. 5.

70. *Ibid.*

71. *New Introductory Lectures,* Lec. 3.

72. *Ibid.*

73. *Ibid.*

74. *Problems of Anxiety,* Chap. 3.

75. The general outlines of what follows is dependent upon Freud, *An Outline,* but some of the details are derived from other sources. For example, Freud originally described only one oral phase, but this and other stages were elaborated and, as Freud accepted them, these elaborations are presented.

76. K. ABRAHAM, *Selected Papers on Psychoanalysis.* London: Hogarth, 1927.

77. *Three Essays.*

78. Anna Freud, Some Remarks on Infant Observation. In Ruth S. Eissler *et al.* (eds.), *Psychoanalytic Studies of the Child.* (Vol. 2) New York: International, 1947, 11–30.

79. *An Outline,* Chap. 4.

80. *Question of Lay Analysis,* Chap. 3.

81. G. S. BLUM, *Psychoanalytic Theories of Personality.* New York: McGraw Hill, 1953, pp. 46–47. (Reprinted by permission.)

82. FENICHEL, *op. cit.*

83. *Ibid.*

84. *New Introductory Lectures,* Lec. 6.

85. RUTH L. MUNROE, *Schools of Psychoanalytic Thought.* New York: Dryden, 1955.

86. *Ibid.*

87. *New Introductory Lectures,* Lec. 3.

88. *Ibid.*

89. *An Outline,* Chap. 8.

90. *Ibid.,* Chap. 1.

91. FENICHEL, *op. cit.*

92. ANNA FREUD, *Ego and Mechanisms, op. cit.*

93. FENICHEL, *op. cit.*

94. *Mosses and Monotheism,* part III, sec. II.

95. PHYLLIS BOTTOME, *Alfred Adler, a Biography.* (New York: Putnam's, 1939) This has been considered standard for many years. It must, however, be supplemented by a more recent statement which fills in some of the gaps and makes some corrections. This is the account by C. Furtmüller (*vide* ref. 96, pp. 311–393).

96. H. L. ANSBACHER & ROWENA R. ANSBACHER (eds.), *Superiority and Social Interest: a Collection of Later Writings by Alfred Adler.* Evanston: Northwestern University Press, 1964. (1928–1937) Editorial introduction.

97. FURTMULLER, *op. cit.;* A. H. Maslow, Was Adler a Disciple of Freud? (A note.) *J. Indiv. Psychol.,* 1962, 18, 125: H. L. Ansbacher, Was Adler a Disciple of Freud? (A reply.) *J. Indiv. Psychol.,* 1962, 18, 126–135: E. Federn, Was Adler a Disciple of Freud? (A Freudian view.) *J. Indiv. Psychol.,* 1963, 19, 80–82.

98. H. L. ANSBACHER & ROWENA R. ANSBACHER (Editors & Annotators) *The Individual Psychology of Alfred Adler: a Systematic Presentation in Selections from his Writings.* New York: Basic, 1956. (1907–1937) pp. 23–35. (1907)

99. *Ibid.,* pp. 45–52. (1910)

100. R. DREIKURS, *Fundamentals of Adlerian Psychology.* Philadelphia: Chilton, 1950.

101. A. ADLER, Die sexuelle problem in der Erziehung, *Die neue, Gesellschaft,* 1905, 1, 360–362.

102. K. M. COLBY, On the Disagreement between Freud and Adler, *Amer. Imago.,* 1951, 2, 229–238.

103. DREIKURS, *op. cit.*

104. H. VAIHINGER, *The Psychology of "As If."* New York: Harcourt, Brace, 1925. (1911) (Sections excerpted in Ansbacher & Ansbacher, *Individual Psychology,* 77–87.)

105. A. ADLER, *The Neurotic Constitution.* New York: Moffat-Yard, 1917.

106. *Individual Psychology.*

107. *Neurotic Constitution.*

108. *Individual Psychology.*

109. A. ADLER, *What Life Should Mean to You.* New York: Blue Ribbon, 1937; H. L. Ansbacher, The Structure of Individual Psychology. In B. B. Wolman & E. Nagel (eds.), *Scientific Psychology: Principles & Approaches.* New York: Basic, 1965, pp. 340–364.

110. *Ibid.*

111. A. ADLER, *The Science of Living.* Philadelphia: Chilton, 1929.

112. *What Life Should Mean to You.*

113. ORGLER, *op. cit.*

114. *Individual Psychology.*

115. A. ADLER, Individual Psychology. In C. Murchison (ed.), *Psychologies of 1930.* Worcester: Clark University Press, 1930, pp. 395–405.

116. JOLANDE JACOBI, *The Psychology of C. G. Jung.* (rev. ed.) New Haven: Yale University Press, 1951; Frieda Fordham, *An Introduction to Jung's Psychology.* London: Penguin, 1953.

117. C. G. JUNG, *Memories, Dreams, Reflections.* New York: Pantheon, 1961, p. 84.

118. C. G. JUNG, On the Psychology and Pathology of So-Called Occult Phenomena. In *Psychiatric Studies*. New York: Pantheon, 1957.

119. FORDHAM, *op. cit.*

120. R. A. CLARK, Jung and Freud: a Chapter in Psychoanalytic History, *Amer. J. Psychother.*, 1955, 9, 605–611.

121. C. G. JUNG, *Studies in Word Association*. New York: Moffat-Yard, 1919.

122. C. G. JUNG, Psychological Factors in Human Behavior. In *The Structure and Dynamics of Psyche*. (Vol. 8) New York: Pantheon, 1960, p. 121.

123. C. G. JUNG, *The Psychology of Dementia Praecox*. (Translated by A. A. Brill.) New York: Mental and Nervous Disease Publishing, 1908.

124. C. G. JUNG, The Psychology of the Unconscious. In *Two Essays on Analytical Psychology*. (Vol. 7) New York: Pantheon, 1953.

125. C. G. JUNG, The Theory of Psychoanalysis. In *Freud and Psychoanalysis*. (Vol. 4) New York: Pantheon, 1961.

126. C. G. JUNG, The Concept of Libido. In *Symbols of Transformation*. (Vol. 5) New York: Pantheon, 1956, p. 137.

127. *Memories, Dreams, Reflections*, p. 168.

128. *Theory of Psychoanalysis*.

129. C. G. JUNG, Psychological Types. In *Contributions to Analytical Psychology*. London: Kegan Paul, 1928.

130. *Ibid.*

131. *Ibid.*

132. *Ibid.*

133. CLARK, *op. cit.*

134. C. G. JUNG, *Psychology and Alchemy*. (Vol. 12) New York: Pantheon, 1953.

135. *Ibid.*, p. 23.

136. C. G. JUNG, *The Undiscovered Self*. Boston: Little, Brown, 1957.

137. JACOBI, *op. cit.*, foreword.

138. *Psychological Types*.

139. *Ibid.*, p. 303.

140. H. GRAY & J. B. WHEELWRIGHT, Jung's Psychological Types, Including the Four Functions, *J. Gen. Psychol.*, 1945, 33, 265–284.

141. FORDHAM, *op. cit.*

142. GRAY and WHEELWRIGHT, *op. cit.*

143. *Psychological Types*.

144. C. G. JUNG, The Conscious Mind, the Unconscious and the Individuation. In *Archetypes and the Collective Unconscious*. (Vol. 9, part 1) New York: Pantheon, 1959.

145. BLUM, *op. cit.*

146. C. G. Jung, Instinct and the Unconscious. In *The Structure and Dynamics of the Psyche.* (Vol. 8) New York: Pantheon, 1960, p. 138.

147. C. G. Jung, On the Nature of the Psyche. In *The Structure and Dynamics of the Psyche.* (Vol. 8) New York: Pantheon, 1960.

148. *Ibid.;* Instinct and the Unconscious, pp. 137–138.

149. *Ibid.*

150. C. G. Jung, Mind and the Earth. In *Contributions to Analytical Psychology.* London: Kegan Paul, 1928, p. 110.

151. *Instinct and the Unconscious,* p. 133.

152. *Psychological Types.*

153. *Mind and the Earth.*

154. *Ibid.*

155. *Instinct and the Unconscious.*

156. *Mind and the Earth.*

157. C. G. Jung, Introduction to Kranefeldt's Secret Ways of the Mind. In *Freud and Psychoanalysis.* (Vol. 4) New York: Pantheon, 1961, p. 329.

158. *Psychology of the Unconscious.*

159. C. G. Jung, *Modern Man in Search of a Soul.* New York: Harcourt, Brace, 1933.

160. *Mind and the Earth.*

161. *Memories, Dreams, Reflections,* p. 386.

162. C. G. Jung, The Relations Between the Ego and the Unconscious. In *Two Essays in Analytical Psychology.* (Vol. 7) New York: Pantheon, 1953, p. 175.

163. *On the Nature of the Psyche.*

164. *Psychology and Alchemy.*

165. *Contributions to Analytical Psychology.*

166. *On the Nature of the Psyche.*

167. C. G. Jung, *Analytical Psychology.* New York: Moffat-Yard, 1916.

CHAPTER 21

PSYCHOLOGY UNTIL 1945

IN CARRYING to completion the work of the great psychologists a temporal unevenness has resulted. Some accounts of the phases of the history of psychology ended as long ago as the first decade of the century, others were carried further to the end of World War II and some even beyond. In this chapter, consideration will be given to psychological events of historic importance up to about 1945, or, if continuity calls for it, somewhat beyond this date. Linguistic, not national boundaries will be followed; German psychology includes Austrian and Swiss, French psychology, Belgian and Swiss nationals. It is fitting first to return to Leipzig after Wundt's retirement.

GERMAN PSYCHOLOGY

It was Felix E. Krueger (1874–1948) who succeeded Wundt in 1917 to that oldest of psychology's chairs, the one at Leipzig. Disregarding certain nuances of difference, he established what has been called *Ganzheitspsychologie*,[1] totality psychology, holistic psychology and the Leipzig Gestalt School. German psychologists had always referred to Gestalt psychology in terms of reference to its original university setting. Thus the work of Wertheimer, Koffka, and Köhler was referred to as that of the Berlin Gestalt School. The Leipzig Gestalt School accepted the integrated whole or Gestalt concept, but they owed perhaps as much or more to the oldest of Gestalt Schools, that at Graz in Austria. (See page 438.) They accused the Berlin School of limiting themselves to cognitive processes with a consequent neglect of the all embracing totality of the life of feeling. Moreover, they placed considerably more emphasis upon understanding psychological phenomena in the light of their development and insisted that the scope of psychology be broadened to include social and cultural factors.

Perception in the more rigorous Berlin Gestalt tradition is the theme of the research of the senior living German psychologist, Wolfgang Metzger, now at the University of Münster, but earlier at Berlin. His statement of the current status of Gestalt psychology is the most orthodox and systematic treatise that is available in any language.[2]

In the second and third decades of this century three prominent views of personality made their appearance. Eduard Spranger (1882–1963), a philosopher at the University of Berlin, is well known on both sides of the Atlantic for his work, first published in 1913, on personality types expressed in terms of attitudes or values.[3] The work of Ernst Kretchmer[4] (1888–1964) on physique and character that first appeared in book form in 1921, if anything, is better known in the United States. It is unfortunate that the available English translation is so out of date as to give only a caricature of his views.[5] Undoubtedly the world's foremost graphologist was Ludwig Klages (1872–1956) and his most celebrated book, first appearing in 1916, *Handscrift und Charakter*[6] was to go through at least 25 editions in the next forty years.[7] Suspect in the United States because of its intuitive character, graphology, then and now, is widely used in Europe extending well beyond the confines of Germany, both as an individual tool of appraisal and, more commonly, in conjunction with other devices.

It was in 1920 that a pioneer social psychologist, Walther Moede[8] (1888–1958), a professor at Berlin's technical institute, published the results of his valiant effort to introduce the social variable into standard experiments. An example is his comparison of the absolute threshold for sound, not just for one, but for two, three, four or more subjects while observing one another, their involuntary movements when watching others move an arm, association singly and with others, and so on. The work, never translated, did not have the impact in the United States it deserved, except in the work of F. H. Allport.

A typical European approach to personality is characterology. A definition of Thomae catches at least some aspects of what is meant when he defines character "as the structural aspect of personality, the inner conditions of overt behavior that are, to a certain extent, constant."[9] An approach to characterology still widely current in German psychology is stratification theory—actually a variety of approaches which stress a hierarchy or hegemony among distinct mental processes. The leadership in stratification theory may be said to have been shared by two German psychologists, Erich Rothacker (1888–1965), formerly of Bonn, and Philipp Lersch of Munich, who published simultaneously and independently in 1938.[10] The debt to Freud's theory of ego, super ego and id is both obvious and acknowledged.[11] A debt to philosophical ontology, although not obvious, is also not unexpected. But an appeal to brain research is perhaps a surprise. Here the emphasis is upon the different psychological functions found in the new brain (cerebrum) and the old brain (brain stem). The theories of stratified levels of personality calls not for development as a steady growth but the superposition of one layer of personality on another.[12] They also hold that psychology occupies a position between the natural and social sciences and is by no means exclusively confined to experimental methods.

One Swiss psychologist must be mentioned. Influenced both by Freud and Jung, Hermann Rorschach[13] (1884–1922) carried out many clinical studies with his ink-blots between 1911 and 1921. Although for years similar material had been used in the study of imagination, Rorschach's contribution was to conceive of these blots as a means of studying personality by the analysis of the projections made to them.

French Psychology

The University of Paris with which are affiliated in intricate ways the Sorbonne, the College of France and the Ecole Pratique des Hautes Etudes, has dominated psychology in France to an extent almost inconceivable in the United States with its ten or so universities of at least roughly the same degree of excellence.

The dominant figure in French psychology from 1910, when he succeeded Binet as head of the psychology laboratory at the Sorbonne and assumed the editorship of *L'Année Psychologique*, to his death a few short years ago, was Henri Piéron (1881–1964). He had been trained in philosophy and in physiology, but was explicit that it was work in physiology that had the greater influence.[14]

Some years before Watson's pronouncements on the matter, he had insisted that behavior or conduct is the only proper subject of psychological investigation with which he would combine a physiological substratum. This did not mean he would have abandoned psychology and become a physiologist. Both the total reaction of the organism (psychology) and the partial reactions of the organism (physiology) are essential. His books exercised considerable influence.[15] One on the senses, with emphasis upon sense physiology, is a standard reference. Other aspects of his work are referred to later.

In certain respects Albert Michotte[16] (1881–1965) of Louvain, where he taught from 1905 to 1956, was to Belgian what Piéron was to French psychology. Of almost identical ages both in birth and death, they both published over a span of sixty years and both dominated psychology in their respective countries. However, in their research interests and their attitude toward psychological problems they parted company.

Michotte had worked a half year under Wundt at Leipzig and another half year with Külpe at Würzburg, while teaching experimental psychology at Louvain the other half years. His Würzburg experience led to his being occupied for the period before the First World War in problems of volition, using Külpe's approach of systematic experimental introspection. However, the evidence amassed during this period by Wundt, Titchener and others on the inadequacy of the method led him to abandon this approach. After the War, he turned to problems of perception of movement and rhythm with introspective reports, if used, being limited to reports of the presence or absence of the phenomena in question.

It was his studies of the perception of causality which were instituted by his interest in Gestalt principles that attracted greatest international interest. Michotte took up the Humean problem of the conditions which prompt us to believe a sequence of events is causally connected. The action used was simple but effective—one thing seems to hit another and thereby "cause" it to move. A rotating disc behind a slit, with appropriately painted stripes, allowed systematic variation of time, position and velocity. Phenomenological overtones to his work are apparent in that he conceived his work as showing that the fundamental structures of the phenomenal world are linked with identifiable conditions of stimulation. "Causality," "reality" and "permanence" (i.e., of the world), he contended, are at least preshadowed at the level of perception. These studies culminated in a book first published in French in 1946 and now available in English.[17]

Swiss-French psychology had been initiated by Theodore Flournoy (1854–1920) who had studied with Wundt.[18] In 1893, he opened a laboratory at Geneva, the first to be attached to a faculty of science. One of his students was his cousin, Edouard Claparède[19] (1873–1940). In 1901 they founded the *Archives de Psychologie.* Claparède established in 1912 the Jean Jacques Rousseau Institute for the study of the school child and a little later was given a professorship at Geneva.

The greatest of all Swiss psychologists, Jean Piaget,[20] became interested in natural history while still very young (his first paper was published in a local scientific journal when he was ten years of age). Work with mollusks and their classification, the maintenance of copious notebooks, study of philosophy and science, a religious crisis, the publication of a novel and a doctorate in science followed all before he was twenty-three. In 1918, he left for Germany to study psychology and psychiatry. During the next two years he studied at the Sorbonne and, on becoming acquainted with Simon, Binet's collaborator, he worked in his laboratory school ostensibly on the standardization of Burt's tests for reasoning, but actually exploring the reasons for each particular child's failures and exposing children to verbal tasks involving concrete relations of cause and effect. Submission of a psychological article (his third) to Claparède for publication in the *Archives* resulted in a call to be the Director of Studies at the Institute, Jean Jacques Rousseau. So in 1921, he moved to Geneva where he has continued to work to this very day. At present he is Professor of Psychology, Director of the Psychological Section of the Institute of Education and Director of the Center for Genetic Epistemology, and Editor of the *Archives de Psychologie.*

Author of perhaps 30 books and a proportionate number of monographs and articles (to say nothing about the hundreds of studies his contentions have stirred in others) his enormous productivity defies adequate summary or even citation in short compass. To complicate matters still further, Piaget writes as if each new book was read only by those who had faithfully read and digested his previous works.

The first of two broad phases to his work centered on the development of the cognitive abilities of the child. (For the second phase, see page 578.) He followed the conversational method first used in Simon's school, proceeding in a clinical-genetic fashion that would liberate the child's thinking so that he could show not what he does, but what he could do if given the opportunity. The mass of information he has revealed about cognitive development of how the child forms concepts of space, time, number, reasoning, and causality was extremely revealing of the mental processes of the child. His blithe, seemingly almost unpremediated excursions into the child's intellectual development do show an overall plan, that of studying the stages by which a particular form of cognitive process is individuated from experience, how it changes with further experience, and yet how it is still related to previous stages.

PSYCHOLOGY IN GREAT BRITAIN[21]

As we have seen from Chapter 14, experimental psychology was slow in being established in British universities. During the earlier part of the period now under discussion, laboratories and laboratory work were at their beginning while chairs (*i.e.*, professorships) in psychology, so important as sources of academic power, were yet to be established. That at Manchester in 1919 was the first of these, with a living psychologist, Tom H. Pear, the first incumbent. Charles Spearman held the Grote Chair of Mind and Logic at University College, London, until 1928; only then was the title changed to Psychology. Cambridge had its first chair in 1931, while Oxford was to wait until 1946. The British Psychological Society,[22] founded in 1901, still had less than 100 members in 1918 (although in part this was due to very restrictive requirements for membership). At the outbreak of the Second World War, the total lecturing staff in psychology at British universities numbered about thirty.[23] As a consequence, work by physiologists and statisticians loomed large in these years. Names, such as Hughlings-Jackson (see page 314), Sherrington, Head, and Spearman come to mind as representative of the period and of these only Spearman was a psychologist. This is reflected in the account to follow.

The long lifetime of Sir Charles Sherrington (1857–1952),[24] Nobel prize laureate, covered much of the period that saw the emergence of modern psychology. As Professor of Physiology, first at Liverpool (1895–1913) and then at Oxford (1913–1935), he not only carried on distinguished work in neurophysiology, but he also lent his prestige and facilities to the developing field of psychology. He did much to establish the bases of our knowledge of neural functioning. His major work, *The Integrative Action of the Nervous System*,[25] first appeared in 1906 and was reprinted in 1947. In it the reflex was examined, not as it functions in isolation, but as the unit of functional integration in which the reflex came under control of higher levels of neural action. His task was to work out the mechanisms involved in this integration. The discovery of reciprocal innervation led to his working out many of the details of excitation and inhibition, particularly showing that the latter, too, is an activity. In his Liverpool Laboratory, psychologists served as research men and lecturers as did Robert S. Woodworth and Cyril Burt.

Henry Head (1861–1940), a disciple of Hughlings-Jackson and Sherrington's friend and contemporary, clarified for sensation what the latter had done for reflex action. Moreover, he, too, worked directly with psychologists—not only with W. H. R. Rivers, mentioned in a moment, but, years later, F. C. Bartlett. (See page 526.) In 1905 and 1908 Head,[26] with W. H. R. Rivers (1864–1922), ethnologist and early teacher of experimental psychology at Cambridge, published research on cutaneous sensibility of injured nerves and found that a dissolution, in Jackson's meaning of the term, occurred. This was done by Head cutting nerves in his arm and studying the loss and return of sensibility. On the basis of these and other observations,[27] he postulated three levels of sensibility—"deep" sensibility, responsive to pressure and movement, "proto-pathic" sensibility, responsive to extremes of heat and cold and pain, and "epicritic" sensibility, accurate and discriminating for all forms of cutaneous stimulation. These levels of sensibility were considered as supporting the Jacksonian doctrine of evolutionary levels.

His other major research concerned speech disorders and culminated in *Aphasia and Kindred Disorders of Speech*[28] which appeared in 1926. One facet of the work was his concept of vigilance[29] used to account for that level of efficient alertness which maintains automatic actions under control. Lowered vigilance occurred when neural disorders or debilitating disease caused loss of this controlling function. For example, a sick child loses vigilance when he wets the bed, heretofore prevented because of control by a spinal reflex. Not developed by him in detail, this concept stimulated later research pro and con.

With the passing of Sherrington and Head this tradition of physiological work intertwined with psychological aspects did not cease. It has been continued by Edgar G. Adrian who worked on the refractory period of the nerve fiber and more generally, as the title of one of his major works indicates, on *The Mechanism of Nervous Action.*[30] He took advantage of the availability of vacuum tubes to amplify the small electrical charges that corresponded to individual nerve impulse passage. It led to his conclusion that no radical differences in the nature of the nerve impulses existed from either different kinds of sense organs or from different parts of the brain.

After a considerable period of reading and reflection while in the military service, Charles E. Spearman (1863–1945) at the age of 36 decided that the field he wished to pursue was psychology.[31] So at the beginning of this century he turned to Leipzig and a degree with Wundt, Krueger, and Wirth. Although he admired Wundt as a person, he did not have the same feeling toward his work which he characterized as being too centered in sensation. The several years that followed his degree he spent in more or less casual but intensive post-doctoral work with Külpe, Müller and with physiologists. In 1907, he accepted appointment at the University College, London and in 1911 was made professor, a position he held until 1931.

He saw his major task as no less than finding the fundamental laws of psychology.[32] While familiar with the doctrine of association and its claim to establishing such laws, but he was not happy with their formulation. He believed what the associationist had ignored was the mental power of knowing relations and generating items of knowledge not known before. Old relations in new situations, he believed, are capable of generalizing new plans of behavior. In point of time, this theory came after some earlier work he had done in statistics for which it supplied the theoretical substratum. Inspired in part by Galton's work, in 1904 he published two seminal papers.[33] In the first of these, he provided a necessary safe guard for the correlational analysis of mental traits by showing the need for taking into account and making allowance for the degree of reliability of the measurements. This was a precaution heretofore unappreciated. In the second paper, he stated his conclusion based on statistical study of intercorrelations of test scores of a heterogenous group of school children that all intellectual tasks partake of a single capacity, general intelligence, or "G," plus whatever capacities are specific to each of the tests involved. This was the famous two factor theory of intelligence which was to be the center of vigorous study, pro and con, for many years to come.

Central to his factor theory was what he termed the hierarchy of the specific intelligences, i.e., a systematic inter-relation of the correlation coefficients "such as to allow the table of correlations to be arranged with the highest values in one corner and with the other values regularly decreasing in both horizontal and vertical directions." [34]

The Abilities of Man,[35] published in 1927, contains the most comprehensive account of the work he and his associates had done, along with a vigorous criticism of what he called "rival doctrines." After demonstrating to his satisfaction that G and s exist, he proceeds to relate them to response speed, attention, perseveration, conation, and the like. It was on the basis of its scope, as he saw it, which led him to write for the *Psychologies of 1930,*[36] an article in which G is offered as a school to end schools, since he claimed application of the general theory of two factors isolate the factors, while use of the sub-theories explains them. In England the history of factor analysis can be told in terms of the reaction of others to his proposals and findings.

While serving as Wilde Reader in Mental Philosophy at Oxford, William Brown (1881–1952) took the position that, although Spearman had made an epoch-making advance in his studies of factor analysis, he nevertheless must disagree with his interpretation of the significance of the hierarchical order in matrices of correlation coefficients. When Brown turned more and more to his interest in abnormal psychology and psychiatry, he was joined in this critique by Godfrey H. Thomson (1881–1955) who collaborated with him in the second and third editions of *The Essentials of Mental Measurement.*[37] The gist of their argument was that the hierarchical order could be produced by random overlap of group factors without any general factor being present. Thomson, located at Edinburgh University from 1925 on, continued this effort in a very successful general and remarkably non-partison statement of factor analysis, *The Factorial Analysis of Human Ability.*[38] He also concerned himself with the development of tests of intelligence and evaluation of the educational significance of intelligence[39] and a general furtherance of educational psychology.

For many years Charles S. Myers (1873–1946)[40] was associated with Cambridge University where, against considerable opposition, he advanced the cause of experimental psychology. An atmosphere of extreme conservatism and opposition to psychology still existed. Although a Lecturer and Director of the Psychological Laboratory, which had been founded and first directed by W. H. R. Rivers in 1897, Myers did not achieve a professorship. His laboratory did help to train many of the next generation of leading British psychologists (*e.g.*, F. C. Bartlett and C. Burt).

Myer's experiences in the First World War turned his interests toward industrial psychology and in 1922 he transferred to London to direct the National Institute of Industrial Psychology.[41] He also very ably served in reshaping the policies of the British Psychological Society so as to give recognition to practitioners in psychology, thus considerably increasing membership. Not the least of his services was to provide a textbook of experimental psychology[42] on which two decades of British psychologists were trained (with later editions co-authored by F. C. Bartlett).

Beginning in 1931, and for many years thereafter, the chair of psychology at Cambridge University was held by Sir Frederic C. Bartlett.[43] Directing as he did one of the very few British advanced graduate programs, Bartlett exercised tremendous administrative and educational influence. For about a quarter century he edited the *British Journal of Psychology*. In his laboratory were trained many of the present holders of chairs in British universities.

As for personal research, a major study, *Remembering*, significantly bore the sub-title—*A study in experimental and social psychology*.[44] He tells us that early in his career he became dissatisfied with the use of nonsense syllables on various grounds—that these stimuli are still meaningful, that their use creates an artificial situation, and that on the response side their use ignores the influence of subjective attitude toward the material. Consequently, for his research, material from every-day life was used. Following up on some of Head's physiological theorizing concerning postural change, Bartlett and some of his students after him insisted that past experiences were not replicated. Instead they give rise to a personal schema, a model of ourselves, which constantly changes, but with which we meet subsequent experiences.[45]

Bartlett had been a student of W. H. R. Rivers and C. S. Myers and shows their influence in his social and experimental work. More than once,[46] he comments on the difficulty of pinning down what Cambridge, or his own psychology, is precisely. One element certainly is the combination of social and experimental psychology. Moreover, it is neither statistical nor extremely objective, methodologically speaking, while still appreciative of the physiological bases of psychological study.

In view of Bartlett's importance in shaping the thinking of British psychology (other than in the statistical area), it might be well to pause and examine the other major intellectual influences at work. James Ward (see page 317) had died as recently as 1925, and his evolutionary views and his conception of mind as active was still part of the thinking of most British psychologists. Another potent influence was William McDougall. Long after his departure for the United States in 1920, he influenced British psychology, particularly through his *Social Psychology*, reprinted twenty-four times between its first appearance in 1908 and McDougall's death in 1938.[47] Both "instinct" and "sentiment" were concepts much used by British psychologists. Psychology, as the science of mental life, was still an entirely acceptable definition. The existence of a conscious self was accepted as central by all psychologists. Cognition and will were still favorable subjects of research.

The successor to Spearman at University College, London, Sir Cyril Burt,[48] came to the post with the most varied background of interests and experience of any British psychologist since Galton, himself. He had been a student of McDougall's at Oxford who, knowing of his interest in the work of the then still living Galton, encouraged him in standardizing tests. A period at Würzburg, and at Liverpool with Sherrington when he taught medical students and continued research on tests, followed. His experiences in the next twenty years in one way or another involved work with mental tests and statistical procedures as a clinical psychologist, in the first official British child guidance clinic, in governmental agencies during World War I, the National Institute of Industrial Psychology, the Industrial Health Research Board, the London School of Hygiene, the London Day Training College (a teacher's college) and for the London County Council. In 1931, he was appointed to the chair at the University College, a post he held for 20 years. His research was similarily varied, but true to the statistical tradition his most important work was *The Factors of the Mind*[49] published in 1941. He took the position that all factor methods are either approximations to or linear transformations of the same set of theoretical values. Consequently, reconciliation among the methods is possible. In considerable measure this represents the present position.

James Drever, Sr. (1873–1950) for many years represented Scottish (as differentiated from British) psychology.[50] Trained at Edinburgh (and later at London) he represented psychology at the only one of four Scottish universities at which psychology was then on equal footing with the other arts subjects.

Financial circumstances had required him to spend many years teaching school. This, coupled with the pioneering reforms in Scottish education, including the requirement that all teachers receive training in psychology (this innovation was as early as 1905), brought him an appointment in education, and, in a few years, a laboratory in educational psychology. His interests, however, were considerably broader than this might seem to imply since he did much work in general psychology, such as that he carried out on instinct.[51] After World War I, he transferred to the Psychology Department and in 1931, was made professor of psychology, the third such chair in the British Isles. While continuing his other interests, he added those of juvenile delinquency and the psychology of the deaf.[52] In 1944 he was succeeded in the chair by his son, James Drever, Jr.

It was not until 1946, just beyond the period under consideration, that a chair in psychology was established at Oxford. The first holder, an Oxford man, George Humphrey (1889–1966)[53] and a Canadian, with teaching experience there and in the United States, did what he could to fight the good fight. On reaching Emeritus status, however, he retired to Cambridge. His *Nature of Learning* was written during his Canadian period, but his *Thinking: An Introduction to its Experimental Psychology,* was begun in Britain (in 1934) and finished on his return.[54]

RUSSIAN AND SOVIET PSYCHOLOGY

Russian psychology, too, had its Wundtian, G. I. Chelpanov (1862–1936), who had not only received his training at Leipzig but also later visited American and German laboratories. He served as director of the Psychological Institute of Moscow which was founded in 1911 and he founded the first Russian psychological journal.

An assistant to Chelpanov, Konstantin N. Kornilov (1879–1957) remained on at Moscow University weathering several changes in the ideological climate. In the twenties, he developed a psychology in line with dialectical materialism which he called reactology.[55] Following Marx, social existence determines consciousness. Psychic life cannot be reduced to simple mechanistic motion. Hence, reactology was not confined to mere behavior, it centered on the subjective content of reactions. This view, dominant for a time, had a rapid demise. In the early thirties, the communist cell of Moscow University reached the conclusion that reactology was too passive for the activism of Lenin, Marx, and Engels. Although reactology disappeared with hardly a trace, Kornilov did not. He returned to educational psychology and shifted his locus to the Institute of Pedagogy. As early as 1934,[56] he published a textbook for teacher's colleges and over the years in collaboration with others, he wrote a series of textbooks and continued as a senior Soviet psychologist until his death in 1957.

Research on conflict or disorganization of human behavior was carried out during the twenties by A. R. Luria, using hand movements and associative responses into which conflict situations were interjected as, when under hypnosis, the subject was instructed to think of some indecent word as the response. This work was translated into English in the early thirties[57] and established its author as the senior Soviet psychologist in American eyes.

Another psychologist who became rather well-known at the same time was L. S. Vygotsky (1896–1934), who published in the United States an article about his test of concept formation in 1934, the year of his death.[58] His more general and theoretical statement concerning the relation of thought and language in intellectual development was posthumously published. Many years later it was translated into English.[59]

During this period the Pavlovian tradition as a field of physiology was still very active, expressed, for example, in the work of Konstantin M. Bykov (1886–1959).[60] Psychologists, however, were not involved in this research since it was considered to be the province of physiologists.

In the thirties, political pressures were very strong as exemplified in criticisms by Luria[61] of western or bourgeois psychology as primitively biological or idealistically oriented. It was in 1936 that a decree of the Central Committee condemned mental testing[62] and it largely disappeared. In the early forties military efforts were paramount.

PSYCHOLOGY IN JAPAN[63]

Psychology was introduced in Japan in the last decade of the previous and the first decades of this century by Yujiro Matora (1858–1912) and Matataro Matsumoto (1865–1943). Matora, primarily a theoretician and the first professor of psychology at Tokyo University, was succeeded in that post in 1913 by Matsumoto who in the course of his long life trained practically all the senior psychologists of Japan. In these early years, the influence of Wundt and Titchener was strong. However, applied work of an experimental sort was also introduced by Matsumoto. From the twenties through the forties Gestalt psychology, German characterology and, to a lesser extent, American influences were at work. By 1935, there were several journals and at the fifth meeting of the Japanese Psychological Association that year an attendance of 126 persons. There was interruption of the growth from about that time through the end of World War II.

PSYCHOLOGY IN THE UNITED STATES

Some of the earlier national accounts stressed the dominance of a particular department of psychology and even a particular member of that department. The much greater number both of psychologists and of departments, the lack within a department of a rigid hierarchical organization with the other psychologists not subordinate to the "professor," the presence of several professors in a department, all worked against these kinds of personal and departmental dominance being prominent features of the American scene. In the account to follow, that approach gives way in the main to that of examining crucial research areas and some of the men concerned with them.

Psychology in the United States has already been examined against the background of the development of the schools—functional, Gestalt, behaviorist, and the rest. But during these same years there were other psychologists whose research removed them to some extent from the clamor of tongues. For this was the period of Boring and his major historical publication, of Lashley and his studies of the role of the brain in learning, of Thurstone and his factor analytic approach to psychometrics, and only a little later, of Allport and his studies and reflections about personality, of Lewin and his field theory approach to social psychology, of Murphy and his pioneer systematizations of social psychology, and of Murray and his integration of many intellectual currents into an approach to personality. There were also research programs that did have relationship to behaviorism. For it was in the thirties and forties that Hull and Guthrie carried out many of their studies in learning. But it is the research in learning, and not the behavioristic nuances, that is more important. Only one man will be discussed in a setting of the larger theoretical currents, the characteristically mellow, "later" behavioristic approach of Tolman. Toward the end of this period, operationism and related concepts came to be accepted by many psychologists as an orientating attitude in planning and conducting research in which Tolman and others had a part.

Order of presentation of areas of research has been guided by chronological considerations with events reaching farther back into the past, resulting in earlier discussion of a particular area.

Clinical Psychology[64]

Clinical psychology, as we know it in the United States, had its proximal beginnings even before the present century.

Lightner Witmer (1867–1956), trained at Leipzig, must be mentioned, not for his research but for an event—in 1896 he founded at the University of Pennsylvania the first psychological clinic. Its very presence did much to make the clinical method, an expression he coined, an authentic approach for the coming generations of psychologists who would use diagnostic and therapeutic approaches with clients or patients.[65] However, the clinic that Witmer organized more closely resembled what later came to be called psycho-educational clinics than it does the modern child guidance clinic.

This was the innovation of William Healy[66] (1869–1963) who headed the first child guidance clinic organized in 1909 in Chicago at what is now known as the Institute for Juvenile Research. From the very beginning two members of the team, Healy as psychiatrist and Grace M. Fernald as psychologist (shortly to be replaced by Augusta Bronner who subsequently became his wife) functioned together. Psychiatric social work service, originally carried on by part-time workers from cooperating agencies, was replaced in a few years by a full-time social worker, completing the essential child guidance team. Originally a center for the treatment of delinquent children, the recognition that nondelinquent but emotionally disturbed children could be treated by the same means, led this and other clinics that were soon established to broaden their acceptance policies to include these children. After a few years, Healy and Bronner left Chicago for Boston and the Judge Baker Clinic where they carried on their extensive definitive research on delinquency.[67]

A pioneer account of clinic practice made its appearance a few years later. Its author was Frederic Lyman Wells[68] (1884–1964), a student of Woodworth at Columbia, who served as clinical psychologist, first at McLean Hospital in Waverly, Massachusetts, and then at the Boston Psychopathic Hospital. Active as he was in affairs of the American Psychological Association from about 1911 onward, it was his book of 1927, *Mental Tests in Clinical Practice*,[69] which became prophetic of modern practice in clinical psychology. His scornful picture of the rigid psychometrician performing his rites in an identical fashion, case after case, in order to propitiate the savage gods, and his plea for flexible use of tests, not to yield scores as it did for the "mental testers," but in order to understand a person, reflects these attitudes admirably.

The next major development took place some years later. Although there had been a few lonely pioneer psychologist-psychotherapists and remedial workers, it was Carl R. Rogers[70] who made psychotherapy an authentic field of psychological practice and research by his demonstration that a psychologist would make original contributions to both phases. In 1942, when *Counseling and Psychotherapy*[71] appeared, he was a professor at Ohio State. Previously he had received his graduate training at Teacher's College, Columbia and had spent 12 years in Rochester, New York, in child guidance clinic activities.

Although the practice phase, the non-directive or client-centered approaches to psychotherapy itself was very significant, it can be argued that even more important was his demonstration that the clinical impressions of the transcribed psychotherapeutic hours could be quantified and significant research performed.

Physiological Psychology

Both a considerable advance and a severe set-back for physiological psychology came from the same series of researches by one man, Karl S. Lashley.

The way for the work of Lashley was prepared by Shepard Ivory Franz (1874–1933).[72] About 1900, Franz had originated the combination of the method of the study of animal learning with that of surgical extirpation of brain tissue which he used in a series of studies. Typical was the study published in 1915[73] in which he attacked that most firmly established of all "facts" of localization, Fritsch and Hitzig's localization of motor functions. (See page 246.) His results showed that there was a considerable lack of precision to cerebral localization. His findings, however, were hardly seen as more than negative; no more general significance was attached to them.

Research performed by Karl S. Lashley[74] (1890–1958) first with Franz at St. Elizabeth's Hospital, then at the University of Minnesota, and then under the auspices of the Behavior Research Fund in Chicago, led to an appointment at the University of Chicago, and in 1935 to a call to Harvard directly at President Conant's behest, who was seeking, the story has it, "the greatest psychologist in the world."

What was this research that brought on this rapid academic rise, to say nothing of the presidency of the APA and membership in the National Academy of Science, before he was forty years of age? It concerned the problem of the effect of differential extirpation of the rat's cerebral cortex upon intelligence (learning ability). To appreciate the significance of this rather pedestrian-sounding problem, it is necessary to refer to the then current neurophysiological interpretation of learning. At that time learning was seen as a matter of isolated neurones and synaptic resistances forming reflex paths with detailed localization of function occurring in the cerebral cortex. The accepted rough model of the brain's function was that of the electrical switchboard. Begun about 1920, Lashley's research culminated in his 1929 publication, *Brain Mechanisms and Intelligence.*[75] In it he reported overwhelming evidence for much less localization of function in the cortex than had heretofore been accepted and further demonstrated that large lesions effect learning more than small lesions. For these results, he supplied a conceptual framework, involving "equipotentiality" and "mass action." Evidence for modes of organization, rather than for isolated single specific pathways and reactions had been found.

A wide-spread misconception of the significance of his results came about partly at least due to Lashley's manner of presenting his results. He was interpreted as saying that what happens in the nervous system is guided by mass action, that when any area of the cortex is removed another area can carry out its functions. What, under this interpretation, is left for physiological psychology to do? Based on a general acquaintance with his findings, an anti- or a-physiological trend set in, and psychologists lost interest in physiological research and even came to see the nervous system as irrelevant to psychology. "Behavior theorists," to use a loose but sufficiently apt term, could trace part of their scepticism concerning physiology directly back to Lashley's work. I say "part" because, after all, they did make tremendous progress in their studies of behavior with a DNS (disregarded nervous system).

This loose interpretation ignored what a more careful examination of his results show. He did not deny localization in the summary fashion attributed to him. What he was saying was that localization was both less precise and different from what previously had been conceived—and considerably more complicated. In some cases equipotentiality held, in others, it did not; mass action was not always a factor. Mass action and equipotentiality are most evident in complex problems, less so in simple ones, which leaves plenty of scope for physiological research thereafter.

History of Psychology

Edwin G. Boring[76] for many years Professor of Psychology, Director of the Psychological Laboratory and Chairman of the Department at Harvard University, was perhaps the last psychologist who could make his area of research that of experimental psychology in the inclusive meaning of the term. Between 1912 and 1929 he published research on audition, animal behavior, dementia praecox, educational psychology, organ and alimentary sensations, thermal sensitivity, the psychology of testimony, cutaneous sensations, psychophysics, vision, drive sleep, psychometrics, statistics, psychological examining, intelligence, facial expression, psychic research, the psychology of science, olfaction, and memory. It is no wonder than that this widest of backgrounds of any psychologist in the United States prepared him to write the definitive A History of Experimental Psychology,[77] which first appeared in 1929 to be revised in 1950.

As practically every psychologist knows, he had taken his graduate work at Cornell with Titchener. His Ph.D. in 1914 was followed by a few more years at Cornell, a move to Clark University for three years and then an appointment at Harvard in 1922. Forty-six years later, he still maintains an office in William James Hall. In short compass it is impossible to do justice to the depth and erudition of his *History* which maintains the position of dominance to this very day. One comment will have to suffice, it is to this volume that German psychologists turn for the history of their own heritage.

Applied Psychology

Applied psychology in sporadic practice and in primitive theorization had existed for some time and the beginnings for various facets could be traced to events before this period. A just claim for inclusion of many psychologists could be made but attention will be focused on the work of but two of its pioneers—Walter Bingham and E. K. Strong, Jr.

After graduate training in psychology at Chicago and teaching for some years at Dartmouth, Walter Van Dyke Bingham[78] (1880–1952) was invited to accept directorship of the program at the Carnegie Institute of Technology and for the period between 1915 and 1924 he was Professor of Psychology and Director of the Division of Applied Psychology. Shortly afterward, L. L. Thurstone joined him and, on a temporary basis, Walter Dill Scott, and still later E. K. Strong, Jr.

For this decade, there is no question that the staff of the Carnegie Institute, either locally in work involving research in the analysis of occupational interests, in selection of salesmen, educational admission, and curricular problems, or during World War I, in Washington and elsewhere, carrying out personnel selection procedures for the Army, was the center for research in these areas of applied psychology. As a result of an administrative reorganization in 1924 this venture came to an end, and Bingham went on to various posts with an industrial personnel research organization, with the Psychological Corporation, with industrial consulting practice, and when World War II was iminent, a return to governmental service. Bingham's most durable publications have been those devoted to interviewing and aptitude testing.[79]

E. K. Strong, Jr.[80] (1884–1963) of Stanford University who had studied with Cattell and Thorndike at Columbia, and as just mentioned, had been a faculty member at Carnegie Institute of Technology, first published the Strong Vocational Interest Blank in 1927. It has been a tool of research and practice ever since with Strong, himself, as the tireless and, by far, the most prolific investigator.[81] Although he retired in 1949, he continued working with the inventory to the year before his death. Scales were added at various times, a revision was made in 1938 and still another (of the Men's Form) in 1966. It continues to be the most used measure in its area of applicability.

Social Psychology

Prior to this period social psychology had consisted of a man retiring to his study to spin out a system for which empirical illustrations were then selected. A few modern textbooks depending upon the instinct concept, such as McDougall's, which enjoyed the popularity in England mentioned earlier, had appeared, but they still merited the description just given.

A pioneer student of social psychology is Floyd H. Allport, a Harvard Ph.D., then at the University of North Carolina, and later at Syracuse University for many years, who was the first to try to introduce systematically the "behavior" viewpoint into the field as he substituted prepotent reactions for instincts. Guided by whatever research evidence was available, his book, *Social Psychology*,[82] published in 1924, did much to bring systematic order and, considering the relative lack of research evidence, did much to set out many of the divisions of the field acceptable today. Above all, he established the position that social psychology is concerned with the behavior of the *individual* in various social settings.

Gardner Murphy's graduate training was received at Harvard and at Columbia where he took his Ph.D. in 1923.[83] He was associated with Columbia until 1940, when he moved to the College of the City of New York. Although he published in the history of psychology,[84] it was his work in social psychology that marked his Columbia days.[85] His already-formed decision to make it his specialization, his teaching responsibilities, and his share in the overall graduate program at Columbia directed him toward this area. He came to the field with an already firmly established eclecticism which included the conviction that findings from both the biological and the social sciences were important to social psychology, and writing, as he did, when the social psychological experimental literature had grown enormously since Allport had been writing a few short years before. It became a challenge to him to utilize in some comprehensive fashion both the social and biological research literature. This resulted in his definitive *Experimental Social Psychology* of 1931, revised in 1937[86] with the collaboration of not only his wife, who had participated in the original venture, but also Theodore M. Newcomb. Personality development, which Murphy is convinced is an integral aspect of social psychology, became increasingly of concern, but belongs in the period after 1945.

Otto Klineberg, for many years at Columbia University, after taking his degree there, and now at the University of Paris, published in 1935 his *Negro Intelligence and Selective Migration.*[87] This research study set the pattern for the modern conception of the influence of the environment upon intellectual prowess. Although only one among a rapidly increasing number of studies, it was carried out by Klineberg with such care as still to be timely and pertinent.

Kurt Lewin (1890–1947) did graduate work at Berlin and his thinking bears definite relation to that school of Gestalt psychology. However, his later views, especially those formulated after he arrived in the United States in 1932, are sufficiently distinctive to merit separate discussion. While teaching at the State University of Iowa and then as Director of the Research Center for Group Dynamics at the Massachusetts Institute of Technology, he established what has come to be known as field theory. His point of view is most conveniently summarized in the posthumously published collection of his writings, *Field Theory in Social Science,*[88] edited by Dorwin Cartwright. What is field theory? He characterized it as "a method of analysing causal relations and of building scientific constructs."[89] The psychological field is always contemporaneous. If past experiences are still effective, they are part of that field. The psychological task, then, was to identify the general variables that determine behavior at a given moment of time. In the life space (the psychological, as differentiated from the physical environment) of the individual the various psychological phenomena are interdependent. In the view of a considerable number of social psychologists, Lewin made a conceptually illuminating success of applying his method and these concepts to such problems as "intention," "frustration," "regression," "resistance," and "conflict." The very nature of the problems listed also serves to emphasize that field theory extends beyond the boundaries of social psychology.

Child Psychology

Child psychology was going through a period in which there was much industrious and careful fact gathering by a multitude of men. It is fitting to discuss the most industrious of all, Arnold Gesell.

Trained in psychology at Clark University and in medicine, Arnold Gesell[90] (1880–1961) after a somewhat late start settled down to a remarkably rapid tempo of research on child growth and development. Author of 15 or more books on the subject, it is difficult to make a selection. They differ little in method, which was meticulously described child behavior with extensive but not exclusive dependence in cinema-analysis. Study in a controlled environment with precise stimulus conditions was also characteristic. The studies, then, differed primarily in the particular form of behavior under scrutiny, or in the age range under consideration. Perhaps his *Atlas of Infant Behavior*,[91] published in 1934, will serve, since it contains a truly stupendous amount of data. However, his *Child Development*,[92] a reprinting of two of his books, originally published in the forties, serves better as an introduction.

Factor Analysis

To a considerable extent factor analytic research in the United States was derived from the earlier work that had taken place in Great Britain. In this area of research at least one man in the United States reached the stature of Spearman, Thomson, and Burt. This was L. L. Thurstone.

L. L. Thurstone[93] had taken a degree in electrical engineering at Cornell, had worked as an assistant to Thomas Edison and had taught engineering, before he turned to graduate work in psychology in 1914, studying both at Chicago and the Carnegie Institute of Technology. He had done so, he tells us, so as to pursue an interest he had developed in studying learning as a scientific problem. However, somewhere along the line his interest shifted to factor analysis and psychometrics.

After teaching seven years at Carnegie Institute of Technology and carrying out some research in Washington, he returned to the University of Chicago where his interests in factor analysis came to the fore. Instead of repeating Spearman's question about the presence and absence of a general factor, he asked how many factors must be postulated in order to account for a matrix of correlations. Consequently he saw no reason to call one factor more general than another. In this setting the G of Spearman came to be seen as a "second order" factor emerging in correlational study only after the first order multiple-factors. It was the multiple-factors he obtained, not G, which he considered in order to account for the obtained correlations. By and large, however, his results are not so much considered in opposition to those of Spearman as they are an extension of his work. His principle publication was the *Vectors of Mind*,[94] published in 1935. As he continued to work with his approach, it became more and more complex and the data he had collected more and more extensive. As a consequence, the earlier book was rewritten in more extended form to appear in 1947 with a new title, *Multiple-Factor Analysis*.[95]

Personality

Personality was and is an amorphous field, to which it is hard to set boundaries or even to say precisely what it includes. But in the thirties great strides were made toward bringing order and clarity in the field in the attempt at integration of its various widely scattered aspects by Gordon W. Allport and a program of research in depth by Henry A. Murray.

Gordon W. Allport[96] (1887–1967) graduated from Harvard in 1919. He had come to college with an already formed conviction that guidance of conduct was, for him, to be what I would describe, drawing upon Roget's *Thesaurus*, as "diffusive sympathetic affections." It is significant in this connection that his first faculty appointment at Harvard in 1924 was an instructor in social ethics and his last before final retirement in 1967 was a professor of social ethics. For the intervening years, except for a short digression to Robert College of Istanbul and to Dartmouth, he was in the Psychology Department at Harvard (and, on its reorganization and split, the Department of Social Relations).

Within psychology, he found that his social interests best related to the question of personality and how it should be studied. With really remarkable consistency he has maintained this focus from his doctoral dissertation on traits of personality in relation to social diagnosis and his first article on the topic of personality and character. "Trait" and "Organization" and "Development" characterize his approach; the individual's characteristics cannot be divorced from the pattern they form as they both show development over time. It was his *Personality: A Psychological Interpretation*,[97] which appeared in 1937, that established the modern concept of personality as an area of thought and investigation. Later works, extending in time beyond 1945, followed the same path. In the finest sense of the term his work has been eclectic. If he has not succeeded in integrating the diverse strands of personality, it has not been for lack of devotion to the task or of ability, but because the field is not yet ready for it.

Henry A. Murray,[98] Director of the Psychological Clinic and professor at Harvard, arrived at his faculty appointment at Harvard in 1926 by a series of idiosyncratic intellectual experiences which perhaps ideally fitted him for the work he has carried on. After graduating from Harvard in 1915, with one and a half lectures (by Professor Munsterberg), thus completing his formal training in psychology, there followed medical school, a surgical internship, years of biochemical research, a short but important relationship with Jung, and then the Harvard appointment.

He has always worn his theories personally, a point recognized in his own categorization in the *History of Psychology in Autobiography* in which the first two references mentioned are labeled "Autobiographical and Theoretical."[99] Although proceeded in point of time by his first publication on *The Thematic Apperception Technique*,[100] his *Explorations in Personality*,[101] published in 1938, recounted the work he and a considerable staff of unusually talented associates (including Erik H. Erikson, Donald W. Mackinnon, Saul Rosenzweig, and Robert W. White) carried out. They used an in-depth approach in a multi-pronged simultaneous attack upon as many aspects of personality as their resources afforded. Harvard undergraduate subjects were assessed by several investigators, each working independently and each using his own particular technique. The data from all sources on a particular individual was interpreted by the one investigator before the assembled group of the investigators who criticized his efforts. Discussion continued until a consensus was obtained. This procedure was used for all forty subjects. These results, in turn, were subjected to a synthetical interpretation which was based not only upon Freud's system but also the contributions of such diverse theorists as Jung, McDougall, Adler, and Lewin. From this came a conceptual system for assessing a personality in terms of his motives (needs) and the environmental forces bearing upon him (press). It was from the results of this study that much of his later work emerged.

Learning

This generation of research workers on learning had to come to terms with the findings of Thorndike (see page 414) on trial and error learning and the law of effect and those of Pavlov (see page 409) on conditioning and the influence of contiguity and reinforcement. It came to be seen that the crucial issue was the essentiality for learning of either reinforcement or contiguity. The work of Clark Hull supported the former, the work of Edwin Guthrie the latter.

It was during his years at Yale University that Clark L. Hull[102] (1884–1952) carried out his collaborative investigations of learning which made reinforcement central. He had received his graduate training at Wisconsin and had taught there before moving to Yale University as a research professor in 1929. At Yale, his weekly research seminar became one of the major training grounds for many of the present generation of eminent men whose work is mentioned in the *Epilogue.* Either in connection with the seminar or through other means, Kenneth W. Spence, Neal Miller, John Dollard, Robert Sears, Ernest Hilgard, and O. H. Mowrer were associated with him.

The basic statement of the theory of behavior proposed by Hull is given in his *Principles of Behavior*[103] published in 1943. It was modified in his *Essential of Behavior*[104] of 1951 and extended in A *Behavior System*[105] of 1952, published the year of his death.

In his autobiography he stated that he:

came to the definite conclusion around 1930 that psychology is a true natural science; that its primary laws are expressible quantitatively by means of a moderate number of ordinary equations; that all the complex behavior of single individuals will ultimately be derivable as secondary laws from (1) these primary laws together with (2) the conditions under which behavior occurs; and that all the behavior of groups as a whole, *i.e.*, strictly social behavior as such, may similarly be derived as quantitative laws from the same primary equations.[106]

To implement these aims of objectivity and quantitativity he developed statements about learning in terms of postulates, corollaries and equations in a hypothetico-deductive framework using carefully defined symbols. A postulate or corollary led to the formulation of empirical predictions for a particular kind of learning situation, such as, multidirectional maze learning.

After two preliminary postulates his third had to do with the key principle of primary reinforcement. To quote:

Whenever an effector activity (R) is closely associated with a stimulus afferent impulse or trace (s) and the conjunction is closely associated with the rapid diminution in the motivational stimulus (S_D or S_G), there will result an increment (Δ) to a tendency for that stimulus to evoke that response.[107]

Another of his postulates, which numbered 17 in all, had to do with habit formation, utilizing the variable of the number of reinforcements. Others concerned primary motivation or drive, stimulus generalization, reaction potential and experimental extinction.

His theoretical formulations lead to many empirically testable propositions and a tremendous amount of research, which it is impossible to summarize here. One or two conclusions may be briefly mentioned.[108] Contiguous repetition does no more than generate inhibition; all improvement in learning depends upon reinforcement and the basic paradigm for reinforcement rests in need reduction, either positive (food) or negative (escape from injury). Reward and punishment have the same primary reinforcing quality.

Edwin R. Guthrie,[109] (1886–1959) from 1914 until retirement in 1946 at the University of Washington, would make learning dependent upon contiguity of stimulus and response. His training at the University of Pennsylvania had been primarily in philosophy and his thesis in symbolic logic. His interest in psychology and behaviorism came from philosophy, especially after hearing E. A. Singer read a paper on minds as an observable object. His early collaboration on an elementary textbook with Stevenson Smith, a behavioristically oriented colleague, served as part of his post doctoral training in psychology.

It is fitting that it was a person trained as a philosopher who kept association doctrine alive; since his basic principle of learning was that of contiguity, restated in conditioning terminology—two events, stimulus and response, temporally contiguous, is the single sufficient condition for learning.

He even insisted that repetition is not necessary. A single, contiguous occurrence is sufficient. To answer the obvious question of why, often it seems to take many trials for learning to occur, he answered by indicating that the same complex of stimuli is not present on each trial. The simplest learning situation is, in reality, so highly complex as to be different in each trial. Hence, each time the response is made, the stimulus situation is slightly, but for his position, crucially different. All that repeated trials do is to bring about an increase in the number of cues which have been conditioned to response. If the stimulus situation had been identical, then one trial would have sufficed.

Motivation, although often present, is not a necessary condition of learning. When present, it is a part of the present stimulus pattern and thus enters into learning. But motivation is but one kind of stimulus condition; its absence does not prevent learning.

His first paper[110] on this topic concerned conditioning as a principle of learning. In it he mapped out much of this theoretical system but without presenting the evidence. Thereafter, he sought evidence and was not at all hesitant to use anecdotal material open to him as had his associationistic forbears before him, and to press into service research by others which seemed to support his position. He never had many students so that very few research studies were conducted under his auspices. In 1935 his book *Psychology of Learning* appeared, which was to be revised in 1952.[111]

Guthrie and Horton's study[112] of cats in a puzzle box will serve as the source for an illustration of the type of evidence marshalled. While they found the expected trial and error behavior, they also observed what they called "stereotypy." This was the strong tendency for cats to repeat the precise movements leading up to and including the escape movement. These routines were repeated by individual cats, each with his own routine, trial after trial. This they interpreted as evidence in favor of contiguity learning. The pattern of escape movements is repeated because it eventually removes the animal from the box, thereby preventing new and contradictory associations from being formed. Variation from the pattern, which appeared as new solutions, could also be interpreted by the contiguity principle. Entering the box from a slightly different direction or angle set up what was essentially a new learning situation which required a new escape response.

Operationism and Positivism

In the United States during these decades the most influential new theoretical orientation was provided by operationism. It was the work of a Harvard physicist, Percy W. Bridgman[113] (1882–1961), published in 1927, which served to trigger this interest and acceptance. In physical study he argued that a concept was the same as the corresponding set of operations by which it was found. An illustration he gave is that of length. What is length? To find out, we perform certain operations and "the concept is synomymous with the corresponding set of operations."[114] Psychology was ready for operationism, so much so, that four years before Bridgman, E. G. Boring,[115] reflecting an already widely held cliché, wrote a paper for a national magazine in which he pointed out that it could be argued that "Intelligence is what intelligence tests test," an operational definition before operationism. The climate of opinion on this and other grounds was such as to be receptive to operationism.

S. S. Stevens[116] in a 1935 paper issued a call to psychologists to adopt "an operational base of psychology" to quote the title of his paper. This was followed in 1939 by a book by Carroll C. Pratt[117] which gave the history of operationism and considered its implications for psychology. About this time, operationism had been seized on avidly and a flood of articles began to appear. Besides the rigor this theory introduced into psychologists' research activities, it provided a graceful retreat from the excesses of the "schools" which by this time were embarrassing psychologists.

Operationism is wider than a behavioristic outlook. It can be and is used in situations where conscious experience was traditionally considered to be involved, as in studies of sensation and perception, and it could even use mentalistic terms, provided they are operationally defined. A research situation is arranged, the observer reports what he sees—the perception is the reaction. The subjective had been translated into the objective because they were now public operations. From the operational reports of one investigation another research worker can go and do likewise, thus verifying or not, as the case may be, that the operations lead to the claimed result. Operationally, consciousness becomes discriminative behavior.

Operationism, itself, had a relation with positivism, more specifically to a particular approach to the philosophy of science, logical empiricism, which at about this time was attracting considerable interest in the United States, with the arrival in the United States of European refugee philosophers of science, especially those who had been associated with the so-called Vienna circle, which included Rudolf Carnap and Herbert Feigl.

It was again S. S. Stevens who first acquainted American psychologists with this particular orientation. He mentioned it in the paper devoted to the operational basis of psychology already referred to, and more explicitly in a paper a year later,[118] where for example, he showed, following Bridgman's lead, that the relativity theory associated with the name of Einstein arose from fundamentally the same problem and reached the same solution—that the observer needs some way to come to terms with the operations which went into the determination of his research findings and that he, Einstein, was dealing with operations and not physical properties.

With acceptance of operationism and to some extent of positivism, psychology's relation with physics was made respectable. There was a relation too with an influential point of view in philosophy of science. From the same perspective, since psychological observations enter into *all* scientific endeavor, due to the scientist's position inevitably being that of an observer, then psychology, as Stevens argued, was propaedeutic to all science. Although the last point was not taken too seriously, all this gave psychology what seemed to be a more assured position in the scientific hierarchy. But more important than the theoreticians' comforting sense of unity with the other sciences and with the philosophy of science, was that it gave the research man a tool.

The concept of the intervening variable appeared at about the same time. Tolman[119] referred briefly to "operational behaviorism" as early as 1936 as representing his view, but did so in a relatively obscure source of publication so it could not have had the effect of Stevens' papers of this same period. The central theme of this paper was that of the functional and mathematical dependencies of "intervening variables" upon the other variables. He then pointed out the necessity of using operational means of specifying these intervening variables. Discussion of intervening variables in his presidential address[120] before the American Psychological Association, published in 1938, gave his position the wider audience that his earlier paper lacked. Thereafter, the concept of intervening variables was integrated with operationism in a way which made the two central to theoretical endeavors of the time.

Later Behaviorism

When viewed from the perspective of the schools, both Hull and Guthrie were "later" behaviorists. This is saying that they were members of the postpioneer generation who, while accepting many of the tenets of behaviorism, concerned themselves much more with a particular research area, in this case learning, rather than engaging in general polemics, in favor of the adoption of a behavioristic outlook upon matters psychological. Since they devoted most of their efforts to the study of learning, their work was discussed in that setting. Moreover, neither was really too enthusiastic about the doctrinaire aspects of behaviorism. Hull, in fact, rather avoided calling himself a behaviorist.

Edward C. Tolman was so versatile that a good case could be made for discussing him in the setting of learning. However, his behaviorism, his molarism and his purposiveness outweigh his contributions to the cognitive theory of learning, that has variously been described as involving sign-Gestalts, sign-significances, or expectancies.[121] His autobiographical statement[122] finds him stressing in his work, not learning, but a formulation of these other concepts. This was done, however, in a fashion much less militant and strident than was the case with the earlier generation of behaviorists.

Edward Chace Tolman (1886–1961) had been a graduate student at Harvard. In the main, his training had been in the Titchenarian vein and his encounter with Watson's *Behavior* in Yerke's course in comparative psychology was both a stimulus and a relief for he had already been troubled about the inadequacies of introspection. He took his degree in 1915, taught briefly at Northwestern, and in 1918 moved to the University of California at Berkeley where he remained. On arrival at Berkeley, his choice of a new course to teach was comparative psychology and he was soon embarked on research in learning in rats. He felt that Watson had over-simplified notions of stimulus and response, and influenced by his exposure to Gestalt (he had spent some time in Giessen with Koffka), he began to develop his particular views of psychology. Since he conceived psychology as dealing with something larger than muscle contractions—with behavior as behavior, as he stated it—it was not surprising that he borrowed from his philosophy teacher at Harvard, R. B. Perry, the notion that purpose and cognition, while essential to understanding behavior, are still essentially descriptive in nature.

With this as some of the background, he published in 1932 his *Purposive Behavior in Animals and Men.*[123] One should say immediately that "purposive" was being used in the descriptive sense already mentioned. In more detail, he saw it as an urge to get to or away from a type of goal object, shown by persistence and the tendency to use the shortest route. By taking this position he was calling attention to such matters as the readily observable fact that if, on reaching the food box, the rat finds no food, he tries other ways of finding it. A series of trials, not a single trial, shows that there is elimination of blind alleys and the adoption finally of the shortest possible route—the animals is learning a route to a goal, the means to an end. "Learning the maze" is, for Tolman, decisive evidence of goal seeking. This definitely was *not* a teleological use for the term. In contrast to molecular behavior which had to do with the underlying physiological activity, Tolman emphasized the molar behavior of men and animals acting in respects to ends.

REFERENCES*

1. F. Krueger, *Über Entwicklungspsychologie, ihre sachliche und geschichtliche Norwendigkeit.* Leipzig: Engelmann, 1915. F. Sander, Structure, Totality of Experience, and Gestalt. In C. Murchison (ed.), *Psychologies of 1930.* Worcester, Mass.: Clark University Press, 1930, pp. 188–204.

2. W. Metzger, *Psychologie: Die Entwicklung ihrer Grundannahmen seit der Einführung des Experiment.* (2. Aufl.) Darmstadt: Steinkopff, 1954.

3. E. Spranger, *Lebensformen.* (8. Aufl.) Tübingen: Niemeyer, 1950, p. 17 (1913) E. Spranger, *Types of Men: the Psychology and Ethics of Personality.* (Translation 5th German ed.) Halle: Niemeyer, 1928, (1913).

4. E. Kretschmer, *Körperbau und Charakter.* (23rd-24th ed.) Berlin: Springer, 1961. (1921)

5. H. J. Eysenck, Cyclothymia and Schizothymia as a Dimension of Personality. (I. Historical review; II. Experimental.) *J. Personal.,* 1950, 19, 123–152; 1952, 20, 345–384.

6. L. Klages, *Handschrift und Charakter.* (24. Aufl.) Bonn: Bouvier, 1956. (1916)

7. Speaking of 25 editions for Klages' book gives me the opportunity to indicate that often a new German edition is nothing more than a new printing without change of content. It also allows me to apologize for sometimes failing to give the latest edition to a particular book in the German literature.

8. W. Moede, *Experimentelle Massenpsychologie.* Leipzig: Hirzel, 1920.

9. H. Thomae, Problems of Character Change. In H. P. David & H. von Bracken (eds.), *Perspectives in Personality Theory.* New York: Basic, 1957, pp. 242–255. P. 243.

10. E. Rothacker, *Die Schichten der Personlichkeit.* (5. Aufl.) Bonn: Bouvier, 1952. (1938); P. Lersch, *Aufbau der Person.* (7. Aufl.) München: Barth, 1956. (1938)

11. P. Lersch, The Levels of the Mind. In H. P. David & H. von Bracken (eds.), *Perspectives in Personality Theory.* New York: Basic, 1957, 212–217.

12. A. R. Gilbert, On the Stratification of Personality. In H. P. David & H. von Bracken (eds.), *Perspectives in Personality Theory.* New York: Basic, 1957, pp. 218–241.

13. H. Rorschach, *Psychodiagnostics: A Diagnostic Test Based on Perception.* New York: Grune & Stratton, 1942. (1921); H. Ellenberger, The Life and Work of Hermann Rorschach (1884–1922), *Bull. Menninger Clin.,* 1954, 18, 173–219.

* See page 16 for description of reference style.

14.   H. Piéron. Henri Piéron. In E. G. Boring *et al.*, (eds.), *A History of Psychology in Autobiography.* (Vol. 4) Worcester, Mass.: Clark University Press, 1952, pp. 257–278.

15.   H. Piéron, *Aux Sources de la connaissance: le sensation, guide de vie.* (3.éd.) Paris: Librarie Gallimard, 1955. (1945); H. Piéron, *The Sensations, their Functions, Processes, and Mechanisms.* New Haven, Conn.: Yale University Press, 1952.

16.   A. Michotte, Albert Michotte van den Berck. In E. G. Boring (ed.), *op. cit.,* Vol. 4, 213–236.

17.   A. Michotte, *The Perception of Causality.* (2nd ed.) New York: Basic, 1963. (1946)

18.   H. F. Ellenberger, The Scope of Swiss Psychology. In H. P. David & H. von Bracken (eds.) *Perspectives in Personality Theory.* New York: Basic, 1957, pp. 44–64.

19.   E. Claparède, Edoaurd Claparède. In C. Murchison (ed.), *A History of Psychology in Autobiography.* (Vol. 1) Worcester, Mass.: Clark University Press, 1930, pp. 63–97.

20.   J. Piaget. Jean Piaget. In E. G. Boring, *et al.*, (eds.), *A History of Psychology in Autobiography.* (Vol. 4) Worcester, Mass.: Clark University Press, 1952, pp. 237–256; J. Piaget, *The Language and Thought of the Child.* New York: Humanities Press, 1926; J. Piaget, *Judgment and Reasoning in the Child.* New York: Harcourt, Brace, 1928; J. Piaget, *The Child's Conception of Physical Causality.* New York: Harcourt, Brace, 1930.

21.   A relevant history of British psychology that can be recommended is that by L. S. Hearnshaw, *A Short History of British Psychology: 1840–1940.* (New York: Barnes & Noble, 1964)

22.   Beatrice Edgell, The British Psychological Society, *Brit. J. Psychol.,* 1947, 37, 113–132.

23.   Hearnshaw, *op. cit.,* p. 208.

24.   R. Granit, *Charles Scott Sherrington: An Appraisal.* London: Nelson, 1966.

25.   C. Sherrington, *The Integrative Action of the Nervous System.* New Haven, Conn.: Yale University Press, 1947. (1906)

26.   H. Head, W. H. R. Rivers & J. Sherren, The Afferent Nervous System from a New Aspect, *Brain,* 1905, 28, 99–115; H. Head & W. H. R. Rivers, A Human Experiment in Nerve Division, *Brain,* 1908, 31, 323–450.

27.   H. Head, *Studies in Neurology.* (Vol. 1) London: Frowde, Hodder & Stoughton, 1920.

28.   H. Head, *Aphasia and Kindred Disorders of Speech.* (2 vols.) Cambridge: Cambridge University Press, 1926.

29.   *Ibid.,* Vol. 1, pp. 479–487. (Herrnstein & Boring Excerpt 52)

30.   E. D. Adrian, *The Mechanisms of Nervous Action: the Activity of the Sense Organs.* Oxford: Clarenden, 1932.

31. C. Spearman, C. Spearman. In C. Murchison (ed.), *A History of Psychology in Autobiography.* (Vol. 1) Worcester, Mass.: Clark University Press, 1930, pp. 299–333.

32. *Ibid.*

33. C. Spearman, The Proof and Measurement of Association Between Two Things, *Amer. J. Psychol.,* 1904, 15, 72–101; C. E. Spearman, General Intelligence, Objectively Determined and Measured, *Amer. J. Psychol.,* 1904, 15, 201–293. (Herrnstein & Boring Excerpt 85)

34. *Autobiography,* p. 321.

35. C. Spearman, *The Abilities of Man: Their Nature and Measurement.* New York: Macmillan, 1927.

36. C. Spearman, 'G' and after—a School to End Schools. In C. Murchison, (ed.), *Psychologies of 1930.* Worcester, Mass.: Clark University Press, 1930, pp. 339–366.

37. W. Brown & G. H. Thomson, *The Essentials of Mental Measurement.* (3rd ed.) Cambridge, Eng.: Cambridge University Press, 1925. (1911)

38. G. H. Thomson, *The Factorial Analysis of Human Ability.* (4th ed.) London: University of London Press, 1950.

39. G. Thomson, The Trend of National Intelligence, *Eugen. Rev.,* 1946, 38, 9–18.

40. C. S. Myers, Charles Samuel Myers, In C. Murchison (ed.), *History of Psychology in Autobiography.* (Vol. 3) Worcester, Mass.: Clark University Press, 1936, pp. 215–230.

41. H. J. Welch & C. S. Myers, *Ten Years of Industrial Psychology: an Account of the First Decade of the National Institute of Industrial Psychology.* London: Pitman, 1932.

42. C. S. Myers & F. C. Bartlett, *Textbook of Experimental Psychology.* (3rd ed.) Cambridge: Cambridge University Press, 1925. (1909)

43. F. C. Bartlett, Frederic Charles Bartlett. In C. Murchison (ed.), *op. cit.,* Vol. 3, pp. 39–52.

44. F. C. Bartlett, *Remembering: a Study in Experimental and Social Psychology.* New York: Macmillan, 1932.

45. *Remembering,* pp. 199ff.

46. *Autobiography,* p. 40, 42.

47. Hearnshaw, *op. cit.,* p. 212.

48. C. Burt, Cyril Burt. In E. G. Boring, *et al.* (eds.), *History of Psychology in Autobiography.* (Vol. 4) Worcester, Mass.: Clark University Press, 1952, pp. 53–73.

49. C. Burt, *The Factors of the Mind: an Introduction to Factor Analysis in Psychology.* New York: Macmillan, 1941.

50. J. Drever, James Drever. In C. Murchison, (ed.), *History of Psychology in Autobiography.* (Vol. 2) Worcester, Mass.: Clark University Press, 1932, pp. 17–34.

51. J. Drever, *Instinct in Man: a Contribution to the Psychology of Education.* (2nd ed.) London: Cambridge University Press, 1921. (1917); J. Drever, The Classification of the Instincts, *Brit. J. Psychol.,* 1924, 14, 248–255.

52. J. Drever & May Collins, *Performance Tests of Intelligence: a Series of Nonlinguistic Tests for Deaf and Normal Children.* Edinburgh: Oliver & Boyd. 1936.

53. G. Humphrey, Five Years in the Oxford Chair, *Brit. J. Psychol.,* 1953, 44, 381–383.

54. G. Humphrey, *The Nature of Learning.* New York: Harcourt, Brace, 1933; G. Humphrey, *Thinking: an Introduction to its Experimental Psychology.* New York: Wiley, 1951.

55. K. N. Kornilov, Psychology in the Light of Dialectic Materialism. In C. Murchison (ed.), *Psychologies of 1930.* Worcester, Mass.: Clark University Press, 1930, pp. 243–278; G. Razran, K. N. Kornilov, Theoretical and Experimental Psychologist, *Science,* 1958, 128, 74–75.

56. K. N. Kornilov, *Psikhologia.* Moscow: GIZ, 1934.

57. A. R. Luria, *The Nature of Human Conflict.* (Translated by W. Horsley Gantt) New York: Liveright. 1932.

58. L. S. Vigotsky, Thought in Schizophrenia, *Arch. Neurol. Psychiat.,* Chicago: 1934, 31, 1063–1077.

59. L. Vygotsky, *Thought and Language.* (Translated by Eugenia Hanfmann & Gertrude Vakar) Cambridge: M.I.T. Press, 1962. (1934)

60. K. M. Bykov, *The Cerebral Cortex and the Internal Organs.* (Edited and translated from 3rd Russian ed. by W. Horsley Gantt) New York: Chemical Publishing, 1957.

61. A. R. Luria, Krizis burzhuaznoy psikhologii, *Psikhologia,* 1932, 1–2, 63–97.

62. R. A. Bauer, (ed.) *Some Views on Soviet Psychology.* Washington, D. C.: American Psychological Association, 1962.

63. K. Sato & C. H. Graham, Psychology in Japan, *Psychol. Bull.,* 1954, 51, 443–464; H. Misiak & Virginia S. Sexton, *History of Psychology: an Overview.* New York: Grune & Stratton, 1966, pp. 281–298.

64. R. I. Watson, A Brief History of Clinical Psychology, *Psychol. Bull.,* 1953, 50, 321–346. [Reprinted in I. N. Mensh (ed.), *Clinical Psychology: Science and Profession.* New York: Macmillan, 1966, pp. 68–104.]

65. L. Witmer, Clinical Psychology. *Psychol. Clin.,* 1907, 1, 1–9.

66. W. Healy & Augusta Bronner, The Child Guidance Clinic: Birth and Growth of an Idea. In Lawson G. Lowrey, (ed.) *Orthopsychiatry: 1923–1948: Retrospect and Prospect.* New York: American Orthopsychiatric Association, 1948, pp. 14–49.

67. W. Healy & Augusta F. Bronner, *New Light on Delinquency and its Treatment.* New Haven, Conn.: Yale University Press, 1936; W. Healy & Augusta F. Bronner, *Treatment and What Happened Afterward.* Boston: Judge Baker Guidance Center, 1939.

68. L. F. Shaffer, Frederic Lyman Wells: 1884–1964. *Amer. J. Psychol.*, 1964, 77, 679–682.

69. F. L. Wells, *Mental Tests in Clinical Practice*. Yonkers, N. Y.: World Book, 1927.

70. C. R. Rogers, Carl R. Rogers. In E. G. Boring & G. Lindzey (eds.), *A History of Psychology in Autobiography*. (Vol. 5) New York: Appleton-Century-Crofts, 1967, pp. 343–384.

71. C. R. Rogers, *Counseling and Psychotherapy: Newer Concepts in Practice*. Boston: Houghton Mifflin, 1942.

72. S. I. Franz, Shepard Ivory Franz. In C. Murchison (ed.), *A History of Psychology in Autobiography*. (Vol. 2) Worcester: Clark University Press, 1932, 89–113.

73. S. I. Franz, Variations in the Distribution of the Motor Centers, *Psychol. Monogr.*, 1915, 19, No. 81. (Herrnstein & Boring Excerpt No. 50)

74. D. O. Hebb, Karl Spencer Lashley: 1890–1958, *Amer. J. Psychol.*, 1959, 72, 142–150.

75. K. S. Lashley, *Brain Mechanisms and Intelligence: a Quantitative Study of Injuries to the Brain*. New York: Dover, 1963. (1929) (Herrnstein & Boring Excerpt No. 51)

76. E. G. Boring, Edwin Garrigues Boring. In E. G. Boring et al. (eds.), *A History of Psychology in Autobiography*. (Vol. 4) Worcester, Mass.: Clark University Press, 1952, pp. 27–52.

77. E. G. Boring, *A History of Experimental Psychology*. (2nd ed.) New York: Appleton-Century-Crofts, 1950. (1929)

78. W. V. D. Bingham, Walter Van Dyke Bingham. In E. G. Boring et al. (eds.), *A History of Psychology in Autobiography*. (Vol. 4) Worcester, Mass.: Clark University Press, 1952, pp. 1–26.

79. W. V. D. Bingham & B. V. Moore (with the collaboration of J. W. Gustad) *How to Interview*. (4th rev. ed.) New York: Harper, 1959. (1931); W. V. D. Bingham, *Aptitudes and Aptitude Testing*. New York: Harper, 1937.

80. D. P. Campbell, The Strong Vocational Interest Blank: 1927–1967. In P. McReynolds (ed.), *Advances in Psychological Assessment*, Palo Alto, Calif.: Science and Behavior Books (to be published).

81. E. K. Strong, Jr., *Change of Interests with Age*. Stanford, Calif.: Stanford University Press, 1931; E. K. Strong, Jr. *Vocational Interests of Men and Women*. Stanford, Calif.: Stanford University Press, 1943; E. K. Strong, Jr. *Vocational Interests 18 years after College*. Minneapolis: University of Minnesota Press, 1955.

82. F. H. Allport, *Social Psychology*. Boston: Houghton Mifflin, 1924.

83. G. Murphy, Gardner Murphy. In E. G. Boring & G. Lindzey (eds.), *A History of Psychology in Autobiography*. (Vol. 5) New York: Appleton-Century-Crofts, 1967, pp. 255–282.

84. G. Murphy, *Historical Introduction to Modern Psychology*. (rev. ed.) New York: Harcourt Brace, 1949. (1929)

85. G. Murphy, Lois B. Murphy, & T. M. Newcomb, *Experimental Social Psychology: an Interpretation of Research Upon the Socialization of the Individual*. (rev. ed.) New York: Harper, 1937. (1931)

86. *Ibid.*

87. O. Klineberg, *Negro Intelligence and Selective Migration*. New York: Columbia University Press, 1935.

88. K. Lewin, *Field Theory in Social Science: Selected Theoretical Papers*. (D. Cartwright ed.) New York: Harper, 1951.

89. K. Lewin, Defining the 'Field at a Given Time', *Psychol. Rev.*, 1943, 50, 292–310. In *Field Theory*, ibid., p. 45.

90. A. Gesell, Arnold Gesell. In E. G. Boring *et al.* (eds.), *A History of Psychology in Autobiography*. (Vol. 4) Worcester, Mass.: Clark University Press, 1952, pp. 123–142.

91. A. Gesell, *An Atlas of Infant Behavior: a Systematic Delineation of the Forms and Early Growth of Human Behavior Patterns*. Vol. 1: *Normative Series*. (With H. Thompson and C. S. Amatruda) Vol. 2: *Naturalistic Series*. (With A. V. Keliher, F. L. Ilg and J. J. Carlson) New Haven: Yale University Press, 1934.

92. A. Gesell, & F. L. Ilg, *Child Development, an Introduction to the Study of Human Growth*. New York: Harper, 1949.

93. L. L. Thurstone, L. L. Thurstone. In E. G. Boring, *et al.* (eds.), *A History of Psychology in Autobiography*. (Vol. 4) Worcester, Mass.: Clark University Press, 1952, pp. 295–321.

94. L. L. Thurstone, *Multiple-Factor Analysis; a Development and Expansion of the Vectors of Mind*. Chicago: University of Chicago Press, 1947.

95. L. L. Thurstone, *The Vectors of Mind; Multiple-Factor Analysis for the Isolation of Primary Traits*. Chicago: University of Chicago Press, 1935.

96. G. W. Allport Gordon W. Allport. In E. G. Boring & G. Lindzey (eds.), *A History of Psychology in Autobiography*. (Vol. 5) New York: Appleton-Century-Crofts, 1967, pp. 3–25.

97. G. W. Allport, *Personality: a Psychological Interpretation*. New York: Holt, Rinehart & Winston, 1937.

98. H. A. Murray, Henry A. Murray. In E. G. Boring & G. Lindzey (eds.), *A History of Psychology in Autobiography*. (Vol. 5) New York: Appleton-Century-Crofts, 1967, pp. 285–310.

99. *Ibid.*, p. 308.

100. Christiana D. Morgan & H. A. Murray, A Method for Investigating Fantasies: the Thematic Apperception Test, *Arch. Neurol. Psychiat.*, 1935, 34, 289–306.

101. H. A. Murray, *Explorations in Personality: a Clinical and Experimental Study of Fifty Men of College Age*. New York: Oxford University Press, 1938.

102. C. L. HULL, Clark L. Hull, In E. G. Boring, *et al.* (eds.), *A History of Psychology in Autobiography.* (Vol. 4) Worcester, Mass.: Clark University Press, 1952, pp. 143–162.

103. C. L. HULL, *Principles of Behavior: an Introduction to Behavior Theory.* New York: Appleton-Century-Crofts, 1943.

104. C. L. HULL, *Essentials of Behavior.* New Haven, Conn.: Yale University Press, 1951.

105. C. L. HULL, *A Behavior System; an Introduction to Behavior Theory Concerning the Individual Organism.* New Haven, Conn.: Yale University Press, 1952.

106. *Autobiography,* p. 155.

107. *Behavior System,* pp. 5–6.

108. E. R. HILGARD & G. H. BOWER. *Theories of Learning.* (3rd ed.) New York: Appleton-Century-Crofts, 1966. (1948)

109. E. R. GUTHRIE, *The Psychology of Learning.* (rev. ed.) New York: Harper, 1952. (1935)

110. E. R. GUTHRIE, Conditioning as a Principle of Learning, *Psychol. Rev.,* 1930, 37, 412–428.

111. *Psychology of Learning.*

112. E. R. GUTHRIE & G. P. HORTON, *Cats in a Puzzle Box.* New York: Rinehart, 1946.

113. P. W. BRIDGMAN, *The Logic of Modern Physics.* New York: Macmillan, 1927.

114. *Ibid.,* p. 36.

115. E. G. BORING, Intelligence as the Tests Test It, *New Repub.,* 1923, 34, 35–36. (Reprinted in E. G. Boring, *History, Psychology and Science: Selected Papers.* R. I. Watson & D. T. Campbell, eds., New York: Wiley, 1963, pp. 187–189.)

116. S. S. STEVENS, The Operational Basis of Psychology, *Amer. J. Psychol.,* 1935, 47, 323–330.

117. C. C. PRATT, *The Logic of Modern Psychology.* New York: Macmillan, 1939.

118. S. S. STEVENS, Psychology: the Propaedeutic Science, *Phil. Sci.,* 1936, 3, 90–103.

119. E. C. TOLMAN, Operational Behaviorism and Current Trends in Psychology, *Proc. 25th Anniv. Celebr. Inaug. Grad. Stud. Univ. So. Calif.* Los Angeles: Univ. So. Calif. Press, 1936, pp. 89–103.

120. E. C. TOLMAN, The Determiners of Behavior at a Choice Point, *Psychol. Rev.,* 1938, 45, 1–41.

121. An excellent secondary account may be found in Hilgard & Bower, *Theories of Learning, op. cit.,* Chap. 7.

122. E. C. TOLMAN, Edward Chace Tolman. In E. G. Boring, *et al.* (eds.), *A History of Psychology in Autobiography.* (Vol. 4) Worcester, Mass.: Clark University Press, 1952, pp. 323–339.

123. E. C. TOLMAN, *Purposive Behavior in Animals and Men.* New York: Century, 1932.

JUST YESTERDAY

To CONSIDER "just yesterday" in psychology comes dangerously close to implying omniscience and to confuse history with prophecy. It is the path of caution to consider trends, not men. Psychology's men of today are too close to us, too close, in fact, to permit more than this. There are other reasons for emphasizing trends, not contemporary leaders. Closer proximity and the presence of a great number of contemporary psychologists makes the individual seem less important. Moreover, presentation of trends has the virtue of allowing brevity, which the spirit of an epilogue demands. Above all, presentation in this form serves as a belated reminder that too little emphasis has been given to the rank and file among psychologists. Advancement of science proceeds through the patient work of the many as well as through that of the eminent few. Inevitably, too broad strokes of the brush will be used. Nuances that finer detail would permit must be sacrificed. While most of the men who are to be mentioned are considered of senior stature, one must caution that a much larger group of individuals might have been selected. Men and national trends (which are given brief mention) are subordinated to three themes—theoretical currents, professional developments, and research activities.

NATIONAL TRENDS

Only a brief consideration of national events of historic importance need be offered before these three themes are taken up with thereafter only minimal attention to national boundaries.

Psychology in Western Europe

Continental psychology (thus excluding Great Britain) is more qualitative, more subjective, and more concerned with wholes than is psychology in the United States. This is tantamount to saying that European psychologists are relatively uninfluenced by Watson and the others who have held to a methodologically objective view.

Phenomenology is still a strong intellectual current. It will be remembered that it is founded upon what might be called a faith in the validity of observation. Phenomena, to the observer, are what they are. In keeping with this attitude, a psychological test is often a means of refining observation, a means of accumulating experiences, not a method for collecting scores for later statistical manipulation. In personality study, an analysis of style rather than measurement of definitely established characteristics marks the work. This phenomenological emphasis reinforces what would be considered in the United States a lack of rigorous logic in their research.

It is not surprising that laboratory studies of the traditional kind seem to have decreased markedly in number, both as compared to their own past and to the present situation in the United States. Effects so minute as to require elaborate statistical manipulation are only rarely of interest to them. However, insistence upon more exactly controlled research is making some inroads, especially through the work of the younger men who studied in the U. S. The number of professional chairs in the universities is still relatively small. The laboratory equipment and the technical means at their disposal are still reduced. The tie with philosophy is still strong, a minor in that subject often being required from the prospective psychologist.

The stress on learning problems, so obvious in the United States, is absent. On the other hand, in contrast to the United States, there is considerably more research interest in problems of the will, in aesthetics, in graphology, and in expressive movements in general. A certain amount of research in perceptual problems is carried on, especially that cast in the phenomenological mold. There is also continued interest in a particular kind of personality study, referred to previously as characterology.

Psychology in Germany shows these same trends. In an international symposium devoted to national trends in psychology, German psychology was characterized by Wolfgang Metzger[1] as showing an emphasis on personality theory, especially typology, on phenomenalism with an associated distrust of purely empiricistic views. The Germans showed a reserve about elementaristic reduction and an even stronger reserve concerning objectivism. The losses through exile and the civilian and military casualities of the War had a particularly crippling effect. German psychology is only slowly recovering from the circumstances prevailing before and during World War II.[2] Lack of independent psychology departments, which continue to function as parts of larger faculties—either of the humanities or of the natural sciences—which for very different reasons may view psychology askance, is still a handicap in their further development. One particular account of German psychology is admirable for its catholicity and lack of doctrinaire emphasis. This is in the compact volume edited by Peter R. Hofstätter[3] of Hamburg and part of the famous Fischer "Lexikon" series. Reviews of the present status of German psychology are available in English.[4]

In France, Professor Piéron continued active until the time of his death in 1964. The successor to Piéron both at the Sorbonne and as editor of *L'Année Psychologique* and to his position of dominance in experimental psychology has been Paul Fraisse. The professor and director of the Laboratory of General Neurophysiology of the College of France and (loosely translated) "co-editor" of *L'Année Psychologique,* Alfred Fessard in his work on the neurophysiological bases of memory and learning carries on with the physiological aspect. A summary of the history of French psychology, by Maurice Reuchlin[5] of the Ecole Pratique des Hautes Etudes, is available from the international symposium mentioned before.

Psychology in Great Britain[6]

In British psychology the major general development is probably the increase in the number of graduate students and the opening of several new universities in various parts of England. Wider latitude for individualized programs, rather than the following of the traditions of "Oxbridge" seem apparent. It is, however, too early to assess their effect. A new generation of younger psychologists occupy the forty or so chairs. Leadership then is not so concentrated as it had been in the immediate past.

In research, as reflected in the later discussion (see pages 571–581), Britain has made considerable strides since World War II in a relatively wide number of fields. In many respects it resembles psychology in the United States, but with less emphasis upon a militant objectivism and less interest in making learning the central issue. In test development, its work is perhaps as rigorous as that in the United States. In this and other ways, there is much greater similarity between psychological interests in Britain and the United States than of either country with that of the continent.

Psychology in the Soviet Union

As a discipline, psychology was officially called to task in 1950 for not paying sufficient attention to the teachings of Pavlov.[7] His work, heretofore, had been considered as exclusively in the area of the physiology of higher nervous activity with research carried out in the faculties of biology and very definitely outside of psychology. So rapidly did an adjustment take place in the thinking of psychologists that within two years Soviet psychologists held a Pavlovian session of their own. This decree shows that Soviet psychology clearly is under state control. However, in evaluating its effect, we have been assured by at least one of our Soviet specialists, Gregory Razran[8] of Queens, that this change, of course, does not materially interfere with the empirical extension of psychology.

Based on the number of papers delivered at the National Congress[9] between 1959 and 1963 psychological research more than doubled in that period. The 1963 papers were almost equally divided between "applied educational research" and "basic research." In turn, the basic research could be subdivided into three approximately equal areas—engineering and information theory, traditional experimental, and comparative psychology.

In recent years, we have not lacked for English translations. *The Annual Review of Psychology* publishes periodic assessments.[10] A journal in the English language, *Soviet Psychology and Psychiatry,* translates pertinent articles. It has just been split so that now each of the two fields has a journal of its own. In 1966 there was a special issue worth mentioning specifically. Josef Brozek[11] of Lehigh and others reported on current psychological work, gave bibliographies and reported on the books translated. Between 1964 and 1966 thirty-four monographs and books were translated from the Russian. A two volume statement of psychological science is also available in English.[12]

Psychology in Japan[13]

With about 2,000 psychologists, Japan is third in number after only the United States and the United Kingdom. There are several journals, active scientific meetings, a considerable number of university centers and much research productivity. This growth is intimately related to a renovation and modernization of the Japanese educational system. Today the influence of psychology from the United States is stronger than it was in the past, but they have also developed their own characteristic research and theoretical interests. One manifestation is the interest in personality theory attempting to unify Western and Eastern thought, particulary Zen-Buddhist traditions.[14]

Psychology in the United States

There already have been indications that the United States has taken the lead in psychological science. Although by no means the only index of this leadership, more than half the world's 50,000 psychologists are to be found in the United States. From that meeting in 1892 of a handful of psychologists at the behest of G. Stanley Hall in Worcester, Massachusetts, the members of the American Psychological Association had grown by 1945, the year after the historical account closed, to a respectable 4500. In somewhat more than twenty years since then, the number has exceeded 25,000. With increased numbers has come a tendency toward increased specialization. Sheer size has forced upon the Association the separation into divisions organized around some general or specialized scientific or professional interest. Representative of the former are the divisions devoted to experimental psychology, evaluation and measurement, developmental psychology, personality, and social psychology. Representative of the latter are the divisions devoted to teaching, clinical, industrial, educational, and school psychology.

Growth in the United States of the number of psychological journals, the chief source for reports of research, has continued vigorously. From the *American Journal of Psychology* and the *Psychological Review* of the eighties and nineties, the journals have increased to twelve owned by the American Psychological Association. Another fifty journals are considered to be of sufficient interest to psychologists for their publishers to offer special rates. Including the literature from abroad, *The Psychological Abstracts* in 1967 reported on 17,000 individual reports of research and opinion, judged by its editor to be of interest to psychologists. Other indications show that the quantity of research not merely is increasing; the rate is a positively accelerated one, *i.e.*, as time passes, the rate of increase also increases, not merely the sheer number of studies. Of books there is no end. In 1967, the journal of reviews, *Contemporary Psychology*, received 840 books that their publishers hoped would be acceptable for review. Disregarding half of them as either trash or the result of a mistaken view of that which would interest psychologists would still leave about 420 books that might have been reviewed. It is plausible to assume that foreign language books in psychology, not all of which are sent to *Contemporary Psychology*, would number another 100 worthwhile volumes. To keep up with the literature of the entire field of psychology would require reading 47 articles and a book and-a-half every day. Small wonder that the specialization within psychology, has come into being in America to a much greater degree than in other countries.

The major national differences that characterize psychology in the United States have been indicated in the setting of comparison with other countries. Already mentioned as relatively stronger in the United States are quantitative and objective trends, the stress on part functions, the lessened ties with philosophy, the emphasis upon traditional laboratory studies, the stress upon the effect of environmental influence, and the emphasis upon use of statistics. Other national differences will be taken up in the setting of theoretical currents and research activities.

INTERNATIONAL ENTERPRISES

There are certain international endeavors that should be mentioned. Oldest in point of time are the International Congresses of Psychology, the first of which took place in Paris as long ago as 1889. They now take place at three-year intervals and since 1951 have been organized by the International Union of Psychological Science, which includes among its constituent members national associations of psychology. Attendance has been quite popular. Any one from the United States who has attended the last few Congresses will not claim he lacked for compatriots.

The International Union, according to a past president, Roger W. Russell[15] of Indiana, aims to improve communications among psychologists of all nations, encourage exchange of research workers and students, and to collaborate with other international organizations on matters of mutual interest. It has sponsored a directory and a journal. The second edition of the *International Directory of Psychologists,*[16] which appeared in 1966 under their auspices, lists biographical data for psychologists exclusive of the U. S. A. Twenty thousand questionaires were mailed out and some eight thousand replies received. The *International Journal of Psychology* began publication in 1966 under the editorship of G. de Montmollin of the Centre National de la Rercherche Scientifique, Paris.

Two other journals serve the same ends, although in more specific ways. *Acta Psychologica* commenced publication in Amsterdam in 1935 and serves as the forum for European psychology. Periodic accounts of current research in the various European countries is a feature. *Psychologia* is an international Oriental journal of psychology, which began publication in 1951 in Kyoto with Koji Sato as editor. It serves as a channel of communication between East and West, and as a forum for international discussions.

The American Psychological Association[17] also sponsored in collaboration with the International Union an exhaustive study of the opportunities for advanced training and research throughout the world.

Other organizations of psychologists extend beyond national boundaries. The International Association of Applied Psychology, founded in 1920, functions in the same manner as the International Congresses. The Inter-American Society, founded in 1951, promotes communication among psychologists in North and South America. Even the American Psychological Association is international in that Canadian nationals are admitted freely.

THEORETICAL CURRENTS

While theory and research are inseparably related, for one without the other is sterile, it is nevertheless possible for review and evaluative purposes to distinguish by degree of emphasis. Some of the major theoretical currents will be considered here; current research activity is taken up later.

Recent decades have seen the dissolution of the schools, although at differential rates. Titchenarian structuralism we have already seen disappear after it had served its purpose. Functionalism disappeared as a school, to be replaced by a functional spirit. Behaviorism and Gestalt have more than blurred the boundaries they once set up. Psychoanalysis is the most distinguished exception but, as we shall see, active thought is being given to the issue of rapproachment with academic psychology. Claims to be able to order all psychological data to one system are no longer made. Instead, this is seen as a goal of present activity.

After the examination of changes in the schools, one by one, attention will be given to the humanistic influences, the existential approach, and the phenomenological method and theory, all of which characteristic theoretical developments are international in scope.

Functionalism

There had been a functional spirit before there was a self-conscious school of functional psychology, and this spirit was to live on after Dewey, Angell, and Carr, and to mention Europeans, Brentano and Claparède. Many modern-day psychologists without professed allegiance to any school of psychology are often closest in spirit to the functionalists in their stress on activities as utilities, on acceptance of the application of psychology, and upon the contingent meaning of function. This functional cast of modern psychology was reinforced by Watson's adherence to it, despite his opposition to functionalism as a school. Contemporary functionalism is most clearly expressed in studies of learning,[18] although it is characteristic that research workers in this tradition do not have an explicit system to be worked out and appraised as such.

Gestalt Psychology

There are differences of opinion among psychologists about the present status of Gestalt psychology. In varying degrees, Gestalt theses about perception have been absorbed in psychology, not to the exclusion of other views, such as those derived from contemporary learning theory, but to the extent that they serve to remind psychologists that there are configurations, patterns, and equipotentialities involved in perception. As an experimental phenomenon, there is no longer any question that the whole cannot be reduced to its parts and that the parts are changed in different contexts. Non-Gestalt psychologists would say that what was unique and worthwhile within the movement has merged with psychology as a whole. Gestalt psychologists, including Köhler,[19] are not so sure that the assimilation has been quite so successful. They point to the continued appeal to additive connectionism on the part of some psychologists as a flagrant instance of non-integration. Another one of the new beginnings in psychology has become merged as part of the field in large measure but, just as there are articulated objects within a larger field, Gestalt thinking is still distinguishable from that field. Attempts of non-Gestalt psychologists to translate Gestalt concepts into the terms appropriate for other approaches have recently been critically examined by Mary Henle[20] and found to be unsuccessful.

Whether it be meant as a source of praise or as a means of disparagement, it is generally agreed that Gestalt psychology has helped very much to keep alive conscious experience as a legitimate interest of psychology. The status of the systematic views of Köhler have recently been examined.[21] Important in itself, it is relevant at this juncture because it shows how Köhler regarded psychology as both a science of behavior *and* experience. Experiences, rather than responses, are correlated with stimulus variables.

Fritz Heider[22] of Kansas, who took his degree at Graz in Austria and was associated with Koffka at Smith, has developed Gestalt psychology through the study of social perception and interpersonal relations.

In the United States, a younger generation of psychologists with strong allegiance to Gestalt principles has come to the fore. One of them is Mary Henle of the New School of Social Research whose critique of attempts at translation of Gestalt concepts to those of other approaches has already been mentioned. She also edited a valuable collection of recent papers on Gestalt approaches to general theory, cognitive processes, social psychology and motivation, and expression and art.[23] The other living psychologists, whose papers are included, are three of the leading psychologists working in the Gestalt tradition. Rudolf Arnheim of Sarah Lawrence works primarily with problems of aesthetics, Solomon E. Asch of Rutgers University, Newark branch, with social psychological problems, and Hans Wallach of Swarthmore with perceptual and cognitive problems.

In the setting of the larger problem of the kinds of theoretical constructs employed by psychologists of various persuasions, Kenneth W. Spence[24] critically examined Gestalt usages. Other analyses are also available.[25]

In Germany, Wolfgang Metzger of Münster continues as senior representative of the Berlin School. His new edition of *Gesetze der Sehens*,[26] which appeared in 1953 with much new data, is particularly important. Edwin Rausch[27] of Frankfurt, a younger representative, has investigated the influence of distortions upon visual configurations, finding a tendency for them to be perceived in such fashion that they are eliminated.

Representatives of the Leipzig School are Friedrich Sander,[28] recently retired from Bonn, and Albert Wellek[29] of Mainz, both still very active. The latter continues the school's tradition, for example, studying the relation of totality psychology to stratification theory, in a setting which would combine with it a humanistic and philosophical plea for maintaining a breadth to psychology. Experiment, to Wellek, has its place, but it is a relatively limited one.

Psychoanalysis

In most respects Freudian psychoanalysis still stands apart from the main body of psychological science. Its origin in the treatment of adult neurotics, its investigatory method of free association, its insistence upon the primacy of unconscious sexual factors, its development of its own terminology, and its derivation of personnel from the ranks of physicians show how this separation came about and how it is maintained.

Quite possibly the most important theoretical development in psychoanalysis since Freud's death in 1939, has been the expansion of the conception of the ego. Although other theoreticians contributed to this, the work of a particular trio of psychoanalysts, Heinz Hartmann, Rudolf M. Loewenstein and Ernst Kris (1900–1957), is most prominent.[30] In classic psychoanalytic theory the ego was considered as derived from and securing its energy from the id. This contention is now qualified by extending the sources both for its derivation and its energy. The ego is seen as less at the mercy of the id and some autonomous aspects are even attributed to it. Both id and ego are seen as arising from a more or less undifferentiated substratum, instead of the ego arising from the id alone. This autonomy of the ego permits some independence from instinctual demands and allows learning in the more usual and conventional sense to be relevant. Development, then, is not entirely an id-instigated matter. The ego, moreover, is to be defined by its functions—control of motility, perception, reality-testing, and thinking. This allows some psychological functioning to be of a conflict-free nature and less a ceaseless struggle against primative id forces. Conflict-free avenues of adaptation to reality, instead of being peripheral, are now central, and every adaptation or instance of learning need not be attributed to conflict and related means of functioning. This opens the way for rapproachment between psychoanalysis and psychology in general.

Some psychologists have contributed to the theory of psychoanalysis as well as interpreting it in a fashion that would bring out its relation to the general, non-analytic psychology. The papers of David Rapaport[31] (1911–1960) of Stockbridge, are outstanding in his effort to make psychoanalysis a complete and unified theory of individual and social behavior coextensive with psychology. Robert R. Holt and George S. Klein of New York University have worked toward the same end.[32] Integration of psychoanalysis with psychology and anthropology has been attempted with special success in the field of child development by Erik H. Erikson[33] of Harvard, another prominent psychologist-psychoanalyst.

The two world leaders of child psychoanalysis, Melanie Klein[34] (1882–1960) and Anna Freud[35] have practiced and taught in London for many years. John Carl Flugel (1884–1955) at University College, London, was both an academic psychologist and a psychoanalyst and in some measure bridged the two fields. A psychoanalytical society was founded in Paris in 1924 and psychoanalysts occupy chairs at the Sorbonne.[36] It has less influence in Germany, although not unknown.

Freud and his followers originally had been convinced of the validity of their contentions by the sheer wealth of supporting data they found in case after case. Become psychoanalysts, they said to critics, come and do likewise, and you, too, will be convinced. In reply, the non-psychoanalytically oriented psychologist is apt to ask that they go beyond this piling up of positive instances and apply much more frequently than they have in the past the method of experiment. Admittedly, this is a difficult task, but it is necessary before psychoanalysis becomes an integral part of the main stream of psychology.

As various surveys show, there has been no lack of attempts at experimental verification of psychoanalytic propositions as well as an extensive literature examining the extent to which psychoanalysis meets and does not meet the canons of the scientific method. These critics include E. R. Hilgard and Robert R. Sears of Stanford, and B. F. Skinner of Harvard.[37] They are not psychoanalytically oriented, of course, but show varying degrees of sympathy. Others, writing more from a psychoanalytic allegiance, such as Merton Gill, Lawrence Kubie and Heinz Hartmann,[38] have emphasized the relation of theory to method in an attempt at reconciliation. A valiant attempt in depth to integrate Hull's learning theory and some aspects of psychoanalysis was made by John Dollard and Neal E. Miller of Yale.[39]

Some psychologists contend that almost all of the research studies are at fault in that in most instances they do not measure what they purported to be measuring and even when the results support psychoanalytic contentions, it is not clear that it is any more than an analogous relationship. Reliable general secondary sources are available.[40]

The Neo-Freudians

The so-called Neo-Freudians show two major characteristic differences from modern psychoanalysts in the major Freudian tradition. While accepting many Freudian tenets, they also decisively reject other salient features of Freudian thinking. They also put much more emphasis on the influence of social factors upon personality development. Karen Horney[41] (1885–1952) has been most explicit on points of agreement and disagreement. She accepted the doctrine of unconscious motivation, strict determinism, the pervasive influence of emotion upon formation of attitudes and behavior, and the concepts of conflict and repression. On the other hand, she believed the libido theory to be unsubstantiated, that needs grow, not out of instincts, but out of a child's need to cope with a difficult environment; that the Oedipus Complex is not a biological imperative, but something which stems from a describable condition in the family environment; penis envy, as such, is rejected, while the phenomena which are subsumed under this rubric are seen as being aroused in women by the superior status given to masculine qualities in our culture.

A contemporary Neo-Freudian, Erich Fromm,[42] sees man as primarily a social creature whose major characteristic is precisely his independence from instincts. Although influenced by Freudian psycho-sexual stages, he sees character structure most adequately defined in terms of social characteristics, and develops such concepts as that of the receptive person, the exploitative individual, the marketing personality.

The Neo-Adlerians

Alfred Adler anticipated the psychological temper of the times in emphasizing the influence of social factors upon personality and development. To be more specific, it will be remembered that Adler emphasized ego functions, denied the primacy of the sexual, insisted that attention be given to the individual unity of each person, would have psychology look upon man from an ethical point of view and counseled taking a more active role in psychotherapy. One of the more general reasons that psychologists have been responsive to Adlerian thinking is its strong functional character. In these emphases, Adler was prophetic of much current thinking, not only among Adlerians but also among neo-Freudians and many other psychologists. In these respects, as time passed, the followers of Freud moved closer and closer to these views of Adler without surrendering their more specifically Freudian tenets.

Although her evaluation may be more than usually colored by personal feelings, Alexandra, Adler's daughter, claims that the theory of Individual Psychotherapy has changed relatively little.[43] She, therefore, looks to and writes about applications in psychotherapy, such as its use in conjunction with drugs.

While it may be that no radical innovation has been introduced in psychotherapy or, even in the principles upon which it is based, there is no question that greater systematization of principles has been introduced since Adler. This was exhibited in Chapter 20 by the greater order brought into Adlerian concepts by the Ansbachers. (See page 494.) An even more recent effort by H. L. Ansbacher[44] of the University of Vermont shows the continued progress made in this area. Without doing violence to Adler's thinking, he shows that there can be expanded interpretation, which places it in a newer framework, as is the case with the interpretation of the fictional goal as an heuristic device or a construction on the part of the psychologist interpreter so as to provide himself and the patient with a conceptual tool to help modify the latter's behavior. The unconscious, too, is seen to be largely a similar construction.

Individual psychology today shows either an easy adaptability to other positions or, as its protagonists would claim, anticipations of the development of other current trends. Existentialism, for example, in the person of a prominent Viennese existential psychotherapist, Viktor E. Frankl, is claimed as a pupil of Adler [45] In a more general vein, it is argued that Adlerian thinking and existential analysis are fundamentally related because both are phenomenological, holistic, and idiographic.[46]

For all of these reasons present-day interests among psychologists has increased. Formally organized groups are to be found, particularly in New York, Chicago and Los Angeles. There is a flourishing journal, the *Journal of Individual Psychology*, with Ansbacher as editor. Editorially, it has broadened its scope recently to include related phenomenological, field, and socially-oriented approaches. The Chicago group includes among its members a leading Adlerian psychotherapist, Rudolf Dreikurs, who has written extensively on the subject.[47] In New York, there is also an Alfred Adler Institute with Helene Papenek, M.D., as director, who is a specialist in group therapy.[48] Some interest may be found on the Continent as well,[49] but leadership has obviously shifted to the United States.

While systematic controlled research is not entirely absent, particularly that on various facets of the question of the psychological influence of sibling position, there is no question that a greater research orientation, other than clinical, is still very much needed, as illustrated recently with specific research suggestions.[50]

The Neo-Jungians

The number of individuals interested in analytical psychology has shown a considerable increase. Jung's books are popular, and comments in magazines and newspapers has brought his name before the public. There are three formal institutes—in Zurich,[51] London, and New York. There are other clubs and societies in London, on the West Coast and in Chicago. In 1955, the first Jungian journal was founded in London, the *Journal of Analytic Psychology*. In 1958, the first international congress was held in Zurich. His influence upon scholars in diversified fields has been great. As varied individuals as the theologian, Paul Tillich; the historian, Arnold Toynbee;[52] the novelist, Philip Wylie; the critic and author, Lewis Mumford, and the anthropologist, Paul Radin, acknowledge they have an intellectual debt to Jung and his views.

And yet from psychologists there is silence. Relevant articles, even in criticism, are almost non-existent. So far as I am aware only one eminent psychologist, Henry A. Murray, has acknowledged a debt to Jung. How is this divergence to be accounted for? Aside from research of Jung's earlier and admittedly less theoretically important work in word association and introversion-extroversion, almost no research has been conducted in the major psychological tradition. Essentially the validity that Jung sought and the neo-Jungians continue to seek is that of mutual corroboration of psychological, archeological, anthropological, and mythological material. Instances of cross comparison are sought and woven into an intricate tapestry. No way for research, as psychologists understand the term, has yet been found. Until this can be accomplished, Jungian thinking will stand apart.

Humanistic Influences

A humanistic strain is evident in contemporary psychology even in the United States. Humanism is more evocative of a mood or of an attitudinal stance than anything more precise. It is fitting, then, that it does not keep mannered company for its lack of exclusiveness is precisely what it stands for. And the first step toward humanism for psychologists is a realization that science is not all that matters. A variety of psychologists have been calling for the leaven that is humanism. Some of the more representative are John Cohen of Manchester, Albert Wellek of Mainz, Gordon Allport of Harvard, Carl Rogers of Western Behavioral Science Institute, Abraham Maslow of Brandeis, and Adrian van Kaam of Duquesne.[53] Examination of their reasons for this call shows that they do so for very divergent reasons, although in one way or another they are pleas for an added breath to psychology. It should be added that the majority of psychologists meet this appeal with profound indifference.

The Existential Approach

Similarly attitudinal to humanism, and not without significant overlapping of allegiance, is the approach known as the existential. It is sometimes discussed as a philosophical psychology, not only because it has intellectual roots in that array of philosophical doctrines, which is true, but also because it is conceived as not going beyond philosophy, which is not true. As a leading protagonist, Adrian van Kaam[54] of Duequesne, puts it, existential psychology regards existential philosophy as consisting of hypothetical constructs from which testable propositions may be deduced. So far, this is more a statement of policy rather than of accomplishment.

A useful introduction specifically for psychologists is available, edited by Rollo May[55] to which sympathetic critics not entirely committed to position (Maslow, Rogers, Allport) contribute papers. The first systematic and methodological textbook has appeared.[56]

The Phenomenological Method and Theory

The phenomenological approach in its more pristine form is singled out as a theoretical trend, rather than treated merely as one method used in current research activity. This is done in deference to the fact that in the United States, at least, such a distinction is made. Differentiated at least to some extent from its more controlled use among Gestalt psychologists, and by James Gibson and other research workers in perception, a variety of other significant but more impressionistic studies have appeared.

Bearing the subtitle, "a psychological critique," a study of the imagination by the prominent French existentialist, Jean-Paul Sartre,[57] is more psychologically oriented than most of his work. The interpretations of imagination in associationism, Ribot, and Binet, and the Würzburg School are discussed and found wanting. In France, there was also the work on philosophical and phenomenological psychology by Maurice Merleau-Ponty[58] (1908–1961) late of the Sorbonne.

In the Netherlands and in Belgium, although more closely resembling the rigorous use, the phenomenological significance of pain and of perception were studied respectively by Frederijk J. J. Buytendijk[59] of Utrecht and Albert Michotte[60] of Louvain. Turning to Germany, Karl Mierke[61] of Kiel examined phenomenologically needs, habits, and conscience as factors of motivation.

Neo-Behaviorism

From the original doctrinaire appeal by the first generation of Behaviorists, Watson, Weiss, Meyer and the rest, psychology had passed through the stage of the "later" behaviorists. (See page 543.) The present period is that of the neo-behaviorists. Edward Chace Tolman, considered as a "later" behaviorist, now emerges as a neo-behaviorist. Other leading neo-behaviorists are Kenneth W. Spence (1907–1967) late of Iowa and Texas, and B. F. Skinner of Harvard.

As a general point of view, behaviorism has been accepted by most psychologists in the United States today. It might even be referred to as the prevailing eclecticism. There are also somewhat more carefully articulated and self-conscious formulations, the neo-behaviorisms, which owe an acknowledged debt to Watson to be sure, but carefully specify that their positions are to be differentiated from Watsonian behaviorism. In general, neo-behaviorists, with the exception of B. F. Skinner, show an increased liberalization in methods used, in problems studied, and in attitude towards those who do not agree with them.

The language of intervening variables, it will be remembered, had been coined by Tolman as a later behaviorist. Similarly, Hull, Skinner, and Spence involved themselves in some relationship to this way of conceptualizing their work as behavioristically oriented psychologists (as did other psychologists of the prevailing eclecticism). In the early forties, a variety of concepts, "symbolic constructs," "hypothetical constructs" and "hypothetical entities," in some rough way related to Tolman's intervening variables were being used more or less interchangeably, thus creating considerable confusion.

In 1948, Kenneth MacCorquodale and Paul E. Meehl[62] published an extremely significant paper that attempted (and later events showed, in some measure, succeeded) to bring order into this confusion of terms. They made the distinction between hypothetical constructs which involve hypothesizing a process or event which is itself not observable (such as events within the nervous system), and intervening variables which do not involve such hypothetization but abstract the empirical relationships without surplus meaning being involved.

Tolman, more than others, represents the neo-behaviorist position. He shared in the widely held opinion that "grandiose" systems, such as his own, are at least temporarily out of step with the present.[63] The title he chose for his article in the Koch volumes was the "Principles of Purposive Behavior," and yet the article is devoted almost exclusively to specification of his position on learning. There is no mention of behaviorism as a system other than his sceptical comment just mentioned. The structure of his system is stated in terms of independent variables (past and present), intervening variables (means-end readiness, and expectation, and perceptions) and dependent variables. His intervening variables, he cheerfully admitted, share in the surplus meaning of the hypothetical constructs as the term is used by MacCorquodale and Meehl.

Kenneth W. Spence, too, uses the variable approach in formulating his view of behaviorism.[64] This is stated in terms of response variables, stimulus variables, hypothetical state variables (the intervening variables of Tolman) and (possibly) organic variables leading to different types of empirical relationship which yield empirical and hypothetical laws.

In many ways B. F. Skinner shows a more militant and certainly less "liberal" point of view about how to behave as a psychologist. Overall theories are premature, according to Skinner, even intervening variables which had been tolerated by Skinner in his early work of 1938,[65] he argued against in his *Science and Human Behavior of 1953.*[66] The variables we have available for scientific analysis, are operations performed upon the organism from without, such as water deprivation and a kind of behavior, say, drinking. The inner condition, "thirst" (what would be called a hypothetical construct) is useless in trying to control behavior because we cannot manipulate it as we can the operation from without *i.e.*, the water deprivation. Skinner[67] would do away with all such intermediaries entirely. Since theories depend upon these intermediaries, it is quite logical that he would also dispense with theories. Psychology as a field, he held, is still inadequate for theorizing and we must collect more data, much more data. The nearest approach to a theory he tolerates is the assumption that there is order to be found in behavioral data. Functional analysis of these data with a single kind of organism, with adequate controls, but dispensing with statistics except for counting, since statistics hide more than they reveal, characterize the way he carries out research.

In varying degrees, and in different patterns of acceptance, psychologists not identified with the schools, share these attitudes, tools, concepts and aspirations. In so doing, psychology again moves toward an agreement about what constitutes psychological science and thus toward maturity.

PROFESSIONAL DEVELOPMENTS[68]

Psychology, in its professional aspects, makes contact with the general public, with business, with governmental agencies, and with representatives of other professions, such as psychiatrists. Because of these responsibilities, the hallmarks of a profession have developed. There is emphasis on a high level of training being obtained before one is permitted to practice. As in any profession, the standards are imposed by psychologists themselves upon all colleagues offering services to individuals and organizations outside of academic walls. An emphasis upon clinical psychology, the largest professional group, will be found in what follows.

In the United States a speciality board, akin to those in the medical specialties, determines those who will be identified as advanced, professional specialists. After examining the applicant's prior education and experience (Ph.D. in the speciality in question and five years experience in that speciality), this board administers written and oral examinations. A successful candidate receives a diploma which certifies to his right to call himself a specialist. About 1400 psychologists hold the Diplomate in Clinical Psychology, and several hundred in the other areas. In 1947, a Committee on Clinical Training of the American Psychological Association, chaired by David Shakow, now at the National Institute of Mental Health, supplied the basic guide lines of the training program. Intended as suggestive, all too often it was taken too literally as Shakow's evaluation of its effect shows in a report seventeen years later. By 1949 some experience had been gained and 1500 persons were in 60 graduate schools. The first of a series of conferences (extending over the next fifteen years) was held that year and a report issued. The Boulder Conference was edited by Victor C. Raimy of Colorado. This report had a very great influence upon subsequent developments.

Standards of professional training are now maintained by cooperation between the graduate schools and an independent evaluation agency set up and staffed by psychologists. Professional training takes place under the auspices of the same graduate schools that offer training for academic posts. There are various cooperative research and training functions organized through the Veteran's Administration, the United States Public Health Service, and other federal and state offices. The relationship of psychologists as a professional group to other professional groups, such as physicians and, especially, psychiatrists, has been and continues to be the concern of representatives of the professions concerned. A code of ethics based upon patient collection of specific concrete instances has been developed and adopted. Concern with ethics has been continuous since a Code was published in 1953. A relatively recent statement is also available.

Legislation working toward the legal control of psychological practice have been passed by many states, generally at the initiative of psychologists themselves. In these and other ways, psychology has become a profession as well as a science.

Thousands of clinical psychologists in the United States are concerned with the diagnosis and treatment of disturbed patients. The task of diagnosis is not that of merely attaching a label of this or that kind of disorder. Rather, the diagnostic task is to ascertain the individual's personality dynamics, his motives, his ways of behaving and experiencing which make him a disturbed person, his concept of himself, his psychological assets which may be tapped in treatment, and his ways of relating to others in his environment. This task the clinical psychologist performs by utilizing test devices, interviewing techniques, and observation.

In the late twenties and thirties, the Rorschach Technique was introduced in the United States. One of the pioneers was Samuel J. Beck who practiced in Chicago for many years. It was seized on avidly and an abundance or a redundance of studies resulted. It is viewed somewhat less enthusiastically today because of accumulating doubt about its validity when examined by conventional research means, and yet clinicians, who use it for some time and develop skills in interpretation, continue to insist on its considerable value.

Besides the Rorschach, diagnostic techniques in wide usage include the Stanford-Binet, the Wechsler-Bellevue Intelligence Scale and the Thematic Apperception Technique. A whole host of structured and projective devices are also utilized, but these four tend to be the most widely used.

From this diagnostic case study emerges a dynamic picture of the individual on the basis of which the treatment phase is planned in broad outline. Although there were a few lonely pioneers, clinical psychologists as a group first began to practice psychotherapy after World War II. Many of them followed procedures first initiated by psychiatrists and psychoanalysts. Original work in developing new approaches to treatment by psychologists were not slow in coming. In this task, the approach of Carl Rogers' client-centered therapy became rather widely used in certain centers, and was the source of much continuing research. So-called "behavior therapy," based on learning principles and therefore of interest to more academically-minded clinical psychologists has recently become a very active field, primarily on research and incidentally of treatment. A volume by Joseph Wolpe gives one version of this approach. With full recognition that psychotherapy started as an art and still is primarily an artistic process, an earnest attempt is being made to bring it within the realm of science.

Often clinical psychologists work in close collaboration with psychiatrists and other medical personnel, especially in the setting of hospitals and out-patient clinics. Less frequently, clinical psychologists enter into private practice in which their livelihood depends upon the patients who come to them either on their own or by referral.

The balance, or rather, the presumed lack of balance between professional and scientific influences in the field is currently a source of concern to some psychologists. In their eyes, the appliers of psychology have sacrificed their scientific birthright, with a consequent stultification of research advance. Other psychologists take the position that the accentuation of professional activities by psychologists has resulted in a mutual stimulation for psychology as a science and as a profession. Today, this rests as an unresolved issue within the field.

One of the controversial areas in which the clinical and the statistical approaches to the study of these problems came into sharp focus is the problem of their relative accuracy in prediction. The study on this problem by Paul E. Meehl of Minnesota is especially noteworthy.

Although clinical psychology has shown the greatest absolute and relative growth in the United States, a beginning, indeed more than that, has been taking place in other countries. In West Germany a professional training program is in full swing. A diploma requires several years of work in a professional area of psychology. This diploma is granted at all of the West German universities. European diagnostic testing practices have been presented by Richard Meili of Bern and Robert Heiss of Freiburg. In Great Britain, although there are some clinical psychologists who work in mental hospitals, they are, by and large, confined to psychological testing and conduct very little psychotherapy. Very recently an interest in behavior therapy has changed the situation somewhat.

Research Activities

In 1959, research activity in psychology reached a new high point. This was the year that three important series of reports on research began to make their appearance. Plans to survey the methodological, theoretical, and empirical status of psychological science in the United States from about 1930 to the time of publication had been begun in 1952 by the American Psychological Association. Sigmund Koch, then of Duke University, served as editor with the support of an advisory panel drawn from the Association. Eighty carefully chosen contributors to *Psychology: A Study of a Science*[69] were each invited to write on a specialized topic to which he was judged as having made a direct and substantial contribution. Since practically no refusals occurred, the men selected were clearly of first rank in the judgment of their peers on the advisory panel. Six of the planned seven volumes appeared between 1959 and 1963. Only the evaluative summary by the editor is unavailable at the present time. In the same year, the first volumes of a twelve-volume German series also made their appearance. This *Handbuch der Psychologie*[70] is under the editorial supervision of Philipp Lersch of Munich, and Friedrich Sander and Hans Thomae of Bonn. Each volume has its own editor or editors and is devoted to a special aspect of the field. In 1959, still another series with some articles by psychologists, *A Handbook of Physiology*,[71] published by the American Physiological Society, under the editorship of John Field, began to make its appearance. These three series are similar in that they are attempts to assess the research activities up to the time of writing.[72]

As might be inferred from the increased quantification in present-day psychology, statistical techniques have increased in sophistication, precision, and scope from the days of Galton and Pearson and the "co-relation" technique. A wealth of procedures are now available to the point that some psychologists specialize in working on statistical problems as such. Consequently, for advances in this facet of the field, psychology is indebted not only to mathematical statisticians, but also to psychologist-statisticians. The statistical tools now available extend into a great number of fields referred to as mathematical models, probability theory, non-parametric statistics, and scaling. They must be neglected, however, in the account to follow, which will survey substantive research activities.

Physiological Psychology[73]

In most of the countries under consideration, physiological psychology is in a flourishing state despite the relatively small number of research men who make it their speciality. In the United States over half of the present psychologist members of the National Academy of Science are identified primarily with physiological psychology in general, or sensory physiology in particular.

Working in the areas that bring them close to neurology and physiology are Karl H. Pribram of Stanford, Floyd Ratliff of Rockefeller (although also working in the neurophysiology of vision) and Donald B. Lindsley of UCLA, who collaborates in much of his research with H. W. Magoun on consciousness in relation to brain function.

Working in a German holistic tradition, but independently of the Gestalt schools, was Kurt Goldstein (1878–1965), who did much of his later research in the United States. His neurological experience, especially with brain injuries, which led to his publication of *The Organism*, stresses that, whenever evaluation of one aspect of behavioral functioning is made, the condition of the organism in its totality must be considered.

Turning to other countries, Oliver L. Zangwill of Cambridge, beside carrying on his own research in physiological psychology with attention to cerebral dominance, directs research of a considerable number of students. A. R. Luria of Moscow, the Soviet Union's most distinguished physiological psychologist, continues to publish with his latest reports already available in English. Alfred Fessard of the University of Paris continues the tradition of Piéron but centers on such matters as brain potentials and the neurophysiological bases of memory and learning.

Work in psychopharmacology is very active. An authoritative summarization of the psychological effects of drugs has been prepared by Herbert Lippert of Munich, and Roger W. Russell of Indiana recently published a review that chronologically supplements the earlier one by Lippert.

Psychophysics and Sensory Processes[74]

Following the grand tradition of Fechner, S. Smith Stevens of Harvard, since the early thirties, both as a graduate student and as a faculty member, has been working in psychophysics primarily through the study of pitch, frequency and loudness of tones. His singleness of purpose was signalized just a couple of years ago by his title being changed to Professor of Psychophysics. In a broader area, he did much to clarify for the psychologist the various kinds of scales of measurement available for use and thereby helped to avoid their misuse. His work on this was conveniently brought together in his opening chapter of the *Handbook of Experimental Psychology*, which he also edited. At Paris in one of his late publications, Piéron turned to the question of whether or not subjective scales can provide the basis for a new psychophysical law.

For work in the sensory processes the United States takes the lead. Only a few outstanding people can be mentioned. Clarence H. Graham of Columbia has worked for many years on vision, and recently reported on research on color theory, including evaluation of the classical theories of Young, Helmholtz and Hering, as well as the more recent theorists. The papers on audition of Georg von Békésy, Nobel prize winner, formerly of Harvard and now at Hawaii, have been translated and made available. They concern cochlear mechanics, auditory thresholds, spatial attributes of hearing and problems of auditory distortion. William D. Neff of Indiana has specialized in the neural bases of sensory discrimination. Frank A. Geldard of Princeton performed an extremely useful service by preparing a general summarization of knowledge of all the sense modalities. However, much work had been done since his book appeared in 1953. Although work in vision and audition is most extensive, Carl Pfaffman of Rockefeller has specialized in the sense of taste and recently used that modality as a model for a S-R system.

Some work in sensory physiology is conducted in Germany. For example, Richard Jung and Hans Kornhuber of Freiburg edited the papers given at a 1961 symposium concerning both objective and subjective sensory aspects of the visual system.

Perception[75]

Psychologists in all national groups show an interest in perceptual research. In fact, if physiological psychology be omitted from consideration as allied with a more mature science, perceptual psychology is the closest we have to an area showing an international commonality of interest. Even the pure phenomenological phase, discussed earlier, is beginning to show this commonality.

Perhaps the senior student of visual perception in the United States is James J. Gibson of Cornell, who not only recently reported on perception as the function of stimulation, a problem that has been a major concern to him, but has also written a recent book on the closely related issue of the senses as perceptual systems. On the continent, equally outstanding and rigorous work on visual perception has been performed by Ivo Kohler of Innsbruck. Floyd H. Allport of Syracuse has published a masterly account of the various theories of perception.

Perception in relation to some other psychological problem areas have been the research themes of three psychologists—Donald E. Broadbent of Cambridge, and its relation to communication; Leo J. Postman of California at Berkeley and its relation to learning; and William H. Ittelson of Brooklyn and its relation to the transactional process.

On the continent, Wolfgang Metzger of Münster, mentioned so often before, has integrated the material on perception in an important volume he edited in the "Handbuch" series. Paul Fraisse of the Sorbonne continues his work in perception, including studies of the perception of time and of rhythm.

In Great Britain interest in perception, particularly visual perception, is very strong. Magdalen D. Vernon of Reading has been at work on visual perception for most of her career. N. S. Sutherland of Sussex has conducted research in visual discrimination both in human and non-human species. Visual perception is also a research specialization of Arthur Summerfield of London. R. W. Pickford of Glasgow specializes in color vision. As a member of a collaborative team with a philosopher and a biologist an integrated survey of perception from these three points of view has been published.

Learning[76]

The approaches to learning of Hull, Tolman (already discussed), and Guthrie continue to receive attention. Guthrie has reported his mature views on contiguity and Frank A. Logan of New Mexico for the Koch volume accepted responsibility for presenting what he called "The Hull-Spence" approach. Kenneth W. Spence not only extended Hull's research, while modifying his view in some particulars, but also served as a stimulating collaborator with him. At first, Spence concentrated on discrimination learning and then he turned to the investigation of the assumptions of a theory he had formulated concerning very simple learning.

O. Hobart Mowrer of Illinois has attempted integration of reinforcement and contiguity as aspects of an unified approach to learning. His earlier "two factor theory" of learning assigned a separate role to contiguity, as in Pavlovian classical conditioning, and another to reinforcement as in Thorndike's trial and error learning. The former supposedly account for sign learning, the latter for solution learning. However, he later reconsidered this, and in 1956 advanced a second version in which conditioning was made central.

B. F. Skinner of Harvard, encountered before in the discussion of neo-behaviorism, has outstripped all of his rival specialists in learning in the amount of enthusiasm he has stirred in other research workers who follow his lead both in the positions sketched in earlier discussion, and in what he and his students have incorporated in the name of their division of the American

Psychological Association, "The Experimental Analysis of Behavior." The same group has also sponsored a journal. His studies of animal performance used rats conditioned to bar pressing, and, later, pigeons conditioned to pecking at a spot. The particular kind of conditioning with which he worked, operant conditioning, he defined in his *Schedules of Reinforcement* as follows:

Operant condition (1) As operation: arranging the reinforcement of a response possessing specified properties, or, more specifically, arranging that a given reinforcer follow the emission of a given response. (2) As process: the resulting increase in the rate of occurrence of responses possessing these properties.

It should be noted that it is reinforcement of response that is under discussion. Instead of reinforcement being correlated with stimuli, in operant conditioning the response is correlated with reinforcement. Pressing the lever by the rat leads to food, not the sight of the lever (or the sound of a bell as in classical conditioning).

Statistical models of learning give another group of approaches to learning that have been of much recent interest. William K. Estes of Stanford, Robert R. Bush of Pennsylvania, and F. Mosteller have taken the lead in this particular area.

Other research workers have related learning to other psychological problems—Neal E. Miller of Rockefeller University to conflict, motivation and social aspects, and more generally, Donald O. Hebb of McGill to a neuropsychological theory of behavior, and in a less theoretical fashion, Robert Galambos of Yale and Clifford T. Morgan of California at Santa Barbara to a physical basis for learning.

Conditioning in relation to learning is in itself a problem of its relation so it is appropriate to mention that Gregory A. Kimble of Duke has recently revised the standard volume, *Conditioning and Learning* of Ernest R. Hilgard of Stanford and Donald G. Marquis of M.I.T.

Many specialists in the study of learning no longer look to formulating learning theory in some fashion that all learning will be accounted for at one stroke. But even this does not bring out the full degree of specialization. A smaller patch of the territory of learning is selected as a consequence of his limited problem—animal learning, instrumental learning, human verbal learning, or human motor learning. Research specialists in learning do share in common the tacit assumption that if one works thoroughly in the area of the study of learning, other problems that they neglect, once seen in the perspective of a thoroughly documented study of learning, will be more readily coped with thereafter. They do not deny that there are other problems in psychology. Rather, they see behavior most fruitfully studied as problems in learning. Benton J. Underwood of Northwestern with his twenty-five or more carefully articulated papers on verbal learning is an important and typical illustration.

Work outside of the United States is neither as prevalent nor, speaking generally, of similar significance. Especially noteworthy, however, is a critical analysis of various behavior theories by Donald E. Broadbent of Cambridge. Another exception is the work of Poland's leading psychologist, Jerzy Konorski of Warsaw who follows the physiological grand tradition in which research is carried on that attempts to bridge the gap between Pavlov and Sherrington. Rudolf Bergius of Munich has edited in the "Handbuch" series, the German view of learning. In order to fill out the volume, the learning chapters were combined with those on thinking.

Engineering Psychology, Work and Skill[77]

High levels of rigor combined with extensiveness have been reached in recent years in research in engineering psychology, work and skill. In the United States Franklin V. Taylor (1910–1960), late of the U.S. Naval Research Laboratory and Paul M. Fitts of Michigan are leading research men in engineering psychology. Work abroad is similarly of high quality. Henri Piéron had been active all throughout his career in fostering psychotechnology. He edited a multi-volumed series of which the one on methodology is especially worthwhile. The effect of aging on human performance has been studied by A. T. Welford of Cambridge, while engineering psychology is one of the fields of Donald E. Broadbent of the same university. Arthur Mayer of Mannheim and Bernard Herwig of Braunschweig edited the volume in the "Handbuch" series on the psychology of work and social influences on the work environment.

Motivation[78]

Motivational factors, of course, are given an important place in learning theory and research. While Ernest R. Hilgard of Stanford has conducted research and writing over a much wider area, his extensive knowledge prepared him to summarize in a balanced fashion the existing state of the research relating motivation and learning. Clifford T. Morgan of California at Santa Barbara has presented evidence for a physiologically oriented theory of mechanisms of motivation.

The influence of exploratory and epistemic (knowledge-seeking) behavior upon motivation has been of considerable research interest. Daniel E. Berlyne of Toronto is a leading exponent. The work of Harlow, examined when animal research is considered, also emphasizes external motivation.

Charles N. Cofer of Pennsylvania State and Mortimer H. Appley of York have written a very useful summary of an enormous literature on motivation as such. Hans J. Eysenck of London has recently become interested in motivation and with his usual vigor has conducted and directed research eventuating in a recently published book. Hans Thomae of Bonn also writes and edits on the topic of motivation.

Intelligence[79]

Aspects of intelligence have been discussed in previous chapters but still other significant areas of research activity remain. Work on various aspects of the structure of intelligence and the role and nature of creativity as found by statistical manipulation of test scores is the province of Joy P. Guilford of Southern California. J. McVicker Hunt of Illinois has marshalled evidence on the effect of early experience upon subsequent intellectual development. He concludes that the concept of fixed intelligence and predetermined development are, to say the least, suspect, and that a person's behavior repertory is largely a function of opportunity for experience. In the tradition of Binet, Pierre Oléron of Paris stresses the role of proliferation of reactions to perception, and the utilization of symbols in the development of intellectual activities. Ward C. Halstead of Chicago works on the relation of brain functioning and intelligence.

Cognition, Thinking and Communication[80]

There are a good many facets to this complex array of complex topics. Work in the United States is again of high quality. Thinking as expressed in problem solving is an area of research where rigorous methodology is found. An excellent collection of readings, including his own studies and those influenced by him, has been published by Carl P. Duncan of Northwestern. A provocative approach, which has stirred considerable research, has been advanced by Leon Festinger of Stanford. He has argued for a general theory of the significance of inconsistency in thinking and reactions to it, in what he calls cognitive dissonance. Psycholinguistics, the study of relations between communication and the characteristics of the person communicating, has been the province of Charles E. Osgood of Illinois and George A. Miller of Harvard.

Soviet work must be mentioned. The cognitive processes expressed in developmental terms, language usage, the thought processes and information processing has been the concern of the current leading Soviet psychologist, Alexei N. Leontiev, his country's spokesman at International Congresses, professor and head of the Department at Moscow University and recipient of the Lenin Prize for Science. The pathology of thinking is the province of another member of the Moscow department, Blyuma Zeigarnik, who many years before had been at Leipzig and whose name gives that of the "Zeigarnik" effect.

In Switzerland, Jean Piaget continues his provocative, stimulating work. However, in recent years he has devoted more and more attention to its second major phase. (See page 522 for the first phase.) This is work in so-called genetic epistemology, an attempt at integration of psychology and epistemological philosophy, with the central theme being the study of the way in which the individual constructs his knowledge during the course of his development. Related problems of the philosophy of science, such as application of the techniques of symbolic logic to thought structures, also has received his attention. An excellent secondary account, available for both phases, has been prepared by John H. Flavell of Minnesota.

Personality[81]

Over the years, Henry A. Murray and Gordon W. Allport of Harvard have continued to refine and extend their influential theories of personality. Personality theories have also come from others who worked in different fields before 1945. Gardner Murphy of the Menninger Foundation, noted for his work in social psychology, later turned to personality theory and research. Significant of the consistency of his point of view from his work in social psychology, his principle work in personality bears the subtitle "a biosocial approach to origins and structure." Carl R. Rogers of Western Behavioral Science Institute, mentioned before in connection with research and practice of psychotherapy, drew on this experience to develop a theory of personality and interpersonal relationships in which he stressed the role of the self-concept in self-actualization.

Raymond B. Cattell of Illinois has devoted many years to applying multivariate statistical procedures to personally devised instruments for the measurement of personality and has emerged with a theory which is in constant state of change and refinement as his research continues.

In the United States during the present decade, enthusiasm for projective devices as measures of personality has been somewhat chastened and more restrained. This is due to the sharply critical conclusions that emerged from rigorous study, despite protests from protagonists that many of the studies were inappropriate.

In Great Britain, a rigorous experimental approach to the dimensional study of behavior, particularly personality assessment, is very prominent at the University of London and the associated Maudsley Hospital under the direction of Hans J. Eysenck. By and large, the research is programatic in that he and his associates deal with research around a common objective on which the entire organization participates. Factor analysis is the favorite statistical device. There are, of course, psychologists working in Britain in the statistical-measurement tradition of Burt and Thomson with Philip E. Vernon of London an outstanding example. He has concerned himself with personality assessment as well as with other fields.

French concepts of characterology, including Wallon's contribution and the philosophy of René Le Senne (1882–1954), are sympathetically examined and placed in a more psychological framework by René Zazzo of the École des Hautes Études. A self-realization theory of personality, with emphasis upon contact with Christian philosophy, is an effort of Joseph Nuttin of Louvain.

Interest in characterology continues unabated, particularly in Germany and Austria. A general statement by Hubert Rohracher of Vienna has been extremely popular. An attempt to reconcile the American and German approaches of personality has been given Hans Thomae of Bonn. Along with Philipp Lersch of Munich, he also edits the "Handbuch" volume. A masterly appraisal of contrasting trends in European and American psychology is available from G. W. Allport of Harvard. A bibliography of relevant literature with stress on European sources by Henry P. David of the International Research Institute, American Institute for Research, is also available.

Social Psychology[82]

Social psychology is an amorphous field into which order has penetrated little more than it had when Floyd Allport produced his systematic account more than forty years ago. This is clearly recognized in a series of efforts to integrate research and theory in some coherent framework. Donald T. Campbell of Northwestern in his research on social attitudes and other acquired behavioral dispositions aims at integrating the work from the behavioristic and phenomenological camps. Muzafer Sherif of Pennsylvania State, a specialist in group research, was called upon in his article in a Koch volume to try to bring some order in relating social psychology to cognate social disciplines and to bring out the indications of convergence among them. In the same series, Solomon E. Asch of Rutgers, Newark Branch, has explored the steps necessary to arrive at a more systematic view of the field. Authors of textbooks in the field with some attempt at system are David Krech and Richard Crutchfield of California at Berkeley, and Michael Argyle of Oxford.

Research on more specific problems have resulted in important publications. Neal E. Miller of Rockefeller and John Dollard of Yale have clarified the role of imitation in learning, thereby helping to bridge the gap between social psychology and learning. Herbert A. Simon of Carnegie Institute of Technology, a specialist in organizational behavior including human problem solving and decision making in that setting, has more generally concerned himself with the relations of economics and psychology. That characteristically German approach, folk psychology, has been summarized by Willy Hellpach (1877–1955), late of Heidelberg.

Child Psychology[83]

Robert R. Sears of Stanford and his associates have done considerable important research in child psychology of which their *Patterns of Child Rearing* is typical. Theirs was a necessarily large scale study of what happens in the interaction of mother and child in the process of rearing the child in our contemporary culture. Above all, it is distinguished by the fact that they were not deterred in dealing with a complex problem by an equally complex interlocking series of measures and hypotheses. This work is but part of a program of research.

Leonard Carmichael, when at Tufts, represented the tradition of studying the young as a species in a laboratory setting. He was a specialist in ontogenetic development and a considerable number of his studies are of lasting significance.

Piaget's studies of child psychology, especially the earlier ones, by American standards, were quantitatively unsound and based on far too few subjects. Many of his pronouncements on child experience and behavior served as a challenge for more careful research by others. Often his statements were found, not so much wrong, as to be stated much too sharply as to the age ranges involved. The review by Flavell is again very useful.

There is some work abroad. That in England is frequently set in a psychoanalytic framework. In France, René Zazzo of the École des Hautes Études does research on child development which shows the influence of both Binet and Piaget. Hans Thomae of Bonn edits the heterogenous volume devoted to developmental psychology in the German series.

Animal Psychology[84]

Work in animal psychology can be considered as falling into two categories of emphasis, that in which focus is more on the study of the animal as such or that in which the animal is seen more as a convenient means of study of some other psychological problem.

A relatively clear-cut illustration of the former is the careful assemblage of research material on the rat by Norman L. Munn, formerly of Bowdoin, and now of Adelaide. Studies of animal psychology by Pieron and by George C. Drew of London are also of this nature. This is also the case with ethology, the study by zoologists of animals in their natural habitat with particular emphasis on instinct or on a species' specific behavior, which is now international. When psychologists in the United States became interested, however, they immediately took the problem into the laboratory, as did Eckhard Hess of Chicago in his studies of imprinting.

Falling more in the latter category are studies of sensory and perceptual behavior of monkeys by Heinrich Kluver of Chicago and the primate studies of Harry Harlow of Wisconsin with emphasis on the role of external motivation.

Tomorrow

Someday psychology may achieve the hallmark of a mature science—the disappearance of theoretical schisms and national trends which serve to divide rather than to unite a field. The merging of the schools, the greater openness to external influence on the part of psychoanalysts, the greater rigor on the part of the younger European psychologists, and the new humanist emphases in the United States are some of the indications of progress today. Today, throughout all psychology, there is much greater breadth of agreement upon what constitutes psychology as well as upon a body of accepted techniques, data, and hypotheses. There are, of course, still sharp disagreements among psychologists. Present-day disagreements, however, are apt to center on specific points concerning a research problem. This has the inestimable advantage over the situation formerly prevailing in that there is some chance that the point at issue can be submitted to research and evaluation. The present is witnessing a possible merging of these trends into the mainstream of psychology to the mutual strengthening of that goal of history—the future.

REFERENCES*

1. W. Metzger, The Historical Background for National Trends in Psychology: German Psychology, *J. Hist. Behav. Sci.*, 1965, 1, 109–115.

2. *Ibid.*

* See page 16 for description of reference style.

3. P. R. Hofstätter (Hrag.), *Psychologie.* Frankfurt am Main: Fischer, 1957.

4. J. F. Adams, The Status of Psychology in the Universities of Austria and Germany: 1965–1966, *J. Psychol.*, 1966, 63, 117–134; F. Wesley, Assessing German Psychology: 1965, *J. Gen. Psychol.*, 1966, 75, 273–277.

5. M. Reuchlin, The Historical Background for National Trends in Psychology: France, *J. Hist. Behav. Sci.*, 1965, 1, 115–123.

6. Cecily Monchaux & Gertrude H. Keir, British Psychology 1945–1957, *Acta Psychol.* (Amst.), 1961, 18, 120–180.

7. Decree of the Scientific Session of the USSR. Acad. Sci. & USSR Acad. Med. Sci., Devoted to the Problems of the Physiological Theory of Academnician I. P. Pavlov, *Fiziol. zh. SSSR*, 1950, 36, 381–386.

8. G. Razran, Soviet Psychology and Psychophysiology, *Behav. Sci.*, 1959, 4, 35–48.

9. G. Razran, Growth, Scope, and Direction of Current Soviet Psychology: The 1963 All-Union Congress, *Amer. Psychologist*, 1964, 19, 342–347.

10. *E.g.,* J. Brozek, Current Status of Psychology in the USSR, *Annu. Rev. Psychol.*, 1964, 15, 493–594.

11. J. Brozek & J. Hoskovec, Current Soviet Psychology: a Systematic Review, *Soviet Psychol. & Psychiat.*, 1966, 4, 16–44; J. Brozek, J. Hoskovec, & D. Slobin. Review in English of Recent Soviet Psychology: A Bibliography. *Soviet Psychol. & Psychiat.*, 1966, 4, 95–99; J. Brozek & J. Hoskovec, Soviet Psychology in English: Translations of Books, *Soviet Psychol. & Psychiat.*, 1966, 4, 100–104.

12. B. G. Anan'yev, *et al.*, (eds.). *Psychological Science in the USSR.* (2 vols.) Washington, D. C.: U.S. Joint Publications Research Service, 1961, 1962.

13. Y. Tanaka, Status of Japanese Experimental Psychology, *Annu. Rev. Psychol.*, 1966, 17, 233–272.

14. K. Sato, *Psychology of Personality.* (rev. ed.) Tokyo: Sogensha, 1953.

15. R. W. Russell, The International Union of Psychological Science. *Internat. J. Psychol.*, 1966, 1, 65–72.

16. H. C. J. Duijker & E. H. Jacobson, (eds.), *International Directory of Psychologists.* (2nd ed.) Assen, the Netherlands: Royal Vangorcum, 1966.

17. American Psychological Association. *International Opportunities for Advanced Training and Research in Psychology.* Washington, D. C.: American Psychological Association, 1966.

18. E. R. Hilgard & G. H. Bower, *Theories of Learning.* (3rd ed.) New York: Appleton-Century-Crofts, 1966, Chap. 10, Functionalism.

19. W. Köhler, Gestalt Psychology Today, *Amer. Psychologist*, 1959, 14, 727–734.

20. Mary Henle, On Gestalt Psychology. In B. B. Wolman & E. Nagel (eds.), *Scientific Psychology: Principles & Approaches.* New York: Basic, 1965, pp. 276–292.

21. W. C. H. PRENTICE, The Systematic Psychology of Wolfgang Köhler. In S. Koch (ed.), *Psychology: a Study of Science* (Study 1). *Conceptual and Systematic,* (Vol. 1). *Sensory, Perceptual and Physiological Formulations.* New York: McGraw-Hill, 1959, pp. 427–455.

22. F. HEIDER, *Psychology of Interpersonal Relations.* New York: Wiley, 1958.

23. MARY HENLE (ed.), *Documents of Gestalt Psychology.* Berkeley: University of California Press, 1961.

24. K. W. SPENCE, Types of Constructs in Psychology. (The Nature of Theory Construction in Contemporary Psychology. *Psychol. Rev.,* 1944, 51, 47–68.) In M. H. Marx (ed.), *Theories in Contemporary Psychology.* New York: Macmillan, 1963, pp. 162–178.

25. G. BERGMANN, Theoretical Psychology, *Annu. Rev. Psychol.,* 1953, 4, 435–458, (esp. pp. 447–456); L. Postman & K. Riley, A Critique of Köhler's Theory of Association, *Psychol. Rev.,* 1957, 64, 61–72.

26. W. METZGER, *Gesetze des Sehens* (2. aufl.) Frankfurt: Kramer, 1953. (1936)

27. E. RAUSCH, *Struktur und Metrik figural-optischer Wahrnehmung.* Frankfurt-a-M: Kramer, 1952.

28. F. SANDER & H. VOLKELT, *Ganzheits psychologie: Grundlagen Ergebnisse, Anwendugen.* Munich: Beck, 1962.

29. A. WELLEK, *Ganzheitspsychologie und Strukturtheorie.* Bern: Francke, 1955.

30. H. HARTMANN, Ego Psychology and the Problem of Adaptation. In D. Rapaport (ed.), *Organization and Pathology of Thought.* New York: Columbia University Press, 1951, pp. 362–398; H. Hartmann. Comments on the Psychoanalytic Theory of the Ego, *Psychoanal. Stud. Child,* 1950, 5, 74–95; H. Hartmann, E. Kris and R. M. Loewenstein, Comments on the Formation of Psychic Structure, *Psychoanal. Stud. Child,* 1947, 2, 11–38; H. Hartmann, *Essays on Ego Psychology.* New York: International Universities Press, 1964; H. Hartmann, The Mutual Influences in the Development of the Ego and the Id, *Psychoanal. Stud. Child,* 1952, 7, 9–30.

31. M. M. GILL, (ed.), *The Collected Papers of David Rapaport.* New York: Basic, 1967; D. Rapaport, The Structure of Psychoanalytic Theory: a Systematizing Attempt. In S. Koch (ed.), *Psychology: a Study of a Science.* (Vol. 3) New York: McGraw-Hill, 1959, pp. 55–183.

32. R. R. HOLT, Ego Autonomy Re-evaluated, *Inter. J. Psychoanal.,* 1965, 46, 151–167; G. S. Klein, Consciousness in Psychoanalytic Theory: Some Implications for Current Research in Perception, *J. Amer. Psychoanal. Assoc.,* 1959, 7, 5–34.

33. E. H. ERIKSON, *Childhood and Society.* New York: Norton, 1950.

34. MELANIE KLEIN, *Contributions to Psychoanalysis, 1921–1945.* London: Hogarth Press, 1948.

35. ANNA FREUD, *The Ego and the Mechanisms of Defense.* New York: International Universities Press, 1946 (1935); Anna Freud, *The Psycho-analytical Treatment of Children.* London: Image, 1946.

36. REUCHLIN, *op. cit.*

37. E. R. HILGARD, Impulsive Versus Realistic Thinking: an Examination of the Distinction Between Primary and Secondary Processes in Thought, *Psychol. Bull.*, 1962, 59, 477–488; R. R. Sears, Survey of Objective Studies of Psychoanalytic Concepts, *Soc. Sci. Res. Coun. Bull.*, 1943, 51, 156; B. F. Skinner, Critique of Psychoanalytic Concepts and Theories, *Sci. Mon.*, 1954, 79 302–307.

38. M. GILL, The Present State of Psychoanalytic Theory, *J. Abnorm. Soc. Psychol.*, 1959, 58, 1–8; L. S. Kubie, Psychoanalysis and Scientific Method, *J. Nerv. Ment. Dis.*, 1960, 131, 495–512; H. Hartmann, Psychoanalysis as a Scientific Theory. In S. Hook (ed.), *Psychoanalysis, Scientific Method and Philosophy*. New York: Grove, 1959, pp. 3–37.

39. J. DOLLARD & N. E. MILLER, *Personality and Psychotherapy*. New York: McGraw-Hill, 1950.

40. RUTH L. MUNROE, *Schools of Psychoanalytic Thought: an Exposition, Critique and Attempt at Integration*. New York: Dryden, 1955; G. S. Blum, *Psychoanalytic Theories of Personality*. New York: McGraw-Hill, 1953.

41. KAREN HORNEY, *New Ways in Psychoanalysis*. New York: Norton, 1939; Karen Horney, *The Neurotic Personality of our Time*. New York: Norton, 1937.

42. E. FROMM, *Man for Himself, an Inquiry into the Psychology of Ethics*. New York: Rinehart, 1947; E. Fromm, *Sane Society*. New York: Rinehart, 1955; R. I. Evans, *Dialogue with Erich Fromm*. New York: Harper & Row, 1966.

43. ALEXANDRA ADLER, Adlerian Psychotherapy and Recent Trends, *J. Indiv. Psychol.*, 1963, 19, 55–60.

44. H. L. ANSBACHER, The Structure of Individual Psychology. In B. B. Wolman & E. Nagel (eds.), *Scientific Psychology: Principles and Approaches*. New York: Basic, 1965, pp. 340–364.

45. F. BIRNBAUM, Frankl's Existential Psychology from the Viewpoint of Individual Psychology, *J. Indiv. Psychol.*, 1961, 17, 162–166.

46. W. VAN DUSEN, Adler and Existence Analysis. *J. Indiv. Psychol.*, 1959, 15, 100–111.

47. R. DREIKURS, Goals of Psychotherapy. In A. R. Mahrer (ed.), *The Goals of Psychotherapy*. New York: Appleton-Century-Crofts, 1967, pp. 221–237.

48. HELENE PAPANEK, Alfred Adler. In A. M. Freedman & H. I. Kaplan (eds.), *Comprehensive Textbook of Psychiatry*. Baltimore: Williams & Wilkins, 1967, pp. 320–327.

49. A. BORNEMANN & H. L. ANSBACHER, Individual Psychology in Germany, *Indiv. Psychol. Bull.*, 1949, 7, 30–32.

50. J. B. ROTTER, An Analysis of Adlerian Psychology from a Research Orientation, *J. Indiv. Psychol.*, 1962, 18, 3–11.

51. E. W. ARLUCH, Training Facilities of the C. M. Jung Institute, Zurich, *Amer. Psychologist*, 1960, 15, 626–629.

52. A. TOYNBEE, The Value of C. G. Jung's Work for Historians, *J. Analyt. Psychol.*, 1956, 1, 193–194.

53. J. Cohen, *Humanistic Psychology*. London: Allen Unwin, 1958; A. Wellek, Mathematics and Intuition, the Relationship between Psychology and Philosophy Reconsidered, *Acta psychologica*, 1964, 22, 413–429; G. W. Allport, Scientific Models and Human Morals, *Psychol. Rev.*, 1947, 54, 182–192; C. R. Rogers, Some Questions and Challenges Facing a Humanistic Psychology. *J. Humanistic Psychol.*, 1965, 5, 1–5; A. van Kaam, Existential and Humanistic Psychology, *Rev. Existential Psychol. & Psychiat.*, 1965, 5, 291–296; A. H. Maslow, Humanistic Science and Transcendent Experiences. *J. Humanistic Psychol.*, 1965, 5, 219–227.

54. A. van Kaam, Clinical Implications of Heidegger's Concepts of Will, Decision and Responsibility, *Rev. Existent. Psychol. & Psychiat.*, 205–216.

55. R. May (ed.), *Existential Psychology*. New York: Random, 1961.

56. A van Kaam, *Existential Foundations of Psychology*. Pittsburgh: Duquesne University Press, 1966.

57. J. P. Sartre, *Imagination: a Psychological Critique*. Translated by F. Williams. Ann Arbor: University of Michigan Press, 1962; P. J. R. Dempsey, *The Psychology of Sartre*. Cork: Cork University Press, 1950.

58. M. Merleau-Ponty, *The Structure of Behavior*. Boston: Beacon, 1963; M. Merleau-Ponty, 'Les Sciences de l'homme et la phenomenologie,' *Bull. de Psychologie*. 1964, 18, 141–170.

59. F. J. J. Buytendijk, *Pain—its Modes and Functions*. Chicago: University of Chicago Press, 1962. (1943)

60. A. Michotte, (ed.) *Causalité; permanence et réalité phénoménales*. Louvain: Publications Universitairès, 1962.

61. K. Mierke, *Wille und Leistung*. Göttingen; Verlag für Psychologie, 1955.

62. K. Mac Corquodale & P. E. Meehl, On a Distinction Between Hypothetical Constructs and Intervening Variables, *Psychol. Rev.*, 1948, 55, 95–107.

63. E. C. Tolman, Principle of Purposive Behavior. In S. Koch (ed.), *Psychology, a Study of a Science*. (Vol. 2) New York: McGraw-Hill, 1959, pp. 92–157.

64. K. W. Spence, The Methods and Postulates of 'Behaviorism', *Psychol. Rev.*, 1948, 55, 67–78.

65. B. F. Skinner, *The Behavior of Organisms: an Experimental Analysis*. New York: Appleton-Century-Crofts, 1938.

66. B. F. Skinner, *Science and Human Behavior*. New York: Macmillan, 1953.

67. B. F. Skinner, Behaviorism at Fifty, *Science*, 1963, 140, 951–958. (Also in T. Wann (ed.), *Behaviorism and Phenomenology: Contrasting Bases for Modern Psychology*. Chicago: University of Chicago Press, 1964, pp. 79–108.)

68. American Psychological Association. Ethical Standards of Psychologists, *Amer. Psychologist*, 1963, 18, 56–60; T. G. Andrews & M. Dreese, Military Utilization of Psychologists during World War II, *Amer. Psychologist*, 1948, 3, 533–538; S. J. Beck, *et al.*, *Rorschach's Test*: I. *Basic Processes*. (3rd ed.) New York: Grune & Stratton, 1961; S. J. Beck, *Rorschach's Test*: II. *a Variety of Personality Pictures*. New York: Grune & Stratton, 1945; S. J. Beck, *Rorschach's test*. III. *Advances in Interpretation*. New York: Grune & Stratton,

1952; L. Blank & H. P. David, *Sourcebook for Training in Clinical Psychology.* New York: Springer, 1964; S. H. Britt, & Jane D. Morgan, Military Psychologists in World War II, *Amer. Psychologist,* 1946, 1, 423–437; K. E. Clark (ed.), *America's Psychologists,* Washington, D. C.: American Psychological Association, 1957; H. P. David (ed.), *International Trends in Mental Health.* New York; McGraw-Hill, 1966; H. P. David, *International Resources in Clinical Psychology.* New York: McGraw-Hill, 1964; S. C. Ericksen, Responsibilities of Psychological Science to Professional Psychology, *Amer. Psychologist,* 1966, 21, 950–953; H. Eysenck, (ed.), *Experiments in Behavior Therapy: Readings in Modern Methods of Treatment of Mental Disorders Derived from Learning Theory.* New York: Macmillan, 1964; R. Heiss (ed.), "Psychologische Diagnostik." In P. Lersch *et al.,* (eds.), *Handbuch, der Psychologie,* (Vol. 3) Göttingen: Verlag für Psychologie, 1963; P. E. Meehl, *Clinical versus Statistical Prediction: a Theoretical Analysis and Review of the Evidence.* Minneapolis, Minn.: University of Minnesota Press, 1954; R. Meili, *Lehrbuch der psychologische Diagnostik.* (3rd ed.) Bern: Huber, 1955; V. C. Raimy, (ed.), *Training in Clinical Psychology.* New York: Prentice Hall, 1950; C. R. Rogers, *Client-Centered Therapy: its Current Practice, Implications and Theory.* Boston: Houghton Mifflin, 1951; D. Shakow, Seventeen Years Later: Clinical Psychology in Light of the 1947 Committee on Training in Clinical Psychology Report, *Amer. Psychologist,* 1965, 20, 353–362; D. Shakow, (Chm.) Recommended Graduate Training Program in Clinical Psychology, *Amer. Psychologist,* 1947, 2, 539–558; R. I. Watson, A Brief History of Clinical Psychology, *Psychol. Bull.,* 1953, 50, 321–346 (Reprinted in I. N. Mensh (ed.), *Clinical Psychology: Science and Profession.* New York: Macmillan, 1966, pp. 68–104); D. Wechsler, *The Measurement and Appraisal of Adult Intelligence.* (4th ed.) Baltimore: Williams & Wilkins, 1958 (1939); J. Wolpe, *Psychotherapy by Reciprocal Inhibition.* Stanford: Stanford University Press, 1958.

69. S. Koch (ed.), *Psychology: a Study of a Science.* (6 vols.) New York: McGraw-Hill, 1959–1962.

70. P. Lersch *et al.,* (ed.), *Handbuch der Psychologie.* (12 vols.) Göttingen, Verlag für Psychologie, 1959–1967.

71. J. Field, (ed.) *Handbook of Physiology. Section I.: Neurophysiology.* (Vols. 1–3) Washington, D. C.: American Physiological Society, 1959–1962.

72. The presence of these series, especially the first two, has considerably lightened the task of selecting citations to American and German research. Since they are review articles, it must be made explicit that many classic books and articles, indeed often the very ones that made the scientific reputation of the psychologist which resulted in his being asked to participate, are *not* cited. However, the reviews lead directly to these other important sources. Citation of the German literature takes the form of mention of the volume and its editor rather than the authors of specific papers, or of the general editors. Unfortunately, similar sources are not available for the other national literatures and Russian and Japanese are not properly represented. Representativeness of the work for the research area and eminence of the individual for work in that area guided selection. For every one mentioned, there are

undoubtedly many others that plausibly could have been mentioned, especially for workers in allied disciplines.

73. A. FESSARD, Brain Potentials and Rhythms-Introduction. In J. Field (ed.), *Handbook, op. cit.*, Vol. 1, pp. 255–259; K. Goldstein, *The Organism.* Berlin: Beacon Press, 1963. (1934); D. B. Lindsley, Attention, Consciousness, Sleep and Wakefulness. In J. Field (ed.), *Handbook, op. cit.* Vol. 3, pp. 1553–1593; H. Lippert, *Einfuhrung in die Pharmako-psychologie.* Bern: Huber, 1959; A. R. Luria, *Human Brain and Psychological Processes.* New York: Harper, 1966. (1963); A. R. Luria, *Higher Cortical Functions in Man.* (Translated by B. Haigh) New York: Basic, 1966. (1962); K. H. Pribram, Interrelations of Psychology and the Neurological Disciplines. In S. Koch (ed.), *Psychology, op. cit.*, Vol. 4, pp. 119–157; F. Ratliff, Some Interrelations among Physics, Physiology, and Psychology in the Study of Vision. In S. Koch (ed.), *Psychology, op. cit.*, Vol. 4, pp. 417–482; R. W. Russell, Psychopharmacology. In P. R. Farnsworth, *et al.* (eds.), *Annu. Rev. Psychol.*, 15, 87–114; O. L. Zangwill, Psychological Research in the Field of Neurology. In C. A. Mace, and P. E. Vernon, (eds.), *Current Trends in British Psychology.* London: Methuen, 1953.

74. F. A. GELDARD, *The Human Senses.* New York: Wiley, 1953; C. H. Graham, Color Theory. In S. Koch, (ed.), *Psychology, op. cit.*, Vol. 1, pp. 145–287. R. Jung & H. Kornhuber, (eds.) *Neurophysiologie und Psychophysik des visuellen Systems.* Berlin: Springer, 1961; W. D. Neff, Sensory Discrimination, In J. Field, (ed.), *Handbook, op. cit.*, Vol. 3, pp. 1447–1470; C. Pfaffman, Studies of the Sense of Taste as a Model S-R System. In S. Koch (ed.), *Psychology, op. cit.*, Vol. 4, pp. 380–416; H. Piéron, Les échelles subjectives. Peuvent-elles fournir la base d'une nouvelle loi psychophysique? *L'Année Psychologique*, 1959, 59, 1–34; S. S. Stevens, The Attributes of Tones, *Proc. Nat. Acad. Sci.*, Washington, D. C.: 1934, 20, 457–459; S. S. Stevens, Volume and Intensity of Tones, *Amer. J. Psychol.*, 1934, 46, 397–408; S. S. Stevens, A Scale for the Measurement of a Psychological Magnitude: Loudness, *Psychol. Rev.*, 1936, 43, 405–416; S. S. Stevens, Mathematics, Measurement and Psychophysics. In S. S. Stevens (ed.), *Handbook of Experimental Psychology.* New York: Wiley, 1951, pp. 1–49; G. von Békésy, *Experiments in Hearing.* (Translated & Edited by E. G. Wever) New York: McGraw-Hill, 1960.

75. F. H. ALLPORT, *Theories of Perception and the Concept of Structure.* New York: Wiley, 1955; D. E. Broadbent, *Perception and Communication.* New York: Pergamon Press, 1958; P. Fraisse, *Les structures rhythmiques: étude psychologique.* Louvain: Publications Universitaires de Louvain, 1956; P. Fraisse, *The Psychology of Time.* (Translated by Jennifer Leith) New York: Harper & Row, 1963; J. J. Gibson, Perception as a Function of Stimulation. In S. Koch (ed.), *Psychology, op. cit.*, Vol. 1, pp. 456–501; J. J. Gibson. *The Senses Considered as Perceptual Systems.* Boston: Houghton Mifflin, 1966; W. H. Ittelson, Perception and Transactional Psychology. In S. Koch (ed.), *Psychology, op. cit.*, Vol. 4, pp. 660–704; I. Kohler, *Ueber Aufbau und Wandlungen der Wahrnehmungswelt.* Vienna: Rohrer, 1951; W. Metzger, (ed.), Allgemeine Psychologie 1: Der aufbau des Erkennens, 1. Hälfte: Bewusstelin

und Wahrnehmung. In P. Lersch *et al.*, (eds.), *Handbuch, op. cit.;* L. Postman, Perception and Learning. In S. Koch (ed.), *Psychology, op. cit.*, Vol. 5, pp. 30–113. A. Summerfield, & K. M. Miller, Visual Illusion and Figural After-Effect, with and without Fixation, *Quart. J. Exp. Psychol.*, 1955, 7, 149–158; N. S. Sutherland, Figural After-Effects, Retinal Size, and Apparent Size, *Quart. J. Exp. Psychol.*, 1959, 6, 35–44; N. S. Sutherland, Visual Discrimination of Orientation by Octopus, *Brit. J. Psychol.*, 1957, 48, 55–70; M. D. Vernon, *A Further Study of Visual Perception.* London: Cambridge University Press, 1952; M. D. Vernon, *The Psychology of Perception.* Baltimore: Penguin, 1962; G. M. Wyburn, R. W. Pickford & R. J. Hirst, *Human Senses and Perception.* Toronto: University of Toronto Press, 1964.

76. R. Bergius (ed.), Allgemeine Psychologie 1: Der Aufbau des Erkennens, 2 Hälfte: Lernen und Denken. In P. Lersch, *et al.*, *Handbuch, op. cit.;* D. E. Broadbent, *Behavior.* New York: Basic, 1961; R. R. Bush & F. Mosteller, *Stochastic Models for Learning.* New York: Wiley, 1955; W. K. Estes, The Statistical Approach to Learning Theory. In S. Koch (ed.), *Psychology, op. cit.*, Vol. 2, pp. 380–491, R. Galambos and C. T. Morgan, The Neural Basis of Learning. In J. Field (ed.), *Handbook, op. cit.* Vol. 3, pp. 1471–1499; E. R. Guthrie, Association by Contiguity. In S. Koch (ed.), *Psychology, op. cit.*, Vol. 2, pp. 158–195; D. O. Hebb, A Neuropsychological Theory. In S. Koch (ed.), *Psychology, op. cit.*, Vol. 1, pp. 622–643; G. A. Kimble (Revisor), *Hilgard and Marquis Conditioning and Learning.* (2nd. ed.), New York: Appleton-Century-Crofts, 1961 (1940); J. Konorski, *Conditioned Reflexes and Neuron Organization.* (Translated by S. Garrig) Cambridge: Cambridge University Press, 1948; F. A. Logan, The Hull-Spence Approach. In S. Koch (ed.), *Psychology, op. cit.*, Vol. 2, pp. 293–358; N. E. Miller, Behavior, Motivation, and Social Learning. In S. Koch (ed.), *Psychology, op. cit.*, Vol. 2, pp. 196–292; O. H. Mowrer, *Learning Theory and Behavior.* New York: Wiley, 1960; O. H. Mowrer, *Learning Theory and the Symbolic Processes.* New York: Wiley, 1960; B. F. Skinner & C. B. Ferster, *Schedules of Reinforcement.* New York: Appleton-Century-Crofts, 1957; B. F. Skinner, *Science and Human Behavior. op. cit.;* B. F. Skinner, *Verbal Behavior.* New York: Appleton-Century-Crofts, 1957; B. F. Skinner, *The Behavior of Organisms: an Experimental Analysis, op. cit.;* B. J. Underwood, Ten Years of Massed Practice on Distributed Practice, *Psychol. Rev.*, 1961, 68, 229–247.

77. D. E. Broadbent, Perceptual Defense and the Engineering Psychologist, *Bull. Brit. Psychol. Soc.*, 1965, 18, 1–15; P. M. Fitts, Engineering Psychology. In S. Koch (ed.), *Psychology, op. cit.*, Vol. 5, pp. 908–933; A. Mayer & B. Herwig, (eds.), Betreibpsychologie. In P. Lersch *et al.* (eds.), *Handbuch, op. cit.;* H. Piéron, P. Pichot, J. M. Faverage & J. Stoetzel, *Methodologie psychotechnique: Traité de psychologie appliquée.* Livre 2. Paris: Presses Universitaires de France, 1951; F. V. Taylor, Human Engineering and Psychology. In S. Koch (ed.), *Psychology, op. cit.*, Vol. 5, pp. 831–907; A. T. Welford, *et al. Skill and Age; an Experimental Approach.* New York: Oxford University Press, 1951.

78. D. E. BERLYNE, Motivational Problems Raised by Exploratory and Epistemic Behavior. In S. Koch (ed.), *Psychology, op. cit.*, Vol. 5, pp. 284–364; C. N. Cofer & M. H. Appley, *Motivation: Theory and Research*. New York: Wiley, 1964; H. J. Eysenck, *Experiments in Motivation*. New York: Macmillan, 1964; E. R. Hilgard, Motivation in Learning Theory. In S. Koch (ed.), *Psychology, op. cit.*, Vol. 5, pp. 253–283; C. T. Morgan, Physiological Theory of Drive. In S. Koch (ed.), *Psychology, op. cit.*, Vol. 1, pp. 644–671; H. Thomae (ed.), Allgemeine Psychologie II: Motivationslehre. In P. Lersch *et al.* (eds.), *Handbuch, op. cit.*

79. J. P. GUILFORD, The Structure of Intellect, *Psychol. Bull.*, 1956, 53, 267–293; J. P. Guilford, Three Faces of Intellect, *Amer. Psychologist*, 1959, 14, 469–479; J. P. Guilford, Intelligence; 1965 Model, *Amer. Psychologist*, 1966, 21, 20–26; W. C. Halstead, *Brain and Intelligence*. Chicago: University of Chicago Press, 1947; J. McV. Hunt, *Intelligence and Experience*. New York: Ronald, 1961; P. Oléron, *Les activités intellectuelles*. Paris: Presses Universitaires de France, 1964.

80. C. P. DUNCAN (ed.), *Thinking: Current Experimental Studies*. Philadelphia Lippincott, 1967; L. Festinger, *A Theory of Cognitive Dissonance*. Evanston: Row, Peterson, 1957; J. H. Flavell, *The Developmental Psychology of Jean Piaget*. Princeton: Van Nostrand, 1963; A. N. Leontiev, *The Origin and Initial Development of Language*. Moscow: Akad. Nauk, USSR, 1963; G. Miller, *The Psychology of Communication*. New York: Basic, 1967; C. E. Osgood, Psycholinguistics. In S. Koch (ed.), *Psychology, op. cit.*, Vol. 6, pp. 244–316; J. Piaget, Psychology & Philosophy. In B. B. Wolman & E. Nagel (eds.), *Scientific Psychology: Principles and Approaches*. New York: Basic, 1965, pp. 28–43; Blyuma V. Zeigarnik, *The Pathology of Thinking*, New York: Plenum, 1965 (1962).

81. G. W. ALLPORT, European and American Theories of Personality. In H. P. David & H. von Bracken, (eds.), *Perspectives in Personality Theory*. New York: Basic, 1957, pp. 3–24; G. W. Allport, *Pattern and Growth in Personality*. New York: Holt, Rinehart & Winston, 1961; R. B. Cattell, Personality Theory Growing from Multivariate Quantitative Research. In S. Koch (ed.), *Psychology, op. cit.*, Vol. 3, pp. 257–327; H. P. David, Selected Annotated Bibliography. In H. P. David & H. von Bracken (eds.), *Perspectives in Personality Theory, op. cit.*, pp. 385–418; H. J. Eysenck, *Dimensions of Personality*. London: Routledge, 1947; H. J. Eysenck, *The Scientific Study of Personality*. New York: Macmillan, 1952; R. LaSenne, *Traité de caracterologie*, Paris: Presses Universitaires de France, 1945; P. Lersch & H. Thomae (eds.), Persönlichkeitsforschung und Persönlichkeitstheorie. In P. Lersch *et al.* (eds.), *Handbuch, op. cit.*, Vol. 4; G. Murphy, *Personality; a Biosocial Approach to Origins and Structure*. New York: Harper, 1947; H. A. Murray, Preparations for the Scaffold of a Comprehensive System. In S. Koch (ed.), *Psychology, op. cit.*, Vol. 3, pp. 7–54; J. Nuttin, *Psychoanalysis and Personality: a Dynamic Theory of Normal Personality*. (3rd ed.) (Translated by G. Lamb) New York: New American Library, 1962 (1953); C. R. Rogers, A Theory of Therapy,

Personality and Interpersonal Relationships as Developed in the Client-Centered Framework. In S. Koch (ed.), *Psychology, op. cit.,* Vol. 3, pp. 184–256; H. Rohracher, *Kleine Charakterkunde* (7 Aufl.) Wien: Urban & Schwarzenberg, 1956; H. Thomae, *Persönlichkeit: Eine dynamische Interpretation.* (2nd ed.) Bonn: Bouvier, 1955; P. E. Vernon, *Personality Assessment: a Critical Survey.* New York: Wiley, 1964; R. Zazzo, Current French Concepts of Characterology and the Study of Character. In H. P. David & H. von Bracken (eds.), *Perspectives in Personality Theory, op. cit.,* pp. 101–108.

82.   M. Argyle, *The Scientific Study of Social Behaviour.* London: Methuen, 1957; S. E. Asch, A Perspective in Social Psychology. In S. Koch (ed.), *Psychology, op. cit.,* Vol. 3, pp. 363–383; D. T. Campbell, Social Attitudes and Other Acquired Behavioral Dispositions. In S. Koch (ed.), *Psychology, op. cit.,* Vol. 6, pp. 94–172; W. Hellpach, *Einführung in die Völkerpsychologie.* Stuttgart: Enke, 1954; D. Krech, R. S. Crutchfield & E. L. Ballachey, *Individual in Society: a Textbook of Social Psychology.* New York: McGraw-Hill, 1962 (1948); N. E. Miller, & J. Dollard, *Social Learning and Imitation.* New Haven: Yale University Press, 1941; M. Sherif, Social Psychology: Problems and Trends in Interdisciplinary Relationships. In S. Koch (ed.), *Psychology, op. cit.,* Vol. 6, pp. 30–93; H. A. Simon, Economics and Psychology. In S. Koch (ed.), *Psychology, op. cit.,* Vol. 6, pp. 685–723.

83.   L. Carmichael, Ontogenetic Development. In S. S. Stevens (ed.), *Handbook of Experimental Psychology.* New York: Wiley, 1951, pp. 281–303; J. H. Flavell, *The Development Psychology of Jean Piaget.* Princeton: Van Nostrand, 1963; R. R. Sears, Eleanore E. Maccoby, & H. Levin, *Patterns of Child Rearing.* Evanston, Ill.: Row, Peterson, 1957; H. Thomae (ed.), Entwicklungspsychologie. In P. Lersch, *et al.* (eds.), *Handbuch, op. cit.;* R. Zazzo, *Conduites et conscience: I. Psychologie de l'enfant et méthode génétique.* Neuchâtel, Switzerland: Delachaux & Niestle, 1962.

84.   G. C. Drew & F. H. George, Studies of Animal Learning. In C. H. Mace & P. E. Vernon, *Current Trends in British Psychology.* London: Methuen, 1953; H. F. Harlow, Learning Set and Error Factor Theory. In S. Koch (ed.), *Psychology, op. cit.,* Vol. 2, pp. 492–537; E. H. Hess, Imprinting: an Effect of Early Experience, Imprinting Determines Later Social Behavior in Animals, *Science,* 1959, 130, 133–141; H. Kluver, *Behavior Mechanisms in Monkeys.* Chicago: Phoenix, 1933; H. L. Munn, *Handbook of Psychological Research on the Rat: an Introduction to Animal Psychology.* Boston: Houghton Mifflin, 1950; H. Piéron, Psychologie zoologique. In G. Dumas (ed.), *Nouveau traité de psychologie.* Paris: Presses Universitaires de France, 1941.

INDEX OF NAMES

° Page numbers citing references will be followed by "ref." in order to distinguish them from text citations.

INDEX OF SUBJECTS